MW01076894

FOUNDATIONS OF COUPLES, MARRIAGE, AND FAMILY COUNSELING

David Capuzzi
Mark D. Stauffer

WILEY

Cover Design: Wiley
Cover Illustration: ©iStock.com/mxtama

This book is printed on acid-free paper. ♾

Published by John Wiley & Sons, Inc., Hoboken, New Jersey.
Published simultaneously in Canada.

For general information on our other products and services please contact our Customer Care Department within the United States at (800) 762-2974, outside the United States at (317) 572-3993, or fax (317) 572-4002.

Wiley publishes in a variety of print and electronic formats and by print-on-demand. Some material included with standard print versions of this book may not be included in e-books or in print-on-demand. If this book refers to media such as a CD or DVD that is not included in the version you purchased, you may download this material at http://booksupport.wiley.com. For more information about Wiley products, visit www.wiley.com.

Library of Congress Cataloging-in-Publication Data:

Foundations of couples, marriage, and family counseling / [edited by]
David Capuzzi, Mark D. Stauffer.
pages cm
Includes bibliographical references.
ISBN 978-1-118-71099-9 (cloth : alk. paper)
ISBN 978-1-118-71122-4 (pdf)
ISBN 978-1-118-71078-4 (epub)
1. Family counseling. 2. Vocational guidance. I. Capuzzi, Dave, editor of compilation. II. Stauffer, Mark D., editor of compilation.
HV697.F68 2015
362.82'86—dc23

2014018429

Printed in the United States of America

10 9 8 7 6 5 4 3 2 1

Contents

Preface

Whether you are entering the field of couples, marriage, and family counseling or are a counselor who wants to be better prepared for working with couples and families, this text provides a foundational basis. *Foundations of Couples, Marriage, and Family Counseling* addresses real-life clinical concerns while providing the necessary information to keep up to date with trends in the profession and also evolving standards of professional organizations, accrediting bodies, and licensure boards. Counselors in school, mental health, rehabilitation, hospital, private practice, and a variety of other settings must be thoroughly prepared to support couples and families in their quest to be healthy, functional, and unimpaired. As the counseling profession has matured, more and more emphasis has been placed on the importance of preparing counselors to work holistically and synthesize knowledge domains from mental health, developmental, and systemic perspectives.

This textbook draws on specialized knowledge for each contributed chapter. It is written for use in graduate-level preparation programs for counselors. Requirements of the Council for the Accreditation of Counseling and Related Educational Programs (CACREP) and other certification associations have led many university programs in counselor education to require or recommend a foundations course in couples, marriage, and family counseling for all students regardless of specialization (school, mental health, rehabilitation, career, student personnel, etc.).

Although the text addresses the history, theory, and research related to couples, marriage, and family counseling, at least half of the emphasis in the book is placed on techniques and skills needed by the practitioner. In addition, topics connected with diversity issues; concrete reference to assessment tools; research; filial play therapy; sexuality and gender issues; addictions; violence, abuse, and trauma; and divorce and other loss issues make the book engaging and of high interest to the readership. Writers who are experienced in couples, marriage, and family counseling were asked to contribute to the text so that the reader is provided with not only theory and research, but also with applications that are pertinent to the role of the practicing, licensed counselor. This book also reflects the view of the editors that counselors must be prepared in a comprehensive and holistic manner because couples and family issues are so often the reasons clients seek the assistance of professional counselors.

The book is unique in both format and content. The contributed format provides state-of-the-art information by experts who are nationally recognized for their expertise, research, and publications related to couples, marriage, and family counseling. The content provides readers with areas not always addressed in introductory texts. Both the format and content enhance the readability and interest for the reader and should engage and motivate graduate students in counseling and aligned professions, as well as those enrolled in upper-division undergraduate courses.

The book is designed for students who are taking a preliminary course and presents a comprehensive overview of the foundations for couples, marriage, and family counseling, the skills and techniques needed, and special issues in couples, marriage, and family counseling. We know that one text cannot adequately address all the factors that comprise the complex and holistic aspects of assisting clients who seek the help of a counselor. We have, however, attempted to provide our readers with a broad perspective based on current professional literature and the rapidly changing world we live in at this juncture of the new millennium. The following overview highlights the major features of the text.

OVERVIEW

Many chapters contain case studies that illustrate the practical applications of the concepts presented. Most chapters refer the reader to websites containing information that supplements the information already presented. Professors may want to make use of the PowerPoints developed for each of the chapters, as well as the instructor's manual that can be used to develop quizzes and exams on the book's content and provides ideas for individual and small-group class assignments.

The text is divided into the following four parts: Essential Knowledge and Skills; Theories: History, Concepts, and Techniques; Couples Work; and Special Issues.

Part One: Essential Knowledge and Skills (Chapters 1 through 5) begins with information on variations in family systems and family life cycles and provides the reader with the contextual background needed to assimilate subsequent chapters. Chapters focus on using community genograms to position culture and context in family therapy; diversity and intercultural work; using research and evaluation approaches; and legal, ethical, and professional issues.

Part Two: Theories: History, Concepts, and Techniques (Chapters 6 through 11) presents information about psychodynamic, experiential and humanistic, Bowenian, structural, strategic and systemic, and behavioral approaches and applications to actual cases and case studies. All of these chapters provide overviews and introduce readers to the skills and techniques that can be used in the couples and family counseling process.

Part Three: Couples Work (Chapters 12 through 14) presents information relative to key issues and interventions in couples counseling, sexuality and gender in couples counseling, and counseling couples using life cycle and narrative therapy lenses. These chapters highlight information that has relevance and application to diverse contexts.

Part Four: Special Issues (Chapters 15 through 18) discusses filial play therapy and other issues related to parenting; addictions and family therapy; violence, abuse, and trauma in family therapy; and divorce and other loss issues in family therapy.

Every attempt has been made by the editors and contributors to provide the reader with current information in each of the areas of focus. It is our hope that *Foundations of Couples, Marriage, and Family Counseling* will provide the beginning student counselor with the basics needed for follow-up courses and supervised practice in the arena of couples and family work with clients.

ACKNOWLEDGMENTS

We would like to thank the 32 authors who contributed their expertise, knowledge, and experience in the development of this textbook. Publications occur within the context of the authors' lives and families. We would like to thank our families and the families of the authors who provided the freedom and encouragement to make this endeavor possible. Special thanks to those authors who contributed while also dealing with matters of life and death. Our thanks are also directed to members of the Wiley team, Senior Editor Rachel Livsey and Senior Editorial Assistant Amanda Orenstein, for their encouragement and assistance with peer review, copyediting, and, ultimately, the publication of the book.

PART 1

Essential Knowledge and Skills

CHAPTER 1

Variations in Family Systems and Family Life Cycles

David Capuzzi, Mark D. Stauffer, and Nicholaus Erber

Walden University

It is only during the past 40 to 50 years that couples, marriage, and family counseling and therapy have garnered the full attention of practitioners in the helping professions. Although Alfred Adler's work with families and communities began in Vienna 100 years ago, most of the emphasis in counseling, psychology, social work, and psychiatry has been on working with clients on an individual basis (Bitter, 2014). Starting with the work of Sigmund Freud, practitioners drew from the tenets of Jungian, existential, person-centered, gestalt, behavioral, cognitive-behavioral, rational emotive, reality, feminist, solution-focused, narrative, brief, dialectical, and numerous other theories that all primarily focused on one-to-one counseling and psychotherapy (Capuzzi & Gross, 2011; Corey, 2013). Most of these theories were based on values associated with individualism, autonomy, independence, and free choice and, for the most part, were well received in Western cultures (Bitter, 2014). In the 1950s and 1960s, family therapists and the application of systems theory began to challenge these notions.

SIDEBAR 1.1

Working with a family, especially when it is the entire family, results in a group counseling situation. The dynamics occurring in a family group session have both similarities and differences with those occurring in a group comprised of individuals who are not part of a family. If someone who was not a counseling professional, or who was new to the profession of counseling, asked you to describe the similarities and differences, what would you say?

One of the greatest challenges, if not transformations, a family therapist must make is to think systemically when observing, assessing, conceptualizing, and intervening within a family system. To undergo this transformation is to cultivate a dynamic systemic view rather than the linear cause–effect view that is predominant in Western culture. Most counselors understand that working with couples and families is quite different from individual counseling and psychotherapy because the client unit is not just the individual, but can be a dyad, a subgroup of a family, an entire family, or even multigenerational families. A more nuanced understanding is that a family counselor works with the family system even when there is only one individual in the therapy room. In addition, the counselor must think systemically throughout counseling in order to meet the client from his or her worldview. Unlike Western cultures, in collectivist cultures, interdependence, family connectedness, hierarchies of relationships, and even ancestral perspectives guide and inform the daily experiences of people. Adept counselors and therapists in Western cultures have realized that individuals cannot be viewed in isolation from the people and systems (family, neighborhood, school, work, social–recreational, church, etc.) with which they interact daily. Counselors and therapists have appropriately adopted systemic models as conceptual frameworks for couples and family counseling and place less reliance on theories designed for individual counseling and psychotherapy.

SIDEBAR 1.2

Systemic thinking directs the focus of the counselor or therapist away from the individual and individual problems toward relationships and relationship issues between individuals. A linear cause–effect reality does not exist, and the emphasis is on reciprocity and shared responsibility. The counselor does not ask *why*, but makes observations holistically to try to figure out what is going on between and among the members of the family. Patterns and power hierarchies are more important than intrapsychic and historical reasons for the behavior of family members.

Theorists, researchers, and practitioners such as Nathan Ackerman, Gregory Bateson, Murray Bowen, Oscar Christensen, Rudolf Dreikurs, Jay Haley, Don Jackson, Cloe Madanes, Monica McGoldrick, Virginia Satir, and Carl Whitaker are just a few of those associated with the development of the foundation for systemic work with couples and families. Currently, counselors and therapists are also beginning to incorporate the positions of professionals such as Tom Anderson, Harlene Anderson, Insoo Kim Berg, Steve de Shazer, David Epston, Kenneth Gergen, Harold Goolishian, William O'Hanlon, Michele Weiner-Davis, and Michael White in their efforts to assist couples and families seeking assistance (Bitter, 2014). Doing so has further expanded viewpoints about family systems and life cycles.

Before proceeding to a discussion of the differences between family function and dysfunction, the variations in family systems, the issues members of those systems may bring to a counselor or therapist, and some information about the life cycle of a family and needs often connected to this life cycle, it is important to point out that couples, marriage, and family counselors receive their training from programs with differing orientations. There are couples, marriage, and family counselors who receive their education and supervised practice in graduate programs accredited by the Commission on Accreditation for Marriage and Family Therapy Education (COAMFTE), the accrediting body for the American Association for Marriage and Family Therapy (AAMFT). There are also couples, marriage, and family counselors who receive their training in counselor education programs accredited by the Council for Accreditation of Counseling and Related Educational Programs (CACREP) and who are members of the International Association of Marriage and Family Counselors (IAMFC), which is a division of the American Counseling Association.

SIDEBAR 1.3

Identify a journal published by AAMFT and compare it with a journal published by IAMFC. What similarities and differences can you identify?

FUNCTIONAL AND DYSFUNCTIONAL FAMILIES

If the readers of this textbook were to survey the literature written during the past 30 or 40 years about what makes a family function well, they would discover a myriad of definitions, descriptions, and variations related to the topic of a healthy family system. So what are the characteristics of a family system that promote functioning, health, and well-being? The authors of this chapter found James Bitter's (2014) comments interesting and pertinent to the topic of functional versus dysfunctional families. He pointed out that family system theorists have used words such as functional, dysfunctional, healthy or unhealthy, normal or abnormal for decades, and he believes that, over time, these terms have taken on a pejorative connotation. He defines a *functional* family as a family in which family processes are successful in meeting the normal developmental demands as well the abnormal and unexpected stressors experienced by most families. He defines a *dysfunctional* family as one in which there has been a breakdown in coping or in which the family continues to engage in patterns that are no longer successful. What distinguishes Bitter's viewpoint is that he prefers to identify family processes or relational patterns as dysfunctional to avoid stigmatizing the family by labeling it as dysfunctional. The authors subscribe to this approach to understanding family dynamics and add that labeling a family or family member is not helpful; instead, professionals should try to understand and address patterns, behaviors, communication, and other elements of the family system that are unhealthy at a certain point in time in the family context.

Much has been written about functional versus dysfunctional characteristics of a family system. For example, Gladding (2007) listed the following functional characteristics:

- Commitment to the family and its individuals
- Appreciation for each other (i.e., a social connection)
- Willingness to spend time together
- Effective communication patterns
- High degree of religious/spiritual orientation
- Ability to deal with crisis in a positive manner (i.e., adaptability)
- Encouragement of individuals
- Clear roles (pp. 32–33)

Becvar and Becvar (2000), on the other hand, prefer to discuss family functionality in terms of process dimensions. They discuss healthy families as those in which there is a focus of authority that has been established and supported as time has passed, a set of rules that is established and consistently followed, an ample amount of nurturing, effective and clear child-rearing and couple maintenance expectations, a set of goals for the family and the individuals in the family, and enough flexibility and adaptability for the family to cope with developmental issues and unexpected crises.

A solid body of research suggests that family system dysfunction affects individual mental health and psychopathology and vice versa. Family system dysfunction leads to internalizing and externalizing family symptoms; for example, when unclear family boundaries create childhood anxiety and a child from that family, as an adult, carries the family symptom of producing anxiety in interpersonal relationships (Pagani, Japel, Vaillancourt, Côté, & Tremblay, 2008). To note how tangled this becomes in a system, Pinheiro and colleagues (2006) provide this comment on examination of cocaine addiction and family dysfunction: "The symptomatic child . . . becomes the 'battlefield' that keeps the issues of the mother–father relationship in denial, originating intergenerational alliances that separate parents, stimulate the competition between them, and predispose the child to alcohol and drug abuse" (p. 308). The centrality of the family in a culture may heighten or mediate the interplay between family system functioning and individual mental health. For example, research by Chen, Wu, and Bond (2009) suggests that not only is suicidality heightened when there is family distress or fighting but also such family discord may affect Chinese adolescents even more because of the centrality and weighted importance of family in Chinese cultures.

Although working with multiple members of the identified family may complicate conceptualizing therapeutic intervention, it also may provide reasonable avenues for positive change from the same therapeutic investment. One criticism of individual counseling is that the individual leaves counseling and often returns to the system that is not collaborating in therapy, placing the individual solely responsible for systemic shift. Furthermore, with one person in session it is harder for the therapist to explore all the family members' perspectives and conceptual frameworks.

VARIATIONS IN FAMILY SYSTEMS

The definition of what constitutes a family and a family system is ever changing and varies from culture to culture. In the past, European Americans defined *family* as including only those related by blood, and it was identified as the *nuclear family*. Other groups, such as African Americans, defined family in terms of a network of kin as well as community, and included anyone who was psychologically connected and categorized as a friend of long standing. Asian Americans include ancestors and all descendants in their definition of what constitutes a family (Gladding, 2007).

In 2010, the U.S. Census Bureau defined *family* as

> a group of two people or more (one of whom is the householder) related by birth, marriage, or adoption and residing together; all such people (including related subfamily members) are considered as members of one family. Beginning with the 1980 Current Population Survey, unrelated subfamilies (referred to in the past as secondary families) are no longer included in the count of families, nor are the members of unrelated subfamilies included in the count of family members. The number of families is equal to the number of family households; however, the count of family members differs from the count of family household members because family household members include any non-relatives living in the household.

As you might surmise, it is difficult to arrive at a definition of what constitutes a family. For the purposes of this book, our definition will be comprehensive and will include those who are connected via birth or psychological, economic, or historical ties. This definition includes those who marry or never marry, have children or never have children, adopt, are gay or lesbian, or families that are comprised of some other alternative constellation of individuals.

Turning the clock backward illustrates the changing nature of how people in the United States have perceived the definition of a family, especially when contrasted with current thinking about families and family systems.

Flashback to the 1950s

Sixty years ago there were not as many accepted family forms as there are today. Typically, families could be categorized into three subgroups, which are discussed next.

The Nuclear Family

A nuclear family consisted of a husband, a wife, and their children. Usually the husband worked outside the home and the wife worked inside the home, assuming a large percentage of the responsibility for parenting, completing household chores, and making sure the needs of all family members were met. This family form was idealized through television shows such as *The Adventures of Ozzie and Harriet* (which ran from 1952 to 1966) and *Leave It to Beaver* (which ran from 1957 to 1963). Generally, the characters that were promoted and popularized on television were the career-focused husband as the decision maker and the wife who was well-groomed at all times, supportive of her husband's efforts, and an excellent hostess, especially of events that would serve to promote her husband's movement up a career ladder. The image of a dual-career family or a unmarried couple living together with children was not promoted or even discussed to any great extent.

The Divorced Family

During the 1950s, divorce was an option, but it was not really approved of in the United States. The rising divorce rates in the 1960s and 1970s changed people's attitudes about permanent separation (Cherlin, 2010). In a divorced family, women were typically the custodial parents to any children resulting from the marriage. Women were likely to receive child support and alimony for a defined period of time, and they joined the workforce, moved back to their parents' homes with their children, or both. In many cases, as is true today, the family stayed in contact with the former spouse, who participated in parenting the children, at least to some extent. Divorced women were not well received and were referred to, askance, as *divorcées*. Although many divorced women remarried, others found that they were perceived to be flawed and not the best prospects for marriage.

The Stepfamily or Blended Family

In a stepfamily, or blended family, at least one of the two people who marry have children from a previous marriage. In the 1950s and 1960s, the term *stepfamily* was used; the term *blended family*, which has a more positive connotation, was not in wide usage until much later.

At the time, many people assumed that a stepparent could not parent as well as a birth parent, even if the stepparent was more stable and grounded and was very fond of the children brought into the family via marriage. The depiction of stepparents in fairy tales as unaffectionate and unaccepting of their spouse's children did not alleviate this misperception. As time has passed, Americans' views of family forms and constellations have changed dramatically.

Fast Forward to 2015 and Beyond

One way of tracking the changing views of what constitutes family in America would be to watch episodes of *Modern Family*. This television show debuted in 2009 and is an ensemble comedy that revolves around the experiences of three very different families: (1) a post-midlife man (Jay), his second (much younger) wife, her son from a previous relationship, and a son they had together; (2) Jay's daughter, her husband, and their three children; and (3) Jay's son, his husband, and their adopted daughter. The series chronicles the ups and downs of parenting (including parents talking to their teenagers about safe sex), marriage, and family relationships, and features a very accepting depiction of same-sex parenting.

SIDEBAR 1.4

Locate and watch some episodes of *The Golden Girls*. Would you classify the three women who shared a home in this television series as a family?

This is a very different depiction of families in America than would have been portrayed 60 years ago and is illustrative of the many family forms or types that exist today and are described next.

The Single-Parent Family

In a single-parent family, either a mother or father is raising children without a partner. During the past 30 years, divorce and nonmarital childbearing have dramatically increased the proportion of single-parent families in the United States (Wojtkiewicz & Holtzman, 2011). This change has precipitated a myriad of research on the short- and long-term effects of single parenting on the family system and the well-being of children raised in single-parent families (Golombok & Badger, 2010; Parent, Jones, Forehand, Cuellar, & Shoulberg, 2013).

Researchers and clinicians frequently refer to the difficulties and issues that many single-parent families face (Hornberger, Zabriskie, & Freeman, 2010). These issues are often related to the structure of the family (Parent et al., 2013) and whether it is headed by father or mother and whether the single-parent status is because of never marrying, divorce, death, military service, or some other reason. Financial insecurity, higher stress levels, school dropout, early childbearing, and nonmarital births have all been linked to single parenting (Wojtkiewicz & Holtzman, 2011). There is a lot of conflicting research, however, about whether single parenting really does negatively affect the children raised by a single mother or father (Hornberger et al., 2010). Some research shows that the children in single-parent families fare very well if they experience closeness as a family and feel a sense of accomplishment because they work through their difficulties.

The following case study illustrates some of the possible dilemmas a single parent might face. As you read it, think about what could be accomplished in counseling and how some of the described difficulties could be addressed and dealt with so the family would benefit and feel a sense of accomplishment.

The Case of Amy and James

Amy is the mother of James, a 5-year-old boy. Amy had James after a brief relationship with James's father, whom she is still in regular contact with to share custody of James.

Amy and James live in a small two-bedroom apartment that Amy found through another single-mother friend. Amy has several other friends who are also single parents. Amy works two part-time jobs and lives paycheck to paycheck. She receives some benefits from the Department of Social Services, such as food assistance, day care, and medical benefits, which help her make ends meet.

James started school this year, and Amy is going through a big adjustment. She had to take time off work to get him enrolled, which means she will lose a day's pay. James was nervous about starting school and Amy wanted to be there on his first day, but she had to be at work so he went to school from day care. As James progresses through kindergarten, Amy finds it difficult to help him with his homework because she is always working to provide for the two of them. James also has some difficulties in school, especially when other kids ask about his dad and why his mom and dad don't live together. James doesn't have an explanation to give.

Amy also struggles to have a social life as a single mother. She would like to go on dates, but she is worried that people will think badly of her for dating. Amy would like to go out for drinks with her friends after work for a short break, but she is worried she will be looked at negatively for going out. Amy often feels stuck because there is no end in sight for how hard she has to work to maintain a home for her and James. Amy seeks the help of a counselor to deal with the stressors of day-to-day life as a single parent.

If you were the counselor, how would you work with Amy and what goals would you hope to develop for the counseling process? Would you want James's dad to participate in the counseling process with Amy? At what point would you suggest that that couples counseling take place? How could you reframe the situation so Amy and James feel a sense of pride in working through their issues?

The Child-Free Family

This type of family results when a couple makes a conscious decision not to have children, or they cannot have children because of infertility or health-related reasons (Gladding, 2007). In 2007, Daniel Gilbert represented the thinking of many American couples when he wrote the best-selling book *Stumbling on Happiness*, in which he discussed the fact that many couples decide not to have children for personal, economic, career, and a variety of other reasons. This decision would have been considered almost bizarre in the 1950s, but increasing numbers of couples are making the decision not to have children because they feel it is congruent with who they are and that it would not be in the best interests of children.

Despite the decision to be childless, there is always the possibility that child-free couples will face many challenges from those around them (Pelton & Hertlein, 2011). Assumptions that the couple is infertile, dislikes children, disapproves of adoption or foster parenting, or that the individuals had unhappy childhoods are just a few of the attitudes the couple may be faced with and asked to explain. Many child-free couples encounter pressure, disapproval, and ostracism by their peers who are raising children. In addition, some child-free couples mourn the lack of a family as they age and question their earlier decision to remain childless. Although this type of family system is becoming more and more common in the United States and other countries, many child-free couples seek counseling because of pressures they experience.

The Same-Sex Couple Family

There is an abundance of recent research on the topic of same-sex couples with or without children (Armesto & Shapiro, 2011; Berkowitz, 2011; Byrn & Holcomb, 2012; Mallon, 2011; Parker, Tambling, & Franklin, 2011). As noted by Ausbrooks and Russell (2011), it is estimated that one in three lesbian couples and one in five gay couples are raising children. This, too, is a departure from what existed 60 years ago and is representative of the heterogeneity (Berkowitz, 2011) that characterizes contemporary American families.

SIDEBAR 1.5

Same-sex families were not in the public eye during the first half of the 20th century. If you were talking with someone born in the 1930s or 1940s and attempting to explain or describe that such a combination of adults and children constitutes a family, what would you say? How would you answer the person's questions about how the children would respond to inquiries they might receive about who was their father and who was their mother?

In addition, of the 250,000 children living in U.S. households headed by same-sex couples, 4.2% were either adopted or are foster children (Berkowitz, 2011); this also represents a development that is different than what existed in the past. Recently, three very interesting books, *Who's Your Daddy? And Other Writings on Queer Parenting* (Epstein, 2009), *Gay and Lesbian Parents and Their Children: Research on the Family Life Cycle* (Goldberg, 2010), and *Becoming Parent: Lesbians, Gay Men, and Family* (Riggs, 2007), address the topic in ways that might interest the readers of this book and highlight some of the issues faced by these couples. Gay and lesbian families are gaining more social acceptance in recent years as evidenced by the depiction of these types of families in mainstream television sitcoms and real-life situations. Despite this, gay and lesbian families continue to experience stigma and discrimination that increase stressors to family dynamics.

Living Apart Together Families

These families consist of couples who are married or in marriage-like relationships (with or without children) but who live in different households (Cherlin, 2010). Reports from national statistical agencies in the United States, Britain, Canada, and France indicate that living apart together relationships are relatively common, but they also suggest difficulties in conceptualizing and measuring the phenomenon (Cherlin, 2010). Much more research is needed about how the individuals in these family systems interact and communicate, since this type of family constitutes a growing demographic in the United States and in many other countries.

The Dual-Career Family

In dual-career families, each partner places a high priority on his or her career advancement and mobility. As noted by Gladding (2007), more than half of couples with children have careers to which they are highly committed. Some dual-career couples live apart and commute (living apart together) in order to satisfy their career aspirations. Some dual-income families are known as DINKS—dual income, no kids (Gladding, 2007).

The Netflix series *House of Cards* is a contemporary depiction of a dual-career family and the issues precipitated when two very career-minded individuals become a couple. The series is an interesting rendition of the issues such couples sometime face, the efforts members of such a dyad may make in order to foster and preserve their career aspirations, and the pressures and issues that such striving creates in the relationship. Kevin Spacey and Robin Wright do an excellent job of portraying a dual career couple caught up in the politics of the White House and the power wielded by those with money and influence in the Washington, DC, area of our country.

SIDEBAR 1.6

Watch a few episodes of *House of Cards* and list what rules you think the two main married characters followed in their relationship. What kinds of values do you think provide the underpinnings for how they view their careers and how they make career-related decisions?

An Aging Family

Aging families, characterized as headed by individuals aged 65 years or older, are often involved in the launching or relaunching of adult children, caring for their much older parents, planning for and transitioning to retirement, long-term marriages or partnerships, the loss of a spouse or partner, grandparenting, and, quite often, acting as parents to their grandchildren. Living on a diminished income and coping with the loss of lifelong friends are other adjustments that may need to be made by aging families.

Because the demographics of the United States are rapidly changing and the percentage of older adults in our country can be expected to continuously increase, counselors can expect to have more older adult clients than in the past.

The Multigenerational Family

In this type of family, more than one generation lives within the same household. Many young couples, whether married or cohabiting, live for a period of time in the household of one of their parents at the beginning of their union (Ghodsee & Bernardi, 2012). Goldenberg and Goldenberg (2002) estimated that by the year 2020, many American families will be comprised of four generations in a single household. Other examples of multigenerational households might include immigrants living with relatives during the time they adjust to a different culture and locate work, several generations living together because of a housing shortage or the high cost of housing, or unmarried mothers and their children living in their parents' homes. During periods of economic turndown, the number of multigenerational households can be expected to increase as families are forced out of their homes because of foreclosure after job losses.

As the reader might guess, a multigenerational living arrangement can lead to conflicts and other relational issues that need to be addressed, as illustrated in the following case study.

The Case of Joseph and Kalee Joseph and Kalee are a married couple in their 30s and they have three children: Brian, age 10; Alyssa, age 8; and Kyle, age 4. Joseph works in heating and cooling as a skilled worker, and Kalee works as a hairstylist. Several months ago, Joseph's parents fell into some financial problems and had to move in to Joseph and Kalee's house. Together, the family of seven lives in a three-bedroom house with an attached suite that Joseph built for his parents.

Joseph and Kalee both typically work normal business hours, but occasionally Joseph is called out on emergency repair jobs, and Kalee sometimes works late to accommodate her clientele. When Joseph's parents first moved in, space was limited, and the family had some difficulty adjusting. Together they solved this by pooling their resources and building the attached suite on the house. This was an almost ideal situation because Joseph's parents were able to provide live-in child care if Joseph or Kalee was unable to be home on time.

After several months, however, things were not going so smoothly. Joseph's father, Robert, had taken more and more of a paternal role in his grandchildren's lives. Robert was often disciplining the kids before Joseph or Kalee could intervene, and the adults in the household had very different disciplinary approaches to raising children. Joseph and Kalee both spoke with Robert and his wife, Mary, on several occasions, but the discussions seemed to go nowhere. The entire family presents to counseling to devise a plan so they can all live under one roof without damaging relationships.

If you were the counselor for this family, how do you think you would begin the session? Would you suggest goals for the family counseling process, or would you ask the family to establish goals for themselves? Why or why not? What, if anything, do you anticipate would be difficult for this family to discuss?

The Military Family

An estimated 3.5 million Americans comprise the active duty and reserve military armed forces in the United States (Office of the Deputy Under Secretary of Defense, 2012). Currently, there is increasing concern about lack of support for those returning after deployment and attempting to reintegrate into the mainstream of community and family life, as well as into the workforce. Military families face the same issues that other families face, but often resolution of these issues is complicated because of deployment and redeployment experiences.

The Transgender Family

A transgender family may be comprised of both adults and children. Often a transgender family is one in which one of the adults has decided to transition to the opposite gender. Such a transition can be confusing to many (e.g., the children in the family, neighbors, relatives, coworkers), and changing gender can precipitate the need for counseling connected with a variety of issues that were not previously part of the family dynamics. Because this is a type of family system that many people know little about, the following case study may prove helpful.

The Case of John and Melissa John has always felt as though he did not have the correct body and that he should be a woman. He remembers going to sleep as a child and hoping he would wake up a girl. John learned to push these feelings down, and he became hypermasculine. Eventually John married Melissa, and they had two children, RJ and Becky.

John shared his feelings with Melissa when they got married, but his feelings seemed to be put on hold when they got pregnant. John later decided he would like to start transitioning, but thought he would wait until RJ was 18 years old. However, they got pregnant again, and John was both happy and frustrated.

Once Becky was 11, John decided he would like to begin transitioning. He talked to Melissa, and together they told the kids. RJ (then 22) was immediately defensive and stormed out with his girlfriend, and they stayed away for a couple days. Becky cried a lot, but then started asking a lot of questions. John found a counselor to work with as he started the transition process. John eventually chose the female name Jennifer and began taking on a female persona.

The process of the transition was difficult and lengthy. Jennifer went through the courts to change her name and started taking hormones. Jennifer also began wearing female clothes and coming out to her coworkers, friends, and family. As Jennifer's identity became more prominent, her marriage to Melissa began to weaken. Melissa does not have good memories of the marriage and now does not know how to feel about Jennifer's transition. Melissa and Jennifer come to counseling to work on their relationship and determine the new roles in the relationship, or even if the relationship will continue. Jennifer would very much like to remain in the relationship, but Melissa is having trouble with the idea of having a wife instead of a husband. The stress is also taking its toll on the relationships with the kids. The entire family decides to go to counseling for help.

Do you think you would be able to counsel such a family? Why or why not? If you felt you could not do a competent job on behalf of this family, what would you do and how would this decision relate to the ACA code of ethics?

All of the previously described family types experience family life cycles over time. The next section provides a generalized description of what many families experience. As one might expect, however, no single description can account for variations caused by individual family characteristics and changes in society.

THE FAMILY LIFE CYCLE

Family life cycle theory describes the developmental stages a family usually experiences as time passes (Berge, Loth, Hanson, Croll-Lampert, & Neumark-Sztainer, 2011). A number of researchers and theorists have addressed the topic of the family life cycle; Evelyn Duvall (1977) was one of the first to draw this topic to the attention of practitioners. Duvall's model was based on the concept of the traditional nuclear family so popular in the 1950s and 1960s. Other professionals (Becvar & Becvar, 2000; Carter & McGoldrick, 1999; Gladding, 2007) have also addressed this topic.

One of the dilemmas inherent in describing the life cycle of a family is the fact that most depictions are stage theories and are linear in nature and those practicing couples, marriage, and family counseling think systemically and interactively. Stage theories, although helpful in assessing critical tasks that are usually experienced during a specified period of time, do not completely address the interpersonal relationships, power hierarchies, and family rules, and they provide only a snapshot of what transpires at a given time. In addition, they do not take into account the couple or family's interaction with the systems around them, variances from family to family, the impact of culture, and the many forms or types of families found in the United States and other countries today. That being said, subsequent discussion of the topic will provide the reader with an outline of the normal, developmental stages of the family life cycle and the tasks and issues that need to be addressed at each stage.

The Single, Unattached, Young Adult

This stage is characterized by the necessity of facing the critical task of differentiating from the family of origin and developing a new relationship with parents. Both the young adult and parents may experience some starts and stops as the young adult transitions to a more independent lifestyle and parents adjust to letting go of control. The young adult may further develop peer relationships, experiment with the establishment of a career, and assess whether a marital relationship is the option of choice.

Many young adults choose to live with someone of the same or opposite sex and gain experience with maintaining a day-to-day relationship with the same person. This is very different than what the norm was 50 or 60 years ago, and it provides couples with a rehearsal prior to making a marriage commitment. It is during this time that some young adults experience pressure to marry, which can be internally, as well as externally, imposed. In some cases, issues connected with lack of ability to separate from the family of origin or with difficulty in maintaining even short-term relationships can precipitate the need for counseling.

The New Couple

In the past, this second stage of the family life cycle could easily be labeled "the newly married couple," but because so many couples live together without being married, such a label would be a misnomer today. This is the stage during which both individuals adjust to what they think will be a long-term relationship, work through their idealized perceptions of each other, make room for their partner in each of their families of origin, and further develop career goals.

This stage could last anywhere from a few months to a few years and often involves a series of role modification expectations. Marriage may or may not occur during this early stage of the family life cycle, and, based on the laws in a particular state, if a marriage does take place, it could be between two people of the same or opposite genders. Issues, if they arise, can relate to a myriad of topics inclusive of changing perceptions and roles, lack of acceptance in families of origin, the beginnings of career competition between the individuals in the relationship, and conflicts over the importance of making a marriage commitment.

SIDEBAR 1.7

Interview a new couple and ask them about some of the adjustments they have had to make since moving in together. These could be related to living together, pressures experienced from their respective families, and so on. Ask them to identify which of these adjustments could precipitate a decision to seek couples counseling. Evaluate whether you think you could counsel a couple around the identified area. What kind of supervision do you think you would need?

Families With Very Young Children

Starting a family requires changes in routine, loss of freedom, the escalation of responsibility, and an alteration of lifestyle. One way of describing this stage would be to point out that the marital or couples system has to be adjusted to make room for a parenting role. In addition, the extended family must adjust to grandparenting during this stage. New parents, more likely than not, experience fatigue, a changed social calendar and less time available to spend with friends, interruption of career-related work habits, and the necessity to alter financial and other priorities.

Parenting requires around-the-clock responsibility for child care and safety. Unlike many of the neighborhoods of the 1950s and 1960s, neighborhoods today may be too traffic and crime ridden to allow children the free, unsupervised run of the neighborhood, and parents must drive children to activities and monitor many children's activities on a full-time basis. Many couples make play dates with parents of other children in their desire to make sure their preschool-aged children engage in age-appropriate activities with peers. Any of these responsibilities associated with child rearing could precipitate the need for couples or family counseling.

Families With School-Age Children

Allowing children to establish connections that parents are not involved in monitoring on a full-time basis often presents the biggest challenge for parents of children who are entering preschool, kindergarten, or first grade. Parents often have trouble letting go, even if children are only at school for part of the day, because up to this point, parents may have been with their children on a full-time basis. Even though most parents want to support their children's educational progress and extended socialization opportunities with peers, they worry about how the child will fare at school and may even experience feelings of loss. These feelings of loss may relate to the absence of the child in the home or under parental supervision on a full- or part-time basis, or they may relate to generalized feelings of loss of control. In many instances, parents experience even more demands on their time as the children express interest in participating in an increasing number of activities. Parents sometimes lose touch with each other as these demands crescendo.

As might be expected during this stage of the life cycle of a family, parents may struggle to balance responsibilities between work and home, and conflicts over child supervision can occur with more frequency as parental stress escalates. Sometimes one member of the parental dyad begins to feel overburdened, and confusion or arguments over whose career has priority may occur, especially if each adult is quite committed to climbing a career ladder. It is not unusual for any of these areas to precipitate the need for counseling.

Families With Adolescent Children

Adolescence can be a time of turmoil as children adjust to changing bodies and emotions. At times, parents attempt to delay this period of their child's development, especially during the "tween" years (ages 10 to 12), because seeing children mature can make parents more aware of the passage of time. Often parents spend time assessing their own achievements and career progress, and past feelings of uncertainty can be rekindled. Parents may simultaneously be dealing with their children's demands for independence and the realization that they themselves are now middle aged. Parents may have difficulty with the fact that they cannot expect to control everything their child says and does and maintain the set boundaries and limits of the past.

It is also during this period of time that parents may be expected to take responsibility for their own parents as the normal aging process limits the their autonomy or changes in physical or mental health create complications that must be addressed. Every reader of this book has heard the term *sandwich generation*, applied to the squeeze experienced by adults who are simultaneously parenting their own children and looking after aging parents. If anything, responsibility and stress escalate even more during this time in the life cycle of a family. Sometimes watching the capacities of aging parents diminish precipitates concern about individuals' own aging and vulnerability. Although many families experiencing this developmental stage cope well because of a history of good communication with one another, excellent time management skills, and grounded personalities, it is during this stage that many couples begin distancing themselves from each other and find that they need counseling if the relationship is to endure.

SIDEBAR 1.8

Now that you have read all but the last two descriptions of the stages of the life cycle of a family, identify the stage that was most challenging for you and share your thoughts about this with someone in your class. What were some of the adjustments or issues you faced and how did you cope with them? Do you think you are equipped to assist a family with similar adjustment issues? Why or why not? What do you need to do to be as prepared as possible? Ask a partner to share his or her feelings on the same questions.

Families With Children Who Are Launching or Leaving the Nest

Releasing children who are leaving for college, the military, or the workforce or who are entering relationships presents other challenges to families in this stage of the family life cycle. Finances may be of great concern because of the escalating cost of obtaining a college education. Many parents and their children go deeply in debt during this time period unless they have been setting money aside since their children were quite young. Parents of a child who has chosen to enter the military worry about deployment and whether their child will be injured far away from home or, even worse, killed in the line of duty. Parents of a child who enters a live-in relationship at a young age and prior to completing college or vocational preparation often worry about the financial well-being of their young adult child and feel obligated to contribute financially. When a young adult enters the workforce immediately after high school graduation, parents may be concerned about the potential for advancement and financial security of their child.

Families in Retirement and Later Life

During this stage, the family is usually comprised of a couple in their last years of employment or in retirement. The age range is 62 to 65 or older, although recent fluctuations in the financial markets have resulted in the postponement of what used to be the typical retirement age. In general, the ages of 65 to 74 are considered the "young old," 75 to 84 the "old old," and 85 and older the "oldest old." Currently, because of increasing longevity and the increasing percentage of the older adult population in the United States, older couples or widowed individuals may experience a myriad of problems because of factors such as:

- Loss of identity after retirement
- Dwindling finances and buying power
- Decreasing energy
- Grief reactions after the death of a spouse, partner, or long-term friend

- Chronic or terminal illness
- Escalating costs connected with assisted living facilities and skilled nursing care

There are many dilemmas that aging families face for which the assistance of a counselor could prove helpful. The following case study provides an illustration of what a family counselor or therapist may encounter.

The Case of Hattie and Felix

Hattie and Felix are a couple in their 70s and they have been married over 40 years. Felix retired from a blue-collar job working in a lumber company, and Hattie has been a homemaker since she married Felix. Hattie and Felix have lived in the same house for 30 years and it is paid off, but the neighborhood is not as nice as it once was, and the value of their home has dropped considerably. Many of their friends and neighbors have passed away or moved into assisted living, and they do not know very many people in their neighborhood anymore. Felix's parents are both deceased, as well as Hattie's father. Hattie's mother lives in assisted living and is barely able to afford this on her social security. Hattie and Felix lost a lot of their retirement in poor financial decisions and now primarily depend on social security as well. Finances between the three adults are often shared to make up differences.

Hattie and Felix have two adult children: Kim, age 39, and Greg, age 36. Kim is married to David and they have one son, Brayden, age 3. Kim and David live several hours away in a larger city. Greg is unmarried and working on his doctorate in another state. Hattie and Felix do not get to see their children or their grandchild except on holidays, because their children are busy and have family and professional commitments.

Recently, Felix was diagnosed with prostate cancer and is reluctant to proceed with care. He often experiences sleepless nights and feels tired all day, most days of the week. Felix has become short-tempered with Hattie and has not disclosed his diagnosis to her as of yet. He is worried about medical costs because neither of them has signed up for their Medicare supplemental coverage and they would be responsible for a large portion of the cost of treatment. Hattie has been talking with Kim, her daughter, about how Felix has been acting, and Kim called the counseling office to make an appointment. All three adults, Kim, Hattie, and Felix, present to the first session.

If you were the counselor for this family, it is unlikely that you would know, at the time counseling began, about Felix's diagnosis. How would you begin working with this family and what might you hope to accomplish?

Additional Factors Affecting the Life Cycle of a Family

There are issues that may arise in the life cycle of a family in addition to those previously discussed. For example, the birth of a child with a disability could require the family to develop specific coping skills for each stage of the family's life cycle. Parents may experience feelings of grief, loss, and self-blame when the infant or very young child is diagnosed with a disability. The necessity for special education and other school-related support may cause parents and siblings to wish their child or sibling was just like other children who did not need accommodations. Delayed exiting from the K–12 educational system could precipitate resentment and feelings of being different. As another example, the onset of a chronic or terminal illness of family member may precipitate issues around responsibility for caregiving and caregiver fatigue, medical expenses, reduction in family income, and the overall quality of family life.

The varying traditions of certain ethnic or racial groups can also be a complicating factor connected with one or more stages of the family life cycle. The following case study is one example.

The Case of an Interracial Family

Javier is from Argentina and Sakiya is from Japan. They met while in graduate school in the United States and decided to stay in the country. They originally lived in an urban area with a lot of diversity, but they decided to move into a suburban area once they got married and wanted to start having children. The neighborhood they moved into is primarily White and African American. They both feel disconnected from their culture because of the lack of cultural similarities in their current community.

Javier and Sakiya's children are 3 and 5 years old. One time when Javier had the children with him at a grocery store, a woman stopped him on his way out and asked if the children were his. Another time, when both parents were at the school to register their older child for school, the school administrator asked where they adopted their children.

Javier and Sakiya struggle with a decision to see a counselor because they both feel families should handle their own issues, but for different reasons. Javier feels the individual family unit should handle the issue, while Sakiya feels they should both talk to her parents. After many lengthy talks and arguments, the couple decides to seek help from a counselor.

Given what you know about multicultural competencies and issues, what principles would guide you as you worked with his couple?

SUMMARY

Couples, marriage, and family counseling is a rapidly growing specialization within the profession of counseling. Because working with a couple or a family focuses on relational issues and the patterns of relating that family members employ, emphasis during the counseling and therapy process is systemic and holistic rather than linear and individual. The theory and research that a couple, marriage, and family counselor draws from is quite different than the classic theories developed for use in classic individual counseling and psychotherapy. The requisite education and supervised practice required for family counseling can be obtained from programs subscribing to the standards promoted by either the IAMFC or the AAMFT.

Whether a family engages in relational patterns that are functional or dysfunctional, the types of family systems that a counselor may encounter in 2015 and beyond are quite varied and diverse when compared to what were typical and acceptable 50 or 60 years ago in the United States. Even though stage theories only provide a general idea of what families experience during a specific period of the developmental cycle, counselors can anticipate the kinds of adjustments and issues that families may need to address in the context of counseling, depending on how they cope with those life cycle challenges.

USEFUL WEBSITES

The following websites provide additional information relating to chapter topics.

http://www.helpguide.org/mental/blended_families_stepfamilies.htm
http://blended-families.com/
http://www.rainbowrumpus.org/
http://www.lgbtfamilies.info/Welcome.html
http://www.algbtic.org/
http://www.aarp.org/home-family/caregiving/
http://www.aoa.gov/AoARoot/Index.aspx
http://www.grandparents.com/family-and-relationships/family-matters/when-families-live-together
http://www.grandparents.com/american-grandparents-association
http://www.aamft.org
http://www.iamfconline.org/
http://www.pflag.org

REFERENCES

Armesto, J. C., & Shapiro, E. R. (2011). Adoptive gay fathers: Transformations of the masculine homosexual self. *Journal of GLBT Family Studies*, 7(1–2), 72–92.

Ausbrooks, A. R., & Russell, A. (2011). Gay and lesbian family building: A strengths perspective of transracial adoption. *Journal of GLBT Family Studies*, 7(3), 201–216.

Becvar, D. S., & Becvar, R. J. (2000). *Family therapy: A systemic integration* (4th ed.). Boston, MA: Allyn & Bacon.

Berge, J. M., Loth, K., Hanson, C., Croll-Lampert, J., & Neumark-Sztainer, D. (2011). Family life cycle transitions and the onset of eating disorders: A retrospective grounded theory approach. *Journal of Clinical Nursing*, *21*(9–10), 1355–1363.

Berkowitz, D. (2011). "It was the Cadillac of adoption agencies": Intersections of social class, race, and sexuality in gay men's adoption narratives. *Journal of GLBT Family Studies*, 7(1–2), 109–131.

Bitter, J. R. (2014). *Theory and practice of family therapy and counseling*. Belmont, CA: Cengage.

Byrn, M. P., & Holcomb, M. L. (2012). Same-sex divorce in a DoMa state. *Family Court Review*, *50*(2), 214–221. doi:10.1111/j.1744-1617.2012.01445.x

Capuzzi, D., & Gross, D. R. (2011). *Counseling and psychotherapy* (5th ed.). Alexandria, VA: American Counseling Association.

Carter, B., & McGoldrick, M. (1999). *The expanded family life cycle* (3rd ed.). Boston: Allyn & Bacon.

Chen, S., Wu, W. H., & Bond, M. (2009). Linking family dysfunction to suicidal ideation: Mediating roles of self-views and world-views. *Asian Journal of Social Psychology*, *12*(2), 133–144. doi:10.1111/j.1467-839X.2009.01280.x

Cherlin, A. J. (2010). Demographic trends in the United States: A review of research in the 2000s. *Journal of Marriage and Family*, 72, 403–419. doi:10.1111/j.1741-3737.2010.00710.x

Corey, G. (2013). *Theory and practice of counseling and psychotherapy* (9th ed.). Belmont, CA: Cengage.

Duvall, E. (1977). *Marriage and family development* (5th ed.). Philadelphia, PA: Lippincott.

Epstein, R. (2009). *Who's your daddy? And other writings on queer parenting*. Toronto, CA: Sumach Press.

Ghodsee, K., & Bernardi, L. (2012). Starting a family at your parents' house: Multigenerational households and below replacement fertility in urban Bulgaria. *Journal of Comparative Family Studies*, *43*(3), 439–459.

Gilbert, D. (2007). *Stumbling on happiness*. New York, NY: Vintage Books.

Gladding, S. T. (2007). *Family therapy: History, theory, and practice* (4th ed.). Upper Saddle River, NJ: Pearson.

Goldberg, A. E. (2010). *Gay and lesbian parents and their children: Research on the family life cycle*. Washington, DC: American Psychological Association.

Goldenberg, H., & Goldenberg, I. (2002). *Counseling today's families* (4th ed.). Pacific Grove, CA: Brooks/Cole.

Golombok, S., & Badger, S. (2010). Children raised in mother-headed families from infancy: A follow-up of children of lesbian and single heterosexual mothers, at early adulthood. *Human Reproduction*, *25*(1), 150–157. doi:10.1093/humrep/dep345

Hornberger, L. B., Zabriskie, R. B., & Freeman, P. (2010). Contributions of family leisure to family functioning among single-parent families. *Leisure Sciences*, *32*(2), 143–161. doi:10.1080/01490400903547153

Mallon, G. P. (2011). The home study assessment process for gay, lesbian, bisexual, and transgender prospective foster and adoptive families. *Journal of GLBT Family Studies*, *7*(1–2), 9–29. doi:10.1080/1550428X.2011.537229

Office of the Deputy Under Secretary of Defense (Military Community and Family Policy). (2012, November). *2011 demographics: Profile of the military community*. Retrieved from http://www.militaryonesource.mil/12038/MOS/Reports/2011_Demographics_Report.pdf

Pagani, L., Japel, C., Vaillancourt, T., Côté, S., & Tremblay, R. (2008). Links between life course trajectories of family dysfunction and anxiety during middle childhood. *Journal of Abnormal Child Psychology*, *36*(1), 41–53. doi:10.1007/s10802-007-9158-8

Parent, J., Jones, D. J., Forehand, R., Cuellar, J., & Shoulberg, E. K. (2013). The role of coparents in African American single-mother families: The indirect effect of coparent identity on youth psychosocial adjustment. *Journal of Family Psychology*, *27*(2), 252–262. doi:10.1037/a0031477

Parker, M. L., Tambling, R. B., & Franklin, L. L. (2011). Family therapy with GLBT youths: Kite in flight revisited. *Journal of GLBT Family Studies*, *7*(4), 368–387.

Pelton, S. L., & Hertlein, K. M. (2011). A proposed life cycle for voluntary childfree couples. *Journal of Feminist Family Therapy: An International Forum*, *23*(1), 39–53.

Pinheiro, R., Pinheiro, K., da Silva Magalhães, P., Horta, B., da Silva, R., Sousa, P., & Fleming, M. (2006). Cocaine addiction and family dysfunction: A case-control study in southern Brazil. *Substance Use & Misuse*, *41*(3), 307–316. doi:10.1080/10826080500409167

Riggs, D. W. (2007). *Becoming parent: Lesbians, gay men, and family*. Tenneriffe, Australia: Post Pressed.

U.S. Census Bureau. (2010). *Current population survey (CPS)—definitions*. Retrieved from http://www.census.gov/cps/about/cpsdef.html

Wojtkiewicz, R. A., & Holtzman, M. (2011). Family structure and college graduation: Is the stepparent effect more negative than the single parent effect? *Sociological Spectrum*, *31*(4), 498–521. doi:10.1080/02732173.2011.574048

CHAPTER

2

Using Community Genograms to Position Culture and Context in Family Therapy

Sandra A. Rigazio-DiGilio and Hyeseong Kang

University of Connecticut

INTRODUCTION

Family counselors view issues of health, distress, and disorder from an ecosystemic perspective that encompasses individuals as they develop within families that reside within intercultural communities. Individuals, families, and communities are seen as both unique systems and as participants in wider interactive systems. Subscribing to this perspective has direct implications for counselors and counselors-in-training. First, they need a *conceptual framework* that incorporates individuals, families, and communities and the relevant cultural and contextual factors operating within and across these systems. Second, they need a *therapeutic framework* with guidelines for weighing the relevance of each system and of each factor with respect to the difficulties that clients experience. Third, they need a *therapeutic approach* for accessing resources and facilitating change within and across these systems (Rigazio-DiGilio, 2000). These implications can be daunting, and various tools exist that counselors can use to understand and intervene within the multiple layers of human and systemic existence.

This chapter introduces one such tool: the community genogram (Rigazio-DiGilio, Ivey, Kunkler-Peck, & Grady, 2005), a graphic interactive assessment and treatment device used by counselors and clients (i.e., individuals, partners, families, significant others, or wider systems and networks directly or indirectly participating in the therapeutic process) to collaboratively explore cultural and contextual factors that have contributed and are contributing to the difficulties prompting treatment. By using community genograms, counselors and clients can examine how difficulties develop over time and across contexts and can identify and activate relevant individual, family, and community resources. Specifically, this chapter: (a) focuses on using community genograms to understand clients as they develop over time and across the various communities within which they live, and (b) provides guidelines and examples for how to construct and use basic community genograms in ways that bring clients' multiple lived experiences to the forefront of the therapeutic exchange and that identify client, therapy, and community strengths and capacities that can be brought to bear throughout counseling. To position the community genogram within the wider backdrop of graphic devices, we begin with a review of some mainstream approaches that served as a basis for its construction and use.

MAKING THE INVISIBLE VISIBLE: THE EVOLUTION OF GENOGRAMS

> The counselor's theoretical assumptions about the nature and origin of emotional illness serve as a blueprint that guides his [/her] thinking and actions during psychotherapy.
>
> —Bowen, 1976, p. 42

Bowen introduced the *family diagram* in the late 1950s, a method for visually arranging information about extended family systems over several generations to demonstrate relational patterns and emotional processes for objective review and examination (Bowen, 1966). He designed it as a therapeutic approach that was consistent with the theory he developed through his clinical research with families (Bowen, 1978). The *process* used for gathering and discussing information reflected Bowen's assumptions about how change occurs, and the *content* represented in the diagram reflected the eight constructs core to his theory (see Chapter 8).

Over a decade later, the term *genogram* was introduced (Guerin & Fogarty, 1972) and soon became the common nomenclature used to classify graphic devices derived from Bowen's original work. The most recognized among these is the *family genogram*, which provided guidelines for constructing three-generational graphics in ways that enabled counselors and clients to examine patterns and worldviews transmitted from one generation to the next (McGoldrick & Gerson, 1985; McGoldrick, Gerson, & Petry, 2008).

Here we present the basic components of family genograms and provide an illustrative case example. This is followed by brief descriptions of two alternative formats that, along with the family genogram, have informed the construction of the community genogram.

Family Genograms

> [Family] genograms should be seen as a roadmap that, by highlighting certain characteristics of the terrain, guides us through the complex territory of family life.
>
> —McGoldrick et al., 2008, p. 19

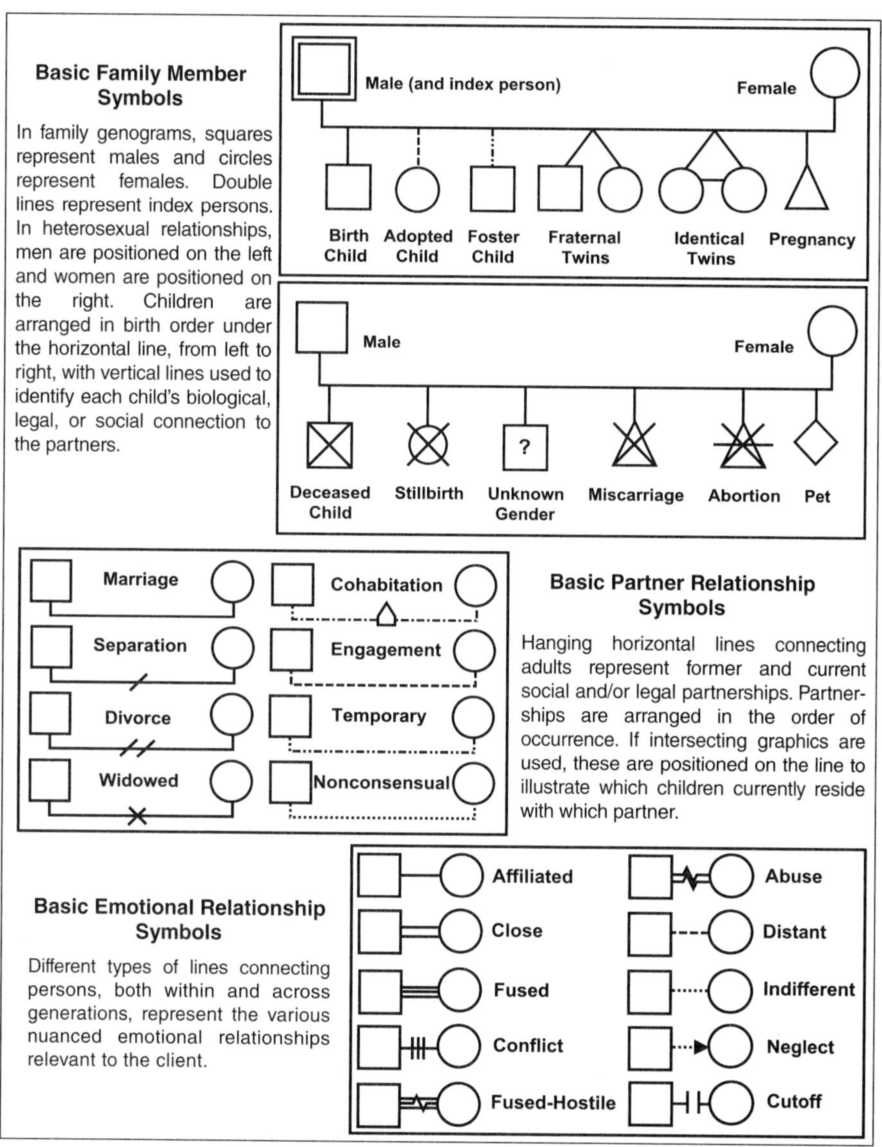

Figure 2.1 Illustrative Family Genogram Symbols and Rules

McGoldrick and Gerson (1985) introduced guidelines for conducting family genogram interviews, along with a set of symbols (see Figure 2.1) for visually arranging the information gathered from the family. The resultant family genogram could be used to illustrate how interactional patterns, emotional processes, and dominant themes take form, transmit, and replicate over at least three generations of an extended family system (McGoldrick et al., 2008).

The basic elements of a family genogram consist of information about the structure of the family and about relevant emotional processes and themes as depicted by the *index person* (i.e., the person from whose perspective the genogram is constructed). Information gathered typically includes: (a) family demographics; (b) biological, legal, and social connections; (c) significant life events and stressors; and (d) emotional relationships among family members. The graphic serves as a common point of reference for counselors and clients to examine presenting concerns from a broader temporal and contextual lens.

Illustrative Family Genogram: Donna

Donna (age 50) sought therapy to understand the circumstances surrounding her adoption and to determine whether to pursue stronger ties with members of her birth families. The rules and symbols depicted in Figure 2.1 were used to identify members of Donna's birth and adoptive families over three generations and to illustrate connections and emotional relationships that had been and are significant to her.

As illustrated in Figure 2.2, Jewel was unmarried when she gave birth to Donna at age 21. Despite marriage requests by Donna's birth father (Michael), Jewel conceded to her mother's expectations and relinquished parental rights. Michael and Jewel severed ties at that time. In addition, Jewel's relationship with her brother became and remained highly conflictual until Jewel's death at age 45.

After Jewel began her nursing career, she married Jordon, a professor. Together, they raised two birth children until their deaths, which occurred one year apart. Their children hold professional positions and have not had any significant partnerships. Michael married soon after Donna's adoption. He and his wife worked at the post office until her death at age 55 and his retirement at age 65.

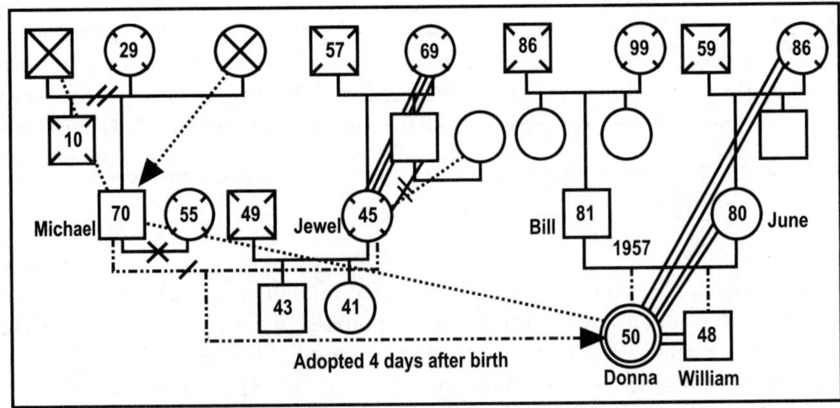

Figure 2.2 Illustrative Family Genogram: Donna

Bill and June adopted Donna four days after her birth, and William soon after. Donna positioned herself with her adoptive family members to illustrate her love and regard for them.

At age 22, Donna searched for her birth parents. By the time she located Jewel, she had already passed. She learned this from Jewel's brother, who agreed to speak with her and to arrange for her to meet with Jewel's biological children. The meetings with Jewel's brother, sister-in-law, and biological children were contentious, as this was the first time the children learned of Donna, and the stories told by Jewel's brother to explain her presence were threaded with negative overtones. Learning of her mother's passing and participating in these exchanges were emotionally draining experiences for Donna and delayed her search for Michael. At the time she began therapy, she had recently connected with him, and they were meeting approximately once or twice a year.

The family genogram was used throughout treatment. First, it helped identify options Donna could pursue to learn more about the circumstances of her adoption. She chose to prepare for meetings with Michael by developing questions to fit her current perceptions of his temperament and their distant relationship. Second, it was used as a backdrop to examine the stories Michael shared. This examination revealed how the intersection of core family values transmitted to Jewel through her mother (e.g., education and career) and societal norms dominant at the time of Donna's birth (e.g., pressure for unwed mothers to relinquish parental rights) limited Jewel's options. The examination also highlighted how significant losses throughout Michael's life (see Figure 2.2) served to shape his current disposition. Secondary gains that came out of the way she chose to approach Michael were the sense of comfort he felt to share stories and the sense of empathy these stories engendered in Donna. These emotions extended the foundation upon which they could build their relationship, prompting more frequent contact.

Donna then decided to make another attempt to reconnect with Jewel's children, using the same approach she relied on with Michael to solicit and share stories. She saw this as an experience that would inform her decision about whether to pursue stronger ties. Reviewing their stories through the same intergenerational lens revealed significant obstacles. First, her appearance several years prior reignited the uncle's hostile feelings toward his sister, which served to taint the stories told when they first met, as well as his responses to questions Jewel's children asked after those meetings. Thus, efforts to share multiple perspectives based on what Donna had learned were less than successful. Second, Jewel's life choices upheld intergenerational values that appeared to be directly transmitted to her children, as evidenced by their professional achievements and their disregard for others who did not accomplish the same—including Donna.

The last sessions were used to review the totality of Donna's genogram in relation to her therapy goals. She now identified Michael as a member of her family and looked forward to building stronger ties. She did not identify with the relationships, themes, and stories transmitted to Jewel's biological children by their uncle and did not feel appreciated or welcomed by them. Thus, Donna chose not to pursue stronger ties at this time.

SIDEBAR 2.1 CREATING AND INTERPRETING FAMILY GENOGRAMS

It is important for counselors to understand how their own life experiences influence their perceptions of the clients they serve. This increases their ability to listen to client stories without interpreting these from their own lenses. Family genograms can be used to help counselors understand their own families, learn ways to carefully listen to client stories, and practice organizing client information into pictures of extended family systems over the course of several generations.

Two students will be partnered to complete this exercise. Each student will:

- Request and review a free 14-day trial of GenoPro® (1996–2014), which provides more information, symbols, and instructions for creating and interpreting family genograms: http://www.genopro.com/free
- Obtain information from their family members to help them construct their own family genograms.
- Take turns serving as interviewers and interviewees. As interviewers, ask for information that can be used to create a family genogram for the interviewee (recording is recommended).
- Independently review the family genogram made by the interviewer. Indicate accurate and less accurate portrayals of information shared, and highlight familiar and new information about patterns, relationships, and themes that stand out.
- Discuss the independent reviews with their partners.

Submit reviewed family genograms and one-page reactions about the experiences of: (a) constructing these, (b) reviewing these, (c) practicing empathic listening and accurately arranging information heard within a visual display of a family genogram, (d) reflecting on ways personal lenses might impact empathic listening skills, and (e) reflecting on ways to use family genograms with clients.

Eco-Maps

Understanding interactions between families and their environments is a longstanding social work tradition. Hartman, a social worker and family counselor, developed eco-maps as a method for diagramming the ecological system of a family. These diagrams provide holistic insight into ways to coordinate services and resources for clients (Hartman, 1978).

Using genogram and other diagrammatic symbols, eco-maps illustrate: (a) the current composition and structure of a family, (b) the outside systems surrounding a family and the degree of influence each system has with respect to client difficulties, (c) the nature and type of connections between relevant systems and the family as a whole or specific family members (e.g., confirming or disconfirming perceptions, constraining or facilitative resources), and (d) the nature and type of connections occurring across the network of systems involved with the family. By visually diagramming these conditions, counselors and clients can examine the supportive connections to build on, the conflictual connections requiring mediation, and the gaps in connections that could be bridged to mobilize resources (Hartman, 1979).

Cultural Genograms

Because cultural experiences and values affect worldviews, attitudes, and behaviors multidimensionally, it is essential to understand the multiple aspects of clients' sociocultural identities. Hardy and Laszloffy (1995) developed cultural genograms to "promote cultural awareness and sensitivity by helping trainees understand their cultural identities" (p. 228). Cultural genograms: (a) illustrate how various aspects of culture influence families, and (b) help trainees explore how various aspects of their cultural identities inform their therapeutic style and effectiveness (Keiley et al., 2002; Warde, 2012). Although they were originally designed as a training tool, cultural genograms have been extended for use with clients (e.g., DeMaria, Weeks, & Blumer, 2014). As a therapeutic approach, it enables counselors to better understand clients' culturally constructed realities and discover how cultural experiences might impact clients' changing worldviews.

Genogram Variations

Efforts have been made to modify family genograms to account for larger cultural contexts and to consider how factors such as gender, ethnicity, and power contribute to the emergence, definition, and management of client difficulties (Becvar, 2005). For example, there are genograms that consider spirituality (e.g., Hodge, 2001) and other salient aspects of one's cultural identity, address wider systems (e.g., Kosutic et al., 2009), target underserved populations (e.g., Chen-Hayes, 2003) and specific clinical issues (e.g., Jordan, 2006), explore the intersectionality of multiple sociocultural identities across various contexts (e.g., Enns, 2010), and incorporate theoretical advances into therapeutic approaches (e.g., Goodman, 2013).

Some modified versions provide structured protocols intended to render reliable clinical information considered relevant for assessment and treatment planning, sometimes from one therapeutic lens, treatment modality, or manualized approach. According to Platt and Skowron (2013), such efforts make it possible to advance research on multigenerational family processes. Other versions provide collaborative semistructured or open-ended protocols intended to engage clients in selecting and illustrating relevant information in an order and manner meaningful to them. According to Fowers (1990), such collaborative approaches increase client participation in defining, managing, and monitoring treatment, which are factors known to be significant predictors of positive therapeutic outcomes (e.g., Friedlander, Escudero, & Heatherington, 2006).

COMMUNITY GENOGRAMS: CAPTURING THE COMPLEXITY OF CULTURE AND CONTEXT

> Community genograms are used to explore clients' cultural legacies, important episodes in clients' contextual and developmental histories, and untapped resources for change.
>
> —Rigazio-DiGilio et al., 2005, p. 11

The community genogram is derived from two concepts. First, the term *genogram* reinforces the importance of legacies and traditions for individuals and families, as these evolve over time. Second, the term *community* reinforces the importance of positioning these legacies and traditions within the wider interactive system comprised of individuals, families, and the wider community networks within which they have lived and now reside. Thus, community genograms widen the scope of assessment and the territory of intervention by expanding the understanding of clients within social and historical contexts.

Examining a graphic of this wider terrain makes it possible to identify: (a) relevant cultural and contextual factors that influence how clients come to understand and participate in their current communities, (b) factors now serving to constrain or enhance effective functioning across the multiple life spaces within which clients reside, and (c) positive strengths and resources existing within these wider terrains. Such examinations provide a multidimensional, nonpathological, and contextually contingent portrayal of the wider contexts within which client difficulties are embedded. This portrayal can reveal paths within the wider terrain that can be navigated to address clients' difficulties. By moving culture and context from the margins to the center of assessment and treatment, it becomes possible to generate multiple perspectives about the difficulties being experienced and to consider multiple options for accessing and activating strengths and resources that have been less available or underutilized within and across clients' multiple life spaces. These expanded visions also reveal issues directly related to: (a) clients' *sense-of-self, self-in-relation, and self-in-context*; (b) intra- and extrafamilial alliances and affiliations; (c) community and cultural resources; and (d) developmental and contextual histories.

Human and Systemic Development-in-Context: An Ecosystemic Perspective

The theory undergirding community genograms assumes that human and systemic development are best understood within a biopsychosocial/ecological framework comprised of a full spectrum of factors, from genetically determined processes to overarching cultural constructions (see Figure 2.3). The theory holds that

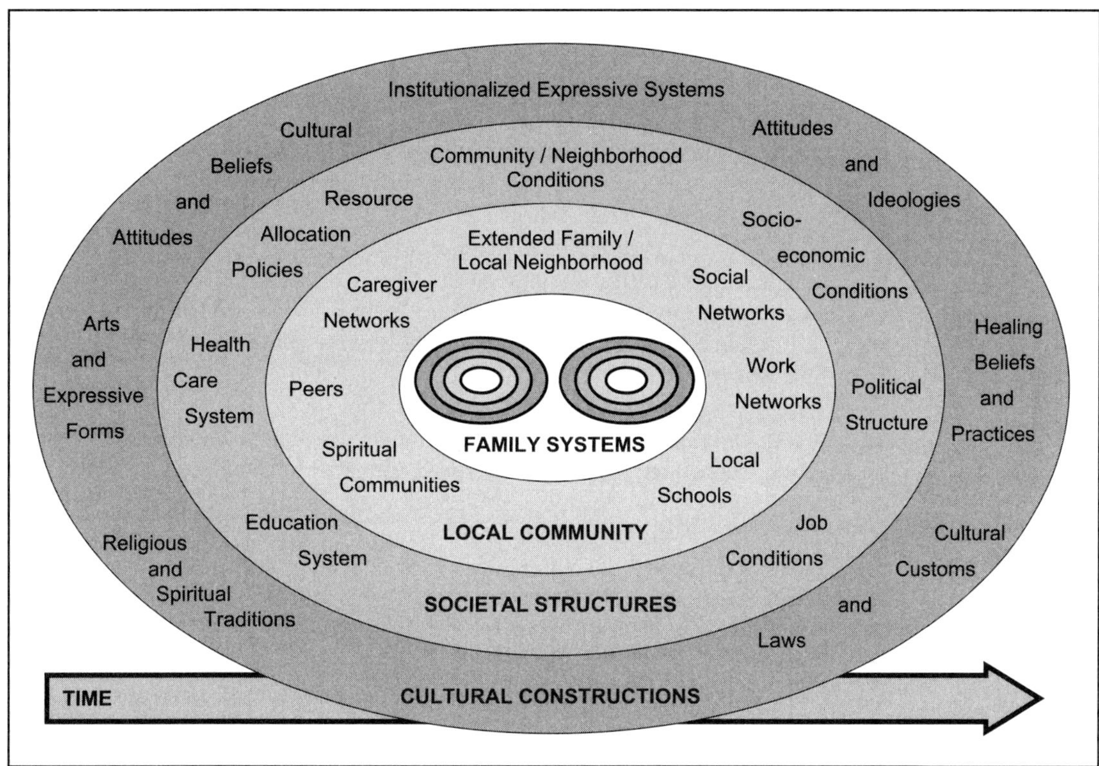

Figure 2.3 An Ecosystemic Life Span Perspective

individuals are embedded within family systems, which, in turn, are embedded in local communities positioned within geopolitical societal structures that are impacted by overarching cultural constructions. Where individuals and families have been and are currently positioned in relation to the dominant societal structures and cultural constructions shaping local communities significantly impacts their lived experiences and their conceptualizations of self, self-in-relation, and self-in-context.

Figure 2.3 consists of four concentric circles positioned on a timeline to represent the ecosystemic life span perspective. *Family systems*, located in the center, represent the patterns of interaction among members that have shaped and are shaping the shared narratives that define family members and the family as a whole. These intrafamilial dynamics have profound effects on the ways in which individuals and families experience, understand, and participate in their multiple life spaces.

As family members develop, the boundaries of the family extend to include various systems within the *local community* that influence different aspects of members' possibilities while constraining others. Families must attend to the psychosocial needs of their members and their own needs and cultural mores while balancing their participation within these systems.

The *societal structures* include dominant institutional, professional, and political systems impacting the ways in which communities are perceived and resources are allocated. These systems help define the expectations, beliefs, and practices that influence individual and family perceptions of everyday life and quality of life. If good schools, rich employment opportunities, full quality health care access, and ample resources are available, the probability of family members doing well increases. Conversely, when schools are underfunded, employment possibilities are slim, health care is variable, and resources are scarce, the probability of family members doing well diminishes.

The potential constraints and opportunities individuals and families experience also are influenced by the dominant *cultural constructions* of the time. Specific to clients, this overarching domain fundamentally shapes definitions of health, classifications of distress and disorder, and credible systems of management.

All four domains are evident every time clients enter treatment. Thus, subscribing to an ecosystemic life span perspective that widens the scope of assessment and the territory of intervention is a necessary first step toward becoming a family counselor. The community genogram is one tool counselors and counselors-in-training can use toward developing this perspective.

BASIC COMPONENTS OF STANDARD COMMUNITY GENOGRAMS

> To work with any individual or relationship without awareness of their unique developmental histories, family backgrounds, and cultural heritage in truth is to lessen their particularity and dignity.
>
> —Ivey and Ivey, 1999, p. 486

The standard community genogram takes the form of a star diagram that arranges information about: (a) clients, (b) influential family members and subsystems, (c) significant others and groups, (d) major cultural and community systems and events, and (e) particular client experiences within an ecosystemic framework. This diagram illustrates the predominant culture and society clients reside within or others they have previously navigated at significant points over the course of their life span.

As counselors and clients collaboratively develop graphic displays for particular life phases, a common point of reference emerges that is used to examine the ways in which relationships with relevant persons and positions within relevant systems contribute to, exacerbate, or help to alleviate the difficulties clients are experiencing when they enter therapy.

Individual Star Diagram

Figure 2.4 presents the basic components of an individual star diagram. Clients are positioned at the center of the star. The *embayments* surrounding the star comprise contexts deemed relevant by clients. The shape of each embayment illustrates how

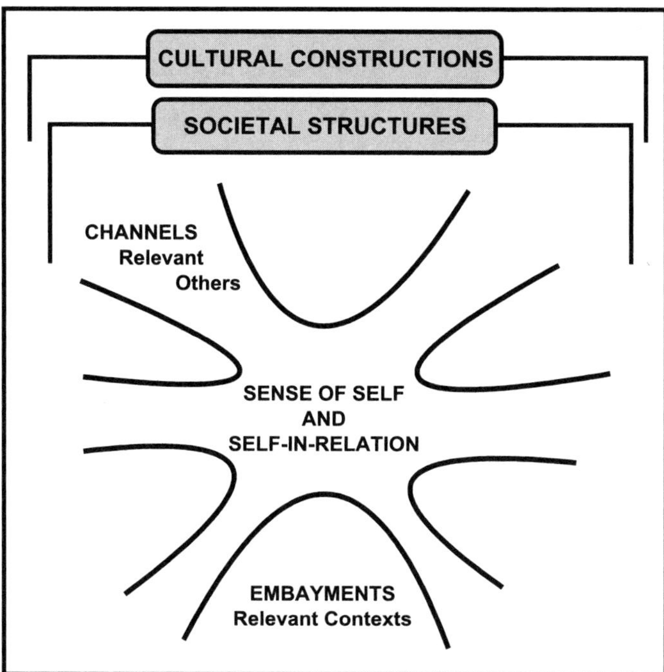

Figure 2.4 Basic Components of Individual Star Diagram

clients perceive the significance of each context. Others participating in these wider contexts who are significant to clients are situated at the end points of the star. The *channels* connecting these significant others to the client are depicted as broad, narrow, or closed off to illustrate how clients perceive the nature and scope of their exchange. Together, embayments and channels demonstrate how clients are uniquely positioned within wider contexts and the ways in which they navigate these contexts and those participating within these contexts.

Illustrative Individual Star Diagram: Ashley

After raising her children as a single parent, Ashley (age 78) reluctantly agreed to relocate to an assisted-living facility. She began therapy after a depressive episode, which was defined as an indication that the facility was not a conducive place for her. The embayments within her individual star diagram (see Figure 2.5) represent five events/circumstances she perceived as either positively or negatively impinging on her sense of connectedness to others and her sense of well-being (e.g., financial difficulties, physical impairment, family traditions and dynamics, religious beliefs, and new living situation). Ashley additionally identified shifting relationships as disconcerting, especially with regard to her two oldest children and her old friends. These are represented by the narrow channels connecting her to these two significant groups.

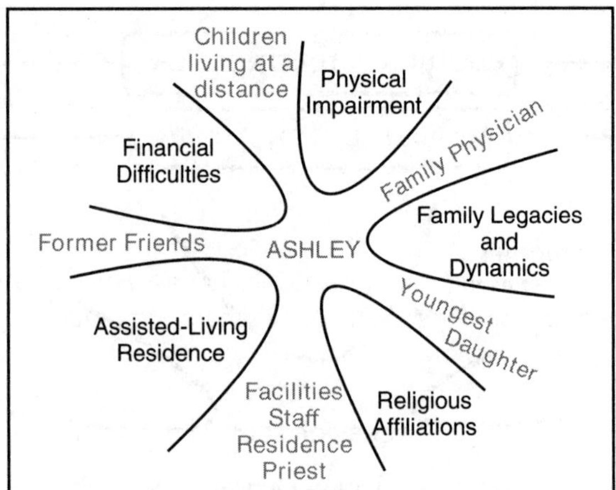

Figure 2.5 Illustrative Individual Star Diagram: Ashley

An examination of her community genogram emphasizes how the circumstances represented in three embayments (i.e., assisted-living residence, financial situation, and physical impairment) contribute to her sense of isolation. Using this aspect of the visual picture, Ashley could understand how social connections, physical challenges, and family traditions and dynamics all intersected and influenced her lack of connectedness to her new community.

Other visually available information emphasized the relationships that had not shifted (i.e., her relationship with her youngest daughter and with her long-term physician), which provided a small sense of comfort for her. In addition, the graphic emphasized how certain circumstances (i.e., assisted-living residence, religious affiliation) were prompting shifts in relationships that seemed more promising.

SIDEBAR 2.2 CONSTRUCTING YOUR OWN INDIVIDUAL STAR DIAGRAM

> By experiencing, naming, reflecting upon, and analyzing our narratives, the connection within our self-in-relation and family-in-relation contexts becomes more evident, and we develop a more profound appreciation of the interwoven fabric of our lives.
>
> —Rigazio-DiGilio et al., 2005, p. 71

This exercise provides an opportunity to move from theory to practice by creating a community genogram using the individual star diagram to visually represent a significant time period in your own life. For this activity:

- Select a time in your life when your cultural identity truly broadened.
- Use a large sheet of paper to visually represent your broad culture and community for the time period selected.

- Draw a large circle that represents your specific life space within the larger community. It can be positioned anywhere on the paper, depending on how you perceive your position for the time period selected.
- Place yourself at the center of your circle, designating the middle of the individual star diagram you will create.
- Working along the outer edge of the circle, write in the names of the significant persons (e.g., mother, minister, best friend) or groups (e.g., parents, siblings, friends, teachers, community groups) who were influential during the time period selected.
- Place them around the circle to represent their relationships with one another.
- Place the most important and significant influences and experiences within the embayments protruding from the outer circumference into the middle of the circle.
- The size and length of each embayment should represent the degree of significance these influences and experiences had for the time period selected.
- As you draw these embayments, consider the channels that are being formed, taking care to represent the degree to which you were interacting with, influencing, and being influenced by the individuals, relationships, and groups you identified.
- Write a one-page narrative describing what you have attempted to illustrate in your individual star diagram.

Relational Star Diagram

Figure 2.6 presents the basic components of a relational star diagram, which is used with individuals who together form a relational system (e.g., partners, families, therapeutic relationships). Members belonging to the relational system are first represented within their own individual star diagram, which includes: (a) *embayments* to depict the degree of significance they ascribe to contexts that are relevant to them, and (b) *channels* to depict the nature and scope of their exchanges with significant others participating in these contexts. These individual stars are then brought together in a graphic that illustrates how members identify: (a) the relevant contexts and significant others that comprise their relational system (e.g., the embayments and channels contained in the gray area depicted in Figure 2.6); (b) the relevant contexts and significant others that, while contributing to a member's sense of self, are not directly contained within the relational system (e.g., the embayments and channels that fall outside of the gray area); and (c) the contexts that are relevant to both members in different ways and through different affiliations (e.g., the embayments and channels that are partially positioned within the gray area). Thus, the relational star illustrates relevant contexts and significant

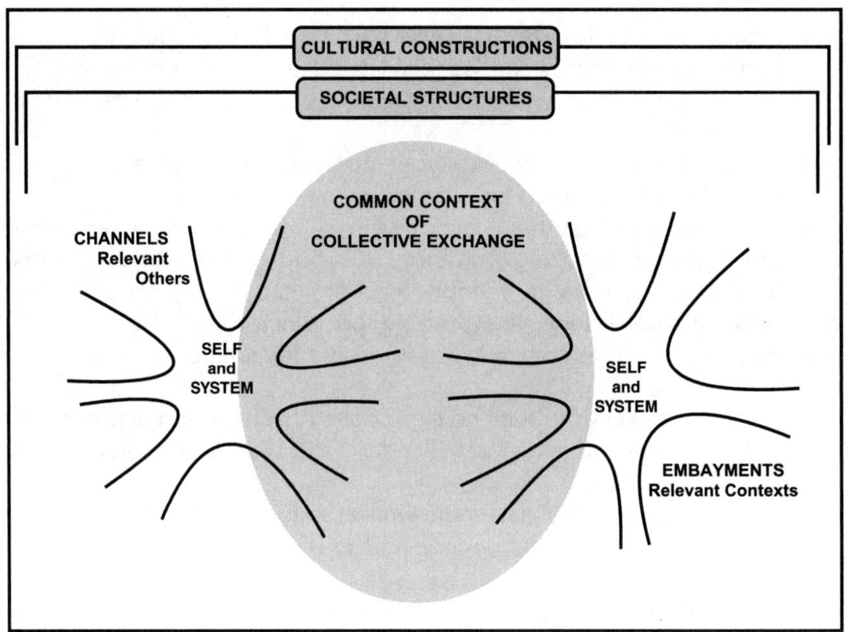

Figure 2.6 Basic Components of Relational Star Diagram

others that contribute to the ways in which members define their sense-of-self and sense of self-in-relation to others, both inside and outside of the relational system.

Illustrative Relational Star Diagram: Dana and Minsoo

At the time Dana and Minsoo entered therapy, they had been married for 23 years and raised two children, Yunseo (age 21) and Hyeon (age 17). Figure 2.7 presents their star diagram developed during treatment, which is referred to later in the chapter. We introduce the diagram here for two reasons. The first is to illustrate the amount of information that can be arranged in a relational star so that the multidimensional cultural and contextual factors portrayed remain in the foreground throughout the counseling process. The second is to emphasize the range of factors family counselors need to consider so that seemingly idiosyncratic individual, partner, and family beliefs that are, in fact, expressions of larger heritages and practices can be recognized as such and accounted for in treatment.

Core aspects of Minsoo and Dana's diagram reflect values and beliefs that took form in South Korea as families learned ways to adapt to and overcome tremendous hardships across centuries of foreign invasions, internal power struggles, rebellions, and more. These values and practices are metaphorically expressed in artistic and folkloric traditions that reflect wider cultural constructions defining the resilient capacities of this small nation. Thus, it would be expected that core elements of their current diagram would be represented in

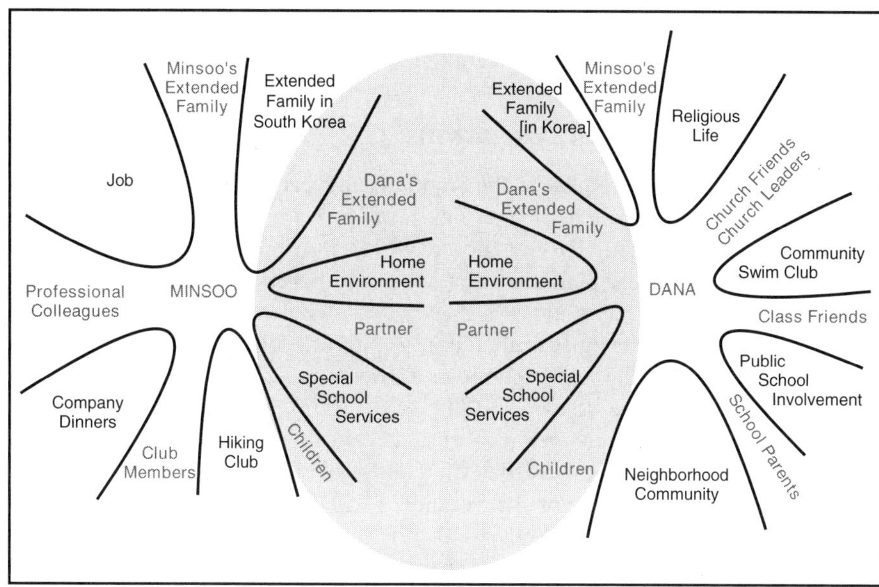

Figure 2.7 Illustrative Relational Star Diagram: Dana and Minsoo

narratives about their earlier lives. This can be seen when one juxtaposes elements of a story shared about their circumstances 15 years earlier with the visual graphic depicted in Figure 2.7. At that time, the family moved to the United States in pursuit of Minsoo's MBA degree. After receiving his degree, Minsoo accepted a position in Korea while Dana remained for 3 more years so their children could complete U.S. educational programs. In Korea, parents of transnational families who live apart for the purpose of securing quality education for their children are referred to as *kirogi* (wild geese) families. This unique family makeup is increasing among Korean middle- and upper-class families imbued with aspirations for education in a globalized world.

Stories shared included examples of how they worked within their separate local communities during this time. For example, Minsoo worked exceptionally hard in order to cover his family's living and tuition expenses. This required the devotion of his energies to his job, where he spent 12 to 14 hours a day. This, combined with his absence in the day-to-day lives of his family, contributed to a sense of loneliness and isolation, prompting him to become more involved with work colleagues and recreational activities. Dana's efforts to create a home and community environment for their children included becoming involved with neighborhood families raising children similar in age to Yunseo and Hyeon. As with Minsoo, her isolation from him and the extended family prompted her to affiliate with her church community and to engage in recreational activities. She also made connections with Hyeon's teachers by participating in volunteer positions at his school, in an effort to support their son when unanticipated and increasing learning challenges alienated him from his peers and Dana. Despite their best efforts to follow honored traditions, Dana and the children had to return home prematurely due to financial constraints and Hyeon's difficulties in the U.S. educational system.

Community Genogram Variations

Although star diagrams represent the standard approach for visualizing complex intersectionalities involving an array of cultural and contextual factors, the actual graphics used are limited only by the creativity and imagination of clients and counselors. Similar to star diagrams, graphic variations encourage clients to depict and narrate their life stories in ways that are most meaningful to them (Becvar, 2005). These can range from abstract ideas to concrete objects and should carefully consider the clients' life experiences and the language they use during the therapeutic exchange (see Rigazio-DiGilio et al., 2005). For example, all members of the Rojas family constantly referred to their "unproductive circles of communication." Drawing from this narrative, the counselor suggested that they consider creating a community genogram using circles or wheels. Because the parents owned a used car dealership, members decided to construct a graphic using the wheels of a car. As members acted together on the graphic, they noticed that the predominant theme of "what goes around, comes around," which they all believed constrained productive conversation and decision making, was only one of several themes depicted in their final design, allowing other less familiar themes to gain prominence. One theme that served to expand perceptions and options referred to wheels that rotated in a counteractive fashion, allowing drivers to discover different routes that now seemed plausible to travel.

USING COMMUNITY GENOGRAMS TO EXTEND CLIENT PERSPECTIVES

Community genograms provide a method and format for counselors and clients to consider ways in which cultural and contextual factors have contributed and are contributing to the difficulties prompting therapy. The fundamental goal is to introduce a wider context that facilitates a shift in clients' perceptions of themselves as *encapsulated identified patients* to people who are experiencing difficulties that are inextricably intertwined with forces in their wider sociocultural environment. Doing so strengthens their sense of self-in-relation and extends their focus to include resources in their wider environment. Community genograms portray vast amounts of client information in a concise, usable, and personalized format that serves as a common point of reference for counselors and clients to carefully consider issues generally not positioned in the foreground of family treatment. By capturing salient cultural and contextual information that can be interpreted in multiple ways and by multiple persons, community genograms can be used continuously throughout treatment to identify and activate new resources. It is generally acknowledged that relevant cultural and contextual factors identified early on in therapy can easily fade to the background as immediate concerns compete for attention during the therapeutic process. Many counselors prominently display these graphics over the course of therapy so that relevant factors within the broader contexts are always accessible and can be easily retrieved.

When used in the early stages of assessment, community genograms uncover numerous options to consider. In treatment, the systemic and contextual aspects of community genograms can be used to stimulate discussion, exploration, enhancement, and transformation of intrafamilial and extrafamilial relationships. By analyzing the graphics, clients are moved from relying on familiar perspectives and ways of functioning to new perspectives that open a wide array of options to guide solution-oriented points of view and actions for change. Through these explorations, clients enhance their sense of self-in-relation and family-in-relation and begin to think differently about their presenting problems and about using untapped community resources. The use of community genograms as an interactive assessment and treatment device is explained next.

Phase 1: Orientation

Most clients will not be familiar with community genograms, so orienting them to the process is an important first step. Oftentimes, counselors share their own community genograms, focusing on key relationships and experiences from their past that contributed to their decision to become a counselor. This introduces the information that will be explored, demonstrates what a community genogram will look like, and actually facilitates the joining process. Others introduce sample genograms to illustrate the kinds of information discussed and displayed and to share ways this information can be useful in understanding how their difficulties emerged and in identifying potential untapped personal, familial, and community resources for change.

Phase 2: Constructing Community Genograms

Counselors begin by posing questions that encourage clients to share their understanding of the issues they wish to explore about themselves and about the issues that prompted treatment in an order and manner that is meaningful to them. As the therapeutic exchange unfolds, counselors' questions are directed toward gaining broader perspectives by attending to the contexts (embayments) and significant others (channels) clients identify as important sources of support or as contributors to their stress. As the visual display generated by these discussions begins to take form, vantage points are introduced that elicit extended perspectives about how difficulties take form and that introduce broader paths to consider as part of the change process.

Phase 3: Positive Asset Search

In this phase, a positive asset search is conducted to uncover resources within the broader terrain portrayed by the graphic display. By exploring the nuances of each embayment and channel, counselors and clients discover explicit and implicit resources previously not accounted for that could be accessed and activated as part of a comprehensive treatment plan. The search generally increases client ownership of strengths they already possess, and it reveals the ways in which counseling can extend beyond the confines of the office as counselors and clients work together to activate cultural and community resources that were previously unseen or inaccessible.

SIDEBAR 2.3 THE POSITIVE ASSET SEARCH

During stressful periods there is often a tendency to focus on the negative aspects of our circumstances, making it hard to identify and examine cultural, community, family, and personal strengths and resources we could access during these times. This often occurs in therapy. Therefore, counselors need to practice ways to hold sustained dialogues that go beyond simply naming strengths and resources to recalling and experiencing how these may have been accessed and activated in other stressful circumstances. For this activity:

- Return to the individual star diagram you created. Focus on one single positive experience that occurred within one of the embayments you identified that significantly influenced the ways in which/the degree to which your cultural identity broadened. Write a brief story about this one specific experience.
- Once you complete this story, focus on one specific relational exchange that occurred with a significant person you identified in your individual star diagram who was a key to your becoming more aware of your cultural identity. Write a brief story about this one specific relational exchange.
- Review your written stories and briefly describe what occurred for you as you recalled the details of these two key experiences.
- Finally, reflect on the ways in which you might help clients to participate in their own sustained positive asset search.

Phase 4: Expressing the Negative Stories

During this phase, counselors and clients consider the wider cultural, institutional, community, and/or family forces that may have contributed or are now contributing to the evolution, maintenance, and management of the difficulties clients are experiencing. These discussions serve to determine whether options exist (beyond accessing and activating resources identified in the previous phase) to challenge reified definitions of clients' particular circumstances. Transparent conversations about the wider forces shaping how client difficulties are perceived and addressed in their local communities are critical to the deconstruction of the encapsulated identified patient and the reconstruction of their sense of self-in-relation. Oftentimes this is a theme to which clients return, taking advocacy roles for others experiencing similar forms of oppression and discrimination.

Phase 5: Promoting Reflective Consciousness

Community genograms are returned to throughout several points in counseling to monitor which multiple perspectives and options were best tailored to the realities of the client's environment. This process reinforces the ways in which examining the cultural, personal, and situational factors that influence difficulties facilitates multiple perspectives and options for change. A counseling process that provides the opportunities to monitor progress and reflect on progress achieved makes it more probable that clients will refrain from familiar perspectives that offer limited resources and will continue the practice of using a broader perspective to identify and navigate options for change.

The ultimate goal of therapy is the liberation of consciousness. It emphasizes the importance of expanding personal, family, group, and organizational consciousness at the place of self-in-relation, family-in-relation, and organization-in-relation. This results in therapy that is not only ultimately contextual in orientation, but also draws on traditional methods of healing from many cultures.

Illustrative Relational Client: Dana and Minsoo

We return now to Dana and Minsoo, whose community genogram was introduced earlier to illustrate the relational star diagram (see Figure 2.7). Dana and Minsoo began therapy due to the increasing disagreements occurring between them regarding their son's defiant behaviors, his inability to adapt to the Korean school system, and the school system's inability to adapt to his learning style. The process of coconstructing the genogram facilitated discussions about their shared and individual perceptions of Hyeon's circumstances, as well as other circumstances they were navigating at this point in time. The relevant contexts and significant others that comprised their relational system are situated within the common contexts of collective exchange (see the gray shaded area in Figure 2.7). Relevant contexts and significant others not directly contained within the relational system are positioned outside of this gray area. Finally, contexts relevant to both members in different ways and through different affiliations are partially positioned within the gray area.

Once the genogram was constructed, Dana and Minsoo focused their attention on relationships they had with significant others. Minsoo stated that his coworkers have been his second family ever since he lived alone as a *goose father*, reflected by the wide embayments to the left of Minsoo in the relational star diagram. The narrow channels between Minsoo and other family members (e.g., his wife, children, and relatives) represent closed-off relationships with significant family members. Dana's close relationships with her children and neighbors are reflected by the open channels within her individual star, and her distant relationship with Minsoo is represented as a narrow channel.

Focusing on the strengths found in the gray area, Dana and Minsoo began an exploration of their relationship. They first shared that they loved each other deeply and enjoyed each other's company at home and with others. They valued what each had accomplished outside the home and respected the ways they were both involved in their communities. The more constraining aspects of their relationship were then examined. They shared that their spousal relationship was constricted by their concerns over schooling for their son, their chores of daily living, and the increasing needs of elder members within each of their respective extended families. They also shared stories about their history, specifically focusing on the circumstances each had to navigate when the children were young and the family lived apart. They quickly noticed the similarities between the ways they functioned with regard to the circumstances they faced when the children were young and the ways they were now navigating their current circumstances. This led to explorations about their different approaches to dealing with stress, specifically Dana's concentrated time with her children and Minsoo's concentrated time at work. One new theme surfaced: how Minsoo's worry about the family's loss of honor (due to Hyeon's school problems) intruded on his having an authentic relationship with Hyeon. The analysis eventually moved beyond the gray area as Minsoo and Dana began to share their different lived experiences outside of their home. Both agreed that Minsoo's involvement with the hiking club and Dana's participation in the swim club were outside activities they wanted to continue.

Ongoing conversations about independent activities were critical, given that much of their time was spent apart. Both described this active listening as similar to courting, and they enjoyed learning about one another in ways they had not been able to in the past. They became aware of the less-known worlds each had established and discovered new significant themes that influenced their relationship. For example, both were surprised by the dissimilar ways they sought emotional support and honor for the family and the similar ways they adjusted to their personal lives without their partners. Three years of separation brought out disparate coping strategies: Dana relied on her neighbors, church friends, and other fellow mothers for help with emotional and relational problems, while Minsoo relieved his stress by working and spending time with his colleagues. They also were startled by how excluded Minsoo was from Dana and the children and about the sadness they both felt regarding their inability to turn to one another to share stories about their daily lives. These conversations increased their sense of empathy for one another and their desire to learn more about one another. The stories shared through the construction of their genogram and those generated by their mutual curiosity regarding lived experiences beyond the gray area increased their empathy for one another, as well as their desire to continue courting. Thus, stories shared during and after constructing their genogram informed the objectives they set for treatment. With minimal direction from the counselor, Minsoo and Dana defined the following goals: (a) to engage in more storytelling, (b) to establish a united front to deal with conflicts between Minsoo and Hyeon, and (c) to find resources to better serve their son's needs in systems more familiar with his learning challenges. The relational star diagram served as a starting point for Dana and Minsoo to look at the broader territory, to assume more personal responsibility for their unique perspectives, and to begin to build on collective stories, the first of which was to partner in their efforts toward identifying an educational system more tailored to Hyeon's needs.

USING COMMUNITY GENOGRAMS AS CONSULTANTS AND ADVOCATES

As the focus of therapy shifts from the individual client to the wider community, the work of the family counselor also changes. Today, family counselors provide services as advocates and consultants to schools, businesses, governmental agencies, and community organizations. This contextualizes the work of the advocate and the consultant and creates an opportunity to promote organizational consciousness in which the goal is to expand the sense of self-in-relationship and organization-in-relation. To provide effective and relevant services in these broader contexts, family counselors must have a strong knowledge base about the multiple definitions of culture and a deep understanding about how culture impacts all members of the organization, so that organizational and institutional resources can be focused on developing the individuals, families, and groups within their boundaries. Community genograms can inform the work of family counselors engaged in consultation and advocacy by providing clinical tools to map the wider sociocultural environments they navigate to effect change for clients and communities. These tools empower the family counselor to accurately monitor the changing client affiliations over time.

Consultation and advocacy work at the wider community level is extremely complex. Whether working with a small community group or a large multinational corporation, the importance of accounting for contextual and cultural issues cannot be overstated. How individuals develop their cultural identities within the organization will require that the consultant and the advocate pay attention to shifts in relationships within and across groups, giving specific attention to interactions between the dominant and subordinate groups.

Consultants and advocates must be prepared to engage with numerous concerned parties, often with competing agendas and decision-making practices. Herein are the two greatest strengths community genograms offer to consultants and advocates: its ecosystemic perspective and its attention to the intersectionalities of salient aspects of client cultural identities within and across various contexts. Using community genograms, advocates and consultants can design interventions tailored to specific groups and individuals of interest. When assuming the role of advocate, the counselor can plan a public relations effort that is based on knowledge about the key stakeholders involved in the project. The consultant can use community genograms to elicit important information about the particular parties involved in the consultation. For both services, planning is a very important skill.

Consultants can use community genograms to represent all key participants to be sure to surface their concerns and issues. This graphic can then become a charter for the work, detailing the needs and interests of all participants. This becomes a common point of reference, especially when it is made available for review every time a meeting is held. Advocates usually work in the wider community/society domain to effect change for a particular client. Often these clients have been oppressed and underserved, and the consultant and advocate are working to change the status quo. It is evident that where persons, families, and groups are positioned in the wider social structure significantly determines the quality of life they experience. It is the job of the consultant and the advocate to alter this arrangement and reduce the disparity between dominant and subordinate groups.

Because of the public nature of this work, any change effected on behalf of a particular client has the potential to be extended to others in the same situation. Community genograms can assist the advocate by keeping track of the many needs of the client, other members of the client group, partners, and members of the public sector that may need to be involved to bring about the social justice changes in policy, law, or organizational governing rules.

Extending the Boundaries of the Therapeutic Exchange

> We remain timid in our visions of what interventions we are capable of and of where interventions should begin and be located. . . . We have little trouble growing to expect the best to come from our interactions with families, yet do not seem ready to imagine that we can be effective on a wider scale.
>
> —Rigazio-DiGilio, Locke, and Ivey, 1997, p. 250

Both counselors and clients bring their individual and collective heritage and contextual influences into the immediacy of the therapeutic exchange. Counselors, therefore, need to be sensitive to the ways these factors impact their assessment and treatment of clients. As well, counselors need to be alert to the ways dominant beliefs held by the institutions, communities, and wider sociocultural contexts within which they work directly influence the issues they bring to the foreground, relegate to the background, or do not address in their work with clients. Finally, counselors need to consider what is not being discussed in sessions that may offer untapped resources to access in therapy.

The power of community genograms to expand our encapsulated perceptions and to support community-based change is illustrated in Figure 2.8, an institutional star diagram constructed by a counselor (Kevin) and client (Maya) during their meetings with a consultant in a university-based counseling center. The consultant met with them after Maya reported little relief of her depressive symptoms and her sense of isolation in the counseling relationship.

The institutional star diagram visually portrayed information about Maya that was both familiar and unfamiliar to Kevin. Salient information highlighted the many forms of discrimination she experiences as an international student (e.g., U.S. immigration laws preventing her access to required internships) with significant ambulatory challenges (e.g., structural barriers preventing her access to required classes and university resources) that impact her academic progress and emotional well-being.

Information that was identified but not explored in counseling is depicted by the embayments and channels of Maya's individual star that fall within or partially within the shaded area of the diagram (see Figure 2.8). This information included stories related to: (a) Maya's experience as an international student, (b) the

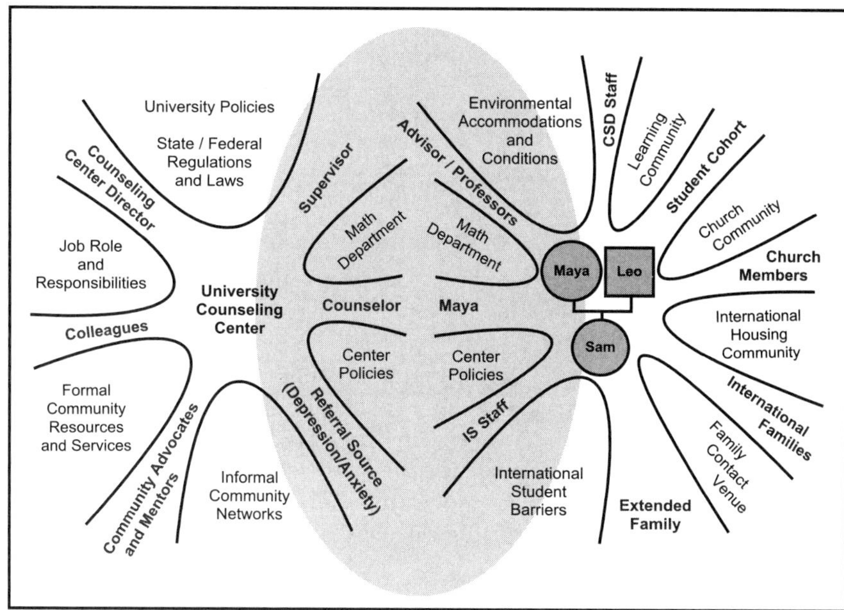

Figure 2.8 Illustrative Institutional Star Diagram: Kevin and Maya

environmental obstacles she encounters daily as a student with significant ambulatory challenges, (c) the positive relationships she has with her major advisor and with the staff at the university's International Center, (d) the difficulties she experiences being seen and responded to as a student with diverse needs in a large academic department, and (f) the limitations of university policies regarding student access to the university counseling center.

Information that was not shared falls outside of the shaded area in the figure. Illustrative information included stories about: (a) the stressors and supports located in Maya's extended family; (b) her experiences with international families around the university, members of her church community, members of her learning community, and staff members at the Center for Students with Disabilities; (c) constraints she experiences as an international student; (d) difficulties she has finding time for quality communication with her relatives in Nigeria; and (e) troubles she has acquiring university-supported housing that can accommodate her physical circumstances.

The graphic of Kevin's working community also revealed information that was part of the counseling exchange and information that was beyond the boundaries of this relationship. The latter information included: (a) the guidance and support he finds in his relationships with the counseling center's director and his colleagues, (b) local community resources that could be made part of the counseling exchange, and (c) possible ways to navigate the wider legal and policy environments.

A broad review of the genogram set the stage for conversations about the sense of isolation Maya experienced in the counseling relationship, a first step in rebuilding the counselor/client alliance. For example, conversations included stories about: (a) the ways in which experiences related to discrimination and environmental barriers were quickly relegated to secondary concerns given the counselor's admitted inability to navigate such issues, and (b) how the narrowing of the territory of assessment concomitantly shifted Kevin's assessment of Maya's symptoms as more related to intellectual deficits than institutional and environmental barriers and as more representative of personal excuses than the day-to-day realities of her lived experiences.

A more specific examination of the embayments and channels partially included in the shaded areas provided a common point of reference for discussions about the challenges Maya faces every day when attempting to navigate options for obtaining the education and degree that brought her to the United States. For example, Maya shared stories about the ways her physical circumstances (which required the use of an elaborate wheelchair) prevented her access to transportation, buildings where required classes were held, library facilities, student resource centers, and the like. These conversations expanded Kevin's ability to understand Maya's symptoms as natural and logical consequences of the discriminatory policies and environmental obstacles disrupting her academic progress. As important, the conversations increased his sense of empathy for Maya and his sense of responsibility for the countless times others, and he himself, intentionally or unintentionally framed Maya's representation of her difficulties as intellectual deficits or as excuses for her academic delays and emotional distress. Finally, these exchanges broadened his understanding of the ways such perceptions of Maya, and of other students facing similar circumstances, perpetuated dominant beliefs that contributed to university delays to comply with standards required by the Americans with Disabilities Act (ADA) that would ensure all admitted students equal access to the resources and opportunities necessary to obtain a quality education.

Conversations that expanded the territory of assessment enabled Kevin and Maya to reposition the realities of the institutional and environmental barriers impacting Maya's academic success and emotional well-being as core factors to be addressed in counseling. This, in turn, revealed wider territories for intervention that drew distinctions between students needing accommodations for mobility and students needing accommodations for intellectual challenges. An extended and collaborative treatment plan was designed that expanded Kevin's role to include both in-session support and advocacy work with Maya to meet her immediate needs and, later, with members of the university and wider community to influence university policies and supports for Maya and other international students with significant physical challenges.

Given that Kevin was able to accurately represent the scope of his competence, he sought out, with the consultant's assistance, an adjunct faculty member and licensed therapist who had experienced similar discrimination and barriers while pursuing his doctoral degree. This therapist provided coaching to Maya (a role he assumes with many students addressing similar circumstances) to successfully open more access to university and community resources and to gain better forms of international communication.

Concomitantly, Kevin and Maya met with the chair of her department to discuss training the licensed therapist could provide to faculty and teaching assistants about appropriate accommodations for Maya and several other students with significant physical limitations. Additionally, they arranged a meeting with the chair and the International Center to discuss ways of revising the language for internship requirements that was tailored to U.S. immigration laws.

When Maya was in her second academic year, she returned to work with Kevin on the second goal they identified after meeting with the consultant. Together, they established a university-sanctioned committee, including students, staff from the Center for Students with Disabilities, faculty, and community leaders dedicated to the mission of raising administrative awareness about and commitment to reallocating funding to include more resources to support the intent of the ADA for the entire student body, and especially for international students with significant physical challenges.

Providing therapy in the name of social justice often requires that the goals and processes of counseling be different from traditional forms of treatment. Counselors need to understand how the wider sociocultural environment can be factored into treatment to maximize the benefits for clients and other community members. Once clients' untapped resources are acknowledged in treatment, the focus can shift from internal work with clients alone to advocating for clients in the wider community.

Community genograms are one tool counselors can use to bring out these hidden resources and map successful treatment goals. If the goal of treatment is to enable clients to create viable new identities that account for contextual and cultural variables, then counseling must seek to realign power differentials that have historically served to marginalize clients positioned outside of the mainstream. Counselors need to move beyond a predominant focus on clients' interpersonal mental phenomena; become more knowledgeable about the multiple and interacting social, political, and economic barriers that impede personal development; and gain the competencies to work for change in the wider community.

SUMMARY

This chapter presented information about the use of community genograms to promote client change and to guide community-based interventions. The standard community genogram template, the star diagram, was offered as one method counselors can use with clients to gather, organize, and present complex multidimensional cultural and contextual factors in ways that make these factors accessible throughout treatment. The star diagram and its variations are limited only by the creativity and imagination of clients and counselors to coconstruct visuals that represent their families and the systems that surround them. By surfacing these variables early in treatment, counselors not only promote a heightened level of client engagement but also generate clinical data they can use to formulate working hypotheses about the nature of the client's issues. Community genograms add new dimensions to the therapeutic dialogue for both clients and counselors.

Benefits for clients using community genograms include an enhanced understanding of their sense of self-in-relationship within a wider community context. Clients are able to refer to these variables throughout treatment so they can examine how the difficulties they face developed over time and across multiple contexts and locations. Community genograms bring clients' multiple lived experiences to the forefront of the therapeutic exchange and identify client, therapy, and community strengths and capacities that can be brought to bear throughout counseling. By bringing out these strengths and capacities in an easily understood fashion, clients are empowered to exercise more influence in the therapeutic relationship. Finally, community genograms can serve as an organizing blueprint to launch community-based advocacy activities in ways that promote social justice.

The power of the community genogram lies in the fact that clients have control over what they include in the graphic, they are the major contributors in the process during the session, and they can quickly and graphically see the connections between and among disparate events and situations by referring to the genogram. By increasing clients' control over content, interpretation, and connections, meaning is enhanced. They are able to discuss topics that are important to them and see links to other situations and developmental issues that help demonstrate continuity and change. The analysis of the community genogram helps them move from the familiar perspectives that offer limited resources to new perspectives that open a wide array of options to guide enlightened points of view and actions.

For counselors, community genograms offer a versatile assessment and treatment device that can be used to determine the relevant cultural and contextual factors operating within and across the wider cultural contexts that contribute to clients' presenting issues. These will need to be considered in a comprehensive treatment plan that is culturally relevant and sensitive to the multiple life spaces of the client. It provides guidelines for analyzing the relevance of each system and the level of influence significant others exercise when interacting with the client. Further, it can be used to determine where to intervene in the wider life space of the client and to identify when to make such interventions. The community genogram helps counselors to consider alternative pathways for the client to pursue and to activate underutilized and less visible resources in support of the treatment goals.

Given the process-oriented nature of constructing and examining community genograms, this interactive graphic device can be incorporated easily into the work of counselors having widely differing theoretical orientations. The broad terrain of information covered provides counselors with a wealth of information that can be drawn from to conceptualize and approach the difficulties clients bring to treatment in ways that are consistent with their theoretical orientation and therapeutic approach.

REFERENCES

Becvar, D. (2005). Forward. In S. Rigazio-DiGilio, A. Ivey, K. Kunkler-Peck, & L. Grady (Eds.), *Community genograms: Using individual, family and cultural* narratives with clients (pp. ix–x). New York, NY: Teacher's College Press.

Bowen, M. (1966). The use of family theory in clinical practice. *Comprehensive Psychiatry*, 7, 345–374.

Bowen, M. (1976). Theory in practice of psychotherapy. In P. Guerin (Ed.), *Family therapy: Theory and practice* (pp. 42–90). New York, NY: Gardner Press.

Bowen, M. (1978). *Family therapy in clinical practice*. New York, NY: Aronson.

Chen-Hayes, S. (2003). The sexual orientation, gender identity, and gender expression genogram. In J. Whitman & C. Boyd (Eds.), *The counselor's notebook for lesbian, gay, and bisexual clients* (pp. 166–173). Binghamton, NY: Haworth Clinical Practice Press.

DeMaria, R., Weeks, G., & Blumer, M. (2014). *Focused genograms: Intergenerational assessment of individuals, couples, and families* (2nd ed.). New York, NY: Routledge.

Enns, C. (2010). Locational feminisms and feminist social identity analysis. *Professional Psychology: Research and Practice*, *41*, 333–339. doi:10.1037/a0020260

Fowers, B. (1990). An interactional approach to standardized marital assessment: A literature review. *Family Relations*, *39*, 368–377. doi:10.2307/585215

Friedlander, M., Escudero, V., & Heatherington, L. (2006). *Therapeutic alliances in couple and family therapy: An empirically informed guide to practice*. Washington, DC: American Psychological Association. doi:10.1037/11410-000

Goodman, R. (2013). The transgenerational trauma and resilience genogram. *Counselling Psychology Quarterly*, *26*, 386–405. doi:10.1080/09515070.2013.820172

Guerin, P., & Fogarty, T. (1972). Studying your own family. In M. Mendelsohn, A. Ferber, & A. Napier (Eds.), *The book of family therapy* (pp. 445–467). New York, NY: Science House.

Hardy, K., & Laszloffy, T. (1995). The cultural genogram: Key to training culturally competent family counselors. *Journal of Marital and Family Therapy*, *21*, 227–237. doi:10.1111/j.1752-0606.1995.tb00158.x

Hartman, A. (1978). Diagrammatic assessment of family relationships. *Social Casework*, *59*, 465–476.

Hartman, A. (1979). *Finding families: An ecological approach to family assessment*. Beverly Hills, CA: SAGE.

Hodge, D. R. (2001). Spiritual genograms: A generational approach to assessing spirituality. *Families in Society*, *82*, 35–48.

Ivey, A., & Ivey, M. (1999). Toward a developmental diagnostic and statistical manual: The vitality of a contextual framework. *Journal of Counseling and Development*, 77, 484–490.

Jordan, K. (2006). The scripto-trauma genogram: An innovative technique for working with trauma survivors' intrusive memories. *Brief Treatment and Crisis Intervention*, *6*, 36–51.

Keiley, M., Dolbin, M., Hill, J., Karuppaswamy, N., Liu, T., Natrajan, R., . . . Robinson, P. (2002). The cultural genogram: Experiences from within a marriage and family therapy training program. *Journal of Marital and Family Therapy*, *28*, 165–178. doi:10.1111/j.1752-0606.2002.tb00354.x

Kosutic, I., Garcia, M., Graves, T., Barnett, F., Hall, J., Haley, E., & Kaiser, B. (2009). The critical genogram: A tool for promoting critical consciousness. *Journal of Feminist Family Therapy*, *21*, 151–176. doi:10.1080/08952830903079037

McGoldrick, M., & Gerson, R. (1985). *Genograms in family assessment*. New York, NY: Norton.

McGoldrick, M., Gerson, R., & Petry, S. (2008). *Genograms: Assessment and intervention* (3rd ed.). New York, NY: Norton.

Platt, L., & Skowron, E. (2013). The family genogram interview: Reliability and validity of a new interview protocol. *Family Journal*, *21*, 35–45. doi:10.1177/1066480712456817

Rigazio-DiGilio, S. (2000). Relational diagnosis. *Journal of Clinical Psychology*, *56*, 1017–1036.

Rigazio-DiGilio, S., Ivey, A., Kunkler-Peck, K., and Grady, L. (2005). *Community genograms: Using individual, family and cultural narratives with clients*. New York, NY: Teacher's College Press.

Rigazio-DiGilio, S., Locke, D., & Ivey, A. (1997). Continuing the postmodern dialogue: Enhancing and contextualizing multiple voices. *Journal of Mental Health Counseling, 19*, 233–255.

Warde, B. (2012). The cultural genogram: Enhancing the cultural competency of social work students. *Social Work Education, 31*, 570–586. doi:10.1080/02615479.2011.593623

CHAPTER 3

Diversity and Intercultural Work in Family Counseling

Brian Canfield

Southern Arkansas University

Families exist in various cultural contexts in a variety of structures, such as single-parent, same-sex, blended, and extended families. The traditional nuclear family is an increasingly rare model. It is estimated that less than 3% of the population of the United States resides in White European, middle-class, Protestant, heterosexual family households that have two school-age children, a stay-at-home mother, and a father who is the primary breadwinner (McGoldrick, 1998.)

The world is an increasingly interconnected place. The expanding trend toward urbanization has brought people from various groups and cultures into closer proximity. The increase in intercultural interaction presents challenges for family counselors who are routinely called upon to work with clients from different cultural backgrounds. In the 21st century, it is possible for those who have the means to travel to any location on earth within a matter of days, if not hours. Yet despite increased intercultural connections, the world remains a disparate mosaic of various nationalities, ethnicities, religions, languages, and cultures. Although we share many qualities common to the human condition, such as birth, family, and death, there are a multitude of differences that serve to categorize and divide people.

Differences, or more importantly the meaning people attribute to differences, have both enriched the human experience and resulted in a great deal of suffering, both historically and in the present context. It is the essential job of a family counselor to help individuals, couples, and families bring about desired change—to help a client family and its members move from where they are to where they would like to be. Whether providing information and support or working to ameliorate emotional pain and suffering, family counselors strive to improve the quality of life and relationships for their clients.

In the early years of family counseling theory and practice development, considerations of culture were largely absent from the narrative of working with couples and families (Bitter, 2009). This chapter draws on extensive clinical work with individuals, couples, and families who self-identify as members of specific cultural groups residing within the United States, as well as clinical work with individuals, couples, and families living in Europe, Asia, Africa, Australia, and the Middle East.

Family counselors recognize the critical importance of possessing knowledge and skills necessary to provide an ethical and competent standard of care to clients regardless of the cultural affiliation or identity of the client. This chapter provides a perspective on diversity and intercultural considerations in family counseling, including a therapeutic conceptual frame and specific strategies for assisting clients in accomplishing their goals in counseling.

People from various cultural backgrounds are increasingly residing in cities and towns outside of their communities of origin. These migratory movements, sometimes temporary and sometimes permanent, occur for a variety of reasons. For some families, geographical relocations are voluntary, sought in the pursuit of greater economic opportunity or an enhanced quality of life. For other persons, such relocations are involuntary, undertaken out of safety concerns to escape societal instability or conflict.

Regardless of the reasons, persons from various cultural backgrounds increasingly find them themselves living in an area that is culturally different from that of their culture of origin. Such relocations present challenges for the first generation of relocated adults and their children, and subsequent generations often find themselves challenged in making adjustments to a new community that differs from their cultural points of reference.

Although the cultural "rules" may differ in terms of how events and life challenges are interpreted and addressed, people from various cultural groups and backgrounds often experience similar life stressors, such as economic challenges, work-related issues, health concerns, martial or relationship conflict, parent–child issues, and the care and support of aging family members.

SIDEBAR 3.1 LIFE STRESSORS: EXPERIENCES THAT SHAPE VALUES AND BELIEFS

Reflecting on your life up to this point, list the notable experiences in life that you feel have influenced and shaped your values, attitudes, beliefs, and experiences. What meaning did you attribute to each of these experiences, and in what way did the experiences change your perspective?

There is broad acceptance, as evidenced by various professional organization and institutional codes of ethical conduct, regarding the importance of intercultural knowledge and skill proficiency. The concepts presented in this chapter approach intercultural family counseling from a conceptual framework of applied cybernetics, emphasizing the interrelationship between the family counselor and the client family as the primary catalyst for bringing about desired changes (Becvar, Canfield, & Becvar, 1997).

GOALS

Professional counseling associations recognize the importance of cultural understanding and competency when working with clients. These considerations apply to all clients, but are of particular importance when the client and family counselor hold different cultural identities. The code of ethics of the American Counseling Association (2005) states that "association members recognize diversity and embrace a cross-cultural approach in support of the worth, dignity, potential, and uniqueness of people within their social and cultural contexts" (p. 3).

In addition to issues of language, cultural considerations require that counselors have a grasp of the nuances of communication styles that may differ between cultural groups (ACA, 2005, p. 4). Family counselors have an ethical responsibility to protect the welfare of a client. To this end, professional ethics require that "counselors gain knowledge, personal awareness, sensitivity, and skills pertinent to working with a diverse client population." In addition, counselors must "recognize that culture affects the manner in which clients' problems are defined. Clients' socio-economic and cultural experiences are considered when diagnosing mental disorders" (ACA, 2005, p. 12).

An awareness of these ethical responsibilities promotes client welfare, particularly in a family context in which the sometimes competing needs of multiple people often emerge. This ensures that clients are not unintentionally harmed due to cultural generalizations, historical prejudices, or cultural differences that might lead to counselor bias and substandard care.

Similarly, the Council for Accreditation of Counseling and Related Educational Programs (CACREP) holds multicultural and cross-cultural competency as a core requirement of counselor training program accreditation (CACREP, 2009). Educational standards illuminate the importance of social and cultural diversity and require knowledge of the "cultural context of relationships, issues, and trends in a multicultural society," as well as knowledge of "characteristics and concerns within and among diverse groups nationally and internationally" (p. 10).

Educational standards not only require an understanding of client cultural issues, but also an understanding on the part of counselors-in-training with regard to counselor cultural self-awareness (CACREP, 2009, p. 10).

In consideration of these ethical and educational standards, a culturally competent family counselor possesses knowledge and skills for working effectively with clients who are culturally different from the family counselor in some aspect. The intercultural family counseling perspective outlined in this chapter holds that successful counseling goes beyond a focus solely on the client, recognizing the systemic nature and cybernetic process of family counseling—the interrelationship between counselor and client irrespective of cultural identity. Intercultural family counseling competency does not only reflect knowledge, but also an attitudinal disposition.

The overarching goal of this chapter is to provide or expand knowledge of diversity and intercultural issues for counselors and therapists who work with couples and families. Many of the concepts discussed apply equally to work with individual clients using a family systems–based therapeutic approach. Specific family counseling strategies and techniques will be presented for use in an intercultural counseling context. This chapter addresses some of the unique ethical considerations that arise when working with diversity issues and clients who differ from the family counselor in some cultural aspect. Specific goals include the following:

- Awareness of cultural identity and diversity issues and implications for family counseling, particularly when working with couples and families who differ from the counselor in some cultural aspect
- Understanding family counselor cultural identity and self-awareness and its potential impact on the counseling relationship and therapeutic outcomes
- Developing a therapeutic approach for helping couples and families bring about desired changes within an intercultural family counseling context
- Presentation of selected family counseling strategies and techniques for facilitating desired change when cultural differences exist between the client and family counselor
- Awareness of some of the unique legal and ethical responsibilities inherent in working with a diverse client population

BACKGROUND

Worldwide, culturally homogeneous communities are increasingly less common, particularly within larger urban areas. As such, it is unlikely that the cultural identity and attributes of a family counselor practicing in a particular community will align with the cultural characteristics of all members residing in that community. Invariably, the family counselor will be called on to work with individuals, couples, and families who differ from the family counselor in one or more essential cultural characteristics.

Humans share many common attributes and life experiences, but they may also differ in many respects. Some of those differences may be merely incidental, while others may hold profound significance in the formation and maintenance of cultural identity. Depending on the meaning attributed to similarities and differences, one may initially feel closer to some people and more distant toward others. Obvious similarities and differences often shape the initial impressions that one person has of another. This exists in almost all human relationships, including the counselor–client relationship.

One narrative regarding cultural diversity is the quintessentially American ideal of society being a cultural melting pot, a concept personified in the Latin motto "E pluribus unum" (translated as "one made out of many") found on the Great Seal of the United States. This was selected in 1776 by the founding fathers of the newly independent United States of America and was officially adopted as the national motto in 1782 (U.S. State Department, 2003). Although it initially described the unification of the American colonies into a cohesive nation, the motto evolved into an aspirational statement about the cultural assimilation of various immigrant groups.

SIDEBAR 3.2 CULTURAL ASSIMILATION: MELTING POT OR CULTURAL UNIQUENESS?

In considering the assimilation of a family who immigrates to a new country, what you do consider to be essential responsibilities? Should the family members learn the dominant language of the host country and adopt the values and customs of the community? Or should the family be free to retain their own cultural identity? What do you consider to be the pros and cons of these responsibilities?

An alternate narrative holds that the world is a mosaic of interacting cultural groups and influences. In most developed nations and emerging countries, professional counselors are called on to address a wide range of concerns within a multicultural and intercultural context. Particularly in economically developed and relatively stable regions of the world, such as North America and Europe, immigration continues to alter the cultural demographics of many nations and communities (United Nations, 2013).

MAJOR CONSTRUCTS

There are many theoretical and clinical models that may be used by a competent counselor to help a client. Almost every approach will prove useful and effective with some clients in some situations. However, no counseling approach will be effective with every client in every situation. A challenge for the family counselor is to identify and use a conceptual model and therapeutic approach to family counseling that maximizes the likelihood for helping the client and minimizes potential risk. Counseling may be viewed as an intrusive activity. Inviting a family counselor—an outsider—into the family's relational system is often an immense barrier for members of some cultural groups in their desire to receive help.

Particularly among member of cultures that place a premium on privacy or self-sufficiency, the well-intentioned efforts and benevolent role of the family counselor may not be readily understood or welcomed. While the potential benefits of counseling are well-known to the family counselor, some family members may hold a different view of the counseling process based on past experiences or cultural values.

Applied cybernetics provides a useful conceptual framework for working with clients, regardless of cultural identity. At the core of cybernetic theory and its application to the family counseling process is the recognition that human relationships—couples, families, groups, extended families, or therapeutic systems—are mutually defined and constructed by members of that relationship system (Becvar et al., 1997). Central to this perspective is a recognition that all human roles and relationships are interactive, recursive, and self-sustaining in nature. For any role, by logical necessity, there exists a corresponding and complementary role. For example, the role of teacher requires the logical complementary role of student. This concept of logical role complementarity exists in all human relationships; some examples are parent–child, seller–buyer, lawyer–client, thief–victim, police officer–offender, husband–wife, and doctor–patient. In understanding role complementarity, it is helpful to recognize that one role does not necessarily create its logical role complement. However, a logical complement must exist in order to establish and maintain any relational role; for example, a bully does not exist in the absence of someone being bullied. This concept of logical role complementarity is essential to understanding the relational nature of the family counseling process from a cybernetic perspective (Becvar et al., 1997).

Unlike traditional approaches that typically view the client as a self-contained unit reflecting symptoms, pathology, or dysfunction, an approach that uses the concepts of applied cybernetics holds that the worldview and cultural attributes of the family counselor are inextricably interconnected to those of the client family. While family members are interacting and engaging in self-maintaining complementary roles, the family counselor "joins" the family system and participates in a complementary role to the client family. From this perspective, recognizing the co-constructed nature of family relationships, as well as the family counseling relationship, is often useful in understanding how each member of the family system contributes to bringing about desired change (Becvar et al., 1997).

The recursive nature of the relationship between the client family and family counselor serves to co-create a narrative about the reasons and issues that prompted the family to seek help, as well as an understanding about problem formation, maintenance, and amelioration. Equally important, this co-constructed narrative about the counseling process establishes a therapeutic context in which desired change can take place by specifying the respective roles and responsibilities of the family counselor and members within the client family.

SIDEBAR 3.3 FAMILY COUNSELOR AND CLIENT FAMILY COLLABORATION

In seeking help from a qualified family counselor, there is an implicit expectation that the family will help bring about needed changes. To what extent do you see the role of the family counselor as a consultant to the client family, rather than as an expert with all the answers and solutions? As the family counselor, how would you balance family expectations without imposing your values and solutions onto the family?

What Constitutes Family Cultural Identity?

Having experienced discrimination while living in England, a Turkish friend asked an American acquaintance: "Do you consider me to be White?" The American colleague's response to this question was: "I'm not really sure what you mean by White; I consider you to be Turkish." A conversation ensued about identity, prejudice, discrimination, and the politics of race. For the culturally sensitive family counselor, the salient question may not be identifying someone's race, ethnicity, or cultural identity, as if such labels hold some inherent and immutable meaning, but rather exploring the meaning a person attributes to such identity.

Historically, the concept of race has been used to exclude and oppress others—a means of exerting power and advancing a particular social or political agenda. One narrative holds that racism is historically and predominantly a "White" offense—a vestige of colonialism. Although such a narrative has some basis in historical facts, it is incomplete and misleading in many respects. White racial identity, and the concept of "White privilege" providing direct and indirect access to the power structure of a predominantly White society, is a historical and contemporary reality for many people. However, racism and oppression have no boundaries with regard to skin color or cultural membership.

Defining Culture

The human ability to survive and flourish reflects the capacity of people to teach and learn from one another. *Culture* refers to the institutions, traditions, and rituals by which collective knowledge is maintained and conveyed to subsequent generations.

Parsing humanity into various groups based on some characteristic or a set of characteristics is both useful and problematic. A client's cultural identity, however defined, often provides a sense of community with others who share similar values, beliefs, or attributes. Cultural identity is also by its nature exclusionary, creating a sense of separateness and division between people from different cultural groups or backgrounds.

Because it is essentially a social construct, defining culture can be a challenging task. Clients differ in terms of how they identify with others. For example, in south Louisiana, the term *Cajun* originally referred to French-speaking descendants of the Acadian French settlers who were deported from Canada in the 18th century by conquering British forces and exiled to the French colony of Louisiana. There remains a strong cultural Cajun identity in parts of south Louisiana, but increasingly, heredity has little to do with Cajun cultural identity. Today, many Cajuns are descendants of German, English, Spanish, or African ancestors. A person may be considered part of the Cajun culture by virtue of being born and growing up in a Cajun southern Louisiana community, regardless of ethnicity (Dorman, 2003).

Several years ago, the author accompanied a group of counseling students to England for a summer study-abroad program. Among the students were five African American females from Louisiana. Being culturally curious and somewhat extroverted counselors-in-training, the American students quickly connected with a group of graduate students from the African nation of Nigeria who were pursuing graduate studies in the United Kingdom. The African students included the American students in a variety of social activities—excursions, parties, and a wedding reception. Following several weeks of social interaction, one of the American students commented in a group class discussion,"I really like the African students. They are very nice and they look like me, but we are very different in so many ways." She went on to explain that she preferred the music, food, and attitudes of her home state of Louisiana, rather than those of her new African friends.

From this cultural immersion experience with a group of Nigerian students, several of the participant African American students began to question their long-held narrative about their cultural identity (i.e., "I am an African American") and came to view their cultural identity in broader terms having less to do with the physical characteristics of race and more to do with the shared lifestyle and experiences.

Common criteria often identify members of a particular culture. Such demographic variables, in and of themselves, have no meaning beyond what a person attributes to them. For one person, same-sex sexual preference or orientation may be a central and defining aspect of his or her cultural identity (e.g., gay or lesbian). However, for another person, their same-sex sexual orientation may be merely incidental to their identity and cultural sense of self. This same person may consider ethnicity or religious affiliation as a more important cultural identifier.

Though by no means all-inclusive, some of the personal qualities, attributes, and other factors that may be used in some contexts as a basis for establishing cultural identity include: language; racial identity; religious affiliation or belief; ethnicity; nationality; national origin; sexual orientation or preference; occupational status; education level; socioeconomic status (e.g., billionaires, blue-collar workers); physical appearance (e.g., fashion model, tall people, obese people); intelligence (e.g., Mensa member); political/philosophical orientation (e.g., conservative, libertarian); social group membership (e.g., motorcycle gang, Free Mason, fraternity or sorority member); shared customs, traditions, or rituals; tribal or clan identity; family organization or structure (e.g., commune); shared values, beliefs, or philosophy; gender; age group; shared preference in food (e.g., vegetarian); shared preference in music or cultural activities; similar clothing choices or appearance (e.g., goth); recreational interests (e.g., hunter, fisher); common interest or participation in sports; school identity; shared physical attributes or limitations; and/or shared history of oppression.

The challenge in selecting any factor as a basis for establishing cultural identity is to recognize which factor, or set of factors, is an essential element of the cultural identity of a particular person or group and which are merely incidental or irrelevant. Although language and race often emerge as distinctive cultural identifiers, in some contexts a shared religious affiliation or sexual orientation may hold a more central role in understanding a client's cultural sense of self.

In working with clients in an intercultural context, it is essential that the family counselor gain an understanding of the meaning their clients may place on their cultural identities and avoid assumptions or generalizations. Does the difference between whether someone is European or Asian, for example, hold a particular central meaning, or is it inconsequential and eclipsed by other, more meaningful factors?

A family counselor should respect the basic client right to self-identify in terms of cultural identity and resist the temptation to label a client based on seemingly apparent factors that some may attribute to cultural identity. In working with a client family, gaining an understanding of the importance the client places on a particular quality or characteristic is essential. For example, a family counselor might ask: "What place does your Catholic faith hold in your life?" For some clients, their Catholic religious identity may be merely incidental. For others, such as a devout believer, priest, or nun, their Catholic religious identity may be the central factor in their cultural self-identity.

SIDEBAR 3.4 CULTURAL IDENTITY: HOW DO YOU SEE YOURSELF?

What other factors contribute to how you self-identify in terms of your cultural identity? From what cultural, ethnic, and racial groups are you descended? List all of these cultural identity influences and the meaning you attribute to each of these influences.

Cultural Values and Intercultural Counseling

Although beliefs, values, ideas, and attitudes may evolve over the course of life due to education, life experiences, and exposure to new ideas, our initial cultural belief system provides a reference point to which subsequent life experiences, concepts, and ideas are compared. Although a person can change a belief, one can never fully escape the profound influence of the cultural identity of their cultural family of origin. Even in so-called liberal societies that encourage a wide range of beliefs and ideas, people are still imprinted by the values of that culture. For example, the capacity for people within a particular society to value diversity and accept a multitude of beliefs is merely a reflection of a cultural value and belief that values diversity and encourages the expression of multiple perspectives.

All societies and communities have mechanisms for shaping and controlling the conduct of their members. Individual members are expected to conform to the general standards of the society in which they live. To ensure compliance with cultural norms, various mechanisms of social control exist. Social control is necessary to maintain a stable society by ensuring that individuals within that society conform to expected standards of conduct. Individuals who deviate from the cultural values of the community in which they live are typically punished to some extent. This reality presents a challenge to the family counselor at practical, ethical, and moral levels.

Recognizing that clients who violate the rules of society may suffer within that society, to what extent does the family counselor work to protect and guide the client, either explicitly or implicitly, toward conforming to the expectations of society? Because human societies and cultures may differ in what they believe and value, to what baseline standard should family counselors align their work—to that of the cultural majority, to the personal values of the family counselor, or to the expressed values of the client?

All people possess a set of core beliefs—notions about how things are, or at least how things should be. Beginning in childhood, a client's worldview is informed from cultural customs. Client views may be explicit or implicit and include such things as religious or spiritual beliefs and practices, philosophy, customs, marital and family roles, and parenting practices. They also include an array of social and moral rules for distinguishing right from wrong as well as acceptable and unacceptable conduct for members within the family or group.

Acceptance of individual and group differences is an ethical responsibility of all counselors. Counselors may not discriminate on the basis of "race, religion, creed, national origin, ethnicity, or sexual orientation" (ACA, 2005, p. 10). Although a moral and ethical value that respects diversity in both individuals and groups may seem self-evident to a professional counselor, this concept challenges many counselors-in-training because it often compels an examination and comparison of the family counselor's own values and beliefs and how they may differ from the values and beliefs of a client with a different cultural identity or orientation.

Depending on the context, social and cultural rules may be codified in law, or they may take the form of social customs. The consequences of violating social rules may vary greatly. In some cases, violations warrant disapproval or admonishment. In other instances, violations may result in imprisonment or even death.

Conflict can occur when a person of one cultural group interacts with a person of a different cultural group, particularly when cultural values greatly differ. The more different or oppositional the worldviews, the greater the potential for conflict or misunderstanding. This reality is exacerbated when the client is a member of one cultural group and the family counselor is a member of a divergently different cultural group.

Multiculturalism is a concept informed by postmodern thought, which holds that the understanding of any phenomenon reflects the reference biases of the observer. Such observer-imposed validity rejects the notion of an immutable objective standard and supports the general tenet that the validity or value of any cultural belief reflects the cultural bias of the observer. The term *intercultural* differs from the term *multicultural* in that it emphasizes the interactive parity between individuals of different cultural groups. Such interaction is the essence of a collaborative family counseling relationship.

Ethically, family counselors refrain from attempting to impose, either directly or indirectly, their personal values and beliefs on their clients. This ethical responsibility can present a challenge. It is possible that a counselor may encounter conflict between ethical responsibilities and community values. For example, the International Association of Marriage and Family Counselors (IAMFC) code of ethics states: "Marriage and family counselors do not engage in activities which violate the legal standards of their community" (2005, p. 11). How can a family counselor ethically support a client and advocate for basic human rights without influencing or endorsing a client's choice that violates the values or offends the sensibilities of the counselor or the predominant values of a community? For example, how might a family counselor address the following issues?

- The practice of polygamy is considered culturally acceptable in some communities and has been widely practiced for many generations in many cultures. Although polygamous marriage is illegal in the United States and Mexico, it is practiced informally in some communities in both countries. How might a family counselor approach this issue should it arise in the course of counseling?
- In some cultures, gender roles are clearly defined and often rigid and relatively inflexible. How might a family counselor address such issues without violating cultural norms?
- Many societies hold increasingly liberal attitudes toward same-sex relationships. However, in some communities and regions of the world, such as East Africa and parts of the Middle East, same-sex relationships are illegal

and violate community values. In light of such cultural considerations, how might a counselor best help a family from Uganda or Saudi Arabia struggling with concerns about the sexual orientation, identity, or behavior of a son or daughter?

TECHNIQUES

The ability of the family counselor and the client family to form a collaborative relationship is essential to a successful counseling outcome. Establishing this collaborative relationship requires the family counselor to identify and accomplish certain tasks. Although they are presented in a sequential order, many of these counselor tasks are ongoing throughout the family counseling process and may be accomplished concurrently.

Task 1: Making a Connection

An initial task in working with any client, but one that is particularly important when a client is culturally different from the family counselor, is establishing a connection with that client. The process of connecting with the client family begins the moment they walk through the door. Initial contact may involve an initial greeting or inquiry about travel to the office or confirming the convenience of the scheduled appointment time. Such an inquiry may appear incidental, but it conveys an initial level of interest and concern about the family. Rather than beginning the session talking about the presenting complaint or problem, it is often useful to ask some initial questions to find out about the family's recent activities and the interests of individual family members. Examples of questions the family counselor might ask to establish an initial connection might include:

- It would be helpful to me to know a little bit about your family. Tell me what each of you like to do aside from work or school.
- What is your favorite subject in school?
- What sport do you most enjoy?
- Do you work outside of the home?

Depending on the responses of various family members, the family counselor may choose to provide appropriate personal disclosure to help establish or strengthen a connection with selected family members. The family counselor should avoid any personal disclosure that contradicts the disclosure of a client (for example, "So you enjoy watching soccer? I find it boring myself; I'm more of a football fan"). While factual, such disclosures serve no useful purpose in the family counseling process. Examples of connecting disclosures that often help the family counselor join with the clients might include:

- I thought the last game was incredible. Like you, I'm also a big fan of the New Orleans Saints.
- Like your father, my dad was a blue-collar worker.

- My wife was also a stay-at-home mom for many years. She reminds me it is probably one of the most demanding jobs on the planet.
- I've always enjoyed trying new foods. Do have any secret for making a gumbo?

Although such opening questions during the initial counseling consultation session may appear to invite innocuous discussion on random topics, they have a clear therapeutic intent. Such questions serve as a sociometric technique for gathering information while simultaneously building a connection with the client based on areas of common interest or experience.

Given the structured, professional nature of the client–counselor relationship, nothing the family counselor presents, says, or does in relation to the client should be random. Everything about the family counselor—mannerisms, personal appearance, office decor, content and nature of questions, and personal disclosures—should have a clear and deliberate purpose. This joining technique is both initial and ongoing and intended to establish and maintain a connection with the client family members.

SIDEBAR 3.5 MAKING A CONNECTION WITH THE FAMILY

If you were a new client meeting a family counselor for the first time, what would you consider to be the most effective things the family counselor could do to establish a personal connection with you? As the client, what behaviors would you consider most important in this process? What might the family counselor say or do that would result in making such a connection? What might the family counselor say or do that would have the opposite effect and result in your feeling disconnected from the counselor?

Task 2: Alignment and Support of Family Members

Many clients, particularly those who identify as belonging to a minority culture, may have experienced bias, prejudice, or discrimination in their interactions with members of other cultural groups. This reality can have a direct impact and complicate the counseling relationship when the family counselor is perceived as a member of such a cultural group.

In addition, although some clients may not have personally experienced or recognized notable incidents of discrimination, there may still be significant vicarious sensitivity due to generalized persecution of family members or close friends. For clients whose families have experienced political oppression, expulsion, or even extermination, the meaning clients attribute to cultural differences can have profound implications for their perceived place and role in society. For example, a counselor who identifies as Jewish may find it challenging to overcome the negative perceptions some Muslim clients may hold of Jews. Similarly, a middle-aged White male counselor may be challenged in his efforts to effectively overcome historical barriers of prejudice and racism in joining with an African American family.

With respect to the attitudes, values, and beliefs of the family counselor, such generalizations may be unwarranted and unfair, but they are often very real. It is necessary that the family counselor address and overcome any such perceptual differences that may precede the counseling relationship or that may emerge during the course of the counseling process. One strategy is for the counselor to directly address any possible concerns about cultural differences: "When you walked into room and saw that I was a 50-year-old White guy, what was your first impression of me? Have you ever had a similar experience—that people make assumptions about you based on appearance (or age, gender, etc.)?"

Task 3: Establishing the Purpose and Goals of Family Counseling

An essential but often overlooked task is clarifying the purpose and goal of family counseling. A central question to be answered is: Why is the family here? It is sometimes erroneously assumed that the goal of the client family is the removal of a presenting symptom or complaint. Although this is sometimes correct, in other situations the goal of the client is unknown or vague, or the complaint is merely a symptom of a larger issue. It is common when working with couples or families that various family members have differing—sometimes conflicting—priorities as to the desired goal or outcome.

In gaining a mutual understanding and agreement as to the family's purpose and goal for participating in counseling, the following questions are often useful:

- Who would like to tell me what brings you here today? (Ask each family member in turn.)
- How may I be of help to you?
- What would you like to see come out of our meeting today?
- What do you *not* want to see come out of today's meeting?
- When will you know that counseling has succeeded and our work here is done?

In further establishing the individual agendas and goals of family counseling, it is often useful at the end of the initial session to give each family member a homework assignment to be completed before the next counseling session. This assignment asks each family member to do the following, separately and without conferring with other family members:

> This week I would like for you to write down three or four things that you would like to see different in your family. This may be something you would like be different in yourself, something different with another family member, or something different among all family members. Give this some thought and bring your written list to our next session. For now, it is important that you keep this information to yourself; I ask that you *do not* share your list with any other family member.

At the next family counseling session, the family counselor will review each list and identify common goals that emerge. The family counselor will then engage the family in a discussion as to whether the identified goal or goals might be an appropriate shared goal on which the family may wish to focus its efforts for change, at least initially. Illuminating a specific goal or goals does not preclude addressing additional issues that may emerge over the course of family counseling or changing goals, as appropriate. However, it provides an initial tangible goal or set of goals upon which the family may wish to focus. Identifying and setting goals for family counseling conveys a sense of shared ownership among family members.

Task 4: Defining and Clarifying the Role of the "Helper"

Counseling is a professional relationship in which a qualified counseling professional uses his or her knowledge and skills to assist the client in bringing about desired change. The practice of counseling, and similar mental health professions such as psychology, psychiatry, and social work, seeks to alleviate human pain and suffering by improving individual functioning and the quality of relationships. Counseling is only the latest incarnation of a long-standing tradition of "human helping." All human cultures recognize certain individuals within a community who serve in this helping role (Pesek, Helton, & Nair, 2006). Titles (e.g., shaman, priest, traiteur, healer) differ, as do methods and techniques, but all of these helping roles share in common the purpose of attempting to ameliorate human problems and suffering. All people, regardless of cultural identity, encounter problems in living and problems endemic to the human condition. As such, counseling as a catalyst for change holds a potential to assist people across cultures.

Depending on cultural expectations, some clients will enter family counseling with preconceived notions about the counseling process and the role of the family counselor. For example, in some Asian cultures it is assumed that the counselor is the "expert" who holds all of the answers to the family's problems. Similar to a physician treating an illness or injury, some or all members of the client family may assume that it is the role of family members to simply present the problem and the family counselor will dispense advice and directives that will result in a desired change or outcome. Such an initial belief about the process of counseling is understandable, particularly when the cultural expectations of a client view the role of the family counselor as the expert. Such client families often prefer more directive therapeutic approaches and may not respond well to seemingly passive and reflective counseling approaches and may even view the family counselor as lacking competence.

Because members of various cultural groups may hold divergent notions as to the appropriate and proper role of the family counselor, it is essential that the role of the family counselor be discussed and clarified. Some family members may hold a mistaken belief that the family counselor has the ability to unilaterally fix the problem. A common parental request might be, "I want you to work with my teenage daughter and make her stop using drugs." Intercultural family counseling emphasizes the collaborative nature of the counseling relationship in which the client family and counselor work as a team to address identified areas of concern and mutually agreed upon goals.

As such, an essential task to be addressed in the family counseling process is clarifying the role of the family counselor. The family counselor should take time during the initial session to explain to the family how the counselor envisages his or her role as a helper to the family. Operationalizing terms might include objective expert, consultant, or coach—essentially any role title that fits the family's cultural narrative and conveys that the family counselor is there to assist the family in accomplishing their desired goals. The family counselor should be unequivocal that he or she is not capable of unilaterally solving the family's problem and that this primary responsibility belongs to the family. Concurrently, the family counselor should convey that he or she will be active in assisting the client family to bring about desired changes by illuminating existing behavioral patterns and attitudes and supporting the family in implementing alternatives.

Task 5: Conveying Interest and Curiosity

A useful position for the family counselor to hold when working with any client, but particularly with a client who is culturally different from the family counselor, is one of curiosity and inquiry. Because the education and status of the family counselor are already known to the client to some extent, this counseling tactic does not diminish the expertise of the family counselor. Rather, it serves to create a collaborative relationship. The nature of this collaborative position conveys the reality that the client is the expert with regard to the particular situation—relationships, needs, and desired changes. This focus, in which the counselor holds expert authority by virtue of position and the client family holds expert authority regarding their life circumstances, places the family counselor and client family on an equal basis in terms of cocreating the family counseling relationship and taking mutual responsibility for its success.

Task 6: Working With the Family to Accomplish Goals

Clearly defining the role of the family counselor and the roles of family members to ensure a successful outcome to the counseling process is essential. This is particularly important when client cultural expectations may hold erroneous assumptions regarding the scope and role of the family counselor in fixing the client's problem. Framing family counseling as a collaborative relationship between the counselor and the client minimizes such misunderstandings. This strategy places the responsibility for change with family members. However, it also emphasizes the role of the family counselor as a knowledgeable resource—an ally who joins the family system and works actively with family members to recognize dysfunctional behavioral patterns and problematic family roles and structure and to create circumstances to bring about desired changes.

In bringing about desired change, it is the role of the family counselor to have an array of intervention strategies that are capable of producing desired changes.

The specific theoretical orientation of the family counselor is less important than the capacity of the family counselor to join and work with the family in a collaborative manner.

LIMITATIONS

As with any type of helping endeavor, family counseling is not a panacea for the human condition—nor is it appropriate in all circumstances. Contextual factors should be examined and considered by the potential client family and family counselor before entering into in a family counseling relationship. Do members of the client family believe that the counseling process holds potential to help the family with its concern or problem?

Often, this consideration is self-selecting because most people will never seek counseling services if they do not believe at some level that such services are potentially helpful. In a family counseling setting, there is the potential that one or more family members believe counseling can be useful and helpful, but other family members may be highly skeptical. In instances in which a client holds an inflexible belief that counseling (in general) and family counseling are not useful or potentially useful, the client should be supported in pursuing other resources, with the caveat that if circumstances change, the counselor is still available to help.

Family counseling as an outpatient intervention is not advised when the level of functioning of one or more family members presents a clear or immediate danger to human life. Examples of this would a family member with homicidal or suicidal ideation with high-risk intentionality, or the diminished functioning of a family member due to a life-threatening situation such as an eating disorder, psychotic symptoms, or severe depression. Some families may lack the organizational structure and resources to support and protect a high-risk family member on a day-to-day basis between counseling sessions. In such cases, referral to professional or community resources that provide necessary support are indicated, such as hospitalization or structured living environments. Inpatient family counseling can also be useful for immediate crisis stabilization.

SIDEBAR 3.6 LIMITATIONS OF FAMILY COUNSELING: HOW WOULD YOU REFER A FAMILY MEMBER FOR INPATIENT HELP?

When encountering a family in which an individual family member is too unstable (e.g., life-threatening diminished functioning or high risk for acting on suicidal thoughts), how you would discuss with the family the need for referral to an inpatient facility to better support the at-risk family member? How might you coordinate ongoing family counseling in light of the hospitalization of a family member?

SUMMARY

Effective intercultural family counseling requires that the counselor possess a basic knowledge and understanding of the client family's cultural orientation. The extent to which the family counselor can join with the client family and become part of a collaborative effort to create desired change presents unique challenges, particularly when the family counselor and client family stem from notably different cultural reference groups. However, such differences can be overcome when the family counselor utilizes an understanding of cultural differences to help the family collectively define the presenting problem issue, develop common goals, and develop a strategy for desired change.

USEFUL WEBSITES AND LINKS

The following websites provide additional information relating to the chapter topics.

American Counseling Association
http://www.counseling.org
American Association for Marriage and Family Therapy
http://www.aamft.org
Association for Counselor Education and Supervision
http://www.acesonline.net
American Mental Health Counselors Association
http://www.amhca.org
Association for Lesbian, Gay, Bisexual, and Transgender Issues in Counseling
http://www.algbtic.org
Association for Multicultural Counseling and Development
http://www.multiculturalcounseling.org
Association for Spiritual, Ethical, and Religious Values in Counseling
http://www.aservic.org
Center for Multicultural Mental Health Research
http://www.multiculturalmentalhealth.org
Center for Multilingual Multicultural Research
http://www.bcf.usc.edu
Consortium for Multicultural Psychology Research
http://www.psychology.msu.edu/cmpr
Ecohealth
http://www.springerlink.com
International Association of Marriage and Family Counselors
http://www.iamfconline.org
The World Fact Book
http://www.cia.gov/library/publications/the-world-factbook
United Nations Data
http://www.data.un.org

U.S. Department of Health and Human Services
http://www.ncadi.samhsa.gov

REFERENCES

American Counseling Association (ACA). (2005). *Code of ethics and standards of practice*. Alexandria, VA: Author.

Becvar, R., Canfield, B., and Becvar, D. (1997). *Group work: Cybernetic, constructivist, and social constructionist perspectives*. Denver, CO: Love Publishing.

Bitter, J. R. (2009). *Theory and practice of family therapy and counseling*. Belmont, CA: Brooks/Cole.

Council for Accreditation of Counseling and Related Programs (CACREP). (2009). *2009 standards*. Retrieved from http://www.cacrep.org/2009standards.html

Dorman, J. H. (2003). The Cajuns: Ethnogenesis and the shaping of group consciousness. In G. R. Conrad (Ed.), *The Cajuns: Essays on their history and culture*. Lafayette, LA: Center for Louisiana Studies.

International Association of Marriage and Family Counselors (IAMFC). (2005). *IAMFC code of ethics*. Alexandria, VA: Author.

McGoldrick, M. (1998). *Re-visioning family therapy: Race, culture, and gender in clinical practice*. New York, NY: Guilford Press.

Pesek, T., Helton, L., & Nair, M. (2006). Healing across cultures: Learning from traditions. *EcoHealth*, *3*(2), 114–118.

United Nations, Department of Economic and Social Affairs. (2013). *International migration*. New York, NY: Author.

U.S. State Department, Bureau of Public Affairs. (2003). *The Great Seal of the United States*. Washington, DC: Author.

CHAPTER 4

Effectively Using Research and Assessment in Couples and Family Therapy

Brandé Flamez
Lamar University

Janet Froeschle Hicks
Texas Tech University

Ashley Clark
Commonwealth of Virginia Department for Aging and Rehabilitative Services

The systemic nature and dynamics of couples and family therapy require interplay between research and assessment. Inconsistencies between practicing counselors and those conducting research give rise to concerns about the practicality and efficacy of the information obtained. Research is intended to provide the tools and information necessary to move from theoretical underpinnings to clinical practice, but it is often performed by those in academic institutions who do the least amount of clinical service (Oka & Whiting, 2013). Brock, Whiting, Matern, and Fife (2009) noted the importance of establishing family counselors as credible and knowledgeable professionals; this requires bridging the gap between those who conduct research and those who employ interventions. Failure to address this gap in communication and understanding, as well as to train clinicians to conduct and employ research effectively, potentially results in unethical and even overreaching services. Developing methods that allow family counselors to contribute their experiences and understanding to research, as well as finding a way to employ that research in practice, is therefore necessary in conducting counseling services, including therapeutic family services. Because a gap between researchers and clinicians exists among various social science professions (Brock et al., 2009), the importance of employing evidence-based interventions cannot be ignored.

Topics affecting couples and families, such as substance abuse, domestic abuse, behavior disorders, marital discord, sexual issues, and a variety of other mental health paradigms, have been assessed and researched within the family setting since the emergence of couples counseling in the 1930s and family counseling in the 1940s (Sprenkle, 2003). Research in the area of family counseling grew following World War II. For example, pioneer practitioners such as Nathan Ackerman, Virginia Satir, John Gottman, Salvador Minuchin, Carl Whitaker, Jay Haley, Gregory Bateson, Murray Bowen, and numerous others changed the way family therapy was viewed and conducted (Rasheed, Rasheed, & Marley, 2011). Interestingly, assessment also played a crucial role in this early research. According to Rhodes (2012), however, family therapy as a profession has historically been resistant to the integration of research into practice, especially over the past decade and a half. Specifically, Rhodes noted "our history has been defined, in many ways, by a struggle to become less deterministic, more collaborative and more respective of the power we yield as therapists" (p. 173). With growing integration of research in similar professions, including individual counseling, a substantial shift in openness to exploring ways to establish accountability and credibility resulted in only a recent acceptance of the importance of research in practice. As such, a growing amount of family therapy research literature began to appear.

Although acceptance of the instrumental value of research in family therapy serves as one piece of the puzzle, knowing how and when to integrate the information is just as important. As a result, the systematic nature of couples and family therapy requires interplay between research and assessment. According to Nichols and Tafuri (2013), family counselors use both indirect observations and more direct tools not only to uncover the interactional components of the presenting problem but also to establish the factors that indicate the necessity of interventions. Therefore, assessment involves more than information gathering and instead focuses on a conceptualization of the family components, which have resulted in the identified issues. As Oka and Whiting (2013) noted, this inquiry has not only served as the basis for research questioning but also provides counselors with a clear understanding of what activities and interventions may be beneficial.

Given an overwhelming push within social sciences to compensate for questions regarding the field's scientific value and the push for use of evidence-based interventions, integration of research and assessment, as well as collaboration between researchers and clinicians, has gained growing importance. As Nichols and Tafuri (2013) noted, knowledge and implementation of assessment methods and research findings in family therapy is a crucial component of ethical and effective practice. As a result, this chapter offers information on family therapy research, including its importance, findings, and design types, followed by information on assessment methods, standardized designs for individuals, and specific assessments for couples and families.

SIDEBAR 4.1 RESEARCH, ASSESSMENT, AND EVIDENCE-BASED TREATMENT

Research and assessment are integral and often inseparable parts of family counseling theory. Think about the family counseling theories you studied. How has research influenced each of the theories? Is formal or informal assessment used in these theories? In what ways are research and assessment integrated when using these theories? Given your knowledge on each theory, which ones are evidence based? Would some theories be easier to research than others? Explain your answers.

THE ROLE OF RESEARCH IN EFFECTIVE FAMILY THERAPY

The International Association of Marriage and Family Counselors (IAMFC) established continued research relative to the efficacy of treatment approaches in addressing issues presented by clients as an expectation for ethical practice (Hendricks, Bradley, Southern, Oliver, & Birdsall, 2011). According to the American Association for Marriage and Family Therapy (AAMFT, 2013), research serves as the fundamental crux of the viability, integrity, and credibility of family counseling, with studies demonstrating increased effectiveness of family therapy in the treatment of specific behavioral and mental health issues. Focused on obtaining a better understanding of the divergence in conventional family systems from those in prior decades, researchers over the past several years have sought to uncover how family counselors can provide services effectively to a more diverse community. Cherlin (2010) concluded that the deterioration of the traditional family structure (increased rates of divorce, children born out of wedlock, blended families, dual-income households, and cohabitation outside marriage) requires further research to increase understanding and effective treatment of resulting issues.

Brock et al. (2009) identified that the onset of family therapy literature was fraught with suppositions and unsupported ideas, bringing into question the efficacy of treatment approaches. As the authors noted, such research has the potential to mislead the population and cast a shadow of doubt on the profession. By conducting honest research that focuses on the issues often resulting in the disintegration of the family structure, counselors can increase preparedness for addressing such concerns in treatment. Furthermore, the establishment of this research has resulted in the formulation of improved theories and will continue to guide practice. Sanderson et al. (2009) noted that it is through this lens of research that family therapy has grown as a distinct and formidable profession. With an increased focus on research integrity, family therapists have distinguished themselves from other similar professionals.

SIDEBAR 4.2

The following statement is taken from this chapter:

> The deterioration of the traditional family structure (including increased rates of divorce, children born out of wedlock, blended families, dual-income households, and cohabitation outside marriage) requires further research to increase understanding and effective treatment of resulting issues (Cherlin, 2010).

While considering the aforementioned issues affecting the nontraditional family, think of ways you might address the following family currently going through a divorce. Mr. and Mrs. Hernandez were married 10 years and have two sons, aged 8 and 6. Mr. Hernandez does not want to divorce his wife but has come to accept the fact that he is homosexual. Mrs. Hernandez is distraught and feels Mr. Hernandez has lied to her for years. What specific issues in this case need additional research if counselors are to be helpful? As a counselor, how would you help this family?

CONCLUSIONS DRAWN IN FAMILY THERAPY RESEARCH

An influx of researchers within the realm of family therapy has sought to establish evidence-based practice to increase clinical effectiveness while reducing the amount of time and resources wasted (both for the clients and the counselor) on ineffective services. Carr (2010) noted that it is through the variations in studies related to positive outcomes of family systems therapy in the efficient treatment of diverse individuals that mounting support of family systems implementation has occurred. Credibility of these studies, coupled with continual evaluation of ways in which to improve treatment outcomes, continues to strengthen the reputation of family systems approaches to counseling.

Given the increasing focus within the marriage and family literature on conducting honest and ethical research studies to support the effectiveness of family systems therapeutic models, it is imperative that family counselors become knowledgeable of the most recent research findings. In attempting to establish a thorough collection of research within the field of marriage and family counseling, several research channels were consulted, including the *Journal of Marriage and Family Therapy*, the *Family Journal*, the *Journal of Family Issues*, the *American Journal of Family Therapy*, and *Contemporary Family Therapy*. Results of this investigation uncovered several themes within family systems research:

- Marriage and family therapy are effective in addressing issues such as adolescent developmental disabilities (Tomasello, Manning, & Dulmus, 2010) and behavioral issues (Lee et al., 2009; Roberts, Mazzucchelli, Studman, & Sanders, 2006).

- Family therapy has been demonstrated to be more effective than individual therapy in increasing communication and reducing discrepancies in perception between parents and children (Guo & Slesnick, 2013).
- In situations of low-conflict divorce, family therapy increases effective coparenting skills (Ramisch, McVicker, & Sahin, 2009).
- Family interventions among family members of an individual with a significant physical illness are associated with increased coping skills (Shields, Finley, Chawla, & Meadors, 2012).
- Family involvement in treatment for individuals with substance abuse disorders is associated with higher levels of treatment success (Matheson & Lukic, 2011; Rowe, 2012).
- Adolescent issues have been linked to familial factors (Baldwin, Christian, Berkeljon, & Shadish, 2012).
- Approaches that incorporate the family systems illness model in the treatment of individuals with severe depression have been demonstrated to be effective (Beach & Whisman, 2012; Lemmens, Eisler, Migerode, Heireman, & Demyttenaere, 2007).
- Despite being rooted in strong Western values and norms, family therapy approaches have been adapted to work with individuals of diverse cultural backgrounds (Seponski, Bermudez, & Lewis, 2013).
- Proposal of evidence-based treatment methods in family therapy is categorized on a three-tier system of "'evidence-informed,' to 'evidence-based,' to 'evidence-based and ready for dissemination and transportation within diverse community settings'" (Sexton et al., 2011, p. 377).
- Family therapy has been shown to be more cost effective than individual or mixed psychotherapy, despite having similar results (Russell Crane & Payne, 2011).
- Research has supported the potential efficacy of family therapy in addressing a variety of presenting issues and diagnoses including anorexia nervosa (Smith & Cook-Cottone, 2011), anxiety (Chambless, 2012), posttraumatic stress disorder (Monson, Macdonald, & Brown-Bowers, 2012), and schizophrenia (Smerud & Rosenfarb, 2011).
- Father participation in family therapy was associated with greater outcomes (Bagner, 2013).
- Despite previous research indicating no increased benefit of using a cotherapy approach in marriage and family counseling (Mehlman, Baucom, & Anderson, 1983), Hendrix, Fournier, and Briggs (2001) argued that cotherapy was reported more effective, including a reduced dropout rate compared to individual therapy, especially when cotherapists were teamed appropriately.

In developing evidence-based support of couples and family therapy, researchers appear to overwhelmingly support an integrative method to family therapy that relies on the presence of a strong therapeutic foundation. It is through this relationship and engagement of multiple members of the family system that

Steinglass (2009) noted that family therapy will be most effective. The following integrative family systems approaches have been suggested in the literature:

- Systemic motivational theory, proposed by Steinglass (2009), integrates aspects of motivational interviewing and systems theory focused on the family members of individuals with substance abuse disorders who are involved in the care and treatment of the individual.
- Integrative brief solution-focused family therapy combines elements of other therapeutic approaches to overcome challenges presented by using a purely solution-focused approach (Beyebach, 2009).
- Integrative problem-centered metaframeworks therapy provides the blueprint to overcome traditional challenges faced in the integration of evidence-based practices into family therapy, including the need to bring cultural variables and considerations into the multifunction framework (Breunlin, Pinsof, & Russell, 2011).
- Multidimensional family therapy (MDFT), which utilizes diverse techniques including psychoeducation and developmentally based interventions, has been successfully employed with adolescents in the juvenile justice system (Marvel, Rowe, Colon-Perez, Diclemente, & Liddle, 2009).
- Gardner, Burr, and Wiedower (2006) identified that despite substantial misconceptions about the ethics of brief strategic family therapy, the integration of multiple approaches to addressing the complex issues that develop in family members is an effective approach to targeting individual issues.

The various research studies noted here, as well as the countless others that have been published in the last several years, demonstrate continued challenges in the assessment of the efficacy of family systems approaches and raise questions about how to incorporate diversity as a means to increase outcomes across multiple populations. Through the utilization of research procedures, marriage and family therapists continue to establish the field as a viable and necessary component of counseling in which systems, as opposed to individuals, are targeted.

Research Methods: Qualitative, Quantitative, and Mixed

Creswell (2013) noted research can be categorized into one of three fundamental research processes: qualitative, quantitative, and mixed methods. Although these processes are generally established as separate entities, the flexibility and approaches within each method result in some potential overlap. In situations in which a researcher wishes to explore complex meanings of human social problems, for example, qualitative methods are likely to be employed. According to Creswell, these studies are often more naturalistic and flexible in approach and use inductive means of inquiry that allow the research to work from participant responses to create a more thematic understanding of the data. In simpler terms, such research is assessed to focus more on words than numbers.

Whereas qualitative research is often criticized for its methodological rigor (Ryan-Nicholls & Will, 2009), quantitative methods of inquiry are often regarded as more systematic in nature. According to Creswell (2013), quantitative studies are often conducted when the researcher seeks to explain or identify relationships between several variables. As opposed to qualitative studies, which take on a more inductive approach, quantitative studies are more deductive in nature, with the researcher laying out a series of hypotheses regarding how the results of the study will answer the research questions. In such studies, the establishment of a hypothesis regarding the outcome of the results is met by a systematic procedure in order to reduce the effects of extraneous variables as potential explanations. As a result, studies that employ quantitative methods are likely to occur in less naturalistic environments, resulting in an increased potential for such studies to be repeated.

Although studies that employ qualitative and quantitative methods may occur independently of each other, some research questions allow for researchers to examine a phenomenon by employing both methods in the same study. According to Creswell (2013), mixed methods designs provide researchers the opportunity to explore issues that will benefit from conjoint explanations of words and numbers. Although they receive less focus in the literature, mixed methods studies serve as a systematic merging of both elements to provide a more comprehensive understanding of a given phenomenon.

RESEARCH METHODS IN FAMILY THERAPY

Matching the diversity of family treatment approaches and clients, researchers in family therapy have incorporated not only qualitative and quantitative inquiries but also mixed method approaches. According to Sprenkle (2012), despite a heavy reliance on quantitative research methods in family therapy, the existence of qualitative inquiries provides the opportunity to gain rich and in-depth information regarding the subjective experience of family members and participants. Creswell (2013) described qualitative methods obtained through multiple methods, including interviews, focus groups, and observations. Subjective experiences are then transformed into themes for meaning. The information obtained through qualitative methods and presentation of material, therefore, provides an opportunity to evaluate programs and procedures.

Despite receiving less attention within the overall body of family therapy literature, qualitative research has been utilized within research to target various perceptions regarding the counseling experience. In fact, qualitative research has targeted parental experiences of children who are in counseling services, uncovering greater rates of treatment completion when parents felt that they were an instrumental part of the process (Sheridan, Peterson, & Rosen, 2010). Results of this study indicate the importance for the family counselor to engage with all members in order to develop a strong therapeutic relationship and increase the opportunity for treatment success. Other qualitative studies have targeted obtaining an increased understanding of the underlying dynamics at play in family counseling. Van Parys and Rober (2013), for example, investigated the experiences of children who had at least one parent diagnosed with severe depression. Results of this study revealed an inherent need among these children placed in a caregiving role to receive positive affirmation in session and noted the potential role that the child may take on in the counseling relationship. Implications of these findings are necessary to determining the most effective ways of approaching the client. In addition to focusing on perceptions of participants both as a result of and prior to the counseling relationship, qualitative research has also investigated the experiences of counselors providing family therapy to increase support and training and reduce counselor burn out. Baker-Ericzén, Jenkins, and Haine-Schlagel (2013), for example, exposed factors such as poor support, lack of family engagement, and complexity of presenting issues as areas of high frustration for counselors. Implications for these results include evaluation of support among the profession in adequately preparing counselors for family work.

Whereas qualitative research provides information necessary to incorporating change and feedback, quantitative research is often referred to as a method that transforms human experience into numbers (Duffy & Chenail, 2008). Given the systematic nature in which quantitative studies are completed, including controlling for extraneous variables, these studies are repeatable and generalizable. Sprenkle (2012) noted that quantitative research in family therapy has been somewhat static over time, with a primary focus on the areas of "conduct disorder/delinquency, adolescent and adult drug abuse, childhood and adolescent disorders (not including conduct disorders/drug abuse), family psycho-education (FPE) for major mental illness, alcoholism, couple distress, relationship education, affective disorders, IPV [intimate partner violence], and chronic illness" (p. 3). Sprenkle cautioned about the credence provided to these articles, noting that the researchers often have a stake in the outcome of their proposed research. Despite this caution, these quantitative studies have demonstrated a reduction in reported symptoms when addressed through a quantitative approach. Repetition of these studies by researchers without a direct stake in the procedures will likely increase the credibility of these studies.

Bridging the gap between the largely inductive approach to qualitative inquiry and the deductive approach to quantitative research, an increase in mixed methods studies can be found within the literature. Referring to the importance of randomized clinical trials (RCT) in establishing evidence of efficacy, Sprenkle (2012) described the potential benefits of merging elements of both approaches in order to gain the scope of information allotted through qualitative means while maintaining a sense of external validity offered through quantitative means. Unfortunately, Gambrel and Butler (2013) revealed that often mixed methods studies are not reported as such, decreasing the perceived impact of such studies in family therapy. Understanding the processes involved in mixed methods research is therefore necessary to ensuring appropriate representation in research. As Weisner and Fiese (2011) noted, mixed methods research is a systematic gathering of qualitative and quantitative research for the purpose of examining a phenomenon. The development of both words and numbers, for example, must serve a purpose of gaining a more in-depth understanding of processes in play within the therapeutic relationship. Given the relative infancy of the employment of mixed methods in family therapy research and the underrepresentation by researchers who utilize mixed methods approaches but do not title them as such, additional investigation is needed to understand the roles that mixed method approaches have had in defining family theoretical approaches.

As the field of family counseling continues to grow and evolve relative to a focus on evidence-based interventions, the role of research will continue to play a large role. Whether undertaking a more subjective evaluation to understand perceptions and experience, or a more objective approach to examining relationships between variables, qualitative, quantitative, and mixed methods research approaches all present as important elements of the profession. Understanding ways to effectively evaluate family therapy outcomes requires a clear understanding of these research designs.

Effectively Evaluating Couples and Families

Although substantial attention has been placed on the difficulties faced by those attempting to conduct research on the effectiveness of family therapy, including the complexities of issues presented in the family environment, few studies provide clear direction regarding how to develop research to evaluate outcomes. Evans, Turner, and Trotter (2012) argued that preliminary decisions on research methods must involve an understanding of the modalities of intervention and the purposes of these modalities. For example, the employment of structural family therapy envisions structural change, while experiential family therapy focuses on increasing individual self-awareness and self-esteem. Understanding the intended scope and purpose of the study is necessary in developing the research design. Cognitive-behavioral therapeutic approaches in family systems, for example, are likely to require a more quantitative approach to examining efficacy, whereas experiential family therapy likely would benefit from qualitative evaluation.

Creswell (2013) established three considerations that lay the foundation for which design to implement in a research study. Specifically, the researcher must understand his or her philosophical worldview, the course of inquiry that fits the worldview, and the method(s) that complement the two factors. Creswell noted that qualitative research often involves either postpositive, interpretive, or critical methodological approaches. In holding this worldview, phenomena are understood in the social environments in which they occur. On the other hand, positivist worldviews lend themselves to a more quantitative approach to research. Collection of data is therefore focused on information that either is numerical in nature or can be transformed into numerical information (Creswell, 2013). In situations in which questions of why and how exist, mixed methods approaches may be employed.

As with any research study, establishment of a representative sample is necessary to ensure that the research meets the standards set forth in the IAMFC code of ethics (Hendricks et al., 2011). Failure to ensure that samples clearly reflect the population of interest results in the portrayal of misleading information. According to Tuckett (2004), establishing a specific number of participants needed for qualitative research is nearly impossible because qualitative research requires saturation of information as opposed to a specific number of people. Determining sample size for quantitative research, on the other hand, requires understanding of the population size, the number of variables of study, and the researcher's desired accuracy (Creswell, 2013).

SIDEBAR 4.3

Qualitative and quantitative research methods are important tools used to advance family counseling services. Qualitative methods can be used to discover information about unknown dynamics within the family culture. Quantitative methods are useful when hypotheses are predetermined and probabilities can be mathematically interpreted. Which method would be most appropriate for the following scenario?

The Green family consists of Mr. Green, age 38, Mrs. Green, age 35, and their daughter Liz, age 13. Mrs. Green states that Mr. Green has no empathy for her situation. She has been diagnosed with cancer, has been through major surgery, and is currently undergoing chemotherapy. Mr. Green states that Mrs. Green is no longer attractive, fusses at him "constantly," and he, therefore, works 17 hours per day. Liz seems angry but will not talk during sessions.

Which research methods would a counselor use to learn more about the unknown dynamics in this family? How would you conduct this research? How would a counselor use qualitative and/or quantitative methods to determine the efficacy of the treatment this family receives?

Given the presence of diverse philosophical foundations, integration of various counseling interventions, a reliance on multiple research methods, and variance in desired treatment outcomes, various instruments may be used. These instruments include the qualitative approaches of interviewing, observations, and focus groups, as well as quantitative methods such as surveys and pretest and posttest measures. Evans et al. (2012) noted that instruments used in individual counseling can often be employed in family therapy research.

Overall, research regarding family therapy is a compilation of research involving individuals with a broader focus on the family system as opposed to the person. As such, researchers must make decisions regarding the methods and instruments used based on the availability of information on the phenomenon and the research questions being answered. Given the standard for evidence-based classifications, utilization of instruments in family research requires the same expectations concerning validity and reliability or credibility as other studies.

In order to meet the guidelines set forth by the IAMFC (Hendricks et al., 2011) regarding delivery of ethical and effective family therapeutic services, clinicians must understand the importance of research. Because research serves as the foundation for evidence-based practice, understanding the presenting issues within the family system is necessary in order to determine which evidence-based interventions may be effectively employed. As such, assessment skills within family counseling provide the means to meet the expectations of IAMFC.

ASSESSMENT IN FAMILY THERAPY

Now that we have discussed the importance of family therapy research, let's turn our focus toward discussing assessment, which is the process by which counselors gather the information they need to form a holistic view of their clients and the problems with which they present. For the remaining sections of this chapter, we focus on assessment methods, standardized designs for individuals, and specific assessments for couples and families.

What Is Assessment?

When individual clients, couples, or families present for therapy, they do so with individual perceptions, ideas, and stories. Despite any discrepancies, the counselor is tasked with gaining a clear understanding of the presenting problems. According to Watson and Flamez (2014), the method for this information-gathering process is *assessment*. Whether through informal or formal means, as discussed further in this chapter, counselors gain important information from this process that sets the stage for how they conceive the client's reason for seeking counseling services.

Purpose of Assessment

Assessment serves an instrumental function within family counseling. In fact, Deacon and Piercy (2001) go as far as to argue that "family therapy without assessment is like a car trip without a map" (p. 355). Without a clear understanding of the family history and dynamics, the family counselor does not possess the tools to work effectively with the family for positive outcomes. Specifically, Deacon and Piercy noted that the purpose of assessment is to know where the family has been, their current location, and where they wish to go. By gaining a picture of the presenting problem, roles of the family members, interactional patterns, systemic resources, and desired outcomes, the family counselor can support the family in developing their own road map to success.

Reliability and Validity

Given the importance of the assessment process in family counseling, it is equally important to ensure that the formal or informal methods used in obtaining information for assessment are appropriate and reliable. Watson and Flamez (2014) noted that when choosing an instrument to be used for assessment, the counselor must first verify the reliability of the instrument. The term *reliability* is used to describe the ability for the test data to be reproduced. Higher reliability estimates therefore indicate that if provided the instrument more than once, an individual would score significantly similar if external factors are considered. As such, increased reliability scores indicate more trustworthy assessments.

Whereas reliability addresses the ability of test scores to be reproduced, the term *validity* is used to evaluate the potential for an instrument to be interpreted accurately within given populations. As such, the validity of an instrument is not a measure of quality but instead a measure of how accurately scores would apply in a given context (Watson & Flamez, 2014). Therefore, interpretation of instruments' validity applied to specific clients or situations relies on consideration of the published research on the given population.

Selecting, Administering, Scoring, and Reporting Assessment Results

Decisions regarding what instruments to use or how to integrate assessment results depend on numerous factors beyond reliability and validity. Understanding why assessments are needed and how results will be used is also important in the decision as to what instrument to employ. After narrowing down the type of assessment needed, the counselor must then proceed to resources to gain more information about specific instruments and how they need to be employed (Watson & Flamez, 2014). There are several sources that can be accessed to learn more about existing tests and their various advantages and disadvantages across counseling settings, including the *Mental Measurements Yearbook* (*MMY*; Spies, Carlson, & Geisinger, 2010); *Tests in Print* (*TIP*, 8th ed.; Murphy, Geisinger, Carlson, & Spies, 2011); *Tests: A Comprehensive Reference for Assessments in Psychology, Education, and Business* (Maddox, 2008); *Test Critiques*; peer-reviewed counseling-related journals; and test publisher websites.

Although there are numerous assessments available, one must ensure he or she is qualified to administer, score, and interpret the test. Most test publishers specify the level of qualification one needs to purchase and use their products. According to Watson and Flamez (2014), information regarding the qualifications of administering these tests is often included in professional standards from national counseling organizations, and it is the legal and ethical responsibility of the counselor to ensure that they are followed. Failure to address these expectations may result in a counselor practicing outside his or her own scope of competence, which is an ethical violation. Furthermore, failure to follow the protocols established by specific instruments has the potential to invalidate results.

Scoring of many formal instruments is also established under the instrument's testing guidelines. As such, counselors employing these instruments must also ensure that scoring follows the established guidelines in order to provide the client with the most accurate and ethical feedback. According to Watson and Flamez (2014), this feedback may occur either formally or informally, but it must be framed in a way that most appropriately meets the client's needs.

Informal and Formal Assessments

In identifying methods to employ in the assessment of couples and families for the purpose of setting therapeutic goals and treatment interventions, as well as measuring effectiveness of approaches, family therapists must consider whether a formal or informal assessment method is warranted. Mirroring the potential subjectivity of social understanding regarding human behaviors and interactions, informal assessments provide less structured approaches to understanding family systems. De Mol, Buysse, and Cook (2010) noted that formal assessments, on the other hand, are more structured and based on empirical data, which may be required when validated means are necessary. Understanding the uniqueness of each assessment method is necessary for family counselors in providing effective therapeutic treatment.

Informal Assessments

During the data collection process, informal assessments often serve to provide the family counselor with relevant information necessary to inform the counselor's approach. According to Spinelli (2008), informal assessments are often multitiered approaches that focus on complex and diverse issues. Tools such as observations, interviews, interest inventories, preference questionnaires, and self-assessments, for example, may be employed in the counseling process as an ongoing diagnostic assessment of family functioning. Other informal methods for assessing couples include the genogram (Chapter 2), medical examination, and structural diagrams (Chapter 9).

Conducive to less structured environments, informal assessments are highly subjective in interpretation. Despite this fact, Spinelli (2008) noted that informal assessments, when used, provide an authentic understanding of information that may not be available through more formal means. In family systems, for example, the counselor has the opportunity to observe the interactions between family members in the context in which they occur.

Informal assessment provides the counselor with the opportunity to collect more comprehensive information, especially in the initial stages of treatment. Numerous informal assessments have been developed to support the counselor in gathering important data. Although these tools are often not validated, they often serve as a precursor to more formative assessments. As such, informal assessments are important elements for family counselors to understand and know how to implement.

Formal Assessments

Whereas informal assessments seek to gather a wealth of information in a concise period of time, formative assessments seek to use validated, standardized measurements specific to the phenomenon being evaluated. Given the diversity of issues that may be the focus of family treatment, hundreds if not thousands of formal assessments exist with implications in family counseling. Meyer and Melchert (2011) noted that formal assessments may be used throughout the treatment process and may cover a variety of issues, including coping strategies, marital satisfaction, family cohesion, and stress.

According to Harris (2006), formal assessments are often used by statutory agencies to investigate and evaluate family dynamics to make determinations on outcomes of such issues as child placement. As a result, these assessments have the potential to be seen as more rigid and less personal. More importantly, Lavee and Avisar (2006) uncovered that less than one third of family counselors reported using formal assessment tools in therapeutic practice. This underutilization of formal assessments in family counseling reveals a lack of understanding or confidence among family counselors in employing these techniques.

Evaluation of which formal assessments to employ with family therapy relies heavily on the established reliability and validity estimates of these instruments relative to the specific populations of interest. Specifically, family clinicians must understand whether assessment must be targeted on an individual member of the family system, relationships between couples within a family system, or within the overall family system. As such, the following information serves not only as a guideline of what instruments may be used by family counselors, but also when they may be used. Given the plethora of assessments that exist, however, the list is far from exhaustive.

Because many informal assessments were discussed in previous chapters, the remaining sections of the chapter focus on standardized instruments often used in family and couples counseling. We begin by discussing two common individual assessments, followed by common inventories used for couples and families. We have divided the discussion of inventories for couples and families into three sections: (1) premarital assessments; (2) couple or marital assessments, specifically those targeted on assessing specific problems and stressors and those that assess the quality of the relationship; and (3) family assessments.

USE OF STANDARDIZED ASSESSMENT INSTRUMENTS FOR INDIVIDUALS

Although the central focus of couple and family counselors primarily revolves around increasing the stability of the overarching systems, whether it is the couple or family, individual assessment is often a useful and necessary component of the counselor's role. In fact, Jankowski and Hooper (2012) noted that studies have validated the tenets of Bowen's family systems theory, in which individual thoughts, behaviors, and actions have an impact on the larger systems. As such, treatment of couples and families also requires treatment of individuals within the system. For example, an individual with personal insecurities may seek out ways in which to distrust his or her partner. As a result of these insecurities, the individual may sabotage the therapeutic process if an individual approach is not integrated into the couple or family treatment. Therefore, family counselors must assess the individual needs of family members to ensure that each can benefit from the therapeutic process.

Understanding the importance of assessing or addressing individual needs prior to conjoint family treatment has been the subject of several research studies. In cases of domestic violence, for example, an establishment of potential safety risk factors is required. Harris (2006) summarized the body of research regarding the treatment of couples involved in domestic violence by noting that situations in which moderate to significant abuse was identified or expected required the implementation of individual therapy prior to family therapy being considered. In cases in which an assessment of the level of abuse resulted in findings of minimal current abuse, however, couples therapy was noted to be an effective strategy. Although the case of domestic violence serves as one example of a situation in which individual assessment is warranted, Hussaarts, Roozen, Meyers, van de Wetering, and McCrady (2012) identified that individual assessment is also important relative to substance abuse issues, given the potential for such issues to have a detrimental effect on the family system and the associated resistance of substance-abusing individuals to participating in treatment. In cases of suspected violence and/or substance abuse, individual interviews are warranted prior to a therapist engaging in family work. Although numerous assessments may be considered in family counseling, it would be impossible to provide an exhaustive list. Therefore, a descriptions of only a few individual assessments are provided.

Substance Abuse Subtle Screening Inventory–3

The Substance Abuse Subtle Screening Inventory–3 (SASSI-3) is an effective and useful tool in clinical practice designed to "identify individuals with a high probability of having a substance dependence disorder, even if those individuals do not acknowledge substance misuse or symptoms associated with it" (Miller, Roberts, Brooks, & Lazowski, 1997, p. 2). The SASSI-3 is appropriate for those aged 18 and older who have a minimum 3.2 grade reading level. The instrument takes approximately 15 to 20 minutes to complete and is composed of 93 questions. The instrument is printed on a single sheet paper and has two sides. The SASSI-3 has 10 subscales. The first side that should be administered consists of 67 true–false questions divided into the following eight subscales: symptoms (SYM), obvious attributes (OAT), subtle attributes (SAT), defensiveness (DEF), supplemental addiction measure (SAM), family versus control measure (FAM), correctional (COR), and random answering. These questions are subtle items and help identify individuals with alcohol and other drug use (AOD) who are unable or unwilling to acknowledge the substance use or are minimizing or denying substance use. The other side contains the Face Valid Alcohol (FVA) and Face Valid Other Drugs (FVOD) assessments, which contain 26 face-valid questions on substance use related on a 4-point scale ranging from "never" to "repeatedly." These items require clients to describe the extent and nature of their AOD use. According to Miller et al. (1997), high scores on the either the FVA or FVOD may warrant the need for supervised detoxification.

The Spanish SASSI is also available for individuals aged 18 and older. The Adolescent Substance Abuse Subtle Screening Inventory (SASSI-A2) is available to assess adolescents from ages 12 to 18 who may have a substance use disorder.

Myers-Briggs Type Indicator

The Myers-Briggs Type Indicator (MBTI), developed by Katharine Briggs and her daughter, Elizabeth Myers, measures four dichotomies of individuals' personality preferences (Watson & Flamez, 2014). Available in two different forms, Form M and Form Q, the MBTI is one of the most widely used personality assessments for normally functioning persons. Consisting of 93 forced-answer questions, Form M represents the older of the two versions and takes approximately 15 to 20 minutes to

SIDEBAR 4.4

Natalie and Gwen report much discord within their relationship. After speaking with the couple for a few minutes, the counselor suspects substance abuse. The counselor decides to administer the SASSI-3 to both parties. After administering the assessment, the counselor scores the results and finds that Natalie's FVA scores, symptom scores, and attribute scores are quite high, while her defensiveness scores are low. Gwen's results indicate low FVA scores, symptom scores, and attribute scores, and high defensiveness scores. Using the Substance Abuse Subtle Screening Inventory Scale Descriptions website (http://nbu.bg/webs/clubpsy/Materiali%20za%20kachvane/Library/razlichni%20lekcii%20na%20angliiski/Sassi_scales.pdf), discuss what these results mean and how these results affect the couple's treatment plan. Hint: Which person is acknowledging a problem and ready for treatment? How does this acknowledgment or lack thereof affect the way the counselor approaches couples counseling sessions?

complete. The newer version, Form Q, consists of 144 forced-answer questions, takes 20 to 25 minutes to complete, and increases the targeted age of completion from individuals 14 years and older to those 18 years and older. Dichotomies on the two forms are the same, with measures of interaction patterns (i.e., extraversion versus introversion), ways of perceiving individuals and the environment (i.e., sensing versus intuition), methods of making conclusions (i.e., thinking and feeling), and ways of dealing with people and situations (i.e., judging versus perceiving). As a result of these dichotomies, individuals are categorized into one of 16 psychological types. According to Watson and Flamez (2014), reliability estimates for individual dichotomies fall between .44 and .88, even after more than a year between pretest and posttest.

Although often associated with assessments of individuals, the MBTI may be integrated both into couples and family counseling as a tool for individuals to understand others' personality characteristics and the potential impact of these characteristics on their relationship. In fact, Williams and Tappan (1995) noted that the MBTI has been demonstrated useful within the context of couples counseling because it provides couples the information necessary to compromise effectively based on an understanding of personality characteristics. The education of family members regarding the ways in which others function is one way to increase communication.

INVENTORIES FOR COUPLES AND FAMILY COUNSELING

Whereas individual assessments, such as the MBTI, focus on specific aspects of an individual, couples and family assessments seek to understand interactional patterns in the whole system as opposed to the sum of the parts. According to

Ghanbaripanah and Mustaffa (2012), the complexities associated with couples and family interactions result in additional challenges for the counselor. Despite this complexity, assessment inventories used for couples and families serve the same fundamental purposes relative to individual assessments. Specifically, the use of couples and family therapy assessments is intended to evaluate systems necessary for developing effective treatment plans. Despite underutilization of these formal assessments by family counselors (Lavee & Avisar, 2006), studies have demonstrated the efficacy of couples and family instruments used among various relationship and family types.

Assessment in Premarital Counseling

Despite only a small proportion of marital and family therapists employing formative assessments in therapy (Lavee & Avisar, 2006), Busby, Ivey, Harris, and Ates (2007) noted that nearly 3 out of every 10 couples seek out some type of counseling prior to initiation of divorce. The proportion of couples seeking out premarital guidance compared to the number of counselors reporting integration of formative counseling assessments presents an area of need among the profession. Despite a lack of utilization among family counselors, Wilmoth and Smyser (2012) revealed that clergy members have relied on premarital assessments in the delivery of premarital counseling with noted success. As such, family counselors must become familiar with premarital assessment instruments to support couples in strengthening their interpersonal relationship to promote marriage success. Assessments such as the PREPARE/ENRICH and Taylor-Johnson Temperament Analysis (T-JTA), for example, are two published premarital assessments that may be integrated for the purpose of supporting individuals embarking on the potential for marriage.

PREPARE/ENRICH

PREPARE/ENRICH is a widely known marriage program that was developed more than 30 years ago and designed to increase awareness of relationship strengths and growth areas. To date, over 3 million couples have participated in the PREPARE/ENRICH program (Olson, Olson, & Larson, 2012). PREPARE is for couples preparing for marriage, whereas ENRICH is for married couples. The program is composed of a couples assessment and a psycho-education, solution-focused feedback process by a facilitator. Facilitators include professional counselors, psychologists, social workers, clergy members, and marriage educators who have completed the PREPARE/ENRICH workshop. The assessment part is in its sixth edition.

PREPARE and ENRICH each consist of 125 items designed to measure each person's personality, the relationship strengths, the couple's interpersonal dynamics, their major stressors, and the family system (Olson et al., 2012). PREPARE/ENRICH covers 10 core scales: communication, conflict resolution, partner style and habits, financial management, leisure activities, affection and sexuality, family and friends, children and parenting, relationship roles, and spiritual beliefs. In addition to the 10 scales, PREPARE/ENRICH assesses "a couple's closeness and flexibility, family-of-origin, personal stress, four areas of relationship dynamics, and five factors of personality" (p. 2).

During the second component of PREPARE/ENRICH, facilitators receive a Facilitator's Report (20–25 pages) and the couple is given a Couple's Report (10 pages) and a Couple's Workbook (25 pages) containing 20 couple exercises. The facilitator uses the couple exercises to identify strengths and areas of growth, to strengthen communication skills, to deal with stressors, and to teach conflict resolution using a 10-step model (Olson et al., 2012).

PREPARE and ENRICH report high validity and reliability. The assessments were normed on a large national sample of over 500,000 couples from various ethnic groups.

Taylor-Johnson Temperament Analysis (T-JTA)

The Taylor-Johnson Temperament Analysis (T-JTA) is a widely used personality assessment in premarital and family counseling that helps clients in developing awareness of characteristics that influence interpersonal relationships and building relationships with others (Psychological Publications, 2013). The T-JTA is designed to measure 18 dimensions of personality (9 bipolar traits). The nine bipolar traits include: nervous/composed, depressive/lighthearted, active-social/quiet, expressive-responsive/inhibited, sympathetic/indifferent, subjective/objective, dominant/submissive, hostile/tolerant, and self-disciplined/impulsive. A unique feature of the T-JTA is the "Criss-Cross" testing, in which an individual completes the assessment on himself or herself but also records his or her impressions of the significant other. The Criss-Cross testing provides useful information on the similarities, differences, and dynamics in the relationship. Several different types of reports are available with the assessment that help the counselor identify the individual's strengths and weaknesses, potential problem areas, and misunderstandings between the couple. The T-JTA shaded profile plots percentile scores for each of the couple's traits and includes the clinical designations: excellent, acceptable, improvement desirable, and improvement needed. The interpretive reports are often used to stimulate discussion, promote understanding, and reduce conflict.

Couples or Marital Assessment

The importance of assessment in marital and family therapy extends beyond the use of instruments among premarital couples. In fact, Snyder, Heyman, and Haynes (2005) noted that more individuals reported seeking treatment for marital problems than any other single type of problem, with a majority of individuals surveyed identifying significant periods of turmoil within their marriage. Given the numbers of individuals experiencing marital issues at some point or another within their relationship, as well as the number of individuals seeking couples therapy, couple and family therapists must be familiar with instruments that may be used to assess specific problems and the quality of the relationship.

Snyder et al. (2005) argued that the majority of issues contributing to marital distress can be categorized within one of six domains: (1) cognitive, (2) affective, (3) behavioral, (4) communication, (5) structural, and (6) socioecological. As such, counselors must assess for the potential benefit of employing instruments in these areas. Although specific assessments related to sexual functioning and domestic violence will be described in more detail, numerous assessments addressing potential stressors exist.

Although assessment of specific issues may provide valuable information in the assessment of couples, overall satisfaction or dissatisfaction instruments are also beneficial in the conceptualization of couples for treatment planning. The importance of these assessments is illustrated by Snyder et al. (2005), who reported that studies have concluded higher rates of marital dissatisfaction were correlated with higher levels of extramarital affairs, separation, and divorce. Three existing tools, the Locke-Wallace Martial Adjustment Test, the Dyadic Adjustment Scale, and the Marital Satisfaction Inventory, Revised, are discussed in further detail within this chapter as an illustration of popularly used assessment tools that show evidence of reliability and validity. Although these tools are often used in couples assessments, numerous other assessment instruments exist.

Assessing Specific Problems and Stressors

Derogatis Sexual Functioning Inventory (DSFI)

The Derogatis Sexual Functioning Inventory (DSFI) is an individually administered test of the quality of the current sexual functioning of an individual. The assessment is helpful in providing counselors with extensive information regarding sexual functioning (e.g., drive, body image, sexual satisfaction) and is considered a highly reliable and valid measure of sexual functioning (Derogatis, Lopez, & Zinzeletta, 1988). The test is composed of 254 items using multiple Likert scales and answering yes or no. The items are arranged into 10 scales reflective of the principal components of sexual behavior: information, experiences, drive, attitudes, psychological symptoms, affects, gender role definition, fantasy, body image, and sexual satisfaction (Derogatis, 1979). A total or global summary score for the DSFI called the Sexual Functioning Index (SFI) is reported and represents the respondent's quality of sexual functioning. A Global Sexual Satisfaction Index (GSSI) is also reported, which is the individual's subjective perception of his or her sexual behavior. Test times are between 45 and 60 minutes. The assessment is also available in a computer-administered version in Arabic, Chinese, English, French, French Canadian, Indian, Korean, Norwegian, Spanish, and Turkish.

Revised Conflict Tactics Scales (CTS2)

The Revised Conflict Tactics Scales (CTS2) is the most widely used measure of assessing for domestic violence on a partner in a marital, cohabiting, or dating relationship. The assessment also provides information on the techniques the couple uses to handle conflict within the relationship. The test is composed of 78 questions that assess domestic violence in the form of psychological aggression, physical assault, sexual coercion, and inflicted injury (Straus, 2007). The first 39 items assess the respondent's behavior, and the remaining items assess the behavior of the respondent's partner. An 8-point scale is used to determine how often the behavior has occurred, and these scores produce a "self" and a "partner" score on each of the five subscales: negotiation, physical assault, injury, psychological aggression, and sexual coercion. Administration time is 10 to 15 minutes. High reliability and adequate validity are reported in the manual.

The Conflict Tactics Scales: Parent-Child Version (CTS PC) is used for evaluating parent-to-child violence and child maltreatment. The CTS PC contains 35 items, including questions about the respondent's own experiences as a child as well as behavior with his or her child. The CTS PC yields scores on: nonviolent discipline, physical assault, neglect, psychological aggression, weekly discipline, and sexual abuse.

Assessing the Quality of the Relationship

Locke-Wallace Marital Adjustment Test (MAT)

The Locke-Wallace Marital Adjustment Test (MAT) is one of the oldest assessments used to measure marital satisfaction. According to Locke (1951), marital satisfaction is when "the mates feel satisfied with the marriage and each other, develop common interests and activities and feel that marriage is fulfilling their expectations" (p. 45). The MAT is a paper-and-pencil measurement and contains 15 questions: one question measures global adjustment, eight questions measure areas of disagreement, and six questions measure conflict resolution, cohesion, and communication. Each partner is given a copy as part of the intake process. Clients are first asked to describe their degree of happiness in their present marriage on a scale of "very unhappy" to "perfectly happy." For questions 2 through 9, each partner indicates the extent of agreement or disagreement between him- or herself and his or her mate (e.g., demonstrations of affection: always agree, almost always agree, occasionally disagree, frequently disagree, almost always disagree, or always disagree). For the remaining questions, the client reads statements regarding conflict resolution, cohesion, and communication and is asked to respond. Responses are weighted differently, and scores range from 2 to 158 with a cutoff score of 100. Scores below 100 indicate relationship or marital distress, while scores above the cutoff indicate satisfaction in the relationship.

The MAT was normed on a sample of 236 married couples who were predominantly White and approximately 30 years old. Internal consistency was good and reported at .90 (Locke & Wallace, 1959), and no information was provided on test–retest reliability. Validity studies show high discriminant validity between adjusted and maladjusted couples. Although the purpose of the MAT is to measure marital adjustment, counselors should be aware that some of the items are out of date and this assessment may not be useful for treatment planning where behavioral specificity is important.

Dyadic Adjustment Scale (DAS)

The Dyadic Adjustment Scale (DAS) is one of the most widely used measures of relationship quality and is a helpful tool in determining the degree of dissatisfaction couples experience (Graham, Liu, & Jeziorski, 2006). The DAS is a 32-item, self-report measure of relationship adjustment for people aged 18 and older. The 32 items are mainly 6-point Likert-type rating scales (e.g., always agree to always disagree; all the time to never). The DAS can be administered in about 5 to 10 minutes. Spanier (1976) defined dyadic adjustment as "a process, the outcome of which is determined by the degree of: troublesome dyadic differences; interpersonal tensions and personal anxiety; dyadic satisfaction; dyadic cohesion; and consensus on matters of importance to dyadic functioning" (p. 17). The DAS consists of four subscales: dyadic consensus, dyadic satisfaction, dyadic cohesion, and affective expression.

The dyadic consensus consists of 13 items and measures the degree to which couples agree on matters of importance to the relationship. The dyadic satisfaction consists of 10 items and measures the degree to which couples are satisfied in the relationship. The dyadic cohesion contains 5 items and measures the degree to which couples participate in activities together. The final scale, affective expression, includes 4 items and measures the degree of demonstration of sexual and affection relationships (Spanier, 1976). The scores on the 32 items are added to create a total score ranging from 0 to 150. Higher scores indicate greater positive dyadic adjustment, with a score of 100 used to differentiate between distressed and nondistressed couples. The norm group for the DAS was based on a sample of 218 married individuals and 94 divorced individuals.

The DAS has undergone extensive research and appears in more than 1,000 published studies. Graham et al. (2006) conducted a meta-analysis to examine the internal consistency of the DAS. Although the DAS produced dyadic cohesion, consensus, and satisfaction scores of acceptable internal consistency, the affective expression subscale produced scores with poor reliability. The Revised Dyadic Adjustment Scale (RDAS) is a 14-point scale designed to measure relationship satisfaction but includes only three of the original four subscales: dyadic consensus, dyadic satisfaction, and dyadic cohesion.

Marital Satisfaction Inventory, Revised (MSI-R)

The Marital Satisfaction Inventory, Revised (MSI-R) is a self-report inventory used to assess the nature and extent of conflict and distress within a marriage or relationship (Synder, 1997). The MSI-R is administered prior to the first interview or initial contact. Each partner responds to 150 true–false items or 129 true–false items (if they have no children), and it takes between 20 and 25 minutes. Because items refer to "partner" and "relationship," the test is used with traditional and nontraditional couples. Both individuals' results are displayed on a single profile highlighting the couple's primary concerns and indicating any differences in their perceptions of the nature and extent of conflict within their relationship. Scores are obtained from 13 subscales that cover marital interaction including: affective communication, role orientation, problem-solving communication, aggression, family history of distress, time together, dissatisfaction with children, disagreement about finances, conflict over child rearing, sexual dissatisfaction, and global distress. The global distress scale (GDS) reports "overall dissatisfaction with the relationship" (Synder, 1997, p. 21). There are two additional scales, conventionalization and inconsistency, which indicate tendency to respond in an unrealistic manner or inconsistently. Administering the assessment during the first initial contact not only helps the clients articulate their discontent and any differences between their perceptions of aspects of their relationship, but also allows the counselor to identify any issues that are contributing to individual or family problems (e.g., depression, substance abuse).

The MSI-R was standardized on 1,020 couples stratified on age, geographic location, education, and ethnicity. The MSI-R reliability coefficients suggest the MSI-R scales are relatively stable over time. Excluding the inconsistency scale, the test–retest reliability coefficients range between .74 and .88 with a mean of .79 (Synder, 1997). The MSI-R has been used cross-culturally and comes in a Spanish language test form. In addition to the paper-and-pencil instrument, computer assessment, scoring, and interpretation are available.

Family Assessment Instruments

Although couples instruments are utilized to assess the relational interactions between two parties, evaluation of family dynamics must account for numerous relationships and the overall functioning of the family system. Hayden et al. (1998) noted that through family assessment tools, counselors can gain greater insight into the numerous subsystems that exist within the family. Completion of these assessments provides insight into family strengths, perceptions, and areas of growth. Illustrating aspects of family assessments, the Family Adaptability and Cohesion Evaluation Scale IV, the Family Assessment Measure-III, and the Family Environment Scale are explored in detail. As with other types of assessments, these instruments are only three of the many assessments with application in family counseling.

Family Adaptability and Cohesion Evaluation Scale IV (FACES IV)

The Family Adaptability and Cohesion Evaluation Scale IV (FACES IV) is a family self-report assessment that assesses family cohesion (e.g., emotional bonding members have toward each other) and flexibility (e.g., quality of leadership and organization, relationship rules and negotiations). FACES IV is based on the circumplex model of family functioning which hypothesizes that: "Balanced levels of cohesion and flexibility are most conducive to healthy family functioning. Conversely, unbalanced levels of cohesion and flexibility (very low or very high levels) are associated with problematic family functioning" (Olson, 2011, p. 65).

The assessment is comprised of six scales (two balanced and four unbalanced) with 7 items per scale making a total of 42 items. The two balanced scales are called balanced cohesion and balanced flexibility. The higher these scores, the more positive. The four unbalanced scales include two unbalanced scales for cohesion (e.g., disengaged and enmeshed) and two unbalanced scales for flexibility (e.g., rigid and chaotic). Higher scores are indicative of a problematic family system. All family members over the age of 12 are able to complete the FACES IV. Family members take the test individually and are asked not to consult or discuss the items until they have completed the assessment. In order to make FACES IV more comprehensive, it is recommended that one use the two additional scales, family communication and family satisfaction. The family communication consists of 10 items that assess communication, and the family satisfaction scale includes 10 items that assess how happy family members are with their family.

A variety of scores are calculated. The summation of the six scale scores yields a total raw score, which is converted into a percentage score. Percentage scores for the following six scales are provided: balanced cohesion, balanced flexibility, disengaged, enmeshed, rigid, and chaotic. Cohesion ratio, flexibility ratio, and total circumplex ratio scores are also calculated. According to Olson (2011), the six scales of the FACES IV were reliable and valid. In addition, high levels of concurrent, construct, and discriminant validity were reported.

Family Assessment Measure–III (FAM-III)

The Family Assessment Measure–III (FAM-III) is appropriate for those aged 10 years and older and assesses family strengths, weaknesses, and functioning. The FAM-III provides useful information to the counselor by obtaining a picture of how family members perceive their levels of family interaction with the other family members. The FAM-III includes three forms: a 50-item general scale that examines overall general family health, a 42-item dyadic relationship scale that examines how a family member perceives his or her relationship with another family member, and a 42-item self-rating scale that asks the respondent to rate his or her own functioning within the family (Skinner, Steinhauer, & Santa-Barbara, 2004). Each scale takes approximately 20 minutes to complete. The FAM-III yields scores on seven scales: task accomplishment, role performance, communication, affective expression, involvement, control, and values and norms.

A useful feature of the FAM-III is the ColorPlot Profile of Family Perceptions. This profile allows members to view their own responses and compare other members' scores on the same profile form. It should be noted that the FAM-III was normed on a predominantly White population consisting of 247 nonclinical adults and 65 nonclinical adolescents. Thus, one should take into account cultural and ethnic considerations before administering the FAM-III.

The Brief FAM is a brief form that is often used when time is limited or for preliminary screening. The assessment contains 14 items in each of the three scales. Although the assessment can provide an overall index of family functioning, the Brief FAM does not allow for calculation of subscale scores. If a family scores high on the Brief FAM, the full FAM should be administered to obtain more information concerning family functioning.

Family Environment Scale (FES, Fourth Edition)

The Family Environment Scale (FES, fourth edition) is a useful tool to assess the social environment of the family unit, compare parents' and children's perceptions, and examine issues of importance in family treatment (Moos & Moos, 2009). The FES has been shown to have important applications for program evaluation, including: planning and monitoring family change, assessing the impact of counseling, and strengthening the family unit by helping the family function more effectively (Moos & Moos, 2009).

The FES consists of three forms that measure family members' perceptions of the family: (1) as it is currently (real, Form R), (2) as she or he would prefer it to be in a perfect situation (ideal, Form I), and (3) expectations about family setting (expected, Form E). Each form consists of 90 true–false items. All three forms can be administered individually or in combination to reveal how a person views a family and his or her place in it. For example, some counselors may administer Form I to gain information on family members' value orientations and assess how this changes before and after treatment. Another counselor may give Form I and Form R to understand areas in which the family member may want to see change in the family.

The FES consists of 10 subscales grouped into three dimensions: relationship dimensions (cohesion, expressiveness, and conflict); personal growth dimensions (independence, achievement orientation, intellectual-cultural orientation, active-recreational orientation, and moral-religious emphasis); and systems maintenance and change dimensions (organization and control). According to Moos and Moos (2009), "the relationship and system maintenance dimensions primarily reflect internal family functioning, whereas the personal growth dimensions primarily reflect the linkages between the family and the larger social context" (p. 1). Each subscale score is converted into a standard score and plotted on a graph where the *y*-axis is the standard score and the *x*-axis is the subscales. The scores can be plotted individually or with all members' scores appearing on one graph. To facilitate the interpretation of the profiles, Moos and Moos (2009) have created seven family types: independence oriented, achievement oriented, intellectual-cultural oriented, moral-religious oriented, support oriented, conflict oriented, and disorganized. According to Moos and Moos (2009), "by classifying a family as representative of a more inclusive type, a clinician can compare it with similar families and formulate more accurate prognosis and diagnosis" (p. 19).

Sufficient validity and reliability are reported in the manual. The Children's Version is available for children between the ages of 5 and 11. The Children's Version contains a 30-item pictorial adaptation of the FES.

SIDEBAR 4.5

Phil and Latisha live in a committed relationship and have three children, ages 15, 13, and 8. During a counseling session, Phil states that he and Latisha have a great relationship, but their children exhibit disruptive behavior in the home and the stress is "overwhelming." Charles, their 15-year-old son, starts laughing at his father's comment. When asked to explain his laughter, Charles states that his father is living in a "dream world." How might a counselor use the FES assessment to help this family? What issues might the FES reveal in this family?

SUMMARY

Counselors who provide family therapy services are held not only to the expectations set forth by the American Counseling Association and the IAMFC, but also to the established rules and regulations set forth by AAMFT. In fulfilling these commitments to the credibility, viability, and ethics of the family counseling profession, counselors must understand not only the importance of research but also the ways in which research must be employed. Focusing on these issues, this chapter has addressed issues related both to family counseling research and assessment.

Without research, family therapy would not benefit from the richness of information necessary to be regarded as a formidable profession. As Sanderson et al. (2009) noted, effective family therapy has been guided through the discoveries available by research inquiry and will continue to evolve only through a continued desire for information. Conclusions drawn from these efforts have continued to inform an understanding of family system dynamics.

Similar to other areas of social science, family therapy has been the subject of countless quantitative studies (e.g., Duffy & Chenail, 2008). Despite a heavy reliance in research on quantitative inquiry, qualitative studies (e.g., Sheridan et al., 2010) have provided researchers an opportunity to explore the experiences of individuals within a family system. Although labeled less frequently, mixed methods research may also be employed to drive discovery. Understanding the unique elements of qualitative, quantitative, and mixed methods research, including individual worldviews and study purpose, serves as the fundamental tenet from which such choices are made.

Decades of research in family counseling have resulted in the development of numerous assessment tools not only with implications for families as a whole but also for individuals and couples. Understanding the individual factors as well as the interpersonal dynamics at play is necessary in developing an appropriate and effective treatment plan for therapeutic services. The aforementioned informal and formal assessment instruments serve as the fundamental tools in supporting family counselors with successful therapeutic services.

USEFUL WEBSITES

The following websites provide additional information relating to the chapter topics.

AAMFT Marriage and Family Core Competencies
http://www.aamft.org/imis15/Documents/MFT_Core_Competencie.pdf
Association for Assessment and Research in Counseling
http://aarc-counseling.org
Bowen Center for the Study of the Family
http://www.thebowencenter.org/index.html
Institute for Intercultural Studies: Gregory Bateson
http://www.interculturalstudies.org/Bateson/index.html

International Association of Marriage and Family Counselors
http://www.iamfconline.org
Responsibilities of Users of Standardized Test
http://www.theaaceonline.com/rust.pdf
Standards for Qualifications of Test Users
http://www.theaaceonline.com/standards.pdf
Substance Abuse Subtle Screening Inventory Scale Descriptions
http://nbu.bg/webs/clubpsy/Materiali%20za%20kachvane/Library/razlichni%20lekcii%20na%20angliiski/Sassi_scales.pdf
Test Taker Rights and Responsibilities
http://www.theaaceonline.com/rights.pdf

REFERENCES

American Association for Marriage and Family Therapy (AAMFT). (2013). *AAMFT*. Retrieved from http://www.aamft.org/imis15/Content/about_aamft/foundation.aspx

Bagner, D. M. (2013). Father's role in parent training for children with developmental delay. *Journal of Family Psychology*, *27*(4), 650–657. doi:10.1037/a0033465

Baker-Ericzén, M., Jenkins, M., & Haine-Schlagel, R. (2013). Therapist, parent, and youth perspectives of treatment barriers to family-focused community outpatient mental health Services. *Journal of Child & Family Studies*, *22*(6), 854–868. doi:10.1007/s10826-012-9644-7

Baldwin, S., Christian, S., Berkeljon, A., & Shadish, W. (2012). The effects of family therapies for adolescent delinquency and substance abuse: A meta-analysis. *Journal of Marital and Family Therapy*, *38*(1), 281–304. doi:10.1111/j.1752-0606.2011.00248.x

Beach, S. H., & Whisman, M. A. (2012). Affective disorders. *Journal of Marital and Family Therapy*, *38*(1), 201–219. doi:10.1111/j.1752-0606.2011.00243.x

Beyebach, M. (2009). Integrative brief solution-focused family therapy: A provincial road-map. *Journal of Systemic Therapies*, *28*(3), 18–35.

Breunlin, D. C., Pinsof, W., & Russell, W. P. (2011). Integrative problem-centered metaframeworks therapy I: Core concepts and hypothesizing. *Family Process*, *50*(3), 293–313. doi:10.1111/j.1545-5300.2011.01362.x

Brock, G. W., Whiting, J. B., Matern, B., & Fife, S. T. (2009). Integrity of the marriage and family therapy research literature: Perceptions and recommendations. *Journal of Marriage and Family Therapy*, *35*(2), 248–252. doi:10.1111/j.1752-0606.2009.00109.x

Busby, D. M., Ivey, D. C., Harris, S. M., & Ates, C. (2007). Self-directed, therapist-directed and assessment based interventions for premarital couples. *Family Relations*, *56*(3), 279–290. doi:10.1111/j/1741-3729.2007.00459.x

Carr, A. (2010). Thematic review of family therapy journals 2009. *Journal of Family Therapy*, *32*(4), 409–427. doi:10.1111/j.1467-6427.2010.00524.x

Chambless, D. L. (2012). Adjunctive couple and family intervention for patients with anxiety disorders. *Journal of Clinical Psychology*, *68*(5), 548–560. doi:10.1002/jclp.21851

Cherlin, A. J. (2010). Demographic trends in the United States: A review of research in the 2000s. *Journal of Marriage and Family*, *72*(3), 403–419.

Creswell, J. W. (2013). *Research design: Qualitative, quantitative, and mixed methods approaches* (4th ed.). Thousand Oaks, CA: SAGE.

Deacon, S. A., & Piercy, F. P. (2001). Qualitative methods in family evaluation: Creative assessment techniques. *The American Journal of Family Therapy*, *29*, 355–373.

De Mol, J., Buysse, A., & Cook, W. L. (2010). A family assessment based on the social relations model. *Journal of Family Therapy*, *32*, 259–279.

Derogatis, L. R. (1979). *Sexual Functioning Inventory manual*. Riderwood, MD: Clinical Psychometric Research.

Derogatis, L. R., Lopez, M. C., & Zinzeletta, E. M. (1988). Clinical applications of the DSFI in the assessment of sexual dysfunctions. In R. A. Brown & J. R. Fields (Eds.), *Treatment of sexual problems in individual and couple therapy* (pp. 167–186). Great Neck, NY: PMA Publishing.

Duffy, M., & Chenail, R. J. (2008). Values in qualitative and quantitative research. *Counseling & Values*, *53*(1), 22–38.

Evans, P., Turner, S., & Trotter, C. (2012), *The effectiveness of family and relationship therapy: A review of the literature*. Melbourne, Australia: PACFA.

Gambrel, L., & Butler, J. L., IV. (2013). Mixed methods research in marriage and family therapy: A content analysis. *Journal of Marital & Family Therapy*, *39*(2), 163–181. doi: 10.1111/j.1752-0606.2011.00260.x

Gardner, B., Burr, B., & Wiedower, S. (2006). Reconceptualizing strategic family therapy: Insights from a dynamic systems perspective. *Contemporary Family Therapy: An International Journal*, *28*(3), 339–352. doi:10.1007/s10591-006-9007-x

Ghanbaripanah, A., & Mustaffa, M. S. (2012). The review of family assessment in counseling. *International Journal of Fundamental Psychology & Social Sciences*, *2*(2), 32–35.

Graham, J. M., Liu, Y. J., & Jeziorski, J. L. (2006). The Dyadic Adjustment Scale: A reliability generalization meta-analysis. *Journal of Marriage and Family*, *68*, 701–717.

Guo, X., & Slesnick, N. (2013). Family versus individual therapy: Impact on discrepancies between parents' and adolescents' perceptions over time. *Journal of Marital & Family Therapy*, *39*(2), 182–194. doi:10.1111/j.1752-0606.2012.00301.x

Harris, G. E. (2006). Conjoint therapy and domestic violence: Treating the individuals and the relationship. *Counselling Psychology Quarterly*, *19*(4), 373–379. doi:10.1080/09515070601029533

Hayden, L. C., Schiller, M., Dickstein, S., Seifer, R., Sameroff, S., Miller, I., . . . Rasmussen, S. (1998). Levels of family assessment: I. Family, marital, and parent–child interaction. *Journal of Family Psychology*, *12*(1), 7–22. doi:10.1037/0893-3200.12.1.7

Hendricks, B. E., Bradley, L. J., Southern, S., Oliver, M., & Birdsall, B. (2011). Ethical code for the International Association of Marriage and Family Counselors. *The Family Journal*, *19*, 217–224. doi:10.1177/1066480711400814

Hendrix, C. C., Fournier, D. G., & Briggs, K. (2001). Impact of co-therapy teams on client outcomes and therapist training in marriage and family therapy. *Contemporary Family Therapy: An International Journal*, *23*(1), 63–82. doi:10.1023/A:1007824216363

Hussaarts, P., Roozen, H. G., Meyers, R. J., van de Wetering, B. J., & McCrady, B. S. (2012). Problem areas reported by substance abusing individuals and their concerned significant others. *American Journal of Addiction*, *21*(1), 38–46. doi:10.1111/j.1521-0391.2011.00187.x

Jankowski, P. J., & Hooper, L. M. (2012). Differentiation of self: A validation study of the Bowen theory construct. *Couple and Family Psychology, Research and Practice*, *1*(3), 226–243.

Lavee, Y., & Avisar, Y. (2006). Use of standardized assessment instruments in couple therapy: The role of attitudes and professional factors. *Journal of Marital & Family Therapy*, *32*(2), 233–244.

Lee, M., Greene, G., Hsu, K., Solovey, A., Grove, D., Fraser, J., . . . Teater, B. (2009). Utilizing family strengths and resilience: Integrative family and systems treatment with children and adolescents with severe emotional and behavioral problems. *Family Process*, *48*(3), 395–416. doi:10.1111/j.1545-5300.2009.01291.x

Lemmens, G. D., Eisler, I., Migerode, L., Heireman, M., & Demyttenaere, K. (2007). Family discussion group therapy for major depression: A brief systemic multi-family group intervention for hospitalized patients and their family members. *Journal of Family Therapy*, *29*(1), 49–68. doi:10.1111/j.1467-6427.2007.00369.x

Locke, H., & Wallace, K. (1959). Short marital adjustment and prediction tests: The reliabilityand validity. *Marriage and Family Living*, *21*, 251–255.

Locke, H. J. (1951). *Predicting adjustment in marriage*. New York, NY: Holt.

Maddox, T. (2008). *Tests: A comprehensive reference for assessment in psychology, education, and business* (6th ed.). Austin, TX: PRO-Ed.

Marvel, F., Rowe, C. L., Colon-Perez, L., Diclemente, R. J., & Liddle, H. A. (2009). Multidimensional family therapy HIV/STD risk-reduction intervention: An integrative family-based model for drug-involved juvenile offenders. *Family Process*, *48*(1), 69–84. doi:10.1111/j.1545-5300.2009.01268.x

Matheson, J. L., & Lukic, L. (2011). Family treatment of adolescents and young adults recovering from substance abuse. *Journal of Family Psychotherapy*, *22*(3), 232–246. doi:10.1080/08975353.2011.602620

Mehlman, S. K., Baucom, D. H., & Anderson, D. (1983). Effectiveness of cotherapists versus single therapists and immediate versus delayed treatment in behavioral marital therapy. *Journal of Consulting and Clinical Psychology*, *51*(2), 258–266. doi:10.1037/0022-006X.51.2.258

Meyer, L., & Melchert, T. P. (2011). Examining the content of mental health intake assessments from a biopsychosocial perspective. *Journal of Psychotherapy Integration*, *21*, 70–89.

Miller, F. G., Roberts, J., Brooks, M. K., & Lazowski, L. E. (1997). *SASSI-3 user's guide: A quick reference for administration and scoring*. Bloomington, IN: Baugh Enterprises.

Monson, C. M., Macdonald, A., & Brown-Bowers, A. (2012). Couple/family therapy for posttraumatic stress disorder: Review to facilitate interpretation of VA/DOD clinical practice guideline. *Journal of Rehabilitation Research & Development*, *49*(6), 717–728. doi:10.1682/J.DRR.2011.09.0166

Moos, R. H., & Moos, B. S. (2009). *Family Environment Scale manual and sampler set: Development, applications, and research* (4th ed.). Menlo Park, CA: Mind Garden.

Murphy, L. L., Geisinger, K. F., Carlson, J. F., & Spies, R. A. (2011). *Tests in print VIII*. Lincoln, NE: Buros Institute of Mental Measurements.

Nichols, M., & Tafuri, S. (2013). Techniques of structural family assessment: A qualitative analysis of how experts promote a systemic perspective. *Family Process*, *52*(2), 207–215. doi:10.1111/famp.12025

Oka, M., & Whiting, J. (2013). Bridging the clinician/researcher gap with systemic research: The case for process research, dyadic, and sequential analysis. *Journal of Marital & Family Therapy*, *39*(1), 17–27. doi:10.1111/j.1752-0606.2012.00339.x

Olson, D. (2011). FACES IV and the Circumplex Model: Validation study. *Journal of Marital & Family Therapy*, *3*(1), 64–80.

Olson, D. H., Olson, A. K., & Larson, P. J. (2012). PREPARE-ENRICH program: Overview and new discoveries about couples. *Journal of Family & Community Ministries*, *25*, 30–44.

Psychological Publications. (2013). *Taylor-Johnson Temperament Analysis*. Retrieved from https://www.tjta.com/asp/index.asp

Ramisch, J. L., McVicker, M., & Sahin, Z. (2009). Helping low-conflict divorced parents establish appropriate boundaries using a variation of the miracle question: An integration of solution-focused therapy and structural family therapy. *Journal of Divorce & Remarriage*, *50*(7), 481–495. doi:10.1080/10502550902970587

Rasheed, J. M., Rasheed, M. N., & Marley, J. A. (2011). *Family therapy: Models and techniques*. Thousand Oaks, CA: SAGE.

Rhodes, P. (2012). Nothing to fear? Thoughts on the history of family therapy and the potential contribution of research. *Australian & New Zealand Journal of Family Therapy*, *33*(2), 171–182. doi:10.1017/aft.2012.18

Roberts, C., Mazzucchelli, T., Studman, L., & Sanders, M. (2006). Behavioral family intervention for children with developmental disabilities and behavioral problems. *Journal of Clinical Child and Adolescent Psychology: The Official Journal for the Society of Clinical Child and Adolescent Psychology, American Psychological Association, Division 53*, *35*(2), 180–193.

Rowe, C. (2012). Family therapy for drug abuse: Review and updates 2003–2010. *Journal of Marital and Family Therapy*, *38*(1), 59–81. doi:10.1111/j.1752-0606.2011.00280.x

Russell Crane, D. D., & Payne, S. H. (2011). Individual versus family psychotherapy in managed care: Comparing the costs of treatment by the mental health professions. *Journal of Marital and Family Therapy*, *37*(3), 273–289. doi:10.1111/j.1752-0606.2009.00170.x

Ryan-Nicholls, K., & Will, C. (2009). Rigour in qualitative research: Mechanisms for control. *Nurse Researcher*, *16*(3), 70–85. doi:10.7748/nr2009.04.16.3.70.c6947

Sanderson, J., Kosutic, I., Garcia, M., Melendez, T., Donoghue, J., Perumbilly, S., . . . Anderson, S. (2009). The measurement of outcome variables in couple and family therapy research. *American Journal of Family Therapy*, *37*(3), 239–257.

Seponski, D. M., Bermudez, J., & Lewis, D. C. (2013). Creating culturally responsive family therapy models and research: Introducing the use of responsive evaluation as a method. *Journal of Marital and Family Therapy*, *39*(1), 28–42. doi:10.1111/j.1752-0606.2011.00282.x

Sexton, T., Gordon, K., Gurman, A., Lebow, J., Holtzworth-Munroe, A., & Johnson, S. (2011). Guidelines for classifying evidence-based treatments in couple and family therapy. *Family Process*, *50*(3), 377–392. doi:10.1111/j.1545-5300.2011.01363.x

Sheridan, M., Peterson, B., & Rosen, K. (2010). The experiences of parents of adolescents in family therapy: A qualitative investigation. *Journal of Marital and Family Therapy*, *36*(2), 144–157. doi:10.1111/j.1752-0606.2010.00193.x

Shields, C. G., Finley, M. A., Chawla, N., & Meadors, P. (2012). Couple and family interventions in health problems. *Journal of Marital and Family Therapy*, *38*(1), 265–280. doi:10.1111/j.1752-0606.2011.00269.x

Skinner, H. A., Steinhauer, P. D., & Santa-Barbara, J. (2004). *Family Assessment Measure–III*. Retrieved from http://www.mhs.com/product.aspx?gr=edu&id=overview&prod=famiii - scales

Smerud, P. E., & Rosenfarb, I. S. (2011). The therapeutic alliance and family psychoeducation in the treatment of schizophrenia: An exploratory prospective change process study. *Couple and Family Psychology: Research and Practice*, *1*(S), 85–91. doi:10.1037/2160-4096.1.S.85

Smith, A., & Cook-Cottone, C. (2011). A review of family therapy as an effective intervention for anorexia nervosa in adolescents. *Journal of Clinical Psychology in Medical Settings*, *18*(4), 323–334. doi:10.1007/s10880-011-9262-3

Snyder, D. K., Heyman, R. E., & Haynes, S. N. (2005). Evidence-based approaches to assessing couples. *Psychological Assessment*, *17*(3), 288–307. doi:10.1037/1040-3590.17.3.288

Spanier, G. B. (1976). Measuring dyadic adjustment: New scales for assessing the quality of marriage and similar dyads. *Journal of Marriage and the Family*, *38*, 15–28.

Spies, R. A., Carlson, J. F., & Geisinger, K. F. (2010). *The eighteenth mental measurements yearbook*. Lincoln, NE: Buros Institute of Mental Measurements.

Spinelli, C. (2008). Introduction: The benefits, uses, and practical application of informal assessment procedures. *Reading and Writing Quarterly*, *24*(1), 1–6.

Sprenkle, D. (2012). Intervention research in couple and family therapy: A methodological and substantive review and an introduction to the special issue. *Journal of Marital and Family Therapy*, *38*(1), 3–29. doi:10.1111/j.1752-0606.2011.00271.x

Sprenkle, D. H. (2003). Effectiveness research in marriage and family counseling: Introduction. *Journal of Marital and Family Therapy*, *29*, 85–96.

Steinglass, P. (2009). Systemic-motivational therapy for substance abuse disorders: an integrative model. *Journal of Family Therapy*, *31*(2), 155–174. doi:10.1111/j.1467-6427.2009.00460.x

Straus, M. A. (2007). Conflict Tactics Scale. In N. A. Jackson (Ed.), *Encyclopedia of domestic violence* (pp. 190–197). New York, NY: Routledge.

Synder, D. K. (1997). *Marriage Satisfaction Inventory manual*. Los Angeles, CA: Western Psychological Services.

Tomasello, N. M., Manning, A. R., & Dulmus, C. N. (2010). Family-centered early intervention for infants and toddlers with disabilities. *Journal of Family Social Work*, *13*(2), 163–172.

Tuckett, A. (2004). Qualitative research sampling: The very real complexities. *Nurse Researcher*, *12*(1), 47–61.

Van Parys, H., & Rober, P. (2013). Trying to comfort the parent: A qualitative study of children dealing with parental depression. *Journal of Marital & Family Therapy*, *39*(3), 330–345. doi:10.1111/j.1752-0606.2012.00304.x

Watson, J. C., & Flamez, B. (2014). *Counseling assessment and evaluation: Fundamentals of applied practice*. Thousand Oaks, CA: SAGE.

Weisner, T. S., & Fiese, B. H. (2011). Advances in mixed methods in family psychology: Integrative and applied solutions for family science [Special section]. *Journal of Family Psychology*, *25*(6), 795–798. doi:10.1037/a0026203

Williams, L., & Tappan, T. (1995). The utility of the Myers-Briggs perspective in couples counseling: A clinical framework. *American Journal of Family Therapy*, *23*(4), 367–371. doi:10.1080/01926189508251367

Wilmoth, J. D., & Smyser, S. (2012). A national survey of marriage preparation provided by clergy. *Journal of Couple & Relationship Therapy*, *11*(1), 69–85. doi:10.1080/15332691.2012.639705

CHAPTER 5

Legal, Ethical, and Professional Issues

Melinda Haley

Walden University

The profession of marriage and family therapy (which will be referred to as couples, marriage, and family counseling [CMFC] within this chapter) began in the mid-1900s and by 1970 had become a distinct counseling specialty with a unique design of study (Bradley, Bergen, Ginter, Williams, & Scalise, 2010; Lee & Nichols, 2010). Couples, marriage, and family counseling has burgeoned since the 1970s, and there has been a "50-fold increase in the number of marriage and family therapists" who are practicing (AAMFT, 2013a, p. 1). Today, CMFC is recognized as a profession that has garnered its own respect and is acknowledged by the U.S. federal government (Northey, 2009). However, CMFC is also known as a specialization housed within other helping vocations.

The formulation of CMFC began within many different professions (e.g., counseling, psychology, and social work) and has strong roots in the university land grant programs of the 1800s (Bradley et al., 2010; Lee & Nichols, 2010; West, Hinton, Grames, & Adams, 2013). Due to its strong roots in these other helping professions, many still offer CMFC as a specialization within their practice (e.g., mental health counselors, social workers, psychiatrists, family medicine practitioners, and psychologists).

CMFC is unique and different from other forms of counseling because it is based on preparation that includes theories specific to couples and families and includes the understanding of family and relationship dynamics, such as issues of power and hierarchy, decision making, communication patterns, family roles, and the family life cycle and processes (AAMFT, 2013a; Moore, Hamilton, Crane, & Fawcett, 2011). The profession of CMFC can also differ from other professions that offer couples, marriage, and family therapy as a specialization (e.g., psychiatry and clinical psychology) in that the profession of CMFC does not espouse a medical or pathological model, but rather focuses on family, relationship strengths, and resiliency, and it takes a holistic wellness approach (AAMFT, 2013a; Lee & Nichols, 2010). CMFC therapeutic approaches are usually brief and solution focused with specific, attainable goals (AAMFT, 2013a; Moore et al., 2011). However, counselors who strictly practice as licensed marriage and family therapists (LMFTs) are also similar to other practitioners because they are also trained in psychotherapy and are licensed to diagnose and treat mental health, emotional, behavioral, and relational issues within individual, couple, and family systems (AAMFT, 2013a; Moore et al., 2011).

Today, counselors who practice CMFC can be found in a variety of work settings, which include hospitals, outpatient facilities, the criminal justice system, public and private schools, and even churches (Lee & Nichols, 2010). CMFC is a nationally recognized profession on par with other mental health professions such as psychiatry, psychology, mental health counseling, and social work (Crane & Christenson, 2012; West et al., 2013). In fact, a study by Moore et al. (2011) found that when compared to other professions such as medical doctors, nurses, psychologists, social workers, and other professional counselors, counselors practicing CMFC "had the lowest dropout rates and recidivism and were more cost effective than psychologists, MDs, and nurses" (p. 149).

This chapter discusses some of the ethical, legal, professional, and educational issues unique to the profession or practice of CMFC. The majority of the information in this chapter will equally apply to CMFC as a profession or as a specialty within another profession. Where differences need to be noted, they will be highlighted. The space constraints of this chapter prevent an in-depth discussions on all of the issues pertinent to CMFC; therefore, this chapter highlights those issues deemed most important or those that are most discussed within the current literature.

ETHICAL ISSUES

The American Association for Marriage and Family Therapy (AAMFT) is the largest organization that supports CMFC as a profession, and it has established the ethical code that couples, marriage, and family counselors follow in their practice (AAMFT, 2012a). This original ethical code was developed in 1962, but it has changed and evolved over time to best meet the needs of both counselors and their clients (Aducci & Cole, 2011). The code delineates between behaviors that are conducive to therapy and those that are harmful to a counselor or clients (Harris et al., 2009). A strong ethical code has aided the field of CMFC to become known as being a cost-effective, reliable, and ethical form of counseling (Brock, Whiting, Matern, & Fife, 2009). The scope of this chapter will not allow for a full dissection of the AAMFT ethical code, but some significant issues that have recently been identified in the literature will be discussed. Other professions that offer couples, marriage, and family therapy as a specialty may also follow the ethical codes of the AAMFT, their own professional organization's ethical code (e.g., the American Counseling Association), or they may follow both. Because many of the helping professions' ethical codes are similar in intent and in nature, and to reduce redundancy in the discussion, only the ethical code of the AAMFT will be explored in this chapter.

Multiple Relationships

One of the most controversial aspects of the AAMFT ethical code that has been reported recently in the literature has been multiple relationships with clients or supervisees (Aducci & Cole, 2011; Dallesasse, 2010). A multiple relationship can be defined as a counselor having a relationship with the client, couple, family, or supervisee outside of the therapeutic or supervisory relationship or when the counselor or supervisor has a dual role with the same person (e.g., counseling supervisor and guitar teacher to the same person (Aducci & Cole, 2011; Dallesasse, 2010).

The ethical code can be difficult to discern in such cases, because often there are no black and white recommendations or admonishments. Instead, practitioners are cautioned that such relationships should not be "exploitive" (Aducci & Cole, 2011). As Aducci and Cole pointed out, there is little research that examines whether nonsexual dual relationships are indeed harmful to clients or practitioners, and the code is based more on assumption than on concrete empirical evidence. Dallesasse (2010) asserted that refraining from multiple relationships is aspirational in nature because this can be very difficult to do in some environments and circumstances.

Examples of environments in which dual roles or multiple relationships are difficult to avoid occur when counselors work in rural or small communities. An example of this might be when a CMFC is working with a client who is also that counselor's dentist, because each is the only professional within the community who can perform that service. Another example in which such role conflicts probably occur is within the university environment. In some university programs, doctoral students may take a cross-listed didactic class that includes master's level students. In one setting the doctoral student is a peer, but then the doctoral student may supervise a master's student for the clinical component of the student's training (Dallesasse, 2010). Another example is when a university counseling center counselor has a client and then later has that same client as a student in a class he or she is teaching (Dallesasse, 2010).

SIDEBAR 5.1

Dr. Mary Alison is a licensed marriage and family therapist who works at the local university in the CMFC track. The program in which Dr. Alison is a core faculty member is both CACREP and COAMFTE accredited (for information on accreditation, see the later section in this chapter). The university is located in a rural area. Dr. Alison's husband is seeking a master's degree, also in CMFC. Dr. Alison has been teaching the theories course for the last 5 years, and now her husband is at the place in his program where he needs to take that class. Dr. Alison's class is the only section being offered during the semester in which her husband needs to take it. No one else in the department has taught that course, and the nearest university that offers a class that is comparable is over 3 hours away. What are your thoughts about this dual role? Is this acceptable under the circumstances? Why or why not? What would you recommend the university or program do in response to this dilemma?

Aducci and Cole (2011) have noted that not all cases of multiple relationships or dual roles can be avoided or are harmful, and they have called for increased research and clarification of the code to help practitioners practice ethically in every environment. Regardless of circumstances for the occurrence of a nonsexual dual role or multiple relationship, it is highly recommended that such relationships have "systematic examination, consultation, and documentation" (Dallesasse, 2010, p. 420). See Dallesasse (2010) for an ethical decision-making model to help determine whether a dual or multiple relationship is acceptable. Although it is geared toward college students, this decision model can also aid those working in other environments.

Scholarly Integrity

Brock et al. (2009) have noted that the CMFC profession has focused on preparing well-qualified counselors, but not researchers. Part of this emphasis on counseling can be explained by the fact that many counselors practicing CMFC are trained at the master's level and very few go on to obtain their PhDs, which is considered to be more research focused (Northey & Hodgson, 2008). Therefore, few counselors have received extensive research training in CMFC. Lee and Nichols (2010) are proponents of developing the profession of CMFC to include much more emphasis on accredited doctoral programs and scholarly research. This issue may not be a concern for other professions who offer CMFC as a specialty within their profession and who do receive much more emphasis on research in their training programs (e.g., clinical psychologists).

Scholarship and empirical research within the practice of CMFC as a profession are becoming increasingly important in order to strengthen the field, increase respect, and gain more opportunities for funding (DuPree, White, Meredith, Ruddick, & Anderson, 2009; Karam & Sprenkle, 2010). This is especially true within higher education, due to the current economy and cuts in state financial support to institutions of higher learning (DuPree et al., 2009). Karam and Sprenkle (2010) and Košutić, Sanderson, and Anderson (2012) have noted that there is a grave disconnect between researchers and practitioners in the field and that research needs to become more user-friendly and more relatable to what clinicians are experiencing. Northey and Hodgson (2008) noted this disconnect is often because clinical research is disseminated in various journal articles that can be difficult or time consuming to read or costly to access. Unless the CMFC has subscriptions to multiple journals or has access to a database through a university, access to relevant research is difficult to obtain.

In addition to these issues, there have also been some ethical concerns regarding the state of research within the profession of CMFC (Brock et al., 2009). Brock et al. stated that as of 2001, the AAMFT ethical code did not sufficiently address research integrity. They asserted the code made "no mention of fabrication or falsification of research as violations of the Code" (p. 249), and that the CMFC field has lagged behind other professions in providing rigor, honesty, and integrity in research. As such, they stated the field has suffered. A survey of counselors who practice CMFC conducted by these researchers found that 27% of clinicians had personal experience with some aspect of fabrication or falsification of data, false reporting, or plagiarism (Brock et al., 2009).

Many of the concerns expressed by Brock et al. (2009) have now been addressed within the current AAMFT ethical code (AAMFT, 2012a). The newly revised ethical code does address the veracity of scholarship and mandates that counselors practicing CMFC be "dedicated to high standards of scholarship, present accurate information, and disclose potential conflicts of interest" (Principle III, 3.5) and that they make "efforts to prevent the distortion or misuse of their clinical and research findings" (Principle III, 3.12). In relation to the issue of plagiarism, the code mandates that counselors "who are the authors of books or other materials that are published or distributed do not plagiarize or fail to cite persons to whom credit for original ideas or work is due" (Principle VI, 6.4).

Currently, the AAMFT requires that counselors presenting at state and national conferences provide a statement that the research has had institutional review board (IRB) approval, but it has further been suggested that the actual IRB protocol number be made public on such documents (Brock et al., 2009). Other suggestions include having researchers engage in integrity training and requiring disclosure of any multiple roles or dual relationships between researchers and participants or grantors (Brock et al., 2009).

Multicultural Competence

In a world that is becoming progressively more diverse, it is increasingly more important for counselors and other helping professionals who offer CMFC to evaluate their competence when providing services to clients who are culturally different from themselves (Nixon et al., 2010). Now more than ever, it is understood that *diversity* refers to more than just ethnic culture. Yet, there are still many distinctions related to cultural multiplicity that some may not consider a variable of diversity.

One example is the cultural characteristic of socioeconomic status (Grimes & McElwain, 2008). The beliefs, values, goals, behaviors, thoughts, and practices of an individual with a high socioeconomic status may differ significantly from someone with a low socioeconomic status (Grimes & McElwain, 2008). Another example is the identification of the concept of family. The notion of the "traditional" family, composed of a father, mother, and children, has become quite antiquated, and counselors practicing CMFC must understand the nuances of what family means or how family is identified within the many different cultural contexts (Dias, Chan, Ungvarsky, Oraker, & Cleare-Hoffman, 2011; Hernández & Rankin, 2008). Other examples of diversity within couples, marriage, and family therapy can be related to where a family is in the family life cycle, the age of the parents, the ethnicity of the family, religious preference, sexual orientation, country or region of origin, and a host of other variables. Counselors also need to understand the unique barriers or opportunities that may arise for different cultural groups in order to best provide services (Hall & Sandberg, 2012; Seponski, Bermudez, & Lewis, 2013).

SIDEBAR 5.2

Chan Sitka and his family are recent immigrants from Bhutan who have been in the United States for 1 year. Acculturation stress has impacted the family and caused discord. The six Sitka children are acclimating to U.S. culture much more quickly than Chan or his wife. Chan is fearful that his children are distancing themselves from their culture of origin and insists they maintain their original cultural values. Three of the older children are actively rebellious and are having behavioral issues because they feel caught between two cultural worlds. Chan feels disrespected and devalued as a result of his children's behavior. The school counselor recommended family counseling, and Chan has agreed to give it a try. The school counselor provided the family with a referral to the nearest CMFC. The CMFC counselor is a White female who is 15 years younger than Chan. She was educated in the United States. What cultural issues do you think might be important for the counselor to consider as she works with the Sitka family?

In addition, just as in other forms of counseling, many theories related to couples, marriage, and family counseling have been formed in the United States or other Western countries, and therefore may not be as applicable for families with cultures originating from other geographical areas (Seponski et al., 2013). Therefore, counselors need to become skilled in adapting or modifying their preferred theories for use with culturally diverse couples, individuals, or families (Seponski et al., 2013). In addition, it is important that counselors continue to gain knowledge on this issue through continuing education, experiences of immersion, and talking with their clients to make sure they understand the unique cultural dimensions of each client, couple, or family. The field of CMFC also needs to continue to develop culturally appropriate theories and interventions so that counselors can successfully treat their diverse clientele (Grimes & McElwain, 2008; Seponski et al., 2013).

There are many ethical issues that pertain to the practice of CMFC. However, the issues of multiple relationships and multicultural competence in a world condensed by globalization and scholarly integrity during a time when research within the CMFC field is flourishing are three of the most prominent issues discussed currently in the CMFC literature. For more in-depth information regarding the issues addressed here, readers are directed to Nixon et al. (2009) and Seponski et al. (2013) for thorough discussions regarding how multiculturalism is and can be taught in the CMFC classroom, and to Hernández and Rankin (2008) for an in-depth discussion on training CMFC students to work with clients and families who are lesbian, gay, bisexual, transgender, and questioning (LGBTQ).

Burnout

As with other helping professions, counselors practicing CMFC can be subjected to burnout in the profession (Clark, 2009; Matheson & Rosen, 2012). *Burnout* can be defined as physical, emotional, and cognitive exhaustion due to the demands of the profession, which can manifest in depersonalization and feelings of reduced accomplishment or outright failure (Clark, 2009; Dias et al., 2011). It is estimated that as many as 15% of counselors practicing CMFC will feel burnout at some point in their careers (Clark, 2009), and this can affect their professional, personal, and family lives (Matheson & Rosen, 2012). As with many helping professions, counselors have their share of stressors that contribute to burnout, such as heavy caseloads and a great deal of paperwork, difficult cases, excessive meetings and trainings, administrative duties, role overload, and having a "helping" personality (Matheson & Rosen, 2012, p. 395).

Counselors practicing CMFC can be uniquely affected by a type of burnout called *compassion fatigue*, given the issues that often arise within families (Negash & Sahin, 2011). Compassion fatigue is similar to burnout, but can also share symptoms similar to secondary traumatic stress (Negash & Sahin, 2011). Negash and Sahin described symptoms common with compassion fatigue as "chronic physical and emotional exhaustion, depersonalization, feelings of inequity, irritability, headaches, and weight loss," "negative feelings toward work, life, and others outside the therapeutic relationship," as well as "self-contempt, feelings of low job satisfaction, and psychosomatic problems" (pp. 1–2).

Practitioners have an ethical responsibility to monitor themselves for burnout and compassion fatigue and assess whether symptoms are affecting their treatment protocols and best practices (Negash & Sahin, 2011). Negash and Sahin recommended that practitioners monitor their abilities to interact successfully with others and whether they have changes in sleep patterns, mood, physical activities, or other signs and symptoms of fatigue. Burnout can be resisted or mitigated by engaging in self-care, setting limits on time commitments, reducing caseloads, instituting a balance of work with pleasurable activities, obtaining personal counseling, and accepting support from colleagues (Clark, 2009; Negash & Sahin, 2011). See Negash and Sahin (2011) for a thorough discussion about burnout and compassion fatigue within the field of CMFC.

LEGAL ISSUES

Just as in any profession, counselors must follow the law and ethical codes. According to the AAMFT (2013d), the most common legal issues found among its practitioners are legal subpoenas and issues involving privileged communication, the Health Insurance Portability and Accountability Act (HIPAA), incorporation versus partnership, closing a practice, parental joint custody and the treatment of minors, minor inpatient and outpatient treatment, improper informed consent, maintenance of clinical records, client/therapist sexual attraction, Internet or cyber therapy, duty to report child abuse, maintaining confidentiality, and termination of treatment. The constraints on this chapter prohibit an in-depth discussion on each of these; however, the following additional issues are discussed: HIPAA, licensure, case notes, and malpractice insurance, because these are the most frequently discussed issues within the current literature.

SIDEBAR 5.3

Tammy Sanchez is a master's level, newly licensed marriage and family therapist (LMFT) who just opened a private practice. When Ms. Sanchez organized her office, she installed a program on her laptop that provided a template through which to write her case notes. She has a total of six families, five couples, and 10 individual clients with whom she is currently working. As a part of her licensure requirements and continued professional growth, Ms. Sanchez attends the AAMFT and American Counseling Association (ACA) conferences and takes continuing education classes. When she travels, she takes her laptop; this way she can work on the plane or on breaks between meetings, in order to make the best use of her time. However, her laptop is not password protected and her clinical notes are not encrypted. After you read the following section on legal issues in CMFC, reflect back on whether Ms. Sanchez is correctly protecting her clients' private information.

HIPAA

The Health Insurance Portability and Accountability Act (HIPAA) was proposed in 1996 and went into effect in 2003 (Benefield, Ashkanazi, & Rozensky, 2006) and the latest revision and new compliance changes were effective as of September 23, 2013 (Wheeler, 2013).

HIPAA defined the methods for handling the privacy of clients' oral, paper, and electronic health information with prescribed sanctions for noncompliance from practitioners (Letzring & Snow, 2011; Wheeler, 2013). HIPAA also provided for portability of benefits so that employees would not lose important remunerations as they increasingly began to merge into new jobs or careers (Benefield et al., 2006). HIPAA also intended to reduce health care fraud and reduce costs for consumers (Wise, King, & Miller, 2011).

Contained within HIPAA is the Health Information Technology for Economic and Clinical Health Act (HITECH) of 2009. HITECH protects consumers' electronic health information (Wheeler, 2013). For example, HITECH stipulates that counselors must store electronic data on a password-protected computer with the clinical files encrypted (Wheeler, 2013). Counselors must monitor their clients' protected information. If a counselor identifies a probable breach of protected information, he or she has certain obligations under HITECH. Failure to meet those obligations will result in financial sanctions that could run into the millions of dollars, depending upon the case (Wheeler, 2013). When a potential breach of information is identified, the counselor must perform a risk assessment and then "mitigate breaches and report them to affected clients, the federal government, and in some cases, even to the media" (Wheeler, 2013, p. 1). For more detailed information about both HIPAA and HITECH, see Wheeler (2013).

Wheeler (2013) suggested that practitioners who are not sure if their practice falls under the HIPAA regulations should go to the website for Centers for Medicare and Medicaid Services (http://www.cms.gov). This site has a decision tree to help in making that determination. Another useful source of information regarding HIPAA is the U.S. Department of Health and Human Services.

Licensure

There are two routes to becoming licensed or credentialed to practice couples, marriage, and family counseling: as a profession or as a specialty within a profession. Counselors can become licensed marriage and family therapists (LMFTs) if they choose to practice CMFC as their primary profession. Counselors who are licensed professional counselors (LPC) can add couples, marriage, and family counseling as a specialty. Both processes will be discussed in this section.

CMFC as a Profession

As mentioned previously, to practice as a licensed couples, marriage, and family counselor as a profession, one needs a minimum of a master's degree (Lee & Nichols, 2010). Education and training include: (a) theories specific to systems, couples, and families; (b) a foundation in family science; and (c) a supervised application of skills (Lee & Nichols, 2010). Education for CMFC as a profession has been based on standards developed by the American Association of Marriage Counselors (AAMC), which periodically has undergone revision since 1949 (Lee & Nichols, 2010). Basic competencies include being trained in empirically based theories and emergent trends in family therapy practice and mental health treatment (Lee & Nichols, 2010). Over the past 15 years, education for counselors practicing CMFC has moved from being housed in multidisciplinary programs to being housed in programs that grant degrees specifically in couples, marriage, and family counseling (Bradley et al., 2010).

California was the first state to legislate the profession of couples, marriage, and family counseling (Northey, 2009). Historically, in order to be a licensed CMFC, one had to be a member of the AAMFT and meet their prelicensure criteria (West et al., 2013). This provided "a common core education, a common practicum experience," and "rigorous supervision with a family systems focus" (West et al., 2013, p. 118). Membership with the AAMFT is no longer required, and licensure is now pursued through state licensure boards (Bradley et al., 2010; West et al., 2013). This shifted the responsibility of ensuring the preparation of counselors who seek to practice CMFC from one single, unified entity, and the profession therefore lost its standardization of experience and training. To facilitate this shift and to try to keep more standardization within the state licensure process,

Table 5.1 Main Differences for 2012 in Licensure Requirements for States Compared to the AAMFT Prelicensure Guidelines

AAMFT Prelicensure Guidelines	State Guidelines (Vary by State)
Prescribed CMFC courses: 11	Course requirements: 8–15
Practicum hours: One year, 300 hours of supervised direct client contact	State practicum hours: 180–500 hours
Postgraduate clinical experience: 1,000 hours of direct client contact	State postgraduate clinical experience: 1,000–3,000 hours
Postgraduate supervision: 200 hours, with 100 of these hours coming from individual supervision.	State postgraduate supervision: 75–175 hours
Postgraduate supervisor qualifications: AAMFT approved supervisors only	State postgraduate supervisor qualifications: Only eight states require supervisors to be AAMFT approved

the AAMFT created the Department of Divisional Affairs (DDA) to define the general requirements for licensure from state to state and also created the Association of Marital and Family Therapy Regulatory Board (AMFTRB) (West et al., 2013). The AMFTRB is composed of representatives from each of the state boards that issue licenses to counselors (Northey, 2009).

Even with these safeguards in place, this shift away from the AAMFT licensure process has created quite a bit of variation in requirements for licensure between the states. West et al. (2013) reviewed the requirements for all 50 states and the District of Columbia and found many differences in the number of courses taken, the number of practicum hours needed, the amount of postgraduation clinical hours and supervision required, and the qualifications needed to supervise couples, marriage, and family graduates for licensure. (See Table 5.1.)

While vast differences now exist from state to state in terms of licensure, some generalities include that an applicant must have a minimum of a master's degree and some postgraduate supervised clinical practice. This is the minimum standard in all 50 states (AAMFT, 2013e; Lee & Nichols, 2010). According to the study conducted by West et al. (2013), 33 states meet or exceed the AAMFT-recommended 11-course requirement of classes specific to couples, marriage, and family counseling pursuant to CMFC licensure. Twenty states meet or exceed the AAMFT clinical practicum standard of 1 year (300 hours) of supervised clinical practice. Forty-three states meet or exceed the AAMFT requirement of 1,000 client contact hours specifically with couples and families. Nineteen states meet or exceed the AAMFT requirement of 200 hours of supervision with 100 hours being given in an individual format.

Generally, once supervision is completed, a state licensure exam must be passed. Most states use the national examination for marriage and family therapists that is administered by the Association of Marital and Family Therapy Regulatory Board (AMFTRB) (AAMFT, 2013e; West et al., 2013). This exam is periodically updated by the AMFTRB using a "role delineation survey," which ascertains skills, knowledge, and procedures needed for current practice (Bradley et al., 2010, p. 281). The first national exam was given in 1988. In 2005, a practice exam was developed for potential applicants to help prepare for the exam, with a second practice exam being established in 2007 (West et al., 2013). The only state that currently does not use this national exam is California (Bradley et al., 2010; West et al., 2013). One strong admonishment that came out of the West et al. (2013) study is that although at one time the CMFC profession had the same training and standards regardless of state of practice, now this training varies widely from state to state. However, attempts to standardized training have improved since 2007 (West et al., 2013).

Other recent changes in the licensure process include: (a) greater portability between states when counselors want to move to another location and practice, (b) increased use of criminal background checks by states prior to issuing a license, (c) the move by many states to require a 60-hour master's program, (d) increased coursework in diagnosis, and (e) increased state guidelines regulating online education, cybertherapy, and cybersupervision (West et al., 2013).

As with many professions, licensed counselors who practice CMFC are mandated to continue their education postlicensure (Lee & Nichols, 2010). However, Northey and Hodgson (2008) asserted that continuing education programs are often ineffective in terms of increasing therapeutic skill as they are often "dyadic in nature" and aren't experiential enough to encourage new practices (p. 55). Therefore, further changes may be needed in this area to improve the continued training of these counselors (Northey & Hodgson, 2008).

CMFC as a Specialization

Education for CMFC as a specialty also has strict requirements. An example of such a specialization is one that is offered within counseling programs affiliated with the ACA. This CMFC specialization has been based on knowledge, skills, and practice standards developed by the Council for Accreditation of Counseling and Related Programs (CACREP). The most recent version of the standards was published in 2009. CACREP is an independent organization that is recognized by the Council for Higher Education Accreditation and is the main accrediting body for counseling programs such as clinical mental health, addictions, career, school, and CMFC. Accreditation is further discussed later in this chapter.

Minimum educational requirements for a specialization in marriage, couple, and family counseling include an approved graduate-level counseling degree "with a minimum of 60 semester credit hours or 90 quarter credit hours" (CACREP, 2009, p. 4). Once licensed as a professional counselor, applicants can apply for credentialing in marriage, couple, and family counseling (IAMFC, 2013).

In 1994, in response to concerns about the training of counselors who specialize in CMFC, the International Association of Marriage and Family Counselors (IAMFC), which is a subdivision of the ACA, created the National Credentialing Academy (NCA) (IAMFC, 2013). This credentialing process "grants recognition to professionals who have met predetermined NCA standards in their training and experience, and meet ethical standards in the field" (IAMFC, 2013, para 2). It should be noted that individuals cannot practice professionally solely with an NCA credential; they must also be licensed as counselors by their individual state (IAMFC, 2013). The NCA credential is desired because it asserts to other mental health professionals, agencies, and clients that an individual has met the minimum standards appropriate to the competent practice of CMFC and is qualified to practice it as a specialty (IAMFC, 2013).

Case Notes

Just as in other helping professions, the importance of clinical case notes cannot be overemphasized. Very often it is through case notes that malpractice lawsuits are won or lost (Harris et al., 2009). For more information on malpractice lawsuits, see the section on malpractice insurance in this chapter.

Harris et al. (2009) asserted that case notes are primary in ensuring quality of care to clients and in protecting client rights. They further indicated that the use of good case notes is beneficial when a client returns for counseling or changes to a new therapist. The course of prior treatment can be reviewed before making new clinical decisions. Case consultations are less effective if supervisors or consultants cannot look at the course of treatment via the counselor's case notes, and it is difficult to ascertain clinical progress without proper note taking (Harris et al., 2009).

Despite its importance, some researchers ascertain that many counselors who practice CMFC do not know how to adequately write good case notes, which can leave the counselor vulnerable in legal proceedings (Harris et al., 2009). For example, there may be times in a counselor's career when his or her notes will be subpoenaed by the court. A court order is legally binding, and the CMFC may have little recourse but to turn over that information to the court (Harris et al., 2009). The scope of this chapter will not allow a detailed discussion of what counselors should do in this case, but there are many resources for counselors to help manage legal issues, such as the legal team of the professional organization to which he or she belongs (e.g., the AAMFT).

One potential reason identified for the deficiency of CMFC case notes is the vague way case notes are discussed in the AAMFT ethical code and the fact that there is no standard set by the profession (Harris et al., 2009). For example, the former version of the AAMFT ethical code dictated that case notes should be "accurate and adequate," but no further instruction is given (Harris et al., 2009). The 2012 version of the ethical code simply states that counselors should "maintain accurate and adequate clinical and financial records in accordance with applicable law" (AAMFT, 2012a, Principle III, 3.6). Even the language used by the Commission on Accreditation for Marriage and Family Therapy Education (COAMFTE) is vague, saying only that counselors should "complete case documentation in a timely manner and in accordance with relevant laws and practices" and that they should "write plans and complete other case documentation in accordance with practice setting policies, professional standards, and state/provincial laws" (Harris et al., 2009, p. 383). Therefore, no instruction is given in regard to what should be included in the case notes, and there is a lot of subjectivity in the process

The most popular forms of case notes are the SOAP note (subjective, objective, assessment, plan), the STIPS (signs and symptoms, topics of discussion, interventions, progress, and special client issues), and the DAP (data, assessment, and plan) (Harris et al., 2009). However, many of these forms are based on the medical model and are for use with individual clients, not couples or family systems (Harris et al., 2009). Therefore, complications arise with these formats when treating couples or families, and many beginning counselors struggle with how much information should be inserted into the case notes (Harris et al., 2009). See Harris et al. (2009) for a discussion on what components should be in a good CMFC case note.

SIDEBAR 5.4

Harris et al. (2009) suggested practitioners review local and state laws to determine any idiosyncratic legal mandates regarding clinical case notes. In general, they also made the suggestion that each case note should include: (a) client identifying information, (b) the date services were rendered, (c) counselor degree and licensure information, (d) counselor signature, and (e) billing information. In addition, the accumulation of clinical notes kept in a file should cover the following: (a) information that reflects the process of counseling, (b) the issue or problem the client or family has presented, (c) past information on history of the problem, (d) therapeutic observations, (e) results of objective or subjective assessments or measures, (f) therapeutic recommendations and treatment plan, and (g) client progress to date. Items that should be excluded from case notes or clinical files are: (a) counselor personal opinion or biased information, (b) emotional statements, (c) privileged communication, and (d) counselor personal notes.

Malpractice Insurance

Many counselors receive malpractice insurance (also known as liability insurance) through their employer, but others do not (Walfish & Barnett, 2009). It is important for counselors practicing CMFC to determine their coverage needs and ensure they have adequate insurance, especially since these counselors have increased risk of liability due to working with families and children (Woody, 2008). Some states do not require private practitioners to purchase malpractice insurance, but it is strongly advised that practitioners protect themselves (Walfish & Barnett, 2009; Woody, 2008). Liability insurance provides assistance in the defense of the practitioner should a suit of malpractice be filed. Members of the AAMFT are eligible for group benefits for malpractice insurance policies (Walfish & Barnett, 2009).

There are many nuances to ensure proper liability coverage, so practitioners are encouraged to do their research as to whether they need a "claims made" or "occurrence" policy. A claims made policy only covers the practitioner while he or she is under the insurance policy. Once coverage is terminated, the practitioner is no longer covered, even if a client files a suit during the time the practitioner had insurance (Walfish & Barnett, 2009). In contrast, an occurrence policy remains in effect indefinitely, but is more expensive than a claims made policy (Walfish & Barnett, 2009). For more information about purchasing a malpractice insurance policy, see Walfish and Barnett (2009).

PROFESSIONAL ISSUES

As with the ethical and legal sections of this chapter, space constraints prohibit coverage of every professional issue that applies to the practice and profession of CMFC. This section will review the professional issues of the mental health recovery movement, work settings, lack of diversity within the profession, core competencies, evidence-based practices, advocacy, and professional development.

The Mental Health Recovery Movement

In 2004, the New Freedom Commission recommended changes in how severe and persistent mental health and dual diagnosis issues were treated, which resulted in the U.S. Department of Health and Human Services issuing a statement on mental health recovery (Gehart, 2012). It was recommended that all public mental health organizations adopt an approach based on the principle of recovery using a nonpathologizing, strength-based orientation, which was an ideal fit with the principles of marriage and family therapy (Gehart, 2012). The recovery movement started with a grassroots effort that rebelled against the medical model of pathology and disease and was supported by cross-national research conducted by the World Health Organization (Gehart, 2012). This approach was adopted in other nations in the early 1990s, but the United States didn't adopt this approach until 2004, (Gehart, 2012).

The recovery approach was a paradigm shift from a notion that severe and persistent mental health could be managed but not cured, to a philosophy that although full recovery might not be entirely possible, individuals can reach a place at which (a) symptoms are nonexistent and the individual has a full quality of life, (b) the person can live up to his or her full potential, and (c) the person can embrace wellness in its fullest definition (Gehart, 2012). In addition, this approach gave the person with a mental illness more autonomy and choice in his or her treatment (Gehart, 2012). In the United States, California has led the nation in implementing recovery-based mental health programs in the CMFC field by changing licensure laws that required training in recovery-based approaches (Gehart, 2012). Along with this change in perspective came a change in terminology, with the term *client* being replaced by *consumer* or *service recipient* (Gehart, 2012).

Further, Butler and Zamora (2013) discussed conceptualizing couples and families through the collaborative care model, whereby counselors collaborate with other professionals to treat within a contextual mixture of "biological, psychological, ecological, and spiritual" components of a mental health issue (p. 85). This has created a further paradigm shift in what are considered best practices. It no longer suffices to look at consumers of services one dimensionally. However, these collaborations can cause confusion in terms of limits of confidentiality and legal procedures due to the requirements of different professions (e.g., medical doctors, clergy members, social workers, licensed alcohol and drug counselors) (Butler & Zamora, 2013; Hudgins, Rose, Fifield, & Arnault, 2013).

Work Settings

Counselors practicing CMFC continue to work in a variety of settings, such as private practice, community mental health agencies, in-home therapy, and schools (Gehart, 2012). Counselors at the doctoral level also teach, do research, and consult at universities. In fact, half of all doctoral-level counselors who are licensed and practice CMFC have careers based at universities (Lee & Nichols, 2010). Over the past couple of decades, a shift has occurred, moving many counselors who practice CMFC from private practice and into employment settings and community mental health agencies. It is expected that this trend will continue (Gehart, 2012). Currently, less than 52% of these counselors work in private practice (Bradley et al., 2010). In addition, counseling is increasingly moving out of the office and into the clients' homes or into coffee shops, parks, and malls, mostly based on the individual needs of the client as determined under the recovery model of service provision (Gehart, 2012). The ethical implications of these new settings and approaches have not yet been fully explored (Gehart, 2012).

Bradley et al. (2010) found that more and more practitioners are identifying solely as counselors who practice CMFC exclusively, most have only master's degrees, and they typically fit into the following profile: "Caucasian/non-Hispanic female aged 51 to 60, [works] as a private practitioner, [is] licensed as a marriage and family therapist, [works] mostly with individual clients, and theoretically [relies] upon behavioral therapy, solution-focused therapy, or Bowen family systems" (p. 282).

Lack of Diversity

As indicated by the Bradley et al. (2010) study and supported by Hernández, Taylor, and McDowell (2009), there is a lack of diversity among practitioners of marriage and family therapy. These authors reported that counselors who practice CMFC are predominantly Caucasian (91%) and female (60%) with a mean age of 54. These authors suggested the CMFC profession is undergoing a crisis and that despite the AAMFT and ACA ethical and curricular guidelines for how to address cultural competence for counselors, the lack of diversity among its counselors presents an increased challenge for those counselors practicing CMFC to deliver multiculturally responsive therapy and supervision when so few practitioners are from ethnically diverse populations (Hernández et al., 2009; Innes, 2009).

CMFC supervisees from diverse backgrounds have identified a lack of attention to diversity and cultural issues discussed with Caucasian supervisors, as well as a lack of assistance in helping the supervisees integrate their cultural identities into their professional identities (Hernández et al., 2009). Furthermore, thus far in the field, there has been a lack of interest in developing models of supervision that incorporate diversity variables such as ethnicity, spirituality, or sexual orientation. Rather, the focus remains on a heterosexual, Eurocentric point of view that leaves many CMFC supervisees feeling disempowered and negatively stigmatized (Hernández et al., 2009). In addition, more supervisory abuse of power was reported when the supervisor was from a privileged background, compared to the supervisee (Hernández et al., 2009). Innes (2009) also noted a gender bias prevalent in counselors and faculty of CMFC programs. Many supervisees from diverse backgrounds stated "that they would have liked to have supervisors with critical consciousness in their training" (Hernández et al., 2009, p. 98).

Other scholars disagree with assessment of Hernández et al. Lee and Nichols (2010) believe the field of CMFC is becoming much more diverse, but noted that graduate programs need to engage in more research in order to provide instructors and practitioners who can teach and practice in culturally appropriate ways. Schomburg and Prieto (2011) stated that within the past decade the field of CMFC has placed more emphasis on recruiting diverse graduate students as well as increasing the training and attention to multicultural variables presented by clients. However, they noted that more training is needed to transcend multicultural concepts in application, especially via the treatment plan. They have observed a disconnect between student knowledge of multicultural theories and concepts and students' abilities to practice them.

Along with the noted lack of diversity within the marriage and family therapy field, beginning counselors practicing CMFC also lament the lack of good mentorship, especially for counselors from culturally diverse backgrounds (Hernández et al., 2009). Often culturally diverse counselors have had to seek mentoring relationships from outside the CMFC profession (Hernández et al., 2009). Allanach (2009) and Hair and Fine (2012) deemed mentorship via supervisory relationships essential to the training of competent practitioners because it provides the dual function of socializing the student into the profession. Unlike other professions such as psychology or social work, which offer undergraduate classes to encourage entry into the field, CMFC classes are not usually offered at the undergraduate level (Latty, Angera, & Burns-Jager, 2010). This further hinders a mentoring process for individuals interested in CMFC. Students have to wait until graduate school to get exposure to coursework specific to the CMFC profession. Latty et al. (2010) advocated for CMFC classes at the undergraduate junior and senior level to expose students to the CMFC profession and establish early mentoring relationships with interested students.

Core Competencies

Core competencies have been developed for the practice of CMFC as both a profession and a specialty. This section discusses the core competencies and processes for the AAMFT and the CACREP.

In 2003, due to a growing movement to define a minimum level of competence for licensure in the CMFC profession and to distinguish the profession from other

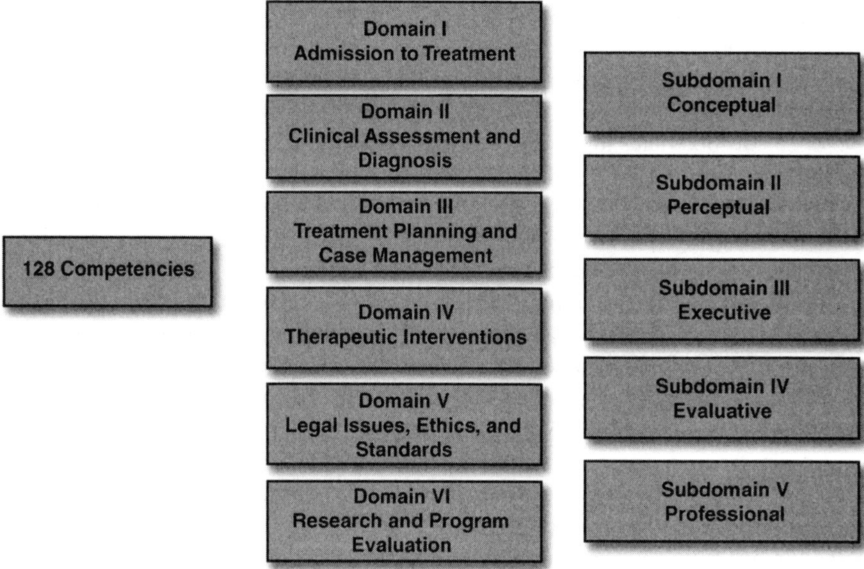

Figure 5.1 AAMFT Breakdown of Competency Domains and Subdomains

types of counseling, the AAMFT created a task force that determined the core competencies for the practice of CMFC (Gehart, 2008; Miller, 2010; Miller & Lambert-Shute, 2009; Miller, Todahl, & Platt, 2010). A second reason for developing the competencies was the rise of managed care organizations that began to make decisions regarding who was competent enough to treat patients or clients as a provider (Miller et al., 2010).

The AAMFT task force produced a compilation of 128 competencies based on the knowledge and skills for successful independent practice. Six core domains were identified: (1) admission to treatment; (2) clinical assessment and diagnosis; (3) treatment planning and case management; (4) therapeutic interventions; (5) legal issues, ethics, and standards; and (6) research and program evaluation. In addition, five subdomains were established: (1) conceptual, (2) perceptual, (3) executive, (4) evaluative, and (5) professional (AAMFT, 2004; Gehart, 2008). In 2006, the COAMFTE implemented the latest version of these standards (Miller, 2010). Many training programs today have developed curriculum around these core competencies to help students prepare for proficient practice (Miller, 2010).

The core competencies were originally met with skepticism from practitioners (Chenail, 2009). There were many complaints that the core competencies were "overly prescriptive, excessively reductionistic, and terribly 'mechanical'" and that students trained under this model would be no more effective than those currently practicing (p. 72). However, some instructors found methods that incorporated the core competencies into instruction with success and fostered a "learner centered approach" that seemed to be conducive to helping students with mastery learning (Chenail, 2009).

As noted previously, concerns also existed regarding the training of those who wished to specialize in CMFC within the profession of counseling. The CACREP developed competencies for the specialization of CMFC that denoted excellence of training. The CACREP (2009) standards defined the crucial knowledge, skills, and practices for competent training within the domains of (a) foundations; (b) counseling, prevention, and intervention; (c) diversity and advocacy; (d) assessment; and (e) research and evaluation.

Another factor in developing the core competencies for both the profession and the specialty is in gatekeeping aspects of the profession. Students who cannot perform at the level of competence will often face remediation, be given additional time to learn skills, or, in the worst-case scenario, face dismissal from their program (Russell, DuPree, Beggs, Peterson, & Anderson, 2007). The core competencies give professors and supervisors firm criteria through which to evaluate potential counselors and pinpoint exact issues in skill development. The goal is to help students remediate any deficits in ability and make sure those entering into the profession are trained to at least the minimal standards of practice (Russell et al., 2007).

Evidence-Based Practice

A related issue to core competency is the formation of evidence-based practice. Like other branches of counseling, the field of CMFC continually strives to engage in evidence-based practice (Brock et al., 2009; Caldwell & Wooley, 2008; Gehart, 2012; Lee & Nichols, 2010; Northey & Hodgson, 2008). The need for such empirical validation has increased due to CMFC's competition with other professions for grant money and insurance reimbursements (Košutić et al., 2012; Miller et al., 2010).

In 1997, the CMFC profession began hosting a series of research conferences espousing the need for more empirically based research to expand the science and practice of CMFC. This focus has strengthened the identity of CMFC and has established it as being separate from other helping professions (Lee & Nichols, 2010). The ensuing research has indicated that CMFC is as effective, and in some cases more effective, than individually based therapies in treating a full range of disorders including: schizophrenia, affective disorders, substance abuse, children's conduct disorders, eating disorders, autism, chronic physical illness, obesity, dementia, and relational issues (AAMFT, 2013a; Crane & Christenson, 2012; Northey & Hodgson, 2008; Moore et al., 2011). Northey and Hodgson (2008) discussed eight evidence-based therapies specific to CMFC: (1) brief strategic family therapy (BSFT), (2) family solutions program (FSP), (3) functional family therapy (FFT), (4) multidimensional family therapy (MDFT), (5) multisystemic family therapy (MST), (6) behavioral couples therapy (BCT), (7) emotionally focused couple therapy (EFT), and (8) Gottman's couple method (GCT).

One noted drawback to evidence-based practices and core competencies is that some practitioners fear that treatment will become rote and prescribed, practitioners will lose their flexibility to consider all the variables of a client's case, and they may further be hindered in using their creativity, intuition, or past experience with a specific cultural group. Couples, marriage, and family counselors do not want therapy to become a "one size fits all" endeavor (Miller et al., 2010; Northey & Hodgson, 2008). Northey and Hodgson (2008) noted that evidence-based treatments often become "manualized," which further constrains creativity in therapy, but helps to maintain "fidelity" to the model (p. 54).

Another noted barrier to incorporating evidence-based treatments into practice is that practitioners need supervision with new models of treatment until they become proficient (Northey & Hodgson, 2008). The cost of hiring a supervisor skilled in the therapy in question can be prohibitive. In addition, although there may be a lot of research supporting the efficacy of a treatment, there is not as much research focused on the best method for training counselors in the evidence-based therapies (Northey & Hodgson, 2008).

Advocacy

Since the early 2000s, issues of social justice and client advocacy have increasingly become an important part of practice and values for counselors practicing CMFC because it is recognized that many client or family issues have systemic or contextual roots (Gehart & Lucas, 2007). It is recognized that intervention at the individual or family level may not be sufficient in all cases (Gehart & Lucas, 2007). Advocacy can be described as a practitioner becoming involved in helping clients with issues of injustice, discrimination, and social and institutional barriers (Gehart & Lucas, 2007). Social justice is related to advocacy because social justice is the outcome hoped for through client advocacy in terms of client rights and equality (Gehart & Lucas, 2007).

Advocacy is also required at the level of the profession. Currently, counselors are involved in various local, state, and national advocacy initiatives through personal commitment and participation via the AAMFT and ACA (AAMFT, 2013c). For example, the AAMFT (2012b) is involved in several federal initiatives that include reimbursement for services or obtaining inclusion as practitioners in Medicare, the Veteran's Administration, the Department of Defense, and K–12 schools.

Professional Development

Lee and Nichols (2010) recommend three professional development trajectories for marriage and family therapists: (1) developing professional maturity, (2) being socialized into the profession, and (3) engaging in family science scholarship. Professional maturity includes engaging in professionalism and appreciation for what it means to be a CMFC and the development of a CMFC-specific identity (Lee & Nichols, 2010). In terms of scholarship, counselors practicing CMFC should be well versed in clinical research, best practices, and empirically validated treatments, as well as be engaged in action research to help develop and strengthen this line of scholarship (Lee & Nichols, 2010). Professional socialization includes the practice of mentoring new counselors and helping them identify their unique place within the helping professions, as well as helping to ground them in the ethics, laws, standards, and competencies of the profession (Lee & Nichols, 2010).

For continued professional development, socialization into the profession, and formation of a solid CMFC identity, it is important for counselors to have active involvement in their professional organizations (Lee & Nichols, 2010). The main organizations for these counselors are the AAMFT, the IAMFC, the American Association of Marriage Counselors (AAMC), and the California Association of Marriage and Family Therapists (CAMFT). The CAMFT is said to have as large a membership as the AAMFT, but that organization only pertains to those practicing in the state of California. The reason the CAMFT has such a large membership is because over half of all licensed counselors practicing CMFT currently reside in that state (Northey, 2009). Other organizations that pertain to these counselors are the American Family Therapy Academy (AFTA) and the International Family Therapy Association (IFTA) (Northey, 2009). Lee and Nichols (2010) stated that involvement in professional organizations helps practitioners build a solid CMFC identity. However, they noted that involvement in these organizations has declined in the last decade.

It has been noted in the literature that it is important for counselors to develop an integrated professional identity that is separate from the other helping professions. It is also important that such an identity incorporate a counselor's cultural identity, adherence to an ethical code, belief in the efficacy of marriage and family counseling, a grounding in a systems perspective, commitment and activity in a professional organization, and a commitment to continuing education due to the increasingly multidisciplinary settings in which many of these work (Hernández et al., 2009; Lee & Nichols, 2010). As noted, a professional identity can be fostered through mentorship, being active within one's professional organization, and in collaborating with one's colleagues (Lee & Nichols, 2010).

There are many professional issues that are important to the profession of CMFC. This chapter has only highlighted a few. Good sources of information for those who are interested in, are preparing for, or are practicing CMFC are the AAMFT and the IAMFC. Professional organizations such as these often have articles that discuss the current status of the field, have support blogs or discussion boards where members can discuss current issues, and hold conferences with presentations on topics important to the current status of the profession.

ACCREDITATION

The Commission on Accreditation for Marriage and Family Therapy Education (COAMFTE) and the Council for Accreditation of Counseling and Related Programs (CACREP) are the accrediting bodies for graduate and postgraduate programs in marriage and family counseling (Lee & Nichols, 2010). Accreditation is a voluntary process for CMFC programs (AAMFT, 2005). Accreditation is desired by programs and students because the process assures that the program and students have either met or exceeded the minimum training standards of the profession (AAMFT, 2005; CACREP, 2013b). These standards are periodically revised to respond to changes in the profession and the needs of the community (AAMFT, 2005).

Accreditation is important to potential employers of counselors wishing to practice CMFT, to licensure boards, and to the public who may use the services of these counselors (AAMFT, 2005). Students who graduate from an accredited program have an easier time (a) documenting their educational activities for licensure, (b) transferring educational credits from one university to another, (c) being accepted into PhD programs in CMFC or a related field, (d) obtaining portability of licensure from one state to another, and (e) becoming employed by the military or the Veteran's Administration (AAMFT, 2005).

Programs generally become accredited through a process whereby the program first does a self-study and reviews their own program as compared to the standards of the accrediting body (e.g., CACREP or COAMFTE). Then programs undergo a peer review process by representatives of the accreditation team from the accreditation body. Each aspect of the program is examined, such as the curriculum, the qualifications of the faculty, the supports for faculty and students, outcome data about retention and graduation rates, and university resources such as the library, financial aid, and student support services (CACREP, 2013a).

The COAMFTE and CACREP are specialized accrediting organizations that ensure quality and standards for graduate programs in CMFC at the master's and doctoral levels, as well as postgraduate clinical training programs for the United States and Canada (AAMFT, 2013b). The COAMFTE accreditation of programs began in 1982, and as of 2007 there were 21 accredited doctoral-level programs (Miller & Lambert-Shute, 2009) and over 100 CMFC-accredited master's-level educational programs (Northey, 2009). In a study conducted by Miller and Lambert-Shute (2009), most doctoral-level students trained in COAMFTE accredited programs felt well trained to competently practice CMFC. Accreditation ensures that students are trained according to the latest standards that are supported by the empirical literature.

SUMMARY

Couples, marriage, and family counseling has a long and varied history that makes it a unique profession separate and different from other helping or mental health professions. This chapter provided some of the history and ethics, legal, and professional issues that separate those that practice CMFC from similar professions. Although this chapter does not cover all areas that are pertinent to the CMFC profession, it draws attention to and gives a purview of contemporary issues currently discussed in the literature. Readers were also directed to supplemental materials to enhance and deepen understanding.

The profession of CMFC is dynamic, and thus standards, competencies, educational objectives, ethics, and legal issues are always evolving. It is recommended that those interested in this profession become, and remain, members of an accompanying professional association such as the AAMFT. These organizations do a good job of keeping students, practitioners, professors, and other interested parties updated on the most current and relevant developments in the field.

USEFUL WEBSITES

The following websites provide additional information relating to the chapter topics.

American Association of Marriage and Family Therapists (AAMFT)
http://www.aamft.org
American Association of Marriage and Family Therapy: Accreditation Resources
http://www.aamft.org/imis15/content/coamfte/Accreditation.aspx
American Association of Marriage and Family Therapists (AAMFT) Code of Ethics
http://www.aamft.org/imis15/content/legal_ethics/code_of_ethics.aspx
American Association of Marriage and Family Therapy: Core Competencies
http://www.aamft.org/imis15/Documents/MFT_Core_Competencie.pdf
Association of Marital and Family Therapy Regulatory Board (AMFTRB)
http://www.amftrb.org
Association of Marital and Family Therapy Regulatory Board (AMFTRB): National Exam
http://www.amftrb.org/exam.cfm
Council for Accreditation of Counseling and Related Educational Programs (CACREP)
http://www.cacrep.org
Commission on Accreditation for Marriage and Family Therapy Education (COAMFTE)
http://www.aamft.org/imis15/content/coamfte/coamfte.aspx
Health Information Portability and Accountability Act (HIPAA)
http://www.hhs.gov/ocr/privacy/index.html
Health Information Technology for Economic and Clinical Health Act
http://www.hhs.gov/ocr/privacy/hipaa/administrative/enforcementrule/hitechenforcementifr.html
International Association of Marriage and Family Counselors (IAMFC)
http://www.iamfconline.org

REFERENCES

Aducci, C. J., & Cole, C. L. (2011). Multiple relationships: Perspectives from training family therapists and clients. *Journal of Systemic Therapies*, *30*(4), 48–63.

Allanach, R. C. (2009, Summer). Role of mentor in the context of clinical supervision. *Annals of the American Psychotherapy Association*, 40–43. Retrieved from http://www.americanpsychotherapy.com/annals

American Association for Marriage and Family Therapy. (2004). *Marriage and family therapy core competencies.* Retrieved from http://www.aamft.org/imis15/Documents/MFT_Core_Competencie.pdf

American Association of Marriage and Family Therapy. (2005). *Commission on accreditation for marriage and family education.* Retrieved from http://www.aamft.org/imis15/Documents/Accreditation_Standards_Version_11.pdf

American Association for Marriage and Family Therapy. (2012a). *Code of ethics.* Retrieved from http://www.aamft.org/imis15/content/legal_ethics/code_of_ethics.aspx

American Association for Marriage and Family Therapy. (2012b). *Federal issues.* Retrieved from http://www.aamft.org/imis15/Content/Advocacy/Federal.aspx

American Association for Marriage and Family Therapy. (2013a). *About AAMFT.* Retrieved from http://www.aamft.org/iMIS15/AAMFT/Press/MFT_Qualifications/Content/About_AAMFT/Qualifications.aspx?hkey=00f76834-705e-4dd9-9dfe-46e6467eb7ca

American Association for Marriage and Family Therapy. (2013b). *Education and accreditation.* Retrieved from http://www.aamft.org/iMIS15/AAMFT

American Association for Marriage and Family Therapy (AAMFT). (2013c). *Federal, state, and private payer advocacy.* Retrieved from http://www.aamft.org/iMIS15/AAMFT/Advocacy/Advocacy_Issues/Content/Advocacy/Advocacy.aspx?hkey=a9abdb52-b6c3-44e0-9bd8-c12308548cd0

American Association for Marriage and Family Therapy (AAMFT). (2013d). *Legal fact sheet.* Retrieved from http://www.aamft.org/imis15/Content/Legal_Ethics/Legal_Fact.aspx

American Association for Marriage and Family Therapy (AAMFT). (2013e). *MFT licensure boards.* Retrieved from http://www.aamft.org/iMIS15/AAMFT/Directories/MFT_Licensing_Boards/Content/Directories/MFT_Licensing_Boards.aspx?hkey=b1033df3-6882-491e-87fd-a75c2f7be070

Benefield, H., Ashkanazi, G., & Rozensky, R. H. (2006). Communication and records: HIPAA issues when working in health care settings. *Professional Psychology Research and Practice*, *37*(3), 273–277. doi:10.1037/0735-7028.37.3.273

Bradley, P. D., Bergen, L. P., Ginter, E. J., Williams, L. M., & Scalise, J. J. (2010). A survey of North American marriage and family practitioners: A role delineation study. *The American Journal of Family Therapy*, *38*, 281–291. doi:10.1080/01926187.2010.493119

Brock, G. W., Whiting, J. B., Matern, B., & Fife, S. T. (2009). Integrity of the marriage and family therapy research literature: Perceptions and recommendations. *Journal of Marital and Family Therapy*, *35*(2), 248–252.

Butler, M. H., & Zamora, J. P. (2013). Ethical and legal concerns for MFTs in the context of clergy-collaborative care: Is what I share really confidential? *The American Journal of Family Therapy*, *41*, 85–109.

Caldwell, B. E., & Wooley, S. R. (2008). Marriage and family therapists' attitudes toward marriage. *Journal of Couple and Relationship Therapy*, 7(4), 321–336. doi:10.1080/15332690802368386

Chenail, R. J. (2009). Learning marriage and family therapy in the time of competencies. *Journal of Systemic Therapies 28*(1), 72–87.

Clark, P. (2009). Resiliency in practicing marriage and family therapy. *Journal of Marital and Family Therapy*, *35*(2), 231–247.

Commission on Accreditation for Marriage and Family Education (COAMFTE). (2005). *Accreditation standards: Graduate and post-graduate marriage and family therapy training programs.* Retrieved from http://www.aamft.org/imis15/Documents/Accreditation_Standards_Version_11.pdf

Council for Accreditation of Counseling and Related Educational Programs (CACREP). (2009). *2009 standards.* Retrieved from http://www.cacrep.org/doc/2009%20Standards%20with%20cover.pdf

Council for Accreditation of Counseling and Related Educational Programs (CACREP). (2013a). *The accreditation process.* Retrieved from http://www.cacrep.org/template/page.cfm?id=49

Council for Accreditation of Counseling and Related Educational Programs (CACREP). (2013b). *Why should I choose accreditation?* Retrieved from http://www.cacrep.org/template/page.cfm?id=12

Crane, D. R., & Christenson, J. D. (2012). A summary report of the cost-effectiveness of the profession and practice of marriage and family therapy. *Contemporary Family Therapy, 34*, 204–216.

Dallesasse, S. L. (2010). Managing nonsexual multiple relationships in university counseling centers: Recommendations for graduate assistants and practicum students. *Ethics and Behavior, 20*(6), 419–428. doi:10.1080/10508422.2010.521440

Dias, J., Chan, A., Ungvarsky, J., Oraker, J., & Cleare-Hoffman, P. (2011). Reflections on marriage and family therapy emergent from international dialogues in China. *The Humanistic Psychologist, 39*, 268–275. doi:10.1080/08873267.2011.592434

DuPree, W. J., White, M. B., Meredith, W. H., Ruddick, L., & Anderson, M. P. (2009). Evaluating scholarship productivity in COAMFTE-accredited Ph.D. programs. *Journal of Marital and Family Therapy, 35*(2), 204–219.

Gehart, D. R. (2008, January). *AAMFT core competencies: History and overview.* Paper presented at the AAMFT California Educator's Forum. Retrieved from http://www.mftcompetencies.org/page13/page14/files/Core%20Comp%20History%20Jan%202008.pdf

Gehart, D. R. (2012). The mental health recovery movement and family therapy, part I: Consumer-led reform of services to persons diagnosed with severe mental illness. *Journal of Marital and Family Therapy, 38*(3), 429–442. doi:10.1111/j.1752-0606.2011.00230.x

Gehart, D. R., & Lucas, B. M. (2007). Client advocacy in marriage and family therapy: A qualitative case study. *Journal of Family Psychotherapy, 18*(1), 39–56.

Grimes, M. E., & McElwain, A. D. (2008). Marriage and family therapy with low-income clients: Professional, ethical, and clinical issues. *Contemporary Family Therapy, 30*, 220–232. doi:10.1007/s10591-008-9071-5

Hair, H. J., & Fine, M. (2012). Social constructionism and supervision: Experiences of AAMFT supervisors and supervised therapists. *Journal of Marital and Family Therapy, 38*(4), 604–620.

Hall, C. A., & Sandberg, J. G. (2012). "We shall overcome": A qualitative exploratory study of the experiences of African Americans who overcame barriers to engage in family therapy. *American Journal of Family Therapy, 40*, 445–458. doi:10.1080/01926187.2011.637486

Harris, S. M., Brown, A., Darkin, J. B., Lucas, B., Riley, L., & Bulham, R. (2009). Are clinical records really that important? The dearth of research and practice guidelines in MFT literature. *The American Journal of Family Therapy, 37*, 373–387. doi:10.1080/01926180902754729

Hernández, P., & Rankin, P., IV. (2008). Relational safety and liberating training spaces: An application with a focus on sexual orientation issues. *Journal of Marital and Family Therapy, 34*(2), 251–264.

Hernández, P., Taylor, B. A., & McDowell, T. (2009). Listening to ethnic minority AAMFT approved supervisors: Reflections on their experiences as supervisees. *Journal of Systemic Therapies*, *28*(1), 88–100.

Hudgins, C., Rose, S., Fifield, P. Y., & Arnault, S. (2013). Navigating the legal and ethical foundations of informed consent and confidentiality in primary care. *Family Systems and Health*, *31*(1), 9–19. doi:10.1037/a0031974

Innes, M. (2009). How do you view your clients in couple therapy? *The Satir Journal*, *3*(1), 20–25.

International Association of Marriage and Family Counselors (IAMFC). (2013). *Counselor credentialing*. Retrieved from http://www.iamfconline.org/public/counselor-credentialing.cfm

Karam, E. A., & Sprenkle, D. H. (2010). The research-informed clinician: A guide to training the next generation. *Journal of Marital and Family Therapy*, *36*(3), 307–319. doi:10.1111/j.1752-0606.2009.00141.x

Košutić, I., Sanderson, J., & Anderson, S. (2012). Who reads outcome research? Outcome research consumption patterns among family therapists. *Contemporary Family Therapy*, *34*, 346–361. doi:10.1007/s10591-012-9192-8

Latty, C. R., Angera, J. J., & Burns-Jager, K. (2010). Socializing undergraduates to the MFT field. *Contemporary Family Therapy*, *32*, 348–359. doi:10.1007/s10591-010-9118-2

Lee, R. E., III, & Nichols, W. C. (2010). The doctoral education of professional marriage and family therapists. *Journal of Marital and Family Therapy*, *36*(3), 259–269. doi:10.1111/j.1752-0606.2009.00158.x

Letzring, T. D., & Snow, M. S. (2011). Mental health practitioners and HIPAA. *International Journal of Play Therapy*, *20*(3), 153–164. doi:10.1037/a0023717

Matheson, J. L., & Rosen, K. H. (2012). Marriage and family therapy faculty members' balance of work and personal life. *Journal of Marital and Family Therapy*, *38*(2), 394–416. doi:10.1111/j.1752-0606.2009.00137.x

Miller, J. K. (2010). Competency-based training: Objective structured clinical exercises (OSCE) in marriage and family therapy. *Journal of Marital and Family Therapy*, *36*(3), 320–332. doi:10.1111/j.1752-0606.2009.00143.x

Miller, J. K., & Lambert-Shute, J. (2009). Career aspirations and perceived level of preparedness among marriage and family therapy doctoral students. *Journal of Marital and Family Therapy*, *35*(4), 466–480. doi:10.1111/j.1752-0606.2009.00150.x

Miller, J. K., Todahl, J. L., & Platt, J. J. (2010). The core competency movement in marriage and family therapy: Key considerations from other disciplines. *Journal of Marital and Family Therapy*, *36*(1), 59–70. doi:10.1111/j.1752-0606.2009.00183.x

Moore, A. M., Hamilton, S., Crane, D. R., & Fawcett, D. (2011). The influence of professional license type on the outcome of family therapy. *American Journal of Family Therapy*, *39*, 149–161. doi:10.1080/01926187.2010.530186

Negash, S., & Sahin, S. (2011). Compassion fatigue in marriage and family therapy: Implications for therapists and clients. *Journal of Marital and Family Therapy*, *37*(1), 1–13. doi:10.1111/j.1752-0606.2009.00147.x

Nixon, D. H., Marcelle-Coney, D., Torres-Greggory, M., Huntley, E., Jacques, C., Pasquet, M., & Ravachi, R. (2010). Creating community: Offering a liberation pedagogical model to facilitate diversity conversations in MFT graduate classrooms. *Journal of Marital and Family Therapy*, *36*(2), 197–211. doi:10.1111/j.1752-0606.2009.00180.x

Northey, W. F., Jr. (2009). The legitimization of marriage and family therapy in the United States: Implications for international recognition. *Journal of Family Psychotherapy*, *20*, 303–318. doi:10.1080/08975350903366253

Northey, W. F., Jr., & Hodgson, J. (2008). Empirical studies in family therapy: Keys to implementing empirically supported therapies. *Journal of Family Psychotherapy*, *19*(1), 50–84. doi:10.1080/08975350801904189

Russell, C. S., DuPree, W. J., Beggs, M. A., Peterson, C. M., & Anderson, M. P. (2007). Responding to remediation and gatekeeping challenges in supervision. *Journal of Marital and Family Therapy*, *33*(2), 227–244.

Schomburg, A. M., & Prieto, L. R. (2011). Trainee multicultural case conceptualization ability and couples therapy. *Journal of Marital and Family Therapy*, *37*, 223–235.

Seponski, D. M., Bermudez, J. M., & Lewis, D. C. (2013). Creating culturally responsive family therapy models and research: Introducing the use of responsive evaluation as a method. *Journal of Marital and Family Therapy*, *39*(1), 28–42. doi:10.1111/j.1752-0606.2011.00282.x

Walfish, S., & Barnett, J. E. (2009). Understanding the insurance needs and options of the independent practitioner. In S. Walfish & J. E. Barnett (Eds.), *Financial success in mental health practice: Essential tools and strategies for practitioners* (pp. 165–180). Washington, DC: American Psychological Association.

West, C., Hinton, W. J., Grames, H., & Adams, M. A. (2013). Marriage and family therapy: Examining the impact of licensure on an evolving profession. *Journal of Marital and Family Therapy*, *39*(1), 112–126.

Wheeler, A. M. (2013). *Tick tock: Heed the HIPAA/HITECH clock.* Retrieved from http://www.counseling.org/docs/ethics/aca-hipaa-hitech-9-23-13-compliance-date.pdf?sfvrsn=4

Wise, R. A., King, A. R., & Miller, J. C. (2011). When HIPAA and FERPA apply to university training clinics. *Training and Education in Professional Psychology*, *5*(1), 48–56. doi:10.1037/a0022857

Woody, R. H. (2008). Obtaining legal counsel for child and family mental health practice. *American Journal of Family Therapy*, *36*, 323–331. doi:10.1080/01926180701686171

PART 2

Theories: History, Concepts, and Techniques

Psychodynamic Theories: Approaches and Applications

Stephanie K. Scott

Walden University

The 20th century saw rapid development in family systems theory. Although Ludwig von Bertalanffy first proposed the concept of general systems theory (GST) in the 1920s, his work continued to evolve through midcentury, culminating in highly influential publications in the 1940s and 1950s. The foundational principles of GST assert that (a) circumstances and events can be evaluated and understood through analysis of dynamic interactions among influential elements, and (b) all systems have shared patterns that reveal key characteristics of that system. These principles proved to be impactful on a broad range of science and challenged researchers and practitioners to consider their fields from a new vantage point.

General systems theory had a significant influence on the developing theoretical models of psychotherapy. Prior to the mid-20th century, mental health treatment focused on the individual and was primarily based in psychoanalytic theory. The contribution of GST fostered a revolution in conceptualization of both client and treatment approaches, challenging providers to consider the system as the client rather than the individual. This paradigm shift, in turn, cultivated the evolution of diverse family and relationship therapy models, with each taking a somewhat different perspective of the relative impacts of individual and systemic forces.

Psychodynamic theory evolved from core concepts of psychoanalysis and was based on the groundbreaking work of both Sigmund Freud and Carl Jung. Psychoanalysis was exclusively an individually oriented treatment approach, centered on enhancing personal awareness and revealing unconscious influences through extensive, time-consuming exploration of the inner self. Participants in this treatment process would often attend therapy several times a week, sometimes for years. Psychodynamics focused more on how these unconscious patterns and constructs manifest in the present and impact behaviors. Through exploration of past influences and identification of unresolved conflicts, clients were encouraged to not only recognize patterns, but also to seek to revise them in the present as a means of alleviating problems and conflicts. Frequency and duration of treatment were reduced under this model as psychodynamics took a more proactive approach to treatment. Despite some differences in theoretical constructs and application, both psychoanalytic and psychodynamic theory "emphasize the causal relationship between early developmental experiences, thoughts, feelings and behaviors that characterize the mental life of adults" (Berzoff, 2011, p. 46). As such, these terms are sometimes used interchangeably, but they are, in fact, different theoretical approaches.

Psychodynamics was significantly impacted by the influences of GST, as its core principles were now being considered from a systemic viewpoint. While psychodynamic therapy focused on unconscious thought processes and their impacts on behavior, psychodynamic family therapy took this concept to a higher order by centering on how these processes impact not only individual behavior but also relational dynamics and dysfunctional family patterns. Treatment under this model included goals of raising individual and system awareness, fostering insight, identifying systemic patterns, rebalancing system deficits, and enhancing relationships. As insight increased, the negative impact of destructive beliefs and patterns decreased, and symptom relief followed.

It is important to note that both psychoanalysis and psychodynamics fell out of favor for some time as newer, more structured, problem-focused therapies were emerging toward the end of the 20th century (Shedler, 2010). Fewer research studies focused on validating the efficacy of psychodynamics, which contributed to the developing assumption that these might be less desirable treatment approaches than other more popular theories. Another factor contributing to the less-than-optimal research support for psychodynamics lies in the difficulty of defining more contemporary approaches. Modern psychodynamics has evolved into an umbrella term, including a spectrum of theoretical approaches in the supportive–expressive continuum of theoretical approaches (Leichsenring, Hille, Weissberg, & Leibing, 2006). Psychodynamic approaches have experienced a resurgence in popularity over the past few decades, with demonstrated efficacy in treating a variety of disorders, including trauma, substance abuse, personality disorders, depression, anxiety, and more (Bell & Khantzian, 1991; Borden, 2000; Bornstein, 2006; Bradley, Greene, Russ, Dutra, & Westen, 2005; Clarkin, Levy, Lenzenweger, & Kernberg, 2004; Crits-Christoph, Connolly Gibbons, Narducci, Schamberger, & Gallop, 2005; Leichsenring, 2005; Maina, Forner, & Bogetto, 2005; Shaver & Mikulincer, 2005). Most research has focused on individual psychodynamic approaches. However, a fair amount has examined efficacies of the couple and family psychodynamics, with considerations for adaptations of models, counter-indications, and optimal treatment circumstances (Dong et al., 2004; Flores & Bernal, 1989; Gold, 2008; Hargrave & Pfitzer, 2003; Messer & Warren, 1995; Nelson & Sullivan, 2007).

In this chapter, a background of the evolution of psychodynamic family therapy is offered, with special attention paid to some of the more influential pioneers. Major constructs, goals, and techniques are discussed, as well as limitations to be considered. Finally, suggested resources for additional study are provided.

BACKGROUND

Many of the most influential figures in family therapy were psychoanalytically trained. Even those whose professional interests would eventually take them farther from their roots, including Murray Bowen and Salvador Minuchin, kept key elements of psychodynamics in their relational theories. The earliest influences on the development of psychodynamic family theory arose from studies observing maternal interactions with children, and those focused on tracking marital interaction patterns. The results of this early research, combined with a refined view of object relations theory, produced a recognition of both intergenerational and intragenerational forces as being at the heart of psychodynamic family therapy.

Nathan Ackerman

Nathan Ackerman is widely credited as being the founder of psychodynamic family therapy. In the mid-20th century, he offered a new construct of families as an emotional unit, and described the dynamic interrelationship of individual and family pathologies (Ackerman, 1956). His groundbreaking 1958 publication, *The Psychodynamics of Family Life*, was the first in the field to focus on the diagnosis and treatment of families. Ackerman proposed a model for understanding family relationships through a psychodynamic framework, which included developing insights into influences on self identity and the self in a social context. In his follow-up work, *Treating the Troubled Family*, Ackerman (1966) provided detailed clinical illustrations of psychodynamic application in family systems. He stressed the importance of family interaction on mental health processes and the necessity of understanding an individual within the context of his or her primary system. Ackerman further identified the influence of the individual on the system, as well as the system on the individual, and the idea that driving forces of each directly impact balance within the system. He further noted:

> In evolving a clinical theory of family, we must deal with three main variables: family organization, family role adaptation, and individual personality. Our aim is to illuminate the participation of the family in the emotional health of its members at every stage of the life cycle: infancy, childhood, adolescence, adulthood and old age. (Ackerman, 1966, p. 40)

Through his studies in working with family systems using a psychodynamic approach, Ackerman was able to understand and describe how family experiences, interpretations, resources, resilience, and development over time contributed to or protected against conflicts and emerging pathologies.

Henry Dicks

In the 1940s, Henry Dicks, a British psychiatrist, headed a team of psychiatric social workers in a couples therapy program that focused on reconciliation in couples referred by divorce court. It was during this time that Dicks first hypothesized a relationship between constructs of ego identity and marital relationship quality. By the 1960s, Dicks had established himself as a pioneer in object relations theory and its application to marital dysfunction. Building on the object relations theory of Fairbairn, Dicks described marriage as a shared process of attribution and projection (Dicks, 1963). He further asserted that mate selection itself was fueled by the drive to find an "ideal object" in a partner. Dicks believed that this unconscious drive led to expectations of conformity to internalized constructs, and that deviations from this conformity were at the root of dysfunction in relationships (Dicks, 1967).

James Framo

James Framo built his relational therapy theory from similar foundations. Using a marital interaction framework and integrating object relations theory, Framo (1981b) offered a family-of-origin-based intergenerational theory. He is credited with recognizing that the partner relationship tends to trigger unresolved attachment issues from childhood caregiver experiences, and conflicts often arise from projection of unconscious beliefs about the self (Framo, 1992). Framo viewed the marital relationship as an opportunity for healing much more directly than Dicks did; he saw the potential not only for growth, but also to alter the likelihood of further transgenerational transmission of faulty constructs (Framo, 1981a, b). Scharff and Scharff (1987) took this idea one step further, asserting that partner choice is both a conscious and an unconscious process, the latter of which is fueled by the quest to heal childhood wounds. In family-of-origin models, treatment focused on helping couples understand how patterns in the marital relationship had foundations in partners' respective childhood experiences (Framo, 1992). The counselor facilitated the revelation of these unconscious motives and perceptions, as well as how these have impacted intimacies throughout the life span. Clients gain an understanding of roots of dysfunction, opening the doors for healing experiences.

Ivan Boszormenyi-Nagy

During this same historical period, Ivan Boszormenyi-Nagy (1987) was developing the foundations of family therapy theory that would later evolve into contextual family therapy (CFT), a comprehensive and integrative model that was both psychodynamic and intergenerational and included elements of individual psychology, systemic interaction, and existentialism. Boszormenyi-Nagy is credited with introducing the concept of "relational reality" (Boszormenyi-Nagy & Krasner, 1986), and he stressed the importance of including unique aspects of individuals into the broader scope of systemic treatment. In many ways, Boszormenyi-Nagy's approach is more complex and encompassing than other psychodynamic family theories because it focuses not only on presenting family issues, but also influences from the past and potential influences on an undefined future. Specific techniques from this theory will be discussed later in this chapter; however, there are two foundational assumptions that should be noted here, as they were a significant contribution to the continued evolution of family therapy theory. In describing the underlying assumptions in clinical work using CFT, Boszormenyi-Nagy and Krasner (1986) wrote:

> The fundamental design for contextual interventions is based on two convictions: (1) That the *consequences* of a person's decisions and actions can affect the lives of all the people who are significantly related to him, and (2) that *satisfactory relating* for one person is inseparable from the responsible consideration of consequences for all of the people to whom he or she is in significant relationship. (p. 8)

Boszormenyi-Nagy's CFT model also included considerations for individual responsibility and accountability within a systemic context, and it was founded on the premise that the self is dependent on reflections of others. The interrelationships between the four "dimensions of reality"—objectifiable facts, systemic interactions, individual psychology, and relational ethics—were the focus of treatment (Boszormenyi-Nagy & Krasner, 1986). It was a model easily adapted to meet specific needs of clients, and it allowed for integration of cultural considerations.

It is interesting to note that Boszormenyi-Nagy and Framo collaborated—along with noted contemporaries Murray Bowen, Gerald Zuk, Nathan Ackerman, and Lyman Wynne—on a highly influential collection of theories and techniques born out of the psychodynamic tradition. The publication of *Intensive Family Therapy* (Boszormenyi-Nagy & Framo, 1965) signified a shift in mental health treatment from one focusing solely on the individual to one in which individuals are viewed within context. In this seminal work, the authors present a "depth family transactional approach" (p. xv) to mental health treatment and stress not only the influence of familial relationships in psychopathology, but also the view of these relationships as essential components and processes in treatment.

John Elderkin Bell

John Elderkin Bell was also a key figure in the shifting focus from an individual psychoanalytic perspective to a more family-focused psychodynamic approach. Bell, a psychoanalytically trained psychologist, concentrated much of his early work on the development of projective techniques in individual psychotherapy (Bell, 1948). He became interested in the systemic psychodynamics, eventually directing much of his clinical practice and research on group dynamics in family systems. Bell was the first to describe families as small groups, stressing the influences of tasks, practices, and constructs on the families' abilities to respond to conflicts and stressors. A primary goal of his therapeutic approach was to facilitate awareness in families regarding how their roles in the system impact each other. In describing the foundation for this approach, Bell (1961) noted:

> The primary intent of the therapist is to accomplish a modification of the functioning and structure of the family as a group. It is assumed that as a consequence modification will be effectuated secondarily in the situation

> of individuals within the family. The method of family therapy emerges, then, from one basic assumption differentiating it from individual therapy: *The family is the unit to be treated.* (p. 6)

Although Bell acknowledged the efficacy of individual psychotherapy, he stressed this systems approach as superior in many ways. While individual therapy can only allow for "symbolic evidence of intrapsychic events" (Bell, 1961, p. 88), family group therapy provides a clinician with an opportunity to experience interactions between family members, offering a better understanding of forces impacting the system. The family is viewed as a whole, with members representing structural components of the system.

Robin Skynner

Robin Skynner, a contemporary of John Bell, was also developing a family therapy theory grounded in group analysis during this period. Based on the groundbreaking work of S. H. Foulkes (1948), who became his mentor and later a clinical partner, Skynner proposed the application of group analysis concepts to family treatment. His model included defined stages of the family group, influences of roles and constructs, and the impact of relational dynamics on the functionality of the family group (Skynner, 1976). Like Bell, Skynner believed the family was the client and the focus of treatment. However, Skynner also stressed the importance of the clinician as an active participant in the therapeutic process, viewing transference and countertransference as critical parts of the therapeutic process, rather than as pitfalls to be avoided (Skynner, 1987).

Skynner outlined three essential functions and responsibilities of the therapist in psychodynamic family group therapy. First, he asserted that the therapist's primary task is to facilitate communication within the group. Recognizing that effective system function relied on harmonious and supportive relationships, Skynner identified effective communication in the family group as being paramount to achievement of this goal and essential to the restoration of balance in the system (Skynner, 1976). Second, Skynner recognized that families, like all groups, function best when there is a clear hierarchy and recognized order to authority within the system. As a means of defining and restoring effectual authoritative structure to the family group, Skynner suggested clinicians need to "intervene and take control of the family situation where necessary, handing back responsibility when a more healthy form of interaction and control has been established by the therapist's example" (p. 54). The third essential task relates to support of overall development and growth. Skynner emphasized the importance of family life stages, as well as the developmental levels of group members. In this model, the therapist must be able to evaluate both of these considerations as they pertain to individuals and to the group as a whole, and to recognize the impact of the family group on its members' achievement of critical developmental tasks.

The classical elements of psychodynamic couples and family work are still practiced today; in fact, contextual family therapy and family-of-origin therapy are widely popular clinical models. However, as was noted earlier, psychodynamics has evolved to include an array of theoretical models under the supportive–expressive continuum and is often also integrated with other theories, such as feminist and narrative therapies. In the next section, key constructs across psychodynamic models are presented and defined, with examples of their utilization in couples and family therapy.

MAJOR CONSTRUCTS

As noted previously, psychodynamic family therapy has its roots in psychoanalytic and systems theories. Combined with a strong influence from object relations and group analysis, psychodynamic approaches seek to uncover unconscious contributors to thoughts and behaviors, dysfunctional defenses, and impacts of these on relationships. Borrowing from object relations theory, psychodynamic family therapy holds that individuals interact in relationships based on expectations formed by earlier experiences. These past experiences create *introjects*: internalized constructs of self in relation to others resulting from those events that create expectation in subsequent interaction. As the individual continues to develop, new experiences are processed based on these constructs, which may be modified or further validated over time.

Contributions from Object Relations Theory

Many constructs foundational to the practice of psychodynamic family therapy have come from object relations theory. Melanie Klein (1946) was the first to propose the idea of *projective identification*, a mechanism by which constructs of self or of self–other are attributed to an external object. *External objects* are most often people to whom the individual has an emotional attachment or with whom there is personal investment. The manner in which these are experienced is dependent on introjects and symbolic representations. External objects can be experienced as (a) ideal, which contributes to gratification and fulfillment; (b) rejecting, which contributes to disappointment and anger, or (c) exciting, which contributes to yearning and desire. Foundations of projective identification begin in infancy and are significantly developed throughout childhood experiences. This is the time that is most rich in symbol formation, which forms the framework for connecting and relating to the outside world.

Fairbairn (1952) proposed the concept of *splitting* based on the manner in which external objects are processed. Building on Freud's original concept of splitting as a defense mechanism, Fairbairn proposed that splitting occurs when the ego seeks to keep positive and negative representations of external objects separated. This generally dissipates early in development as these become integrated. Failure to fully integrate and resolve associated anxiety directly contributes to disruption of identity development and weakens ego strength. As a child develops, experiences and meaning are internalized through introjection and identification, processes that define the self in relation to others, and comprise the earliest foundations of ego identity (Erikson, 1956). An example of these processes can be observed in a child whose mother is excessively critical or abusively punitive. The very young child internalizes a negative construct of the mother role, as well as an unworthy sense of self. These beliefs become core elements of identity on an unconscious level and directly impact the manner in which the child continues to experience the world.

These foundational concepts support attachment theory and solidify its place in psychodynamic family therapy. In simplest terms, this theory asserts that individuals require secure attachments to primary caregivers in order to develop into healthy adults. From an object relations perspective, this means that children need object constancy and positive internalizations to develop secure attachments and a strong ego identity. Similarly, constructive internalizations support separation and individuation, two essential developmental tasks that support identity integration and differentiation. Insecure attachments and poor differentiations contribute directly to conflicts observed in family enmeshments, manifestations of which can be observed in crises and reactions associated with both age-graded and non-normative life events. In addition, poor separation and individuation have a direct negative impact on adult adjustment and adult attachments. Failure to develop an integrated self-identity disrupts the transition of attachments and family life cycle and may result in an emotional attachment to the family of origin that is both dependent and enmeshed.

Parents may contribute to persisting issues in separation and individuation by resisting the recognition of their children as distinct entities. Parental pathology may prevent the acceptance of a child's independence, or of any efforts by that child to develop autonomy. These parents exert more control over children's development and experiences, resulting in individuals who cannot differentiate their own needs from their parents' needs. This is often observed as overly obedient, submissive children whose behaviors are validated by parental approval and the recognition that they are "great kids." However, such children are poorly prepared for the crises of adolescence and, when faced with the first challenges of independence, they will not have the internalized resources to positively progress through these experiences. As young adults, these individuals tend to display emotional volatility and inconsistent relationships.

In fully understanding the impacts of object relations on identity development and relational dynamics, it is important to recognize that introjects develop from subjective interpretations. Ultimately, constructs result not only from the object-associated events but also from the manner in which the individual experiences these events and internalizes meaning. Due to the potential for varying interpretations, wide variations in introjects within the same family system may be observed.

Couple and Family Application

In the practical application of psychodynamic family therapy, key constructs and assumptions must be recognized. First, from an attachment perspective, it is important to recognize that the human drive for caregiver approval and acceptance has a significant impact on identity development and relationships throughout the life span. In childhood, the subjective interpretations of caregiver–child interactions are internalized as identity constructs. In adulthood, these constructs are essential parts of the filter through which relationships are experienced. For example, a wife may believe that her husband only compliments her when he wants something of her. This is a manifestation of projective identification, possibly stemming from an internalized construct of low self-worth that is the result of a detached or destructive experience of caregiver–child interactions in childhood.

From a psychodynamic perspective, the life span development of a couple or family is substantially impacted by the early development of the individuals within the system. Hypothetically, if parents are psychologically healthy, the family will be well-adjusted. If partners bring solid, stable egos into the couple relationship, they are likely to experience minimal interpersonal conflict and enjoy mutual support. Conversely, fragile ego states and negative projections will adversely impact relational dynamics, as well as individual and systemic development. Dicks (1967) described the evidence of these issues in couple systems as *mutual projective identification* and *marital collusion*. He noted the tendency for both partners to project negative introjects onto the other and the cooperative, yet wholly unconscious, manner in which couples will accept these projections and roles. As couples begin to conform to the inner role models of the other, marital bargaining emerges; this is exemplified in role identities within the system. The degree of distress in the relationship is directly related to the functional adaptation of this dynamic.

SIDEBAR 6.1 APPLICATION: STEVE AND SONYA

Steve and Sonya had not been speaking to each other for several days when they first came to counseling. In their initial session, they spoke only to the counselor and not to each other, even avoiding any mutual eye contact. Sonya complained that Steve was overly critical of her, and that nothing she ever did was good enough for him. She added that she always had to be the "bad cop" when disciplining their children, since Steve never held them accountable for anything. Steve reported that Sonya's temper was out of control, and that he could not take it anymore. He wanted her to get help for her outbursts, and to stop her "crazy accusations."

As you begin to conceptualize this case, consider the following:

- How might mutual projective identification be exemplified in this system?
- What collusions can you detect?
- What evidence is there of marital bargaining?

The interactive complicity observed in couple systems is also evident in family systems. As noted previously, projective identification is a process by which an individual perceives an object as though it possessed qualities of the individual's own personality; accompanying emotional reactions are based on these projections. The object will unconsciously collude with the subject's projection, creating externalized conflict, assumptions, distortions, or even scapegoating. Parents often project stress-inducing aspects about themselves onto their children; the children will support these projections by behaving in ways that validate parental fear. For example, a mother may be excessively critical of her adolescent daughter's emerging sexuality, shaming her child with insults and slurs. The adolescent, in turn, may respond with increased desire to dress and behave in a provocative manner, validating the mother's projection of her own internalized sexual shame. Taken even further, this child may become the scapegoat of the family—the "bad one" who is now perceived as the central problem in the family system and is rebellious and irreverent. The mother is relieved of the need to face her own dysfunctional self-construct, live vicariously through her daughter's actions, and still punish her child for her behavior. Repeated episodes of such interaction can have negative impacts on both the child's development and the progression of the family system as a whole.

Projections often contribute to the creation of roles within the family system, underscoring the loyalties associated with these roles (Boszormenyi-Nagy & Krasner, 1986). Loyalties arise from internalized expectations and the collusion of perpetuating the role within the system. The impact is considerable on the system as a whole, and it helps to maintain what can often be very destructive interpersonal patterns. For example, in the previous hypothetical case of the mother–daughter dynamic, the daughter's loyalty to the family system supports her adoption of the "bad girl" role, allowing her mother and other family members to focus on her as "the problem" and not need to address their own dysfunction.

In this transgenerational view, counselors must understand the role of entitlements and ledgers, concepts also derived from Boszormenyi-Nagy's contextual family therapy theory (Boszormenyi-Nagy & Krasner, 1986). *Ledgers* (also called *ledger of merits*) are the system's history of what is provided and what is due—an unwritten record of give and take—and should reflect a general sense of balance. Ledger balances must be viewed intergenerationally, although conflicts arising from imbalances are often visible in a single generation. For example, a parent who as a child experienced a deficit of parental love and attention may find an unconscious drive to seek constant affirmation of his or her worth and value in the family system. In this way, an intergenerational transmission of debt is created, and this supports negative projection in the next generation. This is also an example of destructive entitlement across the system. A key role of the counselor is to help clients understand destructive entitlements and deficits of essential needs such as love and trust not from a perspective of blame, but rather for the sole purpose of enhanced understanding of sources for projection. *Constructive entitlements* exist as well and represent balance and fairness in relationships. Constructive entitlements are earned through reciprocal behavior in relationships and support healthy development of family members.

Relational ethics are also significant factors in the development of loyalties, ledgers, and legacies, and they directly impact entitlements in a system. Relational ethics are concerned with the depth and quality of intra- and intergenerational moral constructs and how these are expressed in a family. Relational ethics are experiential and are based on needs fulfillment and reciprocity. Balance and justice are required across the system. Such balance is more easily attained in horizontal relationships (e.g., partners, siblings) in which members are equals, compared to vertical relationships (e.g., parent–child) in which a power differential exists. As a result, issues of entitlement are more challenging to resolve in the latter as well.

To illustrate how these concepts work together, consider a family system in which there is child abuse. Assuming this dysfunction and its impacts are not effectively dealt with in the first generation, the next generation inherits the "debt" that was created from the negative relational ethics. The ledger is unbalanced, and the individual involved will unconsciously seek to balance that ledger in the next generation. This may manifest in a couple relationship or in a parent–child dynamic, as the wounded child who is now an adult feels entitled to missing aspects from his or her own development. The ledger imbalance from the previous generation unconsciously motivates the individual to demand repayment of emotional debt. Rather than being motivated by constructive entitlement and enjoying balance in love, trust, fairness, and loyalty, this individual will *demand* that these needs be met and compensation made in an unconscious drive to restore balance to the ledger. In essence, the reactions to abuse are far more damaging than the abuse itself (Gold, 2008), and the individual internalizes constructs that become an embedded aspect of identity.

SIDEBAR 6.2 APPLICATION: MIGUEL AND LUZ

Miguel and Luz came to counseling seeking help with their relationship. The precipitating event was a severe argument that precipitated Luz's leaving their house for nearly a week. Luz denied feeling unsafe with Miguel, but rather said that she wanted him to realize what he was going to lose. Miguel felt abandoned by Luz, and he was not sure he could trust her to stand by him through tough times.

As you begin to work with Miguel and Luz, think about what information is needed to complete a case conceptualization through a psychodynamic lens. For example:

- What introjects exist in this system?
- What collusions can you detect?
- How do ledgers and relational ethics impact system dynamics?
- How can balance begin to be restored in this system?

Basic Assumptions

Psychodynamic couples and family therapy is geared primarily toward enhanced understanding of patterns and influences and using this understanding to empower participants toward positive change. Individual and interpersonal functioning are influenced by unresolved conflicts, distorted beliefs, and dysfunctional attachments, and even more so by the unconscious nature of these influences. Unlike more problem-focused and solution-oriented approaches, there is greater meaning placed on insight, awareness, and redefining dysfunctional introjects impacting relationships. As a means of facilitating these changes and working toward goals, several basic assumptions are communicated directly and indirectly throughout the process (adapted from Framo, 1992):

- Focus is not only on the individual, but also on the entire family system.
- Although individual issues may have prompted the clients to seek counseling, system members' individual pathologies are de-emphasized over the functionality of the family dynamics and unique contributions from the family of origin.
- Significant topics and events must be addressed during therapy. Avoidance and denial are expected steps in the process of growth; however, focus must remain on how system members' problems are interconnected.
- Additional conflicts may arise in the process of dealing with presenting issues. These are part of the process and help to shed light on underlying introjects, legacies, and intergenerational dynamics.
- Counselors serve as facilitators, focusing on relationship enhancement over pathology. The counselor serves as a catalyst for growth and provides support for participants' anxieties and tensions that arise from the therapeutic process.

In addition to these assumptions, counselors using psychodynamic theory recognize foundational characteristics of couple and family systems. These attributes help both the counselor and clients understand how the system functions, how change is facilitated, and why challenges may arise during the process. Characteristics of couple and family systems include (adapted from Ackerman, 1958):

- Systems tend toward homeostasis. The system, whether viewed as the couple, a single-generation family, or an intergenerational broader system, maintains relatively stable characteristics. These characteristics may be supportive of development or dysfunctional and pathologic, but they will remain in some state of balance as defined by the system. Homeostasis is resistant to change; therefore, as controlled change is introduced into the system, there must be adequate opportunity for adaptation and recognition of the dynamic impact change can have.
- Defined social roles exist. Social roles are manifestations of the social self and are influenced by circumstance, cultural messages, and internalized constructs of self. From a psychodynamic perspective, they represent the identity of the individual within the context of his or her systems. Social roles often vary depending on the specific system within which the individual is being viewed; the social self adapts to the context, while the inner self remains constant. The social self is therefore dynamic, in constant interaction with the surrounding environment.

- Role complementarity fosters mutual support, dependence, and intimacy. Familial pairs, whether parent–child, partner–partner, or sibling–sibling, exhibit compensatory or counterbalancing behavior in the presence of, or in response to, conflictual circumstances. In positive application, role complementarity can support accommodation and adaptation in familial systems. In negative application, role complementarity can lead to scapegoating and displacement. Conflicts affect the entire system. Past internalized conflict will impact present patterns of conflict in a system. By the same token, present conflicts affect the manner in which past conflicts are viewed and processed. Conflicts can arise at any level within the system and can be individual, intragenerational, or intergenerational in focus. Regardless, both the conflict itself and its resolution will ultimately impact the system as a whole.

Recognition of these features of familial systems is the underpinning of psychodynamic family therapy. Understanding these systems aids in assessment and conceptualization, enhances understanding of presenting issues, and supports identification of treatment goals. Furthermore, counselors may want to consider educating clients on these features at the outset of treatment or during the process, as this can enhance and facilitate the change process. Identifying these foundational elements can also help clients better understand how and why treatment goals begin as broad concepts and are adapted as therapy progresses.

GOALS

Because psychodynamic therapy is awareness oriented, the primary goal of treatment is insight—in most basic terms, the unconscious is brought into the conscious. The counselor acts as both catalyst and active participant in this process, initially focused less on symptom relief and more toward helping the system move forward. A secondary emphasis is placed on working through issues by developing enhanced cognizance and mindfulness and positive progression of the system's developmental phases and tasks. Goals at inception of treatment are broad and open-ended, and relate both to the members individually and the system as a whole. Direction of treatment is adapted as progress occurs, with the general end goal of facilitating an enhanced system dynamic.

Challenges

One of the primary challenges to developing goals using a psychodynamic approach with couples or families is the desire for the system to have symptom relief. Clients are motivated to seek treatment because there is a problem they need help resolving; the indirect and often more time-consuming psychodynamic approach may not seem attractive to them. In addition, clients may be initially resistant to considering their roles in system dysfunction when the problem seems isolated to one member. For example, parents participating in family therapy with their 16-year-old son who was recently suspended for fighting in school may react very defensively to the idea that they had any role in their son's behavior, or that the family as a whole needs to change. Counselors must remember that defensiveness and denial are often part of the process, and they should approach this with sensitivity and support. In such cases, it may be in the best interests of longer-term family success to triage presenting issues, encouraging deeper exploration after symptoms have subsided somewhat. Conversely, counselors may also find that although clients come to counseling motivated by a precipitating event, they also recognize patterns of conflicts and challenges and are open to exploring these. Counselors should try to determine direction and focus within the intake session and develop goals together with clients.

Conceptualization

In consideration of potential challenges, and to facilitate goal development at treatment inception, psychodynamic family counselors may approach the client system much as a counselor from a different theoretical orientation. Clients may want the initial focus to be on symptom reduction; however, in the process of gathering information from system members, the counselor is also observing how symptoms are described and the patterns of communication among members. The counselor must also pay close attention to nuances of dynamics, such as references to recurrences, descriptive metaphors used by the clients, and reactivity to participants' verbalizations and behaviors. This is an information-gathering stage that will lend insight into both goal development and adaptation of interventions to best suit the system. Initially, however, the counselor may choose to focus solely on triage goals such as refining communications across the system and facilitating interpersonal understanding, both of which will support symptom reduction, albeit in the indirect manner that is the hallmark of psychodynamic treatment.

The identification of goals may depend partially on presenting issues, but even more so, it depends on the participants themselves and the relationships between them. Ideally, symptom relief is an almost secondary consideration, and it develops from the improvements in awareness, insight, and dynamics that are part of the treatment process. Framo (1992) described general goals of family-of-origin therapy as focusing on discovery of information, clarification of misinformation, interpretation of perceptions, reacquainting of system figures, and reconstructing relational paradigms. Furthermore, Framo asserted that interacting directly with the family of origin and attending to intergenerational influences help to reduce the impact of internalized constructs. Boszormenyi-Nagy and Sparks (1973) identified treatment goals for contextual family therapy as evolving out of confrontation of emotional conflicts. This was accomplished through recognition of projections, assuming responsibility for the impact of these, recognition of role in system, and rebalancing of dynamics. Such general goals allow clients to reclaim their authentic selves and to respond to their partners and children with mindfulness of the present, rather than with the legacies of the past.

Developing Treatment Goals

With this foundation for conceptualization, the guide map for treatment could be based on the following initial open-ended goals, which are evaluated and revised as treatment progresses:

- Discover and understand presenting issues through a family-of-origin lens.
- Recognize ways in which introjects influence behavioral patterns.
- Understand system coalitions and roles.
- Identify new ways of relating by altering and adapting beliefs.
- Practice awareness and mindfulness of developmentally supportive relational dynamics.

As participants demonstrate progress toward these goals, and as additional issues and considerations are revealed, the following secondary goals develop:

- Improve system functioning and decrease system conflict.
- Improve social function within the system.
- Improve responses to crises.
- Improve system communication.
- Improve relational dynamics across generations of the system.

SIDEBAR 6.3 MEASURABLE GOALS AND PSYCHODYNAMICS

Another challenge to developing goals under this model is the recognition that the psychodynamic approach is, by definition, focused primarily on insight and awareness. Under this model, counselors will focus on identifying introjects and their impact, enhancing relational dynamics, and improving communication—goals that are very difficult to measure. In developing a treatment plan, counselors should consider first identifying measurable goals related to presenting issues. More about this consideration is discussed in the "Limitations" section.

As noted previously, couples or families in treatment may be focused on symptom reduction over lasting growth and development. Certainly, consideration for the client needs comes first. However, psychodynamic family counselors should recognize that the presenting issue is an opportunity to shed light on recurring patterns and underlying influences and to potentially effect long-lasting change beyond simply dealing with a single issue. Presenting issues can serve as flashlights illuminating the pathway of discovery and help to take the couple or family on a journey of enlightenment, empowerment, and self-actualization. Of course, not all clients will want to embark on this journey, and some may prefer the safety of more solution-focused treatment approaches.

TECHNIQUES

Psychodynamic family therapy begins from a position that presenting issues and pathologies have three primary components: intrapsychic, interpersonal, and psychosocial. A comprehensive assessment of each member is essential, with attention paid to individual as well as relational considerations. Often, as part of the assessment process, a counselor will create a genogram of the family system. Genograms are diagrammatic representations of familial systems that include individual pathologies and significant traits, relational dynamics, and potential transmission of issues. The counselor collects information about the current system's presenting issues and relevant information regarding the family of origin. The current generation is the primary focus; however, multiple generations are noted to facilitate awareness of patterns and later to help identify potential introjects. It is important to note that multigenerational participation is not required for effective psychodynamic work, although it is quite helpful and preferred. Counselors using psychodynamic interventions with couples and families can effectively address patterns and unconscious influences directly or indirectly, depending on availability of necessary information and participants.

Under ideal circumstances, psychodynamic family therapy involves two counselors, with one serving a more active role of facilitation and guidance and the other primarily acting as an observer, offering insights as appropriate. This scenario is especially helpful when working with larger family groups, as subtle interactions and nuances of behaviors might be difficult for a single counselor to observe (Framo, 1992; Goldenthal, 1993). Furthermore, the observing counselor may be able to more objectively identify transference and countertransference, both of which are common occurrences in this type of therapy. However, the realities of practice management do not always support this arrangement, which challenges psychodynamic family counselors to develop advanced skills in these areas. Even with these challenges, the psychodynamic family counselor generally employs the most basic counseling techniques: listening, empathizing, observing, and interpreting. In using these techniques, the counselor also approaches the participants using an investigative neutrality, one of the most important features of the clinical process.

SIDEBAR 6.4 NEUTRALITY AND IMPARTIALITY

Investigative neutrality is both a technique and a philosophy in psychodynamic family therapy. It facilitates the analytical and investigative process by supporting clients without the need for solving problems. A related concept is *multidirectional partiality* (Boszormenyi-Nagy & Krasner, 1986), which refers more to the manner of interpersonal interaction with clients. Use of either in psychodynamic work differs from other theoretical approaches in that the counselor actively acknowledges topics and issues from each participant's point of view—even absent family members—while avoiding alignments or bias. Although the net effect is remaining neutral, it differs from the impartiality associated with other theoretical models because the neutrality results from the balancing of temporarily "partial" interactions. Investigative neutrality is a method that facilitates deeper understanding of facts and systemic interactions; however, it is challenging to master and requires considerable practice.

Listening

Strong listening skills are essential for any counselor. However, the psychodynamic family counselor must focus not only on the objectifiable facts shared by clients but also on the subtleties of constructs and patterns, as these give clues to emotional components and ultimately to more unconscious pieces of the family puzzle. Counselors should be attentive, supportive, and use silent encouragers as needed to facilitate communication and the development of therapeutic bonds. Because psychodynamic treatment tends to become a very intimate process, deep levels of trust are essential. Effective listening helps to build that trust by establishing connection at the earliest stages of treatment. It also helps lay the groundwork for case conceptualization. How the system members describe the presenting issue, for example, lends insights into meaning, associated beliefs, and the beginning of pattern recognition.

Unlike many other therapeutic models, Framo (1992) suggested that it is also helpful during early stages of counseling to encourage discussion of family members who are not present. Reasons for the absence help lend insights into the meaning of that family member and his or her role in the system. For example, a deceased family member may be idealized by those present in the session, or a family member who elected not to participate may become a scapegoat in sessions. Listening to the ways in which absent members are described by participants can help the counselor better understand family dynamics and provide additional clues for future observations and interpretations.

Empathy

Empathy in psychodynamic work is often less direct than when used in other theoretical orientations that tend to support an active stance in identifying feelings or providing validation. Instead, psychodynamic counselors convey empathy through immersion in the clients' experiences, conveying understanding as they become part of the client process. When the psychodynamic counselor more directly verbalizes empathy, the purpose is to facilitate understanding, catalyze insights, and clarify meanings for the clients. It is important to note that the depth of emotional connection expressed by the counselor, although less direct than in many other types of therapy, can sometimes trigger both transference and countertransference issues. These are natural parts of the psychodynamic process, however, and will be discussed later in this chapter.

Another aspect of empathy lies in the use of multidirectional partiality. Part listening and part empathizing, this technique fosters connection between client and counselor and conveys a depth of understanding and support. Counselors can validate clients' perspectives and beliefs regarding merited entitlement of basic needs such as love, trust, and safety while being cautious not to take sides concerning specific presenting issues or past conflicts. This is a powerful tool in the establishment of the therapeutic relationship, and it can also serve as a role-modeled behavior for more positive communication among system members.

Observation

A great deal of information comes from observations of clients. Patterns and methods of verbal communication, for example, shed light on both the intellectual and emotional provocations and supports present. Nonverbal communications can convey even more information, but are often less clear. Posture, body language, and eye contact among participants can yield important clues regarding system dynamics. Situational reactions and systemic interactions help the counselor to better understand dynamics in the couple or family, shedding light on the system's organization, alliances, and loyalties. The counselor may want to pay particular attention to the ways in which the clients react to discussion of presenting issues, as well as how such discussion may impact the conflicts themselves.

Another important aspect of observation lies in the proxemics and haptics during a single session, as well as how these might change from one session to another. *Proxemics* refers to the spatial dynamics and arrangements within the system, while *haptics* refers specifically to the physical use of touch. Counselors should observe the space between session participants: Who sits next to whom? Do participants touch to comfort each other? Are there any apparent patterns to this behavior, and does the subject matter being discussed impact these interactions?

Interpretation

Building on listening and observation, the psychodynamic family counselor identifies salient elements of individual psychology of system members, as well as key constructs present in the system as a whole. The counselor conceptualizes emotional displays, communication patterns, and relational ethics, integrating identified constructs from these to facilitate insight in the system. Counselors should also help clients understand the roles existing in the system, both of the system members and of the conflicts themselves, and how these roles are supported by unconscious constructs and repeating systemic patterns. In helping participants recognize these influences on present behaviors and conflicts, change is facilitated through understanding and empowerment. That is, interpretations are not for the purpose of challenging constructs, but rather to assist in the revelation of undiscovered information and associated insights. Counselors may want to limit their interpretations to no more than a few per session, as clients need sufficient time to process and consider the new perspective offered.

It is also important to remember that before providing interpretations and encouraging deeper reflection, there must be trust established in the therapeutic relationship. Framo (1992) cautions against "premature interpretations" (p. 54) and stresses the importance of connecting with the family system on a social level. He noted:

> Certainly, you cannot intervene too quickly, or too deeply; you are in danger of losing the family if you do so. Premature interpretations are considered a sign of inexperience in all psychotherapies; in family-of-origin sessions they are definitely counterproductive. At the same time, one cannot stop being a therapist altogether. The compromise I have found to be most effective is to walk a fine line between being a consultant or facilitator and being a therapist, between guiding the session and yet having family members be accountable for dealing with each other. (p. 54)

A psychodynamic family counselor is very much like a detective—gathering information, making observations, identifying nascent patterns—and must choose the right time and manner in which to share perspectives with the system.

A final consideration on this topic is a word of caution. It is vital for counselors to be aware of potential bias in the interpretation process. Expectations of behavior related to gender, age, cultural heritage, religion, and other areas of diversity have the potential to bias a counselor's interpretations and create inaccurate assumptions. In other words, impartiality is crucial, and interpretations shared should be done with as neutral language as possible, thus allowing the clients to lend meaning to the interpretation through their own worldview. Furthermore, the counselor should periodically evaluate his or her unspoken interpretations to ensure that a high level of objectivity is being maintained throughout the process.

Integration and Session Structure

Psychodynamic family therapy is not a linear process, but rather a recursive, adaptive, and developmental journey with clients. Counselors use the presenting issue or conflict to explore participants' individual experiences of the issue, what emotions are associated with the issue, and the historical significance of those emotions. In couples work, additional attention is paid to how partners trigger each other's historical associations and how this adds meaning to the experience in the present. In family work, this consideration appears in both the horizontal and vertical relationships in the system as both roles and expectations are considered.

A typical session with a couple or family will take place over 45 to 55 minutes (the widely accepted "clinical hour"). The counselor must track and guide the flow of the session and take notice of utilization of time and resources. For example, in an effort to convey multidirectional partiality, it's important to be sure that all participants have sufficient time to express themselves during a session. This might require the counselor to indirectly impose time limits, which can have a negative impact on the overall process. It is also important for the counselor to avoid significant revelations or challenging new integrations too close to the end of a session, as participants should optimally have time to process and reflect before wrapping up a session.

A therapy session under this model typically begins with the counselor asking the couple or family to share presenting issues, conflicts, perceptions, and emotions. As treatment progresses, the opening of sessions becomes less directed, perhaps starting with the counselor asking "Where should we begin today?" Clients may also take the initiative to simply begin on their own terms, having become used to the session format at that point. As the session evolves, the counselor listens attentively, clarifying as needed and lightly probing when appropriate, and actively observes and analyzes session content for patterns, themes, and clues as to insights waiting to be revealed.

Contrary to typical treatment structure, Framo's (1992) family-of-origin therapy is usually conducted in two intensive sessions that are several hours each, over a 2-day period. Although this model supports the treatment brevity so desired by contemporary society, counselors may find it difficult to be reimbursed by third-party payers because the structure deviates from accepted treatment frameworks. As such, using Framo's model in its purest form may have to be limited to private-pay clients or special populations, such as residential treatment environments in which session times may be more malleable. However, treatment elements can surely be adapted and integrated into standard mental health treatment parameters.

Role of Transference and Countertransference

Although frequently considered problematic in other therapeutic approaches, both transference and countertransference have potentially important roles in psychodynamic therapy with couples or families. *Transference* refers to the projection or redirection of emotions, beliefs, and behaviors that were previously associated with one object onto a new object. As it occurs in counseling, this is most often observed as a client's transference onto the counselor in a manner representative of another relationship in the client's life. For example, a client may "parentify" the counselor in an unconscious drive to seek the warmth and approval he or she did not receive in childhood. The counselor may become the new parent of the system, threatening parental authority and disrupting the balance of the system. *Countertransference* refers to the reactions elicited by transference and is generally exhibited by the counselor. The parentified counselor may find him- or herself reacting in a manner that directly fills the client's needs, rather than remaining sufficiently objective so as to explore the underlying causes. Although it is vital for the counselor to be aware of both transference and countertransference occurrences, these can also shed insight on the manner in which the client relates, is perceived, and may contribute to the reactions of others. It is also important to note that although both occurrences are most common between a client and the counselor, they can also occur between two members of a couple or family system. As such, both occurrences warrant further attention, first by acknowledging their existence and second by creating a safe space for exploration.

There are, of course, some dangers associated with both concepts. The potential for either of these to occur increases with the number of participants in treatment, and monitoring may become a daunting task. In addition, when transference or countertransference occurs in session, they can be addressed and processed with the help of the counselor. If they occur outside of session, they may not be recognized and may adversely impact a family system. For example, if during a couple's session transference of unresolved anger is aimed at the counselor and not adequately acknowledged and processed, it could later be transferred to other members of the system, such as one or more children at home. Boszormenyi-Nagy and Krasner (1986) noted that transference can also represent a system member's desire to disengage from the therapeutic process, as he or she focuses on the relationship with the therapist over the relationship with a partner or other family members. Again, it is important to recognize these occurrences when they happen because they can give insight into hurdles to therapeutic progress, resistance, or avoidance.

Challenges

A significant challenge to psychodynamic therapy with couples or families lies in the fact that there are several clients in the room. Individual counseling can elicit strong defenses or cause avoidance or shutting down, even with the most empathetic, supportive counselor. Many clients are simply uncomfortable with the therapeutic process until they feel safe. This issue is magnified considerably in psychodynamic family work, in which individuals are expected to share openly about beliefs and emotions associated with issues. This expectation may increase client anxiety considerably and fuel resistance to the process.

Openness in communication across the system may also contribute to a temporary shift in system dynamics. For example, the mother of an adolescent boy may realize during treatment, following an interpretation shared by the counselor, that she is controlling her son in a manner that impedes his maturation because she is afraid of losing him. She further recognizes that her own mother treated her much the same way. The son, hearing this, becomes angry with his mother, focusing the blame for their conflicts on her parenting deficits. Such anger runs the risk of carrying over outside the session as well and recurring during conflicts outside the session. It is vital for these shifts to be acknowledged and processed with the help of the counselor, and that attempts are made to restore system balance.

Last, it is also important to recognize that while psychodynamic work is founded in past conflicts, the focus remains on present manifestations. Not every family secret must be exposed, every stone overturned, for progress to occur in a system. Recognition of past influences is not about blame, but rather understanding. Insight and awareness foster empowerment. Bringing the unconscious to the conscious where it can be managed, healed, or otherwise positively impacted supports the wellness perspective upon which counseling is founded.

Case Example: The Crane Family

Anne, a 33-year-old Caucasian female, had been in a residential treatment center for approximately 2 weeks when her family was asked to participate in a group session. Anne was the oldest of three children and was in treatment for alcohol addiction. Immediately upon arrival of the family, the counselor noted that Anne's younger sister (18 years old) positioned herself between Anne and their mother, who looked visibly distraught. The younger sister even moved her chair closer to their mother so that she could hold her mother's hand. Anne's father sat on the other side of her mother, and her brother (28 years old) sat on the far side of the father. The counselor opened the session by thanking the family for coming and making small talk to ease the participants. The counselor got the session started by asking each member what they'd like to accomplish during the session. Anne's mother, now crying quietly, stated that she was there for her daughter and didn't have any goals. The father silently agreed. The brother stated that he just wanted his sister to get better. Anne's sister said she agreed with her mother. Noting the resistance and discomfort, the counselor pushed just a bit and asked the family why they thought they were there—a bit deeper question than the initial one. After an extended silence, Anne's mother turned to Anne and asked, "How could you do this to us?" and started to sob uncontrollably. Anne's sister hugged her mother, while Anne simply looked away. The father and brother rolled their eyes at each other and looked uncomfortably at the floor.

Analysis of the Crane Family

Although the above vignette took place over only 15 to 20 minutes, the counselor gathered an enormous amount of information about the Crane family. He listened to the manner in which participants introduced themselves, how they spoke of their attendance, and how they described (or didn't describe) their goals for therapy. The counselor also observed important physical behaviors, such as the distance between Anne and her next closest family member, the sister physically comforting the mother, the father and brother colluding their emotional separation from the events in session, and much more. The counselor also began to get an idea of Anne's role in the family system.

Using a family-of-origin approach, the counselor must now decide the direction to guide this family and how deep further exploration can go. An important consideration would be the amount of time earmarked for family work with this system. Although clients, in most cases, can certainly opt to terminate whenever they choose, it is important to have at least a plan regarding time commitment to the process. It is helpful to make system members aware at the outset, as this counselor did, what the planned treatment time is likely to be. In Anne's case, three 2-hour sessions were planned, so the counselor would likely have sufficient time to explore deeper aspects of historical and current interaction in this system, although perhaps not buried or guarded issues such as history of trauma or abuse. Under this model, specific techniques as counseling moves forward would include interventions designed to reveal the impact of introjects on the system, reauthoring these to a more positive and present-day focus, and improving perceptions across the system. For example, the counselor might ask each family member to share what he or she loves or admires about the others, taking the time to address each member individually. Such an exercise can have an immediate positive impact of system connectivity and give the counselor additional observations, as he or she can observe what is said and how it is received.

Case Example: Mike and Brian

Mike and Brian were a couple in their late 60s who had come to counseling for help with their relationship. During the initial session, Mike shared that Brian had been "depressed" recently and that they were fighting often. Brian agreed that the couple had "been having some problems lately," but denied that he was depressed. Mike reported that Brian did not want to go out and do things together as much as they used to and that their sex life was "nonexistent." Brian reported that he thought their sex life "was age-appropriate" and that Mike was demanding and critical. In gathering information, the counselor learned that Mike and Brian had been together for over 25 years and had raised two children together. Brian was looking forward to sharing their golden years together and had visions of watching grandchildren play in the yard while he and Mike sat side by side on rocking chairs on the front porch. Mike countered that he wasn't ready for rocking chairs and wanted to enjoy the freedom associated with having an empty nest by traveling, socializing with friends, and sharing romantic evenings with his partner. The counselor also observed the dynamics of their communication, which were strained and unsupportive. Mike and Brian sat on the counselor's couch not touching each other in any manner, even when Brian became upset at what he perceived as Mike's harsh judgment. The counselor used multidirectional partiality to connect with each partner, paying close attention to support concerns and perspective and giving validation to respective entitlements. Neither partner felt understood by the other, and they were both quite concerned that their relationship would not survive this phase.

Analysis of Mike and Brian

The counselor used techniques from contextual family therapy to begin to address this couple's issues. First, by using multidirectional partiality, the counselor established connection and support to both clients, while also beginning to role model sympathetic and reassuring communication, which was lacking in the relationship. The counselor also observed important information about system dynamics and began to uncover underlying issues, such as the impact of beliefs of what "should be" in the couple's relationship, carried over from constructs of the past. Most importantly, the counselor recognized deficits in areas of perceived trust, respect, and love in the system. The next steps with this couple would focus on past experiences of these needs in relationships and the sources of deficits. Together, Mike and Brian were able to reshape their internalized constructs, shedding the legacies of the past, and see each other from a here-and-now perspective.

LIMITATIONS

As with any theoretical orientation, there are limits to using psychodynamic therapy in couple and family systems. However, it should be noted that one key limitation lies in a lack of understanding of contemporary psychodynamic models. Although some couples and family therapy models fall clearly under the psychodynamic category, such as those originated by Framo and by Boszormenyi-Nagy, others are offshoots of psychodynamics, retaining important elements while integrating additional considerations and perspectives. For example, even a cursory review of Adlerian family therapy, Bowenian family therapy, and Minuchin's structural family therapy will reveal many foundational similarities to psychodynamics, yet these are considered their own unique approaches. This presents a challenge to researchers who wish to empirically validate the efficacy of psychodynamic work in couple and family systems because it may be difficult to ascertain where psychodynamics end and other models begin. Still, it is important to note that psychodynamics as a broad category does have considerable empirical support (Shedler, 2010). Although there are substantially fewer studies validating psychodynamic systems models, there is quite a bit of research supporting the effectiveness of individual psychodynamic therapy.

In addition to having to clearly define treatment parameters in order to gain empirical support, psychodynamic couple and family therapists have also had to defend criticisms related to cultural considerations. Critics have asserted that psychodynamic models overemphasize influences of gender roles and gender differences and fail to fully integrate the cultural impacts on family dynamics (Hare-Mustin, 1987; Rasheed, Rasheed, & Marley, 2011). Some of this criticism is likely associated with the psychoanalytic roots of psychodynamics, a remnant of early research cohorts being of limited diversity and research analysis reflecting pervasive cultural views of the time. However, it should be noted that contemporary psychodynamic views do not hold such limitations. In fact, because treatment goals and interventions are specific to the unique couple or family system, and because approaches are adapted to the system's distinct needs, psychodynamics can be applied to diverse client family conditions, compositions, contexts, and cultures.

Another potential limitation lies in the perception of psychodynamic treatment. Because it is often confused with psychoanalysis, psychodynamics has at times been considered an outdated and outmoded approach to therapy. It has also been considered too costly to utilize under current realities of third-party payer systems, which are frequently used for reimbursement of services. In reality, psychodynamic approaches can easily fit into the common definition of short-term therapy and rarely involve the lengthy treatment associated with psychoanalysis (Levenson, 2010). Still, counselors using this model should be aware at the outset of treatment what potential time limitations may exist. The structure and depth of interventions can be adapted to the needs of the couple or family.

Third-party payer systems may also influence the use of psychodynamic approaches by requiring a single identified client. Psychodynamic couple and family work focuses on the system itself as the client, which is generally not accepted by third-party payers. Counselors using these approaches while utilizing reimbursements will have to make a compromise in this area, choosing a system member's "presenting issues" upon which to base diagnosis and treatment planning. Although this may go against some basic philosophies of psychodynamic system work, it can also facilitate short-term triage of more pressing issues, allowing the couple or family to then be able to focus on underlying issues and deeper patterns. Similarly, third-party payer systems may influence the development of goals, requiring specific, measurable goals associated with symptom reduction. Again, this conflicts with the foundations of psychodynamic treatment, which focuses on insight and awareness, with symptom reduction considered a secondary benefit arising out of achievement of these tasks during treatment. Counselors using psychodynamics may find themselves having to balance between identifying measurable goals and allowing more systems-focused goals to evolve organically from the counseling process.

Counselors using a psychodynamic approach with couples and families should also be mindful of the level of stability of participants. Messer and Warren (1995) noted that psychodynamics requires an "ability to trust and to share" and "represents a fairly advanced stage of object relations" (p. 77). These two important considerations could rule out clients whose pathology is severe, particularly if the counselor is aware that treatment length may be limited (Messer, 2001). Longer or even open-ended lengths of treatment might still include some limitations in this area. Some systems members may lack sufficient development to completely engage in the process and to fully benefit from a psychodynamic approach. This does not mean that these system members should not participate; however, the counselor must be aware of these limitations, and he or she may need to adapt some interventions as a result.

Another potential limitation related to the system members themselves lies in the availability and cooperation of system members. Logically, the best couple or family work will involve as many system members as possible. However, this may not always be an option. Although psychodynamic system work can still be conducted in the absence of one or more members (Framo, 1992; Goldenthal, 1993), conducting sessions without certain members can also negatively impact perceptions, dynamics, and general therapeutic goals. Furthermore, members who do participate may be reluctant to explore issues along a psychodynamic pathway, and counselors may find their clients hesitant to provide detailed family histories or examine systemic patterns. For example, one or both members of a client couple might avoid discussing family of origin because they do not wish to "blame" parents for their issues. Similarly, parents may resist a psychodynamic systems approach, feeling as though they are being blamed for their children's problems. Concepts such as legacies, entitlements, and projections can put clients in a defensive mode if they are not presented well. It is important for psychodynamic counselors to validate clients' perceptions and resistance, while also stressing the roles of understanding and insight in the psychodynamic counseling process.

Another limitation of psychodynamic work relates to the intensity of the process. Psychodynamic therapy requires the counselor to have a very strong connection to clients as well as intense self-awareness, since the counselor is often an active participant in the process. This can be particularly draining on the counselor, especially in shorter-term treatment, in which interventions can be more powerful and challenging (Levenson, 2010; Rawson, 2005). In addition, although psychodynamic work does include achievement of identified goals, often the full benefit occurs far beyond the termination of treatment. The counselor may not, therefore, have the opportunity to fully observe the benefits to clients, which may have a long-term impact on counselor perceptions and beliefs about his or her own effectiveness. Psychodynamic counselors need to be able to engage with clients intensely and to let go often, two considerations that can be draining to many professionals in the field.

SUMMARY

Psychodynamic couples and family therapy has a firm foundation in psychoanalytic, general systems, and object relations theories. It differs from psychoanalytic therapy in several important ways, including being shorter in duration and involving fewer sessions per week. Psychodynamic family therapy is an insight-oriented treatment approach, with a primary goal of enhancing awareness of past unresolved conflicts and internalized constructs, as well as their influence on present issues. Some psychodynamic systems approaches focus strictly on the system itself, as with Framo's family-of-origin therapy or Bell's family group therapy. Other psychodynamic approaches integrate both individual and familial dynamics, such as Boszormenyi-Nagy's contextual family therapy. In both cases, the family itself is considered "the client." This can be a challenge to using these approaches, as often presenting issues focus on one family member and require immediate attention. A single client may also need to be identified for billing and reimbursement purposes.

The primary tools in a psychodynamic couple and family counselor's toolbox are listening, empathy, observation, and interpretation. The counselor utilizes investigative neutrality and multidirectional partiality to enhance listening and empathy and to convey deep connection to the client. Transference and countertransference are common in psychodynamic treatment and are considered part of the process. Psychodynamic counselors must maintain a high level of self-awareness and insight, so as to use these occurrences to further the client goals and guard against their becoming problematic.

In observing and interpreting information and systemic behaviors, psychodynamic family counselors often act as detectives, uncovering patterns, constructs, and embedded paradigms. Counselors should also pay close attention to collusions, projections, entitlements, and balances across the family system. Clients explore and bring into awareness unconscious thoughts and patterns of behavior. Insights gained from the origins and meanings of these support the secondary goals of symptom reduction and enhanced system interaction.

Psychodynamic couples and family therapy can be used with a wide variety of presenting issues, from basic family conflict to more identified diagnoses and pathologies. However, because it requires an ability to achieve deep insight and self-awareness, this approach is not suitable for every system. Counterindicators include severe pathology, psychosis, and immediate safety issues. Psychodynamic couples and family therapy can also be used with a wide variety of clients because the approach is individualized for the unique system's needs, thus easily integrating cultural and diversity considerations.

USEFUL WEBSITES

The following websites provide additional information relating to chapter topics.

Ackerman Institute for the Family
http://www.ackerman.org
American Family Therapy Academy
http://www.afta.org
National Council on Family Relations
http://www.ncfr.org
Object Relations Family Therapy
http://www.psychotherapy.net/video/object-relations-family-therapy
Psychodynamic Family Therapy
http://psychodynamictherapy.net/category/psychodynamic-therapy-approach

REFERENCES

Ackerman, N. W. (1956). Interlocking pathology in family relationships. In S. Rado & G. Daniels (Eds.), *Changing conceptions of psychoanalytic medicine* (pp. 135–150). New York, NY: Grune & Stratton.

Ackerman, N. W. (1958). *The psychodynamics of family life: Diagnosis and treatment of family relationships*. New York, NY: Basic Books.

Ackerman, N. W. (1966). *Treating the troubled family*. New York, NY: Basic Books.

Bell, C. M., & Khantzian, E. J. (1991). Contemporary psychodynamic perspectives and the disease concept of addiction: Complementary or competing models? *Psychiatric Annals, 21*(5), 273–281.

Bell, J. E. (1948). *Projective techniques: A dynamic approach to the study of the personality*. New York, NY: Longmans, Green and Co.

Bell, J. E. (1961). *Family group therapy*. London, England: Bookstall Publications.

Berzoff, J. (2011). Freud's psychoanalytic concepts. In J. Berzoff, L. M. Ianagan, & P. Hertz (Eds.), *Inside out and outside in: Psychodynamic clinical theory and psychopathology in contemporary multicultural contexts* (pp. 18–47). Lanham, MD: Rowman & Littlefield.

Borden, W. (2000). Contemporary psychoanalysis: Toward a psychodynamically informed social work perspective. *Social Service Review, 74*(3), 352–279.

Bornstein, R. F. (2006). A Freudian construct lost and reclaimed: The psychodynamics of personality pathology. *Psychoanalytic Psychology, 23*(2), 339–353.

Boszormenyi-Nagy, I. (1987). *Foundations of contextual therapy: Collected papers of Ivan Boszormenyi-Nagy, MD*. New York, NY: Brunner/Mazel.

Boszormenyi-Nagy, I., & Framo, J. (Eds.). (1965). *Intensive family therapy: Theoretical and practical aspects*. New York, NY: Harper & Row.

Boszormenyi-Nagy, I., & Krasner, B. R. (1986). *Between give and take: A clinical guide to contextual therapy*. New York, NY: Brunner/Mazel.

Boszormenyi-Nagy, I., & Sparks, G. (1973). *Invisible loyalties: Reciprocity in intergenerational family therapy*. New York, NY: Harper & Row.

Bradley, R., Greene, J., Russ, E., Dutra, L., & Westen, D. (2005). A multidimensional meta-analysis of psychotherapy for PTSD. *American Journal of Psychiatry, 162*, 214–227.

Clarkin, J. F., Levy, K. N., Lenzenweger, M. F., & Kernberg, O. F. (2004). The Personality Disorders Institute/Personality Disorder Research Foundation randomized control trial for borderline personality disorder: Rationale, methods, and patient characteristics. *Journal of Personality Disorders, 18*, 52–72.

Crits-Christoph, P., Connolly Gibbons, M. B., Narducci, J., Schamberger, M., & Gallop, R. (2005). Interpersonal problems and the outcome of interpersonally oriented psychodynamic treatment of GAD. *Psychotherapy: Theory/Research/Practice/Training, 42*, 211–224.

Dicks, H. V. (1963). Object relations theory and marital status. *British Journal of Medical Psychology, 36*, 125–129.

Dicks, H. V. (1967). *Marital tensions*. New York, NY: Basic Books.

Dong, M., Anda, R. F., Felitti, V. J., Dube, S. R., Williamson, D. F., Thompson, T. J., . . . Giles, W. H. (2004). The interrelatedness of multiple forms of childhood abuse, neglect, and household dysfunction. *Child Abuse & Neglect, 28*, 771–784.

Erickson, E. (1956). The problem of ego identity. *Journal of the American Psychoanalytic Association, 4*, 56–121.

Fairbairn, W. D. (1952). *An object relations theory of the personality*. New York, NY: Basic Books.

Flores, O. Y., & Bernal, G. (1989). Contextual family therapy of addiction with Latinos. *Journal of Psychotherapy & the Family, 6*(1/2), 123–142.

Foulkes, S. H. (1948). *Introduction to group-analytic psychotherapy*. London, England: Heinemann.

Framo, J. L. (1981a). Family of origin as a therapeutic resource for adults in marital and family therapy: You can and should go home again. *Family Process, 15*, 193–210.

Framo, J. L. (1981b). The integration of marital therapy with sessions with family of origin. In A. S. Gurman & D. P. Kniskern (Eds.), *Handbook of family therapy* (pp. 133–158). New York, NY: Brunner/Mazel.

Framo, J. L. (1992). *Family-of-origin therapy: An intergenerational approach*. New York, NY: Brunner/Mazel.

Gold, S. N. (2008). Benefits of a contextual approach to understanding and treating complex trauma. *Journal of Trauma & Dissociation, 9*(2), 269–292.

Goldenthal, P. (1993). *Contextual family therapy: Assessment and intervention procedures*. Sarasota, FL: Professional Resource Press.

Hare-Mustin, C. (1987). The problem of gender in family therapy theory. *Family Process, 26*(1), 15–27.

Hargrave, T. D., & Pfitzer, F. (2003). *The new contextual therapy: Guiding the power of give and take*. New York, NY: Brunner-Routledge.

Klein, M. (1946). Notes on some schizoid mechanisms. *The International Journal of Psychoanalysis, 27*, 99–110.

Leichsenring, F. (2005). Are psychodynamic and psychoanalytic therapies effective? A review of empirical data. *International Journal of Psychoanalysis, 86*, 1–26.

Leichsenring, F., Hiller, W., Weissberg, M., & Leibing, E. (2006). Cognitive-behavioral therapy and psychodynamic psychotherapy: Techniques, efficacy, and indications. *American Journal of Psychotherapy, 60*(3), 233–259.

Levenson, H. (2010). *Brief dynamic therapy*. Washington, DC: American Psychological Association.

Maina, G., Forner, F., & Bogetto, F. (2005). Randomized controlled trial comparing brief dynamic and supportive therapy with waiting list condition in minor depressive disorders. *Psychotherapy and Psychosomatics*, *74*, 43–50.

Messer, S. B. (2001). What makes brief psychodynamic therapy time efficient. *Clinical Psychology*, *8*, 5–22.

Messer, S. B., & Warren, C. S. (1995). *Models of brief psychodynamic therapy: A comparative approach*. New York, NY: Guilford Press.

Nelson, T. S., & Sullivan, N. J. (2007). Couple therapy and addictions. *Journal of Couple & Relationship Therapy*, *6*(1/2), 45–56.

Rasheed, J. M., Rasheed, M. N., & Marley, J. A. (2011). *Family therapy: Models and techniques*. Thousand Oaks, CA: SAGE.

Rawson, P. (2005). *Handbook of short-term psychodynamic psychotherapy*. London, England: Karnac.

Scharff, D., & Scharff, J. (1987). *Object relations family therapy*. New York, NY: Jason Aronson.

Shaver, P. R., & Mikulincer, M. (2005). Attachment theory and research: Resurrection of the psychodynamics approach to personality. *Journal of Research in Personality*, *39*(1), 22–45.

Shedler, J. (2010). The efficacy of psychodynamic psychotherapy. *American Psychologist*, *65*(2), 98–109.

Skynner, R. (1976). *One flesh: Separate persons*. London, England: Constable & Company Limited.

Skynner, R. (1987). *Explorations with families: Group analysis and family therapy*. New York, NY: Tavistock/Routledge.

CHAPTER 7

Experiential and Humanistic Theories: Approaches and Applications

Mark B. Scholl
Wake Forest University

Michelle Perepiczka
Walden University

Michael Walsh
University of South Carolina School of Medicine

The humanistic-existential movement of the 1960s, including Gestalt therapy, psychodrama, client-centered therapy, and the encounter group movement, fostered the emergence of experiential and humanistic family approaches (Wetchler & Piercy, 1996). These approaches emphasize the affective or emotional dimensions of the family system. From this perspective, healthy families are ones that are capable of more fully experiencing a range of emotions openly and interact in a lively and spontaneous manner. By contrast, unhealthy families are more rigid, and at times even blocked with regard to their ability to communicate and empathize on an emotional level.

Experiential family approaches are clearly founded on fundamental humanistic tenets including respect for clients' holism, dignity, freedom, right to construct meaning, and capacity for choosing goals (Peluso & Vensel, 2012). These holistic approaches directly contrast with reductionistic problem-focused approaches to family therapy (Wetchler & Piercy, 1996). For example, Virginia Satir took a more holistic view of the family system, asserting that members' behaviors represented their best attempt at coping with a problem, and was quoted as saying, "The problem is not the problem, coping is the problem" (Haber, 2002, p. 24).

In this chapter we present the contributions of three pioneering experiential humanistic family therapists. In addition to their noteworthy theoretical contributions, each of these prominent figures is well known for his or her charismatic personality. First, we discuss Carl Whitaker and present his symbolic-experiential family therapy (SEFT) (Napier & Whitaker, 1978; Whitaker & Bumberry, 1988; Whitaker & Keith, 1981). Second, we discuss Walter Kempler (1973, 1981) and his gestalt family therapy. Finally, we discuss Virginia Satir (1983, 1988) and her approach to experiential family therapy, which was a unique combination of gestalt techniques, psychodrama, and communications analysis.

CARL WHITAKER

The first therapist we discuss is Carl Whitaker, who is very well known for his unconventional and spontaneous approach to joining and working with families.

Background

Carl Whitaker (1912–1995) grew up on a dairy farm in upstate New York. He entered medical school in 1932 and originally trained in the area of obstetrics and gynecology. However, toward the end of his training he decided to switch to psychiatry and completed his residency in a psychiatric hospital. He focused on treating schizophrenia and observed that patients who appeared to have recovered experienced a reemergence of their symptoms after being reunited with their families. This observation led to his focus on treating the family system (Gladding, 2011).

During World War II, Whitaker was assigned to a position in Oak Ridge, Tennessee, counseling workers involved with the top-secret atomic bomb project. In this position he developed his style partly based on Freud's belief that human behaviors, thoughts, and feelings are symbols of the unconscious. At Oak Ridge, he developed symbolic-experiential family therapy (SEFT), as well as a staunch belief in the necessity of working with a cotherapist (Wetchler & Piercy, 1996).

A milestone in Carl Whitaker's career was his appointment as Chairman of the Department of Psychiatry at Emory University in 1946 at the age of 34. At Emory, he further refined his unique approach to working with families. He would join a family system and then adopt an unorthodox freewheeling style in order to assist family members in loosening up their rigid roles and adopting a healthier, authentic way of being. He commonly applied existential principles to the practice of family therapy. For example, rather than viewing anxiety as a pathological symptom, he viewed it as meaningful and intentionally heightened family members' anxiety to increase a family's motivation for change (Connell, 1996). In keeping with his existential influences, he adopted an authentic interpersonal style balancing warmth and nurturance with spontaneity and affective confrontation.

In 1965, he became a professor of psychiatry at the University of Wisconsin. While working in that position, he mentored August Napier, an intern enrolled in the PhD psychology program at the University of North Carolina. *The Family Crucible*, coauthored with Dr. Napier in 1978, provides a vivid illustration of Whitaker's unique approach to family therapy. This book has become highly influential and is a common reading assignment in family therapist training courses.

Whitaker died at his family home in 1995 at the age of 83 after a 2-year illness.

Major Constructs

The major constructs in Carl Whitaker's unique approach to family counseling reflect that he was strongly influenced by both psychoanalytic and existential models of psychotherapy practice.

Symbolism and Metaphor

As a result of his background in psychoanalysis, similar to Freud, Carl Whitaker believed a statement or behavior made by a family member could potentially have both a literal meaning and a latent or symbolic meaning (Whitaker & Ryan, 1989). A primary aim of his was to uncover the unconscious meaning behind the literal meaning. He believed that metaphors were useful for understanding a family because metaphors highlight unstated assumptions of family members (Davies, 2011). For example, there is a session in *The Family Crucible* (Napier & Whitaker, 1978) during which the husband (Dan) criticizes the wife (Carolyn) and she bursts into tears. Whitaker commented that at a certain point Dan was transformed from Carolyn's husband to a symbol representing her critical mother. This was highly significant because Carolyn was unable to continue fighting with her critical mother, and this resulted in an impasse preventing a resolution to the argument. Whitaker also liked to create metaphors as a means of joining and helping a family (Whitaker & Keith, 1981). For example, he commonly used the metaphor of the family as a sports team, and his role was that of a coach responsible for promoting teamwork and enhancing the team's morale.

Symbolic Language

Whitaker believed that symbolic language developed in most close family relationships. For example, in an attempt to engage the husband in dialogue, a wife described her relationship with her husband in the following way: "I just can't talk to him. He loves his tractor more than me. When we fight he usually leaves and goes to work on his tractor" (Connell, 1996, p. 6). Whitaker would use such symbolic language as an opportunity to promote positive change by shifting from metaphor to reality and back again. For example, he might say, "Why don't you trip him the next time he runs to the tractor?" and then, "Why don't you start by teaching him how to give you a hug?" This sequence also illustrates how Whitaker would engage a family in verbal play to enhance flexibility in the family behaviors and roles.

Battle for Structure

Carl Whitaker used the term *battle for structure* to refer to his belief that it was important for the therapist to establish authoritative control early in the process (Wetchler & Piercy, 1996). For example, in *The Family Crucible*, his cotherapist, August Napier, highlights that Whitaker was adamant that the first family therapy session should not begin until all of the family members are present.

Freedom

Consistent with the philosophy of existential humanistic counseling, Whitaker emphasized that once a workable structure had been established, the family should be allowed to determine the course of therapy (sometimes referred to as a *battle for initiative*) (Whitaker & Keith, 1981). He was respectful of the family's right and ability to choose its own direction and goals.

Craziness

Craziness is Whitaker's term for the divergent, playful, creative thinking that families use to solve problems (Wetchler & Piercy, 1996; Whitaker & Keith, 1981). The ability of two or more family members to engage one another through "crazy" behavior and dialogue was, in Whitaker's view, a primary characteristic of a healthy or functioning family. He would model this behavior and use it as a means to enter and engage a family system.

Flight Into Health

Flight into health refers to a tendency for families to terminate therapy prematurely once their anxiety has been reduced (Whitaker & Ryan, 1989). Although premature, this is a positive sign because it indicates that the family has become more autonomous and unified. Consequently, Whitaker asserted that the therapist should not attempt to prevent the family from terminating (Wetchler & Piercy, 1996). He believed the family would return to therapy at a later time, if necessary, with an increased resolve.

Goals

Whitaker and Keith (1981) described the goals of SEFT. They stated they typically have goals at both the system and the individual levels. Their goals are to simultaneously cultivate a sense of belonging among the family members and to also promote the individuality of each family member. They wrote of their intentional efforts to foster the development of a new family culture that included an increased sense of unity. Whitaker and Keith referred to this new culture as a system with increased power and a "team with increased morale" (p. 200). At the same time, they fostered the individuation and self-actualization of the individual family members. Ultimately, they sought to increase the creativity of the family system as well as the creativity of individual members.

Whitaker and Keith (1981) acknowledged that additional goals were commonly identified by the family members. They asserted that the level of investment varies from family to family. Symptom relief, although obvious, may prevent systemic growth and development. They believed that family systems can tolerate the increased anxiety that accompanies symptoms. They framed individual symptoms as systemic problems in order to promote the "development of family nationalism" (p. 200).

Techniques

Whitaker used relatively few techniques in his approach to family therapy. He tended to gently use techniques early in therapy as a means of assessing how the family would respond. Later on, as rapport deepened, he would exert more direct and specific pressure on the family. The following techniques come from a chapter, coauthored by Whitaker, describing SEFT (Whitaker & Keith, 1981).

Redefine Symptoms as Efforts for Growth

In order to depathologize human experience, Whitaker redefined symptoms in the family. For example, a wife's jealousy might be said to indicate that she loves her husband. He also gave the example of redefining a son's psychosis as the son's effort to serve as a Christ-like martyr so the other family members would be saved. The latter example also illustrates Whitaker's belief that humor should be incorporated into these confrontations so that they are not as painful.

Model Fantasy Alternatives to Real-Life Stress

Whitaker proposed that family members should be more playful and defy society's conventions. In a family in which the grandmother complained that she was not being taken seriously by the other family members, Whitaker suggested that she might go to a public dance with her son-in-law. When the grandmother said that she could never do that because of what people would think, Whitaker told her, "That is what makes it so much fun." Ultimately, the son-in-law commented that if the grandmother were more playful, it would make it easier for his "parental" daughter to behave like a carefree child. By teaching family members the use of fantasy in this session, they learned to expand their emotional life and roles without feeling threatened.

Separate Interpersonal Stress and Intrapersonal Fantasy Stress

An example of this occurs in a family therapy session in which Whitaker asked a grandmother whose husband was deceased if she would ever consider remarrying. When she answered no, he asked her how long she thought she had to live. She ventured that she might have 20 years left before her death, and Whitaker suggested that left her with enough time for at least two more marriages. He further suggested that with that much time to live, she should have more fun and act like a teenager instead of a protective mother to her adult daughter. The open discussion of her future death contaminated her intrapersonal fantasy that she must be serious and parental at all times to meet the needs of the family. This discussion of the threatening topic of mortality was freeing for the family because they discovered that such a serious discussion does not lead to tragic consequences.

Add Practical Bits of Intervention

The family therapist can offer suggestions that in other approaches to individual or family therapy might be considered inappropriate or ill-advised. Whitaker believed that the family was strong and intelligent enough to adopt advice it could use, and to ignore recommendations it found to be less helpful. For example, in one therapy session, the mother complained that family members relied on her too much. Whitaker offered that she might decide to leave for a week to take a vacation, and the family members could fend for themselves. He would commonly make a suggestion such as this in a manner that was tongue-in-cheek, believing that the family members would then decide whether to take the suggestion seriously. He did not believe in giving homework assignments, with one noteworthy exception. He insisted that family members avoid discussing their experiences in counseling between sessions.

Augment the Despair of a Family Member

This technique was used so the family members would become united in their emotional support of a suffering family member. For example, Whitaker once said to a grandmother, "If you refuse to have fun and be a bad girl, then your granddaughter won't have anyone to show her how a child is supposed to act. She might go on acting like an adult until she is grown, and miss out on her entire childhood."

Use Affective Confrontation

Whitaker described this as most commonly being used against the parents in defense of the children. For example, he used affective confrontation in situations in which a child was being treated like a scapegoat. In one such interaction, Whitaker initiated a mock wrestling match with an 8-year-old boy. When the parents unjustly criticized their son for engaging in horseplay, Whitaker told them to knock it off.

Treat Children Like Children and Not Like Peers

Whitaker believed in being realistic in interacting with children and teenagers. If children wanted to wrestle, he would enjoy demonstrating that he was physically stronger than they were by overpowering them in a playful wrestling match. Although Whitaker was generally open and accepting, he was not averse to moralizing when a teenager needed to be confronted for inappropriate conduct. This reflected his belief that healthy families are characterized by clear distinctions between appropriate roles for parents and children.

Diversity

Carl Whitaker's symbolic-experiential family therapy has strengths and weaknesses with regard to its usefulness with diverse populations. First of all, with regard to strengths, SEFT emphasizes the priority of establishing rapport with the family member who is the most influential with regard to the family's participation in therapy. A strength of this aspect is that it entails being responsive to cultural differences. That is, whether the most influential family member is the mother, father, or a grandparent, an SEFT therapist would intentionally begin by forming a good working relationship with this family member.

Another strength with regard to working with diverse populations is that SEFT places a high value on experiences and actions as opposed to primarily emphasizing cognitions. Interventions that are playful and entail thinking about family roles in new and unconventional ways potentially appeal to diverse clients because these experiments are playful and humorous. They also have the advantage of being accessible to a diverse range of ages and cognitive abilities. Metaphors and role plays tap into the inherent ability of individuals across cultures to pretend, role play, and imagine possibilities. These inviting approaches can energize a family because they are highly engaging.

Limitations of SEFT, in this regard, are related to the fact that the approach is founded on existential philosophy. SEFT places a high value on individualism, and this aspect might render it less effective with families from a collectivist culture that places more emphasis on a hierarchical system of decision making. There is also an inherent risk that the use of playful language related to family members exchanging roles might unintentionally offend family members from cultures in which freely experimenting with family roles is unacceptable.

Finally, in employing SEFT, Whitaker would present suggestions and recommendations in a playful tongue-in-cheek manner under the assumption that his clients were capable of processing, understanding, and selectively adopting them. However, Whitaker and Keith (1981) acknowledged that this may not hold true for some families. Families from cultures with diverse values, languages, worldviews, and perspectives on the roles of therapists and clients in therapy seem like they, in particular, might have difficulty converting these playful suggestions into their family change process. We recommend that when working with diverse populations, family therapists take more care with regard to processing what occurred during a family counseling session, that they more clearly communicate their recommendations for family change, and that they show respect for the family's ability to decide whether they will adopt recommendations.

Table 7.1 Key Concepts in Carl Whitaker's Symbolic-Experiential Family Therapy

Theoretical Influences	Rogers: Person Centered Yalom: Existential Freud: Psychoanalytic
Constructs	Symbolism and metaphor Symbolic language Battle for structure Freedom Craziness Flight into health
Goals	Increase family anxiety to promote family unity Increase family unity and cohesiveness Cultivate sense of belonging among family members Promote the individuality of family members Promote self-actualization among family members Frame individual symptoms as systemic level symptoms Increase family and individual creativity
Techniques	Redefine symptoms as efforts for growth Model fantasy alternatives to real-life stress Separate interpersonal stress and intrapersonal fantasy stress Augment the despair of a family member Use affective confrontation Treat children like children and not like peers

SIDEBAR 7.1 BEHIND THE CURTAIN: CARL WHITAKER

While employed as a faculty member at Emory University from 1946 to 1955, Carl Whitaker refined his unique approach to working with families. He adopted a spontaneous, unorthodox style he called "therapy of the absurd." His style included challenging social conventions and using affective confrontation with family members. However, Whitaker's colleagues had an adverse reaction to his unorthodox methods and, as a result, he was dismissed from Emory in 1955 (Gale & Long, 1996). In that year, he entered into private practice in the Atlanta area.

SIDEBAR 7.2 QUESTIONS FOR REFLECTION: CARL WHITAKER

1. Think about your family with respect to Carl Whitaker's symbolic-experiential family therapy. What metaphors, if any, do you have in your family of origin?

2. What are some examples of existential themes (e.g., death) that members of your family feel uncomfortable discussing? How might a symbolic-experiential family therapist invite your family to discuss one or more of these themes in a manner that is playful, humorous, or otherwise nonthreatening?
3. Identify one or more "symptoms" exhibited by members of your family of origin. Attempt to redefine each of these symptoms as a systemic problem that the family must solve by working together as a team.
4. What are some examples of roles (e.g., a parent who is always authoritarian, a child who has parental responsibilities) that are rigidly defined? How might these roles be redefined to increase the flexibility of family members?
5. Identify a real-life stressor of your family. How could members be more playful in their approach to addressing that stressor?

SIDEBAR 7.3 QUESTIONS FOR REFLECTION: WALTER KEMPLER

Before reading the following section on Walter Kempler's experiential family therapy, please take a moment to reflect on your own family. Consider the following four questions. While you are reading, notice how your family might interact with a family therapist who takes this type of approach.

1. How does your family communicate to express overt and covert messages?
2. Consider who in your family is close to each other and what combination is more distant. How do these various groupings impact the family?
3. Think back to a time when you were uncomfortable fully expressing yourself to your family members. What was that like for you? What would it be like to be your full self?
4. How does your family go about settling an impasse?

WALTER KEMPLER

Walter Kempler's approach to family therapy, in addition to being inspired by client-centered counseling, is consistent with humanistic counseling due to its holistic nature. He believed that an effective family therapy approach should incorporate affective, behavioral, and cognitive dimensions into a holistic approach to promoting optimal family functioning.

Background

Kempler developed his own form of therapy called *experiential family therapy* in the 1970s (Kempler, 2008). Experiential family therapy was grounded in creating experiential moments in sessions with families to help families increase awareness about their thoughts and feelings, take responsibility, obtain a sense of autonomy, and maintain authenticity to bring about change (Goldenberg & Goldenberg, 2013). Kempler focused on the thoughts and feelings underlying communication in order to obtain a holistic view of what one is communicating. Kempler believed the family as a whole held the key to healing within the family unit, as well as for the individual members. Each family member would contribute to the progress the family would be able to achieve (Kempler, 1982a).

Various humanistic-experiential approaches influenced the creation of experiential family therapy. For instance, Rogers's client-centered therapy influenced Kempler as he adopted the therapeutic core conditions (unconditional positive regard, empathy, and congruence) as well as the high value of the therapeutic relationship as a pillar of therapy (Hougaard, 1994). Also, Kempler incorporated gestalt therapy's emphasis on the here-and-now and experiential exercises with families (Kempler, 2008). Other elements resemble the following concepts from modern theories: Stern's (2004) view of how change occurs in therapy through active participation of a client instead of passive catharsis; Yalom's (1999, 2002) view of a collaborative therapeutic relationship and universal challenges in life (including death, freedom, isolation, and meaninglessness); Spinelli's (1998) view of clients needing to behaviorally do something about their problems in addition to cognitively processing them; and Schibbye's (2005) view of the importance of communication between individuals.

Major Constructs

Experiential family therapy is grounded in multiple constructs that make this particular theory unique with regard to how a therapist assists a family in making positive, forward movement toward their goals. Kempler (1973, 1982a) stated the family unit is important to each individual member and a vital source of life's meaning. Actively preserving and improving the family's communication and dynamics through experience-based therapy is the core emphasis.

In experiential family therapy, each family member is encouraged to be open to expanding one's awareness of oneself and each other (Kempler, 1965, 2008). This would include taking responsibility for one's role in the family and taking responsibility for one's own direction in life. Families are also reminded that each family member has his or her own psychological reality, which means an individual perception of the world as well as the family. Having these concepts in mind while communicating is a helpful starting point for families.

Understanding verbal and nonverbal messages in the family is one essential element (Kempler, 2008). The family is guided in hearing the underlying meaning in what is shared or not shared. They are encouraged to practice identifying the deeper truth in their messages between one another. In a sense, they are challenged to look beyond the surface and discover the underlying messages beneath family members' communication as well as what they are personally truly trying to communicate to others.

The dynamics in the family are also a focal point. More specifically, these dynamics include union and separation in the family. These dynamics inform the family of another layer of communication (Kempler, 2008). *Union* is a dynamic represented in the closeness and sense of connection between individuals, and *separation* takes the form of distance between family members. The family's attention is brought toward identifying subgroups within the family, the roles these subgroups play, and their impact on the family. Integrating the family back together as a whole and reuniting any distant members are significant components for complete family encounters. Further, complete family encounters entail individuals recognizing who others truly are, as well as individuals being their true selves. Authentic meetings are the antithesis of incomplete encounters, which are described as family members being uncomfortable expressing themselves and tensions, or possibly a sense of separation, building in the family.

The following four concepts (Kempler, 2008) play various roles in resolving a family's struggle, and the family's progress toward healing:

1. *Agreement.* This concept refers to a process of being able to accept one another even though family members may not be content with the conflict. This is much like agreeing to disagree, or agreeing to accept differences.
2. *Compromise.* This refers to a mutual agreement that everyone in the family can sustain and live with. This is much like finding a middle or common ground.
3. *Giving up.* This concept refers to a family member letting go of a conflict and fully processing or grieving to achieve full closure and resolution.
4. *Winning.* This term refers to the full resolution of a conflict. In addition, winning is a process in which satisfaction and compromise are fully embraced, and previous emotional or cognitive hardships are no longer experienced.

Goals

When in session, the goal of experiential family therapy is to actively engage each family member in the counseling process so they can experience one another, increase awareness of themselves and the family dynamics, become more united, and practice communication (Kempler, 1965, 2008). Another immediate goal is to increase awareness of different outcomes of healthy and unhealthy family dynamics and communication patterns. Namely, the former tend to sustain existing conflicts, whereas the latter tend to create forward progress and healing for the family (Kempler, 1967).

The overarching goal is to have the family become healthier. A healthy family is characterized by members using authentic forms of communication, supporting one another, accepting one another, and possessing a sense of individual responsibility with regard to both their life paths and the roles played within the family (Kempler, 1973, 1991).

Techniques

To achieve the goals of experiential family therapy, the therapist must be an active participant in the therapy session and take on a directive role. The therapist must be genuine, be personable with the family, build trust, create a safe environment, and be comfortable with honest confrontation in order to deliver honest messages to help the family gain awareness (Kempler, 1967, 1991). The therapist is also responsible for the following:

- Helping the family talk directly about issues and keeping them in the here-and-now by redirecting them when the focus shifts or when resistance begins to develop in the session (Kempler, 1973, 1991).
- Helping the family address issues that may have been ignored for extended periods of time, yet still play an active role in the family dynamics or communication (Kempler, 1991).
- Helping family members identify conflicting needs, such as wanting an improved relationship yet still pushing others away out of fear (Kempler, 2008).
- Helping the family be open and vulnerable with each other in order to ask for what they need or want (Kempler, 1991). Specifically, the therapist is responsible for helping the family identify what they want or need and whom they need something from in a clear and precise manner through which needs can be met.
- Encouraging the family to be emotional and use an affect that matches their verbal message. Releasing the emotions can be healing in itself for the individual expressing the pain as well as for the family members witnessing how the individual has been impacted (Kempler, 1967; Wetchler & Piercy, 1996).
- Emphasizing the family taking action in order to become healthier (Kempler, 1973, 1991).

Diversity

Experiential family therapy embraces diversity and weaves cultural competence throughout each moment with a family (Kempler, 1982b, 1991). Diversity is a core value that the therapist must recognize in the dynamics and communication of the family. Each family is unique, as are each of the individual family members. Diversity is recognized within the family to increase understanding and acceptance, which can help the family develop together and make positive change (Wetchler & Piercy, 1996).

SIDEBAR 7.4 BEHIND THE CURTAIN: WALTER KEMPLER

Walter Kempler, a psychiatrist, was born, educated, and trained in the United States. Kempler received his medical degree from the University of Texas, was trained as a psychoanalyst, and worked as a psychiatrist at the UCLA Neuropsychiatric Institute in the 1950s (Goldenberg & Goldenberg, 2013). Kempler studied with Fritz Perls in the Esalen Training Center in California in the 1960s (Kempler, 2008). The experience with Perls was pivotal because during this time Kempler became more familiar with applied gestalt therapy, learned he had varying ideas from Perls, and applied experience-oriented techniques with families.

Table 7.2 Key Concepts in Walter Kempler's Experiential Family Therapy

Theoretical Influences	Rogers: Person centered Yalom: Existential Perls: Gestalt
Constructs	Positive forward movement toward goals Family unit collaboration to create healing Active experiences in therapy are healing Expand awareness Take responsibility for role in family Understand full messages of family members (verbal and nonverbal) Union (closeness) and separation (distance) in the family Reunite families to have full encounters (genuine) Conflict resolution types: agreement, compromise, giving up, winning
Goals	Increase healthy dynamics Promote active engagement in therapy process Increase awareness of self and family dynamics Unite family Practice healthy, authentic communication Support and accept one another
Techniques	Talk directly and genuinely about concerns in the here-and-now Address ignored conflicts Identify conflicting needs Encourage openness and safety for vulnerability Facilitate expressiveness of emotion Emphasize action

VIRGINIA SATIR

Virginia Satir is another prime example of a therapist whose widespread acclaim was due as much to her appealing personality as it was to the originality of her insights. Consistent with her prizing of the subjective experiences of clients, she drew heavily upon her own background in formulating her unique system of family therapy.

Background

Virginia Satir was born in 1916 to Oscar and Minnie Pagenkopf in Neillsville, Wisconsin. Satir's childhood, which she often described in her teaching, was filled with tales of the roles that she felt her family had played in her own development. As the oldest of five children and the grandchild of German immigrants, family became a critical factor in Satir's life and would later figure prominently in the development of her theories and her approach.

When Virginia was 5 years of age, she developed appendicitis. Her mother, a devout Christian Scientist, refused to take her to a hospital. Finally, her father intervened and took her to the hospital. Unfortunately, Satir's appendix had ruptured in the meantime, and she spent several months in the hospital. When relating this story, Satir often went on to note that she did not blame her mother. Rather, she sought to understand her mother's actions in the larger context of her mother's frame of reference. She also sought to better understand the seeming contradiction of her mother's actions and her obvious love for her daughter. This and other seeming contradictions led the young Virginia to conclude that she needed more information on people's motives. In fact, she often made reference to her decision, at the age of 5, to become "a children's detective of parents." Satir said, "I didn't quite know what I would look for, but I realized a lot went on in families that didn't meet the eye" (Satir, 1988, p. 17).

This "detective approach" came to characterize her later work. Satir often incorporated personal perception and motive into her work, using her own family as both a guide and an example. In one such instance, Satir noted that her grandmothers, both of whom came from privileged backgrounds, married working-class men. She theorized that this breach of social propriety led to her grandparents leaving Germany for the United States. She later came to understand this choice as being the potential root of a feeling of inadequacy on the part of her father, leading to some of his seeming contradictions—such as seeming upset yet claiming things were just fine. She would often point to this story as an example of how individual understanding and context fuel individual human decisions (King, 1989, p. 17).

Satir would also often use stories from her own background growing up on a farm as illustrative material for her concepts and ideas. One such example was the huge black iron pot her family kept on the porch at their farm home. Her mother made all of her own soap, so for some of the year, the pot was used to contain the soap. When threshing crews came through in the summer, they filled it with stew. In other parts of the year, it was used to store manure for the flower beds. In Satir's words: "We came to call it the '3-S pot.' Anyone who wanted to use the pot faced two questions: What is the pot now full of, and how full is it?" Satir later shared the pot story with a family that was seeking a way to express their own feelings of self-concept. The question for the family was whether they had feelings of positive self-esteem or negative self-esteem and the depth of those feelings. They found the story so valuable that they adopted the metaphor of the pot as a tool of expressing their own feelings, and thus a therapeutic metaphor was born (Satir, 1988, pp. 20–21).

Major Constructs

The major constructs in Satir's approach reflect her strong belief in humanistic principles, including honoring the individual's subjective experience, upholding the dignity and self-worth of every individual, empathizing with the individual's needs and goals, and the importance of healthy interpersonal relationships characterized by authenticity and mutual respect.

The Human Validation Model

For Satir, a critical construct was a focus on the development of the potential of each human being in any relationship (Satir & Baldwin, 1983). Key to the realization of this potential, according to Satir, was the relationship between the therapist and the family (Satir & Bitter, 2000). Her approach relies on the genuine caring of the therapist, open communication between the therapist and the family, as well as the importance of spontaneity, risk taking, and emotional experiencing within the counseling relationship. She believed that to develop a human being's full potential, that individual had to be free to genuinely experience and express the full range of his or her emotions. The freer each human being is to experience and express emotion in a given relationship, the better the relationship will function. People, Satir believed, possess both the ability and the tendency to use inner resources to solve problems. Satir believed that this was especially true of families (Satir, 1988). Fundamental to the human validation model was the human capacity to realize full potential by learning new and more adaptive ways of being. Because of her optimistic view of human nature, Satir's vision is fundamentally humanistic.

Family Focus

Critical to Satir's approach was the relationship between two people in a marriage (Satir, 1964). Married relationships that are not harmonious may impact the larger family, producing ripple effects that impair the overall functioning of that family. As part of her "detective work" with families, she came to believe that it was the complex series of perceptions, social expectations, and anticipated behavior patterns that formed the basis of a family's overall coping style. According to Satir, it is often the coping style that becomes disordered, not the individuals within the family. In fact, she asserted, family members are often unaware of how these coping styles influence them and the family as a whole. It is the role of the therapist, as an observer outside of the family's established dynamic, to point out those patterns and help the family to work to effect positive change. As clear as these patterns can be to the therapist, however, she noted that human beings tend to view the world from only their own perspective. A good therapist can help to expand that view and thereby help the person to come closer to her or his full potential. The example she often used was this:

> What I see is not the total reality. Everybody's got a back, but how many people have seen it? Then you get an awareness of the absurdity of thinking all there is in the world is what you see in it. (Mishlove, 1988)

The Presenting Problem as a Myth and a Guide

A related construct, and according to some, a real innovation, was Satir's assertion that the presenting problem was often not the real problem. Rather, she argued, the real problem was the coping strategy used to deal with the presenting problem. The coping strategy used gives clues as to the complex perceptual patterns that form individual personality. It also gives clues as to the ways in which that human being may be able to grow and develop to his or her full potential. Satir believed that a good family therapist, being able to recognize these complex coping strategies, could then help the person to identify the ways in which he or she could more fully experience the feelings in a given situation, thereby releasing multiple action potentials that may have previously been unavailable. In this way, the therapist helps the person to become more fully human (Satir, 1988).

Self-Esteem

Coping strategies are clues to an individual's self-esteem, which was another critical construct in Satir's work. Like the "3-S pot" previously described, Satir noted that self-esteem itself was a value-neutral term whose true value was assigned by each individual. In other words, an individual either has high self-esteem or low self-esteem, as he or she defines it. In Satir's estimation, the perceived level and quality of that esteem is a key indicator of that person's inner thinking as well as his or her interaction with others (Satir, 1972). Self-esteem, according to Satir, is a learned construct gathered from parents' comments and nonverbal behaviors, as well as socially and family-learned norms. As a socially learned construct, she theorized, self-esteem is changeable and adaptable, even in adulthood.

Communication and Maturation

Satir argued that maturity is defined as a state in which an individual is able to clearly communicate his or her self-concept and is fully in charge of self. Further, she asserted, an individual's communication style is a clear indicator of an individual's level of interpersonal functioning (Satir, 1983). For example, an individual who over-generalizes, using terms like "always" and "never" or dichotomous terms like "right" and "wrong," tends to function at a lower level of interpersonal effectiveness due to a divergent and divisive pattern of thinking. This person, instead of fully explaining his or her position and seeking to understand another's position, may become defensive and adversarial, thereby undermining a true and effective exchange of ideas.

Likewise, Satir noted, there are two levels of communication: the denotive level (content) and the metacommunicative level (process or "message about the message"). The content level is simply what was said; for example, "I feel fine." The metacommunicative level includes the nonverbal "way" the message was delivered. Satir argued that human beings, being fundamentally inclined as learners (and social learners at that), will always seek to "match" metacommunicative data with denotive data. For example, if they match "I feel fine" said with a smile and a relaxed posture, then the person will believe in the veracity of the exchange and likely respond with a genuine interaction and message of their own. If, on the other hand, the two types of data are inconsistent (e.g., if a person says "I feel fine" with a grimace and tight posture), the individual is left with a feeling of mistrust and is unlikely to respond with a genuine exchange of ideas, thereby hampering communication and interpersonal functioning (Satir, 1972).

Patterns of Communication

Satir (1988) noted that there are several common defensive patterns or roles that help to define an individual's overall communication style. They are:

- *The placator.* This person agrees with whatever the speaker says and often defers to others' judgment and often seeks others' help. Placators may feel inadequate, and so they do only what others expect of them and do not take initiative.
- *The blamer.* This individual often disagrees and/or accuses the speaker of being at fault. Blamers often feel unsuccessful and lonely.
- *The computer.* This individual is incredibly reasonable and uses logic instead of truly emotionally experiencing a situation. This person often uses logic to emotionally distance him- or herself. The individual often feels vulnerable and uses this position as a form of self-protection or to assert control over a situation.
- *The distractor.* This person often uses language to move the conversation away from the actual topic. Distractors may feel unable to relate effectively to a given situation and may question whether anyone cares. They often appear to be in constant motion and live in fear of stress and confrontation.
- *The congruent communicator.* This person balances fully experiencing a situation with his or her way of communicating. He or she is honest in expressing feelings and is congruent with language, body language, and actions (Satir & Bitter, 2000).

Family as a Microcosm

Satir viewed the family as a complex series of interrelationships, perceptions, and motivations. Like her examples of her own family, Satir theorized that each person, being human and acting in a human way, does things based on her or his own unique understanding. Further, she noted, there are often both spoken and unspoken rules surrounding behavior and expectation that are unique in each family. In this way, Satir theorized, the complex relationships within a family resemble the world as a whole. Understanding and treating the coping styles involved in family dynamics was a critical first step in understanding and being able to treat the ills of the world as a whole. As she noted, "Heal the family and we heal the world" (Laign, 1988).

Goals

The fundamental goal of the human validation model is more than just the elimination of pathological approaches to coping, which was a focus of Satir's early work. Satir expanded her vision to include goals of helping clients redirect energy toward health and optimal functioning (Satir & Baldwin, 1983, p. 207).

Functional communication, according to Satir, was of paramount importance. Functional families, according to Bitter (2013), have four primary characteristics. First, each member is encouraged to have a full and separate life apart from the family, and change is welcomed. Second, differences are viewed as opportunities to expand perspectives and to grow, rather than as attacks on the family system. Third, the family is characterized by freedom of expression, flexibility, and open communication. Fourth, exploration of differences is encouraged and shared jointly among family members.

Satir also identifies the expansion of awareness and growth potential as key goals for family therapy. Key to these efforts is self-esteem development, which leads to enhanced skills in coping with change. It is this ability to cope with change that is critical to long-term success because it removes the need to stay in old, familiar (and sometimes toxic) patterns, which Satir termed the "status quo," and allows families to fully experience and deal effectively with change, thereby getting closer to their full human potential.

Satir's (1988) three main goals of family therapy were:

1. Each family member should be able to report honestly about what he or she sees, hears, feels, and thinks.
2. Decisions in a family are best made by exploring individual needs and negotiating to get those needs met in the group context, as opposed to using "power plays" to get wants met.
3. Differences should be used as growth opportunities within the family.

Techniques

Satir saw the role of the family therapist as one of guiding the family through the process of positive growth by investigating discrepancies and facilitating effective communication. Rather than focusing on specific techniques, Satir felt that the therapist should focus on developing a genuine and congruent relationship with the family while facilitating and encouraging growth and change. The therapist's belief in the potential of change and growth is a critical part of the overall therapy process. The central role of the therapist is to create an atmosphere of support, safety, and human validation (Satir & Bitter, 2000).

Satir felt that one of the advantages of the therapist, being outside of the family dynamic as a whole, was the ability to observe patterns and communication styles that may not be visible to the family members themselves (remember the previous analogy about seeing one's own back). In being able to point out these patterns, the therapist helps the family identify the growth potentials within the family unit.

Additional therapist responsibilities, according to Satir (1988), include: (a) creating a setting in which clients can risk exploring themselves objectively; (b) assisting the family in building self-esteem by identifying past successes as well as present assets; (c) pointing out nonverbal messages, gaps, and discrepancies in communication, opportunities for accountability, and the ways in which past modes of communication have impacted the family dynamics; (d) interpreting messages that may not be clear; and (e) reducing the need for defenses by establishing boundaries and helping families to agree upon healthy roles and functions.

The Status Quo and the Foreign Element: The Satir Change Model

Satir (1988) identified a stage-based process that described the ways in which families make change. She termed this the *Satir Change Model.*

Status Quo

In Satir's estimation, families often find a set of mutually agreed on (often not explicitly, but rather by use and repetition) communication and interaction patterns that come to be the default patterns. This she termed the *status quo.* The status quo will often go unchanged and unchallenged until something, or some event, comes along to disrupt that pattern.

Foreign Element

Satir termed the event that challenges the status quo the *foreign element.* Families change, according to Satir, when (and often only when) the status quo is challenged by a foreign element. This is often an event that leads people to try to employ traditional modes of problem solving but they fail.

Chaos

When traditional modes of problem solving fail, there is often a period of chaos. In this chaos phase, the family resists the potential change and seeks to find ways to continue to employ old patterns of behavior, only experimenting with new ways when forced to do so.

Transformative Idea

It is the introduction of the transformative idea that provides the family the opportunity to identify a growth potential and a new way of doing things that allows for a more congruent and productive approach to the challenge. According to Satir, the transformative idea may come from the therapist, but it is as likely to come from the family itself, with the therapist acting as an idea developer and facilitator.

Diversity

As one of the first women to develop a comprehensive theory of family therapy, Satir brought a fresh perspective. According to Bitter (2013), Satir's approach has been valued by those averse to more traditional forms of family therapy that rely on

Table 7.3 Key Concepts in Virginia Satir's Human Validation Model

Theoretical Influences	Rogers: Person centered Maslow: Realization of human potential
Constructs	Human potential Self-esteem Freedom of expression Coping style is the problem Relationship between the family and therapist is critical Personal perspective and meaning making in decision making
Goals	Realization of human potential Enhancing the full experience of emotion and interactions Enhancing functional communication Enhancing adaptive decision making Expansion of awareness and growth potential Development of self-esteem Moving from the status quo through the transformative idea toward optimal functioning
Techniques/ Role of the Therapist	Create an atmosphere of support, safety, and human validation Develop a genuine and congruent relationship with the family Point out established (and often unnoticed) patterns of family communication and problem solving Help family members mine past successes and present assets for future opportunity Reduce the need for defenses by establishing boundaries and healthy patterns of communication between family members

issues of power. An approach less grounded in power arguably has broader cultural applicability. This is reflected in the current work of her foundation, Satir Global (formerly the AVANTA Foundation).

Satir herself often made reference to her cultural background and multicultural experiences in her work, working with families from all over the world, from Native American Lakota Sioux in South Dakota to many countries in Europe, Asia, and the Pacific Islands (Bitter, 2013, p. 203). Her work has since been adapted in various cultural and organizational contexts, including work with Hispanic families (Bermudez, 2008) and Middle Eastern families (McLendon, 1998), and it has also been associated with multicultural social issues (Callair & McLendon, 1994).

SIDEBAR 7.5 BEHIND THE CURTAIN: VIRGINIA SATIR

Virginia Satir's first job after college was that of a public school teacher in William's Bay, Wisconsin. She found that she did not like the atmosphere of the school, but she became fascinated with the family lives of her students. She began to visit the homes of her students to see if she might elicit some additional support for their education. She later taught all over the United States, all the while being impressed with the role of the family as a whole (Suarez, 2013). This led to her decision to further her education. As she recounts: "I realized that there were a lot of things that needed to be understood that I didn't understand and that's when I decided to find some other place to get education. Somehow I happened on social work school. Someone told me about it; I didn't remember who it was" (Russell, 1990, p. 10).

SIDEBAR 7.6 QUESTIONS FOR REFLECTION: VIRGINIA SATIR

1. Think of someone in your family whose actions you have noticed. What might be his or her personal context? What has happened in his or her life that may influence the meaning the person makes of the world and the way in which he or she makes decisions? This personal and "lived experience"–related context often fuels decision making among family members.
2. Think about how your family solves problems and approaches discussions/communicates. Are there patterns there? Ask someone who knows your family (but is not a part of it) what they see family members do when encountering problems or when communicating. Are there differences between your perceptions and those of someone outside of your family? If so, what are they? It could be that these are some of the hidden coping strategies that your family uses; these tend to be more obvious to outsiders.
3. In your family: (1) Is each member encouraged to have a full and complete life separate from the family? Is change welcomed? (2) Are differences perceived as opportunities to grow as opposed to being perceived as threats to the family? (3) Is the family characterized by freedom of expression, flexibility, and open communication? (4) Is exploration of differences encouraged and shared among family members?

LIMITATIONS

The experiential and humanistic approaches to family therapy were strongly influenced by existential, gestalt, and person-centered approaches to therapy. Limitations of these approaches are closely related to the values and philosophy from these three sources. The approaches of Whitaker, Kempler, and Satir all place a high degree of value on individualism and each family member's capacity for self-actualization (e.g., Satir's transformative idea). However, a limitation of these approaches is lack of acknowledgment that an individual's capacity for self-actualization or transcendence may be impeded by cultural influences such as oppression, racism, and discrimination. Experiential humanistic approaches encourage family members to be authentic in the face of social norms that potentially limit their authentic self-expression. It is important for family therapists to recognize that some cultures may not tolerate a departure from cultural norms, and therefore individuals from some diverse groups may not enjoy the same freedoms or choices that mainstream Americans are commonly afforded.

A second limitation is related to the gestalt and existential perspectives underlying the experiential humanistic approaches. These perspectives entail less formal structure and fewer concrete techniques for working with clients. Experiential humanistic approaches are conducive to creative, spontaneous interventions on the part of the therapist. However, a therapist who is less comfortable with divergent thinking and spontaneous experimentation will not be able to effectively adopt an experiential humanistic approach to family therapy. These approaches would not be a good fit for counselors who possess conventional or conservative interpersonal styles.

A final limitation was mentioned earlier in the section on Carl Whitaker's SEFT. More specifically, Whitaker would provide advice using a tongue-in-cheek style and have faith that a family would be capable of deciding whether to adopt his advice. However, we believe that this type of discernment requires considerable intellectual sophistication. This example points to the fact that the experiential humanistic approaches seem to be best suited for clients who are higher functioning with regard to cognitive abilities. Clients who are cognitively lower functioning, less sophisticated, or have limited command of the counselor's native language may find experiential humanistic approaches less understandable. Counselors may need to make accommodations such as incorporating more structured techniques and more specific explanations when working with these three types of clients.

SUMMARY

Although Whitaker, Kempler, and Satir each had their own distinct style, Wetchler and Piercy (1996) noted their approaches were united by seven shared theoretical assumptions. First, all three had a common goal of assisting clients in becoming more open to their emotions and their inner experiences. Second, they all believed that it was important for family therapists to be genuine with their clients. For example, they advocated for therapists to self-disclose and openly share their emotions in sessions. Third, all three believed that spontaneity was a hallmark of a healthy family system. They sought to promote and model creative, right-brain (sometimes referred to as "crazy") thoughts and behaviors in their clients. Fourth, they all were strongly influenced by traditional existential themes, including a belief that anxiety can signal that an individual is facing a meaningful choice or challenge. They also respected and supported their clients' freedom of choice. Fifth, they emphasized the importance of being fully present in the here-and-now. Full contact with one's inner experience and emotions can only take place in the present. Sixth, they encouraged authentic encounters (Buber, 1970) between family members. They believed that these encounters provide necessary conditions for the therapeutic growth of family members. Seventh, Whitaker, Kempler, and Satir all valued global holistic goals over specific reductionistic goals. Consistent with their emphasis on the individual's inner experience, the goals they espoused were more global outcome goals such as an increased sense of competence, greater self-awareness and self-responsibility, and a heightened sense of well-being.

USEFUL WEBSITES

The following websites provide additional information relating to chapter topics.

Carl Whitaker
Augustus Napier discussing symbolic-experiential family therapy
http://www.youtube.com/watch?v=pIyUqozkbIw
A demonstration of Carl Whitaker using symbolic-experiential family therapy
http://www.youtube.com/watch?v=oOzk-iCeC20
Walter Kempler
The Kempler Institute
http://www.kempler.dk
Virginia Satir
The Satir Global Institute
http://satirglobal.org/about-virginia-satir
Satir discussing coping
http://www.youtube.com/watch?v=gW3KShRdKMo
Satir discussing peace and family
http://www.youtube.com/watch?v=VcnW_3Z0Fm4
A large collection of Satir materials
http://www.oac.cdlib.org/findaid/ark:/13030/ft6q2nb44m

REFERENCES

Andreas, S. (1991). *Virginia Satir, the patterns of her magic*. Palo Alto, CA: Science and Behavior Books.

Bermudez, D. (2008). Adapting Virginia Satir techniques to Hispanic families. *Family Journal, 16*, 51–57.

Bitter, J. R. (2013). *Theory and practice of family therapy and counseling*. Belmont, CA: Brooks/Cole.

Buber, M. (1970). *I and thou*. New York, NY: Scribner's.

Callair, P., & McLendon, J. (1994). A Satir model for multicultural peace. In E. Y. Cross, J. H. Katz, F. A. Miller, & E. W. Seashore (Eds.), *The promise of diversity: Over 40 voices discuss strategies for eliminating discrimination in organizations* (pp. 280–286). New York, NY: McGraw-Hill.

Connell, G. M. (1996). Carl Whitaker: In memoriam. *Journal of Marital and Family Therapy, 22*(1), 3–8. doi:10.1111/j.1752-0606.1996.tb00182.x

Davies, E. W. (2011). Warriors, authors and baseball coaches: The meaning of metaphor in theories of family therapy. *Journal of Family Therapy, 35*(1), 66–88. doi:10.1111/j.1467-6427.2011.00537.x

Gale, J. E., & Long, J. K. (1996). Theoretical foundations of family therapy. In F. P. Piercy, D. H. Sprenkle, & J. L. Wetchler (Eds.), *Family therapy sourcebook* (2nd ed., pp. 1–24). New York, NY: Guilford Press.

Gladding, S. T. (2011). *Family therapy: History, theory, and practice*. Upper Saddle River, NJ: Pearson Education.

Goldenberg, H., & Goldenberg, I. (2013). *Family therapy: An overview* (8th ed.). Belmont, CA: Thomson Higher Education.

Haber, R. (2002). Virginia Satir: An integrated, humanistic approach. *Contemporary Family Therapy, 24*(1), 23–34.

Hougaard, E. (1994). The therapeutic alliance: A conceptual analysis. *Institute of Psychology, 35*, 67–85.

Kempler, W. (1965). Experiential family therapy. *International Journal of Group Psychotherapy, 15*(1), 57–71.

Kempler, W. (1967). The experiential therapeutic encounter. *Psychotherapy: Theory. Research and Practice, 1*(4), 166–172.

Kempler, W. (1973). *Principles of gestalt family therapy: A gestalt-experiential handbook*. Oslo, Norway: A.s Joh. Nordahls Terykkeri.

Kempler, W. (1981). *Experiential psychotherapy with families*. New York, NY: Brunner/Mazel.

Kempler, W. (1982a). *Experiential psychotherapy within families*. New York, NY: Taylor & Francis.

Kempler, W. (1982b). Gestalt family therapy. In A. M. Horne & M. M. Ohlsen (Eds.), *Family counseling and therapy*. Itasca, IL: Peacock.

Kempler, W. (1991). *Experimental psychotherapy within families* (2nd ed.). Odense, Denmark: Kempler Institute.

Kempler, W. (2008). *American men and women of science: A biographical directory of today's leaders in physical, biological, and related sciences*. Detroit, MI: Gale.

King, L. (1989). *Women of power*. Berkeley, CA: Celestial Arts.

Laign, J. (1988). Healing human spirits: Master therapist Virginia Satir. *Focus on Chemically Dependent Families*, October/November, 20–31.

McLendon, J. (1998, Fall). A three day Satir workshop in Cairo, Egypt. *Connections Newsletter, 1*(1).

Mishlove, J. (Producer). (1988). *Virginia Satir: Becoming more fully human* (Thinking Allowed Series) [Videotape] Oakland, CA: Thinking Allowed Productions.

Napier, A. Y., & Whitaker, C. A. (1978). *The family crucible*. New York, NY: Harper & Row.

Peluso, P. R., & Vensel, S. (2012). Humanistic couples counseling. In M. B. Scholl, A. S. McGowan, & J. T. Hansen (Eds.), *Humanistic perspectives on contemporary counseling issues* (pp. 117–140). New York, NY: Routledge.

Russell, D. (1990). *A conversation with Virginia Satir*. Davidson Library Special Collections, University of California–Santa Barbara.

Satir, V. (1972). *Peoplemaking*. Mountain View, CA: Science and Behavior.

Satir, V. (1983). *Conjoint family therapy* (3rd ed.). Palo Alto, CA: Science and Behavior.

Satir, V. (1988). *The new peoplemaking*. Palo Alto, CA: Science and Behavior.

Satir, V., & Baldwin, M. (1983). *Satir step by step: A guide to creating change in families*. Palo Alto, CA: Science and Behavior.

Satir, V. M. (1964). *Conjoint family therapy*. Palo Alto, CA: Science and Behavior.

Satir, V. M., & Bitter, J. R. (2000). The therapist and family therapy: Satir's human validation process model. In A. M. Horne (Ed.), *Family counseling and therapy* (3rd ed., pp. 62–101). Ithaca, IL: F. E. Peacock.

Schibbye, A. L. (2005). *Relationher—et dialektisk perspektiv*. Copenhagen, Denmark: Akademisk Forlag.

Spinelli, E. (1998). Existential encounters with the paranormal and uncanny. *Journal of the Society of Existential Analysis*, *9*(2), 2–17.

Stern, S. B. (2004). Challenges to family engagement: What can multisystemic therapy teach family therapist? *Family Process*, *38*(3), 281–286.

Suarez, M. (2013). *About Virginia Satir*. Retrieved from http://satirglobal.org/about-virginia-satir

Wetchler, J. L., & Piercy, F. P. (1996). Experiential family therapies. In F. P. Piercy, D. H. Sprenkle, & J. L. Wetchler (Eds.), *Family therapy sourcebook* (2nd ed., pp. 79–105). New York, NY: Guilford Press.

Whitaker, C. A., & Bumberry, W. M. (1988). *Dancing with the family: A symbolic-experiential approach*. New York, NY: Brunner/Mazel.

Whitaker, C. A., & Keith, D. V. (1981). Symbolic-experiential family therapy. In A. S. Gurman & D. P. Kniskern (Eds.), *Handbook of family therapy* (Vol. 1, pp. 187–225). New York, NY: Brunner/Mazel.

Whitaker, C. A., & Ryan, M. O. (1989). *Midnight musings of a family therapist*. New York, NY: Norton.

Yalom, I. D. (1999). *The Yalom reader: Selections from the work of a master therapist and storyteller*. New York, NY: Basic Books.

Yalom, I. D. (2002). *The gift of therapy: An open letter to a new generation of therapist and their patients*. New York, NY: Harper Perennial.

CHAPTER 8

Bowenian Family Systems Theory: Approaches and Applications

Dohee Kim-Appel
Ursuline College

Jonathan K. Appel
Tiffin University

The Bowen family systems theory (Bowen, 1976, 1978) is one of the most comprehensive explanations for the development of psychological problems from a systemic and multigenerational perspective (Gurman & Kniskern, 1991; Nichols & Schwartz, 2001). Bowen developed his theory over a lifetime of research on the family as an emotional unit (Gilbert, 1992). Bowen hypothesized that all human emotional problems occur along a single continuum of functioning (Bowen, 1976, 1978). Bowen believed that families varied on a continuum from emotional fusion to differentiation. Optimal family development is thought to take place when family members are relatively differentiated, anxiety is low, and parents are in good emotional contact with their own families of origin. Emotional attachment between spouses often is similar to attachments seen in families of origin. Family development is a process of expansion, contraction, and realignment that supports entry, exit, and development of family members (Nichols & Schwartz, 2001).

The major constructs of Bowen family system theory are: (a) differentiation of self, (b) nuclear family emotional process, (c) multigenerational transmission process, (d) family projection process, (e) interlocking triangles, (f) emotional cutoff, (g) sibling position, and (h) societal emotional process (Bowen, 1976, 1978; Hare, Canada, & Lim, 1998; Kerr, 1984). These concepts not only relate to the constructs of an individual organism's emotional/psychological system but also to the family's emotional/psychological system. This chapter will discuss the conceptual basis for Bowenian systems theory as well as its applications.

BACKGROUND

Biologist Ludwig von Bertalanffy (1950) proposed that the biological concept of a system was a useful framework for studying the phenomena of all sciences. It was at this time the concept of general systems theory was born.

General Systems Theory

General systems theory or systems theory is a conceptual framework that moves beyond the reductionistic and mechanistic tradition in science to focus on linear cause-and-effect relationships. Systems theory frames explanations in terms of wholeness, self-organization, relationships, and interactions between parts. Pattern recognition and events in the environmental context are key notions (Hanson, 1995).

General systems theory has also been used by numerous professional disciples in varying forms within the latter half of the 20th century. An example of this can be seen in the development of the biopsychosocial model in medicine. This model attempts to provide a comprehensive systems-oriented basis for integrating factors in health and illness that range from the molecular-biological to the sociocultural domain (Engels, 1980). Recent developments in this model have even expanded the levels to include the transpersonal/spiritual domain (Sulmasy, 2002). The acceptance of the biopsychosocial model has been slow to displace the contrasting biotechnical model of medicine and psychiatry. This model views illness in a linear fashion—as a mechanistic breakdown of the body "machine." Writers have pointed out that the psychological and emotional functioning can be viewed as a system with roots in biology and embryology, wherein the fertilized egg repeatedly divides into cells that perform different tasks as a means to achieve balance of function, but can be greatly impacted by environmental systems (Papero, 1990).

Systems theory has also been utilized by experts and researchers in the fields of the behavioral sciences (Appel & Kim-Appel, 2010). Systems theory frames explanations in the general principles of wholeness, organization, relationships, reciprocity, and mutual causation. The focus is on the identification of interacting variables and pattern recognition. In this view, identity, personality organization, and mental health symptoms emerge out of a jointly active and dynamic process. Models with these views describe holistic epistemologies that attempt to reflect this complex ontology and thereby avoid reductionism.

General systems theory has been enthusiastically embraced by the field of family therapy and counseling and has offered a unique vantage point from which one can view human experience and behavior. This perspective is embedded within systems theory, which places emphasis on contextual frames of reference, interaction, and the notion of subsystems influencing larger systems of organization. Family systems theory has contributed greatly to the practice of counseling and psychotherapy by (a) identifying processes that can contribute to individual and family problems, and by (b) offering specific interventions to change these processes, thereby improving the family's functioning. In this theory, families are conceptualized as groups/systems of interdependent individuals.

The Family Systems View

The family systems view goes beyond static concepts to take account of the temporal quality of life and the omnipresence of change. Among the key assumptions of this theory that are particularly relevant to family systems are wholeness, feedback, equifinality, and circular causality (Watzlawick, Beavin, & Jackson, 1967). Because systems behave as wholes, change in any one part will cause change in other parts and throughout the entire system. Open systems are regulated by feedback loops or inputs from family members and from the environment. Negative feedback contributes homeostasis by the process of self-regulation and plays an important role in maintaining the stability of relationships. It reduces the tendency toward deviation from the family norms. Positive feedback leads to change when it is used by the family system to amplify a pattern. For learning and growth to occur, families must incorporate positive feedback. All families together must use both forms of feedback to some degree in order to adapt while maintaining their equilibrium in the face of developmental and environmental stresses (Goldenberg & Goldenberg, 1991; Simon, Stierlin, & Wynne, 1985; Watzlawick et al., 1967). *Equifinality* means that the same result may be reached from different beginnings (von Bertalanffy, 1969). In open systems, different initial conditions may lead to the same final result. Family systems theory also recognizes the concept of circular causality. This asserts that systems are constantly modified by recursive circular feedback from multiple sources within and outside of the system; thus, there is no simple linear cause and effect.

BOWEN'S FAMILY SYSTEMS THEORY

Murray Bowen's family systems theory (1966, 1976, 1978) evolved from psychoanalytic theory and has been recognized as one of the most carefully elaborated and comprehensive views of human behavior and its problems of any of the approaches in family systems theories (Anderson & Sabatelli, 1990; Bregman, 1993; Green, 2000; Harvey, Curry, & Bray, 1991; Innes, 1996; Larson & Wilson, 1998; Nichols & Schwartz, 2001; Skowron & Friedlander, 1998; Tuason & Friedlander, 2000). The major assumption of Bowenian family systems theory is that individuals, families, and society in general are all grounded in natural systems theory, which draws from biological and natural sciences and is based on the principles of self-organization, repetition, and formation of patterns (Bowen, 1978). The family system is viewed as a natural system in which interrelationships between family members in the current and past generational family system follow the repetitive patterns of influence within the established emotional system of the family (Kerr & Bowen, 1988; Wetchler & Piercy, 1996).

Bowen, one of the pioneers in the field of family therapy/counseling, contends that the mental health of an individual is strongly influenced by one's family of origin. Bowen's theory moved beyond a simple reductionistic behavioral theory to a complex relationship theory that addresses cognition as well as interpersonal processes (Bowen, 1978). This emphasis on thinking does not deny emotions but acknowledges the importance of self-regulation in the process of differentiation (Friedman, 1991). This is the core goal underlying the Bowenian concept of the differentiation of self. To be self-differentiated, one needs to have the ability to remain one's own person under the pressure of group influences, especially in the face of the intense influences of family life (Bowen, 1978). The Bowenian model stresses the thoughts and feelings of each family member, as well as the larger contextual network of family relationships that shape the lives of the family. Bowen (1978) indicated that there is a natural desire for togetherness as well as the need for separation. Differentiation is achieved when a person can maintain selfhood yet remain part of the family unit. It means that a person has the ability to maintain an emotional connection with significant others while not losing the true integrity of self (Bregman, 1993).

MAJOR CONSTRUCTS

Bowen family systems theory is a theory of behavior that views the family as a basic emotional unit. Bowen family systems theory employs the following major constructs to describe the complex interactions in the unit.

Differentiation of Self

Differentiation of self is one of the most fundamental concepts in Bowen's family systems theory. Differentiation is defined by Bowen as an instinctually rooted life force that "propels each human to become an emotionally separate person with the ability to think, feel and act for self" (Kerr & Bowen, 1988, p. 95). Differentiation is reflected primarily in the system's interactional patterns for maintaining interpersonal distance, with a tolerance for both individuality and intimacy (Farley, 1979; Kantor & Lehr, 1975). This tolerance means balancing (a) emotional and intellectual functioning and (b) intimacy and autonomy in relationships (Bowen, 1976, 1978). Well-differentiated individuals recognize realistic dependence on others in their relationships, but can stay calm and clearheaded enough in the face of conflict or criticism. An example would be a couple recognizing they can agree to disagree about a key parenting issue without it interrupting an important romantic date.

In a family setting, a differentiated individual is regarded as one who has the courage to define self. According to Bowen, these individuals' energies go to changing one's self rather than telling others what to do. These individuals are also aware and respectful of others' opinions and can modify their own opinions accordingly (Innes, 1996). An example of this could be a new parent nondefensively taking parenting advice from his or her own parents. Bowenian theory (Bowen, 1978) describes that most people struggle to separate emotionally from their families of origin and establish individuality (Friedman, 1991). Bowen related this differentiation process to an individual's ability to adapt to life's challenges and reach personal goals (Gilbert, 1992). Bowen (1976, 1978) thought that differentiation was the state of acceptance of who one was, whatever one's values, beliefs, and actions might be. This could mean learning to realistically accept one's flaws and shortcomings as one goes through life. Differentiation also means acting at a rational level when one needs to, and having the capacity for emotionally influenced decision making when desired (Reid & Anderson, 1992). An example of this could be listening to one's feelings about not maintaining a status quo in a relationship that has social benefit but has grown exceedingly destructive. Bray, Harvey, and Williamson (1987) referred to differentiation as a process, which occurs both within the person and external to the person. The process within the person is evidenced by the individual valuing personal decisions and being willing to live with the consequences of those decisions (Reid & Anderson, 1992).

Mental health and adjustment are also seen as functions of one's differentiation. Differentiation is the extent to which one's emotional and intellectual systems are distinguishable (Bowen, 1978). According to Bowen, the more autonomous one's intellect is from automatic emotional forces within the family, the more differentiated one is. Higher levels of differentiation mean better mental health and ego development and strength, and are associated with healthy empowerment in thinking and behavior (including better decision making). This also means that one's emotional boundary is not "fused" with other family members. The concept of boundaries is important in family therapy and can be defined as the invisible lines of demarcation in a family (Piercy & Sprenkle, 1986). Boundaries may be defined, strengthened, loosened, or changed as a result of structural family therapy. Boundaries can range from rigid (extreme separateness) to diffuse (extreme togetherness). Ideally, for optimal functioning, boundaries are clear or distinguishable. An example of rigid boundaries in a family would be family members living separately within the same household. An example of diffuse boundaries in a family would be parents acting as peers to their children. Some clear boundary examples would be to establish rules that include knocking on a door before entering another family member's bedroom or asking permission before borrowing someone's personal items.

According to Bowen (1976, 1978), at the intrapsychic level, differentiation of self is the ability to distinguish thoughts from feelings and to be able to choose between being guided by one's intellect or one's emotions. Greater differentiation has been associated with a greater ability to operate equally well within the emotional or rational dimensions while maintaining autonomy within intimate relationships (Kerr & Bowen, 1988). Poorly differentiated individuals tend to be emotionally needy and highly reactive to others, and are unable to maintain long-term relationships (Kerr & Bowen, 1988).

Within the interpersonal level, differentiation refers to the ability to experience intimacy in relationships while maintaining a healthy independence from others. More differentiated persons are capable of taking the "I-position" in relationships, which means they are able to adhere to a stable, clearly defined sense of self and are less likely to bend to the pressure of others (Nichols, 1987; Skowron, 2000; Skowron & Dendy, 2004; Skowron & Friedlander, 1998). The I-position helps family members say how they think or feel instead of just focusing on what others are doing. This can be an important way to break cycles of reactivity in families. For example, there is a difference when a person states "I wish you could help me more with the chores" versus "You never help me with the chores."

Differentiation of self allows flexible boundaries in relationships, permitting emotional intimacy without fear of engulfment or loss of self (emotional fusion) or the need to detach too much (emotional cutoff). Greater differentiation has been associated with better mental health and relational adjustment (Bray, Williamson, & Malone, 1984; Carpenter, 1990; Cebik, 1988; Craddock, 1983; Fine, 1988; Fleming & Anderson, 1986; Maynard, 1997; Papero, 2000; Skowron, 2000; Skowron, Holmes, & Sabatelli, 2003). On the other hand, highly fused individuals (less differentiated) remained emotionally stuck in the position they occupied in their families of origin throughout their life span (Kerr & Bowen, 1988). Reid and Anderson (1992) theorized that individuals poorly differentiated from their family of origin would have difficulty in attaining a meaningful and coherent life. For example, a lonely, disconnected, middle-aged person who, as the fourth of five children, was often the quiet, ignored, and emotionally isolated child in the corner whose opinions were discounted, has a similar lack of "I-stance" in his/her work and community by not taking a stand, not sharing opinions, allowing people to talk over him/her, and by deferring to others who must have the right answers. What other examples can you think of from your own life of possible fusion and resulting stuckness?

Bowen (1976, 1978) believed that healthy, more differentiated individuals were capable of initiating family change under stress, whereas less differentiated individuals suffer chronic anxiety within stuck families (Carpenter, 1990; Kerr & Bowen, 1988; Skowron & Friedlander, 1988; Skowron, Wester, & Azen, 2004). Bowen (1976, 1978) also theorized that poorly differentiated individuals became dysfunctional under stress and easily evidenced psychological and physical symptoms such as anxiety, somatization, depression, alcoholism, and psychoticism. This theory is illustrated in Figure 8.1. Level of differentiation can be viewed along a continuum of togetherness and individuality (Horne & Hicks, 2002). At the lower levels of differentiation (nearer to zero), one takes on more rigid characteristics within relationships, such as total fusion or total cutoff, and greater psychological distress is also present. This may not be related to actual physical proximity. Members of families may be living many miles away but still be emotionally fused. Furthermore, families living together can be completely disconnected from one another. Both situations could likely be measured as poor differentiation and result in disturbance. However, at the higher levels of differentiation (nearer 100), one would exhibit an absence of pathology, better psychological well-being, and better psychosocial adjustment. Also, individuals at this level would develop healthier emotional intimacy, healthier relationships, and be more likely to maintain healthy emotionality as compared to those at the lower end of the differentiation continuum.

Bowenian theory asserts that the level of differentiation is inversely related to levels of anxiety and, therefore, anxiety is a key mediational variable of a dysfunctional family dynamic (Larson & Wilson, 1998). Individuals with higher levels of differentiation experience less chronic anxiety and are therefore more adaptive to stress (Maynard, 1997). According to Williamson (1982) and Nichols (1984), differentiation of self, which begins as a personal and individual process, is the vehicle of transforming relationships and the entire family system over time.

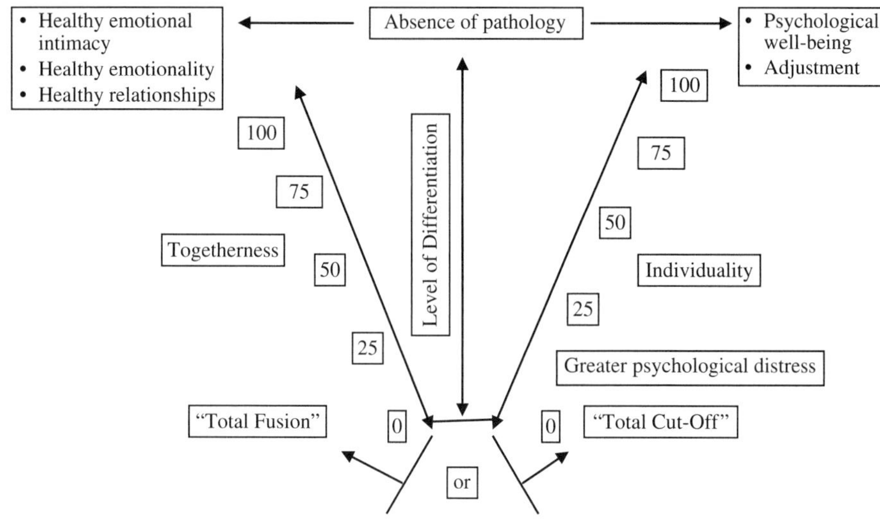

Figure 8.1 The differentiation of self continuum.
Source: Adapted from Horne and Hicks (2002).

Murray Bowen's (1976, 1978) extensive observation of the human family functioning in structured and unstructured settings rests on the concept of differentiation of self (Papero, 2000). Bowen's (1976, 1978) differentiation of self is defined as an emotional detachment or the ability to maintain objectivity by separating affect from cognition (Griffin & Greene, 1999). When referring to well-differentiated families, the construct of differentiation would indicate an age-appropriate balance of familial connectedness and personal autonomy for individual members and their interpersonal transactions. According to Papero (2000), well-differentiated individuals make their decisions and actions based on well-developed sets of internal beliefs and principles that they have thought about carefully and tested in real situations in their lives. Their behaviors, therefore, tolerate differences in others without intense reactive pressure, and thus they can continue to make their decisions and accept responsibility for the outcomes without blaming others, seeing themselves as victims, or being under the control of others. According to Bowen (1976, 1978), highly differentiated individuals and families are thought to demonstrate better psychological adjustment. These individuals are expected to be more satisfied in relationships, better problem solvers, and less anxious (Bray et al., 1984; Carpenter, 1990; Cebik, 1988; Craddock, 1983; Fine, 1988; Fleming & Anderson, 1986; Maynard, 1997; Skowron, 2000). These are the families that enjoy being together, give each other space, and support one another.

At the other end of the continuum, poorly differentiated families or individuals would display a lack of stability, low tolerance for individuality, poor intimacy among family members, anxiety, and rigid behaviors (Anderson & Sabatelli, 1990; Bowen, 1978; Kerr, 1984; Kerr & Bowen, 1988; Stierlin, 1981). Poorly differentiated individuals are also easily overwhelmed by emotionality in their family relationships and tend to engage in fusion or emotional cutoff (Kerr & Bowen, 1988). Highly fused individuals remain emotionally stuck in the position they occupied in their families of origin. This poor adjustment is seen as being repeated in successive generations of families (intergenerational transmission) (Harvey et al., 1991).

Research on Differentiation of Self

It is possible that individuals poorly differentiated from their family of origin would have difficulty in attaining meaningful and coherent lives across the life span (Reid & Anderson, 1992). One would expect poorly differentiated individuals to have greater psychological distress, more problematic relationships, and to show poor psychological adjustment even into later years. Given the centrality of the differentiation of self, it is no surprise that most of the research has focused on this construct.

Bray et al. (1987) indicated that an individual's level of differentiation was a predictor of psychological symptom development, and individuals with a higher level of differentiation produced less life stress in their interpersonal relationships.

Larson and Wilson (1998) researched whether the Bowenian concept of differentiation could be used to explain career decision-making problems in young adults. The authors used a clustered sample of 1,006 college students. They found that the dynamics of fused families, such as emotional dependence and lack of autonomy (which limits independent thinking and acting), were directly related to anxiety. Anxiety was then found to be related to career decision problems. The lack of self-identity and the uncertainty of the future were also found to be related to an external locus of control that contributed to career decision problems. It was concluded that differentiation of self was a useful concept in the investigation of career-related anxiety.

Elieson and Rubin (2001) investigated the relationship between the level of differentiation of self among a clinically depressed sample, a nonpsychiatric sample of students, and Internet users. Findings from this study indicated that clinically depressed individuals showed lower levels of differentiation of self than the student sample. Internet users were found to have the lowest levels of differentiation of self. Within the sample of Internet users, females indicated lower levels of differentiation than males. These results suggest some support for the relationship between differentiation level and depression.

Greene, Hamilton, and Rolling (1986) investigated the relationship between the differentiation of self scale (DOSS) score and 20 various psychiatric diagnoses combined into six general categories. This study utilized 82 inpatients, 28 discharged outpatients from a mental health unit of a hospital, and 61 nonclinical individuals. The authors found that the nonclinical individuals were significantly more highly differentiated than both the inpatients and the discharged outpatients. Even though differences on the DOSS scores were not statistically significant, discharged outpatients scored higher on the DOSS than did inpatients. Greene et al. (1986) concluded that the results of this study supported Bowen's hypothesis on the relationship between differentiation and psychological adjustment (e.g., stress, anxiety).

Maynard (1997) investigated offspring from alcoholic families of origin and nonalcoholic families to explore the relationship of differentiation of self and a measurement of trait anxiety. The results of Maynard's study supported Bowen's (1978) idea of alcoholic families as showing more anxiety among family members. Participants from alcoholic families reported higher levels of state and trait anxiety and lower levels of differentiation of self. Maynard (1997) recommended that the treatment of individuals from an alcoholic family needed to relieve anxiety and support the goal of increasing the level of differentiation of self in the treatment of alcoholism.

Bohlander (1999) examined the relationship of need fulfillment, differentiation of self, and married men's psychological well-being. The author found that differentiation of self, interactional emotional need fulfillment, and sexual need fulfillment exhibited low to moderate linear relationships with psychological well-being. A significant correlational relationship was found between sexual and interactional emotional need fulfillment.

Skowron and Friedlander (1998) presented a study to validate the differentiation of self inventory (DSI). The authors found that higher levels of differentiation of self were associated with lower symptomatic distress. Higher emotional cutoff and reactivity were found to be associated with higher symptomatic distress. It was also found that higher differentiation of self and lower emotional cutoff were also associated with greater marital satisfaction. According to Charles (2001), Skowron and Friedlander succeeded in creating a reliable and valid scale, which tests such core Bowenian concepts as differentiation of self and emotional cutoff. Charles also indicated that the use of large and ethnically diverse samples was a strength of this study. However, Charles (2001) pointed out that the use of a nonrandomized sample and the ratio of subjects (two women for every man) might be a weakness of this study.

Differentiation Studies With Couples Kear (1978) investigated the relationship between differentiation of self and marital attraction and satisfaction using a descriptive and correlational design. A volunteer sample of 30 married couples were found to be more similar in their differentiation of self than randomly paired nonmarried couples within the sample.

Snyder and Smith (1986) found "disruption in the family of origin" was one of the most important characteristics in producing distressed couple types (p. 141). It can be assumed that an individual who has not left home emotionally and who still looks toward family of origin for life's direction may not "own" his or her life or be able to take responsibility for it (Reid & Anderson, 1992). Individuals who remain in satisfying interdependent contact with their families of origin are more likely to establish more satisfying marriages and be more effective problem solvers (Bowen, 1976, 1978).

Day, St. Clair, and Marshall (1997) investigated Bowen's (1978) hypothesis that people marry individuals with similar levels of differentiation of self. They combined Monte Carlo sampling techniques and observational methods of assessing couple similarity. Their research findings did not support Bowen's assertion that people choose spouses at the same level of differentiation of self. The level of individual spousal intimacy was the only evidence of couple similarity.

Bayer and Day (1995) also sought to test the level of differentiation in couples and used an empirical couple typology that measured different facets of differentiation. Results of this study suggested that the level of differentiation was similar and could be a useful dimension in the conceptualization of couple types.

Griffin and Apostal (1993) examined 20 married couples who received training in relationship enhancement skills. These authors wanted to see whether there was a relationship between the effectiveness of the relationship enhancement program in increasing differentiation of self, as well as improvement in basic individual functioning. These authors also examined the relationship between anxiety and differentiation. Results of this study showed significant increases in the level of differentiation of self as well as in basic levels of functioning after the relationship enhancement skill training. There was also a significant increase in the quality of relationships for the sample and a significant negative relationship between differentiation of self and anxiety. These authors suggested basic differentiation could be increased if relationship training increased functioning of self in context of others, which suggests a necessary balance must take place in the self as well as in the larger system.

Skowron (2000) investigated Bowen's (1978) theoretical propositions about the relationship between differentiation of self and the quality of the marital relationship. This research used the DSI and the dyadic adjustment scale (DAS). Results of this study confirmed that 74% of the variance in husband marital adjustment scores and 61% of the variance in wife marital adjustment scores was accounted for by couples' levels of differentiation. Couples who were less reactive, cutoff, or fused with others were better able to take I-positions in relationships and experienced the greatest levels of marital satisfaction, whereas those with less differentiated selves indicated greater marital distress.

Murphy (1999) investigated the relationship between the concept of differentiation of self and marital adjustment. This study's sample was 32 married Asian American couples. Murphy (1999) found the level of differentiation was correlated with marital adjustment. Level of acculturation was also found not to significantly impact the relationship between the level of differentiation and marital adjustment. These results empirically supported that Bowen's (1978) differentiation of self has a similar association with relationship adjustment/satisfaction across cultural lines.

Measurement/Operationalizing of the Differentiation of Self Construct

In order to evaluate/measure the Bowenian concept of differentiation, it has been operationalized in the form of several self-report instruments. Bowen's scale of differentiation (1978) described differences in the functioning of a relationship system based on the degree of emotional separation. Kear (1978) developed the DOSS, which conceptualized differentiation of self using three factors:

(1) separation of thinking and feeling systems, (2) emotional maturity, and (3) emotional autonomy. Unfortunately, construct validity studies of DOSS showed methodological weaknesses, lack of conceptual consistency, ambiguity, and lack of information about sampling, as well as inadequate sample size to confirm a valid and reliable measure of differentiation of self. Also, the DOSS tested only the interpersonal components of differentiation (Skowron & Friedlander, 1998).

Haber (1993) developed the level of differentiation of self scale (LDSS) focusing on the concepts of emotional maturity and emotional dependency. Haber believed that these two factors reflected "Bowen's description of intellectual and emotional system functioning" (Bohlander, 1995, p. 179). However, methodological flaws of the overall findings were sufficient to impede the generalizability of this scale to Bowen's concept of differentiation of self (Griffin & Apostal, 1993).

Bray et al. (1984) developed the personal authority in the family system questionnaire (PAFSQ). These authors included items about the concept of current relationships and behaviors such as individuation, fusion, triangulation, intimacy, personal authority, and intergenerational intimidation. However, they did not address the concept of emotional cutoff, which can occur when adults are faced with the developmental psychosocial task of terminating the intergenerational hierarchical power boundary between individuals and their older parents (Lawson, Gaushell, & Karst, 1993). Poorly differentiated individuals would be unable to successfully complete this development task and would likely be highly emotionally reactive or emotionally disengaged.

Even though all these instruments (DOSS, LDSS, and PAFSQ) contributed important information to the field of marriage and family therapy, they did not completely operationalize the range of interpersonal and intrapsychic components of the differentiation construct (Skowron & Friedlander, 1998).

Hovestadt, Anderson, Piercy, Cochran, and Fine (1985) developed the family-of-origin scale (FOS). The FOS provides adults' past perceptions of their family-of-origin relationships or adolescents' current perceptions of relations with family. A weakness of the FOS is that it focuses only on past relationships with family members with adults. McCollum (1991) developed the emotional cutoff scale (ECS), which measures an individual's emotional attachment to each parent by the degree of cutoff in the relationship (disengagement). However, this instrument only focuses on relationships with parents and did not test the level of differentiation in other relationships.

Skowron and Friedlander (1998), in reviewing previous instruments used for measuring differentiation of self, noted the "methodological limitations," including failure of instruments to include both the "intrapsychic and interpersonal" aspects in differentiation of self (p. 236). In response, Skowron and Friedlander (1998) developed the DSI, which conceptualizes Bowen's differentiation of self as a multidimensional construct. The DSI measures the level of differentiation of self in adults by focusing on their significant relationships, including both intrapsychic and interpersonal variables (thinking–feeling and separateness–togetherness dimensions). The DSI was designed to estimate four distinct aspects of differentiation of self in adults: (1) emotional reactivity (ER), (2) taking the

I-position (IP), (3) emotional cutoff (EC), and (4) fusion with others (FO). The DSI suggests patterns of behavior characteristic of an integrated and differentiated self, which includes increased capacity for influencing one's destiny in life and choosing personal health and well-being in a systemic or holistic sense (Bowen, 1978; Skowron & Friedlander, 1998). Skowron (2000) noted a weakness in the FO subscale, which was reworked for a revised DSI-R scale (Skowron & Schmitt, 2003). The revised DSI-R scale has been confirmed as a psychometrically sound measure of the differentiation of self construct (Jankowski & Hooper, 2012).

Nuclear Family Emotional Process

Bowen introduced the concept of an *undifferentiated family ego mass*, derived from psychoanalysis, to convey the idea of a family that is emotionally "stuck together" in which "a conglomerate emotional oneness . . . exists in all levels of intensity" (Goldenberg & Goldenberg, 1991, p. 171).

According to Bowen, if a nuclear family emotional system is too emotionally fused, the systems will become unstable and members will seek various ways to reduce tension and maintain stability. Members may turn to such means as alcohol, drugs, and/or other symptom development. The greater the nuclear family's fusion, the greater will be the likelihood of anxiety and potential instability, and the greater will be the family's tendency to seek resolution through fighting, distancing, the underfunctioning of one partner, or the acting out of a child (Gilbert, 2006). Undifferentiated individuals experience difficulty managing anxiety and stress. Low levels of differentiation coupled with stress may also increase the emotional fusion between spouses (see Sidebar 8.1).

SIDEBAR 8.1

Emotional fusion is unstable and it tends to produce:

- Overt marital conflict
- Reactive emotional distance
- Physical or emotional symptoms (usually the more-accommodating partner)
- Projection of problems on to children

The nuclear family emotional process describes the patterns of emotional functioning in a single generation. These emotional patterns can also foster and maintain a dysfunctional pattern (steadily unstable) over time, as system anxiety can be passed on to other generations.

Multigenerational Transmission Process

The *multigenerational transmission process* refers to the transmission of family dynamics through projection. This represents the nature and degree of intensity in emotional responses that are passed down from generation to generation (Friedman, 1991). Interactional patterns are transferred from one generation to another. Attitudes, values, beliefs, behaviors, and patterns of interaction are passed along from parents to children over many lifetimes; therefore, certain behaviors can exist within a family through multiple generations. The classic example is unresolved anger toward one's own parents for impulsive angry outbursts and other violent behavior. This abusive behavior is then replicated with one's own children.

Family Projection Process

Projection is when one person attributes to someone else his or her unacceptable thoughts and feelings. Parental projection is a major source for the transmission of family anxiety. Levels of differentiation are affected through generations based on levels of differentiation of partners as they marry. When parents are unable to work through stress or anxiety or other intense emotions, an emotional fusion occurs with parents, projecting the resulting anxiety on to the children. This is classified as the *family projection process*. The child who is the most emotionally attached to parents is likely to be the object of parental projection and, as a result, will have lower levels of differentiation (Bowen, 1978). Bowen also indicates that the lower the level of differentiation of the parents, the more they will rely on the projection process to stabilize the system. This will also increase the likelihood that several children will be emotionally impaired (Goldenberg & Goldenberg, 1991).

Intergenerational Transmission Process Research

Bowenian theory postulates that individual and family functioning are similar across generations. Bowen notes, "Multigenerational emotional process . . . includes emotions, feelings, and subjectively determined attitudes, values, and beliefs that are transmitted from one generation to the next" (Kerr & Bowen, 1988, p. 224). But, based on other dynamics, such as triangulation, family sibling position, and emotional fusion/cutoff, the results can vary among individual members. Thus, it is not surprising that although general research evidence shows that individual and family processes are transmitted, the research is also inconsistent (Miller, Anderson, & Keala, 2004). In a direct test of the multigenerational transmission process, Rosen, Bartle-Haring, and Stith (2001) found that differentiation had a significant mediating role on the transmission process of violence across a generation. Tuason and Friedlander (2000) also investigated whether parents' levels of differentiation predicted those of their children. This study tested several of Bowen's propositions (Bowen, 1978; Kerr & Bowen, 1988) including his most central construct of differentiation of self, but also tested the intergenerational transmission process. Bowen's theory (1978) stated that healthier persons may be able to emotionally and physically separate themselves from their family of origin. However, in some unhealthy families, dysfunctional interactional patterns over many generations are likely to impact current family members and their offspring (Charles, 2001; Sharf, 1996). Tuason and Friedlander (2000) compared a Philippine sample with a U.S. sample, both on the full scale and the subscales of the DSI. Results indicated a parent's level of differentiation did not predict the children's level. However, compared with the U.S. sample, the Philippine sample reported less emotional reactivity, higher I-position functioning, and greater emotional cutoff. These findings suggested that differentiation of self might be uniquely defined in different cultures. Overall, although the findings suggested that the construct of differentiation of self may be a meaningful one in the Philippine culture, the lack of support for the intergenerational hypotheses gave some doubt to Bowen's propositions of human universality about the transmission of differentiation and psychopathology across generations (Tuason & Friedlander, 2000).

Triangles

The concepts of triangles and triangulation are also critical ideas in Bowenian family counseling/therapy. *Triangulation* is the formation of a three-person system, an emotional configuration that is considered the building block of the family system. According to Bowen (1978), this is the smallest stable relationship pattern. The concept of the triangle suggests that when a two-party system becomes unstable because of anxiety, a third person is involved to stabilize them. Diagram A in Figure 8.2 represents an example of a parent under stress drawing an offspring in to create a triangle. This is in contrast to a healthier configuration in diagram B.

All emotionally significant relationships are shadowed by third parties, including relatives, friends, objects, work, and memories. Relationships are dynamic; there are cycles of closeness of distance (see Figure 8.3 for variations of emotional relationships). Triangles are also likely to develop during times of distance. In relationships, the partner who experiences the most distress will often connect with someone else as a way to gain an ally. Sometimes, significant others offer support when they sense anxiety or conflict. The process and structure of triangulation lets off steam, but it also holds conflict in place, remaining unresolved. "Unburdening yourself to a friend will make you feel better. It will also lessen the likelihood that you'll engage the problem at its source" (Nichols & Schwartz, 2001, p. 141). More

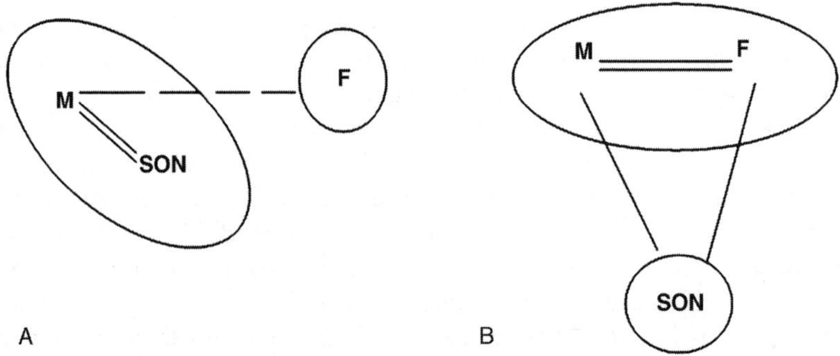

Figure 8.2 Example of triangulation.

Although all families to some extent are described by the emotional bond between the two parents, the **emotional relationship** component can be used to describe the emotional bond between any two individuals in the genealogy tree.

Cutoff / Estranged	A cutoff relationship in which the two individuals have no contact at all, characterized by extreme disengagement and emotional intensity.
Indifferent / Apathetic	An apathetic relationship in which one or both individuals are indifferent to the other.
Distant / Poor	A distant relationship between two individuals. Communication is very limited, usually because of lifestyle differences.
Plain / Normal	A normal relationship. This is not very useful, except to highlight a normal relationship among massive dysfunctional relationships.
Friendship / Close	A close relationship between two individuals who are friends and share secrets.
Intimacy / Very Close	An intimate relationship in which communication is open, uncensored, and without secrets.
Hostile / Conflictual	A hostile relationship in which two individuals have conflicts and argue on major issues.

Figure 8.3 Emotional relationships.

than three people will form into a series of interlocking triangles. Even though triangulation can often help reduce anxiety in a marital relationship or a dyad, Bowenian theory asserts it would increase anxiety in a third person, very often a child within a family system (Bowen, 1978).

Triangulation Research

Miller et al. (2004), in a review of the research, noted the studies that have tested Bowen's concept of triangulation. It is observed that if Bowen's view of triangulation is correct, there should be a significant positive relationship between anxiety and triangulation. There are numerous studies that demonstrate a positive relationship between triangulation and marital distress (Gehring & Marti, 1993; Johnson & Nelson, 1998; West, Hosie, & Zarski, 1987; Wood et al., 1989). Several studies have also assessed the proposed mechanism of parental triangulation increasing the anxiety or distress in an offspring. Larson and Wilson (1998) and Benson, Larson, Wilson, and Demo (1993), in large sample studies, found that intergenerational transmission triangulation was not a significant predictor of anxiety in undergraduates. However, there are several other studies that found a connection between triangulation and negative physical, social, and emotional outcomes (Benson et al., 1993; Protinsky & Gilkey, 1996; Wang & Crane, 2001; West, Zarksi, & Harvill, 1986; Wood et al., 1989).

Emotional Cutoff

Emotional cutoff is a person's attempt to emotionally distance him- or herself from certain members of the family or from the entire family. Although many people have some degree of unresolved emotional attachment to their parents, there are a number of ways to deal with it. Emotional cutoff represents a person's inability to directly resolve issues of emotional fusion, which in turn prevents one from forming a unique identity or satisfying relationships with others. Level of cutoff is influenced by degree of differentiation. The cutoff is an attempt to distance oneself from the emotional field by avoiding contact (Gilbert, 2006). The emotionally cutoff person finds intimacy profoundly threatening.

Sibling Position

Children develop certain fixed personality characteristics based on sibling position in their families. Bowen also believed that family functioning and other variables, such as birth order, influenced roles one had in the family (Gilbert, 2006). Bowen believed that personality characteristics are influenced by sibling position. For instance, older children often are required to be more responsible or have adult roles thrust on them. Sibling conflict may often be the result of triangular relationships (e.g., coalitions with parents can foster sibling antagonism). Bowenian family systems theory suggests that birth order originally influences the triangles found in families. Bowen's theory also asserts that sibling position is a means to assess the level of differentiation, which is transmitted through the multigenerational projection process. Sibling roles, personality patterns, and conflict patterns can be the mirror of unresolved past generational relational configurations. Knowledge of general characteristics plus specific knowledge of a particular family are helpful in predicting what part a child will play in the family emotional system and in predicting family patterns in the next generation.

Sibling Position Research

This aspect of Bowenian family systems theory asserts that sibling position in the family has a great impact on emotional processes. This idea was an expansion of Toman's personality theory, which predicts that family constellation impacts emotional development and personality (Toman, 1976). Miller et al. (2004) note that only two studies attempted to validate Toman's theory directly, with neither supporting his birth order idea. No direct research has been done to date on Bowen's particular view of sibling position. Some do offer indirect support for the notion of sibling position based on the research that supports birth order influencing personality, particularly for first-born children (Eckstein, 2000; Watkins, 1992).

Societal Emotional Process

According to Bowenian family systems theory, emotional processes in families are also influenced by emotional processes in society (and vice versa) (Gilbert, 2006). This process was called *societal emotional process* and includes the social forces of sexism, racism, and poverty. These societal forces can fundamentally influence how families interact with each other. Bowen stated that society is more or less anxious itself, and when there is more anxiety in all people, there is more chaos and institutional breakdown. He originally labeled this process *societal regression* (Bowen, 1978). Bowen's view was that the same processes that occur in a family (differentiation, fusion, cutoff, triangulation, projection, process, etc.) also occur at higher levels of organization, including society as a whole. Thus, a society (or even an agency) could be poorly differentiated, which would result in highly volatile and anxious behaviors from its hierarchy (governance) to its organizational members. The emotional process in society also influences the emotional process in families, like a background influence affecting all families. No direct research has been done on this theoretical construct, but it remains an intriguing idea. An example of a possible societal emotional process could be seen in the increase in crime in the United States in the 1970s and the 1980s. This resulted in emotionally reactive policies of "getting tough on crime," in which the government and the criminal justice system locked up more individuals for longer periods of time (often replacing rehabilitation efforts). This, in turn, contributed to an even further fragmentation of vulnerable families. One also only has to casually view the U.S. governmental reactive need for security functioning in a post-9/11 world to find the intuitive appeal to this idea. What other examples can you identify?

Bowenian Systems Therapy Goals

Bowenian family systems theory offers a unique treatment approach for working with individuals and families in need. The theory will now be examined as a means to offer assessment and counseling strategies and techniques for intervention. A family versus an individual approach and the emotional being of the counselor will also be examined. In the Bowenian model, the therapeutic role is that of a coach or supervisor. Clinical focus is on phenomenology rather than interpretation of others' motivations (Bowen, 1978). The counselor takes on a more equalitarian role of a coach. (See Table 8.1.) He or she asks questions and makes suggestions that the family members discuss and enact with each other. Process questions are asked in an effort to help clients cultivate responses and gain insight into relational patterns. Respect is always given for autonomy. Autonomy is important for all individuals, as it represents the degree of independence that an individual needs to function apart from others in a system. Fusion is the absence of autonomy. Thus, a critical goal of therapy, from a Bowenian perspective, is to help family members

Table 8.1 Goals in a Bowen Family Systems Counseling Approach Therapy

- To increase the level of differentiation of self while remaining in touch with the family system
- Defining and clarifying the relationship between the family members
- Emphasis on understanding the past/present relationships
- Teaching the client to take the "meta-position"
- Detriangulation

differentiate from a family's emotional "togetherness" (Piercy & Sprenkle, 1986). As mentioned, this should be done with awareness and respect for cultural context and cultural and gender-specific norms.

The central premise of the Bowenian model is that lack of differentiation leads to enmeshment with others. Families often need help with issues related to boundaries, enmeshment, and emotional distance. The intense emotional problems within the nuclear family can be resolved only by resolving undifferentiated relationships. Reduction of anxiety and relief from symptoms may occur, but change is not only equated with symptom relief or feeling better but is also measured with an increase in the differentiation level of the family. Frequency of sessions is less important than time in therapy (over time, clients may have a longer time between sessions). Increased time between sessions may reduce dependency.

Ultimately, the counselor seeks to increase each participant's level of differentiation in order to improve adaptiveness (overall with the family and individually).

COUNSELING TECHNIQUES

Genogram Used to Gain Insight

One of the most basic premises of the Bowen approach is that dysfunction in a family is the result of the operation of the family's emotional system over several generations. This suggests that family mapping of patterns and structures could be quite useful. The genogram represents a major tool for assessment of families. The genogram is a visual representation of a family's composition, structure, member characteristics, and relationships. It gives a picture of three or more generations (like a clinical family tree) and notes important family dynamics, rules, patterns, mental health, and even physical health issues. Genograms appeal to clinicians because they are tangible and graphic representations of complex family patterns. The genogram helps both the clinician and the family see the larger picture—that is, to view problems in their current and historical contexts (McGoldrick, Gerson, & Shellenberger, 1999). A genogram lays out problems on paper, allowing one to more easily recognize patterns in family history.

Assessment of differentiation in the family as a whole, as well as in individual family members, is critical because the lower the level of differentiation, the greater the likelihood of problems now and in the future. Areas that may be targeted for assessment include (but are not limited to): marital conflict, triangulation, problematic emotional functioning, and functional impairment.

Calm Questioning

Counselors should be aware that sometimes family counseling is like walking blindfolded into a minefield. In other words, family counseling can be very emotional, with the counselor entering that emotional field. The counselor may slow people down, lower anxiety, and help family members to think. This becomes even more active in couples counseling when conflict is high. The counselor may also use many process questions in counseling, concentrating on the pattern of the family's interaction.

Focusing on One's Role in the Family's Problems Is Critical

Because the counselor in many ways joins the emotional system of the family in the course of the counseling, one must emphasize the differentiation of counselor/therapist. "Bowen has consistently maintained that it is hard for the patient (client) to mature beyond the maturity level of the therapist, no matter how good his or her technique" (Friedman, 1991, p. 138). Ultimately, the capacity to effectively apply Bowenian theory may be a function of the therapist's own differentiation. For instance, if a clinician is recruited into a triangle with a couple and is able to refrain from over-functioning or being emotionally reactive, the clinician can help facilitate change that would not be possible if the two had the same conversation alone. A counselor inducted into a triangle is likely to experience the stress of the couple. This is positional and should be expected. "Maintaining a non-anxious presence . . . is connected to the being of the therapist, not to his or her know-how" (Friedman, 1991, p. 138). Kerr and Bowen (1988) have suggested that learning Bowenian theory requires an emotional chance that is only possible by apprenticing with someone who is a "master" or a disciple of a master.

Minimizing Triangles Within the System

The counselor also needs to be aware of the potential therapy triangle (i.e., the therapist being drawn into a triangle with two or more members of a family). The counselor should try to remain free of emotional entanglements in order to avoid getting stuck or stalemated. Staying detriangled requires a calm tone of voice and talking about facts more than feelings (not taking sides). Under extreme emotional intensity, the counselor may also ask family members to talk to him or her directly to minimize interpersonal tensions. Appropriate clinical supervision is always also a necessary requirement. The counselor may also need to have separate meetings with the adults in the family (i.e., parents). This may be helpful in supporting the needed hierarchy of this subsystem and may promote detriangulation. Relationship experiments may also be encouraged, as the counselor can ask clients to try new behaviors and pay attention and report on the interactional processes and increased insight.

Helping Family Members Develop One-to-One Relationships With Each Other

The counselor using a Bowenian approach seeks to develop clear but connected relationships among family members. This is facilitated by reinforcing the rule that a family member only speaks for him- or herself. Direct communication between each member is also pursued. Each person's "voice" is established within the counseling sessions with the counselor redirecting communication that is monopolizing or too generalized. The counselor may also be required to assist the amplification of the views or interactions of passive members.

Teaching Family Members About the Functioning of Emotional Systems

One of the major roles of the Bowenian counselor is to facilitate self-reflective learning or awareness. Specific feedback on emotional reactions or emotional distancing as they occur in the session (or within the family outside of the session) can serve to increase insight in the process of emotional systems. Bowen himself often avoided directly asking for emotional responses, which he saw as less likely to lead to differentiation of self, preferring mostly to ask for thoughts, reactions, and impressions (Bowen, 1978). Explaining the core tenets of Bowenian family systems theory can be helpful for increased understanding of family process. In addition, a multiple family counseling approach may also be used. This strategy has the counselor working with multiple couples at once. Observing other couples can be very helpful in developing awareness and can offer additional support and modeling.

Promoting Differentiation by Encouraging I-Position Stands During Therapy

In counseling, family members are encouraged to speak directly about their own true personal thoughts and feelings. Family members are asked to speak about how they view the problem without attacking or becoming defensive toward another family member. When a client becomes emotionally overwhelmed, the counselor assesses (with the client) whether he or she is disproportionately absorbing the negative emotions of other members or whether he or she is truly feeling their own feelings. Assertiveness training may also be helpful in establishing the I-position.

Displacement Stories: Tell Stories That Minimize Defensiveness

It is often easier for people to see an emotional or behavioral process in others than within oneself. Using examples through discussion of fictitious families, written stories, or film may help a family safely attend to emotional issues and/or increase awareness of interactional patterns. The same strategies used in the classroom in teaching family systems process (e.g., case examples) can be modified for appropriate use in the counseling practice. Films such as *Ordinary People* or *The Squid and Whale* can be used as an effective way to illuminate common family dynamics.

SIDEBAR 8.2 BOWEN FAMILY SYSTEMS CASE STUDY: YOU BE THE FAMILY COUNSELOR

Paul and Maria came in for marital counseling. You have been assigned to conduct an assessment and make counseling recommendations about how best to proceed.

Describe the case using Bowen family systems theory and develop some hypotheses for the case. Recommend some possible therapeutic approaches/techniques you would use.

Demographics

Maria

Age: 27

Marital status: first marriage

Employment: part-time cashier at grocery store

Paul

Age: 32

Marital status: second marriage

Employment: 12 years as machinist

Their two children: son (Blair), age 8, and daughter (Brittany), age 4

Maria's Family Background

Maria is the middle of three children born to parents who had relocated from Mexico when Maria was 3. She has an older brother and a younger sister. Maria's parents were divorced when Maria was 13. Maria's mother was granted custody of the children at the time of the divorce, and she lived with her mother from age 13 to age 19, when she moved into an apartment with her current spouse. Their first child was born during their cohabitation. Currently, Maria and Paul are "fighting" all the time, and it recently has escalated into "shouting" matches. Paul reports he is very stressed about possible layoffs at work, and he gets annoyed that Maria spends so much time with her mother, who he reports is always over at their house. Their son Blair has begun to act out at school (hitting other children), and many of the couple's fights center around who is at fault for his behavior.

Maria states her father came from a "dysfunctional family." She reports he was verbally and physically abused by his father, and treated Maria similarly. Maria's father was emotionally distant and typically very critical of Maria whenever they interacted. In addition, Maria's grandfather and father abused alcohol heavily. Both were also physically and verbally abusive of their spouses. Maria has grown up around this, having spent time at her grandparents' farm in Mexico in the summers. Maria's father was retired from a job as a laborer in a local factory, but is now deceased. Maria still bears a mixture of unresolved feelings toward her father, mostly anger and sadness that she didn't have a better relationship with him. Maria admits she always wanted her father's approval and feels she was a huge disappointment to him.

Maria's mother comes from a "relatively stable" family. She is the youngest of three, having an older brother and sister. Her parents were married over 30 years. Maria feels her mother has always been very supportive of her, but also acknowledges that Maria was difficult to manage during her preteen and teen years. This caused her mother much frustration and worry, and she now regrets that she put her mother through this. Today, Maria feels her relationship with her mother is very important, and at times Maria feels like her mother is her only friend. Her mother often watches the children while Maria is at work. They often spend many hours together discussing Maria's relationship with Paul in detail, including intimate details of their physical relationship.

Paul's Family Background

Paul reports he comes from a "pretty typical" family. He does report his parents divorced when he was 10, after his father had an affair. Paul says his father was a heavy drinker, but that "was pretty normal" in the neighborhood in which he grew up. Paul's father was a diesel mechanic and had his own business at one time, but he lost it. Paul says he didn't feel particularly close to his father growing up and rarely saw him after his parents divorced. Paul describes his mother as "pretty high strung," and he says she cried very easily. She was a homemaker until Paul's father left, and then she worked as a seamstress. Paul reports his mother died "in a lot of pain" from cancer 3 years ago at age 59. Paul says he hasn't visited his mother's gravesite since the funeral. Paul's father is still alive and at 68 is retired and living "downstate somewhere." Paul was an only child and reports he pretty much kept to himself most of his life, stating that people needed to "learn to rely on themselves." Paul didn't really know his paternal grandfather, but remembers him as a distant cold figure—one that he feared. He did not know his maternal grandparents because they were killed in an auto accident before he was born. He reports his mother was raised by an aunt, who Paul describes as "a real oddball." Paul had little to say about his first marriage, other than to state it was a "real big mistake."

Currently, Paul states that he only wishes to have some "peace" when he gets home from a long day's work, but reports he often gets upset that he has to deal with the "nitpickings" of his wife and mother-in-law.

LIMITATIONS AND FUTURE RESEARCH

Universality of Bowen Family Systems Theory

Bowen (1978) has argued that his theory was universal and would be the same across individuals and across the life span, but there appears to be limited evidence of this. Skowron, Stanley, and Shapiro (2009) found the theory useful in a sample of persons in young adulthood. Kim-Appel, Appel, Parr, and Newman (2007) also found the predictive ability of the self-differentiation construct for mental health measures well into old age.

Some have questioned the universality of Bowen's constructs across gender. Knudson-Martin (1994) criticized the theory for "overvaluing stereotypically male characteristics" (p. 35). Several studies have examined the differences between men's and women's levels of differentiation, with mixed findings. Elieson and Rubin (2001) and Skowron and Friedlander (1998) found no gender differences in the overall level of differentiation (as measured by the DSI). The results for the subcomponents are more mixed. The fusion subscale has demonstrated both a gender difference (Kosek, 1998) and no difference (Skowron & Schmitt, 2003). Numerous studies do show that women score higher on emotional reactivity and the I-position subscales than men (Kosek, 1998; Skowron & Friedlander, 1998; Skowron & Schmitt, 2003). As Bowen's theory suggests, there has been ample research that supports the core idea that low levels of differentiation would be associated with emotional distress (Jankowski & Hooper, 2012). Miller et al. (2004), in a review of the empirical research, concluded: "Although there may be gender differences in some components of differentiation, there are no differences in the overall levels of differentiation" (p. 462).

In examining the universality of Bowen's theory across cultures, Chung and Gale (2006) note that limited research has examined the cross-cultural validity of Bowen's theory, particularly with participants from different countries. In addition, some researchers have questioned the relevance of the construct of differentiation in collectivistic cultures. Markus and Kitayama (1991) suggest that differentiation may be structured differently in collectivist cultures, stating: "This view of the self and relationship between the self and others features the person not as separate from the social context but as more connected and less differentiated from others" (p. 227). Chung and Gale did find self-differentiation to be greater for European Americans than for a Korean sample, and noted that self-differentiation was associated with psychological well-being more strongly in American samples than in Korean counterparts (Chung & Gale, 2006). O'Hara and Meteyard (2011) also suggest two new potential constructs as identified in their research: (1) the significance of an individual's capacity to tolerate interpersonal difference, and (2) the importance of societal expectations on self-differentiation, especially in collectivist cultures.

Emerging Area: Spirituality

There is a growing body of scholarship on the integration of intergenerational family systems theory with spirituality. Jankowski and Vaughn (2009) have noted that "Bowen's system's theory has been an important framework for theorizing about the relationship between individuals' spirituality and their interpersonal functioning" (p. 82). These researchers found Bowen's differentiation of self empirically related to spiritual development, specifically in spiritual practices, including contemplative prayer. A number of scholars have posited a relationship between spiritual maturity and differentiation of self (Balswick, King, & Reimer,

2005; Majerus & Sandage, 2010; Sandage & Harden, 2011; Sandage & Jankowski, 2010). Aspects of mindfulness also appear to be emerging as an area of intersection between Bowen's theory and contemplative or meditative ability (Jankowski & Sandage, 2013; Kim-Appel & Appel, 2013). This area will likely continue to be developed in the years ahead.

SUMMARY

Bowen family systems theory is unique and is a foundational family systems theory. Bowenian theory and practice recognize interplay between biological, genetic, psychological, and sociological factors in determining individual behavior. The Bowenian perspective is also a way of understanding present situations in terms of the influence of past relationships or family histories, and it understands the family as a single emotional unit made up of interlocking relationships existing over many generations. The Bowenian family systems perspective and its applied counseling interventions offer a unique view that highlights important processes that can aid in the support of individuals and families across the life cycle. Increasingly, research has been supportive of Bowenian systems theory and intervention.

Overall, Miller et al. (2004), in a review of the collective basic Bowenian research, conclude that Bowen's theory and the central concept of differentiation of self, in particular, show a promising area for research and practice. While there is much emerging research that supports the efficacy of Bowenian family systems theory (particularly the differentiation of self construct), it does appear that more studies are needed to clarify and validate all of the Bowen family systems theories mechanisms and the role of the theory in therapeutic outcomes. Bowenian family systems theory has been historically one of the most popular theories in the family therapy field, and it continues to gain (and still requires) empirical support to stand the test of time and the rigors of science.

USEFUL WEBSITES

Bowen Center for the Study of the Family
https://www.thebowencenter.org/
Murray Bowen Profile
http://www.abacon.com/famtherapy/bowen.html
The Murray Bowen Archives
http://murraybowenarchives.org/

REFERENCES

Anderson, S. A., & Sabatelli, R. M. (1990). Differentiating differentiation and individuation: Conceptual and operation challenges. *American Journal of Family Therapy*, *18*(1), 32–50.

Appel, J., & Kim-Appel, D. (2010). The multipath approach to personality (MAP): A meta perspective. *Journal of Transpersonal Research*, *2*, 108–115.
Balswick, J. O., King, P. E., & Reimer, K. S. (2005). *The reciprocating self: Human development in theological perspective*. Downers Grove, IL: InterVarsity Press.
Bayer, J. P., & Day, H. D. (1995). An empirical couple typology based on differentiation. *Contemporary Family Therapy*, *17*(2), 265–271.
Benson, M. J., Larson, J. H., Wilson, S. M., & Demo, D. H. (1993). Family of origin influences on late adolescent romantic relationships. *Journal of Marriage and the Family*, *55*, 663–672.
Bohlander, J. R. (1995). Differentiation of self: An examination of the concept. *Issues in Mental Health Nursing*, *16*, 165–184.
Bohlander, R. W. (1999). Differentiation of self, need fulfillment, and psychological well-being in married men. *Psychological Report*, *84*, 1274–1280.
Bowen, M. (1966). The use of family therapy in clinical practice. *Comprehensive Psychotherapy*, 7, 345–374.
Bowen, M. (1976). Theory in the practice of psychotherapy. In P. J. Guerin (Ed.), *Family therapy: Theory and practice* (pp. 42–90). New York, NY: Gardner.
Bowen, M. (1978). *Family therapy in clinical practice*. New York, NY: Jason Aronson.
Bray, J. H., Harvey, D. M., & Williamson, D. S. (1987). Intergenerational family relationship: An evaluation of theory and measurement. *Psychotherapy: Theory, Research, Practice, Training*, *24*(3s), 516–528.
Bray, J. H., Williamson, D. S., & Malone, P. E. (1984). Personal authority in the family system: Development of a questionnaire to measure personal authority in intergenerational family processes. *Journal of Marital and Family Therapy*, *10*, 167–178.
Bregman, O. C. (1993). Bowen theory. *Family Process*, *32*(3), 377–378.
Carpenter, M. C. (1990). A test of Bowen family systems therapy: The relationship of differentiation of self and chronic anxiety. *Dissertation Abstracts International*, *51*, 1791A.
Cebik, R. J. (1988). Adult male maturity and the attainment of personal authority in the family system. *Dynamic Psychotherapy*, *6*(1), 29–36.
Charles, R. (2001). Is there any empirical support for Bowen's concepts of differentiation of self, triangulation, and fusion? *American Journal of Family Therapy*, *29*, 279–292.
Chung, H., & Gale, J. (2006). Family functioning and self-differentiation: A cross-cultural examination. *Contemporary Family Therapy*, *31*, 19–33.
Craddock, A. E. (1983). Family cohesion and adaptability as factors in the etiology of social anxiety. *Australian Journal of Sex, Marriage & Family*, *4*(4), 181–190.
Day, H. D., St. Clair, S., & Marshall, D. (1997). Do people who marry really have the same level of differentiation of self? *Journal of Family Psychology*, *11*, 131–135.
Eckstein, D. (2000). Empirical studies indicating significant birth-order related personality differences. *Journal of Individual Psychology*, *56*, 481–494.
Elieson, M. V., & Rubin, L. J. (2001). Differentiation of self and major depressive disorders: A test of Bowen theory among clinical, traditional, and internet groups. *Family Therapy*, *28*(3), 125–141.
Engels, G. (1980). The clinical application of the biopsychosocial model. *American Journal of Psychiatry*, *137*(5), 535–544.
Farley, J. (1979). Family separation-individuation tolerance: A developmental conceptualization of the nuclear family. *Journal of Marital and Family Therapy*, *5*, 61–67.
Fine, M. (1988). The relationship of perceived health in the family of origin to levels of state and trait anxiety. *Family Therapy*, *15*(1), 51–57.
Fleming, M., & Anderson, S. (1986). Individuation from the family of origin and personal adjustment in late adolescence. *Journal of Marital and Family Therapy*, *12*, 311–315.

Friedman, E. H. (1991). Bowen theory and therapy. In A. S. Gurman & D. P. Kniskern (Eds.), *Handbook of family therapy* (Vol. 2, pp. 134–170). New York, NY: Brunner/Mazel.

Gehring, T. M., & Marti, D. (1993). The family system test: Differences in perception of family structures between nonclinical and clinical children. *Journal of Child Psychology and Psychiatry*, *34*, 363–377.

Gilbert, R. (1992). *Extraordinary relationships: A new way of thinking about human interactions*. Minneapolis, MN: Chronimed.

Gilbert, R. M. (2006). *The eight concepts of Bowen theory*. Falls Church, VA: Leading Systems Press.

Goldenberg, I., & Goldenberg, H. (1991). *Family therapy: An overview* (3rd ed.). Belmont, CA: Brooks/Cole.

Green, R. J. (2000). Lesbians, gay men, and their parents: A critique of LaSala and the prevailing clinical wisdom. *Family Process*, *39*(2), 257–266.

Greene, G. J., Hamilton, N., & Rolling, M. (1986). Differentiation of self and psychiatric diagnosis: An empirical study. *Family Therapy*, *13*(2), 187–194.

Griffin, J. M., & Apostal, R. A. (1993). The influence of relationship enhancement training on differentiation of self. *Journal of Marital & Family Therapy*, *19*(3), 267–272.

Griffin, W. A., & Greene, S. M. (1999). *Models of family therapy: The essential guide*. Philadelphia, PA: Brunner/Mazel.

Gurman, A. S., & Kniskern, D. P. (1991). *Handbook of family therapy* (Vol. 2). Philadelphia, PA: Brunner/Mazel.

Haber, J. (1993). A construct validity study of a differentiation of self scale. *Scholarly Inquiry for Nursing Practice*, *7*(3), 165–178.

Hanson, B. G. (1995). *General systems theory: Beginning with wholes*. Bristol, PA: Taylor & Francis.

Hare, E. R., Canada, R., & Lim, M. G. (1998). Application of Bowen theory with a conflictual couple. *Family Therapy*, *25*(3), 221–226.

Harvey, D., Curry, C., & Bray, J. (1991). Individuation and intimacy in intergenerational relationships and health: Patterns across two generations. *Journal of Family Psychology*, *5*, 204–236.

Horne, K. B., & Hicks, M. W. (2002). All in the family: A belated response to Kundson-Martin's feminist revision of Bowen Theory. *Journal of Marital and Family Therapy*, *28*(1), 103–113.

Hovestadt, A. J., Anderson, W. T., Piercy, F. P., Cochran, S. W., & Fine, M. (1985). A family-of-origin scale. *Journal of Marital and Family Therapy*, *11*, 287–297.

Innes, M. (1996). Connecting Bowen theory with its human origin. *Family Process*, *35*, 487–500.

Jankowski, P., & Vaughn, M. (2009). Differentiation of self and spirituality: Empirical explorations. *Counseling and Values*, *53*, 82–96.

Jankowski, P. J., & Hooper, L. M. (2012). Differentiation of self: A validation study of the Bowen theory construct. *Couple and Family Psychology: Research and Practice*, *1*, 226–243.

Jankowski, P. J., & Sandage, S. J. (2013). Meditative prayer and intercultural competence: Empirical test of a differentiation-based model. *Mindfulness*, *1*(4), 235–253. doi: 10.1007/s12671-012-0189-z

Johnson, P., & Nelson, M. D. (1998). Parental divorce, family functioning, and college student development: An intergenerational perspective. *Journal of College Student Development*, *39*, 355–363.

Kantor, D., & Lehr, W. (1975). *Inside the family*. San Francisco, CA: Jossey-Bass.

Kear, J. (1978). Marital attraction and satisfaction as a function of differentiation of self. *Dissertations Abstracts Intenational*, *47*, 2505.

Kerr, M. E. (1984). Theoretical base for differentiation of self in one's family of origin. *Clinical Supervisor*, *2*, 3–36.

Kerr, M. E., & Bowen, M. (1988). *Family evaluation*. New York, NY: Norton.

Kim-Appel, D., & Appel, J. K. (2013, March). *Mindfulness and differentiation of self*. Research study presentation at the American Counseling Association Conference, Cincinnati, OH.

Kim-Appel, D., Appel, J. K., Parr, P., & Newman, I. (2007). Testing the effectiveness of Bowen's concept of differentiation in predicting psychological distress in individuals age 62 years and older. *The Family Journal: Counseling and Therapy for Couples and Families*, *15*(3), 224–233.

Knudson-Martin, C. (1994). The female voice: Applications to Bowen's family systems theory. *Journal of Marital and Family Therapy*, *20*(1), 35–46.

Kosek, R. B. (1998). Self-differentiation within couples. *Psychological Reports*, *83*, 275–279.

Larson, J. H., & Wilson, S. M. (1998). Family of origin influences on young adult career decision problems: A test of Bowenian theory. *American Journal of Family Therapy*, *26*, 39–53.

Lawson, D., Gaushell, H., & Karst, R. (1993). The age onset of personal authority in the family system. *Journal of Marital and Family Therapy*, *19*(3), 287–292.

Majerus, B. D., & Sandage, S. J. (2010). Differentiation of self and Christian spiritual maturity: Social science and theological integration. *Journal of Psychology and Theology*, *38*, 41–51.

Markus, H. R., & Kitayama, S. (1991). Culture and the self: Implications for cognition, emotion, and motivation. *Psychological Review*, *98*(2), 224–253.

Maynard, S. (1997). Growing up in an alcoholic family system: The effect on anxiety and differentiation of self. *Journal of Substance Abuse*, *9*, 161–170.

McCollum, E. E. (1991). A scale to measure Bowen's concept of emotional cutoff. *Contemporary Family Therapy*, *12*(3), 247–254.

McGoldrick, M., Gerson, R., & Shellenberger, S. (1999). *Genograms: Assessment and intervention* (2nd ed.). New York, NY: W. W. Norton.

Miller, R. B., Anderson, S., & Keala, D. K. (2004). Is Bowen theory valid? A review of basic research. *Journal of Marital and Family Therapy*, *30*, 453–466.

Murphy, F. M. (1999). Is the Bowen theory universal? Level of differentiation of self and marital adjustment among Asian-Americans. *Dissertation Abstracts International: Section B. The Science & Engineering*, *60*(2-B), 0874.

Nichols, M. P. (1984). *Family therapy: Concepts and methods* (1st ed.). Boston, MA: Allyn & Bacon.

Nichols, M. P. (1987). *The self in the system: Expanding the limits of family therapy*. New York, NY: Brunner/Mazel.

Nichols, M. P., & Schwartz, R. C. (2001). Bowen family systems therapy. In M. P. Nichols & R. C. Schwartz (Eds.), *Family therapy: Concepts and methods* (5th ed., pp. 137–171). Boston, MA: Allyn & Bacon.

O'Hara, D. J., & Meteyard, J. D. (2011). Exploring the influence of the intrapersonal capacity to tolerate interpersonal difference as a factor in the differentiation of self and the capacity to tolerate interpersonal difference & societal expectations: An exploratory study. *Asia Pacific Journal of Counseling & Psychotherapy*, *2*(2), 126–137.

Papero, D. V. (1990). *Bowen family systems theory*. Boston, MA: Allyn & Bacon.

Papero, D. V. (2000). Bowen systems theory. In F. M. Dattilio & L. J. Bevilacqua (Eds.), *Comparative treatments for relationship dysfunction* (pp. 25–44). New York, NY: Springer.

Piercy, F. P., & Sprenkle, D. H. (1986). *Family therapy source book*. New York, NY: Guilford Press.

Protinsky, H., & Gilkey, J. K. (1996). An empirical investigation of the construct of personality authority in late adolescent women and their level of college adjustment. *Adolescence*, *31*, 291–296.

Reid, J. K., & Anderson, W. T. (1992). The relationship between personal authority in the family system and discovery of meaning in life. *Contemporary Family Therapy*, *14*(3), 225–240.

Rosen, K. H., Bartle-Haring, S., & Stith, S. M. (2001). Using Bowen theory to enhance understanding of the intergenerational transmission of dating violence. *Journal of Family Issues*, *22*, 124–142.

Sandage, S. J., & Harden, M. G. (2011). Relational spirituality, differentiation of self, and virtue as predictors of intercultural development. *Mental Health, Religion, & Culture*, *14* (8), 819–838. doi:10.1080/13674676.2010.527932

Sandage, S. J., & Jankowski, P. J. (2010). Forgiveness, spiritual instability, mental health symptoms, and well-being: Mediator effects for differentiation of self. *Psychology of Religion and Spirituality*, *2*, 168–180.

Sharf, R. S. (1996). *Theories of psychotherapy and counseling: Concepts and cases*. Pacific Grove, CA: Brooks/Cole.

Simon, F. G., Stierlin, H., & Wynne, L. C. (1985). *The language of family therapy: A systemic vocabulary and sourcebook*. New York, NY: Family Process Press.

Skowron, E. A. (2000). The role of differentiation of self in marital adjustment. *Journal of Counseling Psychology*, *47*(2), 229–237.

Skowron, E. A., & Dendy, A. K. (2004). Differentiation of self and attachment in adulthood: Relational correlates of effortful control. *Contemporary Family Therapy: An International Journal*, *26*(3), 337–357.

Skowron, E. A., & Friedlander, M. L. (1998). The differentiation of self inventory: Development and initial validation. *Journal of Counseling Psychology*, *45*(3), 235–246.

Skowron, E. A., Holmes, S. E., & Sabatelli, R. M. (2003). Deconstructing differentiation: Self regulation, interdependent relating, and well-being in adulthood. *Contemporary Family Therapy: An International Journal*, *25*(1), 111–129.

Skowron, E. A., & Schmitt, T. A. (2003). Assessing interpersonal fusion: Reliability and validity of a new DSI fusion with others subscale. *Journal of Marital and Family Therapy*, *29*(2), 209–222.

Skowron, E. A., Stanley, K. L., & Shapiro, M. D. (2009). A longitudinal perspective on differentiation of self, interpersonal and psychological well-being in young adulthood. *Contemporary Family Therapy: An International Journal*, *31*(1), 3–18.

Skowron, E. A., Wester, S. R., & Azen, R. (2004). Differentiation of self mediates college stress and adjustment. *Journal of Counseling & Development*, *82*(1), 69–78.

Snyder, D. K., & Smith, G. T. (1986). Classification of marital relationships: An empirical Approach. *Journal of Marriage and the Family*, *48*, 137–146.

Stierlin, H. (1981). *Separating parents and adolescents*. New York, NY: Jason Aronson.

Sulmasy, D. P. (2002). A biopsychosocial-spiritual model for the care of patients at the end of life. *Gerontologist*, *3*, 24–33.

Toman, W. (1976). *Family constellation: Its effects on personality and social behavior*. New York, NY: Springer.

Tuason, M. T., & Friedlander, M. L. (2000). Do parents' differentiation levels predict those of their adult children? And other tests of Bowen theory in a Philippine sample. *Journal of Counseling Psychology*, *47*(1), 27–35.

von Bertalanffy, L. (1950). An outline of general system theory. *British Journal for the Philosophy of Science*, *1*, 114–129.

von Bertalanffy, L. (1969). *General system theory*. New York, NY: Braziller.

Wang, L., & Crane, D. R. (2001). The relationship between marital satisfaction, marital stability, nuclear family triangulation and childhood depression. *American Journal of Family Therapy*, *29*, 337–347.

Watkins, C. E. (1992). Birth order research and Adler's theory: A critical review. *Individual Psychology*, *48*, 357–368.

Watzlawick, P., Beavin, J. H., & Jackson, D. D. (1967). *Pragmatics of human communication: A study of interactional patterns, pathologies, and paradoxes*. New York, NY: W. W. Norton.

West, J. D., Hosie, T. W., & Zarski, J. J. (1987). Family dynamics and substance abuse: A preliminary study. *Journal of Counseling and Development*, *65*, 487–490.

West, J. D., Zarski, J. J., & Harvill, R. (1986). The influence of the family triangle on intimacy. *American Mental Health Counselors Association Journal*, *8*, 166–174.

Wetchler, J. L., & Piercy, F. P. (1996). Transgenerational family therapies. In F. P. Piercy, D. H. Sprenkle, J. L. Wetchler, and Associates (Eds.), *Family therapy sourcebook* (2nd ed., pp. 25–49). New York, NY: Guilford Press.

Williamson, D. S. (1982). Personal authority in family experience via termination of the intergenerational hierarchical boundary. *Journal of Marital and Family Therapy*, *8*, 309–323.

Wood, B., Watkins, J. B., Boyle, J. T., Nogueira, J., Zimand, E., & Carroll, L. (1989). The psychosomatic family model: An empirical and theoretical analysis. *Family Process*, *28*, 399–417.

CHAPTER 9

Structural Theory: Approaches and Applications

Shawn P. Parmanand and Esther Benoit
Walden University

THEORETICAL OVERVIEW

The primary goal of structural theory is to help a family, or system, organize in a manner that positively changes the system in question. From a structural perspective, a family system is much more than a group of individuals operating in isolation from one another. This overfocus on individuals can inadvertently be carried by clinicians into family and couples therapy, with "identified clients or patients" deemed to be the direct cause of a family's shared dysfunction. From a systemic and structural perspective, the patterns, interactions, and structure of the family are what bring about function or lack thereof within a system. Family structure is made up of recurring patterns of interaction that help to determine the family's overall organization and functioning. The dynamic relationship between members of a family can provide a clinician with a rich perspective of what occurs within the family, and it is critical to understand and alter this if significant change is to be made within the system.

The structural model further posits that the boundaries and subsystems created within the family are of particular significance. *Boundaries* are defined as unspoken barriers that help to determine the way in which individuals, subsystems, and the family itself interact with others. Boundaries help determine family rules, help to protect individuals and systems, and can range from rigid to diffuse. Subsystems are units within the larger family system that serve specific functions. A few examples of common subsystems in families would be the couple or spousal subsystem, the parental subsystem, and the sibling subsystem. Subsystems within families interact in various ways, and those interactions are mediated by the boundaries between and among different subsystems. Factors such as rule-setting and punishment can be key indicators of a family's current state of functioning. The structural therapist views mental health within a family as the ability of that family to adapt to stressors and challenges based on a healthy structure. Absence of a functional family structure is indicative of struggle within the system. A parental subsystem that consists of one parent who is quick to scold, while the other ignores concerning behavior, is deemed ineffective when it comes to parental governance within the family system. Until the couple creates a true partnership and a united front when rearing children, the attempts to effectively parent their children may prove insufficient.

SIDEBAR 9.1

Take a moment and consider the impact that culture has on family structure, rules, and behavior. What was your cultural upbringing, and how might a structural family therapist view the structure in place in your family of origin? When conceptualizing family functioning, all therapists should be keenly aware of cultural factors and how they might impact the therapeutic relationship and experience. How might you account for culture when taking on the role of a therapist using this theory? How can you ensure that you are respectful when working with all families, no matter their structure and boundaries between relationships?

The therapist's role in structural work is to challenge families to embrace changes in the structure, power, and leadership of the system. As the family evolves into a more balanced yet flexible system, the counselor continues to coach and reinforce the changes being made (Colapinto, 1991). Through direct communication and action between family members, called *enactments*, the family learns to honestly communicate with one another, allowing the therapist to use these interactions as fodder for continued growth within the family.

BACKGROUND: FOUNDERS AND CURRENT PROPONENTS

Salvador Minuchin

Salvador Minuchin was born and raised in Argentina, and he began his professional career as a physician with a focus on pediatrics. In 1948, Israel declared itself a state. As a result, Israel found itself at war with the Arab nations. Minuchin, who is always one for civic duty, spent 18 months as an army doctor for Israel. Following his stint in the military, Minuchin journeyed to the United States to study child psychiatry under the tutelage of Nathan Ackerman. Upon completing his studies in 1952, Minuchin returned to Israel to serve children who had been displaced from the Holocaust. Many of these children had lost the family and structure they had grown accustomed to, and Minuchin quickly noticed the impact the lack of structure had on many of the children with whom he worked. It was during this time that he began seeing the importance of family structure and involvement with regard to mental health and mental illness.

In 1954, Minuchin returned to the United States to begin psychoanalytic training at the William Alanson White Institute, where he studied the interpersonal psychiatry of Harry Stack Sullivan. After completing training, Minuchin began working as an intake coordinator at the Wiltwyck School for delinquent boys in New York City. It was at Wiltwyck that Minuchin suggested to his colleagues—Dick Auerswald, Charlie King, Braulio Montalvo, and Clara Rabinowitz—that they begin seeing and counseling the families of these troubled youth. A majority of the children at the school were from low-income families of African American and Puerto Rican descent from the inner city of New York. Many of these families had problematic and disconnected family structures and, as a result, Minuchin and his colleagues began devising interventions and techniques in hopes of reorganizing family structures to become more healthy, secure, and orderly in nature.

SIDEBAR 9.2

It is clear that Salvador Minuchin's past experiences and clinical work helped to shape his evolving theory and approach to working with families. As burgeoning clinicians, we must be able to draw from our own lived experiences as we create trusting and genuine relationships with our clients. What lived experiences helped to shape who you are, and how might those experiences aid you in understanding and connecting with your clients? How can you continue to use these experiences to grow and meet the needs of the families with whom you work?

Minuchin and his colleagues continued to refine their work over the course of the next few years. It was during this time that Minuchin began to reject the training he had received about classic psychoanalysis when working with this troubled population. Dispelling the notion of passive therapy, new active and intentional techniques were created and demonstrated on family after family. These concrete, brief, and problem-solving techniques were often observed, altered, and transformed as they were implemented in family therapy. In an effort to further develop these techniques, a one-way mirror was installed so each theorist could take turns observing other theorists at work. In 1967, Minuchin and his colleagues published their groundbreaking book, *Families of the Slums* (Minuchin, Montalvo, Guerney, Rosman, & Schumer, 1967), which was based on the work they had done with the impoverished and disadvantaged families with whom they had worked throughout the previous 8 years at Wiltwyck. The book was critically acclaimed and made Minuchin well-known and respected as a therapist on the cutting edge of the systemic movement.

In 1965, Mincuhin was asked to join the Philadelphia Child Guidance Clinic. Minuchin saw this venture as an opportunity to further hone his burgeoning systemic theory. To assist in this process, he invited Jay Haley from Palo Alto, California, and Braulio Montalvo from Wiltwyck. As a result of Minuchin and his colleagues' visionary approach to systemic therapy, the Philadelphia Child Guidance Clinic experienced success and growth. What once was a small clinic consisting of fewer than a dozen staff members prospered into the largest facility of its kind. In time, the clinic became affiliated with the Children's Hospital on the campus of the University of Pennsylvania and employed over 300 individuals in the course of just 10 short years. By the 1970s, structural family therapy had become the most practiced and respected of all systems theories. In 1974, Minuchin published another seminal work entitled *Families and Family Therapy*, which was a compilation of his ideas on how families evolve and change through structural family therapy.

Minuchin displayed a myriad of factors during this time that helped structural theory gain popularity. His unique approach to conceptualizing family dysfunction won over many well-recognized clinicians. Above and beyond the theory itself, Minuchin exhibited a number of personality characteristics that he brought into his tireless work with families and colleagues alike. These personal gifts included a penchant for leadership and responsibility, as well as an ability to push families into thinking and addressing their presenting issues in new and intellectually stimulating ways. Minuchin was also naturally collaborative and encouraging, which meshed nicely with his ability to gently confront the families with whom he worked (Rockinson-Szapkiw, Payne, & West, 2011).

Minuchin later started his own center in New York after leaving Philadelphia in 1981. It was in New York that Minuchin continued to teach, consult, write, and practice his clinical skills for a small group called Family Studies, Inc., before finally retiring in 1996. Minuchin continues to be active in the field, lecturing and educating therapists around the world.

Other Leading Figures

Minuchin created a rich history of working closely with a variety of therapists who contributed to the evolution of structural family theory. Paramount among those therapists is Braulio Montalvo. Montalvo, like Minuchin, committed himself to working with poor, underprivileged, and minority families. Montalvo was important in the growth and rise to prominence of the Philadelphia Child Guidance Clinic. Other instrumental figures in the structural movement include Jorge Colapinto, who serves as director of the Foster Care Project at the Ackerman Institute in New York City, and Marianne Walters, who along with her colleagues (Walters, Carter, Papp, & Silverstein, 1989) advocated for the consideration of gender and gender patterns when conceptualizing family structure within family systems, thus bringing an entirely new focus and understanding to family structure and development. Another prominent clinician is Marion Lindblad-Goldberg who offers structural family training. Lindblad-Goldberg is the head clinician at the now much smaller Philadelphia Child and Family Guidance Training Center. Over the course of several decades, thousands of family therapists were trained at the Philadelphia Child Guidance Center, a testament to the impact and ingenuity of the structural therapy model.

MAJOR CONSTRUCTS

The structural therapy model is clearly organized around several key constructs, which are outlined next.

Introduction to the Theory

Structural family therapy is a contextually focused model that emphasizes structure as the central organizing component of family life. Focusing on context means that therapists view families as embedded within larger systems (including cultural groups, schools, places of employment, and communities of faith) and myriad other factors that contribute to how families organize as functional units. Mental health and wellness come from working with the family structure. Family structure, as viewed by this school, is made up of persistent patterns of interaction that provide families with both covert and overt rules about how, when, and with whom family members relate. Within structural family therapy, the focus is on the entire family system as a whole. Various transactions between and among individuals and subsystems help allude to the overall structure of the family. Transactions between family members are best identified when the family is carrying out those interactions. The structural family therapist might ask questions such as the following to help elucidate typical transactions within a system: Whom do you talk to when you are worried? How do you work out conflict with your sister? At what point does Dad intervene when you are arguing with Mom? Who is the keeper of family secrets? How do you know when Mom is upset? Tell me about a time when your family had to make an important decision—how did you go about that process?

SIDEBAR 9.3

Examples of Covert Rules

- Go to Mom for help with emotional concerns
- Avoid talking to Mary about problems
- Siblings shouldn't rat each other out
- If Dad worked late, don't bother him with questions
- Gender role expectations

Examples of Overt Rules

- Children are not allowed in Mom's room
- Dad has the final say in family arguments
- Try to work out your conflict with siblings before asking for parental intervention
- What happens in the family stays in the family

The family unit is hierarchically organized and contains several interdependent subsystems. More than just the sum of its subsystems, families are conceptualized as dynamic organisms that have internal rules, roles, and boundaries that provide the scaffolding for enduring patterns of family interaction (Minuchin & Fishman, 1981). Within any system, a balance must be struck between stability and change. From a developmental perspective, this theory examines how systems cope with the many transitions inherent in family life. Transactional patterns provide clues about the system's functioning, structure, alignments, and coalitions. When stress overwhelms a system's coping strategies, symptoms manifest as a way to regulate that system. Take, for example, the case of Patricia (age 26) and her sons, Eddie (6) and Tommy (4). Patricia presents for counseling with her family 3 months after the unexpected death of her long-term boyfriend and Tommy's father, Joe. Prior to Joe's death, Patricia describes her family as "getting along just fine," but since then she feels that "everything is falling apart." Joe played the role of family disciplinarian and, according to Patricia, helped to "keep the boys in line." Patricia works part time and is struggling to meet her financial obligations. Joe was the primary earner in the family prior to his death. Patricia reports that both boys have been acting out at home, and that Eddie is starting to act out in school by hitting and shoving other children in his class. Family roles have shifted considerably in a very short time, and the structural therapist would examine with Patricia how those changing roles are influencing the overall functioning within the family. Of note is the shift in subsystems: Patricia is now alone in her parental subsystem and is no longer a member of a couple subsystem. Renegotiating family rules, roles, boundaries, and the family's hierarchical structure will be primary areas of focus in working with them from a structural family therapy perspective. Figure 9.1 provides an illustration of some of the more frequently seen relational boundaries within family systems.

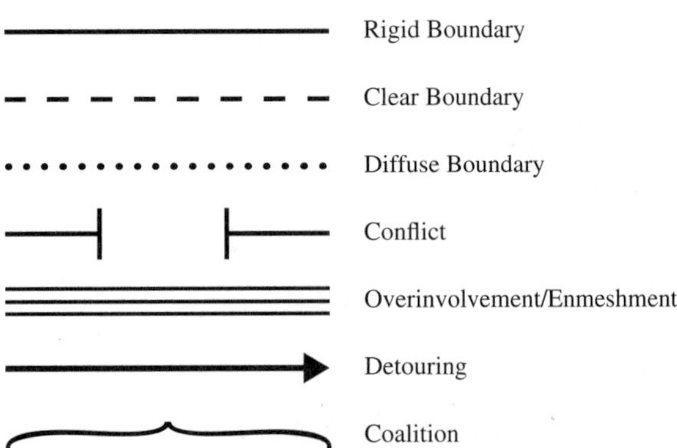

Figure 9.1 Symbols of family structure.
These are some commonly used symbols that help to visually depict elements of family structure. These symbols will be referred to in subsequent figures and will be explored more deeply throughout the chapter.

Family Structure

Family structure helps us identify how and when individuals and subsystems interact. Within family systems, covert or unstated rules exist that act as blueprints for interaction (Minuchin, 1974). The therapist examines the patterns of family interaction created by covert and overt rules as these patterns define and illustrate a family's structure (Colapinto, 1991). Referring back to the example of Patricia, Eddie, and Tommy, a structural therapist might examine a typical interaction and explore the meaning of that interaction with the family. For example, Eddie brings home a note from his teacher requesting a conference with Patricia after Eddie allegedly pushed over a young girl during recess. This is the third conference Patricia has been asked to attend, and she is feeling both overwhelmed and angry. Upon receiving the note, Patricia yells at Eddie and tells him that he cannot watch television for the rest of the week. Later that evening, Tommy is watching television before bed and Patricia gives in to Eddie's pleas to join him. Both Tommy and Eddie are excited to watch TV together and are quite well behaved the remainder of the evening. This pattern of interaction is fairly typical for the family, as Patricia often finds herself "giving in" to one or both boys when she feels tired or overwhelmed. She states that it is often easier to give in because the boys are so much more compliant when she gives in. The structural therapist might explore the effects of this pattern on the family's functioning as it relates to the rules and boundaries within the system. Patricia is undermining her role as disciplinarian and the boundaries around the parental subsystem by being inconsistent in the application of consequences. A covert rule may be communicated to the boys that what Mom says is up for negotiation. This can limit Patricia's effectiveness with regard to the family's overall hierarchical structure (see Figure 9.2).

Figure 9.2 illustrates the diffuse boundaries present between Patricia and her children.

Patterns of interaction between Patricia and Eddie are represented in Figure 9.3.

Family transactional patterns are relatively stable across time and resistant to change. However, as families grow and develop, their needs often change. These changes can cause tension and imbalance within the existing family structure.

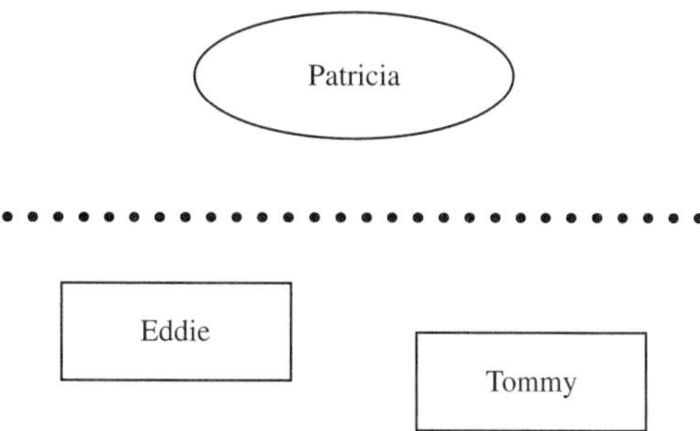

Figure 9.2 Diffuse boundaries.

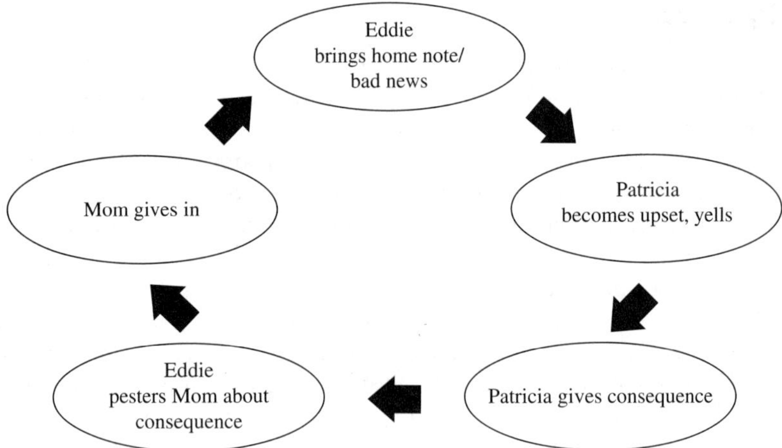

Figure 9.3 Transactional pattern.

Because family systems and structure tend to be fairly resistant to change, developmental transition points can cause significant stress within the family system. Despite the general stability of family structure, it should be noted that it is not completely static. Family structure tends to be dynamic and shifts over time. Families often present for counseling at times of transition, when their system's existing structure is no longer working given their new context and they need support in navigating a more adaptive family structure. Family functioning is related to the family system's ability to respond to the changing developmental needs that occur across the life span. All family systems experience these developmental shifts, during which members renegotiate rules, roles, and boundaries. Rather than pathologizing these struggles, the structural approach views families as inherently competent and unique (Simon, 1995). The assumption of competence suggests that families come to us at points of "stuckness," when their current ways of adapting to stressors are no longer working as well as they did in the past. Minuchin and Nichols suggest that "the basic quest of family therapy is to release unused possibilities" (1993, p. 45). Families have the ability to access this latent potential through the process of enactment within the therapeutic space. The therapist's role is to encourage, facilitate, and motivate the exploration of these alternative interaction strategies.

When we think about day-to-day family life, many different types of interactions or behaviors might come to mind. Think about your own experiences as a member of a family: Do you behave differently with some members of the family than you do with others? Which family members do you turn to with exciting news? As a small child, whom did you turn to for comfort? Who takes care of the basic needs of younger members of the family? These ways of relating to each other as family members help demonstrate how systems are organized. Our patterns of interaction over time create unspoken rules that moderate behavior within the family system. There are two constraints that maintain these patterns: generic/universal rules and idiosyncratic/individualized rules (Minuchin, 1974). Generic or universal rules are those that generally shape family experience and include the need for hierarchical organization within a system. This is typically seen through parents as head of the family system. Generic constraints on family functioning help to maintain the family's existing patterns of interaction and maintain equilibrium. Rules, roles, and patterns emerge and evolve over time and create systemic stability (Minuchin, 1974). In order to observe a family's structure, the therapist must facilitate interaction within the session so that these patterns can be observed.

SIDEBAR 9.4

Transactional patterns may start quite simply. For example, a young child might refuse to get in her car seat when prompted by her father, but does so willingly and easily when her mother asks. Over time, this interaction becomes routine and begins to manifest itself in different situations. A pattern emerges in the family system where mom is seen as an authority figure and dear old dad is disregarded. The key here is understanding that these patterns occur both consciously and unconsciously and are worthy of exploration on the part of the therapist.

Systemic stability, or homeostasis, is a concept rooted in cybernetics and general systems theory. Family systems have a tendency to seek out constancy, even when circumstances change and the system's current methods of coping are not meeting the needs of individual members or the system itself. Within the therapeutic space, the structural counselor, through the use of joining, accommodation, and enactment, works to motivate and encourage family members to practice alternative interaction styles that may better serve their changing developmental and contextual needs.

Subsystems

Several different subsystems exist within the overall structure of a family. These smaller systems within systems can be organized in several ways, including by relationship, gender, interests, and generation. Subsystems help delineate larger family structure by laying out boundaries and rules of engagement within and between other subsystems. Family members occupy various roles within their larger family units, and subsystems help us to better understand how we relate differently depending on the roles and rules of particular family configurations. The three most influential subsystems include spousal/couple, parental, and sibling. These three subsystems will be explored in greater detail here.

Subsystems are formed in order to carry out various family functions. The spousal/couple subsystem can be used to help illustrate the role of complementarity in subsystems. In order to feel a sense of belonging within the couple subsystem, individuals must explore how they will balance individuality and togetherness within their relationship. This subsystem is important as families grow, although it is often given less emphasis by family members, particularly when children are very young. The spousal subsystem serves an important function for the adults in the family because it helps to protect its members from other functions, such as child rearing and work. For single-parent families, the spousal/couple subsystem might consist of any significant adult contacts the parent has. A healthy spousal/couple subsystem can help parents feel supported in the important task of leading their families. It is of critical importance that the therapist exercise caution and multicultural sensitivity when working with a variety of parental and familial structures and subsystems. Recognizing that many family systems will likely present differently, the basic tenets remain that effective subsystems can be created through the seeking out of steady and intentional supporting relationships.

SIDEBAR 9.5

Families often present for counseling during times of transition. Think about how the spousal/couple subsystem might change across the family life cycle, examining the following three life events:

1. A newly partnered couple
2. Addition of the first child to the family system
3. Launching of youngest child from family system

What challenges exist at each of these stages of the family life cycle? Consider the developmental tasks associated with each of these life events. How do these specific tasks influence family structure?

The parental subsystem can be made up of any adults actively engaged in raising the children in a given family system. This unit is tasked with adapting to the varying needs of growing children. The parental subsystem's focus necessarily shifts as children get older, moving from the nurturance of dependent infants and young children, to the control and guidance of older children, to the burgeoning independence of adolescents. Often, families present for counseling when they experience significant developmental changes and their system is struggling to adapt to the changing needs of individual members and subsystems. A well-functioning parental subsystem recognizes the need for children to access their parents or guardians while keeping separate the tasks of children and adults within the larger family system. The boundaries between parents and children are often shaped by culture, family development, and even life stage. Family therapists should pay careful attention to contextual factors when assessing family structure to determine what function current family rules and roles might be playing within diverse systems.

SIDEBAR 9.6

Consider how boundaries might shift within and between subsystems when a new baby enters the family system. Mary recently gave birth to her first baby, Jaden, and finds herself constantly tending to his needs. She is up at all hours of the night, has not had an afternoon to herself in nearly a month, and feels pressure to be a good mom and a good girlfriend to Jim, Jaden's father. Jim complains that since Jaden's birth 3 months ago, Mary has been completely focused on the baby and never makes time for him anymore.

Given the recent life cycle transition Mary, Jim, and Jaden have experienced, it makes sense that the roles and functions within various subsystems would shift. If this family were to come to you for counseling, how would you proceed? In Figure 9.4 you will see an example of a structural family map that indicates several elements of this family's problematic structural organization. Consider how you might alter or rearrange the diagram in an effort to reorganize the system in a more productive way. What cultural considerations might you need to make when forming hypotheses about how to shift a family's structural organization?

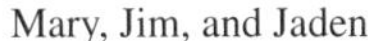

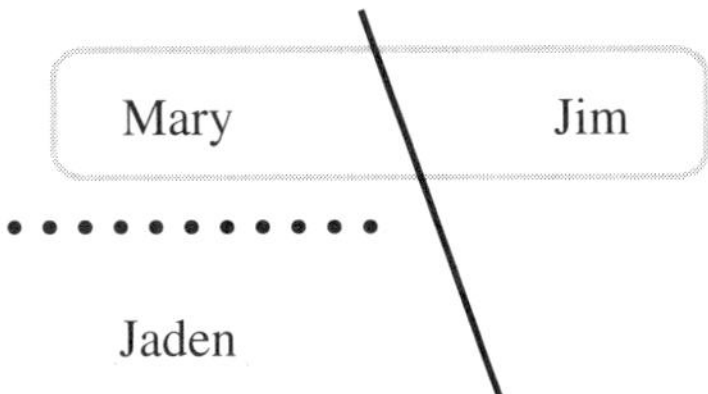

Figure 9.4 Subsystem and boundaries.

Sibling subsystems can be described as a sort of social laboratory for learning about how to interact with others. Our first peer interactions are typically with our siblings, and it is within these relationships that we learn how to negotiate social relationships. Boundaries within the sibling system determine how members engage with each other and to what extent parents or guardians become involved. Because sibling relationships offer an opportunity for social learning within family systems, boundaries should serve a protective function in allowing children the space to work through most interpersonal challenges. Again, contextual factors should be considered when examining any family system, as these will largely influence how families organize themselves. There may be a distinct hierarchy within a sibling subsystem, with older siblings holding more power within the subsystem than younger siblings. Sibling subsystems can also be further delineated by gender, age, interest, or other factors.

Individual family members are often part of multiple subsystems at once. For example, a father can be a member of a parental subsystem and a spousal subsystem. These subsystems act as part of a family's structure and serve specific functions within the larger system. For example, a father may act as a disciplinarian to his children in his role as part of the parental subsystem and as a romantic partner as part of his spousal (couple) subsystem. The functions served by different subsystems must be balanced carefully. As family members grow and change, the system must adapt the function of its subsystems accordingly.

Let's examine the role of subsystems in the Campbell family. Tonya Campbell is a 35-year-old single mother of two boys, Micah (11) and Jerome (15). Tonya lives with her mother, Jackie (54). Together, Tonya and Jackie have raised Micah and Jerome since the boys' father left shortly after Micah's birth. The boys' father, Juan, has not attempted contact since he left 10 years ago. Tonya works the night shift at a local grocery store and also waits tables part time. Jackie is on disability and is at home with the boys before and after school. Tonya has been in a relationship with Renee (42) for 5 years. Renee lives in the apartment across from Jackie and Tonya's and is a consistent presence in the lives of the Campbell boys. Initially, Renee's relationship with Micah and Jerome was strained, but they grew close when Renee stepped in to help care for Jackie when she suffered a minor stroke 2 years ago. Jerome has recently begun struggling in school. His grades have dropped from As and Bs to Cs and Ds, and his teachers have requested a parent–teacher conference. Tonya is concerned that Jerome is focusing too much on his friends and his new girlfriend, Jasmine. Jerome is frustrated that everyone is making "such a big deal" about his grades, and he wishes his mom and grandmother would "back off." Jerome recently confided in Renee that he was sexually active. Renee has not yet shared this information with Tonya because she feels that Tonya would "freak out" and overreact.

Together Tonya and Jackie act as the parental subsystem within their family unit. Renee sometimes steps in to assist with some parenting tasks, helping enforce family rules and limits and assisting Tonya and Jackie in raising Micah and Jerome. Tonya and Renee form this family's couple subsystem. Tonya and Renee would like to move in together when the boys are older and have graduated, but feel it best to keep them in a consistent environment until they have graduated from high school. Their couple subsystem provides them with adult connection and support. Finally, Micah and Jerome comprise the sibling subsystem within the Campbell family. The boys share a room and spend much time together, despite their 4-year age difference. Micah looks up to Jerome and often tries to be like him. Jerome loves Micah, but recently he has become frustrated with his brother's desire to go everywhere that he goes. As Jerome gets older and becomes more independent, the sibling subsystem dynamics and larger family dynamics will shift.

Boundaries

Boundaries within family systems act to manage proximity and hierarchy (Minuchin, 1974). While subsystems help to outline relationships within the larger family structure, boundaries show us how individual members, subsystems, and the larger system function in concert. Clearly defined boundaries are useful in helping to maintain autonomy balanced with a sense of belonging. In times of transition or stress, clear boundaries can serve a protective function for the family system. Boundaries vary in their permeability from rigid to diffuse. Boundary permeability outlines the frequency and nature of contact between and among family members (Minuchin & Fishman, 1981).

Rigid boundaries can be thought of as impermeable—that is, they are not able to be breached or accessed. With rigid boundaries, autonomy is maintained at the expense of nurturance and engagement (Minuchin, 1974). Families run the risk of isolation when exhibiting boundaries within and between systems that are too rigid. Take the example of a child who is bullied at school. The child's parents are unconcerned about the child's fears and instruct the boy to "Just tell your teacher." This is an example of a disengaged/rigid boundary between the family system and the school, and between the parental and child subsystems. Some flexibility is important for the family system to successfully navigate its interactions with external systems and within the system itself. On the other end of the continuum lies the diffuse boundary. Where rigid boundaries are unbending and inflexible, diffuse boundaries are blurred and indistinct. Diffuse boundaries lack the integrity to help a system maintain a clear structure. Hierarchy and differentiation are difficult to establish. Support and care are nurtured at the expense of independence and autonomy. Diffuse boundaries may also be described as *enmeshed*. An example of a diffuse boundary would include the preschooler who comes home upset that he was not selected as the line leader. Mom writes a letter to the school expressing her concern and asks to sit in on next week's class—a classic example of helicopter parenting (when a parent exhibits behavior that might be considered hovering or overinvolved, given the child's current developmental needs) and enmeshment.

Somewhere between rigid and diffuse boundaries is the proverbial "sweet spot," which can only be appropriately determined given the contextual and cultural context of each family situation. An appropriately balanced boundary is described as a clear boundary. Clear boundaries balance elements of separateness and togetherness. Of course, family boundaries shift according to life events. As members of families develop, family subsystems, roles, rules, and boundaries are transformed. When families struggle to make sense of those shifts, they might find themselves in our offices. Our task is to help families identify structural elements and discover alternative ways of interacting that better serve the family's current dynamic. A family does not necessarily exhibit only one type of boundary. Subsystems can compensate for each other, as might be the case in a family in which the couple subsystem is disengaged and the parent–child subsystem is enmeshed. Family members often seek balance within the various roles and relationships of their family system. Assessment of boundaries necessitates the consideration of cultural and contextual influences.

Power, Alignments, and Coalitions

If subsystems represent the various microsystems within a larger family unit and boundaries tell us how those subsystems interact with each other, then alignments and coalitions help us to see how members negotiate power within those family relationships. Alignments are emotional connections between and among family members that indicate the varied levels of support that exist within family relationships. Family members join or oppose each other across various family activities and functions. An example of this can be shown in relation to the Campbell family, discussed previously. Renee and Jerome are aligned in that Renee is demonstrating support for Jerome, and Jerome feels comfortable sharing personal and sensitive information with Renee that he is choosing not to share with his mother, Tonya. Renee has made the decision not to share the information Jerome has disclosed because she agrees with his fear that Tonya will overreact. This alignment demonstrates a sort of coalition between Jerome and Renee. Simply put, a coalition is an alliance against a third member. In this case, neither Jerome nor Renee is actively seeking to undermine Tonya; however, by keeping information from her, the two have aligned in an important way that will undoubtedly impact the overall family system's dynamic.

Alignments and coalitions help family counselors see who has decision-making authority and responsibility within the family system. Power can be thought of as the relative level of influence that one member has over another or over the family system as a whole. Power is both contextual and situational in that members may have varying levels of power in the various roles they play within the family. For example, Tonya and Jackie are quite powerful in the Campbell family system because they are members of the parental subsystem. Tonya and Jackie are able to enforce family rules, set expectations, and follow through on consequences. Jerome can be seen as having less power when we examine his role as a child in this family system. However, when describing the sibling subsystem, Jerome has greater influence and decision-making authority than Micah, illustrating his relative power in that context.

Alliances and coalitions often form in ways that support or challenge the existing family hierarchy and structure. Jerome might align with Renee against Tonya, effectively triangulating their relationship. Triangulation occurs anytime a dyadic interaction aligns against a third party. Triangulation is simply a form of coalition in which an alliance between members has an impact on a third family member. There are several types of alignments and coalitions within families. Certain stable and relatively inflexible alignments can be found in many families. An example of a fixed alliance might include the mother–daughter dyad. This dyad might align itself against a male sibling or parent. Detouring coalitions help aligned pairs hold a third party responsible for challenges within their relationship, deflecting stress on their alliance (Minuchin, 1974).

SIDEBAR 9.7

Take the case of Jorge and Lourdes, a couple in their late 40s with two children, Max (22) and Fatmah (18). Jorge and Lourdes have a strained relationship within their spousal subsystem. Fatmah and Lourdes have a strong mother–daughter alliance. In an example of a detouring coalition,

Jorge and Lourdes begin to place attention on Fatmah and worry about her slipping grades at school (from As to Bs) rather than attending to their own marital conflict. How might you use structural family counseling techniques to examine this coalition and its influence on the overall family structure?

Healthy family structure includes clear boundaries across generations. Typically this will include high levels of parental power and authority. When two parents are involved, a strong alliance between those parents is necessary. Research has shown that families with unbalanced alliances and structures are related to the development of psychopathology in the youth of such systems. The origin of such maladjustment stems from psychological needs of youth being unmet or compromised by an improperly aligned system (Lindahl & Malik, 2011). Furthermore, marital conflict has been shown to impact the relationship parents have with their adolescents, and may be associated with eating disorders experienced by many young women (Blodgett Salafia, Schaefer, & Haugen, 2013). Clear rules and expectations related to family hierarchy help define family structure, which is necessary to avoid such hardships experienced by children in these unaligned systems. Generational boundaries prohibit interference from grandparents and prevent children from taking over parenting.

Codependency

Codependency is a relational pattern in which one member of a subsystem both consciously and unconsciously sabotages the behavior of another member of the subsystem. Often seen with alcoholism, and within couple relationships, one spouse may wish to change his or her spouse's behavior, but rather reinforces the behavior they hope to change. Take, for example, a male spouse who continually calls in to his spouse's employer and requests sick leave for his wife after she drinks to the point of incapacitation the night prior. By mitigating the consequences of her drinking behavior, the male has, in effect, encouraged the behavior to continue. These types of behaviors are often seen in the enmeshed type of families with which Minuchin most commonly worked (Scaturo, 2005).

GOALS

The goal of this therapeutic approach is to implement change in family structure when that structure becomes inoperative and needs to be renegotiated. This model asserts that families need structure, including hierarchy, boundaries, and differentiation between subsystems, to function. Healthy systems demonstrate a wide range of patterns and a relatively expansive repertoire for dealing with change while still maintaining a degree of continuity. Individual symptoms often bring clients to therapy, but they are not necessarily the focus of clinical intervention. Restructuring the family systems with the aim of developing clear boundaries and dealing with underlying conflicts is primary. Structural family therapists believe that individual behavioral changes will only occur when the family's structure has been transformed.

Role of the Counselor

Therapists take on an active and directive role within this model as they work to challenge the family's system in ways that facilitate structural shifts. These structural shifts can be disorienting and stressful for families, so the model necessitates that the clinician strike a balance between support and challenge as family members make sense of the changes within the system (Colapinto, 1991). The structural therapist is active in motivating and facilitating family interactions within session, but the therapeutic process itself places the family at center stage. While the therapist may invite family members to begin exploring new strategies, ultimately the family itself activates the alternatives that will lead to lasting (second order) change (Simon, 1995).

Families often look to solve problems and work on a specific family member's issues when seeking help. A family with young children might present for family counseling to work on their son's acting out behaviors at school. In the context of structural therapy, the focus would move beyond the system's symptom bearer (the son) to the family unit as a whole, attempting to elicit interaction between and among members so the system's structure might be revealed to the therapist.

TECHNIQUES

The following techniques highlight specific strategies that structural family therapists are likely to use in their work with client families.

Joining and Accommodation

As the therapist joins with the family and continually observes and assesses elements of the family's underlying structure, intervention begins. As with any therapeutic approach, the relationship between client and counselor is central to the change process. Rapport building with more than one person at a time can be challenging, and the family therapist must balance connecting with individual members and the system as a whole. When seeking support, families often feel vulnerable and may appear defensive to treatment. The therapist must be mindful to communicate respect not only to the individuals within the family system, but also to the family system's current structure. Addressing parents first is one way of honoring the parental subsystem's hierarchy. The therapist must quickly observe patterns of family interaction to join and accommodate the family's current patterns. Initially, the therapist works to reduce anxiety that may be present within the family because it does not necessarily challenge any potentially problematic interaction patterns. This process is also known as *maintenance.* Joining sets the stage for the therapeutic relationship and must be done with care. Approaching families with respect and genuine interest is equally important to approaching the family with a level of professionalism and direction. Helping families understand what they can expect within the therapeutic space can further clarify the role of the therapist. Joining and accommodation should be done in such a way that the therapist develops a strong relationship with the client family without becoming inducted into that system's patterns. While joining and accommodation are frequently thought of as part of the initial phase of family therapy, the therapeutic relationship should be attended to consistently as the family navigates the change process.

Enactment

Enactment is perhaps the most widely known structural family therapy technique, and it serves as one of the cornerstones of therapeutic practice within this model. This technique is more than an intervention strategy in that it facilitates direct interaction between and among family members within the therapeutic session, placing the family and their interactions (both useful and not) as the point of focus. Before an enactment is facilitated, the therapist observes the family's current patterns of interaction and identifies areas that may be problematic and indicative of larger structural concerns. Once identified, the therapist asks the family to participate in this interactional pattern within the session. For example, a family in which a mother and son are living with the mother's parents present for counseling and the pattern observed includes grandmother and grandson arguing over curfew and mom retreating (and siding with the son). The counselor might suggest to the grandmother and grandson, "Go ahead and discuss curfew the way you would do it at home." The therapist would then move to the periphery and observe and assess the family's interactions. In this example, the therapist might make note of how mom is not involved in the discussion or how the grandson raises his voice to his grandmother and angrily pleads for his mom to "back him up." Enactments often disintegrate and family members become frustrated and look to the therapist in their exasperation. Family members are then encouraged to explore alternative ways of interacting. A therapist might prompt these alternatives by using additional techniques such as using intensity or unbalancing.

Unbalancing

Family systems work hard to maintain homeostasis, and trying new ways of interacting is often quite threatening. After joining and accommodating with a client family, assessing their interactions, and monitoring dysfunctional patterns, counselors actively seek to restructure the family system through intervention. Unbalancing is one way of facilitating the process of restructuring by pointing out patterns that are not functional within the system and asking family members to interact differently. For example, in the case of the Campbell family, the counselor noticed that each week the family would sit in a very specific configuration within the room. Tonya and Jackie sit beside each other, with Micah next to Jackie and Jerome next to Renee. Renee is seated between Jerome and Tonya.

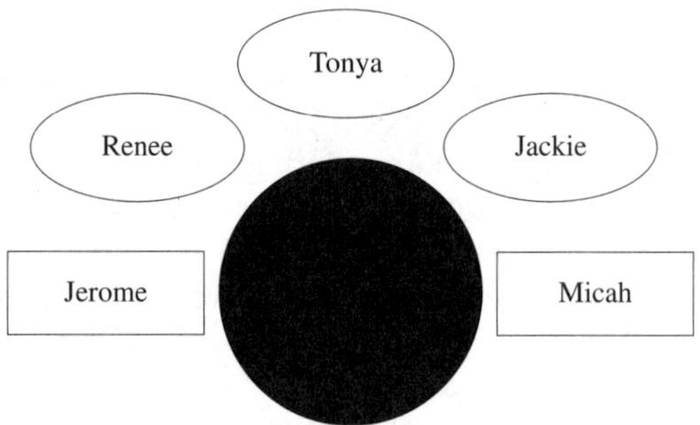

Figure 9.5 Campbell family: Initial seating arrangement.

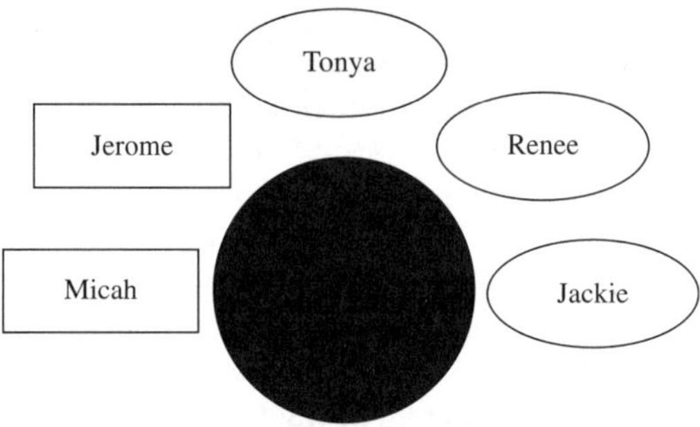

Figure 9.6 Campbell family: Seating arrangement after unbalancing by therapist.

In previous sessions, the counselor has observed the strong alliance between Jerome and Renee and the increased distancing between Tonya and both children. Jackie and Micah appear to be strongly aligned, and Renee and Jerome have formed a strong bond. Tonya is in the middle of this configuration and is frequently blamed for family stress. Seeing these ineffective patterns, the counselor decides to unbalance the system by asking family members to sit in a different configuration to see what that feels like. The following transcript describes a portion of a session with the Campbell family leading up to an unbalancing and boundary-making intervention by the therapist (switching seats within the context of the therapeutic session) (see Figures 9.5 and 9.6).

TONYA: I'm having a hard time getting why things can't just run as smoothly as they used to.

RENEE: I just don't think it's that simple, Tonya.

THERAPIST: What do you mean by that, Renee? Tell me a bit about how things are not simple.

RENEE: Well, they just aren't! I mean, we aren't your typical family, and so we're not going to be able to just put up a picket fence, buy a dog, and get on with life.

TONYA: I never said I wanted that. . . .

RENEE: But you are the one having such a hard time with us, with this, the whole deal.

TONYA: I just think that a son should go to his mother with important things . . . you're not his mom.

RENEE: (Visibly frustrated) Fine. What do you want me to do, turn him away?

THERAPIST: I'm hearing a good deal of frustration between the both of you right now and I'm getting the sense that perhaps things really aren't working out that well in your family at the moment. Tonya, it seems that you and Renee have different ideas around what it means to be part of a family. What does that mean for the two of you as a couple?

TONYA: Well for one, I don't think that we really are a family in the true sense of the word. We don't live together. . . .

RENEE: Yet!

TONYA: You won't even let me talk for a minute without butting in!

THERAPIST: All right, let's go back to that. Tonya, you don't feel as though the five of you are a family.

TONYA: Yeah. I mean, it sounds horrible saying that out loud, but yeah.

JACKIE: (Rolls eyes)

THERAPIST: Jackie, I'm aware of your reaction to all of this and I'm curious, tell me about your ideas about this family.

JACKIE: Well, we are what we are! Who cares what families are supposed to look like. We raise these boys, we care for them. That's enough, isn't it?

TONYA: Yes, we are their family, mom—you and me, mom. I'm not arguing that.

RENEE: (Sarcastically) Well that's just great. Just because I don't live with you all, I'm not in the family, huh?

THERAPIST: Renee, it looks like you've been sent back across the hall to the other apartment just now. What is that like for you?

RENEE: What do you think it's like? It hurts. Obviously.

THERAPIST: Jerome and Micah, I've noticed that you are both sitting here quietly watching as we adults go back and forth. I appreciate you being here to share your views on what is going on for your family right now. So what insight can you share with me so that I can understand life in your family from your perspective? Jerome let's start with you.

JEROME: I don't see what the big deal is.

THERAPIST: All of this, it doesn't seem to you, should be so stressful. . . .

JEROME: Mmmmhmmm. I mean, Renee is part of our life. Deal with it. I mean, you chose to be with her in the first place, it's not like we did that, mom.

TONYA: I never said you did.

JEROME: Whatever.

THERAPIST: So it might seem to you, Jerome, that all of this just is what it is—nothing you can really do about it, and nothing to make a big deal of?

JEROME: Yeah. . . .

TONYA: Well if I had known you felt that way, it would have been nice.

JEROME: Maybe if you would talk to me!

TONYA: I try! You're constantly out with Jasmine or over at Renee's!

JEROME: Well if you didn't work so much. . . .

RENEE: Stop that! You know she does all of that for you and Micah.

THERAPIST: I want to pause for a moment and point out something I noticed just now. Tonya and Jerome, I am hearing that you both want connection, but that there are things getting in the way for both of you. And then, Renee, I saw you step in to defend Tonya. Tell me, is that what usually happens in situations like this one?

RENEE: I mean, yeah, I defend her. She works hard to provide for her boys and sometimes they can be punks; kids should be more respectful.

THERAPIST: Respect is key for you.

RENEE: Yes.

THERAPIST: And Tonya, when Renee defended you just then, what was that like for you?

TONYA: It's frustrating. I feel like they only respond when she does step in. Like I can't keep my own family together.

THERAPIST: So holding it all together on your own is important to you.

TONYA: I guess so.

THERAPIST: And you're feeling like right now that isn't happening.

TONYA: No. It's not. Micah practically sees Gran as his own mother because she's the one who's there when he gets home from school, and it just feels like Jerome is slipping out of reach for me.

THERAPIST: I see that side of things pretty clearly here in the room right now—I'm noticing how Micah is sitting next to you, Jackie . . . and Jerome, you're over here by Renee. Tonya, I wonder what it's like to feel this distance from your kids?

TONYA: I hate it. I feel out of touch.

THERAPIST: Let's see if we can shift things around and try out something a bit different. (See diagram of changed seating arrangements in Figure 9.6.)

The members of various subsystems are not necessarily as important as the boundaries that exist between and among various subsystems. As we have noted with the Campbell case, boundaries act as the invisible parameters of family relationships. The following section explores the role of boundaries within family systems in greater depth.

LIMITATIONS

Despite a plethora of studies detailing the efficacy of the structural approach (Aponte & Van Deusen, 1981; Stanton & Todd, 1979), the theory is not without its limitations. Due to the systemic and familial focus of the theory, it may be possible to neglect an individual's personal distress. The use of refocusing and relabeling techniques may also be deemed as manipulative by many practicing professionals. In addition, the lack of emotive focus for structural family clinicians may be seen as a limitation for those with more of an affective focus in therapy. The lack of feeling integration into sessions may inadvertently send the message to clients that feelings are not a welcome part of the therapeutic journey.

One final limitation involves the role of the counselor in therapy. As a directive change agent within the family, the counselor might foster dependence within the family and usurp their natural ability to problem-solve and effectively work through problems that arise. As a result, the therapist may find him- or herself locked into a position of power, with the family looking to the therapist as the creator of solutions and change. Therapists must be wary of this trap, and work to stay mobile and flexible as the course of therapy progresses.

SUMMARY

The structural approach to family systems work can largely be attributed to the work of Salvador Minuchin and his colleagues. His efforts to study and effectively alter the structure of family systems began at Wiltwyck School and were later perfected at the Philadephia Child Guidance Center. Through Minuchin's work, therapists are better able to fully understand the function and dysfunction that lie within the structure of a family system. Through understanding a family's subsystems, alignments, coalitions, and boundaries, therapists are more able to be purposeful and active in choosing interventions to stabilize the family structure.

The purpose of structural family counseling is to inspire change and insight within the family. Little attention is placed on an identified client when using this theory. Instead, all behavior is conceptualized and understood through the contextual lens of a family's structure. The therapist's charge is to effectively join the family system, thus becoming more privy to the needs within the family structure while simultaneously creating a relationship where direct and sometimes manipulative techniques can be used to shift and realign ineffective family subsystems and structure. Some techniques specific to structural family therapy include family mapping and enactments. Family mapping allows the therapist to effectively map a family's transactional patterns, and enactments are used to allow a family to create conflict-filled situations the therapist can observe. Through this observation, therapists are better able to establish a family's system, subsystems, and current boundary settings. Research shows that structural theory and many of the theory's techniques have proven beneficial in the treatment of schizophrenia, helping those with the diagnosis to avoid relapse and to improve their daily functioning (Yang & Pearson, 2002). The end goal of the structural therapeutic process is fostering a family's ability to problem-solve interactively as the family progresses naturally through its life cycle.

Evidence of a truly changed family lies within the comfort level each individual feels when sharing feelings and frustrations with other members of the system. Roles, rules, and boundaries within the family have a degree of flexibility, and appropriate boundaries are clearly defined. The parental subsystem has particular strength, in that it functions symbiotically and remains in a position of power within the family. Support and healing are hallmarks of the theory, and their creation is of critical importance for the structural family therapist. Facilitating such characteristics within a family can help to bring about long-lasting change in the family system.

USEFUL WEBSITES

The following websites provide additional information relating to chapter topics.

The Minuchin Center
http://www.minuchincenter.org
Philadelphia Child & Family Therapy Training Center
http://philafamily.com
Salvador Minuchin on family therapy
http://www.psychotherapy.net/video/minuchin-family-therapy
More about Salvador Minuchin
http://www.goodtherapy.org/famous-psychologists/salvador-minuchin.html

REFERENCES

Aponte, J. J., & Van Deusen, J. M. (1981). Structural family therapy. In A. S. Gurman & D. P. Kniskern (Eds.), *Handbook of family therapy*. New York, NY: Brunner/Mazel.

Blodgett Salafia, E. H., Schaefer, M. K., & Haugen, E. C. (2013). Connections between marital conflict and adolescent girls' disordered eating: Parent–adolescent relationship quality as a mediator. *Journal of Child and Family Studies*, *22*(4), 1–11. doi:10.1007/s10826-013-9771-9

Colapinto, J. (1991) Structural family therapy. In A. Gurman & D. Kniskern (Eds.), *Handbook of family therapy* (Vol. II). New York, NY: Brunner/Mazel.

Lindahl, K. M., & Malik, N. M. (2011). Marital conflict typology and children's appraisals: The moderating role of family cohesion. *Journal of Family Psychology*, *25*(2), 194–201. doi:10.1037/a0022888

Minuchin, S. (1974). *Families & family therapy*. Cambridge, MA: Harvard University Press.

Minuchin, S., & Fishman, H. C. (1981). *Family therapy techniques*. Cambridge, MA: Harvard University Press.

Minuchin, S., Montalvo, B., Guerney, B. G., Jr., Rosman, B. L., & Schumer, F. (1967). *Families of the slums: An exploration of their structure and treatment*. New York, NY: Basic Books.

Minuchin, S., & Nichols, M. P. (1993). *Family healing: Tales of hope and renewal from family therapy*. New York, NY: Free Press.

Rockinson-Szapkiw, A. J., Payne, L. Z., & West, L. C. (2011). Leadership lessons from Salvador Minuchin. *Family Journal*, *19*(2), 191–197. doi:10.1177/1066480711400159

Scaturo, D. J. (2005). Family therapy: Dilemmas of codependency and family homeostasis. In D. J. Scaturo (Ed.), *Clinical dilemmas in psychotherapy: A transtheoretical approach to psychotherapy integration* (pp. 99–110). Washington, DC: American Psychological Association. doi:10.1037/11110-006

Simon, G. M. (1995). A revisionist rendering of structural family therapy. *Journal of Marital and Family Therapy*, *21*, 17–26.

Stanton, M. D., & Todd, T. (1979). Some outcome results and aspects of structural family therapy with drug addicts. In E. Kaufman & P. Kaufman (Eds.), *The family therapy of drug and alcohol abuse*. New York, NY: Gardner Press.

Walters, M., Carter, B., Papp, P., & Silverstein, O. (1989). *The invisible web: Gender patterns in family relationships*. New York, NY: Guilford Press.

Yang, L., & Pearson, V. J. (2002). Understanding families in their own context: Schizophrenia and structural family therapy in Beijing. *Journal of Family Therapy*, *24*(3), 233–257. doi:10.1111/1467-6427.00214

CHAPTER

10

Strategic and Milan Systemic Theories: Approaches and Applications

Mark D. Stauffer and David Capuzzi

Walden University

BACKGROUND

Three Schools of Strategic Therapy

Within strategic family therapy there are three central models: the Mental Research Institute (MRI) school, the Washington school, and the Milan systemic school. Although distinctions exist between the techniques and goals of these models, all applied a systemic conceptual framework to family therapy. Led by pioneers such as Don Jackson, John Weakland, Cloé Madanes, Paul Watzlawick, and Jay Haley, strategic therapists focused on how families maintained problems through interactional processes and patterns.

Strategic family therapy evolved gradually from its origins in the late 1950s, when it gained a reputation for its unorthodox and unusual therapeutic interventions. Although some questioned the ethics of the uncommon therapeutic processes and practices, the pioneers of strategic family therapy were no doubt devoted to action research to understand the influence of their work with families. Some have questioned whether such criticism was miscast and misunderstanding because of the directive and sometimes intuitive nature of these tailored and complex models of therapy (Gardner, Burr, & Wiedower, 2006). Regardless, red flags do point to the unusual level of expertise and skill required to fully embody this tradition and apply its techniques carefully with clients. This chapter explores the major constructs, goals, roles, processes, techniques, and limitations of strategic family therapy in general, but with a focus on the three main schools.

Strategic family therapy has a strong foundation in Eriksonian principles. For example, the goal for treatment is pragmatic change. As a therapeutic model, it is less concerned with client insight and catharsis. Therapy is tailored and goal directed. In addition, the capability for change is recognized through a present and future frames of reference (Jenkins & Forrest, 1999). As Watzlawick, Weakland, and Fisch (2011) commented in their book *Change: Principles of Problem Formulation and Problem Resolution*, "we can take the situation as it exists here and now, and in spite of our ignorance of its origin and evolution, we do something with (or about) it. In doing this we are asking What? i.e., what is the situation, what is going on here and now?" (p. 81).

Many of the strategic therapy processes, goals, and techniques require that the client family system make significant shifts in their concept of the family and the family problem. All concepts about the nature of family and family problems are derived from conceptual frames that allow the individual and family to make sense of the lived experiences. Whether helpful or not, perceptions about the nature of family, identified problems, and possible solutions to problems are filtered through the conceptual frame. The family may have an unhelpful framework or ineffective methods and conclusions for dealing with the framed problem. Importantly, families often arrive in counseling having exhausted solutions from their frame of the family and problem. Understanding the conceptual framework provides the strategic therapist with a starting point for intervention and rapport with families (Becvar & Becvar, 2000).

SIDEBAR 10.1 THE ALAVI FAMILY CASE EXAMPLE

A recently immigrated family of five (parents, two sons, and a daughter) entered counseling because the daughter is anorectic and won't eat. The father believes she has been spoiled by the "American life" and the vanity of her newfound peers, who are often dieting and giving his daughter modeling magazines. He secretly worries that he has spoiled her, because she is his only daughter and the "baby." The mother secretly blames herself for working away from home; she is unable to "cook appealing meals" and provide a traditional home environment. The parents respond by grounding the daughter from these peers and forcing her to remain at the table until she eats some portion of her food. The two sons don't want to be in counseling and do not understand the need; they are often checked out to their sister's needs and would rather be at home because doctor's visits are seen as boring. The therapist explores with family members the identified family problem, and initially notices that the family rules discourage talk about the move, those they left behind, and unpleasant realities, such as the struggles with acculturation, assimilation, as well as grief and loss. What are the different conceptual frameworks involved in this example?

MAJOR CONSTRUCTS

Generally, family members are seen as acting within a range of interactional behaviors (i.e., principle of redundancy) within the family context. Together the family's behaviors occur in patterns of interaction that are mutually arising, influencing, and perpetuating (i.e., circular causality). Rather than simple cause and effect, circular causality suggests that behavior happens in a contextual and cyclical manner. Most often families and those new to systems thinking have already considered that A (e.g., spousal fighting) causes B (e.g., lack of affection), that A can cause B in a repetitive fashion over time, or that A causes B, which causes C (e.g., divorce ideation), which then causes D (e.g., consideration of therapy) in a chain of cause and effect. In addition, couples sometimes grasp that A causes more of B and then B causes more of A—more fighting promotes less affection, which promotes more fighting, and so on. This is called a *positive feedback loop*. Circular causality is indeed difficult for dualistic linear thinking because we live in a dynamic system that is constantly reshaped in the present moment. Action does not occur in a vacuum of space. Consider the systemic complexity and circular causality in light of recent global climate changes, the outbreak and influence of social media, or even global human population growth. Everyday actions are now influencing local, national, and global systems. Adept strategic therapists understand the family and family systems beyond linear models of causality. In considering the complex nature of circular causality as it relates to family and limits to time available to pursue therapeutic avenues, strategic therapists are first interested in what will pragmatically create change in the system.

In the same way that member actions within a system tend toward the redundant, the entire system seeks a state of balance or homeostasis and resists unbalancing change. This stabilization force occurs in the midst of inevitable change. After all, children leave home, parents die, natural disasters strike, and illness comes. *Negative feedback* is the process by which the system returns to equilibrium by dealing with deviation to the system. For example, returning to the daily schedule and routine helps a family retain order after a loss. From a strategic view, working on one problem provides the potential to shift homeostasis for a symptomatic family toward a healthier pattern. To clarify, symptomatic behavior is often viewed as originating from and being maintained by the complex feedback loops or interactional patterns and not the individual client. The problem may serve a purpose or function in the social context. The problem itself support roles and behaviors in the family and vice versa.

Strategic therapists work with the family to identify solvable problems and then determine therapeutic goals for problem resolution. Across therapeutic schools, there is an underlying notion in counseling that positive change is possible. It is unlikely that a client would freely and effectively participate and persist with therapy if there was not a benefit or a hope that some positive change would come from the effort. Part of counseling is making this underlying assumption a stated value. Strategic therapists often focus on one problem identified by the family system, and then take responsibility to design and apply interventions that will help the family with that problem. Some strategic therapists work on only one problem, whereas others, such as Jay Haley, address other problems after solving the initial family problem. In limiting therapeutic focus to a problem, the problem rather than the family is conceptualized as needing change.

According to various strategic schools, the family problem and homeostasis around the problem are developmentally due to structural, functional, or cybernetic reasons. For example, Haley (1973, 1976) worked with incongruent hierarchies and related power struggles as a structural manifestation of problems, whereas Madanes (1981, 1990) emphasized functional reasons for problems (e.g., child problematic symptoms function as a way of controlling, protecting, gaining desired love, or receiving forgiveness). The MRI school focuses on runaway positive feedback loops and a cybernetic view of problem formulation. As we will examine, variations in problem formulation lead to variations in how these schools and specific therapists might go about problem resolution.

Strategic therapists focus on second-order change rather than first-order change. Both first-order change and second-order change are brought about in strategic therapy. *First-order change* is a change within the system without changing the organizing structure and rules of the system. These are often pragmatic solutions that make sense to the family or have been used successfully to some degree by the family. For example, a therapist helps a family with polarizing gender norms as they deal with a spousal dispute over division of household labor. As facilitated by the therapist, they make a quid pro quo agreement that has been used in the past, which does not challenge the family's conceptual framework regarding the gender division of labor. The wife, Shelly, agrees that she won't let the dishes pile up, if the husband, Deon, splits, stacks, and brings the firewood in regularly. Here the system has not changed, and so it is likely that the same impasse and dispute will arise over the division of labor as a function of the current order, which dictates that men and women have gender-divided duties. Weeks pass and soon Deon gets behind on bringing in the wood, and so to deal with this Shelly tries the usual first-order change solutions: She requests, then "nags" Deon about the "counseling agreement," then shows discomfort by sulking, then copes by talking to friends, and finally, decides to let the dishes become a mess, which Deon says "overstimulates" him and "makes him feel chaotic" because his "mother always kept a clean kitchen."

Second-order change change occurs "when there is a qualitative shift in the system or shift in the frame such that the body of rules governing the structure of that system itself, changes" (Davey, Duncan, Kissil, Davey, & Fish, 2011, p. 101). Second-order change often requires a creative and paradoxical approach to the system creating the problem, often by doing something outside of the family rules. It can seem illogical and irrational, especially when the family uses the conceptual framework that created and sustained the identified problem. As therapists, we could provide an idea of a second-order change for Shelly and Deon, but what intervention might you use to promote or provoke second-order change in this case scenario?

WASHINGTON SCHOOL OF STRATEGIC THERAPY

Background

Several well-known practitioners developed what is known as strategic family therapy, but Jay Haley is one of the most important. Haley studied with three of the most influential theorists in the evolution of family therapy: Gregory Bateson,

Milton Erickson, and Salvador Minuchin. The integration, combination, and influence of their work made Haley's work a unique approach to family therapy. In 1953, Gregory Bateson invited Haley to work with a team in Palo Alto, California, using family therapy to treat and manage schizophrenia. Importantly, this group launched family therapy by applying cybernetic principles to family communication and interactional patterns. Haley (1981) noted that when his project with Bateson ended in 1962, "we had successfully made the shift from describing madness and other symptoms as individual phenomena to describing them as communicative behavior between people" (p. xii). The Bateson Project and team, which included John Weakland and William Fry, would be paramount in the development of family therapy.

As a result of his work with Bateson, Haley was introduced to Milton H. Erickson and became interested in Erickson's hypnotherapeutic communication processes. Under Erickson's supervision from 1954 to 1960, Haley developed his therapeutic skills by close examination and practice of Erickson's model of therapy, which included the use of directives (i.e., clients are directed to act in ways that are counterproductive to their maladaptive behavior). He observed that a client's symptoms were based in incongruent communication patterns, specifically incongruence between overt and covert levels of communication with others. Haley looked beyond simple dyadic relationships by exploring triangular, intergenerational relationships, or, as he called them, *perverse triangles*. Dealing with these in session, he surmised, would provide the client with a sense of control in his or her interpersonal relationships (Haley, 1973, 1976).

In 1962, Haley joined the Mental Research Institute staff, where he was director of family experimentation until 1967. He also became the first editor of the first journal in the field of family therapy, called *Family Process* (http://www.familyprocess.org/about-us/fpjournal), a position he held from 1962 to 1969. It was also during this time that his focus shifted from practicing therapy to performing supervision. In 1967, Haley moved east and directed the Philadelphia Child Guidance Clinic with Salvador Minuchin. Then in 1976, after 10 years at the Philadelphia Child Guidance clinic, Haley moved on to cofound the Family Therapy Institute with Cloé Madanes in Washington, DC, which has since become a major training institute. After the move to Washington, he published two of his most influential books, *Problem Solving Therapy* (1976) and *Leaving Home* (1980).

On top of founding the Family Therapy Institute, Cloé Madanes was critical in forwarding the institute's model of family therapy. She helped shape the modern use of strategic interventions, for example, by introducing the pretend technique as a variation to paradoxical interventions (Madanes, 1981). The pretend technique integrated ideas of play and play therapy with strategic family therapy approaches. In this way, central family problems caused by dual hierarchies and conflicting levels of communication patterns could be shifted with childlike openness and imagination (Haley, 1981). This integrative approach with play can be found in her seminal work, *Strategic Family Therapy* (Madanes, 1981). Recently, Madanes promoted strategic humanism, which examines harmony instead of hierarchy and power struggle.

Additional Constructs

Dysfunctional Hierarchies

The Washington school examined family hierarchy and problems resulting from hierarchy. For example, Madanes (1990) was uniquely concerned with the phenomenon of children adopting symptoms to change parental behaviors and interactions. In this way, children manifested symptomatic problems as a way to deal with incongruent hierarchies. Carl Rogers (1961) described intrapersonal incongruence as a state in which a person is unable to actualize the "real self" because of a superimposed "ideal self." An incongruent hierarchy varies from this in that it is a hierarchy that is inconsistent with a healthy family order. One commonly occurring example of incongruence is when parents have the knowledge, skills, means, social sanctioning, legal duty, and so forth to be decision-making guardians, but the child, through symptomatic behavior, is now "in charge" of the family. Family rules reinforce this hierarchical incongruence, at least until the family is stimulated to change.

At first glance, one might confuse elements of structural family therapy with Haley and Madanes's structural focus on dealing with incongruent hierarchies. Some theorists have advocated for an integration of structural and strategic models of therapy, and in the last decades, more work to bring various schools together has no doubt validated cross-pollination and dialogue (Keim, 2000). To distinguish the two in their focus on structure, structural family therapists focus on the structural boundaries and integrity of the family subsystems. They are more concerned with changing how the family is organized. Strategic family therapists may work on power struggles and hierarchy, but they focus on changing the family interactional processes, patterns, and related functioning (Gladding, 2007).

Roles, Goals, and Process

Roles

As a note to the reader, much of what is described about the various schools in these sections could be applied to each school. In this theoretical yet pragmatic model, the therapist must be flexible, creative, and actively involved. "Strategic therapy isn't a particular approach or therapy, but a name for the types of therapy where the therapist takes direct responsibility for directly influencing people" (Haley, 1973, p. 17). The therapist, in taking responsibility for family-tailored interventions, will use various techniques to provoke change. Haley thought that the healing aspect of the client–therapist relationship involved getting clients to take ownership of their actions and the therapeutic relationship, a process he called *therapeutic paradox*. In other words, a paradox arises because the therapist helps someone to be self-efficacious and self-empowered by way of the therapist affecting and empowering them. Haley also believed that it was far more important to get clients to actively do something about their problems rather than to help them understand why they had these problems. Similarly, the focus is on process rather than, for example, historical context. For example, Haley would ask each member to discuss the family problem and then examine the family interaction about the problem. This would be done before a directive would be given at the end of a session to deal with the interactional pattern and embedded problem (Haley, 1976). This view is shared throughout the schools of strategic therapy.

The counselor, due to the intervention process and the use of directive techniques, is placed in an expert role. This fits the medical model of a practitioner, much like a client entering a medical doctor's office and being prescribed a treatment after the problem has been assessed. The problematic symptom is the focus of treatment, rather than the family, and the counselor is focused on treating the problem through means that may or may not be rationally or fully understood by the patient. This is not to say that the role is authoritarian, because the counselor wants to join with the family in a respectful and cooperative way.

Goals and Process

Generally, strategic family therapy is considered brief, meaning there are a limited number of sessions, often no more than 10. The first session is generally the most important in strategic therapy because it is here that all stages (assessment of the problem, discovery of past attempts, and applying the intervention) occur and rapport is built. In support of this notion, Talmon (2012), in a review of 15 years of family therapy research, noted:

> The first session in psychotherapy is potentially the most therapeutic and often has the greatest influence on the outcome of therapy. . . . The fact that less is very often better in psychotherapy is by now one of the most validated and consistent findings in evidence-based psychotherapy research. (p. 6)

Some therapists work on only one problem, whereas others, like Haley, address additional problems after solving the initial family problem.

At first glance, some strategic interventions seem counterintuitive. They are often paradoxical and may activate a family in a way that does not seem to be causally related to the problem. Interventions are designed to disrupt unhealthy family system homeostasis, allowing family members to incorporate new positive concepts, perceptions, and behaviors. The Washington school, in particular, used the acronym PUSH to describe the problem-defining process (see Sidebar 10.2).

SIDEBAR 10.2 PUSH: PROTECTION, UNIT, SEQUENCE, HIERARCHY

Protection describes the family problem and behaviors that maintain the problem as a form of protective activity. A classic example provided by Madanes is the child who creates a disturbance to unite two divorcing parents in solving the child's problem. *Unit* refers to the triadic, rather than individual, dyadic, or more than triadic, focus of grouping clients for observation in work. Examining less than three negates the ability to observe coalitions, and examining more than three may become taxing to track. *Sequence* is the linear or circular order of the problem pattern. The counselor works to exchange unhelpful and maladaptive patterns with healthier patterns. *Hierarchy* refers to how members play a role and how they function in a given intergenerational system. The strategic therapist examines hierarchy and how shifts in hierarchy can create functional family interaction and membership (Keim, 2000).

Madanes viewed problems as stemming from power and hierarchy such that therapists should work to adjust power in families and change interactional metaphors (Madanes, 1981). Haley (1987) and other strategic therapists (e.g., Watzlawick, Beavin Bavales, & Jackson, 2011) suggested that much of family communication is analogical, rather than digital, because the message is embedded in the context of other messages. "Thus, a piece of communication, including a family's presenting problem, can be seen as a metaphor for the family's current situation (including the family's interactional sequence and structure)" (Young, Negash, & Long, 2009, p. 402).

Madanes (1990), in her book *Sex, Love, and Violence: Strategies for Transformation*, divided reasons into four types: (1) to dominate and to control, (2) to be loved, (3) to love and protect, and (4) to repent and to forgive. Interventions can be tailored to these four categories (Keim, 2000). Counselors apply interventions and then assess responses to those uniquely designed intervention strategies. They weigh effects and potential outcomes (Haley, 1996, 2005). The following are some of the techniques used by the Washington school with a rationale for their use. Because many of the techniques are shared across the three schools, techniques have been placed as representative rather than because they are exclusively used by a specific school.

Washington School Techniques

Directives

One of the techniques of strategic therapy is the use of directives. Directives take various forms, depending on the systemic problem, and require certain conditions of the therapist (see FACE in Sidebar 10.3). In this section we will cover some of them, for example, giving ordeals and rituals, prescribing the presenting problem, and giving paradoxical restraints or paradoxical contracts to clients (Haley, 1973). Haley (1976) discussed two forms of directives: *direct directives* and *indirect directives*. Both make requests of client behavior. Which directive is given depends on the goal of intervention. The direct type of directive provides a clear and overt prompt for some type of behavior on the part of the client. These are more likely to fit within the conceptual framework of the client, be attributed to the counselor's expertise, and "make sense" in their aim. For example, a directive might be given that prompts family members to reunite (Haley, 1976), that asks the family to come up with a solution, or perhaps, that directs a client to employ a strategy that was previously successful in solving a similar problem (Haley, 1973, 1976). Although direct directives are open requests of the client, some fall outside of the conceptual framework and family rules and, therefore, may seem like creative leaps or illogical requests.

SIDEBAR 10.3 REQUIREMENTS OF DIRECTIVE THERAPY

Directives require expertise and a cooperative approach to their application. Keim (2000) suggested that counselors can mistakenly use directives to solve rather than motivate solutions, be insensitive in providing directives, be unclear in providing directives, and fail to develop a strong enough therapeutic alliance to use directives. Keim (p. 180) provided the following FACE map as a guide:

Familiarity: therapist is familiar with the problem and context to a workable degree

Appreciation: having mutual appreciation between client and therapist

Competence: therapist is competent to direct and client is competent to perform the directive and confident in the therapist

Empathy: communicating beyond familiarity with the problem, the therapist communicates the human predicament with compassion and understanding

Indirect directives influence change without a clear and overt request of the client. Often the influence of the therapist is unseen, and the resultant change is often attributed to self or system efficacy by the client. In gently provoking the system toward a second-order change, an indirect directive might reduce the sense of pressure to perform, succeed, or carry through, for example, with homework. An indirect directive might come in the form of a therapist telling a seemingly unrelated story to the family that provides an idea for the family to change.

Using *direct* and *indirect* to describe directives categorizes them by how they are presented to and received by the client. Keim (1993) presented a categorization with three variations related to the function of the directive given. These are primary directives, preparatory directives, and terminal directives. Primary directives are focused on the primary problem. Preparatory directives, while not directly addressing the primary problem, prepare the ground for problem resolution. For example, the counselor gives a directive for the parents of a demanding symptomatic child to engage in a pleasurable activity once a week, which relaxes and unifies the couple, two elements needed to tackle the main symptom. A terminal directive influences therapeutic closure in some way.

Paradoxical Interventions

Although they require a significant level of expertise and training, strategic therapists employ paradoxical interventions to resolve problems for families.

Paradoxical interventions are often applied in the form of directives (Haley, 1973; Madanes, 1981). The therapist understands that family systems are resistant in attempts to maintain stability. Paradoxical interventions lower this resistance. Some key paradoxical interventions are restraining, prescribing the symptom, and redefining the problem through positive connotation.

Restraining *Restraining* is a paradoxical technique that aims at lowering resistance through compliance. The therapist merely states that clients should continue to do exactly as they have been doing. They are to wait or "restrain" themselves from solving the problem, which conveys that they are to refrain from changing. Sometimes this is a simple admonition to "go slow" and consider the consequences of change. Often this is given in combination with an admonition to examine the positive that comes from having the problem. There may also be a warning about getting rid of the problem too quickly because this may undo the benefits of having the problem. For example, Erickson would often encourage a relapse (Haley, 1973) to lower pressure on compliance. When individuals or even families come into counseling for the first time, they have often done so after exhausting attempts to solve the problem in their own way or after having come to an impasse within the family in working on the problem. Failed attempts can lead to a sense of powerlessness and lack of control over problems. Attempts that have not been successful can lead to blame and animosity, but also a loss of hope that the family has control over their ability to resolve a problem. In short, families have tried and come up short. They come to counseling expecting a solution from an expert, while considering their own management of the problem in an inferior way. So, what comes of therapy if a problem is solved and yet the family still believes that they are powerless and not in control of the problem? The technique of restraining helps the family see their real power and the control or lack of control that they do have related to a specific identified problem. Rather than having a dualistic view of a family circumstance and problem, this technique helps the family embody a more systemic mode and a dialectical mode of thinking, thus considering the family from a more complex perspective.

Prescribing the Symptom Prescribing the symptom is a paradoxical intervention in which the unhealthy symptoms of the individual or family are encouraged, sometimes in amplified form. For example, one might prescribe an individual with insomnia to try to stay awake all night (Shoham-Salomon & Rosenthal, 1987). This type of paradox would bind the client by asking him or her to control something (i.e., thinking) that cannot be controlled. This lowers resistance through paradoxical acceptance and allows the client to see in a new light the roles and behaviors he or she maintains.

Amplifying the Problem Contrary to common sense, intentionally removing a solution and thereby making a problem worse can solve a problem. Watzlawick, Weakland, and Fisch (2011) provided this example (shortened here): A couple who came to counseling had overly helpful parents. Although they were good parents, they tended to be interfering and meddling. As had been the pattern, they were not recognizing the autonomy of their son, and now their new daughter-in-law. Throughout his life, the son was readily provided with most needs, including a recent new house, which was chosen by the parents in a more upscale neighborhood than the couple had desired. The therapist instructed the newlyweds to not clean up the house and to leave the car, cupboards, and refrigerator empty prior to the parents' visit. During the visit, the young couple was directed to be polite and respectful, but to not pay for needed groceries, to not mow or do house chores and repairs, and to even watch TV while the parents compulsively helped restore the home. The parents left early, drawing a line with the son conveying their desire for him to be more autonomous.

Ordeals

Haley and Erickson in particular used "ordeals" as a way of changing a client's behavior. To employ the ordeal technique with a client, the counselor creates a difficult task that causes distress for the client "equal to or greater than that caused by the symptom. Usually if the ordeal is not severe enough it can be increased in magnitude until it [is]" (Haley, 1973, p. 6). Having to go through an ordeal to continue the symptomatic behavior decreases the motivation to maintain the problem and increases the desire to surpass it. In one case of Erickson's, an individual was afraid of driving across a state line (Haley, 1973). Erickson gave an ordeal that required the driver to stop a short distance before the state line, get out, and lie in a road ditch, after which the client was to return to the car and drive slightly further and repeat the process. Frustrated, the client resisted the ordeal and drove right through the state line (Haley, 1973). This type of paradoxical intervention requires the client to rebel against the directive. Not all ordeals call for this.

SIDEBAR 10.4 STAGES OF ORDEAL THERAPY (FROM HALEY, 1973, PP. 14–16)

Define the problem clearly: The problem is defined clearly because a consequence must be developed that appropriately fits the problem.

Verify and develop a client's motivation for commitment to change: Ordeals rest on the motivation of the client and a deep desire to solve the problem. Without client motivation, the ordeal will be bypassed. The counselor actively monitors and increases motivation and commitment during the phases of the ordeal technique.

Select an ordeal in collaboration with the client: The counselor will tailor a technique that fits client commitment. It should not be more severe than is necessary for resolving the problem. The ordeal must be beneficial to the person, be morally appropriate in the eyes of the client, have start and end dates, be concretely directing, and be within the client's ability to perform. The client should be directed to apply the ordeal exactly as designed each time and only with symptomatic behaviors.

Give the directive for the ordeal with a rationale: It is not only important to tailor the ordeal, but the counselor must also help the client see the reasonableness of the ordeal. Haley (1973) noted that, for some clients, simply providing a directive without a rationale is possible and maybe preferable.

The ordeal continues until problem resolution: Haley (1973) noted that an ordeal may be kept as a lifelong prevention strategy.

Work with the social context as the ordeal affects the context: When an ordeal is provided, it often creates change within the family and social system. The counselor must then work with the clients to deal with the changes caused by the ordeal.

Pretend Technique

Cloé Madanes extensively used *pretend* as a technique (Madanes, 1981). Its intent is to have the client enact a dysfunctional problem behavior as if it were play or pretend. Pretending in front of the therapist, the client realizes that he or she has more control over the problem than previously thought. Madanes provided pretend techniques as an addition to the list of paradoxical interventions a therapist could use in session to correct power imbalances and change problematic patterns of interaction within the family. Most paradoxical interventions, such as prescribing the symptom or giving an ordeal, have a confrontational element. They are confrontational in that they are not intuitive to the client, but require trusting buy-in with the counselor, for example, when the counselor requires the family to maintain the problematic symptoms that led them to counseling. Pretend allows for exploration and challenge of the central interactional problem while not requiring a professional response. The pretend technique infuses play therapy ideas and mannerisms into the paradoxical intervention (Madanes, 1981).

MENTAL RESEARCH INSTITUTE (MRI) SCHOOL

Background

In 1959, the Mental Research Institute was founded in Palo Alto, California, close to the Stanford University campus and in close connection and quarters with the Palo Alto Medical Research Foundation and the Bateson research project. Started as a nonprofit organization to study interactional processes, MRI stands as one of the most instrumental institutions in family therapy, particularly given its focus on interactional and systemic work with couples and families (see http://www.mri.org). Don Jackson is credited with spearheading the founding of MRI, but he is also known for his instrumental application of systems theory to the family. It was no small task to push a field from a focus on individual mental health in a linear way to conceptualizing mental health in a systemic way. Like Jay Haley, he worked closely with Gregory Bateson and the Bateson research project. Not only was Don Jackson in the forefront in establishing family therapy theory, but he also helped the Mental Research Institute become a premier organization for pioneers in family therapy (see http://www.mri.org/dondjackson/mri.htm). Some of the notable pioneers and influential figures connected to MRI are Paul Watzlawick, Virginia Satir, Jules Riskin, Richard Fisch, John Weakland, Lynn Hoffman, Antonio Ferreira, Janet Bevin Bavelas, Lynn Segal, and Art Bodin.

MRI Additional Constructs

In close connection with Bateson's research project and cybernetics, the MRI model emphasized problem identification and problem resolution by identifying problematic positive feedback loops, examining the rules governing them, and resolving the problem by changing the loops and related family rules. Where the MRI model is keenly aware of feedback loops (in particular, runaway positive feedback loops, discussed earlier), the Washington school and the Milan school tend to focus on structural (i.e., hierarchical power and incongruence) or functional family problems (e.g., symptoms emerging as a function of the family problem). Creating conditions for change to the client's identified problem is primary to all.

MRI Roles, Goals, and Process

Similar to other strategic schools, the therapist is active and creative. In this model, the counselor defines the problem in behavioral language and helps the clients commit to clear behavioral goals related to resolving unhelpful feedback loops. During the phase called *estimation*, the therapist examines how feedback loops are maintained by the family behaviors. Importantly, the therapist does not approach the family as a dysfunctional unit, but rather helps them make second-order changes by interrupting and replacing runaway positive feedback loops through various means.

The therapist will find out what successful and unsuccessful solutions have been tried. Knowing what solutions the family has tried will help the therapist know which strategies to not repeat and which new avenues will create second-order change. Often families create solutions to affect the family problems, but apply the solution to the wrong level. For example, grounding the anorectic child and forbidding her from her friends, in the Alavi case, would be solving the problem at the wrong level. At other times, families create solutions to problems that do not exist, for example, punishing a child for wetting a bed at age 1. In such cases, intervention needs to be applied to the solution, rather than to the problem (Watzlawick, Weakland, et al., 2011). Antithetical to this faulty solution, another type of common solution for clients is doing nothing or ignoring a significant or real problem. As an example, consider how the Alavi family has not only applied a solution at the wrong level, but they have also ignored their grief and loss by disallowing communication.

MRI Techniques

Many of the techniques mentioned in the Washington school section are also used by this school. We add reframing and positioning to those in our discussion of specific techniques.

Reframing

Like many of the techniques in this chapter, reframing is used by all strategic schools in some way or shape. Reframing directly shifts family perspective by providing an alternative view that undermines the current conceptual framework. Families enter counseling with conceptual frameworks that have not helped to resolve the problem, have promoted a limited view of the problem and solutions, and have encouraged solutions for first-order change. To reframe something means to give a different meaning or interpretation to it. For example, a positive connotation can be given to a behavior, thus undermining the negative view of the symptomatic behavior. So, a child's misbehavior is reframed as an attempt to "involve parents" who have been working hard to "provide for and to protect" the family. In this case, the context of the system is changed by providing a new perception that undermines the notion that there is a problem in the first place. Now parental efforts to balance the two needs of providing for family and attention to family are highlighted instead of the misbehavior. This intervention might diminish a positive feedback loop, for example, as child misbehavior increases to gain attention and the father spends more time away (from the misbehavior), where it is easier to focus on work.

"What makes reframing such an effective tool of change is that once we do perceive the alternative class of membership(s) we cannot so easily go back to the trap and the anguish of a former view of 'reality'" (Watzlawick, Weakland, et al., 2011, p. 97). Not only does reframing allow the family to see themselves, situations, and behaviors in a different light (i.e., as new classifications), but it also disenfranchises the old lens. Other theoretical orientations might use reframing and new views of reality to enhance insight and awareness of the problem. Strategic therapists are concerned with pragmatic behavioral change. As a reader, do you believe a therapist has to believe in the reality of what is reframed to use this technique?

Positioning

Positioning is a technique in which the therapist accepts the position of a client and then exaggerates the stance. The intent is to expose the unreasonableness or even absurdity of a belief or concept held by the family. Exaggeration pushes the client to question the conceptual framework connected to the problem. This may be done by holding the position until the family disagrees with the therapist and thereby disagrees with their stance. Along with many of the techniques, such as reframing and positioning, a gentle approach is best to change the view of the system (Watzlawick, Weakland, et al., 2011). If the client states that he or she cannot stand to be in the house as a result of current situation, the therapist might say, "I think even staying a day is too long!" or "It's a completely unbearable situation!"

MILAN SYSTEMIC SCHOOL

Background

A group of Milan family therapists, originally working from a psychoanalytic perspective, were inspired by the work of Jay Haley and began to apply and adapt a strategic approach to working with families. They founded the Center for Family Studies Milan and coined the approach "systemic," after Bateson's work, and began practicing what would become known as *systemic family therapy*. Using applied research processes, the team of Mara Selvini-Palazzoli, Luigi Boscolo, Gianfranco Cecchin, and Guilana Prata refined the Milan systemic family therapy and added unique perspectives and interventions. Uniquely, they conducted research and therapy with teams of four therapists and used novel techniques such as circular questioning and team hypothesizing (Boscolo, Cecchin, Hoffman, & Penn, 1987).

Milan Roles, Goals, and Process

The Milan systemic therapist role stems from a more medical model. Therapists maintain control over certain elements of the session. For example, the therapist might not be transparent about intervention strategy, may ask family members to hold secrets, will end conversations if they are not useful to therapy, and may decide who is to speak at what time in session. The counselor, in this case, is not authoritarian, but still may be assertive by, for example, deciding to dismiss certain members from a future session without explanation to see responses and rectify family games. At times, creating an emotional reaction within the family shifts the problematic pattern and allows the therapist to see the interactional patterns and hierarchy. Milan school therapists also use circular questioning, which stirs the pot with novel probing of the family hypothesis about the selected problem. Congruent with strategic therapy, the counselor does not align with the family's understanding of the problem because the counselor plays a part in creating change that differs from how the family pattern is occurring (Selvini-Palazzoli, Cirillo, Selvini, & Sorrentino, 1989).

Selvini-Palazzoli and colleagues (1989), in the book *Family Game*, provided two metaphors to consider when thinking about their style of therapy. First, the therapist is the "hunter," which directly attempts to dismantle the problematic pattern and the negative family game. There is also the "breeder," meaning the client becomes offspring in taking care of their mental health by following the path of the therapist. This process is seen as similar to most therapeutic modalities in which the therapist is able to work with clients because of their own path to mental health. They then influence as a result of modeling, increased awareness, interpersonal skill, and shared insight. As Selvini-Palazzoli and colleagues (1989) suggested, the therapist team starts as hunters, tracking down the family game, especially in the first few sessions; then they move toward breeder roles as they help, for example, coparents become therapists of their own life. This is often done by unifying parents in a collaborative agreement toward family health through the invariant prescription described later.

Similar to other strategic models, the duration of the work is between 3 and 10 sessions. The family may meet for an extended time in one session but only have sessions once a month. Milan systemic therapy with families involves five stages: presession, session, intercession, intervention, and postsession (Selvini-Palazzoli et al., 1989). During the presession, team members examine the available information and hypothesize about the problem. During the session, they used circular questioning and a unique hypothesizing process (described later) to discover the interactional process and nature of the problem, and to come up with an intervention to replace the "dirty game," as they sometimes called it, with a new family game (Selvini-Palazzoli et al., 1989). The team works at structuring and building rapport by joining. The term *dirty games* describes the family's hidden power struggles and incongruent hierarchies. Often the parental subsystem of the family is stuck in a power stalemate with the family divided along parental lines (e.g., a daughter is angry with one parent on behalf of the the other parent).

During intercession, the family waits while the team meets to discuss interactions and information related to the hypothesis. The therapist (and team) formulate a hypothesis exploring the problem and also the attempts the family has made to solve the problem. Interaction in session helps to confirm, disconfirm, or reshape the hypothesis.

Intervention is the stage in which the team returns and directs the family toward some action for eliminating the identified problem. This means employing one of the techniques described later: invariant/variant prescription, positive connotation, or rituals. In the postsession stage, the team evaluates and plans for future sessions.

As with other types of family therapy, having most of the family in session is important, especially at the start. However, the strategic therapist often excludes certain members to bring about change in the family pattern (Selvini-Palazzoli et al., 1989). For example, the therapists might use an invariant prescription by seeing just the parents in session and implementing a secrecy pact "that invites the couple to start sharing in a new game to play with each other" in a noncompetitive, cotherapeutic mode, marking a "needed autonomy from the first and third generation" (Selvini-Palazzoli et al., 1989, pp. 248–249).

Milan Techniques

Hypothesis

The Milan systemic school is not unique for assessing and coming up with a hypothesis about what is occurring with clients. What makes the technique of hypothesis unique to this school is that hypotheses are collaboratively postulated by and among a team, and then activity in session is directed at confirming or disconfirming the hypotheses to come up with the final intervention. Consider what it would be like to provide therapy to a family for years with a team of four therapists who are also coresearchers! The hypothesis revolves around the conceptual framework of the Milan model for working with client systems. Often this meant hypothesizing about the dirty game or family game in which the symptomatic behavior was maintained by the behaviors of the family. In recalling the Alavi family case from earlier in the chapter, what would change the symptomatic problem of the family? Was the daughter's symptomatic behavior a way of "protecting" the family from the grief and loss of acculturation? Was it meant to draw the mother back home to focus on the sibling subsystem needs? Was it an act of anger to get the family to seek help and to open up disallowed discussion? One of the chief and novel strategies for exploring a hypothesis in session with the family was the use of circular questioning, discussed next.

Circular Questioning

Circular questioning is a signature technique of the Milan group that has since been applied and adapted by various therapeutic orientations and modalities. (See Table 10.1.) The Milan group designed this style of inquiry in trying to find the most "fruitful" method to understand how family members, behaviors, and perceptions are connected. Using circular questioning can provide a rush of novel information for the therapists and family alike as they are both able to see obscured or hidden connections and differences (Selvini-Palazzoli, Boscolo, Cecchin, & Prata, 1980). For example, after a traumatic event, the aunt states that the whole family feels anxious and is beside themselves about the event. With circular questioning the difference in emotion and the severity of the emotion are clearly differentiated, but on the other hand, critical connections and similarities are

Table 10.1 Circular Question Types and Examples

Difference in Perception of Relationship
Who is closer to your sister, your father or mother?
Who is most distant to mother in the family?
Behavior, Attitude, Belief Differences Between People
Of members in your family, who is most likely to storm out? Who is the next likely?
Who shows the most affection to father when he has been sick? Who is next?
Who most believes that the children are in charge of this family?
Difference of Degree (or Severity)
On a scale of 1 to 10, how much do your husband's parents meddle in your life?
To what degree has the grief escalated since the incarceration?
Difference Across Time or Now/Then
When did she start eating differently, before or after your move to the United States?
How long will it take each of you to figure out this problem?
Hypothetical/Future
If your parents split up and moved to different cities, with whom would you move?
How long will it take each of you to do your part of this proposed change?
How might this problem shift for the family in the future?

Source: Adapted from Boscolo et al. (1987) and Brown (1997).

expressed and witnessed. Such a routine might reduce an antigroup habit of speaking for the group as members embrace the likelihood of variation in lived experience. In addition, circular questions can be used therapeutically to help clients see that their behaviors were not only seen by other family members, but also that their behaviors influence the behavior and perceptions of others through circular causality. For example, instead of asking why the son continues to break curfew and come back drunk when the father is on the road working, the therapist asks what the parents' reactions are to the son, what they say to each other and the three younger children when this happens, what the children think about how the parents are responding to the son's episodes, and so on. Furthermore, "the questioning is aimed at creating or maximizing difference and then drawing connections in order to provide information that frames problems in new ways" (Brown, 1997, p. 109).

Circular questioning may force a mode of communication that is uncommon in dysfunctional families, that is, one member of the family commenting and reflecting on the relationship(s) of other members. For example, one might ask a mother-in-law at the first session, "How has your daughter and son-in-law's relationship changed since your granddaughters were born and you moved into help?" Or, to the anorectic daughter in the Alavi family case example, "How has your parents' communication with each other and your brothers changed since the move to this country?" Brown (1997) pointed out that this "triadic modality" may also be extended to one family member's perceptions about nonverbal communications or communication through behavior; for example, "What is your brother saying to your father and/or mother when he comes home late like this?"

Positive Connotation

Positive connotation is a type of paradoxical intervention in that it praises the symptomatic behaviors not only of the identified client, but also of the family in relation to the problem. It does not, however, suggest that the causes of the problem fit with the framework that the family has about the problem. It reframes the problem from a negative to a positive view. Furthermore, positive reinterpretation can be directed at the problem itself or at the underlying process of the problem. For example, a positive connotation might reframe a child's "lying" as "truth telling," or the lying and the parental response to lying as a process of "protecting" the family. Consider Viaro and Leonardi's (1986) competence presupposition, which "explains the therapist's refusal to consider the symptom as a manifestation of illness" (Selvini-Palazzoli et al., 1989, p. 244). Selvini-Palazzoli et al. (1989) stated, "We never consider the patient's behavior compulsory, uncontrollable, or incomprehensible. We always assume individual competence, which implies the existence of behavior obeying to precise motivations and intents" (p. 223). In a review of the literature, Umbelino (2003) suggested that therapists typically used positive connotation for four functional reasons: (1) It places family members on the same complimentary level in the system and so reduces system divisiveness; (2) it allows greater access to the system for current and future work through the act of approval; for example, it may lower reticence to share; (3) it shifts the family's conceptual framework of the problem maintenance from an individual one to a family system one; and (4) it challenges the family with a paradox—"good-behaving" members make a family pattern that requires a "patient." As an example of positive connotation: The therapist praises the tantruming child and the parents responding to the tantrums because they are "creating needed closeness" that is often lacking due to the ever-demanding workplaces of the two-mom, dual-earner household.

Invariant/Variant Prescriptions

As an earlier example depicted, invariant prescription is a method used to strengthen the spousal subsystem so that the symptomatic behaviors, or dirty games, can be eliminated. The invariant prescription creates a space for the parents, for example, to refocus as a team and to not allow other generations, in particular the first generation, to prevent a functioning spousal unit. The variant prescription carries the same purpose as the invariant prescription, but is tailored to the particular conditions and contexts of each family. In addition, prescriptions help to ally the parents with the therapist.

Rituals

Rituals are not new to family or culture; rites of passage (e.g., adulthood and bat mitzvah), spiritual religious celebrations and worship, daily observances such as bedtime and mealtime, seasonal festivals, and other organized processes of peoples help mark the landscape and transitions of family life. "Therapeutic ritual" may be distinguished from "cultural ritual" because therapeutic rituals are not embedded in the long-term history and context of the family and family culture (Richardson, 2012). What do you imagine might be the advantages and disadvantages of long-standing rituals? In your experience, what cultural rituals remain powerful and which feel empty? Sometimes ritual waxes and wanes in meaning and relevance at various developmental stages. What is the experience and meaning of a child celebrating Christmas compared to a young single adult or even a parent of young children?

In the book *Paradox and Counterparadox* (Selvini-Palazzoli, Boscolo, Cecchin, & Prata, 1978), the Milan group introduced the field of family therapy to how therapeutic ritual could be used to enhance or change the interactional patterns of the family. As an example of a prescribed ritual, first, parents are directed to "disappear" from the house on a date once a week. Second, they are not to tell the symptomatic child where they went or what they were doing (Selvini-Palazzoli et al., 1989).

STRATEGIC THERAPY LIMITATIONS

Often the strengths and uniqueness of something add to its limits and potential for problems. Because strategic therapy rests on short-term, tailored interventions that challenge a family's conceptual framework, anything short of a skilled, well-supervised, and maybe even naturally adept therapist might lead to mishandling of clients and harm. Counselors and therapists-in-training would need the direct supervision of someone skilled in strategic family therapy. Keim (2000) pointed out that much of the supervision provided for up-and-coming therapists is found in the universities, and many of the specialized supervision opportunities in strategic therapy shrank during the 1980s shift in managed care. Likewise, Haley (1996) pointed out in his book *Learning and Teaching Therapy* that learning to use directives may mean that a supervisee will need to work directly with a supervisor who has been trained not only in strategic interventions but also in directive therapy, which he considered problematic in an age focused on nondirective therapies.

Much of the criticism at various points in the history of strategic family therapy has come from periods in which the model was in a developmental process or was carried out erringly by less-than-skilled therapeutic application. Designing rituals, circular questioning, reframing, providing paradoxes, and changing systemic patterns require adept sensitivity (Gardner et al., 2006; Keim, 2000).

SUMMARY

Inspired by the work of Gregory Bateson (e.g., cybernetics), the therapeutic genius of Milton Erickson's strategic family therapy uniquely enriched the field as its founders and pioneers applied emerging systems theory to therapeutic work with families. Strategic therapy focuses on brief, goal-directed, here-and-now, second-order changes to interactional patterns. Strategic theory was developed over time with the input of three similar, yet unique, schools of counseling: the Washington school model, the Mental Research Institute (MRI) school model, and the Milan systemic model. Each provided unique techniques in changing family patterns and problem resolution. All schools provided directives to clients and used techniques such as reframing, providing ordeals, restraining change, providing paradoxical interventions, prescribing the symptom, circular questioning, the pretend technique, hypothesis, and giving invariant and variant prescriptions. The Washington and MRI schools continue to support the growth of practitioners.

USEFUL WEBSITES

The following websites provide additional information relating to chapter topics.

Mental Research Institute
http://www.mri.org
Jay Haley on Therapy
http://www.jay-haley-on-therapy.com/index.html
Robbins-Madanes Center for Strategic Intervention
http://robbinsmadanes.com/index.php
The Family Therapy Institute of Washington, DC

http://www.familytherapyinstitute.net
Family Process Journal
http://www.familyprocess.org/about-us/fpjournal
Brown Article on Circular Questioning
http://www.anzjft.com/pages/articles/940.pdf

REFERENCES

Becvar, D. S., & Becvar, R. J. (2000). *Family therapy: A systemic integration* (4th ed.). Boston, MA: Allyn & Bacon.

Boscolo, L., Cecchin, G., Hoffman, L., & Penn, P. (1987). *Milan systemic family therapy*. New York, NY: Basic Books.

Brown, J. (1997). Circular questioning: An introductory guide. *Australian New Zealand Journal of Family Therapy*, *18*(2), 109–114.

Davey, M., Duncan, T., Kissil, K., Davey, A., & Fish, L. (2011). Second-order change in marriage and family therapy: A web-based modified Delphi study. *American Journal of Family Therapy*, *39*(2), 100–111. doi:10.1080/01926187.2010.530929

Gardner, B. C., Burr, B. K., & Wiedower, S. E. (2006). Reconceptualizing strategic family therapy: Insights from a dynamic systems perspective. *Contemporary Family Therapy: An International Journal*, *28*(3), 339–352. doi:10.1007/s10591-006-9007-x

Gladding, S. T. (2007). *Family therapy: History, theory, and practice* (4th ed.). Columbus, OH: Merrill-Prentice Hall.

Haley, J. (1973). *Uncommon therapy: The psychiatric techniques of Milton H. Erickson, M. D.* New York, NY: Norton.

Haley, J. (1976). *Problem-solving therapy: New strategies for effective family therapy*. San Francisco, CA: Jossey-Bass.

Haley, J. (1980). *Leaving home*. San Francisco, CA: Jossey-Bass.

Haley, J. (1981). Forward. In C. Madanes (Ed.), *Strategic family therapy* (pp. xi–xv). San Francisco, CA: Jossey-Bass.

Haley, J. (1987). *Problem solving therapy*. San Francisco, CA: Jossey-Bass.

Haley, J. (1996). *Learning and teaching therapy*. New York, NY: Guilford Press.

Haley, J. (2005). *Strategies of psychotherapy*. Norwalk, CT: Crown House Publishing.

Jenkins, T., & Forrest, A. (1999). Eriksonian approaches to counseling: Toward an assimilated paradigm of practice for the twenty-first century. *Journal of Humanistic Counseling, Education, & Development*, *37*(4), 224–232.

Keim, J. (1993). Triangulation and the art of negotiation. *Journal of Systemic Therapies*, *12*(4), 69–87.

Keim, J. (2000). Strategic family therapy. In A. M. Horne (Ed.), *Family counseling and therapy* (3rd ed., pp. 170–207). Itasca, IL: E. E. Peacock.

Madanes, C. (1981). *Strategic family therapy*. San Francisco, CA: Jossey-Bass.

Madanes, C. (1990). *Sex, love, and violence: Strategies for transformation*. New York, NY: W. W. Norton.

Richardson, C. (2012). Witnessing life transitions with ritual and ceremony in family therapy: Three examples from a metis therapist. *Journal of Systemic Therapies*, *31*(3), 68–78. doi:10.1521/jsyt.2012.31.3.68

Rogers, C. (1961). *On becoming a person. A therapist's view of psychotherapy*. Boston, MA: Houghton Mifflin.

Selvini-Palazzoli, M., Boscolo, L., Cecchin, G., & Prata, G. (1978). *Paradox and counter-paradox: A new model in the therapy of the family in schizophrenic transaction*. New York, NY: Jason Aronson.

Selvini-Palazzoli, M., Boscolo, L., Cecchin, G., & Prata, G. (1980). Hypothesizing-circularity-neutrality: Three guidelines for the conductor of the session. *Family Process, 19*, 3–12.

Selvini-Palazzoli, M., Cirillo, S., Selvini, M., & Sorrentino, A. M. (1989). *Family games: General models of psychotic processes in the family*. New York, NY: Norton.

Shoham-Salomon, V., & Rosenthal, R. (1987). Paradoxical interventions: A meta-analysis. *Journal of Consulting and Clinical Psychology, 55*(1), 22–28. doi:10.1037/0022-006X.55.1.22

Talmon, M. (2012). When less is more: Lessons from 25 years of attempting to maximize the effect of each (and often only) therapeutic encounter. *Australian and New Zealand Journal of Family Therapy, 33*(1), 6–14. doi:10.1017/aft.2012.2

Umbelino, A. (2003). Positive connotation: A short story about the myth. *Journal of Family Psychotherapy, 14*(2), 13.

Viaro, M., & Leonardi, P. (1986). The evolution of an interview technique: A comparison between former and present strategy. *Journal of Strategic & Systemic Therapies, 5*(1–2), 14–30.

Watzlawick, P., Beavin Bavales, J., & Jackson, D. D. (2011). *Pragmatics of human communication: A study of interactional patterns, pathologies and paradox*. New York, NY: W. W. Norton.

Watzlawick, P., Weakland, J. H., & Fisch, R. (2011) *Change: Principles of problem formulation and problem resolution*. New York, NY: W. W. Norton.

Young, T. L., Negash, S. M., & Long, R. M. (2009). Enhancing sexual desire and intimacy via the metaphor of a problem child: Utilizing structural-strategic family therapy. *Journal of Sex & Marital Therapy, 35*(5), 402–417. doi:10.1080/00926230903065971

CHAPTER 11

Behavioral and Cognitive-Behavioral Theories: Approaches and Applications

Marvarene Oliver and Yvonne Castillo

Texas A&M University–Corpus Christi

Behavioral and cognitive-behavioral couple and family therapy are currently generally conceptualized under the broad domain of the cognitive-behavioral approach. Arising initially from behaviorism and later adding information from cognitive psychology and systems thinking, specific frameworks within the broad domain of cognitive-behavioral couple and family therapy (CBC/FT) vary, sometimes significantly. Cognitive-behavioral theorists, scholars, and clinicians give greater or lesser emphasis to variables addressed in theory and practice, depending in part on where they fall on a continuum between a more behavioral or a more cognitive orientation. In addition, specific models vary about how much and in what way systems thinking is considered. While most behavioral and cognitive-behavioral approaches are not strictly considered systemic approaches to working with families, they do share with systems theory an emphasis on rules and communication processes, as well as attention to the reciprocal impact of each family member's behaviors and attitudes on others. Some leading figures in CBC/FT argue that the attention to mutual impact of family members' thoughts, behaviors, and emotions, as well as attention to the context in which families operate, provide a systemic overlay for this approach (Baucom, Epstein, Kirby, & LaTaillade, 2010; Dattilio, 2010). Some approaches (e.g., functional family therapy, integrative behavioral therapy, and some forms of cognitive-behavioral therapy) strongly stress a systemic perspective that cannot easily be dismissed by critics.

However, all cognitive-behavioral approaches share an emphasis on research and clearly outlined goals, ongoing assessment, and treatment interventions. Because of this commitment to a scientific approach, as well as the relative ease of standardizing treatment and measuring outcomes, cognitive-behavioral approaches are the most researched treatments in the arena of couple and family counseling. There have been more studies demonstrating the efficacy of CBC/FT approaches than any other model (Datillio, 2010; Datillio & Epstein, 2005). While other therapies have demonstrated efficacy at least as strong as CBC/FT, the quantity and role of research in CBC/FT is currently unmatched in other approaches (Atkins, Dimidjian, & Christensen, 2003). Not only is CBC/FT well-researched with a sound empirical base, it is among the most-used approaches to couple and family therapy. For instance, Northey (2002), in a national survey of members of the American Association for Marriage and Family Therapy, noted that over 27% of 292 randomly selected therapists identified cognitive-behavioral family therapy (CBFT) as their primary treatment modality, and CBFT was the most frequently cited of all models mentioned.

Distinguishing among variations in CBC/FT theory and practice can be challenging for a number of reasons. Not only are there variations based on closer alignment with behavioral or cognitive elements and the relative importance of a systemic perspective, but there have also been several phases of development of CBC/FT. Each of these has spawned related threads of theory, research, and practice. Each thread provides concepts and principles that are important for the well-trained counselor to understand. In addition, both research and theory may address either couple or family approaches, or both. While couple and family treatments share similarities, they do not always translate precisely from working with couples to working with families. Research is generally clearly demarcated as being with and for couples, or with and for families. Nonetheless, general principles of behavioral and cognitive-behavioral approaches share many similarities, whether working with couples or with families.

BACKGROUND

Counselors who are interested in working from a cognitive-behavioral perspective should be knowledgeable about both behavioral and cognitive therapy and the foundational concepts on which each is based. Behavioral and cognitive-behavioral approaches have their origins in science; the scientific method was critical in the development of the behavioral approach to working with problems, and it remains critical today. The scientific method that characterized early behaviorism remains a critical component of CBC/FT.

First-Wave Approaches

Gurman (2013) conceptualized the development of cognitive and behavioral approaches to couple and family therapy as a series of waves (see Table 11.1). He includes both behavioral and cognitive-behavioral work within the behavioral couple/family therapy (BC/FT) paradigm, and called the earliest period the first wave in the evolution of behavioral therapy's core principles and clinical thought. During the early days of BC/FT, which was closely linked to traditional

Table 11.1 Development of Cognitive and Behavioral Approaches

	Theory	Examples of Major Principles
First wave	Behavioral family therapy (BFT) Traditional behavioral couple therapy (TBCT)	Stimulus-response learning theory Behavior is learned No consideration of internal events, underlying causes, or emotions Skill deficits important
Second wave	Cognitive-behavioral couple therapy (CBCT) Enhanced cognitive-behavioral couple therapy (ECBCT)	Cognitive variables as mediators Stimulus-organism-response theory Internal processes, context, and core themes important
Third wave	Integrative behavioral couple therapy (IBCT) Acceptance and commitment therapy (ACT) Behavioral activation therapy Functional family therapy (FFT) Functional analytic therapy	Importance of self-regulation Recognition of limits of change-oriented interventions Importance of context No class of behavior privileged
Developing third wave	Mindfulness training enhancement to CBCT Integration of dialectical behavior therapy and CBCT	

stimulus-response learning theory, there was no consideration of internal events such as thoughts or emotion because those could not be readily observed, nor was there much attention given to interpersonal processes. A major premise underlying this approach is that all behavior is learned and that people, including families, act according to how they have been reinforced or conditioned. Behavior in the family or couple is maintained by consequences, also called *contingencies*. Unless new behaviors result in consequences that are more desired, they will not be maintained. In addition, the focus is on maladaptive current behaviors as the target of change. From a traditional behavioral perspective, it is not necessary to look for underlying causes; behavior that is not desirable can be extinguished and replaced by more desirable behavior. Finally, many behavioral family therapists believe not everyone in the family has to be treated for change to occur. When one person comes for treatment, he or she is taught new, appropriate, and functional skills. Those who are more systemic in their thinking focus on dyadic relationships, such as parent–child or couple. Today, BC/FT relies on the same theoretical foundation as individual behavior therapy in that it utilizes principles of classical and operant conditioning. However, modeling, attention to cognitive processes and self-regulation, and focus on interactions between family members have been incorporated into behavioral practice. Gerald Patterson, Richard Stuart, and Robert Liberman are generally associated with this first wave of behavioral treatment of couple and family problems.

Richard Stuart and Robert Weiss conducted research on couples in the 1960s. The first publication on behavioral couple therapy (BCT) was written by Stuart (1969), who has been called the founding father of behavioral marital therapy. His later text, *Helping Couples Change: A Social Learning Approach to Marital Therapy* (Stuart, 1980), became a classic that remains widely known and referenced. Stuart (1980) used social exchange theory and operant conditioning principles to increase the ratio of positive behaviors to negative behaviors in couples. He noted that in nondistressed relationships, partners reciprocally exchanged a higher ratio of positive behaviors than negative ones, and initially he coached partners to reward each other using tokens for enacting behaviors that were viewed as positive by each other. Behavioral couple therapists gradually replaced token economies with written contracts and good faith contracts for behavioral exchanges, and added communication and problem-solving skills training. For example, a therapist working with a couple who experiences conflict about the relative importance of work and fun might help the couple devise a contract in which one partner agrees to cleaning the bathrooms once a week. In exchange, the other partner agrees to spend two Saturday afternoons a month doing a fun activity together.

Another key figure in the first wave of BC/FT is Robert Liberman (1970), who utilized social learning principles to work with couples and families. He is often credited with adding strategies of therapist modeling and client behavioral rehearsal of new behaviors to treatment. He also used behavioral analysis of couple and family interaction patterns around presenting problems, and included in his work with couples a focus on unintentional reinforcement of undesirable behavior. In conjunction with colleagues, he reported results of a 10-session behavioral marital group therapy that involved training in communication skills; contingency contracting; increasing recognition, initiation, and acknowledgment of pleasing interactions; and redistributing time spent in recreational and social activities (Liberman, Wheeler, & Sanders, 1976).

Gerald Patterson is often credited with originating behavioral family therapy (BFT) at the Oregon Social Learning Center (OSLC). Patterson (1974) and fellow researchers at the University of Oregon noted the importance of operant conditioning principles in working with children, and studied parental use of reinforcers and punishers to increase a child's desired behaviors and reduce negative ones. Patterson believed that parents and other significant adults could be change agents in the lives of children with behavioral problems, and he identified a number of specific behavioral problems and interventions for correcting them. He was instrumental in writing programmed workbooks for parents' use in helping their children and families modify behavior. The Parent Management Training-Oregon Model, developed by colleagues at the OSLC, is now a widely accepted evidence-based model for promoting prosocial skills and preventing and reducing mild to severe conduct problems in children. In addition, Weiss, Hops, and Patterson (1973) discovered that some parents needed relationship skills in addition to parenting skills, and they applied learning-based principles and methods such as the use of behavioral exchange, contracting for positive experiences, and skills development to the treatment of distressed couples (Atkins et al., 2003; Baucom et al., 2010).

SIDEBAR 11.1 CASE STUDY: HOW CAN JOSHUA GET BACK ON TRACK?

Makayla and Jeremy came for family counseling with their 13-year-old son, Joshua. When Joshua entered middle school 2 years ago, his grades began dropping. Previously a good student, Joshua was now barely passing. Joshua has skipped school a number of times and was sent to a disciplinary campus for 6 weeks. He is frequently several hours late coming home from school. When his father is not home, he is verbally aggressive toward his mother whenever she directs him to do homework or chores. Jeremy has come in from work on several occasions to find his wife in tears and Joshua in his room with his door locked, playing computer games. When Jeremy is at home, Joshua sullenly responds to direction. In session, Jeremy mostly stares at the floor and says he just doesn't want to be treated like a child. As a behavioral family counselor, where will you start?

Although they are not now associated with the first wave of behavioral therapy, at least two others should be included in any discussion of CBC/FT, although each for a different reason. John Gottman, who began his career with an interest in mathematics and earned three of his four degrees with a mathematics emphasis, became interested in psychophysiology and earned a PhD in clinical psychology in 1971. He began his work at the University of Washington in 1986 and established his Family Research Lab, familiarly known as the Love Lab. Thousands of hours of data were collected in the Family Research Lab, including audio and video recordings, use of heart monitors, and information from a chair that monitored fidgeting during different kinds of conversations. He has conducted extensive study on marital stability and divorce prediction, and is known for precision in his research. Even though he is not a cognitive-behavioral theorist, his findings have been important in research of behavioral and cognitive-behavioral approaches to couple and family therapy (e.g., Baucom, Epstein, LaTaillade, & Kirby, 2008; Datillio & Epstein, 2005; Dimidjian, Martell, & Christensen, 2008; Gurman, 2013). Gottman (1999) has identified multiple factors that contribute to relational dissatisfaction, as well as factors that seem to be critical in long-term relational success. For example, couples who are stable and happy regularly make repair attempts when things go awry in their interactions. Repair attempts are used to soften or mend what might otherwise lead to defensiveness or hurt, and are especially important during conflict. On the other hand, couples who are unstable and unhappy have low levels of positivity to negativity in their relationships and higher occurrence of criticism, defensiveness, contempt, and stonewalling.

Neil Jacobson, who started out to be a psychoanalytic and humanistic-oriented clinician, became a behavior therapist after reading the work of Albert Bandura, an influential psychologist and researcher. Jacobson was drawn to the accountability, empiricism, and methodologies associated with the theory. During his academic career, he developed a clinical practice based on research, which helped refine his theoretical contributions to behavioral marital therapy and domestic violence. Work with graduate students also kept him focused on theory. Jacobson indicated that behaviorism is at the base of his theory, but that clinical application is more eclectic. He was intent on bridging the gap between academic research and in-the-trenches, clinical outcome research. Until his death, Jacobson was on the leading edge of the family therapy field and was involved in longitudinal research on couples, including an 8-year study with Gottman concerning male batterers (Jacobson & Gottman, 1998). One major outcome of his meticulous attention to research and refining his way of working with couples was his introduction of integrative behavioral couple therapy (IBCT, discussed later) with Andrew Christensen, his long-time colleague. This orientation represented a major change from traditional behavioral couple therapy (TBCT). It includes the idea that acceptance is as important as behavior change in couple therapy and, in fact, may be more likely to facilitate change with some kinds of relationship problems than a direct focus on change. Jacobson and Christensen wrote a number of articles together and with other colleagues, and Christensen has continued research and writing about work with couples since Jacobson's death in 1999.

Traditional Behavioral Couple Therapy

Traditional behavioral couple therapy (TBCT) was built on two major precepts: (1) that marital dissatisfaction arises when the ratio of rewards to costs is too low, which means there are inadequate behavior-maintaining contingencies, and (2) that partners have deficits in interpersonal skills. In clinical practice, this resulted in an emphasis on increasing positive behavior, decreasing negative behavior, and using reciprocity rather than coercion for behavior change, as well as on providing communication and problem-solving skills training. Therapy from this perspective follows a predictable format, with problem behaviors operationally defined and targeted. Behavioral interventions, such as contingency management and behavioral exchange, are used to decrease negative behaviors and increase positive ones, and skill training in communication and problem solving is provided. Overall, the tone is didactic because the therapeutic process involves much teaching and training.

Critiques of TBCT challenge traditional notions of behavioral theory. As early as the late 1970s, critics noted that BCT of that era did not take into account context (Gurman & Kniskern, 1978; Jacobson & Weiss, 1978). Gurman (2008) stated that poor communication and problem-solving skills serve a defensive function, and noted that couples who do not use such skills with each other nevertheless evidence those same skills in other relationships. Thus, the skill deficits addressed by communications and problem-solving training are not significant enough to warrant explicit instruction for many couples. Rather, the problem to be addressed in therapy is more about how to access skills partners already possess in the context of the relationship. Such arguments aside, change in how TBCT is conceptualized and practiced came largely from research within the field. This is not surprising, because behavior therapy in general strongly values empirical evidence. Research indicated, for example, that gains achieved during treatment were not sustained by a large portion of couples. This information led to various hypotheses about why gains from TBCT are not sustained long term. In clinical practice, it was also evident that some couples do not benefit from change-oriented work, especially those who are not compromising, collaborative, or trusting. Gurman (2013) and others (Christensen et al., 2004; Jacobson & Christensen, 1998) noted that TBCT did not include a mechanism for dealing with what Gottman (1999) called *perpetual problems*, which may account for nearly 70% of what couples regularly argue about. Perpetual problems often include things that involve differences in personality or relationship needs that are experienced as part of one's essential self. For example, one partner may be an introvert and the other an extrovert, which may lead to differences in how each wants to spend leisure time or how much time each wants to spend alone.

Second-Wave Approaches

The emphasis on mediational cognitive variables constitutes the second wave in behavioral therapy (Gurman, 2013), particularly with the development of cognitive theory. As early as the 1950s, some behaviorists began to argue that the stimulus-response cycle as conceived in traditional behavioral psychology was not automatic, but rather was mediated by cognitions. The importance of the one who experienced a stimulus was recognized as a critical part of the cycle (stimulus-organism-response). At about the same time, cognitive theorists and clinicians were proposing their own ideas about how people change. Personal constructs and schemas were recognized as important in understanding how couples and family members gather information, interpret it, and predict events. Thus, therapists who believed the role of cognition was important began working with couples and families about, for example, beliefs they held about what couple or family life should ideally be. Cognitive psychology literature continues to contribute to awareness of potential sources of distortion in client cognitions about events in the family.

Changing the way family members act, as well as their dysfunctional attitudes or beliefs, is central to second-wave approaches. Although goals will vary according to presenting problems and the counselor's particular frame of reference, there are a number of facets that characterize the approaches in this section. Among those are: (a) facilitating the family's ability to see patterns of behavior and understand the interaction among cognitions, emotions, and behavior (Kalodner, 1995); (b) diminishing problem behaviors or interactions and increasing positive ones (Nichols & Schwartz, 2004); and (c) improving each couple or family member's functioning in a way that improves the overall relationship (Weiss & Perry, 2002).

SIDEBAR 11.2 ASSESSMENT: A FOUNDATIONAL COMPONENT OF CBC/FT

Assessment plays a pivotal role in CBC/FT and is an integral part of the therapeutic process. In fact, it isn't really possible to do CBC/FT without it. Assessment begins at or even before the first session and continues until the conclusion of therapy. Assessment is used to monitor progress, refine goals, and determine appropriate interventions. Therapists who practice from a CBC/FT model will vary to some degree in what they assess depending on their particular approach. However, some of the more common purposes of assessment from a CBC/FT perspective are to:

- Establish initial goals and refine them throughout therapy
- Identify behaviors and cognitions that are problematic for the couple or family
- Understand what clients want
- Understand how and why particular problems are impacting the clients' lives
- Monitor progress
- Determine interventions that address problems presented for a particular couple or family
- Set the stage for change

Cognitive-Behavioral Couple Therapy

Cognitive-behavioral couple therapy (CBCT) has its roots in BCT, cognitive therapy, and basic research in cognitive psychology (Baucom et al., 2008). Cognitive-behavioral couple therapy (CBCT) arose from concerns that TBCT was clinically limited because of its lack of attention to internal processes. Cognitive theory was developing as early as the 1960s, and its usefulness in clinical settings was becoming evident in the 1980s. During the 1980s, couple therapists began to attend to cognitive processes such as "attributions, expectancies, assumptions, standards, and schemas with most attention paid to the ways in which such information processing was focally important to intimate relationships" (Gurman, 2013, p. 121). Cognitive-behavioral couple therapy builds on skills-based interventions of BCT that target couple communication and behavior exchanges by directing partners' attention to explanations they construct for each other's behavior and to expectations and standards they hold for their own relationship and for relationships in general (Epstein & Baucom, 2002). Despite several decades of research, CBCT, whether considered a modality of its own or a set of adjunctive procedures to be integrated with other approaches, has only recently become a major force in the field of couple and family therapy (Datillio, 1998, 2001; Datillio & Epstein, 2003).

Cognitive Restructuring Although CBCT is considered a single entity, Gurman (2013) identified three particular emphases in theory and practice. The first, cognitive restructuring, involves core cognitive therapy methods such as identification and modification of partners' automatic thoughts and the use of Socratic questioning to determine evidence for partner attributions about each other and about relationships. For example, some people have an unrealistic or untrue belief that if their partner loves them, then the partner will never let them down or disappoint them. A therapist working with a focus on cognitive restructuring might help an individual identify and change this belief to something that is more helpful and accurate. This approach is the most frequently researched version of behavioral couple therapy.

Couple and Family Schemas A second emphasis in CBCT considers partner schemas (Gurman, 2013). Therapists working with couples and families who focus on schemas pay attention to fundamental central belief structures (schemas), particularly as they relate to beliefs about areas such as intimate relationships, parenting, children, and self-worth. While many CBCT therapists believe schemas are a critical part of couple relationships and work with them in therapy, one particular form of CBCT, couple schema therapy, is significantly different from TBCT and more generic CBCT. The couple schema model includes concepts from object relations and other psychodynamic approaches and encourages immediate experiencing of strong emotions in order to make dominant schemas more accessible.

SIDEBAR 11.3 CASE STUDY: MARIANNA AND ADOLPHO

Marianna and Adolpho have been married for 13 years. When they first married, both worked and shared household responsibilities. They now have two children, ages 7 and 9. When their children were born, they mutually decided that Marianna would stay home "until they were a little older." They have come into counseling because of increasing distance, anger, and conflict between them. Marianna wants to go back to work, and Adolpho wants her to stay at home. He likes their lifestyle and says he doesn't understand why she wants to change it; however, Marianna thinks he just wants her to continue managing most of the household responsibilities, a job that gradually shifted to being primarily hers. Consider some of the schemas that could be relevant to the couple's current distress. Are there beliefs you would be listening for? What are they? What do you need to know about your own schemas?

Enhanced Cognitive-Behavioral Couple Therapy Enhanced cognitive-behavioral couple therapy (ECBCT) is the third and most fully developed emphasis in CBCT. Epstein and Baucom (1990, 2002) expanded their initial cognitive-behavioral approach to include attention to broader patterns and core themes as well as attention to discrete behaviors. They note the importance of individual characteristics and the ways in which individual characteristics impact couple relationships. These authors also recognize the role environmental stressors play in couple relationships. Finally, they give more emphasis to the role of emotion in couple relationships, including the reciprocal impact of emotion on wants, needs, and motives. Epstein and Baucom draw significantly from a variety of theoretical orientations, including emotionally focused therapy and insight-oriented marital therapy, to integrate CBT conceptualizations with an understanding of motives and needs. This approach includes substantial emphasis on increasing positive experiences and emotions rather than focusing primarily on decreasing negatives, as well as consideration of positive experiences beyond the couple relationship itself. Enhanced cognitive-behavioral couple therapy incorporates systems theory, acknowledging the reciprocal relationship between the couple and the environment.

Enhanced cognitive-behavioral couple therapy includes the use of traditional CBCT techniques; however, interventions concerning communication and problem solving are provided as rehabilitative rather than skills training. The distinction is important because, as Epstein and Baucom (2002) pointed out, satisfied couples do not use step-by-step processes for having difficult conversations or solving problems. From a rehabilitative perspective, these interventions are better used as steps to help couples break negative patterns. Once that occurs, the clinician will offer interventions that encourage other ways to more naturally respond to each other. These might include interventions designed to help each partner selectively attend to the other's positive behaviors, interrupt negative inferences each partner may make about the other's intentions, delineate and change problematic expectancy, modify implicit and explicit assumptions about intimate relationships, and challenge maladaptive/inflexible standards for partner behavior. By attending to the couple's interaction with extended family and the community and assessing current relational stressors that originate outside the couple itself, ECBCT also takes a much more comprehensive approach to clinical assessment than had been shown in TBCT's typical emphasis on the immediate interaction of the couple dyad. A particularly striking enhancement of ECBCT is its inclusion of principles of intervention from emotionally focused therapy, especially those that are aimed at deepening affective experience.

According to Gurman (2013), the most clinically significant contribution of ECBCT was the development of principles for the treatment of individual psychological difficulties within couple therapy. When one partner has an individual problem, such as panic disorder, the other partner may be enlisted to help in the therapeutic process. Enhanced cognitive-behavioral couple therapy also examines how an individual's clinical problem affects the couple relationship and how couple interaction may impact an individual's psychiatric disorder. Problematic couple dynamics can complicate the therapeutic process for the individual client, and dysfunctional patterns must be addressed. Finally, ECBCT has been used as a general couple therapy to improve overall couple functioning in areas where dysfunction contributes to the development or maintenance of a disorder.

SIDEBAR 11.4 RESOURCES FOR ASSESSMENTS

There are a number of excellent sources for couple and family assessment. As with assessments used with individual clients, counselors should have a clear rationale for their use with couples and families. In addition, counselors should be aware of the possibility of cultural bias, either in construction or in interpretation of results. Some recent sources of information about couple and family assessment include:

- *Assessment of Couples and Families: Contemporary and Cutting-Edge Strategies* (Sperry, 2004)
- *Handbook of Family Measurement Techniques* (Vols. 1–3) (Touliatos, Perlmutter, & Straus, 2001)
- *Measures for Clinical Practice: A Sourcebook. Vol. 1: Couples, Families, and Children* (4th ed.) (Fischer & Corcoran, 2007)
- *Sourcebook of Marriage and Family Evaluation* (L'Abate & Bagarozzi, 1993).

In addition, *Cognitive-Behavioral Therapy with Couples and Families: A Comprehensive Guide for Clinicians* (Dattilio, 2010) includes an appendix containing a thorough compilation of assessments, as well as an entire chapter about assessment procedures for couples and families.

Third-Wave Approaches

In recent years, there has been an increasing focus on the use of acceptance and mindfulness-based approaches within CBCT (Levin & Hayes, 2009). Gurman (2013) categorized these as the third wave of behavioral therapy. A number of factors resulted in this self-regulation phase (Gurman, 2008), including increasing research demonstrating ceiling effects of standard CBT approaches; the use of CBT approaches in application to problems in living as well as treatment of specific symptoms, such as depression and anxiety; and the influence of Eastern thought on Western mental health perspectives. Among those included by Gurman are acceptance and commitment therapy, behavioral activation therapy, dialectical behavior therapy, functional analytic therapy, and integrative behavioral couple therapy. We believe that functional family therapy also rightfully fits here. Each of these approaches addresses criticisms that previous behavioral approaches are reductionistic and mechanistic because each approach insists that psychological experiences, processes, and events can only be understood in context. Gurman noted that no class of behavior, whether feelings, thoughts, or something else, is privileged in third-wave approaches.

Integrative Behavioral Couple Therapy

Integrative behavioral couple therapy (IBCT) is both contextually based and behavioral (Christensen, Jacobson, & Babcock, 1995; Jacobson & Christensen, 1996, 1998). Arguably the most visible BCT approach, IBCT differs significantly from CBCT's continued emphasis on changing maladaptive behaviors, particularly thoughts, and focuses more attention on functional analysis of behavior. Functional analysis of behavior is concerned with the purposes that behaviors serve. From an IBCT perspective, functional analysis moves beyond identification of events that led to a problem behavior and looks instead for broad classes of behaviors or themes of variables. The IBCT therapist looks for the common theme in groups of behaviors that lead to dissatisfaction in couple relationship. In addition, the IBCT therapist looks for common themes in the dissatisfied partner's reactions, emphasizing that the importance of reaction to ineffective behavior is as critical as the behavior itself to couple satisfaction (Dimidjian et al., 2008).

First published in 1995, IBCT grew out of TBCT (Christensen et al., 1995). While TBCT is one of the most researched treatments for couples and meets the criteria for empirically supported treatments, Jacobson and his colleagues were skeptical of the clinical significance of the approach and published a reanalysis of outcome data on TBCT (Jacobson et al., 1984). Further research revealed that TBCT was more likely to be effective for particular couples (e.g., more committed, younger, less distressed couples who were not emotionally disengaged). Jacobson and Christensen (1996) also noted that for some couples and some problems, TBCT's emphasis on producing change was not effective and could actually add to couples' distress. Jacobson and Christensen concluded that acceptance was the thing that was missing and that acceptance may in itself promote change.

In adding acceptance as an essential part of their approach, Christensen and Jacobson focused significant attention on how a partner views and responds to a behavior that is not desirable in that partner's view, rather than attending solely to behavior change on the part of the individual enacting a behavior that is undesirable to the partner. This view is one that takes into account the reciprocal nature of couple interactions. Working with couples in this way gives recognition to the fact that there are some perpetual or unsolvable problems in couple relationships. In addition, attending to both partners' actions and responses to such problems and including acceptance can mediate increased change in behavior. In addition to a different focus on change, IBCT also differs from TBCT through its emphasis on contingency-shaped, rather than rule-shaped, behavior. Rule-governed interactions mean that a partner is given a rule and punished or reinforced in relation to whether the behavior is performed. Contingency-shaped behavior, on the other hand, is determined by the natural consequences of performing a behavior. Jacobson and Christensen's approach is predicated on the idea that enduring changes are more likely to happen because of shifts in natural consequences, or contingencies. Thus, there is significant time spent in the therapeutic process on creating these shifts (Christensen et al., 2004; Jacobson & Christensen, 1996, 1998).

Working within an IBCT model requires particular skills and attributes, including flexibility and comfort with change. The clinician may function as a coach or teacher, for example, and may use structured and specific communication techniques. However, the highest priority is "maintaining a focus on the case formulation of the couple" (Dimidjian et al., 2008, p. 79). Being a compassionate listener, being attentive to both verbal and nonverbal communication, and being able to remain focused on the couple's central theme despite specific complaints that arise are critical, as is the ability to communicate genuine empathy for each person. Ultimately, the stance of the IBCT therapist is "non-confrontational, validating, and compassionate" (Dimidjian et al., 2008, p. 79).

There are techniques used in IBCT that are used in other approaches as well; however, the rationale for their use may be different (Dimidjian, Martell, & Christensen, 2002, 2008). Empathic joining is used to foster acceptance. The clinician is, in some senses, teaching by doing. Unified detachment is used to help partners get emotional distance from their conflicts by encouraging intellectual analysis of problems, and it is also a way to promote acceptance. Both empathic joining and unified detachment are intended to help partners talk without accusation and to foster greater intimacy and closeness. Interventions aimed at increasing tolerance, and therefore letting go of trying to change each other, are used with problems that are unlikely to be solved and that are not likely to produce more intimacy and closeness, but may also be used with acceptance interventions. Examples of interventions designed to promote tolerance include pointing out positive aspects of negative behavior, practicing negative behavior in session, faking negative behaviors at home between sessions, and promoting self-care. It is important to note that Jacobson and Christensen (1996, 1998) specifically state that there are behaviors that should not be tolerated and that, for couples with particular problems, IBCT is not appropriate. For instance, domestic violence should not be a target of acceptance or tolerance. Behaviors that jeopardize the well-being of either member of the couple should not be a focus of either acceptance or tolerance interventions; thus, another treatment approach should be used.

Change is not ignored in IBCT. Strategies aimed at producing change include behavior exchange, communication training, and problem-solving training. These are typical interventions that are also used in TBCT; however, IBCT clinicians are less likely to insist on particular forms of communication (e.g., "I feel . . . when you . . .") or problem solving and will individualize training to the needs of particular couples, including or excluding elements of typical skills training as appropriate for a particular couple.

Although there are no specific contraindications indicated for IBCT other than domestic violence, Dimidjian et al. (2008) note that it is important that IBCT be conducted in a culturally sensitive and specific manner; thus, clinicians are cautioned to be careful about working with couples with a cultural background outside the clinician's experience or knowledge. Dimidjian et al. indicated that IBCT may require some modification when used with gay, lesbian, and bisexual clients to ensure attention to potential social, cultural, or individual issues around self-acceptance.

Research examining the effectiveness of IBCT has demonstrated that it is an effective approach. A large clinical trial of 134 seriously and chronically distressed couples, for instance, examined results of IBCT and TBCT treatment. Couples in both treatment conditions showed substantial gains that were maintained over a 2-year follow-up; however, results favored IBCT over TBCT, with IBCT couples who stayed together reporting being significantly happier than TBCT couples (Christensen, Atkins, Yi, Baucom, & George, 2006).

Acceptance and Commitment Therapy

As discussed previously, some couples have been found not to benefit from change-oriented approaches. When such approaches are not likely to work, or when partners do not acknowledge there is a problem, acceptance may be a core process that is critical for improving relational distress. In fact, Jacobson and Christensen (1996) indicated that acceptance is critical in any successful marriage. One relatively new approach, acceptance and commitment therapy (ACT; Hayes, Strosahl, & Wilson, 1999), has been suggested for couples to address the reality that there are those for whom change-oriented approaches do not work, in part because partners are not motivated or willing to enter into the therapeutic process (Dattilio & van Hout, 2006). Acceptance and commitment therapy targets avoidance and efforts to control aversive experiences (Hayes et al., 1999), excessive response to cognitive content, and the inability to make and keep commitments to change (Hayes, 2004). Individuals learn how to be mindful of their cognitive and emotional responses to their partner, as well as to their own behavior in the relationship. In addition, couples are helped to clarify values they hold about the relationship and commit to acting in ways consistent with their values, despite unwanted thoughts and feelings that may not be consistent with those values (Peterson, Eifert, Feingold, & Davidson, 2009). Counselors working from an ACT model help couples approach, rather than avoid, thoughts, feelings, and bodily states that are aversive and that are linked with particular relationship patterns and dynamics. A goal is for partners to become more able and willing to approach situations that have been avoided in the past and act in ways that improve relationship satisfaction and intimacy (Peterson et al., 2009).

Functional Family Therapy

Functional family therapy (FFT) was originally developed by James Alexander, Cole Barton, and Bruce Barton. It was first presented as a textbook in 1982 (Alexander & Parsons, 1982), and was more recently described by Sexton (2011). In addition, there have been numerous book chapters and articles describing and reporting on the effectiveness of FFT (e.g., Henggeler & Sheidow, 2002; Sexton, 2011; Sexton & Turner, 2010). Functional family therapy was developed specifically for the purpose of working with families dealing with severe adolescent behavioral problems, with the intent of providing a clinically useful model grounded in research. The approach synthesizes behavioral, cognitive, and systemic thought, but is viewed by its developers as distinct from all of them (Barton & Alexander, 1981). It is an evidenced-based approach that has demonstrated effectiveness in community-based applications with a variety of problems and a wide range of clients. Those who practice FFT in adherence to the model demonstrate profound respect for individual families and each family member, and take pains to learn about the particular contexts in which the family and its individual members live. In addition, those who work from an FFT model are both flexible and creative within specific phases of the therapeutic process, tailoring strategies and techniques to match the individual families with whom they work. It is an approach that requires adherence to the model to be effective, but in a nonmanualized way that recognizes the uniqueness of each family (Barton & Alexander, 1981; Sexton, 2011).

From the FFT perspective, all behavior of individual family members is adaptive and serves a function. No individual in the family is blamed, and the counselor works to understand the functions that behaviors are trying to fulfill for each family member and the family as a whole. In identifying and accepting these functions as important, the counselor seeks to understand meanings of behaviors and interactions in the family. The counselor can then use reframing to help individual family members develop alliances with each other. Alliance within the family is viewed as a requirement for motivation to change current behaviors, as is counselor–client alliance. Further, motivation is not viewed as something with which clients must enter therapy; rather, it is viewed as a result of alliance building that provides family members with the knowledge that they are understood by other family members, can trust each other, and share an idea about how to achieve change. Alliance among family members is often lacking in families in which there is a history of serious behavioral disruptions; thus, FFT emphasizes not only behavior change but also change in family members' subjective attitudes about behaviors. Beginning to establish change in subjective perceptions about other family members, as well as building alliance, are essential tasks of the first phase of treatment (engagement/motivation phase) and continue until completion of therapy (Sexton, 2011).

The second stage of treatment is the behavior change phase. The primary goal of this phase is changing specific behavioral skills of family members, though from a therapeutic rather than a teaching perspective and within a relational context. Immediate concerns are addressed initially, followed by bigger issues involving risk and protective factors. Dealing with risk factors includes both changing those that can be changed as well as building in family protective factors. Skills that may be addressed include parent–child communication, parental supervision, consistency in parenting, problem solving and negotiation, and conflict reduction. Determining which skills are needed and how those should be developed for a specific family with its unique contexts, culture, and history requires an individualized treatment plan to address immediate concerns, set appropriate goals, and fit the relational functions of each family member. Assessment during this phase includes identifying both targets and barriers to change as well as determination of how to match the relational functions of problematic behaviors (Sexton, 2011).

The third and final phase of treatment is designed to generalize, maintain, and support family change. It includes strategies for generalizing skills, maintaining change, and incorporating community and family resources into treatment. Families learn to adapt when new problems arise, be consistent even when using skills that are not completely effective, be realistic in their expectations, and use natural elements of their communities that are helpful as supports when facing normal challenges of family life. Assessment is used to determine interventions that will help family members achieve these goals (Sexton, 2011).

Additional Third-Wave Developments

According to Datillio (2010), mindfulness training is a useful enhancement to cognitive-behavioral therapy as opposed to stand-alone treatment for marital distress. He reviewed research concerning mindfulness practice with couples and linked outcomes of those studies with cognitive-behavioral views of couple distress and relationship satisfaction. Mindfulness is appropriate for enhancing empathy in couples and may be important in lowering levels of relational negativity and avoidance as well as promoting acceptance.

Another emergent approach to working with couples merges dialectical behavior therapy and CBCT (Kirby & Baucom, 2007). The joining of these two approaches is intended to address emotion dysregulation in the context of the couple relationship. Kirby and Baucom (2007) provided a couples group targeting emotion regulation, relationship skills, and the interplay of strong emotions and relationship dynamics. Results indicated that treatment had an impact in several domains, including reduction in depressive symptoms and emotion dysregulation and an increase in relationship satisfaction and confidence in one's partner's ability to regulate emotion.

MAJOR CONSTRUCTS

Many of the major ideas that are foundational in CBC/FT have been addressed in sections describing specific theoretical approaches. However, there are some common elements that are widely understood as basic constructs that counselors working from a CBC/FT model should know.

Contingency Contracting

Contingency contracts are behavioral contracts designed to help people negotiate desirable behavior change. Contracts are specific about who will do what under what conditions and for what reward. Good faith contracts are oral agreements and may be less specific than written contracts.

Cognitive Distortions

Distortions generally come from underlying core beliefs, and are often activated by emotional distress. Examples include mind reading, all-or-nothing thinking, jumping to conclusions, assuming that feelings are facts, disqualifying the positive, and making negative interpretations with no evidence. They may also take the form of irrational beliefs, such as "I must have all of your attention" or "We must always agree."

Reinforcement and Punishment

Operant conditioning involves reinforcement, which is used to increase behavior, and punishment, which is used to decrease behavior. Positive reinforcement introduces a consequence to behavior that is more likely to cause the behavior to occur again. Negative reinforcement occurs when something that is not wanted is taken away following a desired behavior, thus increasing the likelihood of the behavior occurring again. In like manner, positive punishment introduces an aversive consequence to behavior that is intended to reduce the occurrence of the behavior, and negative punishment removes something that is desired or valued in order to reduce the occurrence of the behavior.

Experiential Avoidance

Experiential avoidance is the attempt to avoid experiences, thoughts, feelings, and other internal experiences even when such avoidance causes harm. Avoidance may take the form of attempts at suppression or psychological withdrawal. Third-wave CBC/FT approaches attempt to reduce experiential avoidance in order to provide a way for behavior change to occur.

Automatic Thoughts

Automatic thoughts can be thoughts, images, or memories that are spontaneous responses to events or situations. They tend to be persistent and may seem to come out of nowhere. Automatic thoughts are generally believed to be readily available to the conscious awareness, but may not be noticed by the one experiencing them. They are often described as "just knowing" and may feel true. Automatic thoughts are related to schemas.

Underlying Assumptions

Underlying assumptions are conditional beliefs that can often be phrased as "If . . . then . . ." statements. Underlying beliefs are related to schemas, and are often described as a middle level of belief. Underlying assumptions may be thought of as conditional rules by which an individual operates in the presence of particular events or experiences.

Schemas

Schemas are enduring sets of core beliefs and attitudes about a variety of things, including oneself, other people, relationships, and the world, around which later perceptions are organized. Schemas (or schemata) are activated when a new situation arises that, to the individual, resembles the situations or experiences in which the schema was learned. When a schema is activated, the individual will interpret events through core beliefs that may be inaccurate, resulting in cognitive distortions and misperceptions of reality.

SIDEBAR 11.5 SELF-AWARENESS: WHEN COUPLES AND FAMILIES ARE DIFFERENT FROM YOU

Part of being multiculturally competent in working with couples and families involves being aware of our own biases about the ways couples and families should ideally operate. We can check ourselves by thinking about and discussing questions such as those listed below. What other questions are raised when you think about your responses and listen to responses of others?

- How open am I to going outside my way of thinking about relationships and families?
- In what ways might clinical practices marginalize those who are ethnically or culturally different from the majority culture? From those living in or near poverty?
- What do I need to learn about families that are not like mine in some important way?
- What can I learn from couples and families whose lives are very different from my experience?
- What do I not understand about the multiple contexts in which couples and families live?

TECHNIQUES

There are many specific techniques used in BC/FT and CBC/FT. Some of the most common are briefly described here. Interventions should be chosen intentionally and with purpose. Comprehensive coverage of cognitive-behavioral interventions for use with couples and families are included in texts by Rathus and Sanderson (1999) and Datillio (2010).

Education About the Model

In behavioral and cognitive-behavioral treatment, educating the couple or family is a critical part of intervention. The counselor will present didactic information about the model itself and also about specific concepts. In addition, the use of homework and its importance in the therapeutic process will be addressed. An early homework assignment designed to provide education about the model of therapy might include specific reading assignments that orient clients to concepts that will be emphasized during the course of treatment (Datillo & Epstein, 2005).

Socratic Questioning

During assessment interviews, the counselor may gather information about cognitions and processes that are particular to the family but that cannot be assessed by questionnaires. Socratic questioning is a method of questioning intended to guide discovery on the part of clients. It helps both clients and the counselor to identify clients' core beliefs, including their distorted ideas and attitudes. Socratic questioning can circumvent psychological defenses that may be activated during assessment and treatment. Assisting couple and family members in identifying their own core beliefs or unhelpful attitudes may be more helpful than having those pointed out by the counselor (Beck, 1995; Dattilio, 2000).

Communications Training

Communications training is viewed as an essential component of most approaches to CBC/FT and has long been used in most theoretical approaches to couple and family treatment. In addition to providing guidelines for expressing thoughts, feelings, opinions, preferences, and the like, clients are also given instructions about how to listen effectively and how to let others know they have been heard. Counselors generally model communication skills and provide opportunities to practice in session with the counselor acting as a coach. Improved communication can reduce distorted cognitions and help clients regulate emotion, both in how emotion is experienced and how it is expressed. Communications training is also routinely used in relationship enhancement training.

Problem-Solving Training

Problem-solving training is used to help couples and families learn to approach and deal with problems in an effective manner. Instruction, both verbal and written; behavioral rehearsal; and coaching from the therapist are important parts of the training. At-home practice is assigned, with follow-up in sessions to deal with issues that may arise. Problem-solving training generally involves teaching clients several specific steps that are common to most problem-solving models. These steps might include, for example: (a) clearly identify the problem, (b) generate possible solutions without evaluating them, (c) evaluate and choose an option, (d) put the option into place, and (e) reevaluate.

Behavioral Exchange Agreements

Behavioral exchange is still an important construct in CBC/FT; however, clinicians generally try to avoid having one member's behavior change be dependent on that of another. Unilateral behavior change is encouraged, and didactic information about personal commitment, negative reciprocity, and the ability to control only one's own actions is typically provided to help reduce reluctance to take the first step. For instance, each individual might be asked to identify a behavior that their partner or family members would like to see changed or that would improve the atmosphere in the family, and then to make that change regardless of the actions of others.

Behavioral Rehearsal

Couples and family members are often asked to rehearse specific skills they have learned, and when rehearsal occurs in session, the counselor can model and coach during practice. According to Dattilio (2010), behavioral rehearsal is an essential part of treatment because the counselor gains insight about what couples and family members have understood.

Role Reversal

Spouses or a parent and child may be asked to discuss a problem with each person taking the other's role. Role reversal can help in developing empathic understanding of the other's position and help each person become aware of their own misconceptions about the other. It can also be used as a way for each person to demonstrate a preferred way for the other to behave.

Modification of Cognitions

Changing extreme or distorted cognitions is an important element in CB/FT. A number of methods are used to teach family members to identify automatic thoughts and associated emotions/behaviors. For example, clients may be taught to identify and label cognitive distortions and then be assigned behavioral experiments to test their own predictions in order to help them challenge their distortions. Counselors may ask clients to recollect past interactions and to use role play and imagery to practice acting or thinking in a different way. Thought records forms that have been modified for use with couples and families may be assigned as homework, with clients instructed to record their thoughts about the relationship, including precursors and consequences of their thinking. They may also be challenged to identify more helpful ways of thinking (Dattilio, 2010). Thought stopping is another common technique from CBT that can be used in CB/FT. Clients are instructed to pay attention to how they think, and when they become aware of distorted or unwanted thoughts, to actively tell themselves to stop in order to interrupt dysfunctional thinking patterns.

Identification of Core Beliefs and Schemas

Downward arrow is a particular type of intervention designed to help people discover underlying assumptions and core beliefs behind their automatic thoughts. It is also used to help people who have difficulty in expressing emotion. When an automatic thought is identified, the counselor might ask, "If that were true, what would that mean to you?" Depending on the response, the counselor might ask the same question again. Once identified, schemas and core beliefs about relationships can be changed or modified, or other core beliefs can be encouraged. When working with those who have difficulty with emotional response, the counselor will also coach clients to notice internal cues to their emotions.

LIMITATIONS

One limitation is that most cognitive-behavioral approaches to couple and family therapy can be conducted from a reductionistic or mechanistic stance, particularly by those who are inexperienced in working with couples and families. Lack of attention to family systems, including the multiple contexts in which couples and families live, may result in initial gains followed by a return to pretherapy functioning. Feelings and attitudes do not always change as a result of behavior alteration, and treatment goals may be reached without resolving underlying negative emotions (Nichols & Schwartz, 2004).

With notable exceptions, such as in the case of FFT, there is limited research about outcomes of BC/FT and CBC/FT approaches with couples and families that specifically addresses cultural, ethnic, or other diversity concerns. However, the importance of context together with concentration on client goals can provide some measure of attention to multicultural issues. In addition, several authors have pointed to various aspects of diversity in their research. Baucom et al. (2010) noted that gender, ethnicity, and cultural background can have an effect on a variety of factors in couple relationships. A number of authors have also noted gender differences in how partners respond to relational stress and how partners process information about their relationship (Gottman, 1999; Rankin, Baucom, Clayton, & Daiuto, 1995; Sullivan & Baucom, 2005). In addition, the strong contextual focus of IBCT, ECBCT, and FFT requires significant attention to multiple and overlapping contexts in which people live. Stressors from the environment, such as poverty, violence, and experiences of discrimination, as well as themes and patterns particular to individual families are assessed, with the intention of enabling couples and families to negotiate recurrent problems and build on their strengths (Kelly, 2006; Kelly & Iwamasa, 2005; LaTaillade, 2006).

The emphasis on skills training by some CBC/FT practitioners, whether or not there is evidence that the skill exists and is just not being used, can cause counselors to ignore more salient issues that underlie whatever communication problems may exist. In addition, explicitly focusing on skill deficits, expectations, or attributions may cause some couples to become more aware of characteristics that were previously unknown or overlooked. In addition, some couples are not collaborative or trusting, and change-oriented work does not seem to be effective for those people. Counselors focused on behavior change may not only fail to be helpful but may also be harmful.

Finally, and perhaps most importantly, because the interventions appear to be relatively simple, counselors may use strategies they do not fully understand, unaware that unskilled use can result in significant unintended consequences for the couple or family.

SUMMARY

Rather than a single therapeutic approach, the umbrella of CBC/FT covers a number of specific approaches. This chapter has provided an overview of several of them. Cognitive-behavioral approaches to working with couples and families have repeatedly demonstrated efficacy in treating couple and family issues. In skillful hands, CBC/FT offers a relatively brief approach to treatment that has been demonstrated to improve a variety of presenting problems. It is pragmatic and offers a wide variety of interventions.

USEFUL WEBSITES

The following websites provide additional information relating to the chapter topics.

Association for Behavioral and Cognitive Therapies
http://www.abct.org
National Association of Cognitive-Behavioral Therapists
http://www.nacbt.org
Integrative Behavioral Couple Therapy
http://ibct.psych.ucla.edu
American Association for Marriage and Family Therapy
http://www.aamft.org
International Association of Marriage and Family Counselors
http://www.iamfc.org

REFERENCES

Alexander, J. F., & Parsons, B. V. (1982). *Functional family therapy*. Pacific Grove, CA: Brooks/Cole.

Atkins, D. C., Dimidjian, S., & Christensen, A. (2003). Behavioral couple therapy: Past, present, and future. In T. L. Sexton, G. R. Weeks, & M. S. Robbins (Eds.), *Handbook of family therapy* (pp. 323–347). New York, NY: Routledge.

Barton, C., & Alexander, J. F. (1981). Functional family therapy. In A. Gurman & D. Kniskern (Eds.), *Handbook of family therapy* (pp. 403–443). New York, NY: Brunner/Mazel.

Baucom, D. H., & Epstein, N. (1990). *Cognitive behavioral marital therapy*. New York, NY: Brunner/Mazel.

Baucom, D. H., Epstein, N. B., Kirby, J. S., & LaTaillade, J. J. (2010). Cognitive-behavioral couple therapy. In K. S. Dobson (Ed.), *Handbook of cognitive-behavioral therapies* (3rd ed., pp. 411–444). New York, NY: Guilford Press.

Baucom, D. H., Epstein, N. B., LaTaillade, J. J., & Kirby, J. S. (2008). Cognitive-behavioral couple therapy. In A. S. Gurman (Ed.), *Clinical handbook of couple therapy* (4th ed., pp. 31–72). New York, NY: Guilford Press.

Beck, J. S. (1995). *Cognitive therapy: Basics and beyond.* New York, NY: Guilford Press.

Christensen, A., Atkins, D. C., Berns, S., Wheeler, J., Baucom, D. H., & Simpson, L. (2004). Traditional versus integrative behavioral couple therapy for significantly and stably distressed married couples. *Journal of Consulting and Clinical Psychology*, 72, 176–191.

Christensen, A., Atkins, D. C., Yi, J., Baucom, D. H., & George, W. H. (2006). Couple and individual adjustment for 2 years following a randomized clinical trial comparing traditional versus integrative behavioral couple therapy. *Journal of Consulting and Clinical Psychology*, *74*, 1180–1191.

Christensen, A., Jacobson, N. S., & Babcock, J. (1995). Integrative behavioral couple therapy. In N. S. Jacobson & A. S. Gurman (Eds.), *Clinical handbook of couple therapy* (2nd ed., pp. 31–64). New York, NY: Guilford Press.

Dattilio, F. M. (1998). *Case studies in couple and family therapy: Systemic and cognitive perspectives*. New York, NY: Guilford Press.

Dattilio, F. M. (2000). Families in crisis. In F. M. Dattilio & A. Freeman (Eds.), *Cognitive-behavioral strategies in crisis intervention* (2nd ed., pp. 316–338). New York, NY: Guilford Press.

Dattilio, F. M. (2001). Cognitive-behavioral family therapy: Contemporary myths and misconceptions. *Contemporary Family Therapy*, *23*, 3–18.

Dattilio, F. M. (2010). *Cognitive-behavioral therapy with couples and families: A comprehensive guide for clinicians*. New York, NY: Guilford Press.

Dattilio, F. M., & Epstein, N. B. (2003). Cognitive-behavioral couple and family therapy. In T. L. Sexton, G. R. Weeks, & M. S. Robbins (Eds.), *Handbook of family therapy* (pp. 147–173). New York, NY: Brunner-Routledge.

Dattilio, F. M., & Epstein, N. B. (2005). Introduction to the special section: The role of cognitive-behavioral interventions in couple and family therapy. *Journal of Marital and Family Therapy*, *31*, 7–13.

Dattilio, F. M., & van Hout, G. C. M. (2006). The problem-solving component in cognitive-behavioral couples' therapy. *Journal of Family Psychotherapy*, *17*, 1–19.

Dimidjian, S., Martell, C. R., & Christensen, A. (2002). Integrative behavioral couple therapy. In A. S. Gurman & N. S. Jacobson (Eds.), *Clinical handbook of couple therapy* (3rd ed., pp. 251–277). New York, NY: Guilford Press.

Dimidjian, S., Martell, C. R., & Christensen, A. (2008). Integrative behavioral couple therapy. In A. S. Gurman & N. S. Jacobson (Eds.), *Clinical handbook of couple therapy* (4th ed., pp. 73–103). New York, NY: Guilford Press.

Epstein, N. B., & Baucom, D. H. (2002). *Enhanced cognitive-behavioral therapy for couples: A contextual approach*. Washington, DC: American Psychological Association.

Fischer, J., & Corcoran, K. (2007). *Measures of clinical practice: A sourcebook: Vol. 1. Couples, families, and children* (4th ed.). New York, NY: Oxford University Press.

Gottman, J. M. (1999). *The marriage clinic: A scientifically based marital therapy*. New York, NY: W. W. Norton.

Gurman, A. S. (2008). A framework for the comparative study of couple therapy. In S. Gurman (Ed.), *Clinical handbook of couple therapy* (4th ed., pp. 1–26). New York, NY: Guilford Press.

Gurman, A. S. (2013). Behavioral couple therapy: Building a secure base for therapeutic integration. *Family Process*, *52*, 115–138.

Gurman, A. S., & Kniskern, D. P. (1978). Behavioral marital therapy: II. Empirical perspective. *Family Process*, *17*, 139–148.

Hayes, S. C. (2004). Acceptance and commitment therapy and the new behavior therapies: Mindfulness, acceptance and relationship. In S. C. Hayes, V. M. Follette, & M. M. Linehan (Eds.), *Mindfulness and acceptance: Expanding the cognitive-behavioral tradition* (pp. 1–29). New York, NY: Guilford Press.

Hayes, S. C., Strosahl, K. D., & Wilson, K. G. (1999). *Acceptance and commitment therapy: An experiential approach to behavior change*. New York, NY: Guilford Press.

Henggeler, S. W., & Sheidow, A. J. (2002). Conduct disorder and delinquency. In D. H. Sprenkle (Ed.), *Effectiveness research in marriage and family therapy* (pp. 27–51). Alexandria, VA: American Association for Marriage and Family Therapy.

Jacobson, N. S., & Christensen, A. (1996). *Integrative couple therapy: Promoting acceptance and change*. New York, NY: Norton.

Jacobson, N. S., & Christensen, A. (1998). *Acceptance and change in couple therapy: A therapist's guide to transforming relationships*. New York, NY: Norton.

Jacobson, N. S., Follette, W. C., Revenstorf, D., Baucom, D. H., Hahlweg, K., & Margolin, G. (1984). Variability in outcome and clinical significance of behavioral marital therapy: A reanalysis of outcome data. *Journal of Consulting and Clinical Psychology*, *52*, 497–504.

Jacobson, N. S., & Gottman, J. (1998). *When men batter women: New insights into ending abusive relationships*. New York, NY: Simon & Schuster.

Jacobson, N. S., & Weiss, R. L. (1978). Behavioral marriage therapy. III. The contents of Gurman et al. may be hazardous to our health. *Family Process*, *17*, 149–163.

Kalodner, C. R. (1995). Cognitive-behavioral theories. In D. Capuzzi & D. R. Gross (Eds.), *Counseling and psychotherapy: Theories and interventions* (pp. 353–384). Columbus, OH: Prentice-Hall.

Kelly, S. (2006). Cognitive behavioral therapy with African Americans. In P. A. Hays & G. Y. Iwamasa (Eds.), *Culturally responsive cognitive-behavioral therapy: Assessment, practice, and supervision* (pp. 97–116). Washington, DC: American Psychological Association.

Kelly, S., & Iwamasa, G. Y. (2005). Enhancing behavioral couple therapy: Addressing the therapeutic alliance, hope, and diversity. *Cognitive and Behavioral Practice*, *12*, 102–112.

Kirby, J. S., & Baucom, D. H. (2007). Integrating dialectical behavior therapy and cognitive-behavioral couple therapy: A couples skills group and emotion dysregulation. *Cognitive and Behavioral Practice*, *14*, 394–405.

L'Abate, L., & Bagarozzi, D. A. (1993). *Sourcebook of marriage and family evaluation*. New York, NY: Brunner/Mazel.

LaTaillade, J. J. (2006). Considerations for treatment of African American couple relationships. *Journal of Cognitive Psychotherapy: An International Quarterly*, *20*, 341–358.

Levin, M. E., & Hayes, S. C. (2009). Is acceptance and commitment therapy superior to established treatment comparisons? *Psychotherapy & Psychosomatics*, *78*, 380.

Liberman, R. P. (1970). Behavioral approaches to family and couple therapy. *Journal of Orthopsychiatry*, *40*, 106–118.

Liberman, R. P., Wheeler, E., & Sanders, N. (1976). Behavioral therapy for marital disharmony: An educational approach. *Journal of Marital and Family Therapy*, *2*, 383–395. doi:10.1111/j.1752-0606.1976.tb00433.x

Nichols, M. P., & Schwartz, R. C. (2004). *Family therapy: Concepts and methods* (6th ed.). New York, NY: Pearson.

Northey, W. F. (2002). Characteristics and clinical practices of marriage and family therapists: A national survey. *Journal of Marital and Family Therapy*, *28*, 487–494.

Patterson, G. R. (1974). Interventions for boys with conduct problems: Multiple settings, treatments, and criteria. *Journal of Consulting and Clinical Psychology*, *42*, 471–481.

Peterson, B. D., Eifert, G. H., Feingold, T., & Davidson, S. (2009). Using acceptance and commitment therapy to treat distressed couples: A case study with two couples. *Cognitive and Behavioral Practice*, *16*, 430–442.

Rankin, L. A., Baucom, D. H., Clayton, D. C., & Daiuto, A. D. (1995, November). *Gender differences in the use of relationship schemas versus individual schemas in marriage*. Paper presented at the 29th annual meeting of the Association for the Advancement of Behavior Therapy, Washington, DC.

Rathus, J. H., & Sanderson, W. C. (1999). *Marital distress: Cognitive behavioral interventions for couples*. Northvale, NJ: Jason Aronson.

Sexton, T. L. (2011). Functional family therapy in clinical practice: An evidence-based treatment model for working with troubled adolescents. New York, NY: Routledge.

Sexton, T. L., & Turner, C. W. (2010). The effectiveness of functional family therapy for youth with behavioral problems in a community practice setting. *Journal of Family Psychology*, *24*, 339–348. doi:10.1037/a0019406

Sperry, L. (2004). *Assessment of couples and families: Contemporary and cutting-edge strategies*. New York, NY: Brunner-Routledge.

Stuart, R. B. (1969). Operant-interpersonal treatment for marital discord. *Journal of Clinical and Counseling Psychology*, *33*, 675–682.

Stuart, R. B. (1980). *Helping couples change: A social learning approach to marital therapy*. New York, NY: Guilford Press.

Sullivan, L. J., & Baucom, G. H. (2005). Observational coding of relationship-schematic processing. *Journal of Marital and Family Therapy*, *31*, 31–43.

Touliatos, J., Perlmutter, B. F., & Straus, M. A. (2001). *Handbook of family measurement techniques* (Vols. 1–3). Thousand Oaks, CA: Sage.

Weiss, R. L., Hops, H., & Patterson, G. R. (1973). A framework for conceptualizing marital conflict, a technology for altering it, some data for evaluating it. In L. D. Handy & E. L. Marsh (Eds.), *Behavior change: Methodology, concepts and practice* (pp. 309–342). Champaign, IL: Research Press.

Weiss, R. L., & Perry, B. A. (2002). Behavioral couples therapy. In F. W. Kaslow (Series Ed.) & T. Patterson (Vol. Ed.), *Comprehensive handbook of psychotherapy: Vol. 4. Cognitive behavioral approaches* (pp. 373–394). New York, NY: Wiley.

PART 3

Couples Work

CHAPTER

12

Key Issues and Interventions in Couples Counseling

Montserrat Casado-Kehoe

Palm Beach Atlantic University

Diane Kimball Parker

First Orlando Counseling Center

A variety of issues will bring couples to counseling. This chapter presents an overview of some of the main issues that are common in couples counseling, as well as selected techniques from various theoretical approaches such as creative-experiential therapy, emotion-focused therapy, expressive arts therapies, Gottman's work, solution-focused therapy, Imago therapy, and play therapy.

Couples who come to therapy present with a variety of issues. According to Doss, Simpson, and Christensen (2004), the most common issues reported are communication and lack of affection followed by divorce and separation concerns. However, as therapists we also know that conflict, money, lack of sexual desire, affairs, addictions, infertility, parenting struggles, dealing with a spouse who has a mental illness, or a child with a developmental or physical disability also bring couples to counseling. An assessment of the couple will help the therapist determine the underlying issue(s) the couple may be dealing with and come up with a treatment plan.

In counseling, sometimes a therapist gets to see only one member of the couple, although preferably both partners will come to sessions since it does take both people to change a relationship. Usually, the one who most desires change is the one who calls and makes the appointment. However, working with just one partner can potentially separate the couple even more. Bader (2013) suggested that couples therapists need to take the lead in guiding the couple through the process of therapy. This means standing your ground from the beginning, staying balanced, and involving both partners, known as "sharing the power." It is important for the therapist to establish a relationship and create a safe space with both partners. As a disclaimer, as part of informed consent, the therapist reminds the couple that it is hard work, it is uncomfortable at times, and that both people need to be invested in the process of change. One strategy is to ask each person about their commitment level: How committed are you to working on your marriage and relationship? Love (2001) even differentiates different types of commitment in love. One type is being committed to staying together as a couple. Another is being committed to the relationship and also determined to work on it to make it better. Some couples may be committed to a relationship of coparenting, but not marriage or cohabitation. The therapist will have to assess current levels of commitment and also variations in levels of commitment. Using a scaling question can also be helpful in terms of assessing commitment. For example, the therapist may say, "So, I can see you both would like to have some things different in this relationship. On a scale from 0 to 10, with 0 being not committed at all and 10 being very committed to change, where are each of you?" Some couples enter couples counseling having already decided to end the relationship and want to do it through counseling for better outcomes. For some couples, one may want to end the relationship while the other one is desperately trying to save it. Assessment allows the therapist to see what motivates commitment and couples to counseling. The role of assessment is quite important in couples counseling; the therapist has to determine the actual versus perceived, underlying versus surface, essential versus less essential, and chronic versus acute issues. This creates the question for the therapist: How does one assess a couple? Do you do it through a pathological model that looks for what is wrong with the couple? Or do you use a developmental model that recognizes the various phases of life and stages of a relationship, and the challenges that come along with those in a marriage? The reality is that individual diagnoses do not inform us as to what is going on with a couple. Working with couples requires taking a systemic approach. Couples counseling is about looking in between and discerning what is happening in the individual's context and the couple's context. The therapist will look for the negative cycles and interactive patterns that affect the couple. Goal setting is an important part of treatment so partners can find what they need out of therapy. What is the primary purpose of coming to counseling for each of them? How will they know they have achieved their destination at the end of counseling? How will they describe the end in "action words"? In other words, what needs to happen or change in their relationship?

COUPLES COUNSELING MODELS AND INTERVENTIONS

There is no doubt that childhood family relationships affect the way couples interact with one another. This chapter presents a variety of couples counseling models and interventions that can be used effectively when working with couples.

Attachment Theory and Adult Attachment Styles

Recently there has been a surge of interest in attachment theory and adult attachment styles, bringing insight into a couple's way of relating to each other.

Table 12.1 Three Attachment Styles Identified Through Mary Ainsworth's Strange Situation Experiment

Secure (63% of research participants)	Anxious-Resistant or Ambivalent (16% of research participants)	Avoidant (21% of research participants)
The infant may be upset by the brief separation of the caregiver and appearance of the stranger.	The infant is tremendously upset with caregiver's parting.	The infant frequently appears oblivious or undisturbed by the caregiver's departure.
Upon the return of the caregiver to the room, the infant approaches him/her for support.	Upon the return of the caregiver, the infant is ambivalent in his/her approach for attention and comfort.	Upon return, the infant often avoids the caregiver.
The infant calms quickly, is easily soothed by caregiver's return, and resumes exploration without concern.	The infant is often crying, clingy, and needy, yet appears angry and resistant of the caregiver attempting to quiet.	The infant appears shut down, despondent or indifferent, or is overinvested in their play (observable rote quality).

Source: Adapted from Ainsworth et al. (1978); Levy et al. (2011).

The process of moving couples from a state of disconnection to a place of connection and emotional bonding by addressing underlying attachment dysfunction is viewed as therapeutic and healing by emotionally focused therapists (Johnson, 2008, 2009). Gaining an understanding of attachment theory and adult attachment styles will assist the therapist in working more effectively with couples.

Beginning with the work of John Bowlby, the term *attachment* refers to the manner of relating and connecting within a close relationship, such as between a parent and a child (Bowlby, 1988; Johnson, 2008). It is within this nurturing environment that a child has a felt sense of security, developing skills of emotion regulation and relationship functioning. It is also the ground for personality development. In a secure relationship, the child uses the attachment figure as a safe haven and secure base so that he or she can explore the world, yet seek assurance and safety when distressed.

Mary Ainsworth furthered Bowlby's research by developing the "strange situation," assessing attachment security between an infant and a caregiver (Ainsworth, Blehar, Waters, & Wall, 1978). She discovered three distinct styles of attachment, which were labeled secure, anxious-resistant or ambivalent, and avoidant (see Table 12.1). In further research by Hazan and Shaver (1987), attachment behaviors in adult romantic relationships were explored. Similarities were discovered between romantic partners that had been observed between infants and their caregivers. Adult attachment styles were later named secure, dismissing, preoccupied, and unresolved (Dozier, 1990; Main, Kaplan, & Cassidy, 1985), and these led to further research surrounding main attachment figures, including one's parents, partner, and best friend (Fraley, 2010; Fraley, Waller, & Brennan, 2000b). It was discovered that adults in a secure relationship would use their partner as a safe haven and secure base, seeking assurance and safety when distressed, similar to a

Table 12.2 Summary of Adult Attachment Styles and Characteristics

Secure	Dismissing	Preoccupied
General Characteristics: Open, engaged, collaborative, trusting, proactive.	*General Characteristics*: Resistant, difficulty accepting and asking for help, withdrawing emotionally.	*General Characteristics*: Presents as needy, distressed, and engrossed with life's difficulties. Struggles with emotions.
A securely attached adult can depend on others and have others depend on them; provide and seek support for emotional distress.	An adult with a dismissing attachment style appears to prefer independence over depending on and having others depend on them. They appear aloof, avoiding contact when under emotional distress.	An adult with a preoccupied attachment style is easily angered or frustrated with unmet attachment needs. They appear anxious, demanding, or controlling in an attempt to have their needs met.
Is confident in the support of their partner. More relaxed, at ease in intimacy or closeness.	Gives the impression of being unconcerned or uninterested in close relationships.	Fears not being fully loved and needs to know that their partner is responsive and available to them. This apprehension heightens their anxiety.
Demonstrates a greater level of trust, openness, commitment, endurance, and reciprocal dependence.	Experiences the fear of losing connection, which is expressed through withdrawal or detachment. This withdrawal is an attempt to protect and calm self.	Fears losing connection and is expressed through demanding and clingy behavior in order to gain reassurance or relief from partner.
Is more secure during interactions with their partner, able to perceive the partner's words and actions with greater clarity, without misconstruing their manner of responding to needs. When experiencing their partner's difficult behavior, they are able to express anger in a controlled manner, and work toward resolution and reconnection.	Is more anxious during interactions with their partner, often misconstruing their words and actions, before and during moments of conflict, which leads to increased insecurity.	

Source: Adapted from Brennan, Clark, and Shaver (1998); Fraley (2010); Hazan and Shaver (1987); Johnson (2008); Levy et al. (2011); Paley, Cox, Burchinal, and Payne (1999). (This table was constructed through the adaptation of all these sources.)

parent and child (Hart & Morris, 2003; Johnson, 2008; Levy, Ellison, Scott, & Bernecker, 2011). Insecure adult attachment styles revealed difficulty in the way couples related to each other (see Table 12.2).

When there is a loss of connectedness from attachment figures, responses driven by fear arise. This has been labeled a "primal panic" by neuroscientist Panksepp (Johnson, 2008). This primal panic, felt in the amygdala, is seen in couples and is manifested through demanding or clinging behavior, or through withdrawal and detachment. Because we are wired to seek connection, we experience anxiety and anger when that emotional feeling of connection is lost. This can lead a couple to exhibit and experience reactive instead of responsive behaviors toward each other. However, if the couple can be moved toward a secure attachment bond, they are more apt to hold a more positive view of themselves, handle distress, and mature (Fraley, 2010; Johnson, 2008).

When a couple enters therapy for communication and disconnection issues, it is helpful to look for any attachment injuries and then assist the couple in creating a secure connection by learning to be emotionally available and approachable to each other (Johnson, 2008). Johnson maintains that we are innately wired to connect to someone who provides stable emotional support; it is an interdependency that resembles the parental relationship in which partners are protected, soothed, and nurtured through an emotional bond. Emotionally focused couples therapy endeavors to create and strengthen this emotional bond between partners. Adult attachment screenings can be used to help couples take an objective look at their own attachment style. This frequently leads to a softening toward each other as they understand each other's attachment injury and resulting needs. Chris Fraley (2010), a researcher exploring the role adult attachment has in relationships, has two online screenings that are helpful in the discussion of attachment styles (see Sidebar 12.1). As the couple begins to understand their manner of relating in light of their particular attachment style, the therapist can look for opportunities to identify key moments that can be used to help move them into a healthy, loving adult relationship that is characterized by openness, responsiveness, and accommodating each other (Johnson, 2008).

SIDEBAR 12.1 SELF-AWARENESS: HOW ATTACHMENT STYLE AFFECTS THE THERAPEUTIC RELATIONSHIP

Client attachment injuries are capable of affecting the client–therapist relationship. This can lead to confusion, countertransference, or impatience within the therapist (Levy et al., 2011). Understanding the dynamic of a client's manner of relating can bring deeper insight and compassion, as well as turn difficult interactions into opportunities for client growth. Exploring your own attachment style and understanding its impact on you as a therapist could be a valuable experience. Take the following online attachment surveys to measure your attachment style and manner of relating to those closest in your life, and reflect on your findings:

- Online attachment questionnaire (CRQ/ECR-R) (Fraley, Waller, & Brennan, 2000a), http://www.web-research-design.net/cgi-bin/crq/crq.pl
- Experiences in Close Relationships-Relationship Structures (ECR-RS) questionnaire (Fraley, Heffernan, Vicary, & Brumbaugh, 2011, Fraley et al., 2000b), http://www.yourpersonality.net/relstructures/

Created for Connection

The following case study looks at attachment issues and interventions used to increase connection. John and Erin have been married for 13 years and have two children, Shelly, age 9, and Gregory, age 6. John is a successful architect, quiet and reserved, and enjoys playing golf whenever he has a chance. Erin is a travel agent, outgoing yet anxious, especially when it comes to her children. Gregory has a diagnosis of cerebral palsy, and John struggles over the loss of a normal father–son relationship he dreamed about before having children. John has spent more time away from home in the past 6 months. When he is home, he is irritable, withdrawn, and silent. Erin, in her attempt to draw her husband closer, pursues him through blaming, threatening, and badgering, which is seen during the initial interview through her long list of complaints. John sits on the sofa quietly, not even looking at Erin. When asked for his thoughts, he voices his dissatisfaction in their marriage, stating that life has turned out to be more of a disappointment. Erin is fearful and feels emotionally abandoned. When asked what they would like to accomplish in therapy, they relayed their wish to learn to communicate, become more of a team with their children, and to rekindle feelings of love toward each other.

When working with a couple such as Erin and John, a creative-experiential orientation could be used.

Creative-Experiential Therapy

Creative-experiential couples therapy leads clients through expressing and experiencing their emotions and interactions in creative and meaningful ways. It is believed that clients can heal and change through "experiencing" on an emotional and relational level, which is consistent with emotionally focused theorists (Carson & Casado-Kehoe, 2011; Greenberg, 2011; Greenberg, Rice, & Elliott, 1993). Experiencing changes emotionally and mentally through experiential and creative measures can help heal relationships and facilitate breakthroughs and shifts for the couple. This can result in increased relational abilities, including problem solving, lightheartedness, more give-and-take, and amplified awareness and insight (Carson & Casado-Kehoe, 2011).

The Genogram Intervention

The counselor could explain to John and Erin that a genogram would be useful by bringing bring to light patterns, thoughts, and beliefs generated from their families of origin (Gehart & Tuttle, 2003). Many art therapists have encouraged the development of a creative genogram, recognizing the importance in couples working together, creating and adding their own symbols and drawings (Malchiodi, 2012). To implement this intervention, place a large piece of paper on the wall and lay several colored markers on the table. John and Erin would then be guided through the process of creating their family genogram. This would be referred to occasionally throughout therapy. As they re-create patterns of interaction between their grandparents and parents, they could experience moments of revelation as tenuous and contentious family relationships became exposed. Here is one example:

THERAPIST: I would like the both of you to look at the genogram on the wall. Tell me what you see?

JOHN: I see the difficult relationship between my parents; they did not have a loving relationship. I remember mom was always picking at dad, and in order to get her to stop nagging, he would put his newspaper up to his face and block her out. That would only get her angrier. I don't remember seeing them hug much either. And I see problems with my grandparents too. They would chew each other out in front of us. I remember one day when Grandpa got so angry he left the room and did not come back for hours.

THERAPIST: And what about you, Erin? What do you observe about your family's manner of interacting?

ERIN: My family argued loudly with each other, but it didn't seem too bad because they always made up in front of us. I do remember my mother using sarcasm to spur others into action and my father rolling his eyes at her.

THERAPIST: Do you see any parallels in your manner of relating with each other? How you may have picked up any similar patterns of behavior?

ERIN: I see how I use similar sarcasm and yell a lot.

JOHN: I see how I shut down and get quiet, not speaking at all. I might not use a newspaper, but I feel like I put a wall up there to block her out when it becomes too overwhelming.

This session could end with the counselor inviting John and Erin to describe strengths in their marriage, listing them at the bottom of the paper. As they share their strengths, they could gain insight and understanding that although they have difficulties in their relationship, there are many positive qualities that have been overlooked due to negative interaction patterns developed over the years.

The Mandala Intervention

In couples therapy, it is important for each partner to be able to safely explore his or her emotions in order to move beyond any secondary emotions such as anger, fear, or guilt and covering or masking the true emotion that is being felt (Elliott, Watson, Goldman, & Greenberg, 2004; Greenberg, 2011; Johnson, 2008). According to emotionally focused therapy, it is crucial to reach primary emotions, such as sadness or shame, that are not as easily owned or acknowledged, in order to create a safe emotional connecting experience for couples. A creative intervention using mandalas can be used to help a couple identify the emotions they are feeling. The use of mandalas (Green, Drewes, & Kominski, 2013; Henderson, Rosen, & Mascaro, 2007) has been shown to be effective in the healing process during therapy, and can be adapted to meet the various needs of the client (see Sidebar 12.2).

SIDEBAR 12.2 SELF-AWARENESS: CREATE YOUR OWN HEALING MANDALA

Therapists may be hesitant to incorporate creative-experiential interventions with clients due to lack of exposure or self-confidence. Take some time to create a mandala and experience possible increased inner awareness or insight to a given relationship or situation in your life:

- Prepare by gathering colored pencils, markers or crayons, and a blank sheet of paper.
- Draw a large circle approximately 6 inches in diameter.
- Think about a relationship that you are presently involved in. In the space below the circle, list all the emotions you are feeling when you think of that. You may wish to consult a feelings list to assist you in this process.
- Assign a color to each emotion.
- Color your emotions in the mandala: this may be abstract, symbolic, or realistic.
- Process your creation for new insight and understanding.

An intervention creating a mandala could be used with John and Erin. On a blank sheet of paper, they would be requested to list the emotions they felt when they thought about their relationship, both positive and negative, assigning a color to each of those emotions. They would be directed to draw the listed emotions in their individual mandalas, in any manner they chose. In the sharing that followed, the counselor could gently probe for any primary emotions not yet identified, leading to further discussion and exploration of emotions surrounding their conflict and disconnection. Both John and Erin may be able to accept their individual emotions and begin to verbalize their fears and concerns. They may gain greater awareness in recognizing that their negative pattern of interacting was a cry for connection and safety, as well as a cover-up of the dysfunctional attachment pattern lurking below the surface. An important role of the therapist is to validate their sharing, helping to reframe their emotions in order to facilitate understanding and acceptance.

The Four Horsemen Intervention

It would be valuable for each partner to describe his or her own actions attributing to their difficulties, shifting the focus from their partner to themselves and gaining awareness of their part of the "dance." An emphasis on attachment fears and the vulnerability lying beneath their negative reactive patterns would be helpful. Using Gottman's example of the four horsemen (Gottman & Gottman, 2012) could increase understanding of the destructiveness in their interaction pattern. The four horsemen are listed as criticism, defensiveness, contempt, and stonewalling, or emotionally withdrawing from interacting. It would be important for John and Erin to eliminate these ways of interacting and to replace them with the prescribed antidote.

This excerpt illustrates the implementation of the antidote of "gentle up" for criticism, along with an example of stonewalling:

THERAPIST: Erin, why don't you share with John a concern you have with your children.

ERIN: John, you told me that you would help me with Gregory. You said you would call the school when there was a problem and deal with the principal when it got rough. When I want you to call, you just look at me and walk away. You don't care about Gregory and you don't care about me.

THERAPIST: Erin, by telling John he doesn't care about you or Gregory, you are criticizing his actions and assuming that he does not care. This may get in the way of John listening to you. Will you try again by talking about yourself and how you feel?

ERIN: I'm sorry, John. I do get critical when I get angry. I feel frustrated and all alone in raising Gregory. It is so difficult to deal with teachers who don't have an understanding of what it is like to live with the difficulties of cerebral palsy 24 hours a day. I get overwhelmed and feel alone, especially when you ignore me and walk away.

THERAPIST: How does it make you feel when he walks away?

ERIN: Invisible, all alone.

JOHN: I just feel overwhelmed, unable to do what you want. Instead of yelling, I walk away. I honestly wish I could help more than I do. I see how well you relate to the teachers, but I guess I see how alone you feel in dealing with his disability.

THERAPIST: John, why not ask her what she needs from you in order to make her not feel so alone?

John would be encouraged to see the impact that his stonewalling had on his wife when he acted as if she did not exist when he was disturbed or conflicted over her behavior. He would be encouraged to look for what lies beneath the surface, as well as to increase his availability and responsiveness to his wife. Erin could see how her pointed grasps at connection through criticism were seen as aggressive, with her rage contributing to his retreat into nonresponsiveness.

The Sand Tray Intervention

In Gottman's research, one of the indications cited by couples pursuing a divorce was a lack of positive affect as they withdrew from each other (Gottman & Gottman, 2012). In order to create an atmosphere inviting positive affect, as well as providing an opportunity to generate more insight, compassion, and hope, the therapist could introduce a sand tray intervention with John and Erin. Sand tray therapy has been used to bring understanding to what lies below the surface (Homeyer & Sweeney, 2011; Huckvale, 2011). John and Erin would be asked to choose miniatures from nearby shelves and create scenes in their own sand trays depicting their pattern of interaction. The therapist would observe the manner in which Erin and John chose and placed the miniatures in their respective sand trays. The following is an example of how powerful the processing following the creation of a sand tray can be.

ERIN: (crying gently) I see how I push you away with my sharp words of criticism. I wouldn't want you to be critical of me the way I am with you.

JOHN: (in a soft whisper) I see how turning away from you makes you panic. I can see your anger differently now. I just wanted you to stop, but I see now that it made you feel insecure and not safe.

THERAPIST: John and Erin, I would like you to create a sand tray together showing the way you would like to relate to each other.

During their joint creation of the sand tray, a new attachment pattern of safety and connection could emerge between the two of them. When they complete their tray, they could begin to understand each other's emotional needs at a deeper level than before, possibly experiencing feelings of tenderness and affection evidenced by a change of tone in their voices or gentle hugs. Seeing John and Erin engage with positive emotions would be encouraging, indicating increased connection, and would hopefully continue into the following week. The therapist would check back with them at the next session, looking for any rise in mutual acceptance and responsiveness, along with any softening in Erin's approach or John becoming more emotionally available and responsive.

Communication Techniques

In addition to developing new ways of communication, it is important for couples to understand the role that fear has played in their relationship. According to Bowlby, when an individual experiences dysregulated fear, that fear obstructs and alters successful attempts to connect (Furrow, Johnson, & Bradley, 2011). It would be helpful for John and Erin to learn how to use language in order to promote acceptance and to receive comfort, and to risk moving toward each other in order to build a secure base. They would be encouraged to practice their new skills by scheduling time alone in a nearby café, asking each other questions found in the game "Pocket Ungame: Couples Version." They would be guided to listen to each other, using "I" statements when talking. When one wished to express a concern during their time together, they were urged to use Gottman's skill of "soften startup," by using "I" statements communicating how they felt, sticking to facts, and then stating what they needed in order to resolve the issue (Gottman & Gottman, 2012).

Although John and Erin could experience greater success in connecting, daily problems most likely would trigger old patterns of relating, especially when communication issues revolved around the care of their son. Erin wanted John to be more involved with both their children, and she especially needed his help with Gregory's educational, medical, and social needs. Because both Erin and

John appeared to move toward resolution at a faster pace through creative experiential interventions, an additional experiential intervention involving art could be chosen. They would be asked to schedule a longer session the following week, using the time in between sessions to ponder the parenting issues. The counselor would encourage Erin to reflect on how she felt handling the bulk of Gregory's care, while John would be urged to contemplate on what was holding him back from being more actively involved.

Expressive Arts Collage Intervention

At the next session, the counselor would direct Erin and John in the creation of a collage, offering the couple cut-out pictures, words, and phrases, along with stickers, paper, magazines, scissors, glue, and a file folder for each of them. Erin and John would be instructed to use the outside of the file folder to portray how they expressed their concerns to others over the responsibility and care of their son. On the inside, they would be asked to describe the feelings and thoughts that lay underneath the surface. They would be given 30 minutes to work silently as the therapist observed the emotional states of the couple as they both engrossed themselves in the creation of their folders. When finished, they would be asked to reveal their folders to each other. Here is an example of the dialogue that could follow:

JOHN: On the outside of my folder there is a picture of a man resting his head in his hands in front of a stern-faced judge slamming a gavel down on a podium. This is how I feel when Erin expects me to be involved with Gregory's care. The judge slams his gavel down, saying "Guilty!"

THERAPIST: What are you feeling as you look at that picture, John?

JOHN: I feel anxious and frustrated, like I will not measure up.

THERAPIST: What is on the inside of your folder?

JOHN: This picture of the ostrich and the other things here represent my lack of confidence. I don't have the skill in navigating the educational system, and do not understand what Gregory needs medically. I just want to stick my head in the sand. I am afraid of failing. (turning to Erin) If I fail, I let you down and I let Gregory down. . . . This picture here represents how sad I feel over having a son with cerebral palsy. I feel such loss.

As John shared, Erin reached over to comfort him, and he was able to experience his wife as a secure base, able to handle his emotions and most intimate fears. After processing his folder, Erin was asked her to share hers. She held hers up.

ERIN: I have this picture of Wonder Woman on the cover. She is throwing villains in the air with the flick of a finger. Everyone thinks she is amazing, though she is tired doing it all herself. No one knows what she is really like on the inside and how much she would like another superhero to share the load.

Erin opens up the folder spontaneously and continues to share:

ERIN: I feel like this ox with a heavy yoke on his back. He has to keep doing the work, even though it is tough work. And this is a picture of a person who is walking up a very steep mountain. I feel that way many days, like I'm walking up a big mountain all by myself. I think it would be easier if there was someone on the path with me. We could share the load. But over here (Erin turns to John) is a picture of a young man laughing and enjoying a game of golf with an older man. I want to see you and Gregory connect on a deeper level.

A healing dialogue could be facilitated by the therapist between Erin and John as they shared what they could do together to help their son in the years ahead.

Special Issues With Children

Couples with normally developing children will seek therapy due to concerns surrounding parenting differences as well as specific problems related to their children (Doss et al., 2004). It is also understood that parents caring for children with special needs can experience higher levels of stress and a lower quality of life (Browne & Bramston, 1998). This can lead to more distress in a marriage. As a therapist, it is important to be sensitive to this dynamic when working with couples who have children with special needs. Besides referring parents to appropriate local agencies, therapies, and support groups specific to their child's situation, they often need help in understanding how to obtain assistance at their child's school when difficulties first arise. In an attempt to help reduce the effects of stress, parents may wish to enlist the help of a local advocate who is familiar with educational law and the development of a viable Individual Educational Plan (IEP) or 504 Plan (see Sidebar 12.3). Also of importance is filial therapy, otherwise known as parent training groups, which have been found to help parents tune in, increase acceptance of their child, and increase empathy (Kottman, 2011; Wickstrom, 2010). In helping John and Erin, each of these categories would be discussed with them. John would especially benefit from a child–parent relationship therapy group (Landreth, 2012). As John learned how to interact with Gregory, his ability to enjoy and appreciate the relationship could increase. A well-rounded couples therapist seeks to address all the issues and areas of concern, including parenting, which impact and affect the couple's relationship and even levels of intimacy.

SIDEBAR 12.3 CASE STUDY: PROVIDING THE RESOURCES FOR JOHN AND ERIN

A critical aspect of relieving stress in parents with special needs children is sharing local, regional, and national resources. Parents may not know of the government resources available, such as Medicaid or public school options. Other resources, such as local and state advocacy agencies and specialized attorneys and advocates, assist with issues that seem overwhelming to the parent. Think about the services that a couple may need in order to reduce the stress in their marriage and family. How aware are you of what is available in your community and state?

- State Medicaid, Med-Waiver, or other insurance
- Specialist doctors, therapists, alternative healing professionals
- Public school special education services
- Education advocates assisting with IEP and 504 development, mediating educational disputes
- Legal assistance: guardianship, durable power of attorney
- Disability-specific organizations and support groups
- National and state disability councils and websites

Patterns and Common Issues

Assessment

At the beginning of couples counseling, the therapist assesses how affectionate the couple is, where they are in terms of intimacy, and how much they share with each other emotionally. The therapist can even use an intimacy genogram to assess how the family has developed intimacy patterns (Sherman, 2000), their generational patterns, and what ways they have learned to handle conflict. Johnson (2008) reminds us that marriages that fail do not do so because of their conflict, but because of their lack of emotional responsiveness and lack of affection.

Identifying Dynamics in the Relationship

A common issue in marriage is conflict. An important piece to know is how couples respond to the conflict and what they do after the disagreement is over. The ways in which they handle conflict may help couples reconnect or cause them to distance themselves emotionally. When couples come to counseling, they have been struggling for a while; conflict did not just begin. In fact, most couples do not seek counseling right away; most wait an average of 6 years after dealing with complicated issues before they seek therapy (Doss et al., 2004). As a result of this prolonged wait, couples therapists are often dealing with a pile of issues and a lot of resentment on the part of the couple. Thus, one of the primary goals is to help the couple move away from blaming stances and understand their destructive cycle. Sometimes couples do not even talk to one another when they begin therapy. Thus, it may be helpful to find out how the couple connects or does not. Townsend (2007) reminds us that connection begins the process of love. So, is the couple making a conscious effort to connect or disconnect from one another with the fighting? For some couples, fighting may be a negative way of getting attention from each other and may be a learned pattern from a family of origin. However, connection is a heart-to-heart experience that allows us to engage emotionally with our partners. The therapist wants to promote opportunities that provide connection in and out of therapy.

Identifying the Meaning of *Love*

In couples counseling, couples therapists recommend spending some time clarifying what *love* means to them. What is their definition of love? How does each partner feel loved? It is clear that romantic love is different than deep love. However, each of us feels loved differently. For one person it may be having sex often, which is what makes him or her feel loved. This is also explained by the fact that having sex deepens the love bond due to oxytocin that is released (Love, 2001). For another person, it may be holding hands and going for a walk by the beach. Each person has individual preferences; it is okay to acknowledge those and learn about each partner's likes and desires. Dr. Love has a chemistry inventory that can help couples understand what role chemistry plays in their relationship as a way to understand their partner better. Chemistry is something personal, and it changes with time. Other authors such as Gottman and Gottman (2013) have what they call the "love map" and "opportunity cards" exercise, which allows couples to learn more about each other's worlds as a way to be mindful of their partners. Their research revealed that a positive predictor of marital stability is having an understanding of each other's world—what makes the other person tick. The more that each partner understands the other, the more that they can try to meet each other's needs. Commonly, it is a lack of understanding of the other that makes one want to change his or her partner. In counseling, a couple learns that it is not about changing the partners as much as it is about changing how each one relates to the other partner.

The Miracle Question Intervention

Couples tend to come to counseling complaining about their partners or wondering if they are still in love with their partners. Again, many couples feel they have fallen out of love once the oxytocin goes down and they begin looking at their partners through a different lens (Love, 2001). As a way to get couples to redefine their love images and shift their perspective from a problem-focused one to a solution-focused one, the therapist may ask the couple the "miracle question." This is a technique used in solution-focused therapy that empowers clients to reach into untapped resources and see actions that will take them toward solutions and preferred outcomes (Berg & Dolan, 2001).

The following excerpt illustrates this technique:

THERAPIST: So, Jane and Bill, suppose that when you go home this evening and go to bed, a miracle happens during the night and the problem that brought you here today is gone, all gone. (pause) What would be the first sign in the morning that will let you know that a miracle had happened? What will you be doing? What will be the first indication that would let you know?

BILL: I would wake up in the morning and when I turn around to look at Jane, she would be interested in talking to me, and give me a kiss.

THERAPIST: What about you, Jane? What would it be like for you?

JANE: I would be talking to Bill and he would be interested in me. He would notice me and give me some compliments.

THERAPIST: I see. So, you would each be interested in the other and you would be communicating. Is that right?

The reality is that love allows each partner to see infinite possibilities about the other. Zadra and Yamada (2010) say that when we are in love, we see gifts and possibilities in our partners that nobody else has taken the time to find. Love is what allows us to grow personally, and as a couple, in ways we cannot even imagine (Migerode & Hooghe, 2012).

The Length of Treatment

As one works with couples, the length of treatment will vary depending on the theoretical orientation of the therapist, the level of commitment of the couple to therapy and to saving their marriage, and the specific issues the couple may bring. There are indeed theoretical models that emphasize the need for brief therapy to clients, since many see counseling as a last resort (Hudson & O'Hanlon, 1991). Once the therapist has an understanding of what is going on with the couple and assesses where they are developmentally, it will become more clear what length of time the couple may need to be in therapy. Knowing what goals couples have for therapy will also help the therapist determine what the counseling process may entail. The therapist's aim is to help couples focus on the established goals that will allow them to feel like they can accomplish the vision they had at the beginning. In addition, the therapist helps clients assess how close they are to reaching those goals, and celebrating the small steps along the way is important. Small steps are what make the big changes.

Imago Therapy

Imago therapy believes that people fall in love making unconscious choices about their partners (Hendrix, 2008). They are trying to find the ideal one who will make them complete, heal them, make them happy. They are looking for an image of familiar love unconsciously, as a way to heal their past (Love, 2001). What couples fail to see is the true person in front of them during that time of romance. Hormones are elevated and oxytocin is high, and the thinking brain is not really working. It is in that state of infatuation that many couples confuse being in love with loving a partner. But once the oxytocin drops and reality kicks in, couples have to confront the real person and wake up from that trance state. They may even realize that what brought them together is now pushing them apart. When romantic love ends, true love begins (Love, 2001). But for many couples this is the time they start having problems. They may ask themselves internally, "Who are you? Is this who I married? What was I thinking?" The reality is that they were not thinking, because their thinking brains were not working during the infatuation stage. However, many couples may not seek help right away, or even confront the problem with their partner. They may choose to wait in the muddy waters of conflict until the problems escalate into crisis. At this point, they may decide to seek couples counseling.

Divorce rates are on the rise. It is estimated that 50% to 60% of marriages end in divorce. The reality is that divorce is a traumatic experience for most couples, and even more when there are children involved. A person has decided to marry another person who makes him or her feel complete and who sees the best in him or her, but divorce destroys that dream and the vision of eternal happiness (Baer, 2006). This phenomenon will make some couples engage in couples counseling as they begin the divorce journey or after the divorce while preparing to begin their next relationship. Surprisingly, only about one fourth of divorcing couples actually report having gone to therapy to try to save their marriage, and those who go tend to wait an average of 6 years after problems develop before seeking help (Buongiorno, 1992, as cited in Doss et al., 2004). The reality is that many of those divorces could be spared if couples sought premarital counseling and couples counseling during their marriage. There are some states, such as Minnesota, that require couples to go into couples counseling prior to being able to get a divorce (Doherty, 1999). This movement encourages couples to resolve issues in counseling rather than dissolving the marriage.

Presenting Issues

When couples come to therapy, the therapist wonders if the couple is actually revealing all that is going on in the relationship. For instance, if the husband is abusing alcohol, will the wife share that piece of information or choose to keep it a secret because she has developed a shopping addiction to help her cope with her unhappiness? If one is having an affair, will he or she reveal it or try to triangulate the therapist so the person can be free of the secret? Doss et al. (2004) state that sometimes couples present a different agenda and choose to talk about finances rather than the real issue. With that in mind, how can the therapist really know what is really happening? This is where some couples therapists may choose to use assessments to have an overall view of the relationship, whereas others may rely on that initial interview and what the couple may put forth as the presenting issue. The following case illustrates some of these ideas.

Searching for Trust

Bill and Jane have been married for 15 years and have two children, Sam, age 8, and Leann, age 2. Bill is a lawyer and works many hours. Jane started working part time a couple of years ago, but she is also the primary person who is taking care of the children. It was Bill's idea to get Jane out of the house and back into a part-time job. He had a friend, Mark, who had an independent business and ended up hiring Jane as his secretary. It was 6 months ago that Bill found out that Jane had an affair with his friend Mark. This shook his world, since he thought his marriage was a good one. He is now considering whether he may need to divorce Jane. Understandably so, Bill feels extremely betrayed. Jane is feeling remorseful about the affair and says that she was just feeling lonely. However, deep down it is Bill she loves and wants to be married to. The affair has made her realize that this marriage is more important than she thought. She says that Mark was just a fling and that the affair is over.

The Dialogue Technique

After the initial interview in which the therapist tried to find out the details about what brought Bill and Jane to counseling, she asked what their goals were in therapy. In doing so, she asked both partners independently to write down what the problem was and what they wanted to get out of therapy in order for the counseling experience to be successful. The therapist asked them to write it down in the first person. Once Bill and Jane wrote down their thoughts, the therapist also told them they would be doing a little exercise and asked them to look at one another and state what they wanted to get out of therapy. Their task was to listen to their partner and reflect back what they heard. Hendrix (2008) calls this technique *dialogue*, in which partners learn to listen to the other one and respond empathically to the information presented. It may look like a simple exercise, but it allows couples to really be honest with one another, knowing that their partner will listen and not react to what they are sharing. This exercise deepens intimacy and creates emotional closeness.

Scaling Questions

After Bill and Jane discussed their goals, the therapist asked them a scaling question to assess their level of commitment to working in therapy. Scaling questions are primarily used in solution-focused therapy to help clients pinpoint exactly how high or low they feel in regard to an issue and how to measure progress toward a goal. Scaling allows people to see that change comes in little pieces, and this helps people feel that change is possible (Nelson, 2010).

The therapist asked Bill and Jane this scaling question: "I am wondering, on a scale from 0 to 10, with 0 not being committed at all and 10 being the most committed one can be, where are you in terms of being committed to strengthening this relationship?" Notice the therapist's choice of words; she uses the word *strengthen*, which implies they have some strengths in this marriage—otherwise they would not have survived 15 years together. After the couple tells her their numbers, she may still ask another question. For instance: "Bill, you are saying that right now you feel like you are at a 5 in terms of your commitment to strengthen the relationship. I am wondering, what would need to happen for you to move from a 5 to a 6?" These kinds of questions help clients see that small change is meaningful and that it is within their control. The therapist can also ask the couple an "exception question." Exception questions assume that all couples have successful times, even if they are few. These are times when the problem is not present (Berg & Dolan, 2001). For example, the therapist may say: "Bill and Jane, you have been married 15 years. Tell me about a time that, despite circumstances, you managed to do great as a couple. What were you doing?" This kind of dialogue not only builds hope for the couple, but also lets them know that they can do it again. It is a message of hope in their ability to make it work as a couple. The use of solution-focused therapy techniques helps partners define what their relationship will look like without the problem and the specific steps they are taking in the right direction (Bannink, 2006).

Play Therapy Techniques

The therapist continued the assessment of the couple's desire to change, but decided to use some play therapy techniques to get a better understanding of their internal worlds. In order to do so, she asked the couple to go to the shelf of figurines and to each find a figurine that represented how they felt about the relationship. Bill chose his right away, and he came back to his seat with a look of defeat. He had chosen a caged tiger. Jane brought back a broken seashell. The therapist asked them to tell her what the figurines represented for them. This is always a humbling experience because sometimes clients' interpretations are not what the therapist may think right away; this reminds us that the clients are in charge of their worlds. They are the experts, and the therapist just creates a safe environment for them to share. The beauty of an experiential approach is that it allows the partners to speak metaphorically about what is happening for each of them. By using play techniques, it also brings some distance so couples can feel more comfortable sharing things that make them feel vulnerable. On many occasions, couples are so focused on blaming their partner that they are not checking to see how it is that they feel inside. The couple may be spending too much time reacting rather than problem solving and looking within as a way to own their role of what is happening in the relationship. A great question to get couples to own their part is one used in emotionally focused couples therapy (Johnson, 2004). For example: "Jane, when Bill gets overly involved with work, what do you do?" Or, "When Jane is emotionally unavailable, what do you do, Bill?" One of the greatest things couples can learn in counseling is to understand their own perspectives, and those of their partners, better (Love & Stosny, 2007). Many times couples make assumptions about their partners and do not have a true understanding of what is going on inside the other person. They are in reactivity mode and caught up in their own heads. The therapist may also ask, "What goes on in your head when Bill leaves the room? What do you tell yourself?" The focus is for couples to learn to verbalize those internal dialogues, as well as to develop a better understanding of their partner's feelings and experiences.

Communication Issues and Skill Development

Communication Techniques

Regardless of what issue couples may bring to therapy, most couples therapists will focus on teaching couples some healthy ways to communicate with one another and build intimacy. Basically, the therapist is teaching and modeling the "speaker–listener" technique to couples. Imago therapy calls this *dialogue* (Hendrix, 2008; Love, 2001; Robbins, 2005); others call it *transforming conversations* (Johnson, 2008) or *Videotalk* (Hudson & O'Hanlon, 1991). Rita DeMaria (2010) uses the image of a heart that the speaker puts in the hand of the listener as a reminder that he or she is sharing information from the heart with his or her partner. The heart is a powerful image to engage couples into listening to one another with deep care. Ultimately, the idea is teaching couples to share more of their inner worlds with one another rather than walking on eggshells emotionally and finding ways to distance oneself from the other one. When couples learn to truly listen to their partners, they learn how different their partners are from themselves (Johnson, 2008). The one who listens makes the partner feel heard and understood. Feeling validated by one's partner has a deep impact on the relationship. The person doesn't have to agree with what the partner is saying, but it is crucial that each person can open up to the other emotionally. It is that opening up that makes the relationship grow and mature. The therapist also models for the couple what it means to validate another person as he or she joins the system (Johnson, 2004). When couples feel understood, they are less likely to be emotionally dysregulated.

De-Escalation of Negative Cycles

At the beginning of treatment, emotionally focused couples therapists will focus on assessment and de-escalation of the negative cycles (Johnson, 1999). Emotional safety is another growth-promoting factor that helps couples develop closeness and a desire to be together. Thus, the therapist is constantly engaging the couple in discussions or exercises that promote emotional expression and help them identify feelings and express them in a nonattacking way. If couples do not have the ability to tap into their inner emotions, the therapist may verbalize those feelings for them. A technique that emotionally focused therapists use is "validating underlying emotions," in which the couples counselor speaks for the client (Johnson, 2004). The therapist positions him- or herself close to one partner and speaks for that person, and then asks the client to repeat that interaction with his or her partner. This helps clients develop awareness about their feelings and helps them voice their internal worlds. The therapist listens very carefully to all they say and emphasizes those emotions that are hidden, while helping couples identify their destructive cycle, or their "demon dialogues" (Johnson, 2008). While identifying their cycle, couples learn about primary and secondary emotions and how those are impacting the relationship. Being aware of the cycle can really help a couple de-escalate their level of conflict and later create engagement. At the same time, the therapist helps the couple understand the attachment bond that ties their hearts together as a way to help them reconnect and feel safe (Hart and Morris, 2003; Johnson, 2004). Ultimately, people want to know that their partners care for them, that they will be there for them no matter what the circumstances may be, and they can count on them (Johnson, 2008). Feeling loved and connected are essential needs we have as humans. Thus, our partners not only help us survive, but also thrive. It is in the care of each other that we grow on a personal level.

Developmental Phases

Relationships go through developmental phases and highs and lows. Couples who work at their relationships figure out ways to go through the hard times (Love, 2001). As a therapist, you ask yourself several questions. Where is this couple developmentally? Did they get married recently? Are they still establishing the relationship and negotiating roles and how to separate from their family of origin and friends? Or have they been struggling intimately because they have three kids and their parenting styles collide? Apart from determining their developmental phase, the therapist may ask couples about how they fell in love and the exceptions to their problem: "Tell me how you two met. What let you know she/he was the one?" Or "Tell me about a time when you were doing really well in this relationship. What were you both doing?" These questions have the potential of getting the couple to shift their thinking and be less problem focused.

Most of the time, couples come to therapy complaining about their partners, placing blame on the other. "If only he/she would act differently. If only he/she would respond that way." The therapist may want to ask the couple, "How would each of you would like this relationship to be different?" (Bannink, 2006). But the reality is that couples therapy is about learning how to turn our eyes inward rather than focusing them outward (Johnson, 2004). Each partner plays a role, and the reality is that the other person is not responsible for how we feel. Our partner's actions may trigger something in us, but these are layers of other stuff, past events that are being triggered. And the minute couples can see that real love is about changing oneself, the marriage can change quite drastically (Baer, 2006). There are two main goals for individuals in couples therapy: (1) to understand what is going on inside themselves, and (2) to gain a deeper understanding their partners.

Past Wounds

A variety of theories point toward the idea that the issues we have with our partners are related to experiences we had in childhood. Thus, our partners trigger emotions from the past. For instance, Imago therapy informs us that we are wounded in childhood and we unconsciously attract an image of our caregivers. We search to heal our past wounds with our partners (Hendrix, 2008; Love, 2001).

In session, the therapist asks Bill and Jane to look within to see if there are any connections to their past: "Bill, when she starts talking to you with an angry voice, what happens inside of you? Does it remind you of any other time in your life? What are you feeling and thinking at that time?" Emotionally focused therapy tries to understand our attachment style—how we attached to our parents/caregivers and how that plays a role in our romantic relationships (Johnson, 2004, 2008). Sometimes these patterns emerge clearly when we create a genogram with the couple. Once they develop awareness about their arguing style and ways of connecting, it becomes clearer how they can change their relationship dance.

Creating Safety

A common issue that brings couples to therapy is not being able to see eye to eye and fighting constantly as a way to establish control or getting one's partner to see his or her position. Conflict is inevitable in relationships. But at times, the arguments that couples have keep them from emotionally connecting and instead create an emotional wall because the partners are not listening to one another. Some authors believe that when couples fight they are using the reactive part of their brains out of their own fear and shame. When one is not able to think clearly, it is easier to blame one's partner rather than look within (Love & Stosny, 2007). Gottman's research (2012; Holman & Jarvis, 2003) actually reveals that one of the predictors for success in couples is not lack of conflict, but how the couple handles conflict. In counseling, when couples fight or argue, the therapist needs to know how to actively intervene. Allowing the couple to escalate their fights in therapy is counterproductive and does not teach clients self-regulation, which is a critical skill.

The role of an emotionally focused therapist is being a coach who has the ability to create safety in the session so clients can re-create a safe dialogue at home. The therapist offers a secure bond with both partners that builds attachment, facilitates expression of emotion, and helps the couple identify their fighting dance. It is important for the therapist to let the partners know that his or her role is not to judge them or take sides, but to understand the dynamics that keep the destructive patterns in the relationship going (Hazlett, 2010). In this process, the therapist teaches couples how to fight/argue more effectively. In emotionally focused couples therapy, the therapist tries to understand the bonds that connect couples and then proceeds to teach them skills to argue more effectively. These new skills will prepare them to have conversations rather than fights (May, 2007). During this safe dialogue, the therapist can help the couple see what is deep within each person, which can have a transformative effect. This allows the couple to develop a deeper emotional bond and create intimacy.

Marital Enrichment

Every so often there are couples who come to counseling for marital enrichment. Their marriage is not on the brink or in crisis, but they want a coach to help them grow more in their marriage. The therapist will assess areas for growth, as well as highlight the couple's strengths to create feelings of optimism and hope in the relationship (Warren, 2000). As with any other couple, the first session is focused on building a strong alliance with both partners and assessing and defining what is going on in the relationship, relationally and emotionally. This following excerpt illustrates a couple seeking marital enrichment.

Nick and Shelly have been married for 10 years. They just came back from Hawaii, where they renewed their vows. They came to therapy wanting to work on their marriage. The therapist first asked, "How can I help you? What do you need to happen in this session that would make you feel like your time was worthwhile?" These kinds of questions are solution focused and have the end result in mind.

The couple answered in unison: "Help us grow." This was the ideal couple, in the sense that they were both willing to work and were invested in the process of therapy. When the therapist started assessing their marriage, they were very stable and both wanted to be there for each other. Having empathy for one's partner and wanting the best for the other are signs of a healthy couple. Their emphasis on caring for the other reminded the therapist of Gottman and Gottman's (2013) skill "share fondness and admiration." When couples are able to share the positive aspects of the other, their intimacy levels increase. The therapist gave the couple Gottman's "I appreciate . . ." handout, and they shared traits they admired about each other. Before closing the session, the therapist wanted to explore their dreams together as a couple—what the Gottmans call "making life dreams come true." So, he used an experiential exercise and asked them if they could spend 5 to 10 minutes on the easel writing down a vision of their marriage. What would they like to see happen in 5 years? What is their dream? How would they create something beautiful in their relationship? Shelly took the lead in the creation of their vision, but Nick was also very interactive with Shelly and contributed to the ideas she presented. At the end of the session, the therapist talked with the couple about the idea that a marriage is like a book, with different chapters and an evolving plot. The use of metaphors is another creative way that a therapist can talk to the couple. Metaphors have a visual element that resonates with most people at a deeper level. The therapist can even get couples to draw these images on paper with crayons or create a collage of what they see. These give couples a concrete image that can remind them of their vision. When couples make time to connect emotionally and invest in their emotional bank account (Gottman & Gottman, 2012), it deepens their love for one another, and it helps them build protective factors for when things are not going well in the relationship.

Considerations

Last but not least, those who want to work with couples need to get some specialized training. There are plenty of couples therapists in the field who have had no couples-specific training and are doing more damage than good. Unfortunately, clients are paying the price of having therapists who lack couples training. Doherty (1999) states that only 12% of psychotherapists have had even one course in couples therapy or any supervised experience. Working with couples requires specialized skills and knowledge in couples counseling. When couples come to therapy, they do not know whether the therapist has had specialized training in couples counseling. From an ethical standpoint, all those who have a desire to work with this population should seek specialized training. As therapists, we are responsible for the future of our clients and often the fate of their children. When a couple decides to divorce, this is something they should decide on their own, not because the therapist recommends it. Although some divorces are necessary, some are preventable, and research shows that some marriages could be saved if couples went to therapy (Doherty, 1999). Thus, the couples therapist's role is to help couples fight for the marriage and find ways to help people change so they can have more fulfilling lives and marriages.

SUMMARY

As we have reviewed in this chapter, couples bring a variety of issues to work on when pursuing therapy. The trained couples therapist blends family therapy and individual therapy concepts (Donovan, 1999) with important couples and negotiation skills. These help both partners communicate and engage emotionally on a more adaptive and healthy level, often bringing increased awareness and insight into the counseling process. Also examined was the importance of understanding the role that families of origin, including attachment style, have on the couple's present level of relating and experiencing, as well as looking beyond the initial presenting problem for multifaceted issues hindering the relationship. A variety of theoretical models, key issues, and interventions were discussed that can help couples connect on a deeper level and create a better understanding of each other.

USEFUL WEBSITES

The following websites provide additional information relating to the chapter topics.

American Society of Experiential Therapists
http://www.asetonline.com
Association for Play Therapy
http://www.a4pt.org/ps.index.cfm
Ellyn Bader
http://psychotherapy.net/article/ellyn-bader-couples-therapy
Bill Doherty
http://drbilldoherty.org
Cathy Malchiodi: Art Therapy and Expressive Arts Therapy
http://www.cathymalchiodi.com
Center for Play Therapy (Child Parent Relationship Therapy—CPRT)
http://cpt.unt.edu
Chris Fraley: Overview of Adult Attachment Theory
http://internal.psychology.illinois.edu/~rcfraley/attachment.htm
Empowered to Connect
http://empoweredtoconnect.org
The Focusing Institute: E. T. Gendlin
http://www.focusing.org
The Gottman Institute
http://www.gottman.com
Harville Hendrix and Helen LaKelly Hunt: Imago Therapy
http://harvillehendrix.com
Hold Me Tight: Sue Johnson
http://holdmetight.net

Institute for Solution-Focused Therapy
http://www.solutionfocused.net/solutionfocusedtherapy.html
Institute of Child Development: Trust-Based Relational Intervention Training
http://www.child.tcu.edu
The International Centre for Excellence in Emotionally Focused Therapy
http://iceeft.com
National Dissemination Center for Children with Disabilities
http://nichcy.org
Online Attachment Questionnaire (CRQ/ECR-R)
http://www.web-research-design.net/cgi-bin/crq/crq.pl
Online ECR-Relationship Structures (questionnaire)
http://www.yourpersonality.net/relstructures
Pat Love
http://www.patlove.com
Process-Experiential Therapy
http://www.process-experiential.org
The Relationship Center
http://ritademaria.com
The Marriage Doctor
http://www.marriagedoctor.com
Sandtray Network
http://www.sandtray.org
Solution-Focused Therapy
http://www.goodtherapy.org/Solution_Focused_Therapy.html
Solution-Focused Brief Therapy Association
http://www.sfbta.org/about_sfbt.html
Solution Focused Therapy
http://www.psychpage.com/family/library/sft.htm
Sounds of Encouragement
http://www.soencouragement.org/handlingconflictseminar.htm
Wrightslaw: Special Education Law and Advocacy
http://www.wrightslaw.com

REFERENCES

Ainsworth, M. S., Blehar, M. C., Waters, E., & Wall, S. (1978). *Patterns of attachment: A psychological study of the strange situation*. Oxford, UK: Erlbaum.

Bader, E. (2013). *Getting off to a powerful start in couples therapy*. Retrieved from http://www.psychotherapy.net/article/ellyn-bader-couples-therapy

Baer, G. (2006). *Real love in marriage: The truth about finding genuine happiness now and forever*. New York, NY: Gotham Books.

Bannink, F. (2006). *1001 solution-focused questions*. New York, NY: W. W. Norton.

Berg, I. K., & Dolan, I. (2001). *Tales of solutions: A collection of hope-inspiring stories*. New York: W. W. Norton.

Bowlby, J. (1988). *A secure base: Parent-child attachment and healthy human development*. New York, NY: Basic Books.

Brennan, K. A., Clark, C. L., & Shaver, P. R. (1998). Self-report measurement of adult romantic attachment: An integrative overview. In J. A. Simpson & W. S. Rholes (Eds.), *Attachment theory and close relationships* (pp. 46–76). New York, NY: Guilford Press.

Browne, G., & Bramston, P. (1998). Stress and quality of life in the parents of young people with intellectual disabilities. *Journal of Psychiatric and Mental Health Nursing*, *5*, 415–421.

Carson, D. K., & Casado-Kehoe, M. (2011). Creative/experiential therapy with couples. In D. K. Carson and M. Casado-Kehoe (Eds.), *Case studies in couples therapy: Theory-based approaches* (pp. 229–248). New York, NY: Routledge.

DeMaria, R. (2010, July). *7 stages of marriage*. Paper presented at the Smart Marriages Conference, Orlando, FL.

Doherty, W. J. (1999, July). *How therapy can be hazardous to your marital health*. Paper presented at the Smart Marriages Conference, Orlando, FL.

Donovan, J. M. (Ed.) (1999). *Short-term couple therapy*. New York, NY: Guilford Press.

Doss, B. D., Simpson, L. E., & Christensen, A. (2004). Why do couples seek marital therapy? *Professional Psychology: Research and Practice*, *35*, 608–614.

Dozier, M. (1990). Attachment organization and treatment use for adults with serious psychopathological disorders. *Development and Psychopathology*, *1*(1), 47–60.

Elliott, R., Watson, J. C., Goldman, R. N., & Greenberg, L. S. (2004). *Learning emotion-focused therapy: The process-experiential approach to change*. Washington, DC: American Psychological Association.

Fraley, R. C. (2010). *A brief overview of adult attachment theory and research*. Retrieved from http://internal.psychology.illinois.edu

Fraley, R. C., Heffernan, M. E., Vicary, A. M., & Brumbaugh, C. C. (2011). The experiences in close relationships-relationship structures questionnaire: A method for assessing attachment orientations across relationships. *Psychological Assessment*, *23*, 615–625.

Fraley, R. C., Waller, N. G., & Brennan, K. A. (2000a). *Online attachment questionnaire (CRQ/ECR-R)* http://www.web-research-design.net/cgi-bin/crq/crq.pl

Fraley, R. C., Waller, N. G., & Brennan, K. A. (2000b). Experiences in Close Relationships–Revised (ECR-R). http://www.yourpersonality.net/relstructures/

Furrow, J. L., Johnson, S. M., & Bradley, B. A. (Eds.). (2011). *The emotionally focused casebook: New directions in treating couples*. New York, NY: Taylor & Francis.

Gehart, D. R., & Tuttle, A. R. (2003). *Theory-based treatment planning for marriage and family therapists: Integrating theory and practice*. Belmont, CA: Brooks/Cole Cengage Learning.

Gottman, J. M., & Gottman, J. S. (2012). *Bridging the couple chasm: Gottman couples therapy: A research-based approach*. Seattle, WA: The Gottman Institute.

Gottman, J. M., & Gottman, J. S. (2013). *The art & science of love: A weekend workshop for couples*. Seattle, WA: The Gottman Institute.

Green, E. J., Drewes, A. A., & Kominski, J. M. (2013). Use of mandalas in Jungian play therapy with adolescents diagnosed with ADHD. *International Journal of Play Therapy*, *22*(3), 159–172. doi:10.1037/a0033719

Greenberg, L. S. (2011). *Emotion-focused therapy*. Washington, DC: American Psychological Association.

Greenberg, L. S., Rice, L. N., & Elliott, R. (1993). *Facilitating emotional change: The moment-by-moment process*. New York, NY: Guilford Press.

Hart, A. D., & Morris, S. H. (2003). *Safe haven marriage: Building a relationship you want to come home to*. Nashville, TN: W. Publishing Group.

Hazan, C., & Shaver, P. (1987). Romantic love conceptualized as an attachment process. *Journal of Personality and Social Psychology*, *52*, 511–524.

Hazlett, P. S. (2010). Attunement, disruption and repair: The dance of self and other emotionally focused couple therapy. In A. S. Gurman (Ed.), *Clinical casebook of couple therapy* (pp. 21–43). New York, NY: Guilford Press.

Henderson, P., Rosen, D., & Mascaro, N. (2007). Empirical study on the healing nature of mandalas. *Psychology of Aesthetics, Creativity, and the Arts*, *1*(3), 148–154.

Hendrix, H. (2008). *Getting the love you want: A guide for couples* (20th ed.). New York, NY: Holt Paperback.

Holman, T. B., & Jarvis, M. O. (2003). Hostile, volatile, avoiding, and validating couple-conflict types: An investigation of Gottman's couple-conflict types. *Personal Relationships*, *10*(2), 267–282. doi:10.1111/1475-6811.00049

Homeyer, L. E., & Sweeney, D. S. (2011). *Sandtray therapy: A practical manual* (2nd ed.). New York, NY: Routledge.

Huckvale, K. (2011). Alchemy, sandtray and art psychotherapy: Sifting sands. *International Journal of Art Therapy: Inscape*, *16*(1), 30–40. doi:10.1080/17454832.2011.570272

Hudson, P. O., & O'Hanlon, W. H. (1991). *Rewriting love stories: Brief marital therapy*. New York, NY: W. W. Norton.

Johnson, S. (1999). Emotionally focused couple therapy: Straight to the heart. In J. M. Donovan (Ed.), *Short-term couple therapy* (pp. 31–42). New York, NY: Guilford Press.

Johnson, S. (2004). *The practice of emotionally focused couple therapy* (2nd ed.). New York, NY: Brunner-Routledge.

Johnson, S. (2008). *Hold me tight: Seven conversations for a lifetime of love*. New York, NY: Little, Brown.

Johnson, S. M. (2009). Attachment theory and emotionally focused therapy for individuals and couples. In J. H. Obegi & E. Berant (Eds.), *Attachment theory and research in clinical work with adults* (pp. 410–433). New York, NY: Guilford Press.

Kottman, T. (2011). *Play therapy basics and beyond* (2nd ed.). Alexandria, VA: American Counseling Association.

Landreth, G. L. (2012). *Play therapy: The art of the relationship* (2nd ed.). New York, NY: Taylor & Francis.

Levy, K. N., Ellison, W. D., Scott, L. N., & Bernecker, S. L. (2011). Attachment style. In J. C. Norcross (Ed.), *Psychotherapy relationships that work: Evidence-based responsiveness* (2nd ed.) (pp. 379–386). New York, NY: Oxford University Press.

Love, P. (2001). *The truth about love: The highs, the lows, and how you can make it last forever*. New York, NY: Simon & Schuster.

Love, P., & Stosny, S. (2007). *How to improve your marriage without talking about it*. New York, NY: Broadway Books.

Main, M., Kaplan, N., & Cassidy, J. (1985). Security in infancy, childhood, and adulthood: A move to the level of representation. *Monographs of the Society for Research in Child Development*, *50*(1–2), 66–104.

Malchiodi, C. A. (Ed.). (2012). *Handbook of art therapy* (2nd ed.). New York, NY: Guilford Press.

May, S. M. (2007). *How to argue so your spouse will listen*. Nashville, TN: Thomas Nelson.

Migerode, L., & Hooghe, A. (2012). "I love you." How to understand love in couple therapy? Exploring love in context. *Journal of Family Therapy*, *34*(4), 371–386. doi:10.1111/j.1467-6427.2011.00557.x

Nelson, T. S. (2010). Explanation and description: An integrative, solution-focused case of couple therapy. In A. S. Gurman (Ed.), *Clinical casebook of couple therapy* (pp. 44–66). New York, NY: Guilford Press.

Paley, B., Cox, M. J., Burchinal, M. R., & Payne, C. C. (1999). Attachment and marital functioning: Comparison of spouses with continuous-secure, earned-secure, dismissing, and preoccupied attachment stances. *Journal of Family Psychology*, *13*(4), 580–597.

Robbins, C. (2005). ADHD couple and family relationships: Enhancing communication and understanding through Imago relationship therapy. *Journal of Clinical Psychology*, *61*(5), 565–577. doi:10.1002/jclp.20120

Sherman, R. (2000). The intimacy genogram. In R. Watts (Ed.), *Techniques in marriage and family counseling, Vol. 1* (pp. 81–84). Alexandria, VA: American Counseling Association.

Townsend, J. (2007). *Loving people*. Nashville, TN: Thomas Nelson.

Warren, N. C. (2000). *Catching the rhythm of love: Experience your way to a spectacular marriage*. Nashville, TN: Thomas Nelson.

Wickstrom, A. C. (2010). The development of an advanced filial therapy model. *International Journal of Play Therapy*, *19*(4), 187–197. doi:10.1037/a0020246

Zadra, D., & Yamada, K. (2010). *2: How will you create something beautiful together?* Seattle, WA: Compendium.

CHAPTER

13

Sexuality and Gender in Couples Counseling

Janet Froeschle Hicks

Texas Tech University

Brandé Flamez

Walden University

Gender, sexuality, and intimacy are interrelated and holistic elements within a relationship. Varying hormonal and medical issues, conflicting sexual values and preferences, past sexual experiences, sexual addictions, and sexual orientation are factors that must be considered with regard to a couple's sexual and intimate well-being. Counselors must have adequate training and supervision if they are to help couples maximize intimacy and overcome sexual issues that are often symptoms of a troubled relationship (Goldenberg & Goldenberg, 1991). This chapter offers information on the historical, biological, social, and psychological issues that differentiate sexuality among genders in diverse relationships. Further, sexual behaviors and dysfunction will be discussed, along with techniques and best practices to enhance couple intimacy.

SIDEBAR 13.1 SEXUALITY, CULTURE, AND VALUES

Sexuality is an important aspect within relationships and encompasses a person's attitudes, feelings, perceptions, and values (McCarthy & McCarthy, 2003). Think about your cultural background and things you were taught about sexuality as a child. How do your attitudes, feelings, perceptions, and values affect your own sexuality and biases? What goals might you have for yourself so you become more accepting of diverse couples, genders, styles of sexuality, and sexual behaviors? What are some specific cultural or religious values that might influence a person's or a couple's sexuality in a positive or negative way?

DEFINITIONS OF GENDER AND SEX

In order to make sense of gender and sexuality, a distinction must be made between several terms. *Genetic sex* relates to biology and is determined by chromosomes, whereas *gender* refers to social, psychological, and cultural differences that influence society's perceptions of the individual as being either male or female (Devine & Wolf-Devine, 2003; LeVay & Valente, 2006). While many in society automatically assume a person is either male or female, gender is not so easily defined. For example, the intersexual person cannot be defined dichotomously. *Intersex* refers to a person whose biological sex is unclear or falls on a continuum between male and female (LeVay & Valente, 2006). *Gender identity* goes beyond society's expectations of male/female perceptions to that of the individual defining oneself. For example, a transsexual person's internal perceptions of gender are incongruent with societal gender expectations or *gender roles* (Devine & Wolf-Devine, 2003). Alfred Kinsey (1948; 1953; Kinsey Institute, 2013) believed people did not fall into discrete homosexual or heterosexual categories and created a Heterosexual-Homosexual Rating Scale illustrating this continuum. Kinsey's research found that thoughts and feelings toward the opposite sex could intensify or diminish over time (Kinsey Institute, 2013). While counselors must consider these and other gender issues that affect sexuality and intimacy among diverse couples, helping professionals largely ignored the issue until the late 1980s.

History of Gender and Sexuality

The expression of human sexuality went from a tolerant and relaxed atmosphere prior to the 17th century to a restrained and prudish behavior not to be discussed in public or in front of children during the 19th century. It was during this time the Christian influence infiltrated sexuality, resulting in the censorship of literature to exclude sexual content, phrases, and wording. By the 18th century, sexuality became a political issue used to control lineage, labor markets, and the birth rate. Homosexuality and marriage without parental consent were condemned (Foucault & Hurley, 1990). By the 19th century, women began to participate in birth control via abstinence in order to protect their health and participate in social interests (Glover, 2013). Thus, repression and restraint were part of the sexual culture. Freud believed this sexual repression resulted in hysteria among women (a nervous condition in women believed to cause psychological problems, hallucinations, and/or partial paralysis) (About.com, 2013). It wasn't until Kinsey's research in the early 1900s that the curtain was drawn back and society had to view concepts of normal sexuality.

Alfred Kinsey (1948, 1953) shocked society when he published the results of his studies on sexual behaviors. Kinsey's research intended to collect and disseminate knowledge on both male and female sexual behaviors leading to orgasm. This data, gathered from 1938 to 1963, revealed that approximately half of males and one third of females had participated in coitus by age 19; 11% of males were participating in married anal sex; 48.9% of married men had performed oral sex (cunnilingus); and 30% had received oral stimulation (fellatio). Ninety-two percent of males and 62% of females reported having masturbated. Data indicated that about half of men and 26% of women had participated in extramarital sex at some point in their lives, with 69% of White men revealing they had participated in sexual activities with a prostitute. The most shocking statistic for many, however, was that up to 37% of males and 13% of females reported a same-sex experience in their lifetime. Further, up to 46% of males and 14% of females had engaged in both heterosexual and homosexual activities (Kinsey, 1948, 1953; Kinsey Institute, 2013; LeVay & Valente, 2006).

Following Kinsey's studies and into the early 1970s, public debate emerged regarding the constitution of normal sexual behavior. Empirical data began to dispute the notion that homosexuality was dysfunctional behavior, and a strong political gay/lesbian alliance demanded reform. As a result, the *Diagnostic and Statistical Manual II (DSM-II)* removed homosexuality as a mental disorder and replaced it with the diagnosis, "ego-dystonic homosexuality" in the *DSM-III*. Experts in the field criticized this new diagnosis, and in 1986, homosexuality was removed as a disorder from the *DSM-IV* (American Journal of Psychiatry, 1981; DePaul, Walsh, & Dam, 2009; Herek, 2012). As a result, new perceptions and insight into sexuality and gender emerged.

Despite new insight and less condemnation of homosexuality, the issue of gender as part of sexuality continued to play a minor role in the helping professions. Gender differences were assumed to be minimal and not worthy of consideration. It wasn't until 1988 that the American Association of Marriage and Family Therapists took a first step in understanding gender differences and required accredited programs to include gender issues as part of the university curriculum (Niolon, 2011). Since the late 1980s, more attention has been given to gender issues, sexuality, and diversity, which has led to more discoveries "than [have] been known since the beginning of time" (Hedges, 2011, p. xiv). This knowledge continues to emerge and guides many theoretical interventions and techniques in couples counseling.

Theoretical Background

Several theories attempt to describe the unique sexual behaviors displayed by differing genders. Following are some of the major theories outlined in the literature.

Evolutionary Theory

Evolution is thought to play a role in current male and female mating rituals and mate selection. Raising genetically superior offspring in as great a population as possible was considered the unconscious primary sexual motivation for both genders. This being the case, males were driven to mate with as many fertile females as possible, increasing the chance that their genes would carry on to successive generations. For this reason, evolutionary theorists believe evolution played a hand in the influence of male promiscuity and the heterosexual male's desire to mate with numerous females (Buss & Schmidt, 1993; Petersen & Hyde, 2010).

Because females could only be impregnated and give birth to a limited number of children, they had to be more selective than males when choosing a mate.

Females preferred to mate with the most genetically advantageous males. This meant choosing males who offered the greatest probability of fathering healthy children. Further, because raising and providing for children was a large expense, females were driven to find males who would stay with them for a lengthy time or until children were raised. This meant females often mated with more than one male: one for genetics and another to help nurture children. This theory infers a connection between evolutionary behavior and current female preference for partners with both financial resources and genetic superiority (Buss & Schmidt, 1993; Petersen & Hyde, 2010).

Social Learning Theory

Bandura (1986) proposed that individuals learn new behaviors by watching and analyzing others and imitating their actions. Self-efficacy, or the belief in one's ability to perform a behavior, is believed to result in better performance. This theory can be illustrated by examining the media's influence on sexual behavior. For example, couples watch sexual behaviors, listen to sexual discussions via the media, and imitate this sexual functioning. Social learning theory would imply that couples learn intimate sexual behaviors and values by watching television, reading articles in magazines, and viewing information obtained over the Internet. Because many images and information seen via the media are inaccurate, counselors must counter inaccuracies with information.

Gender Similarity Theory

Gender similarity theory posits that males and females are more similar than different. For example, Petersen and Hyde (2010) state that males and females indicate few differences with regard to cognitive ability, mental health, self-esteem, sexual satisfaction, and sexual behaviors. These researchers contend that although sexual differences are evident with regard to masturbation and attitudes toward casual sex (with males exhibiting a greater occurrence of masturbation and more lenient attitudes toward casual sex than females), differences between genders are so minor they do not present a significant enough difference to require a specific focus.

Social Structural Theory

Social structural theory describes a link between the labor force and its inherent devaluing of women. Because women have less societal power and earn less in the workforce, they must submit to those who have power (males). This power differentiation leads women to subject themselves to becoming sexual objects and to select inferior mates who have power. For this reason, social structural theorists suggest that counselors become aware of power within relationships and encourage mutual partner respect.

Despite numerous theories attempting to understand sexuality, power structures, and gender differences within relationships, much remains unanswered. Are gender differences based solely on biological issues? How do culture and society factor into the process? The next sections discuss these issues and offer knowledge for counselors striving to understand and empathize with each partner in the relationship.

SIDEBAR 13.2 NATURE OR NURTURE

During the 1970s, feminist theorists contended that existing gender differences were based solely on learning and culture. Other researchers contended that biological differences predetermined gender issues such as aggression among boys and submissiveness among girls (LeVay & Valente, 2006). These issues continue to be debated today and are relevant when discussing sexuality. If this premise is applied to infidelity, it can be suggested that either culture and learning or hormones and biological tendencies determine choices that are made. What is your position? Do you think infidelity is a consequence of nature or nurture? Which theories in this chapter agree or disagree with your position?

The Biology of Sex in Relationships

Understanding the physical processes of sexuality aids clients in understanding their own bodies and helps with diagnosis and treatment of sexual disorders (Sanders, 2008). For this reason, William H. Masters and Virginia Johnson studied the sexual response cycles of 382 women and 312 men in an attempt to discover treatment options. Masters and Johnson's research revealed four biological stages that occur for both genders during the sexual experience (Sanders, 2008). The first phase of the human sexual response cycle, excitement, occurs during arousal. Lubrication and swelling of the female genitals and erection of the male genitals prepare the body for sexual activity. The next phase, plateau, is a state of enhanced arousal where the body becomes flushed, heart rate and blood pressure increase, and muscles tense. The third phase, orgasm, describes muscle contractions and a release of sperm by the male. The final phase, resolution, is indicated by a relaxing of muscles, heart rate and blood pressure returning to normal, and a reduction in body swelling (LeVay & Valente, 2006; Pfaff, 2011; Sanders, 2008). Despite this common sexual experience, biological gender differences also exist and influence sexual behavior.

Differing genetic codes and hormonal levels are responsible for the variance between male and female sexual desire and behaviors (Pfaff, 2011). When presented with stimuli (e.g., a visually appealing female), males with adequate levels of testosterone release the hormone, dopamine, in the preoptic area of the brain and become quickly aroused and sexually motivated (Pfaff, 2011). Testosterone, the primary male hormone, adds to the process by intensifying sexual desire and perpetuating more frequent and varied sexual fantasies than does the primary female hormone, estrogen (Berkowitz & Yager-Berkowitz, 2009; Pfaff, 2011). Consequently, it comes as no surprise that most males have heightened libido when compared to females and may enter counseling hoping to increase sexual frequency. Hormonal deficiencies, biological impairments, and psychological issues, however, may impede the process, resulting in low libido (Berkowitz & Yager-Berkowitz, 2009). Because of this, it is important not to stereotype males as being easily aroused or hypersexual.

Women experience hormonal issues much differently than men. The hypothalamus is responsible for determining the timing of puberty. Once this timing has been established, the primary female hormone produced in the ovaries, estrogen, signals the brain that ovulation must occur. A monthly cycle ensues, whereby hormones control the release of an egg that is either fertilized, in which case pregnancy occurs, or disposed of through the menstrual cycle. Studies infer that females show greater sex drive and promiscuous behaviors when estrogen levels are highest or during ovulation (Pfaff, 2011).

Females also experience biological differences due to pregnancy and menopause. While sexual activity is safe in a normal pregnancy, female hormonal levels and the bodily changes that occur during pregnancy may affect the sex drive. In addition, menopause causes a quick decrease in hormonal levels and can lead to low libido and sexual difficulties (Taverner, 2008). Reproduction itself can pose sexual difficulties for heterosexual couples in that both genders may fear pregnancy and resist intimacy in order to avoid the condition. The social expectations of parenthood can have devastating effects on a relationship and sexuality (LeVay & Valente, 2006).

Society's Role in Sexuality

Society plays an important role in influencing sexual differences between men and women. Gender and the unique psychological and sexual issues inherent within each individual are not just biologically based, but may be learned via society and culture. For example, values learned through religion, socialization, trauma, and past sexual experiences all affect sexuality and, therefore, the relationship.

Every culture throughout history has demonstrated some form of cultural and social gender difference (Devine & Wolf-Devine, 2003). For example, males and females have been taught to dress differently, adorn their bodies uniquely, and/or participate in gender-based rituals. In Western societies, male and female children are often taught to play with gender-specific toys by the age of 9 months, or prior to the emergence of gender-related play (Pomerleau, Bolduc, Malcuit, & Cossette, 1990). Eisenberg, Wolchik, Hernandez, and Pasternak (1985) and Katz and Boswell (1986) found that children preferred gender-specific toys over other toys if the aforementioned toys were given to them by parents. It would seem, therefore, that differences in behaviors among genders are not only biologically but also socially and culturally influenced. According to Chodorow (2002), "gender is an individual creation, and there are thus many masculinities and femininities. Each person's gender identity is a fusion of personal and cultural meaning. Gender cannot be seen apart from culture" (p. 237).

Other forms of gender socialization occur in Western society that affect the sexuality, intimacy, and overall relationships of couples. Men have been socialized to hide emotion and weakness and display aggression in order to promote masculinity (Shallcross, 2010). Most men feel pressure to provide for their partner, harbor a need for respect (Feldhahn, 2013), and are more likely to rate their relationships as less satisfactory when dissatisfied with the sexual relationship (Society for Scientific Study of Sexuality, 2007).

Women have been oppressed and treated by society as inferior in many ways. Galen, a second-century Greek physician, stated that women's bodies were inferior to those of men because it was believed that simply having a womb left one vulnerable to hysteria. Even during the 19th century, specialists (including Freud) thought women's health problems came from sexual deprivation and hysteria. Many of these oppressive beliefs, while eliminated from prominent studies in the 20th century, can be seen in the socialization of women today (LeVay & Valente, 2006).

Petersen and Hyde (2010) suggest that men and women are more similar than different with regard to sexuality. These researchers contend that an emphasis on gender differences in sexuality promotes an unhealthy double standard. Men are expected to have high libido and perform on cue, and women experience a double standard inferring female sexuality as degrading. As a result, Petersen and Hyde contend that an emphasis on gender similarities promotes gender equality and acceptance of a greater range of sexual activities. The result is better sexual intimacy among these egalitarian couples.

SIDEBAR 13.3 EGALITARIANISM CASE STUDY

Effective counselors must search within themselves and examine personal gender-role attitudes and stereotypes that help them respond in an egalitarian manner to clients. With this in mind, how would you respond to clients in the following case?

Pedro enters the counseling room and states he doesn't want to be in counseling and is only present for Maria. Maria is distressed because Pedro constantly wants sex and she is exhausted from working all day and taking care of the children. Needless to say, Maria has very little sexual desire. The problem is exacerbated in that Pedro shows little emotion and refuses to discuss Maria's concerns.

How have cultural or societal expectations influenced the sexual difficulties faced by this couple? How might a counselor coming from a true egalitarian stance respond to these issues? Do you have gender-based biases related to this couple's issues? How might you overcome your own biases?

It is important to consider both biological and societal influences when assessing sexual difficulties. Hedges (2011) suggests overcoming gender socialization issues that affect sexuality by (a) helping clients construct broader definitions of "interpersonal narratives," (b) having clients participate in unique erotic experiences (regardless of gender), and (c) assisting clients as they develop new meanings of experiences and sexuality. Counselors who suggest that couples participate in these novel sexual experiences must broaden their sexual definitions and, therefore, have knowledge of and be open minded to different sexual behaviors. The following sections briefly discuss sexual behaviors, intimacy, sexual dysfunction, sexual addiction, affairs, and sexual trauma.

Current Sexual Behaviors

Since the mid-1900s, the public has gradually become more accepting of a larger range of sexual behaviors. Wells and Twenge (2005) conducted a meta-analysis of articles comparing sexual attitudes and behaviors between 1943 and 1999. The 56-year analysis suggested greater numbers of adults were sexually active, participating in oral sex, placing greater acceptance on sex outside of marriage, and experiencing a greater reduction in feelings of guilt associated with sexual activity throughout time. Chandra, Mosher, Copen, and Sionean (2011) compared the sexual practices of adults between the ages of 15 and 44 during the years 2002 and 2006 to 2008. They found that up to 98% of adults between ages 25 and 44 had participated in vaginal intercourse; 90% had participated in oral sex; and between 36% of females and 44% of males had participated in anal sex with a same-sex partner. Reece et al. (2010) surveyed 5,865 adults and adolescents aged 14 to 94 and found that although vaginal sex continued to be the most prevalent sex act, individuals more commonly participated in multiple sexual acts such as oral sex, anal sex, and masturbation. Although the aforementioned studies infer that society has become more accepting of once-condemned sexual behaviors (i.e., oral, anal, and homosexual sex), these liberal attitudes, along with media misrepresentations, make many couples wonder, "Is something wrong if I feel less passion for my partner than I did at the beginning of the relationship? Is our sexuality normal?" The next sections answer these questions through discussions on sexual behavior, intimacy, and sexual dysfunction.

Intimacy

Emotional intimacy plays an important role in sexual and marital satisfaction (Society for Scientific Study of Sexuality, 2007). At the same time, few couples understand what true intimacy is within a relationship. Many remember the lustful passion experienced at the beginning of the relationship and watch media programs inferring that all couples experience deep passion and lust within relationships. It is no wonder, then, that many couples begin to feel their relationship is inadequate and begin to chase the hot passion they once experienced. The truth is this type of lustful passion naturally disappears in a relationship, and trying to recapture it is ineffective (McCarthy & McCarthy, 2003). This may leave you wondering, "If this is the case, then how does one enhance sexuality and what is true intimacy? How does one build this intimacy?"

The Society for the Scientific Study of Sexuality (2007) lists three factors shown to enhance intimacy: communication, egalitarianism, and affection.

Communication is defined as listening and sharing ideas directly and has been found to lower sexual dissatisfaction for couples facing life stressors (i.e., raising children, managing health issues, and aging). Good communication offers each partner the opportunity to express sexual desires and experience personal passions.

The second factor shown to enhance intimacy, egalitarianism, is defined within a relationship as an equitable division of household tasks and power sharing. Niolon (2011) stresses the importance of advocating for the partner who holds no power in the relationship and asks couples to state times when they experience gender-biased thoughts. The Society for the Scientific Study of Sexuality (2007) studied 57 couples who had been married for over 7 years. Findings concluded that the higher the egalitarianism in the relationship, the higher the sexual passion for both partners. At the same time, these researchers suggest adding a degree of distance and autonomy in relationships to increase the element of mystery and desire.

The third factor in creating intimacy, affection, consists of hugging, cuddling, sharing humor, as well as other physical and nonphysical expressions of emotional closeness. Interestingly, expressions of physical affection and egalitarianism have been found to increase intimate communication (Society for Scientific Study of Sexuality (2007). McCarthy and McCarthy (2003) state that partners learn to "think, talk, act, and feel like an intimate team" (p. 10).

Mature relationships become more cohesive by establishing acceptable forms and levels of intimacy. Because all individuals and couples are different, each must communicate needs and arrive at mutually agreed upon styles of intimacy. For example, some prefer a strong friendship, whereas others prefer strong individuation combined with times of closeness. Each person and couple must establish intimacy that meets the emotional needs of each partner (McCarthy & McCarthy, 2003).

Finally, couples must accept that not all sexual experiences are fulfilling and not all intimacy is sexual. Nonsexual intimacy can be the gateway leading to pleasant physical sexual experiences; this cannot be underestimated. McCarthy and McCarthy (2003) state, "The keys to revitalizing marital sexuality are building bridges to desire, increasing intimacy, enjoying non-demand pleasuring, and creating erotic scenarios" (p. 10). Whether couples are overcoming biological dysfunction or battling social and emotional issues that impair sexual desire, couples can experience healthy intimacy. The following section discusses sexual dysfunctions, factors that impair desire, and social poisons that can threaten intimacy and sexuality in relationships.

Sexual Dysfunction

Before the 1970s, little was known about sexual dysfunction (McCarthy & McCarthy, 2003). Since this time, much has been learned about sexuality, its importance in relationships, and sexual functioning. Despite this, sexual dysfunction is still a problem and in fact remains much the same as it did in the 1950s (McCarthy & McCarthy, 2003).

McCarthy and McCarthy (2003) and Berkowitz and Yager-Berkowitz (2009) state that lack of desire and boredom are the primary causes of sexual abstinence.

McCarthy and McCarthy (2003) categorize sexual functioning within relationships using the following terms: nonconsummated, no-sex, low-sex, inhibited sexual desire relationships, and healthy sexual functioning. Nonconsummated relationships are those in which sexual activity has never occurred. No-sex partnerships describe couples who have sex less than 10 times per year, whereas low-sex relationships are the category suggested for those who have sex less than 25 times annually (Berkowitz & Yager-Berkowitz, 2009). Inhibited desire relationships are those in which one partner feels rejected by the other due to low sexual desire. This often leads to a vicious cycle of blaming, guilt, and even less sexual desire among the abstinent partner.

Why would someone choose not to have sex? Berkowitz and Yager-Berkowitz (2009) surveyed 4,000 individuals to try to explain low- or no-sex behaviors. Reasons men gave for abstinence, as well as reasons inferred by women in these sexless relationships, ranged from issues such as boredom, partner's appearance, anger, depression, erectile dysfunction, inhibited ejaculation, exhaustion, a preference for masturbation using pornography, affairs, and sexual orientation confusion. *The Diagnostic and Statistical Manual of Mental Disorders, Fifth Edition* (*DSM-5*; American Psychiatric Association, 2013) delineates diagnoses considered dysfunctional and includes: delayed ejaculation, erectile disorder, female orgasmic disorder, female sexual interest/arousal disorder, genito-pelvic pain/penetration disorder, male hypoactive sexual desire disorder, premature (early) ejaculation, substance/medication induced sexual dysfunction, other specified sexual dysfunction, and unspecified sexual dysfunction (American Psychiatric Association, 2013). For specific diagnostic criteria on each disorder, refer to the *DSM-5*.

Sexual Dysfunction Treatment Considerations

Although the abundance of disorders makes it impossible to delve into the specific treatments for each disorder previously listed, a few common counseling practices are helpful to many experiencing sexual dysfunction. For example, counselors can help couples stay connected by encouraging date nights, fun activities (both erotic and nonerotic), encouraging and teaching good communication strategies, fostering feelings of intimacy through touch, and broadening couples' definitions of sex. Couples who are unable to have sexual intercourse can find new ways to experience sexual activity through oral sex, mutual masturbation, and intimate touching. These strategies can bring intimacy and excitement into the relationship (Berkowitz & Yager-Berkowitz, 2009). Probably the most important thing counselors can do for those diagnosed with a sexual dysfunction is to teach active listening skills that lead to better communication. These communication skills can be used to stop partners from blaming one another for sexual dysfunction and become true loving partners who are a team working on the issue together. Following is a discussion of several sexual behaviors for which the team concept is especially important because individuals may be isolating themselves from their partners by maintaining painful and detrimental secrets. These issues include addictions, affairs, and past sexual trauma.

Internet Addiction

Technology is criticized for introducing sexual confusion, fear, and sexual problems into a new generation of couples (Hedges, 2011). The Internet and smartphones allow never-before-seen sexual practices such as cybersex, sexting, cam sex, instant access to pornography, as well as the ability to meet numerous sexual partners in chat rooms or various other sites. Movies, television programs, and Internet sites depict couples constantly desiring one another and participating in spontaneous sexual activity. These myths and unrealistic images put pressure on couples to perform and may make partners judge one another as sexually inferior.

Another problem connected with technology is decreased sexual desire within the intimate relationship. Compulsive masturbation and perfect images via the Internet create a scenario with which one's partner cannot compete. Further, intimacy and nondemand pleasuring become absent from sexuality. This constant stimulation and focus on performance and quantity in lieu of intimacy and quality increase sexual dysfunction among men as they age (McCarthy & McCarthy, 2003) and may create an addiction from which withdrawal is difficult.

Why would a person who loves their partner prefer pornography over intimate sexual experiences? Hedges (2011) states that some use pornography and Internet sex to compensate for past issues, low self-esteem, and insecurities. "When self-other empathic recognition fails, sexual stimulation often serves to restore, at least momentarily, a sense of safety and well-being" (Hedges, 2011, p. 120). When this happens, sexual activity can become an all-consuming passion, and many refer to it as an addiction.

Sexual Addiction

Approximately 6% of the population exhibits symptoms of a sexual addiction, with men outnumbering women three to one (Carnes, 2009). Carnes (1994) describes a sexual addict as someone who participates regularly in harmful, compulsive, and uncontrollable maladaptive sexual activities. Not all experts condone the use of the word *addict* when describing the dysfunction because the problem goes beyond simply craving sexual activity and is often a coping mechanism for issues such as anxiety, stress, depression, and shame (Goodman, 2001; Hagedorn & Juhnke, 2005; McMillen, 2013). This is further illustrated by the fact that comorbidity has been found to occur between sexual addiction and disorders such as substance abuse, obsessive-compulsion, paranoia, mania, anxiety, and depression (Carnes, 1994; Mayo Clinic, 2011).

According to the Mayo Clinic (2011), causes of sexual addiction are chemical imbalances in the brain; unbalanced hormone levels; medical conditions affecting the brain such as multiple sclerosis, dementia, Huntington's disease, and epilepsy; and changes in the brain's neural circuits. Many who suffer from sexual addictions are victims of sexual abuse, exhibit drug or alcohol abuse, or suffer from another psychological condition (Mayo Clinic, 2011). Regardless of the cause, many need help overcoming dangerous sexual urges that can result in disease, infidelity, and relationship problems (McMillen, 2013).

SIDEBAR 13.4 SEXUAL ADDICTION AND PORNOGRAPHY

Carnes (2009) believes access increases addiction problems. For example, he states the "more casinos the more gambling addictions" and believes Internet access increases opportunity for greater numbers of people to become sexually addicted (p. 1). Do you agree with Carnes that access to pornography in high volume via the Internet creates more addicts and, therefore, sexual difficulties within relationships? Should this problem be called an "addiction" or is it simply a coping mechanism for other stressors?

Sexual Addiction Treatment Considerations

Hagedorn and Juhnke (2005) suggest several steps to take when working with those who present with sexual addictions. First, counselors should perform a thorough assessment and evaluation of the client and couple. Assessments include both interviews and formal assessments. Involving the partner in the assessment and counseling sessions can result in better outcomes.

Next, counselors should plan the treatment. This entails giving feedback about results of the prior assessment and formulating goals that address holistic facets of the addiction, including: relationships, health issues, employment, and legal consequences (Carnes, 1994). Goals may include education about the addiction, self-help groups, addressing denial, and specific assignments.

The next steps in the process include giving appropriate referrals and advocating for the client. Maladaptive sexual behavior is often accompanied by legal and health problems that require professional referrals. Further, these clients need extensive individual counseling as well as couples counseling. Couples counselors can offer referrals to personal counselors who work as part of a treatment team. Advocacy may also be included because community services are limited and managed care can pose an obstacle.

Finally, counseling techniques found effective for use with sexual addicts include psychoeducational techniques, cognitive-behavioral therapies, psychodynamic approaches, support groups, and psychopharmacology (Hagedorn & Juhnke, 2005). Couples counselors build on individual therapy by using similar techniques, focus on building empathy and trust within the relationship, and encourage communication and listening skills. Mostly, counselors need to become aware of their own biases with regard to sexual activity and sexual addictions so they do not impose values on their clients. Society lacks understanding or empathy for sexual addicts and, therefore, counselors must remain open to advocacy while continuing to motivate clients to change maladaptive behaviors (Carnes, 1994).

Emotional and Sexual Affairs

According to statistics, sexual addicts are not the only ones participating in emotional and physical sexual affairs. Whitbourne (2012) states that up to 20%

of adults are unfaithful in their relationships. Finding partners willing to participate in emotional affairs, cybersex, or even physical affairs has become easier as technology has spanned the globe. The following section discusses gender issues and relationship problems that arise as a result of emotional and sexual affairs.

Many couples form open marriages in which each partner agrees to see other sexual interests outside the relationship. Many of these couples are happy in this type of relationship, and this section does not intend to impose values on these couples. According the American Counseling Association (2005) Code of Ethics, counselors "avoid imposing values that are inconsistent with counseling goals. Counselors respect the diversity of clients" (A.4.b., pp. 4–5). As a result, the following discussion is limited to those couples seeking help due to infidelity and for whom infidelity represents a breach in the relationship.

Infidelity comes in many forms. For some, infidelity means only a physical relationship. For others, emotional connections and shared verbal connections and exchanges are viewed as equally harmful. Counselors must view each couple uniquely and work to improve the relationship without imposing personal values or boundaries on the couple. In other words, behaviors that cause harm within the relationship must be managed whether the affair is physical or emotional.

Infidelity affects the entire family system (Scharff, 1998). The betrayed partner feels hurt, deceived, insecure, anxious, agitated, angry, isolated, and abandoned. Many feelings emanate, including an initial loss of identity that occurs with the realization that the partnership was not the trusting relationship once believed. As the betrayed partner attempts to reconcile with this loss of identity, several other personal losses may also emerge, such as lack of self-respect; loss of a sense of specialness; recognition that control has been lost as has as a sense of order and justice in the world; loss of a sense of purpose; loss of relationships with your partner's family and friends; and a questioning of religious principles (Spring, 2006).

The unfaithful partner may feel conflicted, anxious, angry, guilty about hurting others, isolated, hopeless, paralyzed, and disgusted with self. The initial revelation about the affair may bring relief that the secret is in the open, followed by impatience at the time it takes to rebuild trust and connection. This person may also grieve the loss of the lover and miss the excitement and special feelings experienced during the affair. Once the affair is revealed, isolation may set in as children, family members, and friends reject and judge the unfaithful partner. Hopelessness, indecision, and self-disgust set in, and the person wonders if the relationship can be saved (Spring, 2006).

SIDEBAR 13.5 SEXUAL BOUNDARIES

On January 26, 1998, President Bill Clinton (when questioned about a young intern named Monica Lewinsky) stated, "I did not have sex with that woman!" It was later revealed that President Clinton received oral sex from Ms. Lewinsky. Many emphatically stated this was indeed not sex (Miller, 2013).

Many today log onto chat rooms and create friendships. Some even share intimate, romantic words with these friends online. Webcams (special Internet cameras) may be used so these friends can be viewed from afar while talking aloud over a speaker. Some go a step farther and participate in mutual masturbation via webcam.

Which of these acts would you consider sex or cheating if done by your significant other? What are your sexual boundaries within a relationship? Is it fair to judge clients by your sexual values and boundaries?

Infidelity Treatment Considerations

If the partnership is to be saved, counselors must help clients manage indicators that lead to future infidelity. First, clients must explore underlying attitudes about affairs. For example, those who justify infidelity as long as the partner is ignorant of the occurrence may need to reexamine these values and discuss specific issues with their partner. Second, couples may need to discuss the history of deception. For example, numerous infidelities over time may need to be discussed at length, and the consequences of secrets and deceit made clear to both parties. Third, communication between partners must be developed so both feel nonthreatened and open in their ability to discuss difficult issues and values. Fourth, both partners must be taught to actively listen and empathize with the other. It may also be important to discuss triggering events (e.g., deaths, illness, financial problems or shifts, personal failures, transitions) so new ways to manage vulnerabilities can be learned (Scharff, 1998; Spring, 2006).

Several techniques may assist partners with the triggering events listed. For example, partners may explore how early life experiences contributed to the problems undermining the current relationship. Feelings of safety, security, and the ability to express intimacy may be products from childhood (Scharff, 1998). Spring (2006) suggests that couples discuss issues of infidelity that influenced them during their childhood and how those affect them today. Couples then discuss how each partner blames the other for past hurts.

If the relationship is to survive, trust must be rebuilt. This means the affair must be discussed, secrets disclosed, and both parties' behaviors changed (Scharff, 1998). Both partners must determine what information they wish to know and how to disclose. Counselors help clients ask about details that will aid the relationship and avoid unnecessary information that is detrimental. A rule of thumb is for both partners and the counselor to focus on the relationship and not the third party (Spring, 2006). Teaching reflective listening, empathy, and paraphrasing can go a long way toward instilling better communication patterns.

Affairs are not the only sexual issue in which outside and past events cause problems. Following is a discussion on past sexual trauma and interventions to help those dealing with the shame and stress of the phenomenon.

Sexual Trauma

Past sexual trauma affects both males and females in numerous ways, such as marital dissatisfaction (Liang, Williams, & Siegel, 2006), sexual dissatisfaction and sexual disorders (Colangelo & Keefe-Cooperman, 2012), and low sexual arousal (Hodges & Myers, 2010). This is especially concerning because up to 10% of adult men and 20% of adult women have experienced some form of sexual abuse (National Center for Victims of Crime, 2012).

Sexual Trauma Treatment Considerations

Partners who have experienced past sexual trauma should be referred for personal counseling in addition to couples counseling. While outcomes research over the past two decades fails to reveal an empirically supported treatment for child sexual abuse (Colangelo & Keefe-Cooperman, 2012; Hodges & Myers, 2010), several personal counseling methods are suggested in the literature. These therapies include: affect management groups, feminist theory based groups, eye movement desensitization and reprocessing, interpersonal and transaction processing groups, symbolic confrontation groups, wellness models whereby clients retell traumatic experiences, and trauma-based counseling. It is suggested that the victimized client first receive individual counseling to deal with the abuse and then transfer learning to couples counseling.

Once in couples counseling, it is important to build trust in the relationship both sexually and emotionally. Trust can be built through communication, intimate touch, empathy from the significant other once past abuse is revealed, and erotic exercises that slowly create intimacy without pressure for sexual contact (Colangelo & Keefe-Cooperman, 2012; Hodges & Myers, 2010).

The previous section discussed strategies counselors can use when working with clients displaying sexual problems. Each couple is unique, and when using any strategy, each individual and couple must be treated as such. Because couples differ, the following discussion intends to offer suggestions for working with minority couples who have unique issues due to societal oppression.

COUPLE DIFFERENTIATION

Alfred Kinsey (1948) stunned society when his survey revealed that 37% of men had participated in at least one sexual act with another male resulting in orgasm. This challenged the notion that homosexuality was extremely rare and an aberration. In fact, over 3 million people live together in same-sex relationships in the United States, and same-sex relationships can be found in 99.3% of all countries worldwide (Taverner, 2008). This doesn't even take into account transsexual and transgendered individuals for whom prevalence is difficult to determine given few accurate studies revealing information on this diverse group (American Psychological Association, 2013).

In June 2013, the Supreme Court made two decisions that removed impediments faced by same-sex couples wishing to marry. The Supreme Court overturned California's Proposition 8 and invalidated the Defense of Marriage Act (DOMA) that was signed into law by President Bill Clinton in 1996. California's Proposition 8 was placed on a California ballot and intended to forbid same-sex marriage. The voters of California approved the proposition, but a federal judge overturned the ruling. This ruling was appealed to the Supreme Court, which stated that the plaintiffs did not have the authority to challenge the federal judge's ruling (Sherwood, 2013).

DOMA did not allow the federal government to recognize marriages between same-sex couples and, therefore, denied same-sex couples the right to file joint tax returns or collect veteran's benefits, survivorship benefits, and many other federal benefits taken for granted by those in male/female marriages. While this was a positive move for those desiring same-sex marriage and benefits, the ruling did not remove each state's right to determine whether to perform or recognize same-sex marriages (Sherwood, 2013). This left a nation divided on the issue of gay marriage with only 20 states and Washington, DC, issuing marriage licenses to same-sex couples (Wilson, 2014). While court decisions have led to more liberal attitudes about homosexuality and homosexual sexual activity among the general population, discrimination continues to exist in many states, and this affects homosexual couples' relationships (Petersen & Hyde, 2010).

Oppression and discrimination are still evident in that the dominant view in society continues to assume a dichotomous categorization of sexual and gender identity. In reality, sexual and gender identity are complex and must take into account a continuum of preferences and a vast culture of individual differences. One textbook chapter does not allow for an extensive discussion on every type of diverse relationship in existence. As a result, the following section focuses on special concerns and treatment issues that may help lesbian, gay, and bisexual couples.

Special Concerns and Treatment Considerations

Many counselors feel unprepared to work with lesbian, gay, and bisexual couples (Evans, 2003; Evans & Barker, 2010; Grove, 2009). Training is particularly important in the areas of advocacy, sexuality, vocabulary related to homosexuality, and the coming out process (Dermer, Smith, & Barto, 2010). Further, counselors need to be aware of issues such as prejudice and discrimination, self-hatred, judgment, oppression, career issues, and religious and spiritual confusions faced by these diverse couples.

The American Counseling Association has come out with competencies to help inform counselors about concerns of diverse groups (Singh & Burnes, 2010). It is imperative that counselors become familiar with these competencies so they are helpful to lesbian, gay, and bisexual clients. Table 13.1 lists definitions to increase personal knowledge of vocabulary in this area.

Knowledge of identity models that describe the coming out process may be helpful in educating couples counselors because the stage in which each person

Table 13.1 Sexual Minority Definitions

Term	Definition
Homophobia	Fear of homosexuality
Heterosexism	Prejudicial attitudes and actions directed toward sexual minorities
Sexual minority	A person whose sexual orientation is not strictly heterosexual or whose gender identity falls outside current culturally accepted standards
Internalized homophobia	Negatively judging oneself as a result of sexual orientation
Internalized homonegativity	Believing culturally accepted and negative stereotypes about homosexuality
Minority stress	Anxiety and distress experienced due to negative societal messages about sexual orientation
Coming out	The continuous revelation of sexual preference experienced by sexual minorities

Source: Adapted from Dermer et al. (2010); Evans and Barker (2010); Pelton-Sweet and Sherry (2008).

identifies affects personal obstacles and, therefore, romantic intimacy. For example, a client in a stage where sexual orientation is hidden may unintentionally make his or her partner feel unimportant and rejected. Couples counselors can help by educating both parties about identity development, validating the relationship, and advocating for homosexual couples. Table 13.2 gives a generic overview of stages that may occur in the coming out process. The stages are not intended to be linear; rather, they are listed to give some insight into the complexity of the coming out process. The table also lists some common actions taken by clients and counselor responses that may be helpful during the coming out process.

It is important not to judge clients who choose to keep their sexual orientation private. Not everyone has the social supports and self-esteem to experience the coming out process (Pelton-Sweet & Sherry, 2008). At the same time, communication between partners is crucial because this decision also impacts the relationship. For example, higher levels of internalized homophobia in gay men resulted in less sexual satisfaction, and lower levels of internalized homophobia were correlated with greater comfort in their sexual attraction toward the same gender (Rosser, Metz, Bockting, & Buroker, 1997). Further, higher levels of internalized homophobia resulted in decreased sexual satisfaction among sexual minority women (Szymanski, Kashubeck-West, & Meyer, 2008). Firestone (2014) states that women experience guilt when they deviate from the sexual roles portrayed by their mothers. As a result, lesbian women may experience sexual dissatisfaction as a result of guilt, societal, and familial pressures.

Several techniques are discussed in the literature as efficacious for sexual minorities and couples. First, couples can be taught relaxation techniques including couples massage and intimate touch. These techniques help overcome stress caused by internalized homonegativity while also becoming part of intimacy

Table 13.2 Minority Sexual Identity Development

Stage	Actions Taken by Client	Counseling Issues and Appropriate Responses
1. Uncertain feelings and views about sexual orientation	Exploring perceptions of others and examining suppressed feelings	Accurate information giving; continuous awareness of personal bias; build a relationship with client
2. Familiarity	Awareness and acknowledgment of sexual orientation	Empathy; unconditional positive regard; exploration of self-judgment and/or hatred; manage expectations of rejection and discrimination
3. Uncertainty	Acknowledging costs associated with revelations about sexuality	Empathy; unconditional positive regard; validation; role playing
4. Disclosing	Divulging sexual orientation with reliable confidants	Empathy; unconditional positive regard; help manage rejection and judgment of others; validation
5. Revealing sexual orientation to family, work associates, and peers	Divulging sexual orientation publicly and handling societal rejection and prejudice	Empathy; unconditional positive regard; assertiveness training; help manage rejection, discrimination, and oppression; advocacy; validation
6. Advocating	Assisting others as they deal with societal prejudice and oppression and becoming a change agent	Empathy; unconditional positive regard; assertiveness training; help manage rejection, discrimination, and oppression; advocacy; empower

Source: Cass (1979); Plummer (1995).

through touch. Art therapy is a second useful technique for releasing internalized emotions in couples counseling (Pelton-Sweet & Sherry, 2008). Finally, group therapy may be helpful for dealing with religious and sexual orientation value conflicts. Group therapy helps sexual minorities develop self-acceptance and self-identity that can be transferred to a couple's acceptance and a couple's identity (Yarhouse & Beckstead, 2011).

One last strategy deals with inherent career issues that go alongside discrimination and are intertwined with the gay or lesbian person's personal relationship and sexuality. For example, workplace homophobia, explaining the couple's relationship to work associates, partner introductions, and social events can cause turmoil in a relationship. O'Ryan and McFarland (2010) describe using a "teaming up" approach to help couples blend their relationship and career in a method that validates the partner and relationship while also managing discrimination, oppression, and victimization. How much to reveal must be discussed between partners and managed as a team.

Many of these techniques require specialized training to ensure clients receive optimal assistance. Following is information to guide counselors wishing to receive additional education or certifications in sexuality counseling.

COUNSELOR SEXUALITY TRAINING

Competent counselors need specific training in sexuality if they are to ethically work with couples presenting with sexual difficulties. The American Counseling Association (2005) Code of Ethics states,"counselors practice in specialty areas new to them only after receiving appropriate education, training, and supervised experience" (C.2.b., p. 9). Information follows detailing specific certifications counselors can receive in order to become specialized in the area of sexuality.

Specific Training for Counselors

The American Association of Sexuality Educators, Counselors, and Therapists (2004) offers certification for those seeking professional advancement in the areas of teaching, counseling, and therapy. Four different certifications are available, depending on credentials and professional goals: Certified Sexuality Educators, Certified Sexuality Counselors, Certified Sex Therapists, and Supervisors of Sex Therapy. Table 13.3 outlines professional sexuality certification types and requirements.

SUMMARY

Although sexual satisfaction and overall relationship satisfaction are correlated (Society for Scientific Study of Sexuality, 2007), diversity between couples with regard to sexuality makes defining "normal and satisfying sexuality" difficult. Satisfaction, therefore, is subjective and must be weighed differently in each partnership. Gender differences (including those related to biology as well as society and culture) all contribute to or detract from intimacy and healthy relationships. Special training allows counselors to help diverse couples facing challenges such as sexual dysfunction, sexual addictions, infidelity, and oppression. Counselors help clients listen effectively, empathize with one another, and grow in intimacy, sexuality, and relationship contentment.

Table 13.3 AASECT Certification Requirements

Certification Type	Certification Requirements	Educational Requirements	Training Requirements	Supervision/ Consultation Requirements
Certified Sexuality Educators	Membership in AASECT Follow AASECT Code of Ethics	Either bachelor's degree and 4 years experience as a sexuality educator; master's degree plus 3 years experience; or doctoral degree plus 2 years experience as a sexuality educator	90 clock hours of human sexuality education, 10 clock hours of attitudes training, and 60 clock hours sexuality education	25 consultation hours completed with an AASECT-certified sexuality educator
Certified Sexuality Counselors	Membership in AASECT Follow AASECT Code of Ethics	Bachelor's degree in a human service program plus 2 years professional counseling experience	90 clock hours of human sexuality education, 10 clock hours of attitudes training, and 60 clock hours sexuality counseling training	100 clock hours supervised sex counseling and 30 clock hours of supervision with an AASECT-certified sexuality counselor
Certified Sexuality Therapists	Membership in AASECT Follow AASECT Code of Ethics State licensure in psychology, medicine, social work, counseling, nursing, or marriage/family therapy	Master's degree that included psychotherapy component plus 2 years clinical experience, or doctoral degree that included psychotherapy component with 1 year clinical experience	90 clock hours of human sexuality education, 10 clock hours of attitudes training, and 60 clock hours sexuality therapy training	250 clock hours of supervised clinical treatment of clients with sexual concerns and 50 clock hours of supervision with an AASECT-certified supervisor
Certified Supervisor of Sex Therapy	State licensure in psychology, medicine, nursing, social work, marriage/ family therapy		Practiced as an AASECT-certified sex therapist for 3 years	Received 30 hours supervision of clinical sex therapy

Source: American Association of Sexuality Educators, Counselors, and Therapists (2004).

USEFUL WEBSITES

The following websites provide additional information relating to the chapter topics.

ALGBTIC Competencies
http://www.counseling.org/docs/ethics/algbtic-2012-07.pdf
American Association of Sexuality Educators, Counselors, and Therapists
http://www.aasect.org
The Kinsey Institute
http://www.indiana.edu/~kinsey/research/ak-data.html#Scope
The Mayo Clinic: Compulsive Sexual Behavior
http://www.mayoclinic.com/health/compulsive-sexual-behavior/DS00144
National Survey of Sexual Health and Behavior
http://www.nationalsexstudy.indiana.edu/graph.html
Society for the Scientific Study of Sexuality
http://www.sexscience.org/what_sexual_scientists_know
WebMD Sexual Conditions Health Center
http://www.webmd.com/sexual-conditions/features/is-sex-addiction-real

REFERENCES

About.com (2013). *Sigmund Freud-life, work and theories.* Retrieved from http://psychology.about.com/od/sigmundfreud/p/Sigmund_freud.htm

American Association of Sexuality Educators, Counselors, and Therapists. (2004). *Original certification requirements and applications.* Retrieved from http://www.aasect.org/cert_requirements.asp

American Counseling Association. (2005). *American Counseling Association code of ethics.* Retrieved from http://counseling.org/Resources/aca-code-of-ethics.pdf

American Journal of Psychiatry. (1981). The diagnostic status of DSM III and homosexuality in DSM III: A reformulation of the issues. *American Journal of Psychiatry*, *138*, 210–215.

American Psychiatric Association. (2013). *Diagnostic and statistical manual of mental disorders* (5th ed.). Arlington, VA: American Psychiatric Publishing.

American Psychological Association. (2013). *Answers to your questions about transgender people, gender identity, and gender expression.* Retrieved from http://www.apa.org/topics/sexuality/transgender.aspx?item=6#

Bandura, A. (1986). *Social foundations of thought and action: A social cognitive theory*. Englewood Cliffs, NJ: Prentice-Hall.

Berkowitz, B., & Yager-Berkowitz, S. (2009). *Why men stop having sex: Men, the phenomenon of sexless relationships, and what you can do about it.* New York, NY: HarperCollins.

Buss, D. M., & Schmidt, D. P. (1993). Sexual strategies theory: An evolutionary perspective on human mating. *Psychological Review*, *100*, 204–232.

Carnes, P. (1994). *Out of the shadows: Understanding sexual addiction* (2nd ed.). Center City, NM: Hazelden.

Carnes, P. (2009). Sex addiction. *University of Florida Department of Psychiatry Newsletter.* Retrieved from http://apps.psychiatry.ufl.edu/Newsletters/Archive/Carnes/Newsletter.html

Cass, V. (1979). Homosexual identity formation: A theoretical model. *Journal of Homosexuality, 4*, 219–235.

Chandra, A., Mosher, W. D., Copen, C., & Sionean, C. (2011). Sexual behavior, sexual attraction, and sexual identity in the United States: Data from the 2006–2008 National Survey of Family Growth. *National Health Statistics Report, Center for Disease Control* (Report No. 36). Retrieved from http://www.cdc.gov/nchs/data/nhsr/nhsr036.pdf

Chodorow, N. (2002). Gender as a personal and cultural construction. In M. Dimen & V. Goldner (Eds.), *Gender in psychoanalytic space: Between clinic and culture* (pp. 237–261). New York, NY: Other Press.

Colangelo, J. J., & Keefe-Cooperman, K. (2012). Undertanding the impact of childhood sexual abuse on women's sexuality. *Journal of Mental Health Counseling, 34*, 14–37.

DePaul, J., Walsh, M. E., & Dam, U. (2009). The role of school counselors in addressing sexual orientation in schools. *Professional School Counseling, 12*, 300–308.

Dermer, S. B., Smith, S.D., & Barto, K. K. (2010). Identifying and correctly labeling sexual prejudice, discrimination, and oppression. *Journal of Counseling & Development, 88*, 325–331.

Devine, P. E., & Wolf-Devine, C. (2003). *Sex and gender: A spectrum of views*. Belmont, CA: Wadsworth/Thompson.

Eisenberg, N., Wolchik, S. A., Hernandez, R., & Pasternak, J. (1985). Parental socialization of young children's play: A short term longitudinal study. *Child Development, 56*, 1506–1513.

Evans, M. (2003). Christian counselors views on working with gay and lesbian clients: Integrating religious beliefs with counseling ethics. *Counseling & Psychotherapy Research, 3*, 55–60.

Evans, M., & Barker, M. (2010). How do you see me? Coming out in counseling. *British Journal of Guidance & Counselling, 38*, 375–391.

Feldhahn, S. (2013). *For women only*. Colorado Springs, CO: Multnomah.

Firestone, R. (2014). *The 7 factors affecting orgasm in women*. Retrieved from http://www.psychologytoday.com/blog/the-human-experience/201404/7-factors-affecting-orgasm-in-women

Foucault, M., & Hurley, R. (1990). *The history of sexuality* (Vol. 1). New York, NY: Vintage Books.

Glover, L. (2013). Revolutionary conceptions: Women, fertility, and family limitation in America 1760–1820 (review). *Journal of the History of Sexuality, 22*, 173–175. doi:10.1353/sex.2013.0004

Goldenberg, I., & Goldenberg, H. (1991). *Family therapy: An overview*. Pacific Grove, CA: Brooks/Cole.

Goodman, A. (2001). What's in a name? Terminology for designating a syndrome of driven sexual behavior. *Sexual Addiction & Compulsivity, 8*, 191–213.

Grove, J. (2009). How competent are trainee and newly qualified counselors to work with lesbian, gay, and bisexual clients and what do they perceive as their most effective learning experiences? *Counseling & Psychotherapy Research, 9*, 78–85.

Hagedorn, W. B., & Juhnke, G. A. (2005). Treating the sexually addicted client: Establishing a need for increased counselor awareness. *Journal of Addictions & Offender Counseling, 25*, 66–86.

Hedges, L. E. (2011). *Sex in psychotherapy*. New York, NY: Taylor & Francis.

Herek, G. M. (2012). *Facts about homosexuality and mental health*. Retrieved from http://psychology.ucdavis.edu/rainbow/html/facts_mental_health.html

Hodges, E. A., & Myers, J. E. (2010). Counseling adult women survivors of childhood sexual abuse: Benefits of a wellness approach. *Journal of Mental Health Counseling, 32*, 139–154.

Katz, P. A., & Boswell, S. (1986). Flexibility and traditionality in children's gender roles. *Genetic, Social, and General Psychology Monographs, 112*, 103–147.

Kinsey, A. C. (1948). *Sexual behavior in the human male*. Philadelphia, PA: W. B. Saunders; Bloomington, IN: Indiana University Press.

Kinsey, A. C. (1953). *Sexual behavior in the human female*. Philadelphia, PA: W. B. Saunders; Bloomington, IN: Indiana University Press.

Kinsey Institute. (2013). *Data from Alfred Kinsey's studies*. Retrieved from http://www.indiana.edu/~kinsey/research/ak-data.html#Scope

LeVay, S., & Valente, S. M. (2006). *Human sexuality* (2nd ed.). Sunderland, MA: Sinauer Associates.

Liang, B., Williams, L. M., & Siegel, J. A. (2006). Relational outcomes of childhood sexual trauma in female survivors: A longitudinal study. *Journal of Interpersonal Violence, 21*, 41–57.

Mayo Clinic. (2011). *Compulsive sexual behavior*. Retrieved from http://www.Mayoclinic.com/health/compulsive-sexual-behavior/DS00144

McCarthy, B., & McCarthy, E. (2003). *Rekindling desire: A step-by-step approach to help low-sex and no-sex marriages*. New York, NY: Taylor & Francis.

McMillen, M. (2013). *Is sex addiction real?* Retrieved from http://www.webmd.com/sexual-conditions/features/is-sex-addiction-real

Miller, J. (2013). *15 years ago: Bill Clinton's historic denial*. Retrieved from http://www.cbsnews.com/8301-250_162-57565928/15-years-ago-bill-clintons-historic-denial

National Center for Victims of Crime. (2012). *Child sexual abuse statistics*. Retrieved from http://www.victimsofcrime.org/media/reporting-on-child-sexual-abuse/child-sexual-abuse-statistics

Niolon, R. (2011, August). *Gender issues in couples therapy*. Retrieved from http://www.psychpage.com/family/library/gender.html

O'Ryan, L. W., & McFarland, W. P. (2010). A phenomenological exploration of the experiences of dual-career lesbian and gay couples. *Journal of Counseling & Development, 88*, 71–79.

Pelton-Sweet, L. M., & Sherry, A. (2008). Coming out through art: A review of art therapy with LGBT clients. *Journal of the American Art Therapy Association, 25*, 170–176.

Petersen, J. L., & Hyde, J. S. (2010). A meta-analytic review of research on gender differences in sexuality, 1993–2007. *Psychological Bulletin, 136*, 21–38.

Pfaff, D. W. (2011). *Man and woman: An inside story*. New York, NY: Oxford University Press.

Plummer, K. (1995). *Telling sexual stories*. New York, NY: Routledge.

Pomerleau, A., Bolduc, D., Malcuit, G., & Cossette, L. (1990). Pink or blue: Environmental gender stereotypes in the first two years of life. *Sex Roles, 22*, 359–367.

Reece, M., Herbenick, D., Fortenberry, J. D., Sanders, S. A., Schick, V., Dodge, B., & Middlestadt, S. (2010). National survey of sexual health and behavior. *Journal of Sexual Medicine*. Retrieved from http://www.nationalsexstudy.indiana.edu/

Rosser, B. R. S., Metz, M., Bockting, W. O., & Buroker, T. (1997). Sexual difficulties, concerns, and satisfaction in homosexual men: An empirical study with implications for HIV prevention. *Journal of Sex and Marital Therapy, 23*, 61–73.

Sanders, S. A. (2008). Physiology of sex. In W. J. Taverner (Ed.), *Taking sides*. Dubuque, IA: McGraw-Hill.

Scharff, D. E. (1998). *The sexual relationship*. Northvale, NJ: Jason Aronson.

Shallcross, L. (2010, August). Men welcome here. *Counseling Today*, 25–31.

Sherwood, I. H. (2013). *DOMA, California Prop 8 overturned by Supreme Court in victory for same sex marriage.* Retrieved from http://www.latinpost.com/articles/1093/20130626/doma-california-prop-8-overturned-supreme-court-victory-same-sex.htm

Singh, A. A., & Burnes, T. R. (2010, February). ACA endorses ALGBTIC competencies for counseling transgender clients. *Counseling Today*, 52–53.

Society for Scientific Study of Sexuality. (2007). *Sexual satisfaction in committed relationships.* Retrieved from http://www.sexscience.org/dashboard/articleImages/SSSS-SexualSatisfactionInCommittedRelationships.pdf

Spring, J. A. (2006). *After the affair: Healing the pain and rebuilding trust when a partner has been unfaithful.* New York, NY: Harper/Collins.

Szymanski, D. M., Kashubeck-West, S., & Meyer, J. (2008). Internalized heterosexism: A historical and theoretical overview. *Counseling Psychologist*, *36*, 510–524.

Taverner, W. J. (2008). *Taking sides: Clashing views in human sexuality*. Dubuque, IA: McGraw-Hill.

Wells, B. E., & Twenge, J. M. (2005). Changes in young people's sexual behavior and attitudes, 1943–1999: A cross temporal meta-analysis. *Review of General Psychology*, *9*, 249–261.

Whitbourne, S. K. (2012, September). The 8 reasons people cheat on their partners. *Psychology Today*. Retrieved from http://www.psychologytoday.com/blog/fulfillment-any-age/201209/the-eight-reasons-people-cheat-their-partners

Wilson, R. F. (2014). *A closing window*. Retrieved from http://www.libertylawsite.org/feed/

Yarhouse, M. A., & Beckstead, A. L. (2011). Using group therapy to navigate and resolve sexual orientation and religious conflicts. *Counseling and Values*, *56*, 96–120.

CHAPTER

14

Counseling Couples Using Life Cycle and Narrative Therapy Lenses

Colleen R. Logan, Aaron H. Jackson, Lee A. Teufel-Prida, and Dawn M. Wirick

Walden University

CASE STUDY

Larry and Tom, an African American gay couple, are seeking counseling for a number of reasons. Larry and Tom have been together for 15 years. Larry is a successful accountant, and Tom is a soccer coach at a local high school. They have two children, Mary and Stephen. Mary is 6 years old and Stephen is 12. Larry's mother lives with the couple and helps care for the children. Larry is very extroverted, affable, and jovial. Tom sits quietly and listens while Larry speaks. Larry reports that the two main issues for the couple are communication and intimacy. He states that he wishes Tom would talk to him more. He states he is disappointed that he and his mom have to do everything around the house while Tom doesn't take any initiative. He alludes that this is also the same case in the bedroom. He states that Tom never initiates and that it's been over a year since they have been intimate. Larry goes on to say that, in general, the kids are doing well. Stephen does well at school and is very athletic. He plays football, baseball, and soccer. Mary, on the other hand, seems to struggle in school. She is frequently corrected for disruptive behavior. She also struggles with reading and math. Larry states he is not that concerned about Mary because his mother and Stephen can help her with her homework. Larry finishes by exalting and praising his mother. "I don't know what we would do without her, truly," says Larry, "she is such a big part of our family."

Tom reports that he agrees that the primary concerns are sex and communication. Tom feels that he does his best to anticipate Larry's needs and participate in all that goes on at the house. Simply said, Tom feels that he doesn't have a role or really any authority. He starts to weep as he starts to share his perspective. He shares that the first 5 years of their relationship were idyllic. They talked and laughed, went on vacations together, and shared many interests. And then Larry's mother moved in and that was the beginning of the end, according to Tom. First, she ignores the fact that Tom is in an intimate relationship with her son, and she insists on referring to Tom as the "roommate." He goes on to say that he never wanted kids, Larry and his mother did! Yes, he loves the kids, but the way he is treated by Larry's mother and Larry, quite frankly, makes him feel like he is the hired help. Because Tom felt that he never did things "right," he just stopped trying. Tom states that he is willing to give counseling a try, but he doesn't really see the point and he doesn't think the relationship will last. If it weren't for the kids, Tom says sadly, he'd be long gone.

INTRODUCTION

After presenting some pertinent background material, the focus of this chapter is to provide a broad and yet comprehensive overview of how to work with and evaluate family systems using life cycle analysis and narrative therapy. Family systems theory arose out of von Bertalanffy's (1968) concept of general systems theory. Systems theory has its own set of theoretical assumptions that are different from the assumptions associated with individual therapy. Chief among these assumptions is that each part of any given system is interrelated with each and every other part. In addition, these various parts are to some degree interdependent on each other. A *family* is defined as an organization of inter- and intrarelated parts, some of which are internal to the family, and some of which are external to the family (Gladding, 2011). Internal factors include individual interactions between and among the family members, and external factors include various institutions and entities with which the family interacts on a regular basis. Professional counselors working from a family systems perspective consider the family, however defined, in terms of the influence of both internal and external factors.

SIDEBAR 14.1 DEFINITIONS

A systems approach requires that we think about families, presenting problems, and possible solutions in context. It is also helpful to consider the many different influences on any given family. These influences are both internal and external. Internal influences are factors that are within the family. Each family has its own unique history, rules, values, and characteristics. External influences come from the world around us. As systemic counselors, attention is paid to the external influences just as much as the internal things that influence the way a family operates. External influences are factors such as the surrounding community, friendship networks, extended family, politics, and cultural values. Space and time limit a thorough presentation of the many internal and external influential factors that impact family functioning. For a more in-depth understanding and analysis of these factors, see Knoff (1986) and von Bertalanffy (1968).

In general, accurate clinical evaluation requires that counselors thoughtfully and carefully consider all aspects of the presenting problem. Counselors working with couples and families spend time observing, applying what is known (and not known), and then carefully putting together all of the related information in order to conceptualize and determine issues.

Family systems are indeed beautifully complex and difficult to understand. In many cases, it can be said that what appears to be the problem in the family is not the "real" problem that the counselor must consider (Berg & Reuss, 1997; DeJong & Berg, 2001). In other words, sometimes the family views the problem in a completely different way, and it is up to the skilled family counselor to able to see and determine the real issues. It is this set of skills that requires couples and family counselors to be purposeful and intentional when working with families and, in particular, during the evaluation process. This chapter provides guidance on the intensive and critically important process of clinical evaluation, including the unique nature of assessing couples and families, the general differences and similarities between assessing couples and families versus individuals, and general guidelines for the evaluation process.

Individual Versus Family Evaluation

One of the most challenging shifts for emerging counselors who aspire to work with couples and families is the process of moving beyond the idea of simply observing and understanding the individual versus the process of observing and understanding the entire family system. The family as a whole is defined as the primary client, rather than the individuals, and, as such, the family as a whole is subject to evaluation from the very beginning of the counseling relationship.

The difference between individual and family evaluation is really quite clear. According to Corey (2009), the clinical evaluation process for an individual is primarily guided by the *Diagnostic and Statistical Manual of Mental Disorders* (American Psychiatric Association [APA], 2013), now in its fifth edition. Typically, issues and symptoms are matched with diagnostic criteria, which are then attached to specific diagnoses. For example, if an individual meets all of the *DSM* criteria for major depressive disorder, he or she would be given that diagnosis.

Not surprisingly, the process of evaluating and indeed "diagnosing" families is not quite so simple and straightforward. According to Gladding (2011), the *DSM* offers very little guidance in terms of diagnostic criteria and/or specific diagnostic categories for counselors working with families. The *DSM* does, however, provide what are referred to as *V codes*, which provide a diagnostic framework for working with couples and families. These V codes are presented in Section II of *DSM-5* (APA, 2013) under the topic heading of "Other Conditions That May Be a Focus of Clinical Attention." It is of note, however, that these V codes are indicative of an issue that is "not attributable to a mental disorder" (APA, 2013) and, therefore, insurance companies and other third-party payers are reluctant to reimburse counselors for services rendered specifically for those issues. Third-party payers are typically more willing to reimburse clinicians for those diagnoses that are "attributable to a mental disorder." As a result, couples and family counselors are less likely to obtain third-party payment for services.

SIDEBAR 14.2 DIAGNOSTIC CATEGORIES

The fifth edition of the *Diagnostic and Statistical Manual of Mental Disorders* (American Psychiatric Association, 2013) provides helpful diagnostic direction in terms of conceptualizing family-focused diagnoses. The *DSM-5* provides diagnostic categories known as *V codes.* A few of these are summarized here:

V61.20 (Z62.820)—*Parent–child relational problem.* This code may be used when the relationship between the parent(s) and children is causing problems in family functioning, treatment, and so on. Examples of this include problems with parental involvement, cases of a parent being overly protective of a child, or "feelings of sadness, apathy, or anger about the other individual in the relationship" (APA, 2013).

V61.8 (Z62.29) - *Upbringing away from parents.* This code may be used when clinical attention is focused on issues related to a child being raised in a different setting than the home. Children who are raised in foster care and other care facilities or institutions may present with clinically significant concerns; this is applicable in those scenarios if the clinical presentation is related to the aforementioned settings.

V61.03 (Z63.5)—*Disruption of family by separation or divorce.* This code may be used when clinically significant concerns arise out of a situation in which the partners are in the process of separation or divorce.

These are just a few of the V codes available. For a more complete understanding, please refer to Section II of the *DSM-5.*

Focus of Evaluation

The diagnostic criteria for family systems have yet to be set forth in any systematic format; therefore, the diagnosis is heavily influenced by the theoretical perspective of the clinician. For example, a couples and family counselor would not diagnose a family as having obsessive compulsive disorder. The counselor would, however, use diagnostic language to describe what are observed as obsessive and compulsive behaviors within the particular family system. For example, the counselor who adheres to structural family therapy would use terms associated with structural theory to describe and understand the concerns presented during the initial evaluation. To that end, the structural family therapist might conceptualize the family's presenting problem of obsessive and compulsive behaviors in terms of dysfunctional relationships related to poor boundaries, alignment, and abuse and/ or misuse of power.

Family Within Context

Marriage, couples, and family counselors consider the family within the context of all other environmental, social, and cultural arenas. To that end, during the evaluation process, the counselor takes into account and considers such things as the family's historical context, the impact of laws/legal issues, racial and ethnic domains, and interaction with educational or medical institutions. The family is always seen as an integral part of a larger system. In turn, the larger system has an impact on the family, and vice versa. Initially, an emerging couples and family counselor can become overwhelmed with all that can be and should be considered during the initial evaluation process. Rather than succumbing to the enormity of this task, students are asked to remember that couples and family counselors can and do enlist the help of other professionals, such as school counselors, medical practitioners, or spiritual leaders, in an effort to help meet the treatment needs of the family.

Emphasis on Context/Culture

To assess any family without considering its unique nature in terms of the culture of the family would be inappropriate and unprofessional. For more information, review the American Counseling Association (2014) Code of Ethics, American Mental Health Counselors Association (2013) Code of Ethics, and International Association of Marriage and Family Counselors (Hendricks, Bradley, Southern, Oliver, & Birdsall, 2011) Code of Ethics. For the purposes of this chapter, culture can be defined best by Rabin (2005): "[*Culture*] is loosely used to denote a variety of social environmental factors related to ethnic, racial, and class factors" (p. 16). These include poverty, racism, differences in sexual behavior, immigration and resettlement, and acculturation. Cultural content (this is the definition of this concept) in the helping process refers to the specific meanings through which these social phenomena appear, including patterns of individual behavior, interpersonal reactions, and emotions. Cultural variables also include norms regarding gender roles, attitudes about sexuality, identity, and world and self views that run through an almost infinite number of guidelines for daily life behaviors.

The Family Life Cycle as a Concept

The family life cycle is both a concept and an indispensable tool for the couples and family counselor to use when conducting an evaluation of a family. As a concept, the family life cycle posits that families, over the course of their lives, progress and/or transgress through a series of life stages. These stages are described by several different models, each stage being marked by different characteristics, duties, responsibilities, and developmental trends. The underlying assumption is that in order to move on to the next stage, the family must successfully negotiate the tasks of the current stage. Carter and McGoldrick (1999) describe the family life cycle as having six distinct stages, each of which is described in Chapter 1 of this text. A summary of those stages is presented here for the convenience of the reader. For a more detailed description, see Chaper 1.

Stage 1: Young Adults Leaving Home

In this stage, an individual takes the first fledgling steps toward independence. The individual is learning self-care in many different areas, including financial, physical, and emotional well-being. The individual begins to separate from the family of origin, establishing new social connections and enhancing his or her sense of individuality.

Stage 2: The New Couple

This stage denotes the birth of a new family system. Two or more individuals are joining through marriage, partnership, commitment, or other form of agreement to establish themselves as a new familial unit. This new family is establishing itself as a unique organization with its own rules, boundaries, communication style, and value system. In addition, prior relationships with friends and family are being adapted to fit into this new family system. It is a time in which cultures blend and a new family culture begins to arise, one that is unique and separate from the previous familial systems and influences.

Stage 3: Families With New/Young Children

In this stage, new members are introduced into the new family. New family members are added through birth of one or more children. In order to accommodate these new members, the new couple must learn to adjust. The responsibilities of parenting take more time and resources. Finances and personal schedules are altered in an effort to provide the new children with the things they need to thrive. Relationships with extended family members must also be adjusted.

Stage 4: Families With Adolescents

The family is now responsible for launching an adolescent. The child is growing, and with that growth come new developmental tasks for both the child and the family. This stage is marked by an increasing flexibility in boundaries and roles in an effort to accommodate these new developmental tasks. The adolescent is able to provide more self-care, thus providing more flexibility for the parents and grandparents. The primary family may now learn to focus, or refocus, its energies toward career endeavors or other creative undertakings. The primary family may also have time to reconnect as a couple and work on the adult relationship. At the same time, *sandwich family/generation* might characterize this stage. The primary family unit now has children to care for, as well as aging parents or other family members for which to provide care.

Stage 5: Launching Children/Moving On

By now you may have picked up on the trend that these stages are most notably characterized by different family members coming into and leaving the primary familial unit. These entrances and exits become more noticeable during this stage. Children are now leaving the home. The possibility of aging parents passing away increases. A decline in the couple's health may be noted during this stage as well. As children leave the home, the parental subsystem can now be restructured. The relationships with adult children must also be restructured. A new generation is ready to launch and be independent, on their way to starting their own family life cycles.

Stage 6: Families in Later Life

In this stage, the primary family unit is faced with new roles. Parents are becoming grandparents, and their roles are being defined. Aging and its related effects are also noted in this stage. The potential death of one's spouse or partner becomes a reality, and the couple begins to make preparations for the inevitable.

Larry and Tom: Which Life Cycle Stage?

Regarding Larry and Tom, which stage of the family life cycle applies to their family? (Remember, these stages are approximate. Sometimes, clinicians have to find the "best fit" for the family.) Larry and Tom appear to be somewhere between stage 3 and stage 4. In fact, they show characteristics of each stage. They have two children, one of which might be considered an adolescent, and there is an older adult living in the house as well, Larry's mother. There is no indication that Larry's mother requires care, but she certainly does have a major impact on the family system. For example, she struggles with accepting her son's relationship with his male partner, and this is an added strain on the couple's relationship. Mapping out where the couple and/or family is in terms of the family life cycle can provide a wealth of information and insight into the health and well-being of the family system.

The Family Life Cycle as Assessment Tool

How can the family life cycle be used to aid in evaluation and treatment planning? As discussed earlier, each stage is marked by specific characteristics and tasks. The assumption of a stage-based model is that each task associated with each stage must be completed in order for progress to be made. That is, the tasks of the first stages must be successfully negotiated in order for the family system to progress and proceed to the next stage. For counselors working with couples and families, it is helpful to "stage" a client family during the initial evaluation process. By doing so, the clinician can ascertain where the family most closely aligns with the stages of the family life cycle. For example, Larry and Tom closely fit stage 4. Larry and Tom have two children, ages 6 and 12. Now that the family has been staged, it is important to examine and understand the required tasks of this stage, such as the shift in the parent–child relationship in order to afford the adolescent more freedom, as well as the ability to provide more focus on the couple's relationship.

In general, counselors can use the family life cycle tasks to guide both evaluation and initial treatment planning. To that end, the counselor would evaluate the family's progress according to each of the life cycle tasks by asking the following questions:

- How is your family meeting the developmental needs of the children?
- What energies and/or resources need to be redirected toward building and enhancing your relationship as a couple?
- Have you had a conversation with Larry's mom about her roles and responsibilities? Are you in agreement?

The answers to these questions might be helpful in the initial treatment planning process.

Larry and Tom: Presenting Issues From the Family Life Cycle Stage

As was discussed earlier, Larry and Tom are a stage 4 family. On closer examination, the various life cycle challenges they are facing are consistent with the family life cycle model. They are moving ahead with their careers, and they are working toward meeting the developmental needs of both children. In addition, they are in the beginning stages of accommodating an aging parent into their home.

The family life cycle concept is not without its critics. As helpful as it is, it is deficient in some areas. In reality, families will not always fit nicely into any given stage. Families might not progress through the stages in lockstep formation. Therefore, it is wise to consider these stages in a more circular, rather than linear, fashion. For example, a family might be thrust into a given stage without time to prepare for that stage, or a family might be in the new couple stage and still be faced with the tasks associated with prior or later stages. Furthermore, there are important cross-cultural concerns about the family life cycle model. Many families do not fit that description, and the application of this, or any other model of life cycle development, should be taken in the context of the client family's cultural and ethnic background.

Beyond Life Cycle Assessment: The Importance of Theory

When evaluating and treating couples and/or families, one also has a professional responsibility to create and select concrete techniques that best serve the client (Levitt & Bray, 2010). Professional counselors are to operate from a theoretical stance that is congruent with their own philosophy of human change and change processes. Theory, then, provides the foundation for evaluation and treatment. Theories provide a means to understand what one is doing, how one is serving clients, and, most notably, how to explain the counseling process to clients (Levitt & Bray, 2010). Theories reflect clients' realities, counselors' knowledge of what is important, and effective elements of the counseling relationship (Hansen, 2006). Theories help counselors organize clinical data, shed light on complex processes, and provide a conceptual framework for evaluation and interventions (Hansen, 2006).

SIDEBAR 14.3 NARRATIVE THERAPY EXERCISE

Review your perceptions of Tom and Larry's case from the perspective of narrative therapy. How do your own beliefs about their situation impact how you would select a theoretical orientation? How do you see social constructionism, as a philosophical school of thought, impacting how theories such as narrative therapy came into being? Does narrative therapy fit your personal philosophy and worldview?

One way to develop one's own theoretical approach is to consider questions of how people change; what motivates people to behave, think, and feel in the ways that they do; and how someone grows and develops. These elements are foundational and must be considered when developing a theoretical orientation. In addition, one's view of human nature will influence which type of theoretical orientation the counselor decides on and subsequently selects. For example, if the counselor believes that one's internal state (e.g., thoughts) leads to the client's emotional distress, then the counselor will select a theory that specifically focuses on the role of changing thoughts in order to increase mental health and well-being. The techniques that will evolve from this theory will focus on how to work to re-create/reorganize one's internal state, namely, thoughts. Theory provides the "conceptual framework that explains existing observations in particular contexts and generates hypotheses about new observations" (Hansen, 2006, p. 291). Theory, then, provides the foundation for the counselor's conceptualization of the couple and/or family's presenting concerns, primary themes, and which direction(s) the counselor might decide to undertake, according to his or her theoretical orientation.

If one believes that the clients' narratives or stories have impact on their mental health, then the counselor will more likely select a theory that focuses on the stories that clients create. The techniques used with this theory will focus on how the stories one creates can actually be modified if the client is taught how to reconstruct the story line.

Postmodern Background Underlying Narrative Theory and Therapy

In order to comprehend narrative theory and its subsequent therapeutic techniques, it is first essential to outline the philosophical underpinnings of the theory. A primary postmodern school of thought that contributed to narrative therapy's main themes is social constructionism. In social constructionism, meaning is developed through social interaction and the language used in social interaction.

Social Constructionism

Social constructionism focuses on how clients compose their own realities through social interactions (Nichols & Schwartz, 1998). Therefore, theoretically speaking, humans derive meaning from social interaction and the language that is present within these interactions. One of social constructionism's proponents, social psychologist Kenneth Gergen, concluded that not only are humans unable to construct an objective reality, but also the realities constructed are founded within the language systems themselves. In fact, he challenged the notion that historically dominated the psychotherapeutic world, namely, that persons possess innate resources that therapists can draw out (Nichols & Schwartz, 1998). Instead, he contended that realities are reinvented once persons find themselves in new conversational contexts.

This perspective offers several clinical implications for the couples and family therapist. One primary implication is that because everyone's thinking is governed by social interactions, the couple's truths are based on these social constructions. This concept encourages therapists to assist clients in understanding cultural and socially derived meanings that they may be facing in the counseling session. The second implication is that therapy is a "linguistic exercise," in that therapists can lead their clients to new constructions about their problems (Nichols & Schwartz, 1998, p. 324). Third, the postmodern viewpoint of social constructionism implies that the therapeutic process is to be collaborative. Because neither the therapist nor the client brings an objective truth to the session, brand new realities emerge through counseling conversations in which both clients and therapist share meanings through conversation.

Narrative Theory and Therapy

In the family therapy field, social constructionism was welcomed by those therapists who wanted to shift from "changing action into changing meaning" (Nichols & Schwartz, 1998, p. 323). In fact, this postmodern view became the basis for narrative therapy, which emphasized that the therapist's job was to cocreate new realities with clients. As such, counselors are not experts, but instead work with the clients to assist them in understanding that a person's sense of self evolves when interpersonal conversations are "internalized as inner conversations" (Nichols & Schwartz, 1998, p. 324).

Furthermore, it is believed that problems within couples or families are not located within individuals, but rather in points of view individuals possess about themselves and situations (Guise, 2009). Narrative therapy, then, can become a process by which clients can come to reexamine the narratives that govern their lives. The therapist helps the clients to share their stories and then assists the clients in reexamining the stories by which they live.

In addition, narrative therapy created an avenue through which family therapists who wish to address and integrate issues of social justice in their clinical work are able to do so. Clients' self-loathing, lack of optimism, and fear of making changes can follow from internalizing toxic cultural narratives related to their lives and experiences (Nichols & Schwartz, 1998). In fact, narrative therapy has been used to highlight societal impacts of patriarchy, heterosexism, social class, and racism, and to point out to clients how being exposed to these internalized narratives impacts their individual and family narratives. Overall, the goal of narrative therapy is to bring into the open these internalized narratives so they can be replaced with more productive life narratives (Guise, 2009).

The process of rewriting and coconstructing the story begins with "externalizing the problem" (Guise, 2009). In other words, the counselor works to separate the person from the problem. During this process, the counselor and client begin to look more closely at the client's experiences for any ignored components that might contradict the problem-saturated story, paying particular attention to strengths and competencies. Via these conversations, clients continue to rewrite their story lines, which results in an increased sense that they are not solely defined by problems and deficits.

The counselor is interested in hearing the stories so he or she can gain an appreciation of how the client and/or family members view themselves and their issues (e.g., their narrative); then the counselor works with the client or client family to create an alternative narrative. Therefore, narrative therapists ask a series of questions to delineate the impact of the problem. These questions assist the counselor and family in examining and redefining the problem-saturated narrative and working to help to begin reauthoring an alternative, healthier narrative.

Types of Questions

One of the primary questions that a narrative counselor might ask is the deconstruction question, which helps the client externalize the problem. For example, a counselor might ask a question such as: "What does the conflict in your relationship tell you to do?" (Guise, 2009). An opening space question will help the client to uncover unique outcomes; for example: "Has there been a time that insecurity did not take control of your life, even when you thought it would?" A question to extend the story into the future will help to reinforce positive changes; for example: "What will your life be like now that fear of abandonment does not have the upper hand any longer?" Because many clients see themselves as internally possessing or *being* the problem, it is essential for the counselor, as part of the narrative model, to suggest that the self is not a stable entity, but rather is a constitutionalist self that can become deconstructed and reconstructed continuously through interactions (Nichols & Schwartz, 1998). The first goal, then, is to identify and externalize/separate the person from the problem. Then, the client can see the problem as an unwelcome invader that attempts to dominate the person and that person's family. Most importantly, externalizing the problem unites the family against the common enemy or problem instead of placing the blame onto self or others.

In summary, questions form the foundation for discovery of the dominant narrative; then the counselor and the client can work together to deconstruct and reauthor the dominant narrative so that a new narrative will bring a higher quality of contentment to the client and the client family. The following section demonstrates how to apply narrative techniques with Tom and Larry.

Narrative Therapy Applied to Tom and Larry

It is clear that the narratives that Tom and Larry cling to exert an extensively negative impact on their lives and their relationship. Problem-saturated stories (Piercy, Sprenkle, & Wetchler, 1996) affect what Tom and Larry notice in the couple relationship. For example, Larry wishes Tom would talk more and be more active in the relationship, undertake more duties/responsibilities in the home, and initiate intimacy between the two of them. Tom, on the other hand, wants Larry to recognize him as having a role and decision-making power in the relationship. Therefore, Tom tends to cling to his narrative that Larry takes sides with his mom and that their relationship has completely shifted since Larry's mom moved in with them. Larry, however, praises all that his mother does and claims that without her, their family would not be the same. Tom and Larry's problem-saturated narratives center on how each is not receiving from the other, and they tend to solely focus on what is wrong in their relationship. For example, Larry notes that Tom does not talk, and the meaning he attaches to it is that Tom does not care. Tom notes that Larry does not recognize him as being equal in the relationship and concludes that Larry does not respect or honor his voice in the relationship. Both Tom and Larry cling to the problem-saturated story and are not able to see past what is wrong in their relationship. The counselor could assist both Tom and Larry in developing alternative stories and help both see that it is not the other one in the relationship who is the problem, but rather that the problem is the problem itself.

Externalizing the Problem

Using a narrative approach with Larry and Tom would mean that much time would be spent working to gain an understanding of, and appreciation toward, the problem-saturated story. It is important to hear from each partner what he believes are his dominant narratives and then help each one deconstruct the problem-saturated story and coauthor more helpful stories (White & Epston, 1990). Therefore, it would be necessary to separate the person from the problem, or work to externalize the members of the couple from the problem. The therapist could work with Tom to examine more closely the potentially ignored elements that contradict the problem-saturated story, paying close attention to competencies in the relationship (Guise, 2009). The therapist would also work with Larry to help him look more closely at elements within the relationship that contradict his problem-saturated story. As therapy progresses, each person in the couple begins rewriting his story, paying close attention to his competencies as a person and as a person in a committed relationship. The therapist communicates with the couple, both collectively and individually, that he or she is interested in listening to the couple's history to gain appreciation of how the individuals within the couple view themselves and each other. Once the dominant narratives are established, the therapist listens to how individuals view their individual competencies and their competencies as a couple. When the therapist assists the couple in externalizing what they view to be the primary problems in the relationship, they can then work to externalize the problem by asking, "Has there been a time in your relationship when the two of you told the 'lack of communication' to back away from your relationship?" Or, "When the 'lack of intimacy' tries to tell the two of you to distance from one another, how do you work against this external force?" As externalizing the problem progresses in the relationship, questions to extend the story into the future can also be applied, such as: "What will your lives be like now that lack of intimacy does not have the upper hand?" and "How do you see your lives unfolding since you both addressed lack of intimacy together?"

Deconstructing the Dominant Narrative

During this time, the counselor would also work with Tom and Larry to more clearly define how each views the role of being in a nonheterosexual relationship (gay relationship). Because narrative therapy also concerns itself with dominant cultural discourses, it would be important to gauge from Tom and Larry how they may have internalized negative social, political, and cultural messages (Guise, 2009). The counselor could then work with Tom and Larry to deconstruct the dominant cultural discourse and help them rewrite their dominant cultural discourse away from one that emphasizes that being gay is somehow inferior, morally flawed, and not normal.

When assisting Tom and Larry with rewriting the dominant cultural discourse, the counselor could aid them in coming together against their common enemy, namely, how society views their narrative that celebrates and embraces their relationship. Since shame-based issues around their sexuality might be present, the counselor could assist Tom and Larry with uniting against societal views that do not honor relationships that are not heterosexual.

Mapping the Influence of the Problem

Some issues that Tom and Larry present are related to their interactional sequence. For example, Tom and Larry might be engaged in a distance–pursuit pattern in which Larry pursues by desiring to communicate with Tom, while Tom (according to Larry) does not listen to him when he speaks. The therapist can label this interactional sequence as "the rift," and then ask questions related to the rift in their lives. One question that the therapist could ask is, "How does the rift make you believe that the other person is trying to pull away from you?" (Guise, 2009, p. 153). The therapist can ask Larry and Tom how they view the rift and how the two of them can work to silence the rift. When their interactional sequence is defined as an external rift, then the interactional sequence can be externalized and no longer defined as housed within either Larry or Tom, or emanating from either of them.

Reconstructing and Reinforcing a New Narrative

As Tom and Larry uncover their individual competencies and their competencies as a couple, the counselor can assist them in further identifying and broadening their competencies, such as helping them to both see that the rift is the challenge that presents itself in both their intimacy and communication. In addition, the rift can be identified as getting in the way of their effective communication in regard to Larry's mother being present. When Tom and Larry are able to see the rift as the personified entity that inserts itself into their relationship and causes negative impacts, then they will be more likely to decrease the amount of time they spend arguing about who did and did not do what was expected. A question that the counselor could use to ascertain the relative influence of the problem would be: "Since the last session, how much were you in control of the rift, and how much was it in control of you?" Tom and Larry can then reflect on their growing ability to be victorious over the effects of the problem and, in the process, reinforce the notion that the challenges and problems are external to them and not an internal part of either person.

SIDEBAR 14.4 ETHICS OF TERMINATION

Please take a minute to review the following ethical codes regarding termination and the potential for abandonment:

- The American Counseling Association, http://www.counseling.org/resources/aca-code-of-ethics.pdf (specifically A.11)
- The American Mental Health Counselors Association, http://www.amhca.org/assets/news/AMHCA_Code_of_Ethics_2010_w_pagination_cxd_51110.pdf (specifically B.5)

What challenges do you think are associated with ending the counseling relationship with clients?

TERMINATION

Termination is the final phase of counseling. All marriage, couples, and family counselors must attend to the final steps of the counseling process and consider the clinical and ethical implications of ending the counseling relationship. "Psychotherapy termination may be conceptualized as an intentional process that occurs over time when a client has achieved most of the goals of treatment, and/or when psychotherapy must end for other reasons" (Vasquez, Bingham, & Barnett, 2008, p. 653). Specifically, marriage, couples, or family counseling reaches a point that counseling goals have been met and/or the couple or family must end counseling for a particular reason. It is important to consider that the couple and/or family, along with the counselor, is likely to benefit the most from termination if the process is planned and systematic instead of abrupt.

There are generally two primary types of termination: client-initiated termination, which is the most common, and therapist-initiated termination (Rappleyea, Harris, White, & Simon, 2009; Renk & Dinger, 2002). There are various reasons why clients initiate the end phase of counseling, including goal completion or no resolution of identified issue (Lebow, 1995). Leslie (2004) highlights six reasons why a counselor might initiate termination:

1. The client realizes goal accomplishment, which is a natural ending point in the therapeutic process.
2. The client is unable to pay for counseling.
3. The counselor determines the problem is outside his or her scope of competence.
4. The counselor determines that the client is no longer benefiting from counseling.
5. The counselor is unable or unwilling to continue providing counseling.
6. The counselor is no longer employed at the place in which the counseling is provided.

In the case of Larry and Tom, counseling ends as treatment goals are accomplished.

Given that Larry and Tom discussed termination during the initial phase of counseling and understood that counseling would come to an end at some point, counseling termination for this couple seems natural and justified. Family counseling for Larry, Tom, their children, and Larry's mother ends as a result of goal realization. Larry and Tom participated in counseling with a narrative therapy approach. Both Larry and Tom worked on externalizing the problem, mapping the influence of the problem, and reconstructing and reinforcing a new narrative. This new narrative was especially reinforced after several sessions as a family with Larry's mom and the children present. During the family sessions, Larry and Tom were able to practice improved communication as unified partners with a shared narrative that was functional for them as a couple.

Termination Strategies

Regardless of the reason for counseling termination, it is important to follow a systematic process during this final phase of the counseling relationship. Ward (1984) offers specific counseling strategies to following during termination. These strategies are described in more detail as related to the case study of Larry and Tom.

Assessment of Goal Completion and Learning

The clients identify with the counselor the various goals that they accomplished. It is often helpful in evaluating progress to list and measure changes that occurred for the clients. Another technique is to review an early session in the counseling relationship and discuss relative progress on a particular goal.

For Larry and Tom, the counselor made the decision to assess for goal completion by reviewing an initial session in which Larry and Tom argued openly about Larry's mother and were able to list several reasons why their partnership was "not working." As the counselor reviewed this initial session with Larry and Tom, both were able to smile and reflect on why their relationship was not working at the time. Both Larry and Tom discussed with insight the new dialogue they share and how much their perspectives on things have changed.

Closure of Affective and Relationship Issues

Clients and counselors have affective issues around the termination of counseling. Counselors can provide clients an open invitation to discuss feelings of loss, grief, abandonment, and related issues as a way of addressing affective issues and providing an opportunity for appropriate good-byes.

Larry and Tom express to the counselor that they will miss coming to counseling and that they plan to come back if issues arise in the future. Tom discusses that he is surprised to feel some sadness about the end of couples counseling. The counselor openly processes both Larry's and Tom's feelings. Similarly, the counselor provides an opportunity for Larry and Tom to say good-bye and find closure to the counseling relationship.

Preparation for Postcounseling Self-Reliance and Transfer of Learning

What are the client's expectations for transfer of learning to life after counseling? One of the ways to work toward life without counseling and a simple way to achieve termination is to reduce the frequency of sessions. Clients and counselor can assess how counseling gains are maintained outside of counseling and status of self-reliance given goal achievement in counseling.

Larry and Tom expected to improve their intimacy and communication. Although their intimacy and communication have improved greatly, both Larry and Tom now realize that much more effort is needed to maintain healthy intimacy and communication. Larry and Tom feel confident with their new communication style and believe their new narrative is strong and positive.

REFERRAL

Sometimes the end of counseling is not always the end, and a referral to alternative or additional services is needed. Also, the counselor and/or client may deem it appropriate to have periodic counseling sessions to check on whether change was maintained or if old issues resurface.

Referrals can also provide a supplement to current or finished counseling. As a supplement, referrals to various community groups or services can support and enhance wellness that was achieved during the counseling relationship. Based on the case and treatment process of Larry and Tom, no specific referrals were made at termination. However, the counselor did leave the door open for Larry and Tom to return for follow-up couples sessions should any of the issues that were resolved in counseling reemerge.

SUMMARY

In summary, working with couples and families requires a fundamental paradigm shift for counselors in that the focus of evaluation and treatment must move away from the individual and instead focus on the relationships between and among all family members. To do so requires that counselors understand the differences and similarities between assessing individuals versus evaluation of a family as an entire entity. Moreover, treatment of the family is guided by specific theories and techniques and is always reflective of the notion that families operate in context and therefore must be treated as such. Finally, effective termination and referral require counselors to assess that treatment is indeed complete, providing the couple and family with a list of resources should further assistance be required.

USEFUL WEBSITES

The following websites provide additional information relating to the chapter topics.

American Counseling Association (ACA) Code of Ethics
http://www.counseling.org/resources/aca-code-of-ethics.pdf
American Mental Health Counselors Association (AMHCA) Code of Ethics
http://www.amhca.org/assets/news/AMHCA_Code_of_Ethics_2010_w_pagination_cxd_51110.pdf
American Psychiatric Association: DSM-5 Development
http://www.dsm5.org/Pages/Default.aspx
International Association of Marriage and Family Counselors (IAMFC) Ethical Codes
http://www.iamfconline.org/public/department3.cfm

REFERENCES

American Counseling Association. (2014). *Code of ethics.* Retrieved from http://www.counseling.org/docs/ethics/2014-aca-code-of-ethics.pdf?sfvrsn=4

American Mental Health Counselors Association. (2013). *Code of ethics.* Retrieved from http://www.amhca.org/assets/content/AMHCA_Code_of_Ethics_2010_update_1-20-13_COVER.pdf

American Psychiatric Association. (2013). *Diagnostic and statistical manual of mental disorders* (5th ed.). Arlington, VA: American Psychiatric Publishing.

Berg, I. K., & Reuss, N. H. (1997). *Solutions step by step: A substance abuse treatment manual.* New York, NY: Norton.

Carter, B., & McGoldrick, M. (1999). *The expanded family life cycle: Individual, family, and social perspectives.* Boston, MA: Allyn & Bacon.

Corey, G. (2009). *Theory and practice of counseling and psychotherapy* (8th ed.). Belmont, CA: Brooks/Cole.

DeJong, P., & Berg, I. K. (2001). *Interviewing for solutions* (2nd ed.). Pacific Grove, CA: Brooks/Cole.

Gladding, S. T. (2011). *Family therapy: History, theory, and practice* (5th ed). Boston, MA: Pearson.

Goldenberg, H., & Goldenberg, I. (2008). *Family therapy: An overview*. Belmont, CA: Brooks/Cole.

Guise, R. W. (2009). *Study guide for the marriage and family therapy examination*. Jamaica Plain, MA: Family Solutions Corporation.

Hansen, J. T. (2006). Counseling theories within a post-modern epistemology. *Journal of Counseling and Development, 84*, 291–297.

Hendricks, B., Bradley L., Southern, S., Oliver, M., & Birdsall, B. (2011). Ethical code for the International Association of Marriage and Family Counselors. *Family Journal, 19*, 217–224. doi:10.1177/1066480711400814

Knoff, H. M. (Ed.). (1986). *The assessment of child and adolescent personality*. New York, NY: Guilford Press.

Lebow, J. (1995). Open-ended therapy: Termination in marital and family therapy. In R. H. Mikesell, D. D. Lusterman, & S. H. McDaniel (Eds.), *Integrating family therapy: Handbook of family psychology and systems theory* (pp. 73–86). Washington, DC: American Psychological Association.

Leslie, R. S. (2004, May/June). Termination of treatment. *Family Therapy Magazine, 3*(3), 46–48.

Levitt, D. H., & Bray, A. (2010). In B. T. Erford (Ed.), *Theories of counseling. Orientation to the counseling profession: Advocacy, ethics, and essential professional foundations* (pp. 95–123). Upper Saddle River, NJ: Pearson.

Nichols, M. P., & Schwartz, R. C. (1998). *Family therapy: Concepts and methods* (4th ed.). Boston, MA: Allyn & Bacon.

Piercy, F. P., Sprenkle, D. H., & Wetchler, J. L. (Eds.), *Family therapy sourcebook* (2nd ed., pp. 79–105). New York, NY: Guilford Press.

Rabin, C. (Ed.). (2005). *Understanding gender and culture in the helping process*. Belmont, CA: Thomson.

Rappleyea, D. L., Harris, S. M., White, M., & Simon, K. (2009). Termination: Legal and ethical considerations for marriage and family therapists. *American Journal of Family Therapy, 37*, 12–27.

Renk, K., & Dinger, T. M. (2002). Reasons for therapy termination in a university psychology clinic. *Journal of Clinical Psychology, 58*(9), 1173–1181.

Vasquez, M. J. T., Bingham, R. P., & Barnett, J. E. (2008). Psychotherapy termination: Clinical and ethical responsibilities. *Journal of Clinical Psychology: In Session, 64*(5), 653–665.

von Bertalanffy, L. (1968). *General systems theory: Foundations, development, and application*. New York, NY: Braziller.

Ward, D. E. (1984). Termination of individual counseling: Concepts and strategies. *Journal of Counseling and Development, 63*, 21–25.

White, M., & Epston, D. (1990). *Narrative means to a therapeutic end*. New York, NY: Norton.

PART 4

Special Issues

CHAPTER

15

Filial Play Therapy and Other Strategies for Working With Parents

John Sommers-Flanagan, Kirsten W. Murray, and Christina G. Yoshimura

University of Montana

Parents constitute a complex and challenging population. When parents come to counseling or psychotherapy, they bring unique problems that can test the competence of even the most well-seasoned helping professionals (Holcomb-McCoy & Bryan, 2010; Slagt, Deković, de Haan, van den Akker, & Prinzie, 2012). The nature, range, scope, and intensity of parenting problems are immense.

The following case example illustrates the complexity inherent in counseling parents.

Casey and Pat arrive in your office with the intent to discuss concerns about their 6-year-old daughter, Hazel. Initially, they describe their worries about a small behavioral or motor tic that Hazel has developed over the past year. Repeatedly throughout the day and particularly during novel social situations, Hazel cocks her head to the side, rolls her eyes backward, and then brings the knuckle of her right hand upward to her nose. She then presses her knuckle into the side of her nose while scrunching up her face. When Casey or Pat asks her about the purpose of her behavior, she usually reports that her nose "itches on the inside" and that she cannot resist scratching it.

As is often the case with children, Casey and Pat are worried about more than just Hazel's nose-itching behavior. They're also worried about how this behavior will affect Hazel's social development. Hazel will be starting full-day kindergarten in less than a month, and Casey and Pat are terrified that other kindergarten students will pick on her. In addition, as you explore their worries about Hazel's social development, you also discover she's having severe emotional outbursts (i.e., tantrums) and that neither Casey nor Pat seems to have skills for effectively dealing with their daughter's anger.

Not long into your session, both parents also tell you that their relationship is in crisis. Pat's anger has been only marginally in control. Their couple conflicts have become more frequent and more intense. Two weeks prior to their counseling appointment, they were fighting so intensely that their neighbors called the police. Pat was nearly cited for domestic abuse. Then, Pat quickly escalates, claiming that Casey is too "easy" on Hazel and that Hazel just needs more firm and consistent discipline. Pat gives a short monologue on the effectiveness of spanking. Casey responds with tears, disclosing a personal history of physical abuse and adamant opposition to corporal punishment. Casey emphatically states, "I will not let Pat abuse my daughter."

Not surprisingly, all this talk about discipline and abuse may raise emotional issues within the helping professional. You may begin to feel like supporting Casey and chastising Pat—at least up until the point Pat bursts into tears. Pat then begins detailing their financial stressors and the fact that neither of them has had a full-time job over the past year. They're living in run-down, low-income apartments within a neighborhood that both Pat and Casey find frightening. Eventually, Pat discloses that he has a 13-year-old son from a previous relationship. In an effort to escape the tension between himself and his stepfather, Pat's teenage son is intermittently showing up at the apartment late at night after a round of drinking with his buddies. When the appointment ends, you end up with more questions than answers.

We hope this case illustrates how working directly with parents is a unique process that requires special knowledge and skills. Pat and Casey present a profoundly complex scenario—even without adding dimensions related to their sexuality or culture. For example, how might Casey and Pat's parenting and family issues shift if they were a lesbian or gay couple? And how would potential cultural matches or mismatches between the parental dyad and the therapist—or within the parental dyad—affect the therapeutic process and potential outcomes? Obviously, working with Rosa and Miguel or Minkyong and Liang (and all the stereotypes linked to these client names) instead of Casey and Pat might add complexity to the counseling process. Our main point is that you should try not to fool yourself into thinking you can work effectively with parents unless you've obtained specific training for working effectively with parents.

This chapter describes principles, methods, and techniques for counseling parents. It's organized into three parts: (1) parenting problems and theoretical models; (2) general knowledge and skills for working directly with parents; and (3) the history, knowledge, and skills associated with Filial Therapy, a specific play therapy approach to working with parents and children.

PARENTING PROBLEMS AND THEORETICAL MODELS

Parents come to counseling with both common and uncommon problems. Although most parenting and family problems are complex and multidimensional, it can be useful to think of parenting or family problems as primarily involving a focus on one of three areas:

1. A problem ascribed to a parent or parents; examples include excessive parent anger and abusive behavior, the use of ineffective discipline strategies, or a parent with a mental health problem (e.g., clinical depression).
2. A problem ascribed to a child's behavior or problem; examples include a child with a specific developmental disability, a child who is setting fires, or a child with anxiety disorder symptoms.
3. A problem ascribed to maladaptive or suboptimal family interactions; examples include parent–child conflict, parent–parent conflict, and ineffective communication patterns within the family system.

The counseling situation with Pat and Casey included all three of these problem levels (e.g., Pat's flash anger; Hazel's behavioral tic; dysfunctional interactions between and among Pat, Casey, and Hazel). Whether practitioners focus on parent problems, child problems, or family system (or interactional) problems depends, to a large extent, on a given practitioner's theoretical perspective. As with individual counseling, having and adhering to a single theoretical model can provide a helpful guide for practitioners who work with parents (Capuzzi & Gross, 2011). Specifically, family therapy based on family systems, Adlerian, behavioral, solution-focused, attachment theory, and person-centered theory approaches all have at least some empirical support (Sommers-Flanagan & Sommers-Flanagan, 2012). The strength of this empirical support varies depending on parent or family problems. For example, Filial Therapy, the approach featured in this chapter, has broad empirical support across a number of parenting-related child and family problems (VanFleet, 2005). Filial Therapy focuses primarily on dysfunctional interactions between parents and children (Guerney, 1964).

The renowned statistician George E. P. Box once wrote: "Remember that all models are wrong" (Box & Draper, 1987). Because all models are wrong, he suggested that it's more important to focus on the usefulness of various models. This is a very important point, especially when it comes to working with parents and families. The truth is that every parent who comes for help will be coming from a unique and specific parenting and family situation. As a consequence, no single therapeutic model can possibly suffice. Nevertheless, this chapter focuses on general principles for working with parents as well as the play-based Filial Therapy model. We focus on general principles and Filial Therapy because these models have been linked to positive therapeutic outcomes (Sommers-Flanagan, 2007; VanFleet, 2005). However, alternative models that you may find more (or less) useful are also available (Murray, Sommers-Flanagan, & Sommers-Flanagan, 2012). Given the wide range of problems parents can face when raising children, being aware of alternative therapy models is essential.

The Many Problems Parents Face

The range of problems and body of knowledge needed to work with parents is overwhelming. To get you a flavor for specific problems parents will bring to counseling, please read through the following list:

- I'm parenting a child with Down syndrome.
- My triplets are driving me insane.
- My daughter bangs her head on the headboard of her bed every night for about 15 minutes before she goes to sleep. What should I do about that?
- The school is on my case because my son never turns in homework. I make him do his homework every night, but somehow he can't seem to get the homework from home to school. He loses it every day. And now I'm losing it.
- I have a very strong-willed child and I don't know what to do anymore.
- I think my son is possessed by the devil.
- My husband and I can't agree on discipline.
- I haven't had a good night's sleep since my daughter was born 3 years ago. She never sleeps through the night. I can't get her to stay in her room. And at this point, she's totally in charge of the house and I just want to move out.
- I went to a workshop and they said if my son drinks without permission, I should sit him down and have him drink until he starts throwing up. Is that a good idea?
- My daughter won't stop peeing and pooping in the houseplants.
- I think my son has Tourette's.
- I think my daughter has obsessive-compulsive disorder.
- When I was growing up my parents were abusive and I swore to myself I would never hit my children. But now, sometimes, I feel like hitting them. And it's completely freaking me out.
- Do you know anything about problems with sensory motor integration?
- My son has bipolar disorder. Do you know anything about bipolar disorder?
- I think my daughter is using drugs and I don't know what to do.
- You won't believe the crazy and scary kids my son is hanging out with, but when I tell him he can't go out, he just tells me to "F-off" and leaves anyway.
- My neighbor told me that the best way to stop my daughter from biting is to bite her back. And so I tried it, but it didn't feel right. And now she's biting even more. What should I do?
- My daughter is bossy and controlling. I'm worried she'll never have friends.
- If you're like all the other shrinks and you tell me to put a "star chart" up on the fridge, I'm just walking out of here.
- Lately, when I get angry at my children, I can hear my mother's voice coming out of my body and it makes me absolutely hate myself.

This list is only a small sampling of the potential problems parents might articulate when they attend an initial therapy session.

CORE PRINCIPLES FOR WORKING WITH PARENTS

As we've been emphasizing, counseling parents is different from counseling other individuals or couples who seek professional services. This is partly because parents come to counseling with very specific questions and goals, and these questions and goals are explicitly and broadly relational. Further, parent goals and questions typically focus on how to manage, influence, or control specific child behaviors.

Put another way, parents often want immediate knowledge and skills to help them decrease, increase, or eliminate specific child behaviors or problems (Sommers-Flanagan & Sommers-Flanagan, 2011). These behaviors or problems may be occurring within or outside of the family setting.

Principle 1: Experiencing and Expressing Empathy for Parents

Empathy in counseling and psychotherapy is one of the most robust empirical predictors of positive treatment outcomes (Norcross & Lambert, 2011). Although this seems conceptually simple and straightforward, there's an important caveat to remember about empathy as a predictor of positive treatment outcomes. That is, it's the clients' empathy ratings that predict positive treatment outcomes, not the therapists' empathy ratings (Elliott, Bohart, Watson, & Greenberg, 2011). This finding is important for work with all client populations and problems. Specifically, counselors or therapists should observe for indirect signs that clients feel heard and understood; therapists also should intermittently ask clients (directly or via a counseling process questionnaire) if they're feeling heard and understood (Lambert & Shimokawa, 2011).

General Empathy

In the context of working with parents, general empathy (also called *objective empathy*; see Clark, 2010) refers to having empathy for the universal challenge of raising children. This may involve exposure to and appreciation for the ways in which "American" society often expects young women to instantly and competently know how to parent young children. It could involve an appreciation for the shame parents feel when their children misbehave or behave oddly in public settings. General empathy also involves resonating with what parents want from counseling (see Sidebar 15.1).

SIDEBAR 15.1 HAVING EMPATHY FOR WHAT PARENTS WANT

Most parents want their children to live happy, healthy, and misery-free lives. It's helpful to listen for these positive parenting goals and then reflect these goals back to the parents. Following are several examples for how to communicate empathy for what parents want, but you should put these messages into your own words:

- You really want your child to be happy.
- You want your child to have friends and skills for getting along with others.
- You really want your child to stay out of trouble and stay out of jail.

- You're worried your son/daughter might develop an alcohol problem and you want him/her to avoid that painful path in life.

For optimal results, therapists should experience and express empathy for parents—for their general and specific challenges and goals—before offering specific guidance. This will help parents feel listened to and initiate the goal-setting process.

Specific Empathy

When parents come to see a professional, they often have a strong need for the professional to understand or "get" exactly what they're experiencing in their unique home setting. This involves going beyond general empathy for the parenting role and responsibilities. Specific empathy might involve:

- Listening closely to spontaneous stories parents tell about their children. These stories are often an effort to communicate to a professional the depth of a problem or the intensity of a family situation.
- Asking parents to share a story about a troubling family situation and then listening closely to that story.
- Expressing appreciation for the depth, intensity, or intractability of a particular problem behavior (e.g., "That sounds tremendously difficult").
- Universalizing or connecting parental distress with the distress or dilemmas of other parents (e.g., "Getting children to stop hitting can be one of the most challenging situations a parent can face").

Having specific empathy for parents also involves having specific empathy for their doubts about whether counseling or the counselor can be helpful. For example, it's not unusual for parents to say something like: "You don't have any children of your own, do you?" If this occurs, rather than becoming defensive, it's more effective for counselors to empathically resonate with the parents' concerns, validate those concerns, and then follow with an invitation for collaboration. For example:

> It sounds like you have concerns about whether I can be helpful to you. I think these are very reasonable concerns. After all, you hardly know me and you don't know anything about my work and whether I can be effective. But I hope you'll give me a chance to be of help and then you can judge, in the end, whether this experience has been helpful. Does that sound okay to you?

When counselors empathically resonate with parental concerns and then offer an invitation for collaboration, parents nearly always say something like "Yes, I'm open to working with you."

Principle 2: Radical Acceptance

Based partly on person-centered theory and partly on Buddhist philosophy, Marsha Linehan (1993) articulated the concept of radical acceptance as part of her dialectical behavior therapy approach. Similar to other person-centered principles, radical acceptance involves both therapist attitude and skill. Specifically, practitioners who experience and express radical acceptance generally adhere to the following beliefs and guidelines:

- A belief in the dialectical behavior therapy core dialectic: "I accept you as you are and am helping you to change."
- Making an effort to "graciously welcome even the most absurd or offensive [parent] statements with a response like, 'I'm very glad you brought that [topic] up'" (Sommers-Flanagan & Sommers-Flanagan, 2007, p. 275).
- A special emphasis on radical acceptance when clients make comments that are surprising, disagreeable, sexist, racist, or insensitive.
- An active welcoming of any and all comments from parents.
- A letting go of the need to teach parents a new way until the parent is fully ready to receive new and potentially helpful ideas.

Radical acceptance was developed for use with clients diagnosed with borderline personality disorder. It aims to reduce the likelihood of affect dysregulation that can be stimulated in an invalidating family environment. When counselors show radical acceptance, clients are less likely to become affectively dysregulated. Similarly, when counselors immediately judge parents and begin prematurely educating them, parents may become justifiably angry (i.e., affectively dysregulated) and then resist or reject even the most helpful advice.

Principle 3: Collaboration

Collaboration involves two or more people working together to accomplish a common goal. When working with parents, collaboration is very similar to the evidence-based concept of the working alliance or therapeutic relationship (Friedlander, Escudero, Heatherington, & Diamond, 2011). Collaborative practitioners (a) explicitly welcome parents as the best experts on the family situation; (b) de-emphasize their own knowledge and expertise; (c) approach the therapy relationship from a position of not knowing too much, but intent on learning about the parent(s) and child; and (d) offer suggestions or guidance with an experimental mind-set. This encourages both parent and practitioner to observe and discuss how the suggestions or guidance is working.

There are many different counselor behaviors that facilitate or promote collaboration. Examples include:

- Explaining to parents how the counseling/consulting process works: "At first I'll be listening and asking a few questions, and later I'll offer a few suggestions me to be quiet and listen, or offer more ideas, just let me know."

for things you might try out at home. But this is your session and so if you want me to be quiet and listen, or offer more ideas, just let me know."

- Affirming parental expertise: "You know your child better than anyone else."
- Asking for permission before offering advice: "I have some ideas about what might be helpful to you in your family situation. Is it okay with you if I share them with you?"
- Encouraging an experimental mind-set: "Nothing works perfectly for every parent and every child. How about if you try these ideas out and observe how they work, and when we meet next time we can talk about what was more helpful and what was less helpful."

Note how most of these preceding behaviors are designed to empower parents as active participants who are engaged in the counseling process.

Principle 4: Be Therapeutic First and Educational Second

When counselors adopt or embrace an empathic, radically accepting, and collaborative orientation, the fourth principle—be therapeutic first and educational second—becomes a reality. This is because if a counselor is resonating with general and specific parenting challenges, radically accepting whatever parents say, and acting as a helper who collaborates with parent knowledge and expertise, then providing premature educational information simply won't happen. As a means of illustrating how these four core principles can be integrated into a therapeutic conversation with a parent, the following case example and commentary are provided (adapted from Sommers-Flanagan & Sommers-Flanagan, 2011, pp. 12–13).

CASSANDRA: My son is so stubborn. Everything is fine one minute, but if I ask him to do something, he goes ballistic. And then I can't get him to do anything.

COUNSELOR: Some kids seem built to focus on getting what they want. It sounds like your boy is very strong-willed. [The counselor uses a simple initial reflection using common language. This is used to quickly formulate the problem in a way that empathically resonates with the parent's experience.]

CASSANDRA: He's way beyond strong-willed. The other day I asked him to go upstairs and clean his room and he said "No!" [The mom seems to need specific empathy; she wants the counselor to know her son isn't just an ordinary strong-willed boy.]

COUNSELOR: He just refused? What happened then? [The counselor shows appropriate interest and curiosity. This honors the parent's perspective and helps build the collaborative relationship.]

CASSANDRA: I asked him again and then, while standing at the bottom of the stairs, he put his hands on his hips and yelled, "I said *no!* You wanna piece of *me*?!"

COUNSELOR: Wow. You're right. He is in the advanced class on how to be strong-willed. What did you do next? [The counselor accepts and validates the parent's perception of having an exceptionally strong-willed son.]

CASSANDRA: I carried him upstairs and spanked his butt because, at that point, I *did* want a piece of him! [Mom discloses becoming angry and using corporal punishment.]

COUNSELOR: It's funny how often when our kids challenge our authority so directly, like your son did, it really does make us want a piece of them. [The counselor avoids judgment, universalizes, validates, and radically accepts the mom's anger and impulses, but doesn't endorse her behavior.]

CASSANDRA: It sure gets me! [Mom acknowledges that her son can really get to her, but there's still no mention of anger.]

COUNSELOR: I know my next question is a cliché counseling question, but I can't help but wonder how you feel about what happened in that situation. [This is a gentle and self-effacing effort to have the parent focus on herself and perhaps reflect on her emotions and behavior.]

CASSANDRA: I believe he got what he deserved. [Mom doesn't explore her feelings or question her behavior, but instead shows a defensive side; this suggests the counselor may have been premature in trying to get mom to critique her own behavior.]

COUNSELOR: It sounds like you were pretty mad. You were thinking something like, "He's being defiant and so I'm giving him what he deserves." [The counselor provides an empathic response and uses radical acceptance. There's no effort to judge or question whether the son "deserved" physical punishment, which might be a good question, but would be premature and likely close down exploration. The counselor also uses the personal pronoun *I* when reflecting the mom's perspective, which is an example of the Rogerian technique of "walking within."]

CASSANDRA: Yes, I did. But I'm also here because I need to find other ways of dealing with him. I can't keep hauling him up the stairs and spanking him forever. It's unacceptable for him to be disrespectful to me, but I need other options. [Mom responds to radical acceptance and empathy. She opens up and expresses interest in exploring alternatives]

COUNSELOR: That's a great reason for you to be here. Of course, he shouldn't be disrespectful to you. You don't deserve that. But I hear you saying you want options beyond spanking and that's exactly one of the things we can talk about today. [The counselor accepts and validates the mom's perspective—both her reason for seeking a consultation and the fact that she wants respect. Resonating with parents about their hurt over being disrespected can be very powerful.]

CASSANDRA: Thank you. It feels good to talk about this, but I do need other ideas for how to handle my wonderful little monster. [Mom expresses appreciation for the validation and continues to show interest in change.]

This case example illustrates how general and specific empathy, radical acceptance, and collaboration can be used in a therapeutic conversation with a parent. Also, consistent with this general model for working with parents, the counselor embraces the role of not knowing too much and consequently avoids offering education prior to establishing a therapeutic relationship. These four principles for working with parents are consistent with the specific family therapy approach featured in this chapter, Filial Therapy. (To reflect on how to talk with parents about spanking or corporal punishment, see Sidebar 15.2.)

SIDEBAR 15.2 TALKING WITH PARENTS ABOUT SPANKING

Can you imagine talking with parents about spanking? Regardless of your personal view, you should be ready to talk about spanking in a balanced manner. Consider the following:

- Both the American Psychological Association and American Association of Pediatricians are opposed to spanking and other forms of corporal punishment.
- Just because parents use spanking doesn't mean they're bad parents.
- Spanking has many potential negative consequences (see Gershoff, 2002, 2008).
- The only positive consequence of spanking is that it suppresses the undesirable behavior in the moment, but not necessarily in the long term.

If you're sensitive and nonjudgmental, most parents who spank will acknowledge they'd like to learn alternatives.

In the end, it's best to join with parents on their child-rearing goals (e.g., to teach their child self-control) and then work with them to develop alternatives to spanking.

FILIAL THERAPY: A SPECIFIC APPROACH TO WORKING DIRECTLY WITH PARENTS

In the late 1950s and early 1960s, Louise and Bernard Guerney developed Filial Therapy. VanFleet (2011) described the moment and the historical context:

> In the 54 years since Dr. Bernard Guerney walked onto the back porch of his home and suggested the idea of Filial Therapy to his wife, Dr. Louise Guerney, the method has been refined, researched, and disseminated throughout the world. Because the concept was far ahead of its time, it was met with initial criticism. Critics could not quite imagine that parents would be capable of making a difference in their children's lives this way especially because the prevailing view was that parents were the cause of all the child's problems. (p. 16)

Filial Therapy (FT) is a therapeutic method that teaches parents to be the primary change agents for their children through structured, child-guided play sessions. Although theoretically complex, FT can be boiled down to three essential components: *Family therapy* that employs a *play therapy* based *psycho-educational* model.

FT can be, and often is, implemented with individual families and children. However, it was originally designed to be delivered in a group therapy format. Bratton, Ray, Rhine, and Jones (2005) described the traditional group FT treatment protocol:

> Parents are taught basic child-centered play therapy principles and skills and then required to practice these skills under the close supervision of a trained play therapist, in weekly videotaped or live-supervised play sessions with their child. Filial therapy is most often taught in a group setting to provide parents with emotional support in addition to providing them with a balance of didactic and experiential activities to facilitate their learning. (p. 386)

Consistent with the general principles for working with parents described previously in this chapter, filial therapists use a collaborative approach, and FT is not based on the medical model. This fits with Bernard Guerney's original ideas about the etiology of child and family problems. Louise Guerney and Virginia Ryan (2013) described Bernard Guerney's early thinking:

> Guerney had a different explanation for the etiology of problem interactions between parents and children. He assumed that in the majority of cases, rather than parental pathology causing children's problems, parental lack of knowledge and skills of how to interact with their children were the bases of parent-child interaction difficulties. Parents needed to be taught how to motivate their children to make them feel loved and respected. . . . Thus, Guerney wanted to find a way to help parents . . . to learn to interact with their children in positive, supportive ways that would still maintain the necessary control that children need. (p. 16)

Consequently, FT does not identify parent problems as the treatment focus; it also does not target child problems as the treatment focus. Instead, FT employs child-directed play therapy as a means through which child–parent relationships can be improved and strengthened. Improving or strengthening the child–parent relationship is the ultimate goal of FT.

What's in a Name?

The Filial Therapy name is somewhat slippery and deserves a brief explanation. VanFleet (2011) wrote that, in 2003, Louise Guerney asked that the words *Filial Therapy* be capitalized when referring to Filial Therapy in its original form. She also requested that the words *filial therapy* be in lowercase when writers are referring to "significant variations from the original approach" (p. 17). These requests are an acknowledgment of how some practitioners and writers have modified FT.

The most significant FT modification is child–parent relationship therapy (CPRT). Garry Landreth and Sue Bratton (2006) developed CPRT as a distinct form of filial therapy. CPRT is a time-limited (10 session) format. Through their research, practice, and workshop activities, Landreth and Bratton have been credited with substantially contributing to the popularizing and evidence-based status of FT (Daneker & Hunter-Lee, 2006). Although CPRT is a modification of FT and even has a different name, it is, more or less, pure FT.

To make matters slightly more complex, the original Filial Therapy approach is also interchangeably referred to as *filial family therapy* and *filial play therapy*. In addition, on the website for the National Institute of Relationship Enhancement and Center for Couples, Families and Children. Filial Therapy is also referred to as *child relationship enhancement family therapy*. And in some cases and by some practitioners, Filial Therapy is simply referred to as *filial*.

Finally, it should be noted that there are some family or play therapies with names similar to modified FT approaches. For example, parent–child interaction therapy (PCIT) (Eyberg, 1988) is a directive, behavioral approach to treating children's problems. PCIT is not affiliated with or considered a form of FT.

Overall, the FT approach has empirical support and is considered evidence-based. Based on a meta-analysis of 22 studies, Bratton et al. (2005) reported an effect size of $d = 1.15$. Based on Cohen's (1977) guidelines, this is considered a large treatment effect.

Origin and Background

FT as a distinct approach to therapeutic change for children is deeply rooted in play therapy as a more general method. Play therapy operates on the presumption that play is both the work and language of children (Nagera, 1980). Through play, children develop problem-solving skills, rehearse for future situations, and manage emotions (Axline, 1964; Gil, 1994). Play allows children a vehicle for communicating and expressing ideas, desires, and fears for which they lack words. Play can also help children gain confidence in their expressive abilities (Esman, 1983).

Although play therapy can be seen as monolithic and as synonymous with child therapy, many different theory-based play therapy approaches have been developed. Early use of play in therapy began with A. Freud (1928) and Klein's (1932) psychoanalytic play therapy. Several play therapy approaches have also arisen from humanistic, behavioral, and Jungian traditions (Gil, 1994). Although motivations for using play in therapy differ across these traditions, the underlying goal of facilitating and supporting children's expressive abilities is common to most play therapies. Specifically, play therapy allows children an opportunity to communicate thoughts and feelings that might not otherwise be communicated.

During the early 1960s, nondirective or child-centered play therapy influenced the Guerneys as they developed FT. Child-centered play therapy was a therapy application of Carl Rogers's (1957) client-centered therapy. This approach was given a popular boost with the publication of Virginia Axline's (1964) classic book *Dibs: In Search of Self*. As noted previously, FT involves teaching parents how to use very specific child-centered play therapy methods with their children.

Family systems theory is also foundational to FT. The Palo Alto group was instrumental in the 1950s and 1960s in popularizing family work as a viable alternative to individual counseling or psychotherapy. Ackerman (1970) extended this systemic approach to therapy with families and introduced a unique playfulness into his therapy sessions. In addition, Satir (1964) encouraged families to engage in exaggerated role plays with one another. These role plays offered a fictional, play-like means for family members to act out their emotions and struggles.

From these historical roots, Bernard and Louise Guerney developed FT. The Guerneys' conceptualization of FT includes the belief that children can express the otherwise inexpressible through play, and that it is appropriate and potentially helpful to focus on family relationships within a complex system instead of presenting problems. Their play therapy method is notable for at least two reasons. First, they joined Satir (1964) as some of the first therapists to believe that families could work together on their own problems. Play therapy to that point had typically occurred between therapists and children, although parents may have been permitted in the room (a notable exception to this pattern was Safer [1965], who required in conjoint play therapy that parents not only be present, but also participate in child-directed play). These were significant moves away from the primarily intrapersonal therapy processes at the time (Guerney, 2000).

Second, FT included parents as agents for change rather than scapegoating them for children's behavioral or emotional problems. FT's novel move to integrate parents actively into therapy reduced parent noncompliance and promoted receptiveness (Grif, 1983). Specifically, FT shifts the focus away from previous parenting failures and toward incremental skill building. This skill-building focus emphasizes positive goals instead of negative or maladaptive behaviors. It works to remove parental resistance by quieting the presumption of parental pathology as the source of children's problems (Guerney, 2000). L. Guerney and Ryan (2013) described Bernard Guerney's rationale for focusing on parents as the primary agent of change in FT:

> He reasoned that therapeutic change would be more likely and lasting in children if their own parents served as therapists. By taking on the play therapist role, parents would not only be given positive skills, but this role also would create a new perception of their parents on the part of their children. These behavioral and attitudinal changes required of parents in order to conduct play sessions then would be generalized to parent-child relationships in daily life. Simultaneously, the children would experience the positive benefits that accrue from [play therapy] sessions, as they would from any valid therapy. (p. 17)

Several highlights in the evolution of FT are worth noting. In the 1970s, parent training in FT evolved from a full year of training sessions to 5 to 6 months of sessions. These briefer filial training models yielded no significant differences in parent and child outcomes (Guerney, 2000). In the 1980s, the dominance of strict behavioral treatment approaches within academia nearly supplanted all play therapy approaches. Nevertheless, clinical research and practitioner interest continued, and play therapy survived. Subsequently, in the 1990s and 2000s, Landreth and Bratton contributed significantly to FT's status within the helping professions. Currently, it's accurate to say that play therapy has not only survived, but it is thriving across many different professional helping disciplines (Guerney, 2000).

Wickstrom (2010) recently described and advocated an advanced FT model. For parents who already have initial training, she suggested forming small groups of parents along with a group facilitator. These groups not only offer support and camaraderie (typical in group-based FT), but also help further develop and advance core filial play therapy skills. This is achieved through a rotation in which each parent in the group interacts with each child, while the rest of the group observes. Parents are able to develop additional play skills through this process in two ways: (1) They witness other people engaging in play with their own child using play techniques or communication approaches they may have never tried (allowing parents to evaluate the parenting play technique and child's response and consider whether to add this approach or technique to their own parent–child play repertoire); and (2) parents can interact with someone else's child, possibly encountering a different personality or response in that child that can stimulate the learning of new play behaviors and parenting skills. The ultimate goal of this advanced model is to extend parents' play therapy abilities into new settings and interactions outside of regular parent–child playtimes.

Assumptions

There are five basic assumptions of FT:

1. Interpersonal family interactions constitute an important contributor of childhood behavioral and/or emotional maladjustment (Guerney, 1964).
2. When parents improve the nature and quality of their interactions with their children, improvements in parent–child relationships follow (Guerney, Guerney, & Andronico, 1999; Landreth, 2002). This assumption rests on the belief that it is a lack of parental skills, rather than any particular pathology, that primarily contributes to a child's problems (Guerney, 1964). Consequently, building trust, responsiveness, and the opportunity to correct miscommunications and enhance communication between parent and child are essential elements in FT.
3. The play context allows children an atmosphere for communicating (directly or often indirectly) important messages in their natural "language" to parents (Guerney, 1964). This context also allows children to feel heard and understood.
4. Within the context of an improved parent–child relationship, children's anxiety can diminish, self-worth can begin to build, and emotional and behavioral competencies can be generalized to new developmental tasks and feelings (Guerney, 1964).
5. Parental resistance to change is reduced when parents are empowered as change agents for their children, rather than being framed as a problem to be solved or overcome (Guerney, 1964, 2000).

FT focuses on teaching several specific parenting skills. These skills include reflective listening, empathy, limit-setting, enhancement of the child's self-esteem, and use of toys and time to structure productive 30-minute, once-weekly, parent–child play sessions (Landreth, 2002). Parents are introduced to these skills and then engaged in a supervision relationship with a therapist while the skills are practiced. After a supervision period of approximately 10 weeks, parents are sent home with the expectation that they will continue engaging their child in structured play sessions and that skill development and utilization will continue.

Process and Goals

Filial therapists engage parents and children in a specific process that leads toward several goals. These goals are consistent with FT's strength-based and educational focus. Filial therapists use a "socialization-as-intervention" approach as the vehicle or process for therapeutic change and rely on play as the common language for deepening the parent–child relationship (Topham & VanFleet, 2011).

Filial Therapists Make Emotional Connections With Parents

Although FT is psychoeducational, filial therapists do not ignore the therapist–client relationship. In her discussion of empathy and acceptance from the FT perspective, VanFleet (2011) echoes the perspective discussed earlier in this chapter and articulates how filial therapists seek to connect with parents on a deep emotional level:

> Deep understanding of parent feelings typically results in greater engagement in the therapeutic process, enhancing the potential for positive parent change. Empathic listening with parents is not a simple restatement of their thoughts and feelings, rather, it is a commitment to understanding parent feelings at the deepest level possible. An example would be if a parent asserted, "Sometimes I just can't stand that kid. He's hateful!" A response such as "You're upset with him" would be considered empathic, but it fails to reflect the intensity of the parent's feelings. A deeper empathic response would be, "You're furious with him and feel at the end of your rope!" In FT, therapists use empathy and acceptance with parents throughout the process. (p. 8)

If the initial FT goal of connecting with parents is not achieved, parental engagement will be adversely affected and parent resistance will be more likely.

Filial Therapists Seek to Strengthen the Parent–Child Relationship

Successful FT strengthens the parent–child relationship. To accomplish this, parents are trained to be more supportive and attentive via time-limited, child-directed play therapy sessions. The therapist facilitates a structured, child-led opportunity for personal growth. While promoting the parent–child relationship, the therapist uncovers opportunities to both support unconditional acceptance of the child and establish necessary boundaries (Topham & VanFleet, 2011).

Filial Therapists Facilitate Healthy Boundary-Setting

Establishing boundaries in the parent–child relationship during playtime includes: (a) setting limits for the safety of people and property; (b) beginning and ending play sessions in a timely, structured manner; and (c) allowing the child to lead the direction of the play. Striking a balance between setting limits and maintaining a nurturing and empathic environment is at the crux of the FT experience. Allowing parents to be excessively rigid when boundary setting or too unstructured with diffuse boundaries contributes to family environments that become overcorrective and punitive or unstructured and confusing. Neither of these extreme environments helps children feel safe or helps the parent–child relationship to thrive. The goal, to borrow a structural family therapy term, is to encourage implementation of clear boundaries. Therapists help parents soften their rigid ways of being to include more nurturing and warm responses; therapists also strengthen enmeshed and diffuse relationships to help parents hold unified, clear, and consistent limits (Topham & Van Fleet, 2011).

Filial Therapists Help Parents Become More Present

Therapists also seek to improve parents' ability to be fully present with their child, unconditionally accepting their child's feelings and needs in the moment (Topham & VanFleet, 2011). Although it may seem simple, asking a parent to change from an authoritarian or permissive style to a curious and reflective stance may challenge what it means for them to be an active participant in their child's play. This change can be tricky to execute, especially if parents are transitioning from a more directive role or have difficulty setting their own needs and feelings aside during a play session. As support, therapists give direct feedback on attending skills and provide a space for parents to explore what may be preventing them from being fully available during the play session.

FT consultations with parents include time for teaching and building strategies to enhance child-directed play. For example, a consultation may focus on how parents can set aside their own needs and feelings during a play session so they can attend more fully to the child. Perhaps a mother becomes frustrated when her son is absorbed in a drawing and won't answer her questions during their play session. She is convinced the approach isn't working and that her son is only trying to annoy her. The therapist would then intervene, accepting and honoring the mother's frustration while collaborating on strategies that allow her to process her frustrations later and remain present in the moment with her son. These consultations are a place for the therapist to model unconditional acceptance and empathy for parent struggles. When filial therapists experience and express unconditional positive regard toward parents, they're providing a model for how parents can show similar respect, attentiveness, and acceptance toward their children during play therapy interactions (Topham & VanFleet, 2011). This is a parallel process wherein filial therapists experience and express unconditional positive regard toward parents—even during challenging therapy moments—just as parents are expected to display unconditional positive regard toward their children, even when challenging child behaviors emerge.

Filial Therapists Act as Coaches for Parents

The therapist role during FT is aptly described using a coaching metaphor. Therapists are on the sidelines, observing and acting as a source of support and feedback for parents as the parents engage in child-centered play therapy. This shift for therapists can be difficult because the primary therapy relationship is not with the child; the client becomes a family subsystem, rather than an individual. Conceptually, the client becomes the parent–child relationship (Topham & VanFleet, 2011).

As coaches (or supervisors) who provide feedback for parents, the filial therapist's goals are twofold. First, facilitate a collaborative and true partnership with parents. Second, help parents develop skills necessary for nondirective, child-led play (VanFleet, Ryan, & Smith, 2005). Consistent with the general principles for working with parents described previously, filial therapists enter the relationship with parents with humility and patience, remembering that parents understand their child in unique and meaningful ways. Parents' knowledge of their child is valuable and should not be ignored; how they see their child can readily inform treatment plans and interventions for the parent–child relationship. While honoring parents and their struggles, therapists must also be ready to guide them into new ways of being with their children. Giving clear and consistent feedback to parents about how to be more present with their child and establish necessary boundaries requires a balance of firm language that clearly communicates directives, yet also holds enough empathy to honor the vulnerability parents experience when seeking help with their parenting.

Filial Therapists Attend to Subsystems and Individuals

Unlike other systems models that emphasize the whole family system, FT methods focus on parent–child subsystems. As a result, conceptualizations, goals, and interventions are all applied within a single subsystem, with the assumption that change will generalize to larger family dynamics. Often, filial therapists find themselves shifting foci between the individuals and the relationship between them. Topham and VanFleet (2011) described the need for therapists to respond to individual goals such as self-esteem needs and awareness of emotions, while also navigating subsystem goals that enhance the relationship, such as increasing playful interactions between parent and child.

The Four Basic Filial Therapy Skills

There are four basic skills that filial therapists teach parents: (1) focusing on children's feelings and actions—empathy, empathic responding, and tracking;

(2) following children's lead; (3) structuring play sessions; and (4) limiting children's behavior (see Guerney & Ryan, 2013, for many more details and examples).

Focusing on Children's Feelings and Actions—Empathy, Empathic Responding, and Tracking

Filial therapists guide parents to be attuned and responsive to their child during moment-to-moment interactions. Specifically, parents are taught to use (a) basic attending behaviors using tracking statements ("I see you chose to start with the dollhouse today"); (b) paraphrases ("Oh, now we're going to the barn"); and (c) feeling reflections ("That horse is angry"). These reflective listening or tracking skills help parents establish an empathic presence within their child's play, while also maintaining a nondirective stance.

Guerney and Ryan (2013) describe how tracking and empathy go together:

> Leaders also should be aware that tracking alone, without empathy, is insufficient for therapeutic purposes. For example, a parent saying to a child in a play session who is looking very pleased with himself, "You are turning the truck upside down," is tracking an action, but not reflecting a feeling. A fuller empathic response is: "You are really enjoying turning the truck upside down." (p. 107)

Early in the process of learning empathy and tracking skills, parents may feel and appear robotic. Eventually and ultimately, the goal is for parents to be spontaneous and authentic as they convey acceptance of their child. However, some parents may be especially uncomfortable or awkward when expected to engage in imaginary play with children (VanFleet et al., 2005). It can be helpful for filial therapists to encourage parents to give themselves permission to be silly and spiritedly interact in play scenes their child is directing. This can integrate more creativity, humor, fun, and connection into the child-directed play experience.

Following Children's Lead

It can be difficult and challenging for some parents to give up control and follow their child's lead during child-directed play. Nevertheless, this is a crucial skill, and parents receive coaching, feedback, and role modeling to help them embrace and enact this skill. Guerney and Ryan (2013) explain the rationale for following children's lead and describe some of the limits parents must place on their own behavior:

> Parents are trained to fully attend to their children during play sessions and to participate in play sessions, either through actions or words, at their children's invitation. By following their children's lead, parents create a child-led atmosphere, within the well-defined structure and limits of play sessions. Children in turn feel accepted and emotionally secure. During skills training, leaders help parents avoid asking questions of their children,

> and refrain from praising them or suggesting activities to them during play sessions. Yet all of these responses, which are avoided in play sessions, serve important functions in daily life, where parents have the role of stimulating their children, managing their behavior, and educating them. (pp. 107–108)

For parents to follow their child's lead, they must resist their own impulses to say and do things that might direct their interactions with their child. In some cases, a parent might feel upset or bored or angry with the child's play behavior. For example, a child might choose a toy the parent dislikes, ignore the parent during part or all of the play time, or act out embarrassing family dynamics during imaginative play. In each of these situations, it's the parent's job to control his or her impulses and continue with empathic, tracking responses. Parents are asked to control their emotional expression, waiting for group or individual meetings in which their emotional reactions can be met with empathy and support.

A key theme in FT is that although child-centered play is very important, it represents a special time in which children are directing and parents are following. During the rest of the day and week, parents are expected to direct their children in a balanced and healthy manner. Parents are coached to use both the skills they've developed (e.g., empathy and limit-setting), as well as what they learn about their child during child-directed play, to be and become better parents outside their play interactions.

On a conceptual level, parents are guided to be aware of the developmental tasks occurring during play sessions, including problem solving and mastery themes. Therapists also direct parents to remain curious about how a child's play may relate to their internal worlds and life events. Often, children's hopes, fears, anxieties, and needs play out and resolve in the FT process. Play is often a metaphor for children's internal struggles. For example, a parent may tentatively connect a play scenario of a toy cat's fear of going outside to the child's same hesitancy of leaving home to attend school. A child's patterns of behavior during play can also be connected to his or her "outside" experiences. Examples might include regularly seeking adult help before attempting a task (opening Play Doh, reaching for a book, etc.) or becoming stuck in perfection-seeking loops before moving forward in play (drawing and erasing a picture to begin again numerous times or adjusting dollhouse furniture time and time again until it is "perfect"). Therapists can then teach parents behavioral and social learning principles such as shaping, reinforcement, and modeling to address these barriers when they arise outside of the play sessions with their child.

Structuring Skills

Filial therapists use instruction and coaching to help parents structure and set boundaries within and around play sessions. These structuring skills are complex and often overlooked or assumed to be naturally present in all parents. Structuring is the foundation upon which a positive child-directed play session is built. From smoothly opening and ending play sessions, to learning how to manage parameters of time, safety, and logistics, parents use structuring skills to ensure that play is possible and secure. While firmly and consistently setting necessary limits, parents must also be ready to shift their energy to a reflective and curious stance, allowing the child to direct the play session (O'Connor, 2000).

The special time of child-directed play begins with an opening statement. This opening statement creates a boundary around the play time and clarifies parent and child roles. Helping parents deliver this opening statement can generalize to outside therapy. Specifically, as parents learn to structure the child-directed play therapy sessions, they may also learn to be clearer in communicating boundaries and structure outside therapy.

Guerney and Ryan (2013) provide the opening statement for play sessions:

> "[Name of child], this is a very special room [time, place, depending on the space parents use]. You can do ALMOST anything you want.* If you cannot do something, I will tell you." (*This statement may include the optional statement: "You may say anything you want in here.") (p. 114)

Limiting Children's Behavior

In the opening statement for child-directed play, parents are instructed to tell their children, "You can do *almost* anything you want." This is a crucial message. Children cannot do anything they want to do during play, and some children will instantly test their parents to see exactly where the limit lies.

The rules and limits focus on personal safety and basic respect for property or toys. If children cross one of these limits, the parent is coached to use a three-step limit-setting process:

1. Describe the limit: "You may not try to hurt me with a toy or anything else."
2. If the behavior recurs, offer a clear reminder: "Remember, you may not try to hurt me with a toy or anything else; if you do that again, we'll have to leave this area and end our play session right away."
3. If the behavior occurs a third time, immediately end the session: "Remember, I said if you tried to hurt me again that we would end our play session and so now that you chose to do that again, our special play time is over."

Using this three-step limit-setting model serves two main goals. First, it helps create a sense of safety and reasonable limits during play time. Second, as parents use this simple and straightforward method, they learn to generalize this skill to other situations, which can result in decreased nagging and increased children's listening.

Therapist Skills and Techniques

Therapists must be competent in child-centered play therapy before using FT with families. While knowledge and training in play therapy is foundational to practicing FT, additional training and supervision in skills specific to a filial approach are essential (VanFleet et al., 2005). Filial therapists employ specific skills and techniques across a number of contexts. These include:

- Initial assessment and parent training
- Live observation of parent and child play sessions
- Parent consultation sessions

Filial therapists need knowledge for what to teach (child-directed play) and skills for how to best teach it. A knack for the psychoeducational task of providing training and supervision (or coaching) is essential to the filial therapist's skill set (Landreth & Bratton, 2006). Like radical acceptance, this involves accepting parents where they are and encouraging them toward new behaviors. Therapists must keep a moment-to-moment pulse on parent reactions to the therapy and educational process. This helps filial therapists know when to push forward with feedback and when to ebb back and attend to the therapeutic relationship. General empathy for the fact that parents are often vulnerable, full of concern for their child, and battling self-doubt about their parenting abilities as parents is important. If these typical but serious emotions remain ignored, feedback and guidance will easily be received as critique and judgment.

Effective filial therapists also allow space for parents to have and discuss negative reactions. Negative reactions are an unparalleled opportunity for therapists to show empathy, unconditional positive regard, and provide emotional education (Sommers-Flanagan & Sommers-Flanagan, 2011).

When supervising parents, filial therapists rely on modeling play session skills and drawing parents' attention to when these skills appear in sessions with their child. Common coaching or supervision activities include: (a) helping parents identify what they did well, (b) giving voice to any questions or problems that have arisen, and (c) collaboratively exploring potential meanings of play themes (see Sidebar 15.3).

SIDEBAR 15.3 STAYING OUT OF THE WAY AND FOCUSING ON THE MEANING OF CHILDREN'S PLAY

Most practitioners agree that one of the gifts of child-directed play is that it provides a glimpse of children's emotional and psychological struggles. However, to clearly see and appreciate the struggles, parents have to keep their own reactions and issues in check.

We remember a 6-year-old who had her father pretend to be her little brother. She had them run away from home together to get away from their bossy parents who "forced" them to clean their rooms and didn't let them eat candy. During child-directed play, her father wanted to tell her how good she had it at home. Fortunately, he held back that judgment and just validated her perspective. This was essential because even though she had a positive home life, she was still struggling with cleaning up and eating healthy foods. By observing children in free play, you can see what issues they're trying to master.

Filial therapists also help parents generalize play session skills to daily parent–child situations. This may involve selecting a specific skill and assigning a homework task to incorporate it in parenting strategies throughout the week. Filial consultation sessions are also a place to review goals, check in on the child's daily behaviors, and discuss additional parenting skills and strategies.

Structuring the time and process of the FT experience requires presession preparation and organizational skills. Filial therapists need to decide in advance which FT treatment model is most appropriate for a given client. VanFleet has a 16-session model, Landreth and Bratton (2006) have a 10-session model, and Guerney and Ryan describe a 20-week group model. The phases associated with VanFleet's 16-session model are described in Sidebar 15.4.

SIDEBAR 15.4 FILIAL THERAPY PHASES

Filial Therapy (FT) typically includes the following phases (see Daneker & Hunter-Lee, 2006):

- Developmental and background information is gathered in an initial interview; parents are introduced to FT.
- An extended discussion with parent(s) about FT occurs.
- The filial therapist demonstrates child-centered play with parents observing (live or via video).
- Positive feedback, coaching, and encouragement are used to begin teaching parents the four FT skills: (1) structuring; (2) empathic listening; (3) nondirective, child-centered play; and (4) limit-setting.
- Under therapist supervision, parents engage in child-centered play with their child. Discussion and feedback follow.
- Parents practice child-centered play at home. Observations (live or video-based) and journaling are used to provide guidance and feedback.
- Maintenance and support sessions continue with the therapist.
- The therapist facilitates discussions of how FT skills can generalize beyond therapy.
- Follow-ups and booster sessions are provided.

All FT models follow a similar protocol. First, parents are introduced to the model during an initial interview. Second, therapists actively teach parents child-centered play therapy skills through didactic instruction, modeling, practice, feedback, and more practice. Following this training, therapists observe parents in play sessions with children for about four to six sessions (with each play session lasting about 30 minutes). These observation sessions include private consultation, feedback, and supervision. Next, play sessions transition to the home, where there's an even greater emphasis on generalizing filial skills to daily parent–child interactions (Topham & VanFleet, 2011). Some parents make videos of their home-based play sessions and later review them in consultation sessions with the therapist. This eliminates self-report bias and provides richer examples of play interactions between parent and child (VanFleet et al., 2005). Some filial play sessions even incorporate live bug-in-the-ear supervision strategies with the therapist giving immediate direction and encouragement to parents through an earpiece as they engage in a play session with their child.

Applications

FT is typically used with children 2 to 12 years old and their parents (VanFleet, 2005). Early research (e.g., Andronico & Guerney, 1967) found that trained parents develop skills for working with their children that are not discernible from therapist skills. Additionally, FT outcomes include increased maternal satisfaction with children and increased parental empathy for children (Bratton et al., 2005). Researchers have also reported that FT gains are maintained for up to 5 years after the therapy is complete (VanFleet et al., 2005).

Rennie and Landreth (2000) have compiled an extensive list of the various populations that have benefited from play therapy, including two-parent families, foster parents, single parents, incarcerated mothers, incarcerated fathers, parents of mentally challenged children, parents of chronically ill children, parents of children with conduct problems, parents of children with learning difficulties, and non-offending parents of sexually abused children. Van Fleet (2005) also noted that FT has been used with children of divorce, adoptive families, and children with attachment disruptions and disorders. For a more comprehensive list of specialized populations that can benefit from FT, *The Casebook of Filial Therapy* is an excellent resource (VanFleet & Guerney, 2003).

Multicultural Applications

Multicultural applications of FT are on the rise, and there is ample evidence that the core emphasis on healthy and strong family relationships is one that translates well across many ethnicities and environments (see Sidebar 15.5).

SIDEBAR 15.5 WHY FILIAL THERAPY IS A GOOD FIT FOR MULTICULTURAL CLIENTS

VanFleet (2005) described three reasons why FT is cross-culturally sensitive and useful:

1. All children play, given the opportunity to do so. The play emphasis in filial therapy transcends cultural differences to appeal to the innate language of children.
2. Parents, not therapists, are the primary recipients of the communication from children in filial play therapy. The insider view of parents is paramount as the means of interpreting children's play, not the

perspective of an "outsider" therapist who may lack cultural sensitivity and knowledge.

3. Therapists are in partnership with parents and genuinely respect and accept influence from parents. This partnership view of filial therapy is essential to ethnic understanding and provides an openness toward cultural education that other therapeutic approaches may lack.

There have been many reports of multicultural applications of FT. Two research-based examples are briefly summarized.

Jang (2000) reported on FT with Korean parents. Mothers were recruited to either an experimental group (in which mothers participated in an abridged 8-week version of FT training) or a control group (in which mothers received no FT training). Mothers who received FT training ranked higher in acceptance of their children and in encouragement of child self-direction than did nonparticipating mothers. Participating mothers were also more empathic and more involved with their children than nonparticipating mothers. Although these results were both significant and positive, mothers in the FT cohort reported that they continued to meet with one another even after the experiment ended. The educational approach of FT appeared to resonate with Korean cultural values. Learning through group interaction was enthusiastically accepted as a means for bringing more positivity into parent–child interactions.

In contrast, Glover and Landreth (2000) found that a 10-week FT intervention with Native American parents on the Flathead Reservation had mixed results. Again, parents were assigned to either a control group or an FT experimental group. There were modest gains for participating parents: They exhibited more empathy in interactions with their children and allowed their children more self-direction in play than nonparticipating parents. However, the increases in parents' positive behaviors in this study were not as robust as those from parents in many other FT interventions. Glover and Landreth (2000) attributed the less robust findings to low attendance at group play training sessions. It seems that although FT resonated well with the priorities of Native American parents, one cultural barrier to full efficacy may be the priority placed on attending meetings. Attendance was secondary to meeting immediate needs of friends or family members, and 30% of initial participants dropped out of the program. Glover and Landreth reported that lack of full participation in the 10-week session may at least partially explain the minimally positive treatment outcomes.

These two studies imply that FT has positive potential for family-oriented or collectivist cultural groups. However, practitioners who carry on this work may need to be especially open to shifting the intervention format to match specific cultural norms. Glover and Landreth (2000) suggested that perhaps shortening the number of sessions required or introducing food and a more social environment to the sessions might have increased parental attendance on the Flathead Reservation. In other cultures, different adaptations may be necessary to address social norms (e.g., expectations for personal space, for power distance, for preferred eye contact).

Limitations

FT limitations are related to specific client populations, logistics, and resistance.

Client Populations

FT has been used effectively for a variety of different problems and populations. However, it's not recommended as a treatment of choice for perpetrators of physical or sexual abuse and their children. In addition, some parents, perhaps because of religious or cultural perspectives, will flatly refuse to allow their child to direct anything within the family—including 30 minutes of play. Finally, some clients will prefer a different therapy approach. This may be due to a lack of faith in the power and potential of parent–child play or for other unspecified reasons.

Logistics

When engaging in play sessions at home, the family must designate a private space and time where parent and child can play without interruption (Landreth & Bratton, 2006). Parent consultation sessions require similar privacy. Navigating between these contexts and upholding firm boundaries pose logistical or practical challenges. Logistical questions to consider before engaging in FT include: Who will tend to the child(ren) during postplay parent consultations? How might consultation meetings be interpreted or misinterpreted by children? O'Connor (2000) discussed the possibility of children detecting a stronger alliance between the therapist and parents and believing the purpose of the meeting is to "tell on" the child. This perception may need to be addressed for FT to be successful.

When assisting parents in home-based play sessions, similar logistical questions must be considered: Where in your home can you establish a private and consistent play space? How will children respond to parents' special time with another child? Who will care for other children when a parent is engaged in a play session? It is recommended that therapists coconstruct solutions with parents before such challenges arise.

Resistance

Some parents may believe that an approach grounded in play cannot be effective. This skepticism ferments in the idea that play and work are two separate and different tasks (Topham & Wampler, 2008). Fred Rogers may have challenged this idea best, identifying play as the work of childhood. Therapists, then, must discuss and demonstrate the power and potential of therapeutic play. This often means explicitly describing how FT will specifically help the presenting problem.

Parents may also resist the filial process because it doesn't present a "quick fix" to presenting problems. Parents are often exhausted and look to therapists for swift solutions. When engaging parents, filial therapists should express empathy for their skepticism, while also being clear about FT's usual benefits. This involves answering the parents' often unasked question, "What's in it for me?" (VanFleet, 2000). As described in Sidebar 15.6, the answer to that question is "positive change."

SIDEBAR 15.6 ARTICULATING THE NATURE OF FILIAL THERAPY

Filial Therapy is a powerful family therapy technique. Rise VanFleet (2011) has written eloquently and succinctly about the nature and potential of Filial Therapy. She wrote:

> Filial Therapy is a form of family therapy. It is based on a psychoeducational model, not a medical model. . . . It harnesses the power of Play Therapy. It empowers children, parents, and families. It changes children. It changes parents. It changes the family. (p. 16)

What do you think of this Filial Therapy description? Do you think VanFleet captured its essence? What would you add or take away from this definition?

REFERENCES

Ackerman, N. W. (1970). Child participating in family therapy. *Family Process, 9*, 403–410.

Andronico, M. P., & Guerney, B. (1967). The potential application of filial therapy to the school situation. *Journal of School Psychology*, *6*(1), 2–7.

Axline, V. M. (1964). *Dibs in search of self.* New York, NY: Ballantine Books.

Box, G. E. P., & Draper, N. R. (1987). *Empirical model building and response surfaces.* New York, NY: Wiley.

Bratton, S. C., Ray, D., Rhine, T., & Jones, L. (2005). The efficacy of play therapy with children: A meta-analytic review of treatment outcomes. *Professional Psychology: Research and Practice*, *36*(4), 376–390. doi:10.1037/0735-7028.36.4.376

Capuzzi, D., & Gross, D. R. (2011). *Counseling and psychotherapy: Theories and interventions.* Alexandria, VA: American Counseling Association.

Clark, A. J. (2010). Empathy: An integral model in the counseling process. *Journal of Counseling & Development*, *88*, 348–356.

Cohen, J. (1977). *Statistical power analysis for the behavioral sciences* (Rev. ed.). Hillsdale, NJ: Erlbaum.

Daneker, D., & Hunter-Lee, B. (2006). Filial therapy: Culturally sensitive intervention for children and their parents. *Vistas Online*. Alexandria, VA: American Counseling Association.

Elliott, R., Bohart, A. C., Watson, J. C., & Greenberg, L. S. (2011). Empathy. *Psychotherapy*, *48*(1), 43–49. doi:10.1037/a0022187

Esman, A. H. (1983). Psychoanalytic play therapy. In C. E. Schafer & K. O'Conner (Eds.), *Handbook of play therapy* (pp. 11–20). New York, NY: Wiley.

Eyberg, S. (1988). Parent-child interaction therapy: Integration of traditional and behavioral concerns. *Child & Family Behavior Therapy*, *10*(1), 33–46.

Freud, A. (1928). *Introduction to the technique of child analysis*. New York, NY: Nervous Mental Disease Publishing.

Friedlander, M. L., Escudero, V., Heatherington, L., & Diamond, G. M. (2011). Alliance in couple and family therapy. In J. C. Norcross (Ed.), *Psychotherapy relationships that work: Evidence-based responsiveness* (2nd ed., pp. 92–109). New York, NY: Oxford University Press.

Gershoff, E. T. (2002). Corporal punishment by parents and associated child behaviors and experiences: A meta-analytic and theoretical review. *Psychological Bulletin*, *128*(4), 539–579.

Gershoff, E. T. (2008). *Report on physical punishment in the United States: What research tells us about its effects on children*. Columbus, OH: Center for Effective Discipline.

Gil, E. (1994). *Play in family therapy*. New York, NY: Guilford Press.

Glover, G. J., & Landreth, G. L. (2000). Filial therapy with Native Americans on the Flathead Reservation. *International Journal of Play Therapy*, *9*(2), 57–80. doi:10.1037/h0089436

Grif, M. D. (1983). Family play therapy. In C. E. Schafer & K. O'Conner (Eds.), *Handbook of play therapy* (pp. 65–75). New York, NY: Wiley.

Guerney, B. (1964). Filial therapy: Description and rationale. *Journal of Consulting Psychology*, *28*, 304–310.

Guerney, B., Guerney, L., & Andronico, M. (1999). Filial therapy. In C. Schafer (Ed.), *The therapeutic use of child's play* (pp. 553–566). Northvale, NJ: Jason Aronson.

Guerney, L. (2000). Filial therapy in the 21st century. *International Journal of Play Therapy*, *9*(2), 1–17.

Guerney, L., & Ryan, V. (2013). *Group filial therapy: The complete guide to teaching parents to play therapeutically with their children*. London, England: Jessica Kingsley.

Holcomb-McCoy, C., & Bryan, J. (2010). Advocacy and empowerment in parent consultation: Implications for theory and practice. *Journal of Counseling and Development*, *88*, 259–268.

Jang, M. (2000). Effectiveness of filial therapy for Korean parents. *International Journal of Play Therapy*, *9*(2), 39–56. doi:10.1037/h0089435

Klein, M. (1932). *The psychoanalysis of children*. London, England: Hogarth.

Lambert, M. J., & Shimokawa, K. (2011). Collecting client feedback. *Psychotherapy*, *48*(1), 72–79. doi:10.1037/a0022238

Landreth, G., & Bratton, S. (2006). *Child parent relationship therapy (CPRT): A 10-session filial therapy model*. New York, NY: Routledge.

Landreth, G. L. (2002). *Play therapy: The art of the relationship* (2nd ed.). New York, NY: Routledge.

Linehan, M. (1993). *Cognitive behavioral therapy of borderline personality disorder*. New York, NY: Guilford Press.

Murray, K. W., Sommers-Flanagan, J., & Sommers-Flanagan, R. (2012). Family systems theory and therapy. In J. Sommers-Flanagan & R. Sommers-Flanagan (Eds.), *Counseling and psychotherapy theories in context and practice: Skills, strategies, and techniques* (2nd ed., pp. 405–438). Hoboken, NJ: Wiley.

Nagera, H. (1980). Child psychoanalysis. In G. P. Sholevar, R. M. Benton, & B. J. Blinder (Eds.), *Emotional disorder in children and adolescents* (pp. 17–23). New York, NY: Spectrum.

Norcross, J. C., & Lambert, M. J. (2011). Psychotherapy relationships that work II. *Psychotherapy*, *48*(1), 4–8.

O'Connor, K. J. (2000). *The play therapy primer*. New York, NY: Wiley.

Rennie, R., & Landreth, G. (2000). Effects of filial therapy on parent and child behaviors. *International Journal of Play Therapy*, *9*(2), 19–37.

Rogers, C. R. (1957). The necessary and sufficient conditions of therapeutic personality change. *Journal of Consulting Psychology*, *21*, 95–103.

Safer, D. J. (1965). Conjoint play therapy for the young child and his parent. *Archives of General Psychiatry*, *13*(4), 320–326.

Satir, V. (1964). *Conjoint family therapy*. Palo Alto, CA: Science & Behavior Books.

Slagt, M., Deković, M., de Haan, A. D., van den Akker, A. L., & Prinzie, P. (2012). Longitudinal associations between mothers' and fathers' sense of competence and children's externalizing problems: The mediating role of parenting. *Developmental Psychology*, *48*(6), 1554–1562. doi:10.1037/a0027719

Sommers-Flanagan, J. (2007). Single-session consultations for parents: A preliminary investigation. *Family Journal*, *15*, 24–29.

Sommers-Flanagan, J., & Sommers-Flanagan, R. (2007). Our favorite tips for interviewing couples and families. *Psychiatric Clinics of North America*, *30*, 275–281.

Sommers-Flanagan, J., & Sommers-Flanagan, R. (2011). *How to listen so parents will talk and talk so parents will listen*. Hoboken, NJ: Wiley.

Sommers-Flanagan, J., & Sommers-Flanagan, R. (2012). *Counseling and psychotherapy theories in context and practice: Skills, strategies, and techniques* (2nd ed.). Hoboken, NJ: Wiley.

Topham, G. L., & VanFleet, R. (2011). Filial therapy: A structured and straightforward approach to including young children in family therapy. *Australian and New Zealand Journal of Family Therapy*, *32*(2), 144–158.

Topham, G. L., & Wampler, K. S. (2008). Predicting dropout in a filial therapy program for parents and young children. *American Journal of Family Therapy*, *36*, 60–78.

VanFleet, R. (2000). Understanding and overcoming parent resistance to play therapy. *International Journal of Play Therapy*, *1*(9), 35–46.

VanFleet, R. (2005). *Filial therapy: Strengthening parent-child relationships through play*. Sarasota, FL: Professional Resource Press.

VanFleet, R. (2011). *Filial therapy: Strengthening family relationships with the power of play*. In C. Schaefer (Ed.), *Foundations of play therapy* (2nd ed., pp. 153–169). Hoboken, NJ: Wiley.

VanFleet, R., & Guerney, L. (2003). *Casebook of filial therapy*. Boiling Springs, PA: Play Therapy Press.

VanFleet, R., Ryan, S. D., & Smith, S. K. (2005). Filial therapy: A critical review. In L. A. Reddy, T. M. Files-Hall, & C. E. Schaefer (Eds.), *Empirically-based play interventions for children*. Washington, DC: American Psychological Association.

Wickstrom, A. (2010). The development of an advanced filial therapy model. *International Journal of Play Therapy*, *19*(4), 187–197.

CHAPTER

16

Working With Addictions in Family Therapy

Pamela S. Lassiter, Astra B. Czerny, and Kimberly S. Williams

University of North Carolina at Charlotte

The impact of addiction on families can be devastating. Addiction tears apart the very core of family interaction and relationships, leaving members struggling with consequences that often seem too large to bear. Whether the addict in the family is a teenage child or an adult parent, the far-reaching and negative consequences of addictive behavior can impact the legal, financial, social, psychological, and emotional functioning of a family system. The common notion that fixing the addict will fix the problem not only unduly burdens the addicted individual, it also ignores the pervasive and destructive nature of the consequences of addictive behavior to all family members and loved ones. Children of an addicted parent are often left vulnerable as the addict is drawn increasingly away from the family; parents of an addicted teen struggle with protecting their child and minimizing harm while at the same time exercising a tough-love attitude. Either way, the family is impacted and struggles to find balance in spite of the growing storm of addiction that surrounds them.

Addiction can take many forms. While a large portion of the existing literature on addiction is devoted to substance abuse and misuse, an emerging area of study is behavioral or nonsubstance addiction, such as gambling or binge eating disorder. In this chapter, we focus on both substance use and behavioral types of addiction, their impact on family functioning, and the implications for treatment of individuals and their family members.

WHAT IS ADDICTION?

To understand addiction, one must begin with the reward circuitry of the brain. *Addiction* is defined as a "primary, chronic disease of brain reward, motivation, memory and related circuitry" (American Society of Addiction Medicine [ASAM], 2011). Motivation, brain reward circuitry, and memory are genetically conserved phenomena that are driven by our instinctual need for survival. When dependence on a drug or behavior takes over, the brain is essentially "hijacked" and disruption of the normal brain reward circuitry results. This dysfunction can result in biological, psychological, social, and spiritual manifestations.

Addiction is a progressive, chronic disease that cannot be cured and involves cycles of relapse and remission. Without treatment and intervention, addiction can result in disability and premature death. However, with appropriate treatment, structure, and support, including engagement in recovery activities, individuals struggling with addiction can achieve remission and lead fully functional and healthy lives.

PREVALENCE OF ADDICTION IN FAMILIES

Statistics regarding the prevalence of addiction in families are often specific to a single substance. For example, it is estimated that approximately 1 out of every 4 children in the United States is exposed to either alcohol abuse or dependence in a family member (Grant, 2000). While estimates may be hard to make on a global scale, some researchers conservatively calculate that as many as 90 to 100 million adult family members worldwide are affected by some form of substance misuse or abuse (Copello, Templeton, & Powell, 2010; Orford, Velleman, Natera, Templeton, & Copello, 2013). This estimate does not take children into consideration, nor does it account for nonsubstance or behavioral addictions.

The negative effects of alcohol and other drug problems on families are well documented (Casswell, You, & Huckle, 2011; Copello et al., 2010; Ray, Mertens, & Weisner, 2009; Schaefer, 2011). Ray et al. (2009) compared family members of individuals with alcohol and other drug dependent (AODD) problems to family members of individuals with asthma, diabetes, and a control group. The researchers found that family members of individuals with AODD problems were more likely to be diagnosed with depression, substance use disorders, and trauma than family members of individuals with asthma, diabetes, or a control group.

The National Institute of Health estimated that in 2012, 59.6% of women and 71.8% of men had at least one drink and, of those who chose to drink, 28.8% of women and 43.1% of men qualified as binge drinkers (consuming four or more drinks for women and five or more for men in a 2-hour period). The impact on families can be calculated in terms of direct cost, such as the cost of purchasing the substance of choice; indirect costs, such as lost wages due to absenteeism at work; and psychological costs, which may be harder to measure but can include the impact on the mental health of family members (Copello et al., 2010).

IMPACT OF ADDICTION

The existing research that addresses the impact of addiction on family members is small. What research does exist often focuses on the experience of the parents—specifically the mother—and tends to ignore or diminish the role of other family members (Orford et al., 2013). In spite of this, one research team led by Orford, Velleman, and Copello from the United Kingdom gathered 20 years of data on the impact of drug and alcohol addiction on family members. In a summary of their findings, these researchers describe the stressful and negative consequences of living with an addict (Orford, Velleman, Copello, Templeton, & Ibanga, 2010), namely, that the relationship with the relative becomes disagreeable and sometimes aggressive, that conflict over money or possessions often erupts, that family members experience uncertainty and worry about their relative, and that home and family life are often threatened. In addition, these researchers found that social support for family members is often lacking.

While research has shown that addiction can have a negative effect on the functioning of couples and families, the alternative is also true. The quality of marital and family relationships can impact a person's drinking in positive or negative ways, depending on whether the relationship functions in a healthy or an unhealthy manner (Velleman, 2006). While interventions for addicts remain largely individualist in their approach, the fact that families are affected demands that we broaden our approach to substance abuse intervention to include family members and significant others involved with the addict, not just because of the stressful nature of living with a relative's addiction, but because the very nature of the family dynamic can help or hinder treatment outcome.

SUBSTANCE ABUSE VERSUS NONSUBSTANCE ADDICTIONS

Recently, there has been an increase in the literature that addresses nonsubstance or nondrug addiction, often called *behavior addiction* or *process addiction* (Grant, Potenza, Weinstein, & Gorelick, 2010; Karim & Chaudhri, 2012; Smith, 2012). A behavior that becomes repetitive, that can't be stopped, and that ultimately results in feelings of euphoria or a decrease in anxiety can be defined as a process addiction.

In 2011, the American Society of Addiction Medicine revised their definition of addiction to include two new areas: (1) the prescription drug problem and (2) process or behavior addiction (Smith, 2012). Examples of process addictions include gambling, sex, shopping, Internet or video games, work, and food or binge eating. The *DSM-5* (American Psychiatric Association [APA], 2013) now includes pathological gambling under the new category of "Addiction and Related Disorders."

Prior to the publication of the *DSM-5*, researchers and experts, including the International Association of Addictions and Offender Counselors (IAAOC) Committee on Process Addictions, advocated for the inclusion of a new diagnosis, namely, addictive disorders (Hagedorn, 2009). They argued that behavior addictions manifest in similar ways as chemical addictions and that they should be diagnosed and treated in similar ways. However, in spite of the increase in literature addressing the problem of process addictions, the *DSM-5* (APA, 2013) only includes pathological gambling under the new category of "Addiction and Related

Disorders." The debate on whether process addictions can be treated similarly to chemical addictions continues. The fact is, if you are working in the field of addictions counseling, you can expect to see clients with process addictions.

Hagedorn (2009) states that the number of treatment facilities for process addictions is inadequate and underserves the existing need. The number of individuals estimated to struggle with behavior addictions is staggering. For example, Hagedorn estimates that there is one treatment center for every 227,000 individuals struggling with an eating disorder, one facility for every 250,000 individuals struggling with pathological gambling, and one facility for every 1.08 million individuals with sexual addiction.

In addition, it is not uncommon to work with individuals who are struggling with comorbid addictions (polysubstance or a combination of chemical and behavior addiction), individuals who are in recovery from one addiction and who have replaced it with another addiction (for example, someone who quits drinking and begins eating excessively), or family members of chemically addicted individuals who are struggling with process addictions. Knowing how to properly assess process addictions is critical. Not all behaviors that are repetitive qualify as an addiction. For example, a lot of people participate in gambling; however, not all are pathologically addicted to it. According to Goodman (2001), a behavior can be defined as an addiction according to the following definition:

> A behavior that can function both to produce pleasure and to reduce painful affects is employed in a pattern that is characterized by two key features: (1) recurrent failure to control the behavior, and (2) continuation of the behavior despite substantial harmful consequences. (p. 195)

Hagedorn (2009) offers a possible diagnostic criteria for behavioral addictive disorders that includes the manifestation of three or more of the following: tolerance; withdrawal; increased activity over time; unsuccessful efforts to cut down the behavior; a significant amount of time spent on the behavior; other social, occupational, or recreational activities are given up or reduced; and continuing the behavior despite negative effects that are caused by or exacerbated by the behavior.

The inclusion of gambling in the *DSM-5* (APA, 2013) will serve to continue the research and examination of behavior addictions as a subset of broader addictive behaviors. Counselors are well served to be aware of the symptoms and to hone their abilities to properly assess process addictions in addition to chemical addictions.

BIOPSYCHOSOCIAL EPISTEMOLOGY OF ADDICTION

There are many theoretical models that attempt to describe and understand what causes and maintains addiction. Although no one theory completely answers these complex questions, it is important for the counselor to understand his or her own theory of addiction because that theoretical base will ultimately determine what treatment approach is prescribed. For example, the moral model assumes that addicted individuals are choosing to be addicted to an extent that violates cultural norms. From this perspective, they are perceived as irresponsible, evil, wrong, transgressors, and their misbehavior must be punished. Users are not out of control, but are deliberately using drugs and thereby causing purposeful suffering for others. This directly impacts treatment approaches. From this model, the addict can be justifiably blamed and punished, and the prescription for healing involves a return to "traditional" or "family" values. Most approaches to addiction treatment no longer solely subscribe to the moral model, but instead incorporate biological, sociological, and psychological models of addiction epistemology.

Although biological factors such as the brain reward circuitry and genetic predisposition contribute to addiction, they are not alone in creating addictive behaviors. Psychological, sociological, and cultural factors play major roles as well. Such a biopsychosocial view of addictive behaviors allows us to view the addict in a more holistic, person-centered way, while at the same time acknowledging that multiple factors influence an individual's susceptibility to addiction. Preexisting conditions, such as depression, learning style and ability, learned coping behaviors, and family dynamics, play important roles in the development of addictive disorders. It is important that family counselors not take an overly simplistic view of the nature of addiction. One's theory of addictive behavior will directly connect to the treatment a counselor prescribes for the disorder.

SIDEBAR 16.1

John is a 25-year-old White male counselor working at a local addiction treatment and recovery center. John has been assigned a new client, Janelle. Janelle is a 60-year-old African American woman who has been referred to counseling for issues related to her abuse of prescription painkillers. Janelle states that she had knee replacement surgery several years ago and was prescribed oxycodone to help her with the pain. Janelle states that the physician continued to refill her prescription long after her knee had healed. As John speaks with Janelle, he learns that her oldest son recently died in a car accident. Janelle is emotional and appears distraught when she talks about her son. Janelle lives alone and has the support of her friends and family, especially those from her church. However, Janelle seems embarrassed about her drug use and has not disclosed this to anyone. John is not sure how best to help Janelle, especially given the difference in age, race, and gender. As you consider how John can best help Janelle, answer the following questions:

- Why do people start using substances?
- Why do people continue to use substances?
- How do you personally think about addiction?
- What does the word *addiction* mean to you?
- What does treatment have to do with how addiction is perceived?

There are numerous sociological and cultural factors that underlie and contribute to addictive behavior. Cultural considerations can include the way in which alcohol and/or drug consumption has changed over time according to the mores and values of specific groups of individuals. For example, Americans in the 19th century drank 3 times more alcohol per capita than they do today (Heath, 1988), partially due to a lack of safe drinking water. Improvements in water treatment and research on the negative effects of alcohol have helped to change our attitudes regarding excessive drinking. For more information about the history of drinking in America and the social consequences of prohibition, see Ken Burns's documentary entitled *Prohibition* (Burns & Novick, 2011). In addition, the way in which excessive drinking is now seen as a disease versus a moral choice or deviant behavior gives credence to the medical community and to the ability of physicians and mental health professionals to help individuals suffering with addiction.

It is important for the counselor to consider cultural issues for the families they work with in treatment, both in terms of underlying or antecedent factors and in terms of treatment issues. For example, for some cultures anomic depression resulting from historical, racial, or ethnic oppression may be a part of the epistemology of addiction. Gay and lesbian families may have addictions that have been impacted by discrimination and struggles with issues of internalized homonegativity (Singh & Lassiter, 2012). Families with aging parents who may have an addiction problem may be confused about the symptoms of aging and how they mimic the symptoms of addiction (Briggs, Magnus, Lassiter, Patterson, & Smith, 2011). These adult children may be reticent to confront an elderly parent at the end stages of life. Women who are addicted may struggle with internalized shame related to trauma histories or simply use substances to cope with gender role expectations and stress related to multiple roles. It is also important for family counselors to be aware of varying definitions of *family*. For example, Native American families and Latino families may include multiple extended family members who are crucial to understanding the context of addiction and recovery. Lesbian and gay families may include "chosen family" members.

SIDEBAR 16.2

Maria is a 39-year-old single mother who has brought her 15-year-old son in for counseling. Maria is Hispanic but speaks English well enough to be able to communicate. Maria has caught her son, Jose, drinking on several occasions since the death of her husband (Jose's father) 1 year ago. Maria reports that she has two other children at home, a 12-year-old daughter and a 9-year-old son. Maria states that in addition to catching Jose drinking, she has noticed that he is less talkative and that he doesn't seem as eager to hang out with his friends anymore. Maria has a large extended family, and she states that they have also noticed a change in Jose. Maria is worried because she relies on Jose to help her with her younger children since the death of her husband. She has noticed that Jose is more argumentative with her and less willing to help. Maria works as a night manager at a large local hotel. She is worried about leaving Jose alone at night with the responsibility of watching his siblings.

- What underlying sociocultural factors might influence or contribute to addiction for this family?
- How would these cultural factors influence how you would proceed with treatment for Maria, Jose, and their family?

The consumption of alcohol and drugs also serves several sociological functions (Thombs, 2006). For example, alcohol and drugs facilitate social interaction and enhance social bonds by minimizing interpersonal barriers and increasing communication between individuals. They provide a release from everyday responsibilities and social obligations. In addition, the consumption of (or abstinence from) alcohol and other drugs provides opportunities for social or ethnic groups to become more cohesive, increasing identification to the group between members. Finally, for some, the consumption of alcohol and other drugs can be a way of repudiating the values and ideals of the establishment majority. These sociological aspects of drinking can be especially pronounced in adolescents and include social facilitation, stress control, defiance, peer acceptance, and parental control (Thombs & Beck, 1994).

Wurmser (1982) delineates the complexity of the psychological aspect of addiction by describing a primary and secondary view of the addict's behavior. The primary, or surface, view is that of the addiction itself: "The compulsive use of some mind-altering substance and its medical and psychological sequels" (p. 33). The main task here is to end the misuse of the substance. The secondary view sees the substance abuse as a symptom of a much deeper problem of considerable complexity. This deeper problem has to do with the addict's immediate environment, as well as with conscious and unconscious cognitions, affect, and personality. According to Wurmser, it is insufficient to treat either of these views alone. Treating the addiction without addressing the deeper, unconscious layers may result in success in the immediate moment, but generally not in long-lasting recovery. Treating the person without addressing the problem of addiction will not result in satisfactory treatment either. Thus, the trick in working successfully with addicted individuals is to manage both forms of treatment simultaneously.

USING FAMILY THERAPY AS A TREATMENT MODALITY

Empirical evidence supports the use of marriage and family therapy as a successful treatment for addiction. A meta-analysis of 38 controlled studies by O'Farrell and Fals-Stewart (2003) showed that marital and family therapy (MFT) is effective in helping families cope better and in encouraging addicts who are resistant to enter treatment. A follow-up study by O'Farrell and Clements (2012) goes even further to conclude that MFT is an effective intervention, and specifically that Al-Anon and spouse coping skills training help family members cope better. Community reinforcement and family training (CRAFT) was also shown to promote treatment entry for resistant addicts and was successfully implemented in community settings as opposed to clinical research settings. CRAFT is a behavior therapy approach that utilizes positive reinforcement and natural consequences to help get treatment-resistant addicted family members engaged in treatment. CRAFT is evidence based and has a success rate of about 70% (Meyers, Smith, & Lash, 2005). CRAFT has also been shown to be an effective treatment regardless of family ethnicity, specific substance (alcohol or other drugs), or family relationship (spouses or parents). MFT, specifically behavioral couples therapy (BCT), was also shown to be superior in increasing abstinence and improving couples' relationship functioning compared to individual therapy alone.

FAMILY DYNAMICS AND ADDICTION

It is important to understand the effects addiction may have on the dynamics of the family system as a whole, the adaptive roles family members may take to cope with the addiction, and some common terms that may be used to describe relational tendencies in addicted families. While many dynamics may be common to other families, there are some unique patterns in addicted families that may be useful in helping families create change within the system.

Roles

The severe stress brought on by a family member's addictive behaviors works to undermine the roles that family members normally play within the family structure. Alternate roles may be assumed by spouses and children in an attempt to survive the chaos and negative effects of life with an alcoholic parent. Such alternate roles, which are necessary for survival in childhood for children of alcoholics (COAs), can cause problematic behaviors for COAs as adults. Wegscheider (1981) defined five roles that family members often assume in homes with an alcohol-dependent parent: enabler, hero, lost child, mascot, and scapegoat. According to Wegscheider, family members not only experience the negative effects of the alcoholic's behavior but also play a role in maintaining that behavior in an attempt to maintain homeostasis, or equilibrium, in the family. The role of enabler most often describes the spouse of the alcohol-dependent parent. The function of the enabler is to protect the substance-abusing spouse from the negative consequences of his or her actions. While to the observer it may at first seem that the enabler is doing everything possible to stop the spouse's drinking, the result is that the enabler's actions actually promote errant behavior by assuming additional roles (making excuses to friends and employers, driving the spouse when the spouse is incapacitated, etc.) and preventing the spouse from experiencing the consequences of their drinking. The hero child is often the oldest child in the family, who in many ways assumes a "parentified" role in taking care of the family's needs. The hero is accomplished in ways that are pleasing to the family and seeks external validation and general approval of his or her behavior. The lost child, on the other hand, has the job of remaining small and unnoticed by the family, forgoing his or her wants and needs so that the family's energy can remain focused on the addict. The mascot child is the comic relief of the family and often uses humor as a way to ease the tension. Often the mascot is the youngest child in the family and, similar to the lost child, can minimize his or her needs through humor, jokes, and antics. The scapegoat often acts in ways that are the exact opposite of the hero child, but with the similar result of pulling attention away from the family problem. The scapegoat can display maladaptive behaviors that can resemble those of the drinking parent. The scapegoat is often in trouble and provides a distraction for the family members as an alternative to dealing with the drinking parent. The scapegoat is often characterized as angry, as opposed to other members of the family, who tend to keep their emotions internalized.

Similar to Wegscheider's (1981) model of family dynamics, Black (1981) also conceptualized an alternative and similar system for classifying the behavior of family members when an alcoholic parent is present. Black uses the term codependent to describe the alcoholic's spouse and four subsequent child roles: the responsible child as the child who assumes additional roles for the alcoholic parent and family, the adjuster child who changes or adjusts to fit the needs of the family, the placater child who is often more emotional and attempts to diffuse family tension, and the acting out child as the family member who displays the negative behaviors that are often modeled by the parent.

Wegscheider (1981) and Black (1981) conceptualized two models of family survival that specifically relate to a family with an alcoholic parent. It is important to note that these roles should not be seen as rigid or predetermined, and that family members may adopt one or more roles depending on the situation and level of family dysfunction (or function) at any point in time. Vernig (2011) reviewed the difficulties resulting from attempts to operationalize the roles. His conclusion is that the roles are not sufficiently supported by empirical evidence and that attempts to create measures for the roles, which would be needed for further research, have been fraught with poorly designed questionnaires and weak supporting evidence. Finally, the roles have not been studied in families of diverse ethnic and cultural backgrounds or in families that do not meet a traditional, two-parent, heterosexual structure. The strength of Wegscheider's (1981) and Black's (1981) work is in providing a conceptual model for understanding how families might shift roles in order to maintain balance in the wake of a loved one's addiction.

Codependency

Early definitions of the term *codependency* generally addressed a woman's behavior toward her alcoholic husband. The term has been used synonymously with the term *enabling*, in which an individual unintentionally reinforces an undesired behavior (such as drinking) in another person (Whitfield, 1984). The definition of codependency has included the manifestation of issues related to interpersonal boundaries, enmeshed relationships, and a willingness to sacrifice one's own needs in order to meet the needs of another (Cermak, 1986). However, similar to the roles of family functioning for children of adult alcoholics, the term has not been operationalized, and attempts to measure the construct have been rife with difficulties (Stafford, 2001).

Because the term *codependency* has gained popularity in professional and self-help literature and in 12-step meeting (Alcoholics Anonymous, Al-Anon) circles, it has come under scrutiny as a meaningful concept for helping professionals. Stafford (2001) poses four questions that should be kept in mind when using the term:

1. Is the term useful for the distress, low self-esteem, and negative effects that individuals often experience?
2. Could the concept be arbitrary in that it describes a grouping of symptoms that many individuals who have unresolved family of origin issues might experience?
3. Is it ethical to encourage an individual to accept the label "codependent" and seek treatment for the "disease"?
4. Does it make sense to conduct research on treatment interventions for a construct that has yet to be operationalized?

Circular Dynamics (Causality)

Circular causality in family systems theory refers to the reciprocal nature of family interaction and is emphasized over linear causality. Relationships and interactions between and among members of the system include circular feedback loops. Feedback loops are a way to describe the complex nature of family or system interaction; certain behaviors become stimuli that cause other new behaviors to occur. Or, to view it another way, a family member's behavior affects other family members, which can in turn affect the individual. The circular dynamic can seem self-promoting. For example, a wife nags at her husband to stop drinking, and the stress from the nagging causes the husband to drink more. These cycles can be functional or dysfunctional in that they can either help or hinder the family interaction. The previous example is one that hinders family interaction. However, if the wife from the previous example started attending Al-Anon meetings, thereby addressing her own enabling behaviors, she might find that the husband is more likely to consider joining AA and working toward sobriety.

Circular dynamics in family interaction draw attention away from the individual and put it on the functioning of the system and on repeating patterns of behavior. They also put the burden of blame for bad behavior on the system, rather than on any one individual in the family. Thus, each family member contributes to the behavior of other family members, and no single individual, not even the addict, carries the sole burden of blame.

Homeostasis and Addicted Families

Homeostasis refers to the system's need to find balance and stability in the face of change. Viewing family functioning from a systems perspective means that the system itself becomes an entity that is worthy of analysis. That is to say that in the same way an individual seeks balance after developmental growth or change, a system seeks stability so that members can continue to function in predictable ways. Given this definition, it is possible to see even addiction as a behavior that seeks to maintain family balance. If the drinking, gambling, or addictive behavior were to change, then the family would be thrown out of balance and all members would be affected and forced to change as well. It is possible that, given such a scenario, one or more family members might try to sabotage efforts to seek recovery in an attempt to maintain a predictable and familiar stability.

Homeostasis is an important concept to understand when working with addicts and their families. Families need and seek out balance in order to remain stable, even if that stability is dysfunctional or unhealthy. Family members will put up with a certain level of discomfort in order to avoid the upheaval, distress, and chaos that change might bring. Often the addiction serves an important function in the family, such as masking deeper, more personal issues between family members. Addiction can mask marital problems and divert attention away from unexpressed emotions. Recovery from addiction may mean that family members need to address issues that have long been ignored or denied. In functional families, change is incorporated easily into the family system that allows all members to get their needs met. However, in dysfunctional families, change is often met with rigid resistance, and members may find that their needs go unmet. The tendencies toward homeostasis and resistance to change are not static, however, and families can learn to adapt with the help of therapy and family counseling. The challenge, however, is to get the family to agree that change is necessary in order to reach a more satisfactory level of functioning for all family members.

RECRUITMENT OF ADDICTED FAMILIES

Addicted families are often weary of dealing with the consequences of substance abuse in the family system. Many have made multiple attempts to help the addicted family member and many times have suffered personally from the consequences of addiction. They may also see the addicted person through a moral model lens, feeling as though the person should be able to stop using if he or she really wants to and viewing the addictive behavior as intentionally hurtful or mean. Another reason family members might be reluctant to participate in family therapy may be that they themselves are addicted and either in denial or trying to hide their problem. If the identified client gets help, then this person may feel that he or she will also have to get help, or at least stop using. Other family members may be reluctant to come because they feel they might be blamed for the person's addiction or they feel they don't need to change, only the addict needs to change. For these and many other reasons, it may be very difficult to engage families in the treatment process.

Thoughtful recruitment strategies are necessary to help engage as many family members as possible early on in the treatment process. The most important recruitment tool is the counselor. The counselor must believe in family systems work with addicted families. The counselor must believe that he or she cannot be the only person in the therapy room with the client who wants the addict to get help. Because the counselor does not have the history, connection, or rapport with the client that loving family members have, the external motivation and support to become clean and sober will not be there. If the counselor is hesitant in any way to work with the client's family (out of fear, lack of appropriate training, or confidence), the family will not likely engage in treatment, and crucial resources and support may be lost. In cases where there are no family members available to recruit, counselors may be able to find others in the person's life with strong connections to them, such as social service workers, sober peers at work, even probation officers and homeless shelter personnel. Anyone who seems to be emotionally invested in the person's recovery will help.

It is important for the counselor to pay attention to who in the addict's system may have the power and ability to get the person the help they need. Who called for the initial appointment? Who called the emergency help line or who brought them to the initial appointment? This person may be a key motivator for change and may carry the power in the system to recruit other members for help with the addiction. It is likely that if this person had the initial concern and power to get the addicted person to the first session, they might be a key person for whom the client might begin the hard work of recovery.

In some cases, the person identified by the family as the patient may in fact be a "paper tiger" of sorts. For example, a family may come to a counselor out of concern for a child's acting out behavior or even experimentation with substance use. The child's behavior may be an unconscious attempt to get an addicted parent help for their addiction. Through this sacrificial act, the child can at least get the family to a therapist and create hope for change. It is important in these situations for the counselor not to move the focus on to the parent's addiction problem too soon or they may risk losing the family. Timing is crucial after appropriate rapport has been developed and after a thorough assessment of the child's behavior has been conducted. In this situation, the first goal would be to help the parents understand the meaning of the child's behavior.

ASSESSMENT STRATEGIES

Assessment is a crucial core function for addictions counseling and has been defined as "procedures by which a counselor/program identifies and evaluates an individual's strengths, weaknesses, problems and needs for the development of a treatment plan" (ICRC, 1998, pp. 17–18). Along with this definition of addiction assessment are the minimal competency criteria (known as *global criteria*) through which the counselor should approach the assessment process. The global competency for assessment is to:

- Gather relevant history from the client using AODD abuse–appropriate interview techniques.
- Identify methods and procedures for obtaining corroborative information from significant secondary sources regarding clients' AODD abuse and psychosocial history.
- Identify appropriate assessment tools.
- Explain to the client the rationale for the use of assessment techniques in order to facilitate understanding.
- Develop a diagnostic evaluation of the client's substance abuse and any coexisting conditions based on the results of all assessments in order to provide an integrated approach to treatment planning based on the client's strengths, weaknesses, and identified problems and needs. (ICRC, 1998, pp. 17–18)

There are several sources of information for an adequate substance abuse assessment, including assessment interviews with the client and significant others, behavioral observations of the client, physiological instruments (i.e., blood tests, breathalyzers, urine screens), and psychometric instruments focused on addiction (e.g., CAGE, MAST, AUDIT). Please visit the following website to access a database of free screening tools for use with addicted clients: http://www.ncbi.nlm.nih.gov/books/NBK64190

ASSESSMENT AND INITIAL INTERVIEWS

In addition to understanding basic knowledge about addiction, every counselor should know and understand simple evaluation tools that will help assess whether the individual of concern is addicted or at risk for addiction. One of the simplest to use is an instrument called the CAGE (Ewing, 1984), which is an acronym that articulates the four items in the instrument. The C is for *cut down*, the A is for *annoyed*, the G is for *guilty*, and the E is for *eye opener*. An answer of yes to two or more of the following questions indicates the person may have an addiction problem. The questions of the instrument are as follows (Ewing, 1984):

- Have you ever felt you ought to cut down on your drinking?
- Have people annoyed you by criticizing your drinking?
- Have you ever felt bad or guilty about your drinking?
- Have you ever had a drink first thing in the morning (eye opener) to steady your nerves or get rid of a hangover?

Other instruments to consider include the Alcohol Use Disorders Identification Test (AUDIT) (Hodgson et al., 2003) and the Michigan Alcohol Screening Test (MAST) (Selzer, 1971). Please see the resource list at the end of this chapter for more information on screening and assessment tools for substance abuse problems.

SIDEBAR 16.3

Things to remember when conducting an assessment:

- Treat clients with respect.
- Empathize.
- Engage and empower.
- Balance need for accurate info with developing a therapeutic alliance.
- Build trust and rapport.
- Demystify the process.
- Find out who is suffering most in the system.
- Point out hope.

JOINING WITH ADDICTED FAMILIES

Joining with a family begins with the first phone contact and is especially important during the first session. How you conduct the first session sets a tone for that connection, and with an addicted family, that is important for many reasons. Good rapport helps increase the accuracy/trustworthiness of the information you gain about the problem and may ensure engagement of the family for the long haul. Joining and rapport may also increase motivation for sobriety and ultimately help young people with the consequences of addiction in the family. Because shame and guilt are such a large part of addiction, treating all family members with respect is crucial to gaining their confidence in the process.

A therapist "joins" with a family by creating a therapeutic relationship that feels welcoming and unthreatening. This can be done by employing numerous techniques. Some of these are using active listening skills, matching the family's mood or tone, communicating understanding, using their words to describe issues and concerns, supporting individual and family strengths, challenging without judgment the family's view of themselves and the situation, and giving the family hope for change. Joining is a technique that is used consistently throughout the therapeutic relationship. It is important to remember that many addicted individuals are mandated or forced into treatment and as such may feel angry about being confronted regarding their addiction. The therapist must take an understanding stance of the overwhelming emotion and chaos that motivates a family to seek help. This is an important part of the joining process. Edwards (1990) stated that "joining is to therapy as staying on key is to singing—it's a vital part of the activity, not a technique to be used at certain times" (p. 94). The necessary confrontation and challenging of client behaviors cannot occur successfully until the therapist has adequately joined with the identified client and family members.

SEGMENTING

At times, it might be necessary to segment out certain family members for specific reasons. Some of these reasons might include the need for further information about the impact of the addiction problem on family members, the need to do a thorough substance abuse/use assessment, or as a strategy for application of particular interventions. There should always be a good reason for the segmenting of family members. When children are seen separately from their parents, it should always be done with the permission of the parents and with a clear contract with the family about what happens if secret-sharing occurs. For example, a counselor may choose to segment out children in an addicted family who might share information about ongoing neglect or abuse.

Before the segmenting occurs, the clinician should explain the purpose, gain the parent's permission to visit with the children alone, and go over informed consent and the limits of confidentiality again, as well as explain to the family that what is shared in private segmented sessions is open for all in the family to hear. Of course, great caution should be taken in all cases in which abuse or endangerment is possible. If abuse or neglect is reported, it is recommended that the clinician work with the family in a way that is safe, empowering, and that if at all possible maintains the therapeutic relationship. In some cases in which abuse or neglect is present, the family can be supported in collaborating with social services to ensure safety for all vulnerable family members so that change can occur. In cases in which substance use is ongoing in a family's environment and there is a history or potential for abuse or neglect, extreme caution should be taken to not put those vulnerable at greater risk by participation in family therapy. The family counselor should always operate under the rule "safety first."

STAGES OF CHANGE

It is important to consider the stages of change (Prochaska, DiClemente, & Norcross, 1992) when conceptualizing working with an addicted family. The stages of change model encourages us to view change not as an event, but rather a decisional and behavioral process. When they present for treatment, clients can range from those who have never considered changing to those who have already made significant changes. The contribution of this model is that different strategies may need to be employed for different stages of change. The stages of change are: precontemplation, contemplation, preparation, action, maintenance, termination. In the precontemplation stage, the addicted person has no intention of changing his or her behavior. The person has relatively low awareness that there is a problem although others in his or her life may have some awareness that a problem exists. Resistance is at the core of this stage. During the contemplation stage, the client is aware there is a problem and is thinking seriously about changing. He or she is beginning to weigh the pros and cons of changing and evaluating the cost of change. (What will I lose if I change? What will I gain? Is it worth the effort?) Ambivalence is at the core of this stage. At the preparation stage, the addicted person has accepted that change needs to occur and is considering how best to approach it. In some cases he or she has tried but failed within the past year because there was not enough action. During the action phase, the client has begun to put a plan in place and he or she is putting time, energy and effort into changing. In the maintenance phase, the client has developed new behaviors and is able to maintain them for at least 6 months. Because relapse is a part of the recovery process, the client may need to cycle through the stages many times before lasting recovery is maintained.

Assessing readiness for change of a family or addicted family member will help the counselor determine how to approach the family and where to begin in attempting to help the family along in the readiness-for-change process. Different family members might be at different levels of readiness for change. Typically, nonaddicted family members in an addicted system are very ready for the identified patient to change, but are very resistant to change themselves. Therefore, it is important for the clinician to develop strategies to encourage change for all family members and to work with each of them from where they are in the stages of change process.

MOTIVATIONAL INTERVIEWING

Motivational interviewing techniques can be helpful in encouraging and promoting the change process. Motivational interviewing is a directive, client-centered counseling style for eliciting behavior change by helping clients to explore and resolve ambivalence (Miller & Rollnick, 1991). It works well with substance abusers and their families because there is such ambivalence around change. The spirit of motivational interviewing is as follows (Miller & Rollnick, 2002):

- Motivation to change is elicited from the client.
- It is the client's task, not the counselor's, to articulate and resolve his or her ambivalence.
- Direct persuasion is not an effective method for resolving ambivalence.
- The counseling style is generally a quiet and eliciting one.

Use of these strategies from the very beginning of the counseling relationship can enhance motivation for change, encourage joining and rapport building, and encourage resistant family members to more fully engage in the change process.

During the initial phases of treatment, counselors should be assessing sources of motivation for change within the system. It is sometimes helpful to find out from the family who is suffering the most from the person's addiction. The addict usually is the best source for this information, but typically all family members can quickly answer this question. The person who is suffering the most is usually the most invested person in the addict's recovery and can be the linchpin to help motivate the family toward change.

FAMILY INTERVENTIONS PROTOCOLS

Family intervention protocols were originally developed by The Johnson Institute (Faber & Keating-O'Connor, 1991) and involved an orchestrated coercion of the addicted person into treatment by the family under the guidance of a therapist. Research on Johnson-method interventions has found that only 22% of concerned significant others were successful in getting their addicted family member into treatment using this approach (Miller, Meyers, & Tonigan, 1999). Other methods, such as community reinforcement and family training (CRAFT), unilateral family therapy (UFT), and behavioral couples therapy (BFT) have shown better results in getting addicted family members to enter treatment. (For a complete evaluation of the current marriage and family therapies available, see O'Farrell & Fals-Stewart, 2003.) Many clinicians continue to implement family interventions to encourage clients to go into treatment. Training in the intervention protocol is crucial, and great planning must be carried out ahead of time.

FAMILY EDUCATION PROGRAMS

Most treatment programs for substance abuse issues have a family education component. Family education often includes structured group sessions that provide psycho-educational experiences for family members to help encourage awareness and change in the system while the addicted individual seeks treatment for the substance use. Family members are taught about addiction as a disease, the impact of the disease on both the addict and on the family system, the roles family members may be playing in the addiction, and how important it is for family members to change along with the addicted person. For many families, the family education component helps normalize their feelings about the addict and provides a great deal of support for them to move forward in recovery as a unit. The addict may be included or excluded from all or part of the family education experience. Some treatment programs culminate the family education component with single-unit family therapy or with a multiple family therapy group experience.

GOALS FOR THERAPY WITH ADDICTED FAMILIES

Edwards (1990) outlines five goals for using a systems approach to working with addicted families:

1. To increase motivation for recovery
2. To convey the whole-family message
3. To change family patterns that work against recovery
4. To prepare the family for what to expect in early recovery
5. To encourage family members' own long-term support

In the following section, each of these goals is discussed, along with examples of techniques that might be used with families to accomplish the goal.

Increasing Motivation for Recovery: Addiction as Emergency

Because denial is such a strong part of addiction, families will unconsciously conspire to ignore the problem, even in the face of dire consequences such as legal problems, loss of jobs, child neglect and abuse, dangerous and risky behavior, and serious health issues. The system operates under strong covert rules that keep individual family members from talking about the proverbial "elephant in the room." Motivation for change for most of us usually comes when the pain of staying the same is greater than the pain of changing. This assumes, of course, that family members can connect the emotional pain or discomfort they feel with the addiction present in the system. Family therapy can help them make that connection (Edwards, 1998). Despite the struggle created by the addiction, family members will tend to be more comfortable with what they know and have adapted to than they would be if they stepped into the unknown territory of change. A complicating factor for many family members may be their tendency to perceive their enabling behaviors as a demonstration of love and loyalty to the addicted person. The therapist will need to have strategies that help the family members shift their perceptions of the addiction from a chronic issue that they tolerate and adapt to, to one that has a sense of urgency. Framing addiction as an emergency means the therapist helps the family prioritize getting help for the addiction and understanding the consequences of not changing, especially on children within the system. To help with this, the therapist will need to understand basic facts associated with addiction. For example, when working with a family who minimizes their adolescent child's drinking behavior, it would be important for the therapist to know and to help families understand that car crashes are the leading cause of death for teens, and about one-third of those are alcohol related (National Highway Traffic Safety Administration, 2009). See the following list of other salient facts that family therapists working with addicted families should know. Regardless of the strategy, increasing the urgency for change can help the family move beyond comfortable discomfort.

Facts Counselors Working With Addicted Families Should Know

- High school students who use alcohol or other substances are 5 times more likely to drop out of school or believe good grades are not important (Johnston, O'Malley, Bachman, & Schulenberg, 2008).
- In 2009, 4.3 million people aged 12 or older were treated for substance abuse–related issues (U.S. Department of Health and Human Services, 2009).
- Teen alcohol abuse is responsible for about 4,700 deaths each year (CDC, 2012).
- While it is reported that one in five teenagers binge drinks, only 1 in 100 parents believe their teens binge drink (Bonnie & O'Connell, 2004).

- Female alcoholics are more likely to report a history of physical abuse and emotional abuse than nonalcoholic women (U.S. Department of Health and Human Services, 1997).
- According to the U.S. Department of Justice, 61% of domestic violence offenders have substance abuse issues (Collins & Spencer, 2002).
- Common risk factors for becoming drug addicted include, among others, family history and genetics (National Council on Alcoholism and Drug Dependence, n.d.).
- Studies indicate that approximately 700,000 college students are assaulted by students who are under the influence of alcohol (National Council on Alcoholism and Drug Dependence, n.d.).
- A survey of college students estimates that approximately 100,000 students are victims of alcohol-related sexual assault or date rape (National Council on Alcoholism and Drug Dependence, n.d.).

Children can be powerful motivators for change in a family. Although ultimately addicted individuals must enter recovery for themselves, the guilt they may feel over the impact of addiction on children, especially younger children, can be a strong motivator for change. Helping children express their anxiety or hurt about parental addiction can be the deciding influence on a parent's entry into recovery (Edwards, 1998).

Conveying the Whole Family Message

Conveying the whole family message is, in essence, the idea that the problem in the family is not just one person's addiction, but rather that it involves the whole family. All members are affected by the addiction, support the maintenance of the addiction, and have the opportunity to effect change within the system. This is less a technique than it is an approach. It starts when the counselor invites everyone who lives in the home to the first session. The counselor is sending the message that it will take the whole family to make and maintain this change. It would be a daunting task if the counselor was the only person in the therapy room who wanted the addict to change. Most people will not change for complete strangers. Even if the whole family does not show up for family sessions, the counselor can emphasize the importance of a missing member's influence and of hearing his or her opinions, as well as ask present members what the missing member might have to say about particular issues. Often, including missing members in the session in small ways or big ways can result in them attending the subsequent sessions to "set the record straight." Other ways a counselor might convey the whole family message is in the way questions are asked. For example, the family counselor might ask systemic questions like: "Which of your children seems most affected by the impact drinking has had on your relationship with your spouse?" or "How are your children's relationships with each other impacted by your partner's drug use?" Such questions directly emphasize the systemic relationships that impact and support addiction and recovery. Other mechanisms in addiction treatment that emphasize the whole family are family education sessions, which describe typical family roles in addicted families, as well as other family dynamics, through psychoeducational sessions as described earlier in this chapter.

Changing Family Patterns That Work Against Recovery

Edwards (1998) describes four common addicted-family patterns that work against recovery: (1) enabling, (2) conflicts, (3) coalitions, and (4) the peripheral addicted family member. The goal is to help families become aware of these patterns, address them, and help the family find alternatives to those behaviors.

Enabling has been defined as behavior that prevents the addicted person from facing the negative consequences of their behavior (Nowinski, 2003). Examples may include making excuses or covering up for the addicted person so that he or she would not lose a job or suffer other consequences, providing money directly or indirectly for the person to purchase drugs, or perhaps justifying the person's behavior. Although enabling is a common term in addiction treatment and in 12-step groups, it is not useful to use the term early on in work with addicted families because of the resistance and defensiveness it can create (Edwards, 1998). Use of the term *enabling* early on would discount the positive intention of the family member's behavior, which is usually to help or protect the addicted individual, or sometimes ensure the survival of the family as a whole. Instead, it is more useful for the counselor to use descriptors of the enabling behavior, such as: "Your effort to protect your children from the effects of addiction seems to have resulted in great sacrifice on your part." Understanding and acknowledging an enabler's motivation; assisting him or her in exploring how that behavior, although well intentioned, may be helping the addictive behavior continue; and helping to explore alternative ways of helping that might be more effective are important to shifting the enabling dynamic in an addicted family system.

In order to survive, addicted families may form coalitions against the addicted family member. For example, one of the children may unite with one of the parents against the addicted parent. That bond may actually be much stronger than the bond between the parents. Once the addict becomes clean and sober, those coalitions may continue, especially in rigid systems. It will take time for trust to build among family members in the recovery process and for realignment to take place along parental or other appropriate lines. The therapist can help create conversations and interactions that help establish trust, reducing the need for coalitions against a third member in the family. Family sculpting activities might be useful in helping the system identify existing coalitions and other alliances, including the impact those coalitions have on other members. Sculpting may also assist the family in identifying alternative alignments that might be more useful.

Surprisingly, conflicts can become more frequent and more intense in early recovery than they were even in active addiction (Edwards, 1998). Family members may have buried their anger and resentment when they were in active addiction out of self-preservation and out of fear. Once the addicted member becomes sober, family members may feel safe enough to allow themselves to express that anger. Conflict is common in addicted families and is closely related to the tendency to form coalitions. For example, the addicted parent may resent the closeness of the children to the nonaddicted spouse, which evolved as a result of the real or emotional absence of the addicted parent. Once in recovery, the addicted parent may feel the need and right to become a more active parental figure, displacing the role of the nonaddicted parent who may have been compensating for years. This can create resentments, anxiety, and in some families, even a wish that the addicted person would go back to using, where roles were clearly defined and more comfortable.

Drama triangles (Karpman, 1968) and interpersonal games are common in addicted systems. Drama triangles are situations in which one family member may feel attacked by another. In the triangle, the attacker is known as the *persecutor*, and the person being attacked is known as the *victim*. A third family member is then drawn into the conflict and takes sides with the victim, fulfilling the rescuer role. As the rescuer attacks the persecutor, the victim is drawn in and rescues or defends the persecutor. The original persecutor is now treated as the victim, and the original victim is now the rescuer. The original rescuer has now become the perceived persecutor. And the drama goes on and on. As the drama escalates, there are no winners, just hurt and angry feelings. This game is called *uproar*, and the only way to resolve the drama is to remove the rescuer role and allow those in conflict to resolve their issues without interference. Through family counseling, addicted families in recovery can learn how to work with conflict without forming destructive coalitions and without discounting others' abilities to resolve conflicts that come up as a natural part of life.

Isolation or psychological distancing from the family by the addicted member is common. Once the addict begins recovery, that distance may remain out of fear, awkwardness, shame, or in order to avoid conflict and confrontation. If the peripheral addicted family member remains distant from the family, it may work against the family's recovery. The addicted member may not feel needed or have a sense of belonging, creating anger and resentment that may lead to relapse. The recovering family member may also withdraw into a 12-step program, feeling understood in that arena more than at home. The goal of the family counselor is to help with the adjustment issues that arise from the reentry of the addicted person into the family system. The length of this adjustment period will vary from family to family, but it is important that the family feel in control of the pace of this adjustment and acclimation to new roles within the system (Edwards, 1998).

Prepare the Family for Early Recovery

Families new in recovery have unrealistic expectations about how life will be different, believing that all problems will be solved when the addiction stops. Unfortunately, that is when the real work begins. Once sobriety is achieved, the hard work of learning to communicate effectively, reestablishing roles, creating new rules for behavior, and implementing boundaries within the system has to take place. The goal for family therapy in early recovery is to raise the family's awareness about the adjustment issues that may come up and to prepare them for typical reactions and setbacks. The therapeutic assumption is that it is more helpful to inform the family of these potential issues than to have the family suddenly be thrown into crisis when they come up unexpectedly (Edwards, 1998).

Encourage Family Members' Long-Term Support

A counselor working with a family that is early in the recovery process needs to not only prepare the family for what to expect during the early phases, but also help them perceive recovery as a process and not an event. It is a process for the entire system and will require buy-in and support from all members of the system to sustain changes. One way to encourage long-term support is to invite individual family members to seek their own recovery programs. Although the immediate physical consequences of active addiction are gone, many emotional/psychological issues linger long after initial abstinence, such as anger, resentment, anxiety, low self-esteem, guilt, shame, and intimacy problems (Edwards, 1998). At this stage of recovery, the family therapist can encourage nonaddicted family members to take responsibility for their own behaviors and their own growth by encouraging them to attend self-help programs such as Alateen, Al-Anon, Nar-Anon, and Codependents Anonymous (CODA). These and other similar support groups can help individual family members receive support for their own recovery by interacting with other families who have traveled a similar path. Ironically, it is the family member who needs to attend self-help meetings the most who is often the most resistant to going. The therapist cannot make family members attend these ancillary programs, but we can "refer, urge, encourage, cajole, wheedle, and coax" (Edwards, 1998, p. 40) until it becomes more likely to happen. Counselors should always have pamphlets and brochures in their offices about the various self-help programs, including meeting times and locations, so that they can be given to the family. It is strongly recommended that the therapist help the family create a plan of action around long-term support for each member. In families where violence has been a part of their history, safety plans should be in place for each member and for the system as a whole, which must include emergency contacts and crisis resources.

SIDEBAR 16.4

Addiction and family violence often occur simultaneously. It is important to assess for violence with family members individually so they can speak freely about what they are experiencing. In the case of intimate partner violence, joint counseling is generally not recommended. You might need to help family members create a safety plan if they indicate that a family member has violent tendencies. Important components of a safety plan may include:

- Having the phone numbers for police, hotlines, friends, and family who can help close by.

- Creating a code word with a friend or neighbor that can be used when a family member needs help, or asking neighbors to call 911 if they hear angry or violent noises from the home.
- Creating a safe escape plan from the home.
- Removing weapons from the home safely.
- Having a plan on where individuals can go if they do need to escape quickly, such as a local domestic violence shelter.
- Having excuses to leave the home, such as needing to take out the trash, walk the dog, or run to the store.
- Have a copy of important documents either hidden in a vehicle or at a friend or relative's house. Keep a small bag of overnight clothes and toiletries or medication there as well.
- Teach children how to call 911.
- Review the safety plan often with your clients.

A relapse prevention plan is also essential for the family in long-term recovery. This is especially important because studies have found that 20% to 80% of addicts relapse within 1 year following addiction treatment (Marlatt, 1985; NIDA, 2008). Relapse is a part of recovery and must be planned for and ultimately learned from so that the addict and the family can move forward successfully. Relapse can be used not as indication of failure, but rather as a resource to enhance treatment. It is up to the family therapist to help reframe the relapse and to keep the family engaged and moving toward their goals. The experience of relapse can be frightening for many clients who may feel that they have failed and will be judged by clinicians and family members. Helping the family to understand that recovery is a process that will most certainly include experiences of relapse as well as sobriety can minimize the initial reaction that many individuals might have regarding relapse. It is critical that counselors also understand that responding harshly to a client who has relapsed can have a negative impact on treatment fidelity.

TRAINING AND SUPERVISION

Working with addicted families can be rewarding but challenging work. It is crucial that counselors and therapists receive the proper training and supervision in addiction counseling, as well as in family systems theory and technique.

Training

The primary of objective of this chapter has been to highlight the importance of an integrated approach for treating individuals and families with addiction issues. Counselor education programs often employ a curriculum that introduces treatment modalities as distinct to specific areas of counseling. However, becoming an effective counselor requires the ability to blend counseling modalities that address the complex and multidimensional factors that influence an individual's presentation. As such, we encourage counselors to seek training that is appropriate for their particular clients. Counselors who are not educated in systems work or who lack expertise as addictions specialists should seek appropriate training prior to working with individuals and families struggling with substance use. Cotherapy, in which two therapists engage conjointly in the process of counseling with one client or family (Hendrix, Fournier, & Briggs, 2001; Tanner, Gray, & Haaga, 2012), can be beneficial for counselors who have been trained solely as individual therapists. In some cases, one counselor may have training and experience in family therapy but not in working with addicted clients, and the other counselor may be trained in addictions work and not in family therapy. The opportunity to work together can enhance treatment for individual clients and family members. The paired therapists may either possess comparable skills and experience or be engaged in a supervisory relationship (Hoffman & Hoffman, 1981; Tanner et al., 2012). Cotherapy can be helpful for the novice counselor who lacks experience. However, it can also be used by the more experienced counselor to mitigate the intensity and stress that might occur when working with the complexities of family systems and addiction.

Supervision

Supervision is essential for any practitioner working with addiction and families. It should be noted that the use of cotherapy previously mentioned does not replace supervision. It is possible, however, that a supervisor can also work as a cotherapist. If that is not the case, though, additional supervision is recommended, especially for the novice counselor. However, this can apply to anyone practicing as a counselor, regardless of level of expertise.

Your Agency as a System

It is possible that the agency you work for someday will not have a proper understanding of family work and addiction or about how these are best addressed together. As such, you may find yourself in a position of needing to advocate for a family systems perspective when an individual with substance abuse presents. This may also put you in the awkward position of having to effect policy change in the agency you work for. It is best to remember in such situations that there is much to be gained from addressing addiction through the lens of family systems. You may need to take the time to educate your peers on the benefits of family work. We encourage you to consider doing this and to not shy away from addressing the system that supports addiction. If your agency expects you to resort to individual counseling as the only intervention used to address substance use, we hope you will consider advocating for a systems approach by highlighting the benefits of family therapy and advocating for change in the system that you work in.

SUMMARY

In summary, the damage of addiction is pervasive in nature. Although a specific individual is often identified as "addicted," the disease inevitably impacts the family as well. This chapter discusses principles and components of both addictions treatment and family therapy with the intention of proposing a multidimensional view of addiction in families. Counselors must have an understanding of the addictive process not only to address the individual but also to educate and empower the family as well. There are many different forms of addiction, including substance abuse and process or behavioral addictions. Although the manifestation of the various forms of addiction may be similar, the manner in which individuals and families are impacted will vary. Previously mentioned research suggests providing services within the family system in order to promote successful treatment outcomes. Consequently, it is imperative for counselors to also possess a working understanding of family systems as well as addictions counseling.

Thus, this chapter emphasizes an integrated approach of addictions counseling and family counseling as the most effective treatment when addressing addictions in families. Further, this chapter acknowledges the potential challenge for some counselors to implement this integrated approach if they have not received extensive training in certain areas. Supervision and training are encouraged as a means of helping counselors integrate the approaches of addictions and family counseling into their treatment of addicted clients. Doing so will ensure that individuals and their families who are struggling with the disease of addiction will receive optimal treatment that will also ensure the chances for maintained sobriety and success.

USEFUL WEBSITES

The following websites provide additional information relating to the chapter topics.

Alcoholics Anonymous
http://www.aa.org/
Al-Anon Family Groups
http://www.al-anon.alateen.org/
American Association of Marriage and Family Therapy
http://www.aamft.org/iMIS15/AAMFT/
American Counseling Association
http://www.counseling.org/
Narconon International
http://www.narconon.org/
Office of National Drug Control Policy
http://www.whitehouse.gov/ondcp
SAMHSA Division of Workplace Programs
http://beta.samhsa.gov/workplace
Substance Abuse and Mental Health Services Administration
http://www.samhsa.gov/

NonProfitList.org
www.nonprofitlist.org/
United States Department of Education
http://www2.ed.gov/about/offices/list/osdfs/index.html
United States Drug Enforcement Administration
http://www.justice.gov/dea/druginfo/factsheets.shtml

The following websites provide additional information relating to substance use assessments.

National Institute on Alcohol Abuse and Alcoholism
http://pubs.niaaa.nih.gov/publications/arh28-2/78-79.htm
SAMHSA Tip 26: Substance Abuse Among Older Adults
http://store.samhsa.gov/product/TIP-26-Substance-Abuse-Among-Older-Adults/SMA12-3918
SAMHSA Tip 31: Screening and Assessing Adolescents for Substance Use Disorders
http://store.samhsa.gov/product/TIP-31-Screening-and-Assessing-Adolescents-for-Substance-Use-Disorders/SMA12-4079
The Substance Abuse and Subtle Screening Inventory
https://www.sassi.com/

REFERENCES

American Psychiatric Association. (2013). *Diagnostic and statistical manual of mental disorders* (5th ed.). Washington, DC: American Psychiatric Publishing.

American Society of Addiction Medicine. (2011). *The definition of addiction.* Retrieved from http://www.asam.org/advocacy/find-a-policy-statement/view-policy-statement/public-policy-statements/2011/12/15/the-definition-of-addiction

Black, C. (1981). *It will never happen to me!* New York, NY: Ballantine Books.

Bonnie, R. J., & O'Connell, M. E. (Eds.). (2004). *Reducing underage drinking: A collective responsibility.* Retrieved from http://www.nap.edu/openbook.php?isbn=0309089352

Briggs, W., Magnus, G., Lassiter, P., Patterson, A., & Smith, L. (2011). Substance use, misuse, and abuse among older adults: Implications for clinical mental health counselors. *Journal of Mental Health Counseling*, *33*(2), 112–127.

Burns, K., & Novick, L. (2011). *Prohibition*. Retrieved from http://www.pbs.org/kenburns/prohibition/watch-video/#id=2082675582

Casswell, S., You, R. Q., & Huckle, T. (2011). Alcohol's harm to others: Reduced wellbeing and health status for those with heavy drinkers in their lives. *Addiction*, *106*, 1087–1094. doi:10.1111/j.1360-0443.2011.03361.x

Centers for Disease Control and Prevention. (2012). *Alcohol-related disease impact (ARDI)*. Retrieved from http://www.cdc.gov/alcohol/fact-sheets/underage-drinking.htm

Cermak, T. L. (1986). *Diagnosing and treating codependence*. Minneapolis, MN: Johnson Institute Books.

Collins, J. J., & Spencer, D. L. (2002). *Linkage of domestic violence and substance abuse services, research in brief, executive summary*. Retrieved from https://www.ncjrs.gov/pdffiles1/nij/grants/194122.pdf

Copello, A., Templeton, L., & Powell, J. (2010). The impact of addiction on the family: Estimates of prevalence and costs. *Drugs: Education, Prevention, and Policy*, *17*, 63–74. doi:10.3109/09687637.2010.514798

Edwards, J. T. (1990). *Treating chemically dependent families. A practical systems approach for professionals*. Minneapolis, MN: Johnson Institute.

Edwards, J. T. (1998). *Treating chemically dependent families: A practical systems approach for professionals*. Center City, MN: Hazelden.

Ewing, J. A. (1984). Detecting alcoholism: The CAGE questionnaire. *Journal of the American Medical Association*, *252*, 1905–1907.

Faber, E., & Keating-O'Connor, B. (1991). Planned family intervention: Johnson Institute method. *Journal of Chemical Dependency Treatment*, *4*, 61–71.

Goodman, A. (2001). What's in a name? Terminology for designating a syndrome of driven sexual behavior. *Sexual Addiction & Compulsivity*, *8*, 191–213.

Grant, B. F. (2000). Estimates of US children exposed to alcohol abuse and dependence in the family. *American Journal of Public Health*, *90*, 112–115.

Grant, J. E., Potenza, M. N., Weinstein, A., & Gorelick, D. A. (2010). Introduction to behavioral addictions. *American Journal of Drug and Alcohol Abuse*, *36*, 233–241.

Hagedorn, W. B. (2009). The call for a new *Diagnostic and Statistical Manual of Mental Disorders* diagnosis: Addictive disorders. *Journal of Addictions & Offender Counseling*, *29*, 110–127.

Heath, D. B. (1988). Emerging anthropological theory and models of alcohol use and alcoholism. In D. D. Chaudron & D. A. Wilkinson (Eds.), *Theories on alcoholism* (pp. 353–410). Toronto, Canada: Addiction Research Foundation.

Hendrix, C. C., Fournier, D. G., & Briggs, K. (2001). Impact of co-therapy teams on client outcomes and therapist training in marriage and family therapy. *Contemporary Family Therapy: An International Journal*, *23*(1), 63–82.

Hodgson, R. J., John, B., Abbasi, T., Hodgson, R. C., Waller, S., Thom, B., & Newcombe, R. (2003). Fast screening for alcohol misuse. *Addictive Behaviors*, *28*, 1453–1463.

Hoffman, L. W., & Hoffman, H. J. (1981). Husband–wife co-therapy team: Exploration of its development. *Psychotherapy: Theory, Research & Practice*, *18*(2), 217–224.

International Certification and Reciprocity Consortium (ICRC)/Alcohol and Other Drug Abuse. (1998). *Study guide for case presentation method oral interview for alcohol and other drug abuse counselors*. Research Triangle Park, NC: Columbia Assessment Services.

Johnston, L. D., O'Malley, P. M., Bachman, J. G., & Schulenberg, J. E. (2008). Secondary school students. *Monitoring the Future*. Retrieved from http://monitoringthefuture.org/pubs/monographs/vol1_2008.pdf

Karim, R., & Chaudhri, P. (2012). Behavioral addictions: An overview. *Journal of Psychoactive Drugs*, *44*, 5–17. doi:10.1080/02791072.2012.662859

Karpman, S. (1968). Fairy tales and script drama analysis. *Transactional Analysis Bulletin*, 7(26), 39–43.

Marlatt, G. A. (1985). Relapse prevention: Theoretical rationale and overview for the model. In G. A. Marlatt & J. R. Gordon (Eds.), *Relapse prevention: Maintenance strategies in the treatment of addictive behaviors* (pp. 3–70). New York, NY: Guilford Press.

Meyers, R. J., Smith, J. E., & Lash, D. N. (2005). A program for engaging treatment-refusing substance abusers into treatment: CRAFT. *International Journal of Behavioral Consultation and Therapy*, *1*, 90–100.

Miller, W. R., Myers, R. J., & Tonigan, J. S. (1999). Engaging the unmotivated in treatment for alcohol problems: A comparison of three strategies for intervention through family members. *Journal of Consulting and Clinical Psychology*, *67*, 688–697.

Miller, W. R., & Rollnick, S. (1991). *Motivational interviewing: Preparing people to change addictive behavior*. New York, NY: Guilford Press.

Miller, W. R., & Rollnick, S. (2002). *Motivational interviewing* (2nd ed.). New York, NY: Guilford Press.

National Council on Alcoholism and Drug Dependence. (n.d.). *Frequently asked questions and facts*. Retrieved from http://www.ncadd.org/index.php/for-youth/faqsfacts

National Highway Traffic Safety Administration. (2009). *Traffic safety facts 2008: Young drivers*. Retrieved from http://www-nrd.nhtsa.dot.gov/Pubs/811169.PDF

National Institute on Drug Abuse. (2008, July). *Relapse rates for drug addiction are similar to those of other well-characterized chronic illnesses*. Retrieved from http://www.drugabuse.gov/publications/addiction-science/relapse/relapse-rates-drug-addiction-are-similar-to-those-other-well-characterized-chronic-ill

Nowinski, J. (2003). Facilitating 12-step recovery from substance abuse and addiction. In F. Rotgers, J. Morgenstern, & S. Walters (Eds.), *Treating substance abuse: Theory & technique* (pp. 31–66). New York, NY: Guilford Press.

O'Farrell, T. J., & Clements, K. (2012). Review of outcome research on marital and family therapy in treatment for alcoholism. *Journal of Marital and Family Therapy*, *38*, 122–144. doi:10.1111/j.1752-0606.2011.00242.x

O'Farrell, T. J., & Fals-Stewart, W. (2003). Alcohol abuse. *Journal of Marital and Family Therapy*, *29*, 121–146.

Orford, J., Velleman, R., Copello, A., Templeton, L., & Ibanga, A. (2010). The experiences of affected family members: A summary of two decades of qualitative research. *Drugs: Education, Prevention and Policy*, *17*, 44–62. doi:10.3109/09687637.2010.514192

Orford, J., Velleman, R., Natera, R., Templeton, L., & Copello, A. (2013). Addiction in the family is a major but neglected contributor to the global burden of adult ill-health. *Social Science and Medicine*, *78*, 70–77. doi:10.1016/j.socscimed.2012.11.036

Prochaska, J. O., DiClemente, C. C., & Norcross, J. C. (1992). In search of how people change: Application to addictive behaviors. *American Psychologist*, *47*, 1102–1114.

Ray, G. T., Mertens, J. R., & Weisner, C. (2009). Family members of people with alcohol or drug dependence: Health problems and medical cost compared to family members of people with diabetes and asthma. *Addiction*, *104*, 203–214. doi:10.111/j.1360-0443.2008.02447.x

Schaefer, G. (2011). Family functioning in families with alcohol and other drug addiction. *Social Policy Journal of New Zealand*, *37*, 135–151.

Selzer, M. L. (1971). The Michigan Alcoholism Screening Test: The quest for a new diagnostic instrument. *American Journal of Psychiatry*, *127*, 1653–1658.

Singh, A., & Lassiter, P. S. (2012). Lesbian, gay, bisexual, and transgender affirmative addictions treatment. In D. Capuzzi & M. D. Stauffer (Eds.), *Foundations of addiction counseling* (2nd ed.). New York, NY: Prentice Hall.

Smith, D. E. (2012). Editor's note: The process addictions and the new ASAM definition of addiction. *Journal of Psychoactive Drugs*, *44*, 1–4. doi:10.1080/02791072.2012.662105

Stafford, L. L. (2001). Is codependency a meaningful concept? *Issues in Mental Health Nursing*, *22*, 273–286.

Tanner, M. A., Gray, J. J., & Haaga, D. A. F. (2012). Association of cotherapy supervision with client outcomes, attrition, and trainee effectiveness in a psychotherapy training clinic. *Journal of Clinical Psychology*, *68*(12), 1241–1252.

Thombs, D. L. (2006). *Introduction to addictive behaviors* (3rd ed.). New York, NY: Guilford Press.

Thombs, D. L., & Beck, K. H. (1994). The social context of four adolescent drinking patterns. *Health Education Research*, *9*, 13–22.

U.S. Department of Health and Human Services. (1997). *Effects of domestic violence on substance abuse treatment*. Retrieved from http://www.ncbi.nlm.nih.gov/books/NBK64441

U.S. Department of Health and Human Services. (2009). *Results from the 2009 National Survey on Drug Use and Health: Vol. I. Summary of national findings*. Retrieved from http://samhsa.gov/data/NSDUH/2k9NSDUH/2k9Results.htm#2.2

Velleman, R. (2006). The importance of family members in helping problem drinkers achieve their chosen goal. *Addiction Research and Theory*, *14*, 73–85. doi:10.1080/16066350500489311

Vernig, P. M. (2011). Family roles in homes with alcohol-dependent parents: An evidence-based review. *Substance Use and Misuse*, *46*, 535–542. doi:10.3109/10826084.2010.501676

Wegscheider, S. (1981). *Another chance: Hope and health for the alcoholic family*. Palo Alto, CA: Science and Behavior Books.

Whitfield, C. L. (1984). Co-alcoholism: Recognizing a treatable illness. *Family and Community Health*, 7, 16–25.

Wurmser, L. (1982). The question of specific psychopathology in compulsive drug use. *Annals of the New York Academy of Sciences*, *398*, 33–43. doi:10.111/j.1749-6632.1982.tb39471.x

CHAPTER 17

Violence, Abuse, and Trauma in Family Therapy

Danica G. Hays
Old Dominion University

Kevin C. Snow
Old Dominion University

Cassandra G. Pusateri
Youngstown State University

Families and their individual members can encounter trauma across various systems, with acute effects and long-term consequences that often transcend generations. In this chapter, we define key terminology and provide statistics associated with violence, abuse, and trauma; articulate their factors and consequences; discuss diversity considerations; and outline assessment techniques and interventions for individuals, couples, families, groups, and community systems. Finally, we discuss the impact of violence, abuse, and trauma on counselors and provide self-care strategies.

INTRODUCTION TO VIOLENCE, ABUSE, AND TRAUMA

It is important for counselors to be familiar with the terms violence, abuse, and trauma. The World Health Organization (WHO, 2013) defines *violence* as the actual or threatened act of force or power on individuals, groups, or communities that results in psychological harm, maldevelopment, physical injury, or even death. Violence can include physical, psychological, or sexual attacks as well as deprivation or neglect. Further, it may be self-directed (e.g., suicide, self-injury), interpersonal (e.g., family and intimate partner violence, community violence), or collective (e.g., social, economic, or political violence).

Although various forms of abuse exist, we conceptualize *abuse* as forms of domestic violence, which include intimate partner violence, child abuse, elder abuse, and incest. Intimate partner violence (IPV) is actual or threatened abuse against a partner by another partner in a romantic relationship such as a dating relationship, marriage, civil union, or other form of partnership. IPV affects women and men in all racial, ethnic, socioeconomic, and religious groups; however, individuals who are members of multiple oppressed groups (e.g., women of color who also have a low socioeconomic status) are at an increased risk of harm because of their multiple oppressed social positions (Sokoloff & Dupont, 2005). Elder abuse—acts toward individuals aged 65 and older—is a criminal offense in all 50 states, with a majority of states having mandatory reporting laws (Administration on Aging, 2010). In addition, in cases in which older adults are neglecting themselves, some states allow law enforcement to intervene when these individuals refuse services (Forman & McBride, 2010). There are three major types of abuse commonly associated with IPV, child, and elder abuse: physical abuse (e.g., hitting, choking, pushing, throwing objects, disfiguring, burning), emotional abuse (e.g., isolating from family and friends, name-calling, jealousy, stalking, depriving an individual of basic medical, educational, mental health, and other needs), and sexual abuse (e.g., threatened or actual rape, sexual humiliation, exposing or involving children in age-inappropriate sexual content or behaviors). Finally, incest involves sexual intercourse between biological, adoptive, or step family members or close relatives. Cases involving sexual intercourse between siblings who are minors or between consenting adults (e.g., cousin relationships, adult siblings) are traditionally conceptualized as incest. Research indicates that adolescent perpetrators of sibling abuse choose younger victims, harm victims over a lengthier period, and use violence more frequently and severely than adult perpetrators (Cyr, Wright, McDuff, & Perron, 2002).

The Substance Abuse and Mental Health Services Administration (SAMHSA, 2012a) defines *trauma* according to three E's: events, experience, and effects. Specifically, they offer the following working definition for trauma:

> Individual trauma results from an event, series of events, or set of circumstances that is experienced by an individual as physically or emotionally harmful or threatening and that has lasting adverse effects on the individual's functioning and physical, social, emotional, or spiritual well-being. (p. 1)

Individuals do not experience trauma in isolation, and families and communities play an integral role in the healing or exacerbation of trauma. Further, collective trauma can occur for communities, whether one defines that community by geography or shared identity or experience. Examples of collective trauma include natural disasters, political persecution, mass incarceration, school violence, sexism, racism, or terrorism. Individuals within an affected community may jointly respond with hypervigilance, fear, or even acts of resiliency; further, the experience may become infused into cultural norms and narratives that are carried intergenerationally. Whether individual or collective in nature, traumatic events may occur once or repeatedly. They are perceived as traumatic to varying degrees based on individual labels or assigned meanings, with the nature of an event and its perceived level of severity resulting in various short- and long-term effects for individuals and communities.

Based on these definitions of violence, abuse, and trauma, we conceptualize violence as the actual or threatened event, act, or circumstance that results in trauma for individuals, families, and communities. Further, we view abuse as a subset of violence that impacts individuals within family configurations. The following lists present pertinent statistics associated with violence that affects family systems and subsystems.

General Violence

- 1,203,564 violent crimes are estimated to have occurred in the United States in 2011 (U.S. Federal Bureau of Investigations, 2012a).
- 740,000 children and youth are treated in emergency rooms as a result of violence each year (U.S. Department of Health and Human Services, 2010).
- 707,212 people aged 10 to 24 were treated for injuries sustained from physical assaults in 2011 (U.S. Department of Education, 2012).
- 60.6% percent of children surveyed in 2008 witnessed some type of violence: 36.7% witnessed assault, 14.9% assault with a deadly weapon, 6.1% sexual victimization, 9.8% family violence, and 19.2% community violence (U.S. Department of Justice, 2009).

Suicide and Homicide

- The leading causes of death in 2010 for 15- to 24-year-old Americans were unintentional injury, homicide, and suicide (CDC, 2011a).
- 4,828 people aged 10 to 24 were victims of homicide in 2011 (U.S. Department of Education, 2012).
- 14,612 people were murdered in the United States in 2011 (U.S. Federal Bureau of Investigations, 2012a).
- There were 17 homicides of children aged 5 to 18 in schools in the 2009–2010 school year (U.S. Department of Education, 2012).
- Suicide was the 10th leading cause of death in the United States in 2010, with 38,364 completions (CDC, 2011a).
- 19,392 persons in 2010 committed suicide with a firearm; 9,493 by suffocation; and 6,599 by poisoning (CDC, 2011a).

Intimate Partner Violence (IPV)

- Approximately 30% of women and 10% of men have experienced physical violence, sexual assault, and/or stalking (Black et al., 2011).
- IPV affects more than 12 million Americans each year (CDC, 2011b).

- One in four women and one in seven men were victims of IPV in 2010 (CDC, 2011b).
- Approximately 25% of women and 14% of men experienced severe physical violence by an intimate partner (CDC, 2011c).
- 1.3 million women were raped in 2009 (CDC, 2011b).
- 81% of women who have experienced rape, stalking, or IPV report post-traumatic stress disorder symptoms (CDC, 2011b).
- Prevalence rates among adolescents and college students range from 16% to 35% (CDC, 2006), with individuals of multiple oppressed statuses at greater risk for relationship violence, victimization, and/or perpetration.
- Nearly 1.5 million high school students nationwide experience physical dating violence victimization each year (CDC, 2006).
- Among 681 African American and Caucasian adolescents, 61% of males and 63% of females reported emotional abuse in dating relationships (Holt & Espelage, 2005).
- More than 80% of females ages 13 to 17 reported receiving or perpetrating psychological violence (Cyr, McDuff, & Wright, 2006).

Child Abuse

The U.S. Department of Health and Human Services (2011) published a report on child maltreatment and noted the following data in 2010 for 45 reporting states with a population of 75 million children:

- 3.3 million referrals involving maltreatment of 5.9 million children, with over 2.6 million of these cases actually screened.
- Approximately 436,000 (22%) of referrals screened indicated substantiated reports of child abuse.
- With respect to reporting sources, 32.5% of the 2010 reports came from those working with children in clinical and educational settings.
- For unique cases (i.e., those with a singular type of abuse), 78% of the cases related to neglect, 17.6% to physical abuse, and 9.2% to sexual abuse.
- The child fatality rate was 2.07 deaths per 100,000 children; nearly 80% of these involved children under age 4.
- Victimization rates by child's gender were approximately equal (48.5% male, 51.2% female).
- Victimization rates by child's race/ethnicity for three groups reported were 44.8% White, 21.9% African American, and 21.4% Latino; however, African American, Native American, and multiracial populations had the highest rates per 1,000 children (14.6%, 11.0%, and 12.7%, respectively).
- A majority of abusers were parents (81.2%, with 84.2% of these involving biological parents); for abuse involving one parent, 53.6% of perpetrators were female and 45.2% were male.

Elder Abuse

- Estimates of elder abuse frequency for the general elderly population typically range from 2% to 10% depending on type, definition, and degree of reporting;

perpetrators of elder abuse are generally male and can include family members, paid caregivers, or fellow residents in a care facility (Forman & McBride, 2010).

- According to the National Incidence Study on Elder Abuse, approximately 450,000 elderly people experienced abuse in 1996; if self-neglect is included, the number is over 550,000 (National Committee for the Prevention of Elder Abuse, n.d.).

Miscellaneous Community Trauma

- 6,222 hate crimes occurred in the United States in 2011 (U.S. Federal Bureau of Investigations, 2012b).
- 58,179 refugees were admitted into the United States in 2012 (U.S. Department of Homeland Security, 2013).
- 21,292 of the refugees admitted in 2012 were children (U.S. Department of Homeland Security, 2013).
- 29,484 individuals came to the United States in 2012 seeking asylum (U.S. Department of Homeland Security, 2013).
- Nearly 3 million troops have been deployed to Afghanistan and Iraq since wars began, with about 2 million children separated from a parent or guardian (Waliski, Kirchner, Shue, & Bokony, 2012).
- Incidence of PTSD, depression, anxiety, and significant interpersonal problems range from 15% to 35% for military service members postdeployment (Milliken, Auchterlonie, & Hoge, 2007); military children present with emotional and behavioral difficulties above the national average (Chandra et al., 2010), with approximately 17% meeting criteria for a mental health diagnosis (Mansfield, Kaufman, Engel, & Gaynes, 2011).
- In 2011 and 2012 alone, approximately 1,000 Americans were killed and 800,000 were displaced because of natural disasters.

Available research indicates that helping professionals have limited knowledge related to assessing and addressing the dynamics and impact of family violence, often accompanied with negative attitudes when couples and families of minority statuses are involved. For example, research examining attitudes toward abuse in intimate relationships shows heterosexual bias. Although statistics indicate that abuse occurs at similar or higher rates for same-sex couples as compared to heterosexual couples, Brown and Groscup (2009) noted that helping professionals have differing attitudes, with more negative views toward same-sex couples. Further, male-against-female violence—what may be typically considered "normative" IPV—is viewed as more likely to occur, more serious, and thus more difficult for a female partner to escape from, and more credible in general than same-sex relationship violence (Blasko, Winek, & Bieschke, 2007; Poorman, Seelau, & Seelau, 2003). Further, Blasko et al. (2007) noted that marriage and family therapists often place equal blame on partners in same-sex relationships as compared to heterosexual relationships. Often, there may be a lack of professional support or understanding due to heterosexism, lack of knowledge about domestic violence in diverse families, and/or inaccurate statistics due to underreporting from individuals who likely lack adequate resources. Regardless, this differential level of support can significantly impact treatment recommendations, including suggestions for community-based interventions.

In addition to research on IPV, there is some discussion in the literature about school counselor attitudes and competency regarding families experiencing psychological trauma from wars, as well as children exposed to school violence. School counselors report limited knowledge of mental health or physical symptoms of children whose family members are deployed to wars, are generally not aware of issues faced by families of service members, or lack knowledge of resources or outreach activities for these families (Waliski et al., 2012). With respect to school violence, McAdams, Shillingford, and Trice-Black (2011) noted that although 94% of a sample of school counselors reported at least two incidents of school violence, about 82% reported a limited knowledge of violence literature.

Although there seems to be limited training available for preparing to work with family members experiencing violence (Kitzrow, 2002), counselors are to be aware of several psychological and physical symptoms associated with exposure to violence as they prepare to assess and intervene with families. Emotional or psychological symptoms may include the following: shock or denial; anger or mood swings; guilt, shame, and self-blame; depression; suicidality; poor concentration; anxiety, hypervigilance, and fear; social withdrawal; emotional numbness; and poor body image. Clients may also present with physical symptoms such as insomnia or nightmares, fatigue, overactive startle reflex, heart palpitations, aches, pains, and muscle tension. Long-term responses to violence may include chronic mental and physical illness; substance abuse; self-injury; eating disorders; sexual impulsivity and unplanned pregnancy; depression and suicidality; generalized anxiety; interpersonal problems, including issues within families; academic and occupational problems; dissociation from relationships or overwhelming situations; antisocial behaviors and aggression; and mental health disorders such as post-traumatic stress disorder, acute stress disorder, or dissociative disorders (Horton & Cruise, 1997; McLeod, Muldoon, & Hays, 2014; Waliski et al., 2012). Further, those identifying with oppressed statuses (e.g., lower socioeconomic status, racial/ethnic minority, female, sexual minority) often encounter more severe outcomes with fewer community resources (Coker et al., 2002; Hays, Green, Orr, & Flowers, 2007; Horton & Cruise, 1997; Sokoloff & Dupont, 2005).

DIVERSITY CONSIDERATIONS

The American Counseling Association Code of Ethics (ACA, 2014) calls counselors to be aware of and sensitive to the interaction between culture and the therapeutic process. Cultural domains such as race, ethnicity, sexual orientation, immigration status, spirituality, geography, and age can influence the therapeutic relationship and process. In this section, cultural considerations for providing services to individuals, couples, and families who have encountered violence and traumatic events will be discussed. Counselors are encouraged to remember that each client will have a unique cultural identity that could be a combination of several domains. For example, a client may identify as Latino, of the Catholic faith, and from a rural area. When working with all clients, an individualized therapeutic approach is required.

Therapist/Client Matching

The literature outlines the complexity of therapist–client matching with authors indicating that treatment outcomes can be either improved or unaffected by cultural matching (see Cabral & Smith, 2011; Flicker, Waldron, Turner, Brody, & Hyman, 2008; Stracuzzi, Mohr, & Fuertes, 2011). With this said, there are several considerations. Building a strong therapeutic alliance and rapport with diverse clientele is of utmost importance (Cragun & Friedlander, 2012). This includes having an open conversation about therapeutic preferences. For example, Chang and Berk (2009) found that some clients believe there are benefits to having a counselor who is not culturally matched. Furthermore, there could be unforeseen consequences of cultural matching (e.g., cultural segregation) (Flicker et al., 2008). Therefore, counselors should consider the multitude of variables involved in successful therapist–client matching and make intentional decisions about how to move forward with diverse clientele (Horst et al., 2012).

Nontraditional Couples and Families

Although the prevalence of domestic violence among individuals who identify as gay, lesbian, and bisexual is gaining recognition (Messinger, 2011), there remains a shortage of literature available about domestic violence among nontraditional couples and families. Therefore, counselors are encouraged to increase awareness of domestic violence among nontraditional couples and families and market services to meet current needs (Banks & Fedewa, 2012; Basow & Thompson, 2012; McLaughlin, Hatzenbuehler, Xuan, & Conron, 2012). In addition, counselors have reported decreased confidence when working with nontraditional couples and families and are therefore encouraged to seek additional training (Banks & Fedewa, 2012; Basow & Thompson, 2012; Brown & Groscup, 2009). Finally, as with other culturally diverse clients, counselors are encouraged to create an individualized therapeutic plan that addresses concerns specific to the client, couple, and/or family (McLaughlin et al., 2012).

Race and Ethnicity

As indicated earlier in the chapter, individuals who identify as racial and/or ethnic minorities appear to be at an increased risk for violence, abuse, and trauma when compared to individuals who identify as White (see Carbone-Lopez, 2013; Lipsky, Cristofalo, Reed, Caetano, & Roy-Byrne, 2012; Renner & Whitney, 2010). Therefore, the provision of services designed to increase awareness, provide education, and ultimately increase prevention efforts is needed (Carbone-Lopez, 2013; Lipsky et al., 2012). For example, counselors could provide information about legal considerations in IPV cases given that women of color are less likely to obtain a protective order (Durfee & Messing, 2012). In addition, counselors are encouraged to demonstrate sensitivity to the interplay between race/ethnicity and domestic violence by utilizing culturally specific treatment models, incorporating culturally appropriate nontraditional helpers, and learning about cultural barriers to seeking assistance (Carbone-Lopez, 2013; Cho & Kim, 2012; Tehee & Esqueda, 2008). Finally, counselors are encouraged to become social justice advocates by working to eliminate racial and ethnic discrimination (Carbone-Lopez, 2013; Lipsky et al., 2012).

Immigrants and Refugees

Violence, abuse, and trauma may be considered a social or cultural norm for some refugees and immigrants. For example, Gustafson and Iluebbey (2013) found an acceptance of IPV among a group of immigrants from Sudan and confusion associated with the lack of acceptance in the United States. The acculturation process can be stressful and ultimately lead to an increased risk of violence (Gupta et al., 2009; Nilsson, Brown, Russell, & Khamphakdy-Brown, 2008). Furthermore, the way in which violence is perpetrated can be different for refugees and immigrants. For example, language restrictions and threats of deportation may be used to exert control in domestic violence situations (Erez, Adelman, & Gregory, 2009). For every form of violence, abuse, or trauma an immigrant or refugee may present with, counselors are encouraged to adopt a framework that includes learning about cultural norms and perceptions of mental health, being sensitive to cultural barriers, reducing isolation of victims, increasing availability of support, and providing educational opportunities (Erez et al., 2009; Fuchsel, Murphy, & Dufresne, 2012; Gupta et al., 2009; Mahapatra, 2012; Nilsson et al., 2008).

Spirituality

An individual's spirituality can serve as a coping strategy when faced with multiple stressors or promote disempowering thoughts that influence perceptions of violence and help-seeking behaviors (see Benavides, 2012; Bowland, Biswas, Kyriakakis, & Edmond, 2011; Fowler, Faulkner, Learman, & Runnels, 2011; Levitt, Swanger, & Butler, 2008; Yick, 2008). For example, Fowler et al. (2011) found that one's level of spirituality can affect the utilization of and satisfaction with counseling services. Counselors are therefore encouraged to be sensitive to the spiritual needs of clients and collaborate with leaders of various faith communities to ensure that spirituality is appropriately integrated into service provision (Bowland et al., 2011; Fowler et al., 2011; Levitt et al., 2008; Skiff, Horwitz, LaRussa-Trott, Pearson, & Santiago, 2008; Todhunter & Deaton, 2010; Yick, 2008). For example, counselors could provide training to faith community leaders (Bowland et al., 2011), given that many report lacking confidence and preparation for addressing domestic violence (Skiff et al., 2008). Finally, counselors are encouraged to empower clients to challenge disempowering beliefs and engage in social activism to promote positive changes in the larger community (Levitt et al., 2008; Yick, 2008).

Geography

Although there is a dearth of literature about domestic violence in different geographic areas across the United States, counselors are encouraged to engage with diverse geographic communities to expand their understanding of unique service needs (Shuman et al., 2008). For example, there appears to be an increased prevalence of domestic violence in certain geographic areas when compared to others (see Grossman, Hinkley, Kawalski, & Margrave, 2005; Peek-Asa et al., 2011). Counselors are also encouraged to consider the effect geographic location can have on accessibility to services (Hetling & Zhang, 2010). For example, isolation has been identified as a barrier to service utilization among individuals in rural areas (Peek-Asa et al., 2011). It is also important for counselors to consider the culture of the area and its influence on the perception of mental health, domestic violence, and service utilization. Finally, there is a need for increased educational opportunities about domestic violence, healthy relationships, and resources available in diverse geographic areas (Grossman et al., 2005).

Age

Although each state has specific requirements and processes, counselors are considered mandated reporters of suspected or observed child abuse (Child Welfare Information Gateway, 2012). Likewise, every state has laws regarding elder abuse as well as specifications and processes regarding reporting (National Center on Elder Abuse, n.d.). Therefore, it is imperative that counselors become knowledgeable of the laws in their state regarding child and elder abuse, as well as the preferred process for reporting.

Regarding service provision, counselors working with children who have been victims of or have been exposed to domestic violence are encouraged to use a holistic approach that includes all providers involved in the child's treatment (McPherson, Scribano, & Stevens, 2012). When service provision is handled appropriately, counseling can result in a significant decrease in abuse recurrence (Palusci & Ondersma, 2012). Counselors who are providing services to elderly clients are encouraged to provide education about the resources available, raise awareness of domestic violence later in life, and address the stressors that may affect this population (Lundy & Grossman, 2009; Roberto, McCann, & Brossoie, 2013).

Conclusion

In addition to the considerations provided, the importance of demonstrating multicultural counseling competence (MCC) has been mentioned throughout the literature (see Banks & Fedewa, 2012; Brown & Grosup, 2009; Cabral &

Smith, 2011; Chang & Berk, 2009; Cragun & Friedlander, 2012; Horst et al., 2012; Lundy & Grossman, 2009; Stracuzzi et al., 2011). MCC has been recognized as an effective approach for working with clients of diverse cultural backgrounds. Therefore, counselors are encouraged to learn and implement the multicultural counseling competencies originally outlined by Sue, Arredondo, and McDavis (1992).

COUNSELING FAMILIES EXPERIENCING VIOLENCE, ABUSE, AND TRAUMA

With diversity considerations as a backdrop, we begin this section by outlining key assessment areas for counselors to consider. Then, we introduce general stage treatment models for acute (i.e., crisis intervention) and long-term (i.e., trauma recovery) exposure to violence, abuse, and trauma. We conclude this section with several systemic, couples, family, and group-based interventions.

Not surprisingly, there are many approaches to treating IPV and other forms of violence and trauma within counseling and affiliated mental health professions. While it is not possible to list all of these interventions, this section will attempt to highlight some common interventions and direct the reader for further training. We note traditional individual and group therapy remain primary intervention tools in the treatment of violence in families and individuals, along with crisis counseling (Pender, 2012). All counselors should have basic understandings of violence dynamics and treatment because IPV concerns may arise at any time with any client. As with all clinical issues, it is important to use basic counseling skills to provide empathy, support, compassion, attending, understanding, and care.

We give a note of caution prior to reviewing specific interventions. When violence is present in a client's life, safety must be the primary focus of all interventions. The efficacious counselor is to be certain that clients are safe in their lives, and thus advocate or assist clients to establish safety. Counselors know the resources available in a community to provide client safety, whether those are shelters, police, medical facilities, and so on. Assessing for client safety when violence exists is as important as doing suicide assessments when thoughts of harm are present for a client. Consultation, supervision, and referral are key activities in all counseling, especially when violence is a presenting issue.

Assessment of Family Violence, Abuse, and Trauma

Prior to any intervention (excluding acute crises), it is important for counselors working with families to conduct a comprehensive assessment. The nature of the assessment and who is involved are dependent on the type of situation. For example, it is typically not safe for an IPV survivor to be assessed when the abuser is present; however, it may be appropriate to involve several family members during a suicide risk assessment or after community violence. The following are key areas that counselors should assess with family members. It is important to gather information from individual family members when possible to determine any patterns or inconsistencies that may have clinical relevance.

- *Family definitions of violence, abuse, and/or trauma:* In order for counselors to have a more accurate understanding of a traumatic event or occurrence of abuse or violence, they are to ask family members to label and describe the act using their own terminology. In addition, counselors are to solicit information from family members about their knowledge and awareness of violence, abuse, and trauma.
- *Identification of stressors:* Counselors are to have family members describe stressors with which they have been coping. Although families may not directly link stressors to violence, abuse, and trauma, it is important to have them list as many stressors as possible, including academic, occupational, social, economic, psychological, and physical concerns, among others. Then counselors are to gather information about general coping resources individuals have, as well as specific ways of coping with particular stressors. Identifying stressors and coping mechanisms can illuminate how stress impacts individual family members and help determine the individual and collective resources available to assist with stress management.
- *Identification of threats:* Counselors are to evaluate the current threat level for the family as well as its individual family members, because individuals respond to stressors in different ways. For example, it is important to assess family members' current risk of exposure to violence, abuse, and trauma. Some families, based on limited available support, may be at greater risk. In addition, counselors are to evaluate the current risk of harm to self or others. This involves examining individuals' self-reported risk, any plan to harm and the specificity and lethality of that plan, availability of means, any history of harm to self or others, and the level of severity of any current mental disorders or psychological and environmental stressors.
- *Availability of social support:* Social support can be an important protective factor for families. Counselors are to identify individuals in the community whom family members can rely on to help them cope or minimize risk for retraumatization. Community supports might include individuals identifying as culturally similar, support groups, religious institutions, schools or workplaces, neighbors, peers, and professionals, to name a few. Counselors can assist family members in identifying available support networks and understanding how they can be useful in difficult times. In addition, family members might list ways they would like to expand their social networks.
- *History with trauma, violence, and/or abuse:* Counselors are to seek information about historical occurrences that families have encountered. In initial sessions, counselors should gather limited information to avoid retraumatization. Future sessions might involve using more extensive methods of trauma assessment, such as the traumagram or trauma timeline (Figley & Kiser, 2013). The traumagram is similar to the genogram and is used to track the

course of traumatic events for the family or family members. The counselor collects information from each family member (as appropriate) including significant and stressful events with lingering effects, dates and names of those involved, and ratings for the degree of stressfulness at the time of the event, 1 year later, and presently. Then, the counselor views family members' traumagrams together to create a collective chart of traumas while noting patterns in individual and collective reactions and coping skills. The trauma timeline involves family members making a list of traumatic events with start and end dates. Then, the events are placed in chronological order and ranked from least to most stressful (Figley & Kiser, 2013).

Many of these assessment areas can be evaluated with assessment tools. Although it is beyond the scope of this chapter to include a complete list of available quantitative and qualitative tools to evaluate all types of violence, abuse, and trauma affecting families, the following includes a sample of trauma assessments as well as tools useful for monitoring consequences of violence, abuse, and trauma.

Select Violence, Abuse, and Trauma-Related Assessments

Alcohol Use Disorders Identification Test (Babor, Higgins-Biddle, Saunders, & Monteiro, 2001)
Beck Anxiety Inventory (Beck & Steer, 1993)
Beck Depression Inventory-II (Beck, Steer, & Brown, 2003)
Brief Symptom Index (Derogatis, 1993)
CAGE Questionnaire (Ewing, 1984)
Child Dissociative Checklist (Putnam, Helmer, & Trickett, 1993)
Childhood Maltreatment Interview Schedule—Short Form (Briere, 1992)
Child Sexual Behavior Inventory (Friedrich, 1997)
Childhood Trauma Questionnaire (Bernstein & Fink, 1998)
Conflict Tactics Scale Revised (Strauss, Hamby, Boney-McCoy, & Sugarman, 1996)
Lesbian Partner Abuse Scale (McClennen et al., 2002)
Life Events Checklist (Gray, Litz, Hsu, & Lombardo, 2004)
Michigan Alcoholism Screening Test (Evans, 1998)
Parent Report of Child's Reaction to Stress (Fletcher, 1991)
PTSD Checklist (Weathers, Huska, & Keane, 1991)
SAD PERSONS Scale (Patterson, Dohn, Bird, & Patterson, 1983)
Self-Injury Questionnaire (Alexander, 1999)
State-Trait Anger Expression Inventory-2 (Spielberger, 1999)
Suicide Assessment Checklist (Rogers, Alexander, & Subich, 1994)
Teen Screen for Dating Violence (Emelianchik-Key & Hays, 2013)
Trauma Assessment Interview (Hindman, 1989)
Traumatic Events Screening Inventory for Children-Brief Form (Ippen et al., 2002)
Trauma Symptom Checklist for Children (Briere, 1996)
Trauma Symptom Inventory (Briere, 1995)

Crisis Intervention

A *crisis* can be defined as a life event that an individual or family perceives as beyond their ability to cope. Applied to violence, abuse, and trauma within families, crises typically involve acute occurrences that result in a significant state of disequilibrium. Examples include natural or human-made disasters, terrorism, hate crimes, military deployments, recent immigration or asylum, suicides or homicides, or episodes of abuse. In addition to the psychological and physical responses listed earlier, common signs and symptoms are as follows: survivor guilt, inadequacy, feeling overwhelmed, irritability, loss of trust, flashbacks, difficulties in decision making, antisocial acts, changes in activity or communications, hysterical reactions, anger toward God, and sudden resistance to spiritual activities (Greenstone & Leviton, 2011). Greenstone and Leviton (2011) posit six stages of crisis intervention that counselors should consider when working within family systems:

1. *Immediacy:* Act immediately to mitigate anxiety and reduce harm risk.
2. *Control:* Take control to help provide structure for the survivor(s) while presenting with a calm and supportive demeanor.
3. *Assessment:* Evaluate accurately and expeditiously what has caused the crisis, what symptoms receive priority for intervention, and what barriers and resources exist for the family member(s).
4. *Disposition:* Decide how to handle the situation, explore solutions, and mobilize personal resources.
5. *Referral:* Refer as needed to other helping professionals.
6. *Follow-up:* Follow up with family members to ensure they have made contact with the referral.

SIDEBAR 17.1 EFFECTIVE COMMUNICATION WITH FAMILIES IN CRISES

Greenstone and Leviton (2011) offer the following tips when working with individuals in crisis.

- Listen to fully understand what the individual is saying and how he or she is feeling. Clarify as necessary. Attend to both verbal and non-verbal messages.
- Respond descriptively, avoiding judging what the individual is saying.
- Use your own feelings and be clear and specific. Use I statements to reduce a sense of threat.
- Assess needs and discern which issues the individual has control over.
- Make timely responses, prioritizing those issues most important.

Trauma Recovery

In instances in which families encounter pervasive trauma, or when acute interventions are insufficient, counselors should consider long-term trauma recovery. Herman (1997) identified three stages of trauma recovery that may be useful for working with families and individual members. Stage 1 involves *establishing safety* for the individual after a traumatic event. Essentially, counselors help individuals gain control of their internal and external environments to the extent possible. Specifically, counselors help family members meet basic health needs such as sleeping, eating, and exercise; manage PTSD symptoms; control self-destructive behaviors; create a safe living situation and build a support system; and develop a self-protection plan. Stage 2, *remembrance and mourning*, involves counselors continuing to empower and promote the safety of clients while also beginning to reconstruct trauma narratives, transform memories, recover new memories, and mourn and ultimately accept a variety of physical and psychological losses. The final stage, *reconnection*, involves family members developing new selves, relationships, and belief systems, often revisiting Stage 1 tasks. In addition, counselors help families learn new coping skills and reframe the traumatic event (i.e., integration of traumatic events into family and personal narratives).

Systemic-Based Interventions

Violence has an impact beyond the home, workplace, and other settings in which it occurs, and it frequently reaches into the community. As violence moves into the larger community, organizational systems respond to the violence in specific ways to prevent future violence from occurring. Law enforcement is generally the first systemic intervention to violence (Danis, 2003). Police and the court system are regularly involved in providing protection to victims and issuing criminal and civil punishment to perpetrators (Copps Hartley, Renner, & Mackel, 2013). Other first responders, such as paramedics, are frequently involved in the response to IPV and other forms of violence in the community. Only law enforcement can legally intervene in IPV situations, but individual police responses and attitudes toward IPV victims and abusers vary across jurisdictions.

Victims, following incidents of violence, often file a protection from abuse order (PFA) or restraining order (Durfee, 2009). Depending on geographical location, the terminology and process to obtain these protection orders can vary dramatically. All U.S. states have some variation of a legal protection order for individuals involved in intimate or familial relationships to seek protection against an abuser. These orders of protection are legal documents that issue court and law enforcement protection for survivors of violence and/or their immediate family members. Courts issue PFAs for various lengths of time from a few weeks up to 3 years in some jurisdictions. PFAs do not inherently stop violence but do provide legal protection and sanction on the perpetrator including probation, fines, and jail time. Courts may be further involved in domestic relations hearings, custody disputes, divorce proceedings, and related civil legal matters, all of which may deal with aspects of IPV in relationships.

Communities frequently respond to violence, abuse, and trauma in interdisciplinary ways. For example, domestic violence and sexual assault centers in most regions provide emergency shelter, crisis counseling, legal support, and referrals. Some shelters provide long-term clinical treatment for survivors. Many centers are independent nonprofit organizations and thus collaborate with other community organizations, law enforcement, and sometimes businesses and universities to create coalitions and networks of care (Ritchie & Eby, 2007). Many domestic violence and sexual assault shelters are affiliated with area YMCA or YWCA centers. Other programs arise organically from communities to respond to violence and frequently partner with various stakeholders to fund, educate, counsel, and offer support to victims of violence through proactive activities, such as parental education or bullying programs in school settings (Busch-Armendariz, Johnson, Buel, & Lungwitz, 2011). These shelters and crisis counseling centers represent a key frontline approach to treating IPV victims (Roberts & Roberts, 2002). Partnerships between IPV shelters and centers with local hospitals, government agencies, colleges, and other concerned organizations increase the strength of responses and care for trauma victims in a community.

SIDEBAR 17.2 MY WORK WITH FAMILIES AFFECTED BY DOMESTIC VIOLENCE

It is 3:00 a.m. and I am on call for the next few weeks. By day, I see clients in need of support and options for complex domestic violence and sexual assault cases. By night, I take calls of victims in desperate need of safety and legal protection. Frequently that means going to violent scenes, police stations, or hospitals. Often, it means packing families into my car to take them to shelter in the early morning hours. Sometimes they need a completely new life. Sometimes they choose to stay in the home. My job is not to judge but to support.

Couples-Based Interventions

Couples-based counseling for IPV remains a controversial yet growing area of clinical intervention and research (Stover, Meadows, & Kaufman, 2009). Many experts in IPV strongly caution against couples counseling whenever violence is present (Harris, 2006) because there is a risk of increasing the violence when engaging in this intervention. Exploring violence in a couples counseling setting could lead to strong negative feelings for the abuser, such as guilt, shame, embarrassment, frustration, or anger. Once revealed in session, the feelings or thoughts attached to these disclosures could cause escalating retaliatory violence (Babcock, Green, & Robie, 2004).

With this caution in mind, recent research has shown that couples-based counseling can effectively reduce violence for some clients (Harris, 2006; La

Taillade, Epstein, & Werlinich, 2006; Stover et al., 2009). Proper assessment of the level and extent of violence, as well as the presence of substance use in the home, is essential prior to exploring violence within a couples counseling setting. Experts recommend couples counseling only when there is a mild to moderate risk of violence present in the home, there is an absence of substance abuse, and the therapist has separately assessed each partner to fully explore the relationship dynamics in the home, explain the risks of couples counseling, and obtain clear treatment consent from each partner.

Family-Based Interventions

Family-based interventions to violence represent a holistic approach to addressing IPV. Although there is a diverse range of approaches being practiced involving families, each approach shares the theoretical perspective that because violence originates within a home, the interventions should involve as many family members as possible (Cleek, Wofsy, Boyd-Franklin, Mundy, & Howell, 2012; DeVoe, Dean, Traube, & McKay, 2005).

Two such approaches with children are play therapy and filial therapy (Watts & Broaddus, 2002). Children dealing with violence in their lives do not always have the words to express how violence is affecting them. Play therapists use play as a primary tool to explore a child's feelings and thoughts. Play, an activity children naturally do, can be an excellent resource for learning, healing, and growth when used therapeutically. Far from simply sitting down to play with a child, play therapy is a rigorous therapeutic specialty employing specific tools, games, toys, and interventions. Filial therapy takes the practice of play therapy and translates it to the parents of the children experiencing violence. Play therapists educate parents over a period of weekly sessions in the tools and techniques of the modality and give structured play homework assignments to the parents (Kinsworthy & Garza, 2010). Once the training period is over, the play therapist monitors the parental play and works further with the parents to create healing bonds via filial therapy.

Family empowerment programs represent a multiproblem approach to treating issues within the family system (Cleek et al., 2012). There are various models existing under the family empowerment banner, each looking at the array of problems affecting troubled families (e.g., violence, homelessness, addiction, poverty, mental illness, lack of childcare) and developing strategies to address each of these problems from within the family. Parental involvement in groups, educational sessions, and related interventions is an essential component of these family-based intervention programs. The goal is to reduce the overall family stress, alleviate problems, and increase the ability of the family to cope with or be empowered to address the many challenges they face. Some of these models employ an interdisciplinary approach similar to systems-based interventions, incorporating various agencies, mental health facilities, community supports, and universities (Cleek et al., 2012; DeVoe et al., 2005). Tsey et al. (2007) described a grassroots version of family empowerment created by an indigenous population in Australia, meeting the unique needs and challenges of family and personal dynamics present in indigenous cultures within a dominant society. This approach may prove useful in other indigenous populations or be a guide for local communities interested in developing their own empowerment programs to address IPV and family violence.

Resilience-focused brief family therapy (RBFT), which is based on positive psychology and individual psychology principles, is an approach to treating family violence through increasing resilience in the home (Nicoll, 2011). Walsh (2003) defines *resilience* as "the ability to withstand and rebound from disruptive life challenges" (p. 1). RBFT and related resilience-based treatments aim to identify and increase those factors within a family that contribute to rebound from difficult and traumatic events (Czyszczon & Lynch, 2010). Increased family resiliency promotes growth and healing from family stress and trauma as opposed to stagnation, harm, or dysfunction within the family. Family therapists carry out resilience-based treatment in either home-based or outpatient settings.

Group-Based Interventions

Group therapy is a common therapeutic intervention used to treat victims and perpetrators of IPV (Pender, 2012). Counselors often use group interventions and support groups with adult victims and children, sometimes in school settings, as a key method to help clients see the universality of their experience and feel support from other victims. Psychoeducational groups combine educative components with deeper exploration of personal issues, often employing a structured format or curriculum (Babcock et al., 2004). They are less intense than therapy groups. The focus of psychoeducation is on developing new strategies, coping techniques, or behaviors to reduce violence, deal with trauma, or teach prevention skills.

There are several unique forms of group interventions, particularly for the treatment of IPV perpetrators. Counselors utilize these methods in inpatient, correctional, outpatient, and other community-based settings (Hanson, 2002; Yorke, Friedman, & Hurt, 2010). Frequently, the members of these groups are involved in the criminal justice system as part of mandated court or probation treatment requirements. Mandated clients present unique challenges that are surmountable by skilled clinicians.

According to Mills, Barocas, and Ariel (2013), the most popular group-based interventions in the United States for the treatment of violent offenders are batterer's intervention programs (BIPs). There are many BIPs in practice throughout the country, but the Duluth model, or the Domestic Abuse Intervention Project, is the most common (Hanson, 2002). This model is a feminist-based, psychoeducational program that views violence as being rooted in the patriarchal belief system of abusers and the dominant Western society. First developed in 1981 by a collective of agencies in Duluth, Minnesota, the model spread rapidly and formed the basis of most BIPs in existence today. The power-and-control wheel is a tool used frequently by Duluth model adherents looking at the belief and behavioral sources of violence perpetrated by males (Babcock et al., 2004). One male and one female facilitator colead Duluth model programs. Recently, there has been a debate in the research on the effectiveness of Duluth model BIPs in preventing future violence. Recidivism and attrition are major problems within BIPs, and many studies indicate these forms of intervention are only mildly successful. Other researchers, however, show good results or conclude that any effect, however minimal, is beneficial to preventing violence (see Dutton & Corvo, 2007; Gondolf, 2007; Pender, 2012; Schmidt et al., 2007). Other models for BIPs exist beyond the Duluth model, with some incorporating elements from the restorative justice movement, which looks at making reparations of crimes and incorporates victim involvement or testimony into the group intervention (Mills et al., 2013). BIPs vary in length, ranging from 6 to 12 weeks up to 18 months for intensive programs.

Related to BIPs are cognitive-behavioral therapy (CBT) programs, designed from a psychological perspective to treat violence as a primary learned coping skill that can be unlearned in the group setting (Schmidt et al., 2007). This approach views violence as a functional behavioral strategy from the abuser's perspective and seeks to explore the benefits and costs of using violence in this manner. Babcock et al. (2004) argued that this approach is frequently indistinguishable from Duluth model programs, as liberal sharing of CBT techniques and exploration of values and beliefs from patriarchal perspectives exist between the programs. These researchers further state that CBT-based BIPs often go beyond looking at thoughts and behaviors into exploration of feelings with the abusers, such as feelings of jealousy.

Anger management programs make up a large portion of group-based treatment for violent offenders and perpetrators of IPV, yet studies show varying success with this type of intervention (Burt, Patel, Butler, & Gonzalez, 2013). Although no set standard for anger management programs exists, they frequently employ various techniques from BIPs. These programs are generally short-term group interventions, 6 to 12 weeks long, that teach coping skills, relaxation techniques, assertiveness, and related skills. Longer-term intensive programs also exist (SAMHSA, 2012b; Wood, Toyn, & Claypole, 2012). In general, anger management groups are curriculum-based and are led by one or two counselors. Anger management groups are popular within school settings to deal with IPV and bullying, as well as in correctional and mandated treatment settings (Dwivedi & Gupta, 2000; Wood et al., 2012).

POSTSCRIPT: COUNSELOR SELF-CARE

Counselors are ethically bound to be aware of any personal circumstances that may limit their ability to competently provide services (ACA, 2014). When working with family-related issues associated with violence, abuse, and trauma, counselors could be at an increased risk for professional impairment. The terms *compassion fatigue*, *vicarious trauma*, *secondary trauma*, and *burnout* have been used to describe this impairment (see Lawson & Myers, 2010; Maltzman, 2011; Warren, Morgan, Morris, & Morris, 2010). Factors associated with counselor wellness include increased service provision to high-risk clientele and personal levels of stress (see Lawson & Myers, 2010; Wester, Trepal, & Myers, 2009), both of which easily relate to counseling professionals working with individuals and families affected by violence.

To remedy potential or observed impairment, counselors are encouraged to actively participate in self-care (Richards, Campenni, & Muse-Burke, 2010). *Self-care* is defined as "any activity that one does to feel good about oneself. It can be categorized into four groups which include: physical, psychological, spiritual, and support" (Richards et al., 2010, pp. 252–253). These activities could range from the use of creative writing to reflect on professional experiences to meditation and yoga (Maltzman, 2011; Warren et al., 2010). There are several additional recommendations in the literature: incorporation of self-care into organizational structures and academic programs (Richards et al., 2010; Wolf, Thompson, & Smith-Adcock, 2012), mentorship of counseling students and professionals to promote integration of self-care plans and increase accountability (Wester et al., 2009; Wolf et al., 2012), and regular assessment of wellness and self-care practices (Lawson & Myers, 2010; Maltzman, 2011). The following list (Maltzman, 2011; Myers & Sweeney, 2005; Myers, Sweeney, & Witmer, 2000) includes recommendations beyond those just described, to assist with the development of an individualized self-care plan.

Self-Care Recommendations for Counseling Professionals

Recommendations are presented within four domains: emotional, physiological, spiritual, and social. Although it is important that each of these domains be addressed, counselors are encouraged to use this as a framework from which to develop individualized plans.

1. Emotional

   Counselors should be aware of and regulate their emotional states to achieve stability.

   - Be aware of personal stressors and ways to effectively manage those stressors.
   - Affirm sense of worth and control.
   - Regularly reflect on work as a counseling professional.
   - Place realistic expectations on self.
   - Use effective problem-solving skills when faced with professional dilemmas.
   - Maintain an appropriate sense of humor.
   - Create healthy professional boundaries.
   - Appropriately delegate activities to others.
2. Physiological

   Counselors should engage in activities that promote physical health and well-being.

   - Eat a well-balanced diet to ensure the receipt of adequate nutrition.
   - Regularly take part in a preferred exercise regimen.
   - Utilize alternative healing approaches when desired.
3. Spiritual

   Counselors should seek a sense of wholeness by addressing personal spiritual needs.

- Maintain positive thoughts about the present and future.
- Be optimistic about self and environment.
- Use culturally specific helping networks when desired.

4. Social

   Counselors should build social networks within and outside professional environments to ensure adequate personal support.

   - Find an appropriate balance between personal and professional obligations.
   - Identify individuals, familial and otherwise, who are trustworthy and available.
   - Make time to participate in non-work-related activities.
   - Consult with supervisors and colleagues when appropriate.
   - Build peer cohesion and support within the professional environment.

SUMMARY

Counselors encounter families who have experienced violence, abuse, or trauma within family, community, sociopolitical, and historical systems. It is important for counselors to understand the types, prevalence, protective and risk factors, and consequences associated with various forms of violence. We began the chapter by defining violence, abuse, and trauma, conceptualizing violence as an umbrella terminology that includes abuse, with trauma viewed as the individualized label and meaning associated with an event. Then, we presented several statistics on general violence, suicide and homicide, IPV, child abuse, elder abuse, and community trauma. Further, we discussed common symptoms associated with violence, abuse, and trauma.

As a prelude to the discussion of interventions counselors might use, we outlined several diversity considerations such as age, race, ethnicity, nontraditional couples and families, immigrants and refugees, and spirituality. Several interventions were then presented, with a general discussion surrounding key assessment areas and stages of crisis intervention and trauma. The final section included self-care strategies for counselors providing these services.

USEFUL WEBSITES

The following websites provide additional information relating to the chapter topics.

American Red Cross
http://www.redcross.org
National Center for Children Exposed to Violence
http://www.nccev.org/violence/community.html
National Center on Domestic Violence, Trauma, and Mental Health
http://www.nationalcenterdvtraumamh.org/resources/national-domestic-violence-organizations

National Center on Elder Abuse, Administration on Aging
http://www.ncea.aoa.gov
National Coalition Against Domestic Violence
http://www.ncadv.org
National Network to End Domestic Violence
http://www.nnedv.org
National Voluntary Organizations Active in Disaster
http://www.nvoad.org/members
U.S. Department of Health and Human Services, Administration for Children and Families
https://www.childwelfare.gov/pubs/reslist/rl_dsp.cfm?rs_id=21&rate_chno=19-00044
U.S. Department of Justice, Office of Justice Programs
http://www.ojp.usdoj.gov/programs/yvp_resources.htm

REFERENCES

Administration on Aging. (2010). *Older Americans Act*. Retrieved from http://www.aoa.gov/AoA_Programs_OAA/index.aspx

Alexander, A. (1999). *The functions of self-injury and its link to traumatic events in college students* (Doctoral dissertation). Retrieved from UMI Dissertation Services. (UMI No. 9932285).

American Counseling Association. (2014). *ACA code of ethics*. Retrieved from http://www.counseling.org/docs/ethics/2014-aca-code-of-ethics.pdf?sfvrsn=4

Babcock, J. C., Green, C. E., & Robie, C. (2004). Does batterers' treatment work? A meta-analytic review of domestic violence treatment. *Clinical Psychology Review*, *23*, 1023–1053. doi:10.1016/j.cpr.2002.07.001

Babor, T. F., Higgins-Biddle, J. C., Saunders, J. B., & Monteiro, M. G. (2001). *The alcohol use disorders identification test: Guidelines for use in primary care* (2nd ed.). Retrieved from http://whqlibdoc.who.int/hq/2001/who_msd_msb_01.6a.pdf

Banks, J. R., & Fedewa, A. L. (2012). Counselors' attitudes toward domestic violence in same-sex versus opposite-sex relationships. *Journal of Multicultural Counseling and Development*, *40*, 194–205. doi:10.1002/j.2161-1912.2012.00017.x

Basow, S. A., & Thompson, J. (2012). Service providers' reactions to intimate partner violence as a function of victim sexual orientation and type of abuse. *Journal of Interpersonal Violence*, *27*, 1225–1241. doi:10.1177/0886260511425241

Beck, A. T., & Steer, R. A. (1993). *Beck Anxiety Inventory manual*. San Antonio, TX: Psychological Corporation.

Beck, A. T., Steer, R. A., & Brown, G. K. (2003). *Beck Depression Inventory–II manual*. San Antonio, TX: Psychological Corporation.

Benavides, L. E. (2012). A phenomenological study of spirituality as a protective factor for adolescents exposed to domestic violence. *Journal of Social Service Research*, *38*, 165–174. doi:10.1080/01488376.2011.615274

Bernstein, D. P., & Fink, L. (1998). *Childhood Trauma Questionnaire: A retrospective self-report manual*. San Antonio, TX: Psychological Corporation.

Black, M. C., Basile, K. C., Breiding, M. J., Smith, S. G., Walters, M. L., Merrick, M. T., . . . Stevens, M. R. (2011). *The National Intimate Partner and Sexual Violence Survey (NISVS): 2010 summary report*. Atlanta, GA: National Center for Injury Prevention and Control, Centers for Disease Control and Prevention.

Blasko, K. A., Winek, J. L., & Bieschke, K. J. (2007). Therapists' prototypical assessment of domestic violence situations. *Journal of Marital and Family Therapy*, *33*, 258–269. doi:10.1111/j.1752-0606.2007.00020.x

Bowland, S., Biswas, B., Kyriakakis, S., & Edmond, T. (2011). Transcending the negative: Spiritual struggles and resilience in older female trauma survivors. *Journal of Religion, Spirituality, and Aging*, *23*, 318–337. doi:10.1080/15528030.2011.592121

Briere, J. (1992). *Child abuse trauma: Theory and treatment of the lasting effects*. Newbury Park, CA: Sage.

Briere, J. (1995). *Professional manual for the Trauma Symptom Inventory*. Odessa, FL: Psychological Assessment Resources.

Briere, J. (1996). *Professional manual for the Trauma Symptom Checklist for Children*. Odessa, FL: Psychological Assessment Resources.

Brown, M. J., & Groscup, J. (2009). Perceptions of same-sex domestic violence among crisis center staff. *Journal of Family Violence*, *24*, 74–93. doi:10.1007/s10896-008-9212-5

Burt, I., Patel, S. H., Butler, S. K., & Gonzalez, T. (2013). Integrating leadership skills into anger management groups to reduce aggressive behaviors: The LIT model. *Journal of Mental Health Counseling*, *35*, 124–141.

Busch-Armendariz, N. B., Johnson, R. J., Buel, S., & Lungwitz, J. (2011). Building community partnerships to end interpersonal violence: A collaboration of the schools of social work, law, and nursing. *Violence Against Women*, *17*, 1194–1206. doi:10.1177/1077801211419330

Cabral, R. R., & Smith, T. B. (2011). Racial/ethnic matching of clients and therapists in mental health services: A meta-analytic review of preferences, perceptions, and outcomes. *Journal of Counseling Psychology*, *58*, 537–554. doi:10.1037/a0025266

Carbone-Lopez, K. (2013). Across racial/ethnic boundaries: Investigating intimate violence within a national sample. *Journal of Interpersonal Violence*, *28*, 3–24. doi:10.1177/0886260512448850

Centers for Disease Control and Prevention. (2006). *Physical dating violence among high school students—United States, 2003*. Retrieved from http://www.cdc.gov/mmwr/preview/mmwrhtml/mm5519a3.htm

Centers for Disease Control and Prevention. (2011a). *Ten leading causes of death by age group, United States—2010*. Retrieved from http://www.cdc.gov/injury/wisqars/pdf/10LCID_Unintentional_ Deaths_2010-a.pdf

Centers for Disease Control and Prevention. (2011b). *The National Intimate Partner and Sexual Violence Survey (NISVS): 2010 summary report*. Retrieved from http://www.cdc.gov/violenceprevention/pdf/nisvs_report2010-a.pdf

Centers for Disease Control and Prevention. (2011c). *National Intimate Partner and Sexual Violence Survey*. Retrieved from http://www.cdc.gov/ViolencePrevention/pdf/NISVS_Report2010-a.pdf

Chandra, A., Lara-Cinisomo, S., Jaycox, L. H., Tanielian, T., Burns, R. M., Ruder, T., & Bing, H. (2010). Children on the homefront: The experience of children from military families. *Pediatrics*, *125*, 16–25. doi:10.1542/peds2009-1180

Chang, D. F., & Berk, A. (2009). Making cross-racial therapy work: A phenomenological study of clients' experiences of cross-racial therapy. *Journal of Counseling Psychology*, *56*, 521–536. doi:10.1037/a0016905

Child Welfare Information Gateway. (2012). *Mandatory reporters of child abuse and neglect.* Retrieved from https://www.childwelfare.gov/systemwide/laws_policies/statutes/manda.pdf

Cho, H., & Kim, W. J. (2012). Intimate partner violence among Asian Americans and their use of mental health services: Comparisons with White, Black, and Latino victims. *Journal of Immigrant Minority Health, 14*, 809–815. doi:10.1007/s10903-012-9625-3

Cleek, E. N., Wofsy, M., Boyd-Franklin, N., Mundy, B., & Howell, J. (2012). The family empowerment program: An interdisciplinary approach to working with multi-stressed urban families. *Family Process, 51*, 207–217. doi:10.1111/j.1545-5300.2012.01392.x

Coker, A. L., Davis, K. E., Arias, I., Desai, S., Sanderson, M., Brandt, H. M., & Smith, P. H. (2002). Physical and mental health effects of intimate partner violence for men and women. *American Journal of Preventive Medicine, 24*, 260–268. doi:10.1016/S0749-3797(02)00514-7

Copps Hartley, C., Renner, L. M., & Mackel, S. (2013). Civil legal services and domestic violence: Missed service opportunities. *Families in Society, 94*, 15–22. doi:10.1606/1044-3894.4260

Cragun, C. L., & Friedlander, M. L. (2012). Experiences of Christian clients in secular psychotherapy: A mixed-methods investigation. *Journal of Counseling Psychology, 59*, 379–391. doi:10.1037/a0028283

Cyr, M., McDuff, P., & Wright, J. (2006). Prevalence and predictors of dating violence among adolescent female victims of child sexual abuse. *Journal of Interpersonal Violence, 21*, 1000–1017. doi:10.1177/0886260506290201

Cyr, M., Wright, J., McDuff, P., & Perron, A. (2002). Intrafamilial sexual abuse: Brother-sister incest does not differ from father-daughter and stepfather-stepdaughter incest. *Child Abuse and Neglect, 26*, 957–973. doi:10.1016/S0145-2134(02)00365-4

Czyszczon, G., & Lynch, M. (2010). Families in crisis: Resilience-based interventions in in-home family therapy. *Vistas, 10*. Retrieved from http://counselingoutfitters.com/vistas/vistas10/Article_17.pdf

Danis, F. S. (2003). The criminalization of domestic violence: What social workers need to know. *Social Work, 48*, 237–246. doi:10.1093/sw/48.2.237

Derogatis, L. R. (1993). *BSI: Administration, scoring, and procedures for the Brief Symptom Inventory* (3rd ed.). Minneapolis, MN: National Computer Systems.

DeVoe, E. R., Dean, K., Traube, D., & McKay, M. M. (2005). The SURVIVE community project: A family-based intervention to reduce the impact of violence exposures in urban youth. *Journal of Aggression, Maltreatment & Trauma, 11*, 95–116. doi:10.1300/J146v11n04.05

Durfee, A. (2009). Victim narratives, legal representation, and domestic violence civil protection orders. *Feminist Criminology, 4*, 7–31. doi:10.1177/1557085108324961

Durfee, A., & Messing, J. T. (2012). Characteristics related to protection order use among victims of intimate partner violence. *Violence Against Women, 18*, 701–710. doi:10.1177/1077801212454256

Dutton, D., & Corvo, K. (2007). The Duluth model: A data-impervious paradigm and a failed strategy. *Aggression and Violent Behavior, 12*, 658–667. doi:10.1016/j.avb.2007.03.002

Dwivedi, K., & Gupta, A. (2000). "Keeping cool": Anger management through group work. *Support for Learning, 15*, 76–81. doi:10.1111/1467-9604.00150

Emelianchik-Key, K., & Hays, D. G. (2013). *Initial development and validation of the Teen Screen for Dating Violence.* Manuscript submitted for publication.

Erez, E., Adelman, M., & Gregory, C. (2009). Intersections of immigration and domestic violence. *Feminist Criminology, 4*, 32–56. doi:10.1177/1557085108325413

Evans, W. N. (1998). Assessment and diagnosis of the substance use disorders (SUDs). *Journal of Counseling and Development*, *76*, 325–333. doi:10.1002/j.1556-6676.1998.tb02549.x

Ewing, J. A. (1984). Detecting alcoholism: The CAGE Questionnaire. *Journal of the American Medical Association*, *252*, 1905–1907. doi:10.1001/jama.252.14.1905

Figley, C. R., & Kiser, L. J. (2013). *Helping traumatized families* (2nd ed.). New York, NY: Routledge.

Fletcher, K. E. (1991). *Parent report of the child's reaction to stress*. Worcester: University of Massachusetts Medical Center.

Flicker, S. M., Waldron, H. B., Turner, C. W., Brody, J. L., & Hyman, H. (2008). Ethnic matching and treatment outcome with Hispanic and Anglo substance-abusing adolescents in family therapy. *Journal of Family Psychology*, *22*, 439–447. doi:10.1037/0893-3200.22.3.439

Forman, J., & McBride, R. (2010). Counselors' role in preventing abuse in older adults: Clinical, ethical, and legal considerations. *Adultspan*, *9*, 4–13. doi:10.1002/j.2161-0029.2010.tb00067.x

Fowler, D. N., Faulkner, M., Learman, J., & Runnels, R. (2011). The influence of spirituality on service utilization and satisfaction for women residing in a domestic violence shelter. *Violence Against Women*, *17*, 1244–1259. doi:10.1177/1077801211424480

Friedrich, W. N. (1997). *Child Sexual Behavior Inventory*. Lutz, FL: Psychological Assessment Resources.

Fuchsel, C. L., Murphy, S. B., & Dufresne, R. (2012). Domestic violence, culture, and relationship dynamics among immigrant Mexican women. *Affilia: Journal of Women and Social Work*, *27*, 263–274. doi:10.1177/0886109912452403

Gondolf, E. W. (2007). Theoretical and research support for the Duluth model: A reply to Dutton and Corvo. *Aggression and Violent Behavior*, *12*, 644–657. doi:10.1016/j.avb.2007.03.001

Gray, M., Litz, B. T., Hsu, J. L., & Lombardo, T. W. (2004). Psychometric properties of the Life Events Checklist. *Assessment*, *11*, 330–341.

Greenstone, J. L., & Leviton, S. C. (2011). *Elements of crisis intervention: Crises and how to respond to them* (3rd ed.). Belmont, CA: Brooks/Cole.

Grossman, S. F., Hinkley, S., Kawalski, A., & Margrave, C. (2005). Rural versus urban victims of violence: The interplay of race and region. *Journal of Family Violence*, *20*, 71–81. doi:10.1007/s10896-005-3170-y

Gupta, J., Acevedo-Garcia, D., Hemenway, D., Decker, M. R., Raj, A., & Silverman, J. G. (2009). Premigration exposure to political violence and perpetration of intimate partner violence among immigrant men in Boston. *American Journal of Public Health*, *99*, 462–469. doi:10.2105/AJPH.2007.120634

Gustafson, D. T., & Iluebbey, V. (2013). "Traditional discipline" or domestic violence: Participatory action research with a Sudanese refugee community. *Journal of Cultural Diversity*, *20*, 51–56.

Hanson, B. (2002). Interventions for batterers: Program approaches, program tensions. In A. R. Roberts (Ed.), *Handbook of domestic violence intervention strategies* (pp. 419–448). New York, NY: Oxford University Press.

Harris, G. (2006). Conjoint therapy and domestic violence: Treating the individuals and the relationship. *Counseling Psychology Quarterly*, *19*, 373–379. doi:10.1080/09515070601029533

Hays, D. G., Green, E., Orr, J. J., & Flowers, L. (2007). Advocacy counseling for female survivors of partner abuse: Implications for counselor education. *Counselor Education and Supervision*, *46*, 186–198. doi:10.1002/j.1556-6978.2007.tb00024.x

Herman, J. (1997). *Trauma and recovery: The aftermath of violence from domestic abuse to political terror*. New York, NY: Basic Books.

Hetling, A., & Zhang, H. (2010). Domestic violence, poverty, and social services: Does location matter? *Social Science Quarterly*, *91*, 1144–1163. doi:10.1111/j.1540-6237.2010.00725.x

Hindman, J. (1989). *Just before dawn*. Ontario, OR: AlexAndria Associates.

Holt, M. K. & Espelage, D. L. (2005). Social support as a moderator between dating violence victimization and depression/anxiety among African American and Caucasian adolescents. *School Psychology Review*, *34*, 309–328.

Horst, K., Marcos, M., Culver-Turner, R., Amanor-Boadu, Y., Minner, B., Cook, J., & McCollum, E. (2012). The importance of therapist/client ethnic/racial matching in couples treatment for domestic violence. *Contemporary Family Therapy*, *34*, 57–71. doi:10.1007/s10591-012-9174-x

Horton, C. B., & Cruise, T. K. (1997). Clinical assessment of child victims and adult survivors of child maltreatment. *Journal of Counseling and Development*, *76*, 94–104. doi:10.1002/j.1556-6676.1997.tb02381.x

Ippen, C. G., Ford, J., Racusin, R., Acker, M., Bosquet, M., Rogers, K., . . . Edwards, J. (2002). *Traumatic Events Screening Inventory—Parent Report Revised*. Washington, DC: National Center for PTSD.

Kinsworthy, S., & Garza, Y. (2010). Filial therapy with victims of family violence: A phenomenological study. *Journal of Family Violence*, *25*, 423–429. doi:10.1007/s10896-010-9303-y

Kitzrow, M. A. (2002). Survey of CACREP-accredited programs: Training counselors to provide treatment for sexual abuse. *Counselor Education and Supervision*, *42*, 107–118. doi:10.1002/j.1556-6978.2002.tb01803.x

La Taillade, J. J., Epstein, N. B., & Werlinich, C. A. (2006). Conjoint treatment of intimate partner violence: A cognitive behavioral approach. *Journal of Cognitive Psychotherapy*, *20*, 393–410. doi:10.1891/jcpiq-v20i4a005

Lawson, G., & Myers, J. E. (2010). Wellness, professional quality of life, and career-sustaining behaviors: What keeps us well? *Journal of Counseling and Development*, *89*, 163–171. doi:10.1002/j.1556-6678.2011.tb00074.x

Levitt, H. M., Swanger, R. T., & Butler, J. B. (2008). Male perpetrators' perspectives on intimate partner violence, religion, and masculinity. *Sex Roles*, *58*, 435–448. doi:10.1007/s11199-007-9349-3

Lipsky, S., Cristofalo, M., Reed, S., Caetano, R., & Roy-Byrne, P. (2012). Racial and ethnic disparities in police-reported intimate partner violence perpetration: A mixed methods approach. *Journal of Interpersonal Violence*, *27*, 2144–2162. doi:10.1177/0886260511432152

Lundy, M., & Grossman, S. F. (2009). Domestic violence service users: A comparison of older and younger women victims. *Journal of Family Violence*, *24*, 297–309. doi:10.1007/s10896-009-9230-y

Mahapatra, N. (2012). South Asian women in the U.S. and their experience of domestic violence. *Journal of Family Violence*, *27*, 381–390. doi:10.1007/s10896-012-9434-4

Maltzman, S. (2011). An organizational self-care model: Practical suggestions for development and implementation. *Counseling Psychologist*, *39*, 303–319. doi:10.1177/0011000010381790

Mansfield, A. J., Kaufman, J. S., Engel, C. C., & Gaynes, B. N. (2011). Deployment and mental health diagnoses among children of U.S. Army personnel. *Archives of Pediatric Adolescent Medicine*, *165*, 999–1005. doi:10.1001/archpediatrics.2011.123

McAdams, C., Shillingford, M. A., & Trice-Black, S. (2011). Putting research into practice in school violence prevention and intervention: How is school counseling doing? *Journal of School Counseling*, *9*. Retrieved from http://jsc.montana.edu/articles/v9n12.pdf

McClennen, J. C., Summers, A. B., & Daley, J. G. (2002). The Lesbian Partner Abuse Scale. *Research on Social Work Practice*, *12*, 277–292. doi:10.1177/104973150201200205

McLaughlin, K. A., Hatzenbuehler, M. L., Xuan, Z., & Conron, K. J. (2012). Disproportionate exposure to early-life adversity and sexual orientation disparities in psychiatric morbidity. *Child Abuse and Neglect*, *36*, 645–655. doi:10.1016/j.chiabu.2012.07.004

McLeod, A. L., Muldoon, J., & Hays, D. G. (2014). Intimate partner violence. In L. R. Jackson-Cherry & B. T. Erford (Eds.), *Crisis assessment, intervention, and prevention* (2nd ed., pp. 157–191). Boston, MA: Pearson.

McPherson, P., Scribano, P., & Stevens, J. (2012). Barriers to successful treatment completion in child sexual abuse survivors. *Journal of Interpersonal Violence*, *27*, 23–39. doi:10.1177/0886260511416466

Messinger, A. M. (2011). Invisible victims: Same-sex IPV in the National Violence Against Women survey. *Journal of Interpersonal Violence*, *26*, 2228–2243. doi:10.1177/0886260510383023

Milliken, C. S., Auchterlonie, J. L., & Hoge, C. W. (2007). Longitudinal assessment of mental health problems among active and reserve component soldiers returning from the Iraq war. *Journal of the American Medical Association*, *298*, 2141–2148. doi:10.1001/jama.298.18.2141

Mills, L. G., Barocas, B., & Ariel, B. (2013). The next generation of court-mandated domestic violence treatment: A comparison study of batterer intervention and restorative justice programs. *Journal of Experimental Criminology*, *9*, 65–90. doi:10.1007/s11292-012-9164-x

Myers, J. E., & Sweeney, T. J. (2005). The indivisible self: An evidence-based model of wellness (reprint). *Journal of Individual Psychology*, *61*, 269–279.

Myers, J. E., Sweeney, T. J., & Witmer, J. M. (2000). The wheel of wellness counseling for wellness: A holistic model for treatment planning. *Journal of Counseling and Development*, *78*, 251–266. doi:10.1002/j.1556-6676.2000.tb01906.x

National Center on Elder Abuse. (n.d.). *Reporting abuse*. Retrieved from http://www.ncea.aoa.gov/Stop_Abuse/Get_Help/Report/index.aspx

National Committee for the Prevention of Elder Abuse. (n.d.). *What is elder abuse?* Retrieved from http://www.preventelderabuse.org/elderabuse

Nicoll, W. G. (2011). Resilience-focused brief family therapy: An Adlerian approach. *Journal of Individual Psychology*, *67*, 206–221.

Nilsson, J. E., Brown, C., Russell, E. B., & Khamphakdy-Brown, S. (2008). Acculturation, partner violence, and psychological distress in refugee women from Somalia. *Journal of Interpersonal Violence*, *23*, 1654–1663. doi:10.1177/0886260508314310

Palusci, V. J., & Ondersma, S. J. (2012). Services and recurrence after psychological maltreatment confirmed by Child Protective Services. *Child Maltreatment*, *17*, 153–163. doi:10.1177/1077559511433817

Patterson, W. M., Dohn, H. H., Bird, J., & Patterson, G. A. (1983). Evaluation of suicidal patients: The SAD PERSONS Scale. *Psychosomatics*, *24*, 343–349. doi:10.1016/S0033-3182(83)73213-5

Peek-Asa, C., Wallis, A., Harland, K., Beyer, K., Dickey, P., & Saftlas, A. (2011). Rural disparity in domestic violence prevalence and access to resources. *Journal of Women's Health*, *20*, 1743–1749. doi:10.1089/jwh.2011.2891

Pender, R. L. (2012). ASGW best practice guidelines: An evaluation of the Duluth Model. *Journal for Specialists in Group Work*, *37*, 218–231. doi:10.1080/01933922.2011.632813

Poorman, R. P., Seelau, E. P., & Seelau, S. M. (2003). Perceptions of domestic abuse in same-sex relationships and implications for criminal justice and mental health responses. *Violence and Victims*, *18*, 659–669. doi:10.1891/vivi.2003.18.6.659

Putnam, F. W., Helmer, K., & Trickett, P. K. (1993). Development, reliability, and validity of a child dissociation scale. *Child Abuse and Neglect*, *17*, 731–741. doi:10.1016/S0145-2134(08)80004-X

Renner, L. M., & Whitney, S. D. (2010). Examining symmetry in intimate partner violence among young adults using socio-demographic characteristics. *Journal of Family Violence*, *25*, 91–106. doi:10.1007/s10896-009-9273-0

Richards, K. C., Campenni, C. E., & Muse-Burke, J. L. (2010). Self-care and well-being in mental health professionals: The mediating effects of self-awareness and mindfulness. *Journal of Mental Health Counseling*, *32*, 247–264.

Ritchie, D., & Eby, K. (2007). Transcending boundaries: An international, interdisciplinary community partnership to address domestic violence. *Journal of Community Practice*, *15* (1-2), 121–145. doi:10.1300/J125v15n01_06

Roberto, K. A., McCann, B. R., & Brossoie, N. (2013). Intimate partner violence in late life: An analysis of national news reports. *Journal of Elder Abuse and Neglect*, *25*, 230–241. doi:10.1080/08946566.2012.751825

Roberts, A. R., & Roberts, B. S. (2002). A comprehensive model for crisis intervention with battered women and their children. In A. R. Roberts (Ed.), *Handbook of domestic violence intervention strategies* (pp. 365–395). New York, NY: Oxford University Press.

Rogers, J. R., Alexander, R. A., & Subich, L. M. (1994). Development and psychometric analysis of the Suicide Assessment Checklist. *Journal of Mental Health Counseling*, *16*, 352–368.

Schmidt, M., Kolodinsky, J., Carsten, G., Schmidt, F., Larson, M., & MacLachlan, C. (2007). Short term change in attitude and motivating factors to change abusive behavior of male batterers after participating in a group intervention program based on the pro-feminist and cognitive-behavioral approach. *Journal of Family Violence*, *22*, 91–100. doi:10.1007/s10896-007-9064-4

Shuman, R. D., McCauley, J., Waltermaurer, E., Roche, W. P., Hollis, H., Gibbons, A. K., & McNutt, L. A. (2008). Understanding intimate partner violence against women in the rural South. *Violence and Victims*, *23*, 390–405. doi:10.1891/0886-6708.23.3.390

Skiff, D., Horwitz, S. H., LaRussa-Trott, M., Pearson, J., & Santiago, L. (2008). Engaging the clergy in addressing the impact of partner violence in their faith communities. *Journal of Spirituality in Mental Health*, *10*, 101–118. doi:10.1080/19349630802081046

Sokoloff, N. J., & Dupont, I. (2005). Domestic violence at the intersections of race, class, and gender: Challenges and contributions to understanding violence against marginalized women in diverse communities. *Violence Against Women*, *11*, 38–64. doi:10.1177/1077801204271476

Spielberger, C. D. (1999). *State–Trait Anger Expression Inventory–2*. Odessa, FL: Psychological Assessment Resources.

Stover, C. S., Meadows, A. L., & Kaufman, J. (2009). Interventions for intimate partner violence: Review and implications for evidence-based practice. *Professional Psychology: Research & Practice*, *40*, 223–233. doi:10.1037/a0012718

Stracuzzi, T. I., Mohr, J. J., & Fuertes, J. N. (2011). Gay and bisexual male clients' perceptions of counseling: The role of perceived sexual orientation similarity and counselor universal-diverse orientation. *Journal of Counseling Psychology*, *58*, 299–309. doi:10.1037/a0023603

Strauss, M. A., Hamby, S. L., Boney-McCoy, S., & Sugarman, D. B. (1996). The Revised Conflict Tactics Scale (CTS2). *Journal of Family Issues*, *17*, 283–316. doi:10.1177/019251396017003001

Substance Abuse and Mental Health Services Administration. (2012a). *Trauma definition*. Retrieved from http://www.samhsa.gov/traumajustice/traumadefinition/index.aspx

Substance Abuse and Mental Health Services Administration (SAMHSA). (2012b). *Anger management for substance abuse and mental health clients: A cognitive behavioral therapy manual*. (HHS Publication No. SMA 12-4213). Rockville, MD: Department of Health and Human Services.

Sue, D. W., Arredondo, P., & McDavis, R. J. (1992). Multicultural counseling competencies and standards: A call to the profession. *Journal of Counseling and Development*, *70*, 477–486. doi:10.1002/j.1556-6676.1992.tb01642.x

Tehee, M., & Esqueda, C. W. (2008). American Indian and European American women's perceptions of domestic violence. *Journal of Family Violence*, *23*, 25–35. doi:10.1007/s10896-007-9126-7

Todhunter, R. G., & Deaton, J. (2010). The relationship between religious and spiritual factors and the perpetration of intimate partner violence. *Journal of Family Violence*, *25*, 745–753. doi:10.1007/s10896-010-9332-6

Tsey, K., Wilson, A., Haswell-Elkins, M., Whiteside, M., McCalman, J., Cadet-James, Y., & Mark, W. (2007). Empowerment-based research methods: A 10-year approach to enhancing indigenous social and emotional wellbeing. *Australasian Psychiatry*, *15*, S34–S38. doi:10.1080/10398560701701163

U.S. Department of Education. (2012). *Indicators of school crime and safety, 2011*. Retrieved from http://www.bjs.gov/index.cfm?ty=pbdetail&iid=2295

U.S. Department of Health and Human Services. (2010). *Child maltreatment 2008: Summary*. Retrieved from http://www.acf.hhs.gov/programs/cb/resource/child-maltreatment-2008

U.S. Department of Health and Human Services. (2011). *Child maltreatment, 2010*. Retrieved from www.acf.hhs.gov/programs/cb/pubs/cm10/index.htm

U.S. Department of Homeland Security. (2013). *Refugees and asylees: 2012*. Retrieved from http://www.dhs.gov/publication/refugees-and-asylees-2012

U.S. Department of Justice. (2009). *Exposure to violence: A comprehensive national survey*. Retrieved from https://www.ncrjs.gov/pdffiles1/ojjdp/227744.pdf

U.S. Federal Bureau of Investigations. (2012a). *Crime in the United States, 2011*. Retrieved from http://www.fbi.gov/about-us/cjis/ucr/crime-in-theu.s/2011/crime-in-the-u.s.-2011/violent-crime/violent-crime

U.S. Federal Bureau of Investigations. (2012b). *Hate crime statistics, 2011*. Retrieved from http://www.fbi.gov/aboutus/cjis/ucr/hatecrime/2011/narratives/incidents-and-offenses

Waliski, A., Kirchner, J. A., Shue, V. M., & Bokony, P. A. (2012). Psychological traumas of war: Training school counselors as home-front responders. *Journal of Rural Health*, *28*, 348–355. doi:10.1111/j.1748-0361.2012.00404.x

Walsh, F. (2003). Family resilience: A framework for clinical practice. *Family Process*, *42*, 1–18. doi:10.1111/j.1545-5300.2003.00001.x

Warren, J., Morgan, M. M., Morris, L. B., & Morris, T. M. (2010). Breathing words slowly: Creative writing and counselor self-care—the writing workout. *Journal of Creativity in Mental Health*, *5*, 109–124. doi:10.1080/15401383.2010.485074

Watts, R. L., & Broaddus, J. L. (2002). Improving parent-child relationships through filial therapy: An interview with Garry Landreth. *Journal of Counseling and Development*, *80*, 372–378. doi:10.1002/j.1556-6678.2002.tb00202.x

Weathers, F. W., Huska, J. A., & Keane, T. M. (1991). *PCL-C for DSM-IV*. Boston, MA: National Center for PTSD, Behavioral Science Division.

Wester, K. L., Trepal, H. C., & Myers, J. E. (2009). Wellness of counselor educators: An initial look. *Journal of Humanistic Counseling, Education and Development*, *48*, 91–109. doi:10.1002/j.2161-1939.2009.tb00070.x

Wolf, C. P., Thompson, I. A., & Smith-Adcock, S. (2012). Wellness in counselor preparation: Promoting individual well-being. *Journal of Individual Psychology*, *68*, 164–181.

Wood, C., Toyn, S., & Claypole, C. (2012). Delivering group-based treatment programmes for clients in high security settings. *Mental Health Practice*, *16*, 32–36.

World Health Organization. (2013). *Building global commitment to violence prevention*. Retrieved from http://www.who.int/violenceprevention/en

Yick, A. G. (2008). A metasynthesis of qualitative findings on the role of spirituality and religiosity among culturally diverse domestic violence survivors. *Qualitative Health Research*, *18*, 1289–1306. doi:10.1177/1049732308321772

Yorke, N. J., Friedman, B. D., & Hurt, P. (2010). Implementing a batterer's intervention program in a correctional setting: A tertiary prevention model. *Journal of Offender Rehabilitation*, *49*, 456–478. doi:10.1080/10509674.2010.510770

CHAPTER 18

Divorce and Other Loss Issues in Family Therapy

Thelma Duffey

University of Texas at San Antonio

Loss comes upon a family like a thief in the night, taking something or someone dearly loved and treasured and leaving behind confusion and feelings of grief. When couples and families experience a significant loss, their equilibrium is shattered; their sense of normalcy replaced with an unexplainable void. People in grief not only suffer tangible losses; they often suffer abstract losses, like the loss of a dream (Duffey, 2005). Given the diverse coping styles, personalities, developmental maturity, and the frame of reference that each family member carries, and in light of each person's unique relationship with the loss, individual responses to loss vary. Families undergoing periods of loss are challenged to respect the individual grieving styles of its members and to be patient with the periods of emotional disconnection that invariably come, not only with others but often within themselves.

The form and range of losses that families endure are as broad as they are painful. Families suffer concrete losses such as death, divorce, job loss, the loss of a home, and loss of possessions. They suffer intangible losses such as betrayal, trust, illusions, and treasured dreams. In each of these cases, individual family members must negotiate their feelings and experiences in relation to the loss and their relationships with one another. Counselors have the unique privilege of working with couples and families as they negotiate these losses. As they do so, they bring with them education and skills, objectivity and perspective, and their own life circumstances and histories. Collectively, these factors inform a counselor's work with grieving clients.

This chapter provides a family perspective on grief and loss and a brief review of relevant guiding theories that support grief counseling. Illustrated with practical case examples, the chapter provides a framework for a counselor's work with grief issues in a couple and family context. In this chapter you will find some salient factors related to grief, such as gender socialization, cultural variables, stigma, and the role of spirituality, creativity, and the narrative experience in grief work. This chapter details some common loss experiences that couples and families face and introduces theory-based creative interventions. Finally, this chapter incorporates the person of the counselor and offers some means by which counselors can offer compassionate, supportive services while practicing self-care.

THE GRIEF EXPERIENCE

When people experience grief, they often experience feelings of sadness, anger, guilt, insecurity, anxiety, loneliness, and fatigue (Duffey, 2005; Worden, 2009). Many people feel helpless and experience a strained sense of longing when deprived of someone or something they love and want. They may experience physical sensations, such as a shortness of breath, tightness in the stomach, keen distractibility, dry mouth, and a lack of energy (Worden, 2009). Shock, confusion, sleep disturbances, and bewilderment are common symptoms of grief. For many, eating becomes a challenge. People in grief may have difficulty focusing. At times they withdraw from others. They may obsess and ruminate. Grief can bring people to their knees.

When couples or members of a family experience a shared loss, they are challenged to negotiate their feelings in tandem with the feelings of those around them. At times, sharing a loss can bring comfort and respite. Partners and family members are often in positions to uniquely understand the meaning of the loss and its magnitude. Other times, however, conflicting expressions of loss can add distress to an already challenging situation for couples and family members. Differences in personality styles, relational support, spiritual beliefs, and personal histories impact how each person experiences loss. Honoring these differences so each person has the space and time to grieve becomes especially significant.

Family Communication During the Grief Process

One of the greater challenges facing counselors working with grieving couples and families involves meeting the needs of the various members with respect to communication. For example, Miriam and Ray, both 60, recently lost their only son to a drug overdose. They had sought counseling at various points in their marriage and shared an unsteady alliance. Although they loved and depended on one another, their roles with one another were problematic. Roy was authoritarian, and Miriam resented feeling controlled. Miriam was free-spirited and often distracted and, as a result, did not always garner the respect she so wanted. Their gifted and talented son succumbed to drugs at an early age, and Miriam and Ray did all they could to support his recovery. In fact, much of their efforts over the past 20 years involved raising their son and keeping him safe. Now, as they faced the greatest loss of their lives, they looked to one another for the comfort that no one else could readily provide. Unfortunately, the increased communication between them, which felt like comfort for one, felt like pressure and an impossible imposition for the other.

Researchers suggest that grieving couples and families benefit from the opportunity to share their memories and together make sense of their losses (Neimeyer, 2012; Neimeyer, Harris, Winokeur, & Thornton, 2011; Walsh & McGoldrick,

2004). Grief theorists purport that the meaning families make of their losses and the sharing of feelings, thoughts, and memories bring people together, strengthen bonds, and enhance relationships (Neimeyer, 2012; Neimeyer et al., 2011). Indeed, sharing experiences and information is a form of self-disclosure, which can promote intimacy among people (Duffey, Wooten, Lumadue, & Comstock, 2004). However, Hooghe, Neimeyer, and Rober (2011) suggest that shared communication during periods of grief is not always helpful. In fact, they propose that, in some cases, silence may be a healthy and purposeful coping strategy for grieving couples and families as they negotiate their loss.

While Miriam felt a deep need to express her grief with Ray, he felt an opposing need to retreat in silence. Much of their work involved helping Ray come closer to Miriam and share space with her while helping Miriam respect that Ray's grieving style involved some silence and isolation. For periods of time, Miriam would cry alone in her room while Ray would sort through their son's belongings, and in the privacy of his mind, attempt to make sense of his loss. The differences in their coping and their long-standing conflicts as a couple exacerbated an already excruciatingly painful loss and challenged their ability to grieve together. However, as Ray was able to release some control over the daily operations of their home, and as Miriam was able to recognize that Ray's grief looked different than hers, they were both better positioned to enter into a new form of collaboration. Their marriage remained challenged, but they were better able to share space in their grief. Hooghe et al. (2011) recommend that counselors take a more accepting view of silence, stressing that "emotions can be expressed in nonverbal ways" (p. 917). In this case, Ray experienced relief in knowing his retreat into silence could be respected, yet he struggled to allow Miriam more ownership and control in areas that had been historically his domain.

Hooghe et al. (2011) reinforce the idea that some grieving family members may want to be alone with their thoughts and work through their grief in private, and Ray exemplified that construct. Grief communication between family members is a complex process. For example, one person may want to be open to the other but may fear a negative response. Another person may fear feeling like an annoyance and will remain silent. No doubt, grief creates insecurity in the bereaved and within their relationships. However, Niemeyer (2009) contended that as people are able to make meaning of their experiences and share that meaning through the stories they tell, they are better able to connect with one another and make sense of their shared grief (Neimeyer, 2012; Neimeyer et al., 2011).

Further, because sharing stories is an ongoing dialogue between family members, the storytelling process is complex. It involves more than one person's desire to share and another person's willingness or lack of willingness to listen (Hooghe et al., 2011). In that respect, communication is considered dynamic because it occurs in the context of a relationship in flux (Hooghe et al., 2011). Couples and families experience feelings differently at different points in time, so the story shifts depending on how they experience it. Many times, there are few words available at the onset of a grief experience. People need space, and often communicate more effectively over time. However, not all members of a family value sharing their thoughts, feelings, and experiences in the same way. Therefore, counselors can assist each member in considering the diversity of his or her needs during these difficult times (Hooghe et al., 2011).

SIDEBAR 18.1 CASE STUDY: JANE'S SEARCH FOR SPIRITUALITY

Jane, 38, sought counseling following her sister's death to addiction. She is angry at God and overwhelmed with guilt for feeling this anger. Jane is a longtime devout Catholic and is concerned about how her feelings impact her relationship with God. Jane reveals feeling resentful that God took her sister from her. Her counselor, who has a different faith practice than Jane, is aware of the difference in their belief system and is invested in learning more from Jane about her faith. He understands that a person's spiritual and cultural beliefs deeply impact a family's grief process. Imagine you are Jane's counselor. How would you address Jane's conflict between her feelings and her faith? How would you help Jane process her experience?

Culture, Communication, and the Expression of Grief

Cultural norms play a prominent role in the grief experience of couples and families. Couples and families across the nation and around the world grieve daily, and the grief practices within their communities deeply influence how they respond. While this information can be helpful to counselors working with diverse populations, it is equally important that counselors also consider the diversity within cultures and the unique ways that individuals, couples, and families grieve. Moreover, each member of a family is influenced by a multiplicity of cultures to which they belong, including race, ethnicity, socioeconomics, and gender, among others. Understanding the complexity of culture and its relationship to a couple or family's grief process is a key counseling consideration.

Take Beth and Mark, for example, who have been married for 20 years. Beth identifies as Hispanic American and Mark identifies as German American. They come from similar middle-class socioeconomic backgrounds, and as first-born children in their families, they describe themselves and each other as hardworking, responsible, and eager to do well. Indeed, over time they invested in a family-owned business and have dedicated much of their lives to its success. Very recently, however, their family-run bookstore was hit by the economic times. At a point in time when Beth and Mark were preparing to send their three children to college, they not only suffered an unanticipated loss of income, they lost the business they both loved.

While Beth's response to this loss was to move closer to her family, Mark felt more relief as he moved further from his. Differences in their responses could be conceptualized from both cultural and gendered perspectives. The Hispanic culture is collectivistic, and connecting during times of loss is customary (Vazquez & Rosa, 2011). Beth's gender identification also supports nurturing connections during times of loss. Mark, on the other hand, prides himself on his hard work and self-sufficiency, both socially sanctioned values. As Kiselica and Englar-Carlson (2010) note, many men are socialized to appear strong during times of stress. In addition, some men see their primary job as one of "providing for their families" (Kiselica & Englar-Carlson, 2010, p. 278). To lose their socially sanctioned roles could create grief on multiple levels. Many men internalize these roles and interpret disruptions to their livelihood and their own feelings about this loss as weakness and personal vulnerability. This is unfortunate, given the cost not only to the man but also to his relationships and his own healing. Helping men reconcile their losses while retaining their dignity and respecting the influence of culture on their worldviews is an important therapeutic goal.

Along the same vein, Jordan (2010) described how women are often socialized to respond to stress, loss, or grief in socially sanctioned ways. In fact, relational-cultural theory (RCT) posits that women and members of minority cultures move toward connection rather than autonomy (Jordan, 2010) in their growth and development. As a result, and in times of grief, many women expect to both seek out and provide support to their loved ones. If a male partner cannot respond in kind, and instead distances himself from his wife at the same time that she is attempting to reach out to him, both persons can be left with feelings of loneliness and loss. In cases in which one partner in a family has needs that diametrically oppose the needs of the others, these feelings of loss are exacerbated. In cases such as these, one or both partners could feel isolated and misunderstood. Counselors working with grieving couples and families can help them identify and negotiate their unique needs to offer themselves and each other compassion, respect, and opportunities for healing.

Doka and Martin (2010) noted that many women mourn in a manner in which they both seek and provide comfort. This includes finding a support system, comforting others, and recounting their experiences. While some men grieve similarly, other men mourn in a manner in which they may seek to reclaim control, struggle with fears of losing control of their feelings, or seize control in those areas where they can, such as with funeral finances (Doka & Martin, 2010). While considering gender as an important cultural consideration in work with couples and families facing loss, it is incumbent upon counselors to see the unique needs and styles of coping that couples and families bring and to help them understand their own responses and each other's. Culture, then, influences the grief experience of family members and becomes a contributing factor in effective grief counseling. Diversity and culture inform clinical work and provide counselors with nuanced understanding of their clients' grief processes and recovery.

THEORIES OF GRIEF

The literature on grief and loss has evolved considerably from Freud's initial conceptualization of loss and attachment (Marwit & Klass, 1995) to include diverse conceptualizations on bereavement and its implications. From theories that espouse task-oriented (Worden, 1996) and multiphasic processes of grief (Parkes,

1993; Rando, 1993) to those that emphasize meaning-making in the grief journey (Neimeyer, 1999), conceptualizations of bereavement have progressed considerably over the past several decades. The following section describes two foundational theories commonly discussed in the grief and loss literature.

Kübler-Ross Grief Cycle Model

Kübler-Ross (2003) is perhaps best known for her stage theory and grief cycle model. Designed to reflect the experience of bereaved couples and families following the terminal illness or death of a loved one, this model is commonly used with myriad losses that people face. Although presented as a stage theory, it is important for counselors to be aware that people experience these stages nonlinearly rather than resolving one stage and moving into the next one. At times, couples and families may experience concurrent and conflicting emotions. They may feel anger and sadness simultaneously. In fact, bereaved family members may have difficulty identifying their feelings. By understanding that grief is multilayered, counselors can help normalize the mixture of emotions and thoughts that grieving couples and families invariably experience. In that respect, grief models can be helpful for couples and families undergoing diverse forms of loss. The stages of grief as identified by Kübler-Ross offer one such model.

Denial

Denial is a conscious or unconscious resistance to accept circumstances or painful information. Commonly associated with the experience of shock, denial is an initial and natural human response to loss (Kübler-Ross, 1969). Counselors working with couples and families are aware that individual members of a family may experience denial for longer periods of time than others.

In the earlier case, for example, Beth was optimistic about the bookstore's ultimate success, while Mark struggled with doubts about their ability to sustain it. However, she reached a point where the facts seemed to speak for themselves before Mark did. In fact, Mark held on to the idea of resurrecting the business far beyond Beth's comfort level. While Beth was concerned about the degree of loss they would sustain, Mark believed that more effort would yield success. At one point, Mark identified his determination as denial. Until then, Beth and Mark carried not only the unsettling feelings that come from being on different sides of this issue, but they also carried their feelings of grief over their inevitable loss. This was the work they embarked on in grief counseling.

Anger

People display anger in different ways. Some people become angry at others. Other people become angry at themselves. Many people vacillate between both experiences. Anger is generally triggered by feelings of helplessness and desperation (Kübler-Ross, 1969). When people become stuck in anger, they may alienate others, feel victimized, and strike out at people who attempt to become close.

Both Mark and Beth felt considerable anger as they worked toward their decision to close their business. Operating at a financial loss for an unsustainable length of time generated great financial costs. Their money problems derailed important plans for their children and their own retirement. When Beth would create a positive picture of the situation, Mark would feel his anger more deeply. At the same time, when Beth would feel her sadness, Mark would become angrier. The literature on men and masculinity notes that many men express their feelings of depression and sadness through anger (Doka & Martin, 2010). Interestingly, women may also channel their hurt feelings by expressing their anger.

Bargaining

People in the bargaining phase of grief attempt to experience a sense of control. To ward off intense grief, they attempt to bargain with their higher power, if they have one, or with other people when this is possible (Kübler-Ross, 1969). In cases of death, bargaining is short-lived. However, people suffering other losses attempt to "fix" a problem by coming up with potential solutions that are generally dead-end.

Beth and Mark took turns bargaining with their God, with their financial institutions, with themselves, and with each other. Considerable effort in counseling involved identifying and naming this aspect of their grief experience. Although the discussions increased both parties' anxiety at different points, they also helped clarify each person's position, which ultimately led to increased understanding of each other.

Depression

People experiencing grief-related depression feel sadness and regret. They feel insecure and uncertain about their futures. Grief-related depression is normal and expected (Kübler-Ross, 1969). In cases of chronic or complicated grief, depression can become a medical issue.

Neither Mark nor Beth experienced clinical depression. Both, however, experienced deep distress. Beth's depression prompted her to temporarily withdraw from family, which was alarming to Mark. This was uncharacteristic of Beth and concerned him greatly. Mark's depression manifested in angry outbursts while driving. He received a warning ticket for speeding and acknowledged feeling out of control. Counseling involved helping Beth put words to her grief so they would not remain "stuck" in her heart, and helping Mark design a plan of action that made him feel like he had some control over their situation. By doing so, he was better able to connect with his feelings and articulate them.

Acceptance

When people find acceptance, they are better able to view their loss from an objective perspective (Kübler-Ross, 1969). Although they do not resolve their loss, they are able to come to terms with the facts surrounding their experience. Achieving acceptance is a hard-won task.

Beth and Mark reached the acceptance phase within a relatively similar time frame. Even in this stage, both had a mixture of regret and anticipation. Knowing they no longer had a choice, and coming to terms with their feelings, allowed them to take the steps that would move them in a new direction. Acceptance can feel bittersweet when people must release someone or something they wanted to keep in their lives.

Kübler-Ross's model provides a context for couples and families like Beth and Mark to make sense of their feelings and the feelings of their loved ones. Bowlby (1969, 2005) also contributed his influential work on attachment and separation toward the literature on grief and loss.

Bowlby's Attachment Theory

Whereas Kübler-Ross (1969) identified a stage theory perspective on grief, Bowlby approached grief from an attachment–separation perspective. For example, according to Bowlby (1969, 2005), early attachments are pivotal to growth. People learn early on to depend on the attachments that provide security and survival. When people lose these attachments, or when attachments are intermittently reinforced, people become distressed and experience feelings of anxiety and anger (Bowlby, 1969, 2005). Mourning is considered the expression of these emotions. According to Bowlby (1969, 2005), there are four phases of mourning, which we discuss next.

Numbing

Numbing involves the feelings of bewilderment and disbelief surrounding the loss (Bowlby, 1969). Much like Kübler-Ross's stage of denial, this experience provides the bereaved with an initial opportunity to distance from the loss. Numbing is generally followed by acute pain.

When Mark first attended counseling, he presented with a "numb" countenance. This alarmed Beth because she felt disconnected from him and she was afraid they would step deeper into debt. Mark later described this period of time as being in a "fog," which was soon followed by intense anger. Once he was able to work through some anger, he was better able to see the reality of their situation and take steps to address it.

Yearning and Searching

During this phase, the bereaved is aware of the loss and experiences deep feelings of anger and pain. People in this phase search for someone or something to hold responsible for the loss (Bowlby, 1969).

Both Mark and Beth yearned for their lost business and searched for someone to blame, yet they did not blame each other. There are times when couples turn on each other during times of deep grief. Other times, they may turn away from each other while carrying private feelings of betrayal, loss, and disappointment. When couples put words to their experiences, respect the experiences of each other, and work through hard feelings or disappointments, their connection is reinforced. They then can better face reality and deal with the inevitable consequences.

Disorganization

People in this phase begin to accept the reality of the loss, and they connect to the fallout that loss triggers. In this phase, people begin to look at what their lives will look like without the object of their loss (Bowlby, 1969). When Mark and Beth recognized the significance of their losses and the resulting ramifications, they were better able to realistically assess the damage and seek assistance to mitigate it. Couples working in the disorganization phase of grief may feel overwhelmed by the challenges they face, and counseling can help them break these down to a manageable size. Then, they can prioritize their next step and begin the work of reorganization.

Reorganization

This process is characterized by the idea that there is life after loss. People recognize their past affiliations with the loss are gone and make changes that allow them to move forward (Bowlby, 1969). Finally, one of the significant changes that Mark made was to seek employment with a large, multistate retail vendor. Beth enrolled in school and worked part-time in a women's clothing retail shop. While couples experience loss as individuals and a dyad, their family system is also challenged to respond, cope, and adapt to loss and grief.

A FAMILY'S ADAPTATION TO LOSS

Walsh and McGoldrick (2004) identify several variables that influence a family's adaptation to loss related to the death of a loved one. These variables include "the manner of death, the family and social network, family organization, such as flexibility of the family system, family connectedness, sociocultural influences, and the timing of the loss in the family life cycle" (Walsh & McGoldrick, 2004, p. 15). In conceptualizing the family's situation, counselors may consider whether the death was sudden or whether the family member lingered. They may note whether the loss was ambiguous (Boss, 1999, 2004) or disenfranchised (Worden, 2009). Ambiguous loss differs from ordinary loss in that there is no verification of death or no certainty that the person will come back or return to the way they used to be. Ambiguous loss freezes the grief process and prevents closure, paralyzing couple and family functioning. They also consider whether the death was violent, as in the case of suicide or homicide (Walsh & McGoldrick, 2004).

In working with a family's adaptation to loss, counselors consider the strength of the family and its social network (Walsh & McGoldrick, 2004). For example, they consider how supportive networks can help couples and families make meaning of their experiences (Neimeyer, 2012). Counselors assess the state of relationships at the time of death and the compatibility of communication among members. When couples or families experience ongoing conflict in their relationships, these patterns can exacerbate their grief experience, particularly when trust, goodwill, and other essential relational factors are missing. These factors can complicate a couple or family's grief recovery (Stroebe, Schut, & Stroebe, 2005).

Walsh and McGoldrick (2004) also identified a number of factors that influence a family's response to these variables. For example, in the event of a sudden loss, extended family members and friends provide sources of emotional supports. Helping families with the initial crisis by identifying sources of support is important. Given that issues of guilt and regret are common responses to sudden loss, the counselor can work with couples and families to work through these feelings. In cases in which a family member has suffered a prolonged dying process, family members may have expended their resources and may experience guilt feelings, as well. Counselors can support their clients as they reconsider feelings of guilt or misplaced responsibility (Walsh & McGoldrick, 2004). When couples or families experience an ambiguous loss, such as when a family member is missing, unique challenges to grieving families arise (Boss, 1999, 2004) as they attempt to balance the tension between sustaining hope and living with the often debilitating ache of ambiguous loss (Boss, 1999).

COMMON EXPERIENCES OF LOSS IN A FAMILY SYSTEM

Families experience a myriad of losses every day. Some families experience death, divorce, sudden illness, and job loss. They lose children, parents, siblings, and friends. Families cope with miscarriage, family crises, traumas, and injury. They lose their limbs, sight, hearing, and mobility. They lose their loved ones in war and on the home front. Family members experience accidents, homicides, acts of terrorism, and suicides. Families reel from job loss, economic crises, and the onset of a chronic, terminal, or mental illness. Members of a family lose a beloved family pet. They lose their place in an extended family as a result of divorce. At times they lose their homes and friends following a geographical move. Families lose their homes and belongings during natural disasters. Sometimes families can feel they have lost everything.

Although it is beyond the scope of this chapter to address the many losses couples and families experience, here you will find variations on two significant losses regularly faced by couples and families: divorce as it relates to couples, children, and adult children of divorce, and a brief introduction to death in a family. Later, other forms of losses, such as ambiguous, unacknowledged, and stigmatized losses are introduced.

Divorce

Divorce is not only a relatively common reality for some families, but it can also be a source of tremendous grief and family disorganization (Wallerstein, 1991). In addition to legal issues faced by divorcing spouses, such as distribution of assets and child custody and support, families also negotiate a number of emotional, structural, and relational challenges. Dykeman (2003) described how the amount of conflict within a family unit and the degree of cooperation between divorcing parents greatly influence the productive processing of a family's grief experience. For example, in spite of the commonly reported negative effects of divorce on the family, some children actually thrive in family dissolution. Reports indicate that children who fare well during divorce live in homes with clear and caring boundaries and significant support (Dykeman, 2003). Positive parent–child relationships can safeguard family members from damaging residual effects of divorce (Richardson & McCabe, 2001). Access to trusting, emotional connections is integral to resiliency after divorce.

Issues related to the restructuring of marital and parent–child relationships, finances, and adaptation to living apart are each vital aspects of the divorce grief process. Not only must spouses disengage legally, but their grief also involves resolving an "emotional divorce" (Friedlander, Escudero, Heatherington, & Diamond, 2011). In counseling, divorcing spouses identify and address feelings of anger, guilt, and hurt, and do the arduous work of relinquishing their fantasies. Conversely, divorce counseling often involves releasing hopes, dreams, and expectations from the marriage (Duffey, 2005). Counselors can help divorcing spouses face the challenges of single parenting, clarify confusion surrounding new relationships, and reconcile feelings of loss over the last relationship (Klerman, Weissman, Rounsaville, & Chevron, 1994). Counselors can also assist divorcing couples in managing their feelings of loneliness and isolation while finding new sources of support and trust. Counselors can help divorcing couples clarify misconceptions that interfere with forming a productive meaning of their experiences and contribute to exacerbated feelings of blame and guilt.

When children are involved, counseling can support the psychological adjustment for parents so they can coparent effectively. Coming to terms with divorce may involve coping with the lack of a support system, becoming solely responsible for managing a household, and feeling emotionally and logistically overloaded. Divorce-related grief work can help divorcing spouses work through feelings of isolation and rejection, damaged self-esteem, and depression (O'Halloran & Carr, 2000).

A couple or family's spirituality or religious beliefs can also frame how they grieve a divorce (Dyer & Hagedorn, 2013). When couples view marriage as a sacred covenant with a higher being, divorce may be conceptualized as breaking a spiritual or religious pact and be a potentially punishable offense (Dyer & Hagedorn, 2013). If counselors are not aware of the significant influence that a person's spiritual beliefs can carry with respect to divorce, they may not provide adequate support and guidance through divorce-related grief. When counselors respect the cultural, spiritual, and religious perspectives of the family and enter the family's paradigm, they are better equipped to help them work through their divorce-related losses and create a fulfilling life after loss.

Given that at least half of married couples and their families in the United States will experience this loss, it is important to consider how couples grieve during divorce (Duffey, 2005). Simply put, divorce can create havoc in the lives of spouses and children alike. Not only do people lose their relationships, their families, and many times their homes and the lives to which have become accustomed, but they also lose their dreams for a life together (Duffey, 2005).

Divorcing Couples

When people marry, most enter the union with an expectation that they have found the one person with whom they can share mutual trust, love, and respect until the end of time. Spouses build lives together that can lead to deep bonds and shared histories. Although challenges inevitably arise, many couples are able to meet them together. If they experience persistent incompatibilities in personality, worldview, or life goals, however, their resilience in meeting life challenges is less strong.

When a spouse does not have the maturity, ability to compromise, or motivation to consider the needs and wants of the other, conflicts arise. Problems are exacerbated when at least one spouse assumes a self-centered stance, disregarding the needs of the other spouse. If this pattern of disregard continues, it will slowly erode the good feelings in the marriage. Spouses are no longer trusted with goodwill. Family members may feel as if they must walk on eggshells. One or both spouses may abuse substances. A third person could be triangulated into the relationship. At times, this results in a physical affair. Emotional affairs are no less hurtful. Couples become estranged from one another, and their dream can turn into a nightmare.

Other couples experience stressors in their relationships that tear at the very fabric of their lives. Couples whose children suffer from chronic illness, succumb to drugs, or die suddenly must negotiate profound losses together. The strength of the relationship prior to the loss, the means by which they manage stress as individuals, the degree of resources available, and their ability to support one another all influence the trajectory of their marriage. When couples are not able to grieve their losses and sustain their marriage, they enter into what can be a very painful culmination of their relationship: divorce.

Counselors working with divorcing families can help spouses work through some of their hurt, anger, and bitterness. They can help them divorce in ways that preserve the dignity of both people. In spite of the often chaotic and emotional climate during this period, counselors can help couples problem-solve specific family needs. They can help couples find the words to inform their children on their decision to divorce. Counseling can assist couples as they coparent during this turbulent time. Finally, counselors can help couples and their children make meaning out of their experiences and establish a "new normal" (Walsh, 2011).

Children of Divorcing Families

Children whose families are disrupted by divorce often experience confusion and a range of emotions. Many feel angry and betrayed. Some feel abandoned and may lose trust in adults. Some children lose contact with one of their parents, and they may have to adjust to becoming part of a new blended family. At times, these challenges affect children well into adulthood, and their capacities to establish and maintain intimate relationships are thwarted (Kenny, 2000). Counselors can help parents facilitate their children's grief by providing a compassionate connection with a nonparental adult (Rodgers & Rose, 2002).

Family counseling is an excellent forum for children of divorcing families, particularly when there is ongoing family conflict or avoidance of grief (McConnell & Sim, 2000). Family counseling is most effective when parents are motivated and willing to participate in the counseling process. Counseling can help children understand what divorce means for their family and assist them in building resiliency and productive coping skills. Counselors can also help children find words for their thoughts and feelings (Dykeman, 2003). Counseling can provide an environment in which children can rebuild their sense of security (Walsh, 2003).

Counseling becomes particularly important given that children may lose their primary support system when families separate. In some cases, children may also lose their home, school, and their friends should they move. Because divorce can result in an economic decline for the custodial parent, children may lose a familiar and comfortable lifestyle (Kenny, 2000). Counseling, then, becomes a valuable context in which children can express their grief. Although it is important that children feel free to express their feelings in counseling, they may have little trust in adults as a result of their experience with divorce and parental conflict. Compounding matters of trust and safety, children do not have the absolute right to confidentiality (Dykeman, 2003). It is important, then, that counselors inform parents that children must have a degree of privacy within the therapeutic relationship for counseling to prove effective (Johnson, 2011).

During the course of counseling, counselors may recommend that parents communicate with their children about the divorce. Counselors educate parents on how to do so while also supporting the well-being of the child. Children learn best when explanations are age appropriate and do not include excessive details that might increase their confusion or anxiety. Rather, counseling is most effective when counselors focus on offering support, comfort, and clarity. When one spouse discusses the faults of the other parent, counselors can remind them of the harm and added grief children experience when parents attempt to alienate their children from the other parent (Johnson, 2011).

Questions may arise as to whether children incur greater harm when they live in a home with two parents engaged in perpetual conflict or when they become children of divorce. According to Kenny (2000), children respond better to divorce than they would to living in a home high in conflict or violence.

Children of divorce often cope with the changes brought on by divorce successfully, particularly when they are given a safe place to express their feelings. Helping parents to be clear and open with young children is important. When parents communicate mixed messages or leave important information unsaid, children experience anxiety (Walsh, 2003). Bowlby (1969, 2005) describes the reorganization that families undergo after loss. Divorce is among the more disorganizing experiences families face. Counselors can help parents through this reorganization of their lives by developing an age-appropriate explanation for divorce and establishing a cooperative coparenting relationship (Dowling & Elliott, 2012).

Reorganization can involve helping parents develop new roles for each household and establishing positive communication between parents (Lewis, Wallerstein, & Johnson-Reitz, 2004). It also involves managing their feelings in ways that protect their children. Creating appropriate boundaries allows children to remain children rather than risking becoming *parentified*, or an emotional support system for their parents (Garber, 2011). Counseling is a place where children process and make sense of their feelings (Dozier, 2004).

Adult Children of Divorce

Many children function well following their parents' divorce, and counseling can help them make sense of their loss in ways that support their resilience. At the same time, many adult children of divorce carry strengths that support their relationships with others. These include an increased capacity for empathy and a greater understanding of emotions. These adults also possess an increased maturity and greater self-esteem than their counterparts (Wallerstein, 1991).

Other children, however, grow into adulthood with long-term challenges following their parents' divorce (Conway, Christensen, & Herlihy, 2003). When adult children of divorce do struggle, they often describe challenges with emotional intimacy. They may fear abandonment or loss and harbor concerns about betrayal. This can be a primal fear for many. When adult children become involved with people who reinforce their fears and indeed betray or abandon them, their fear is intensified. In less severe cases, adult children of divorce may misinterpret natural marital disagreements as precursors to divorce. They may unrealistically seek perfection in a union. Some withdraw emotionally to maintain their independence, seeking self-preservation (Conway et al., 2003). Although divorce can create problems for some children as they grow into adulthood, effective counseling services can circumvent exacerbation of a child's grief. Counseling can cultivate children's relational strengths of empathy, maturity, self-esteem, and compassion. These strengths may serve them well throughout their lives.

A Child Dies

Often considered the worst possible grief, couples and families who face the death of their child suffer immeasurably (Bissler, 2005). Regardless of the child's age and stage in life, parents expect their children to outlive them. Couples and families suffering this loss often experience prolonged grief (Bissler, 2005), particularly because their lives as they have known them to be will never be the same. This is particularly so when the death is sudden or traumatic (Byers, 2012). Counselors working with couples and families who experience a sudden traumatic death can offer comfort and understanding of the complicating factors that arise with traumatic deaths (Clements, DeRanieri, Vigil, & Benasuttie, 2004). Deaths by homicide or suicide are both shocking and unexpected.

Parents whose children die from violent or tragic circumstances often carry graphic images of their child that can hijack their minds, causing them to obsessively relive the event. One parent grieved that she scolded her son on the morning of his death for taking her car without permission the night before. This parent lamented her last moments with her son and could not stop asking herself and others, "How could this happen? How *did* this happen?" It is common for family members to try to make sense of a loss. This is akin to Kübler-Ross's (1969) stage of denial and Bowlby's (1969) yearning and searching phase of loss. However, their repeated attempts to do so can complicate their process. It is as if to say, "If I can figure out what happened, I can figure out how I could have prevented it." Many couples and families are challenged to work through feelings of guilt and responsibility when their child dies tragically or suddenly, in addition to their already incredible loss.

Survivors may feel overwhelmed by both emotional and practical matters, such as notifying others and preparing for a funeral or burial (Byers, 2012). Counselors can provide psychoeducational materials that can help family members digest information and guide them through their experience. They can also serve as a trusted resource and source of support and connection for bereaved couples and families (Duffey, 2012).

Monica's young daughter, Emily, was diagnosed with cancer 3 years ago. The doctor's report was shocking to Monica, a single parent deeply dedicated to her children and family. Monica described feeling immobilized and physically sick upon hearing the doctor's report. She was beyond grief as she drove home from the appointment wondering how she would tell Emily about her condition; her mind raced while she wondered how she would prepare Emily and her siblings for what was sure to be the greatest battle of their lives.

Emily's illness was slow and painful. Although she had many happy times with her family, she was no longer able to attend school and had few friends. She underwent painful treatments which ultimately proved unsuccessful. Emily's family was forced to see her die a little every day. Couples and families whose loved one suffers a prolonged illness begin mourning at the onset of the illness and grieve what they fear to be an eventual loss. Emily died before her 13th birthday.

Like many parents who face this grueling loss, Monica was speechless following Emily's death. She eventually cried out, "I don't know how to go on living. I have children who need me but I'm dying inside. A part of me just died and I don't know how to live." Given the hopes and dreams that parents have for their children (Duffey, 2005), and given that children represent a parent's hopes and dreams for the future (Bissler, 2005), this loss can be devastating. Indeed, the survivors of loved ones who die unexpectedly face a primal shock to their system. When counselors are connected to their own humanity, and when they are patient and willing to be with the pain of their clients, they can offer the guidance, care, and stability that can make an immeasurable difference in the lives of grieving families.

The death of a child can be even more devastating when families are already experiencing difficult situations such as economic stress, substance abuse, or domestic problems (Anastasi, 2011). Families that have little support, such as single parents, teen parents, gay and lesbian parents, or those living away from extended families, face unique challenges and may benefit from support networks (Anastasi, 2011). Parents who lose the only child they are capable of having because of the mother's age or medical condition face enormous grief challenges.

Amanda, a professional counselor for 20 years, hears of another death involving an adolescent or young adult in her community. In the past year, the lives of five families in her immediate community have been irrevocably changed by the passing of one of their children resulting from automobile accidents, some substance related, and drug overdoses. She hears from a colleague that Brad, a 22-year-old young man and only child was killed in a car accident while returning home from college for the holiday break. Amanda only knows Brad and his family by reputation. He was well-known in the community for his good grades, and his family was known for their good deeds. She relates to Brad's family in that her own children are Brad's age. Regardless of how long Amanda has been a counselor, and in spite of the many people she has counseled through the years, she continues to be shocked by tragedies such as these. They resonate with her not only professionally, but also on a basic human level. When the grieving parents call to make an appointment seeking grief counseling from Amanda, she quietly prays that she can do justice to the family as she prepares to meet the couple who find themselves in the moment blindsided by life.

Like Amanda, counselors working with grieving couples and families carry an important role in people's lives. A counselor's responsibility is to sit with families in their shock, despair, bewilderment, anger, and pain. Their work involves being present, emotionally available, authentic, and informed; it involves practicing self-care. By doing so, they are better able to assist couples and families by connecting with their own needs and their self-compassion.

Grief and Loss in Older Adulthood

Practicing self-compassion is an important skill at any age, and especially so as one reaches older age. In the later stages of a person's life and as adults grow older, they lose important friends and family and suffer their own physical or psychosocial declines. Some older adults experience chronic disease as they age. Concurrently, they may experience the loss of emotional resources that help them cope (Talerico, 2003). These multiple losses not only impact them, but they also impact the families who love and care for them (Anngela-Cole & Busch, 2011).

Couples who love and depend on one another, and who have shared much of their lives together, are particularly impacted when one spouse dies. When spouses enjoy close long-term marriages and lose the care and support of their partners, they can feel isolated and lost and are more prone to intense grief (Ott, Lueger, Kelber, & Progerson, 2007.) This is an all-too-familiar experience for families when one parent loses a long-time spouse.

Take, for example, Kim and Betty, who are in couples counseling working on communication issues and details surrounding launching children and other family concerns. At one pivotal point in the session, as the couple discussed the events of the week, both spouses looked at each other and sighed. Betty went on to describe their distress over his mother's sudden decline. Kim's father and his mother's long-time husband died earlier this year, and the adjustment is understandably difficult. His father was a true patriarch and is sorely missed. In addition, both Kim and Betty feel deep compassion and concern for Kim's mother, who seems lost without him. Moreover, and integral to their counseling work, Betty relates to her mother-in-law's pain. Betty's empathy and awareness of her own aging process connect her with her own fears of loss. This awareness marks a turning point in their counseling work and gives both Kim and Betty context for her current distress and hope for a reasonable resolution. As people age, they often revisit previous grief experiences. And with multiple losses, their grief is compounded. This may be confusing to family members, like Kim, who are confused when their loved ones express grief that appears disproportionate to the situation (Newson, Boelen, Hek, Hofman, & Tiemeier, 2011). In Betty's case, she was relieved to place her current fears and concerns in context and see how they related to previous, more powerful losses.

In addition to the stress of compounded and reinforced loss in older adulthood, some families also manage issues of cognitive decline. With significant numbers of older adults afflicted with Alzheimer's disease and dementia, the emotional strain that family members endure while caring for them can cause serious psychological issues. Family members whose loved ones suffer from this long-term, degenerative disease often experience a nondeath grief at their perceived loss of the person they once knew and loved (Lefley & Wasow, 1994; Lindgren, Connelly, & Gaspar, 1999).

Marian and Joe, both 60 years old, were married 6 years ago, and they are transitioning into retirement. However, over the course of a year, a number of stressors have challenged their relationship and replaced their sense of ease and fun with tension. Single for 25 years prior to this marriage, Joe liked having a lifestyle that required little from him. And although he enthusiastically stepped into a new phase of life with Marian, he found himself quickly challenged with Marian's response to her mother's onset of dementia. Marian missed her relationship with her mother, and Joe saw his fun-loving wife become anxious, upset, and depressed. Joe expressed missing his simple, uncomplicated life and resented "walking on eggshells" around his house. Marian and Joe presented for counseling to work out their conflicts. In the course of the work, they recognized a significant source of stress to be grief-related. Conceptualizing their situation from a grief counseling lens relieved the pressure between the spouses and normalized their experience. Although their couples work also involved developing greater mutuality, patience, and collaboration, identifying grief as a stressor brought clarity to the relationship and helped them focus on ways to move forward together.

SIDEBAR 18.2 CASE STUDY: BARRIERS TO WORKING WITH MEN IN GRIEF

Lillian and David have been married 53 years. Their dream was to retire in the mountains of Colorado. Lillian and David made use of their investments and purchased a home they both loved. As their friends celebrated their time together, the happy couple replied, "We are off to our last great adventure!" Unfortunately, Lillian became ill and died soon thereafter. David had no one to turn to for solace. The couple never had children and neither Lillian nor David was very close to their families. David eventually sought refuge at a local bereavement group for spouses, but became discouraged upon discovering there were no male participants. David did not believe women could relate to his pain, and he was uncomfortable exposing his vulnerability. As a counselor, how could you engage David? Given his developmental and life stage, which factors may be most salient to his grief process?

AMBIGUOUS LOSS

Couples and families suffering an ambiguous loss (Boss, 2004) lack clarity, and in some cases, live with deep anguish and a grueling sense of uncertainty. Ambiguous losses, which come in two forms described next, are commonly experienced by couples and families. The first form of ambiguous loss is seen when family members are physically absent yet psychologically present (Boss, 2004). For example, children with an absent parent experience an ambiguous loss. Although the parent is alive, he or she is not available for the family. This can be the case when family members are missing in the wake of a natural disaster. A loved one may be very much alive in the psyche of their families yet physically absent. The second form of ambiguous loss is seen when members of a family are physically present yet psychologically absent (Boss, 2004). This is seen in couples or families in which loved ones suffer from dementia, depression, eating disorders, or other addictions.

Here the reader will find a conceptualization of the impact of a family member with an eating disorder using the Kübler-Ross model and the five stages of grief. This is followed by a brief discussion on the grief experience of childhood trauma on families using the trauma-focused cognitive-behavioral therapy (TF-CBT) model. Following this discussion is a brief description of common ambiguous losses that family members face.

SIDEBAR 18.3 SELF-AWARENESS: WHAT IS AMBIGUOUS LOSS?

When a family member disappears, as is the case with a kidnapping or a military soldier who is missing in action, the family suffers unimaginable grief. This grief is commonly known as *ambiguous loss.* This loss is particularly devastating because the families are torn between mourning for their loved one and maintaining hope for a reunion. If you were counseling a family suffering ambiguous loss, how would you help the family negotiate this tension? What strengths would you bring to this family that could help them live with the ambiguity of their family crisis? Given the lack of control that comes with ambiguous loss, how would you help them cope?

Eating Disorders as Ambiguous Loss

Eating disorders are among the most complicated issues that counselors see in their offices. Long thought of as a disorder that afflicted young, privileged Caucasian females, eating disorders are now known to affect males and females alike, different races and ethnicities, and various age groups (Becker, Franko, Speck, & Herzog, 2003). Eating disorders are complicated by cultural influences, high comorbidities with other mental health disorders, and severe physical complications. The fact that clients cannot escape from food further complicates recovery, unlike a person suffering from substance abuse who can avoid the drug of choice. The relationship with food is not one that can be severed; rather, clients must come to peace with food and learn to have a healthy relationship with their bodies.

Eating disorders involve various forms of loss. When an individual is in the throes of this disorder, family members experience the loss of relationship. The eating disorder can consume the individual's life to the extent that relationships with loved ones cease to exist. By withdrawing from relationships and life experiences, the individual with an eating disorder attempts to achieve a sense of control (Trepal, Boie, & Kress, 2012). The person whom families once enjoyed and spent time with is no longer available. The family member suffering from an eating disorder often experiences a loss of identity. Part of the recovery journey involves coping with this loss of self.

Given that eating disorders have the highest mortality rate among all mental health disorders, families may face the actual death of a loved one (Arcelus, Mitchell, Wales, & Nielsen, 2011). Approximately 10% of those suffering from anorexia nervosa will eventually die due to eating disorder–related complications (Academy for Eating Disorders, 2010). Although this occurs in extreme cases, families need to be aware that this is a heartbreaking possibility.

SIDEBAR 18.4 PERSONAL REFLECTION AND INTEGRATION

Families with members who have eating disorders suffer numerous losses. Among them is the stigma that can come with eating disorders resulting in anorexia, bulimia, or obesity. Reflect on the messages you hear from society and the media regarding body image. In what ways would your beliefs and attitudes about body image and wellness affect your counseling with couples and families struggling with eating disorders in the family? Consider your gender expectations and whether these would influence your work with clients of any gender who suffer from eating disorders.

Eating Disorders: Stages of Grief in the Therapeutic Process

The five stages of grief outlined by Kübler-Ross (1969) provide an effective tool to conceptualize couples' and families' grief and recovery processes. Although a family member may severely restrict calories, hide food, obsess about his or her appearance, and experience amenorrhea (Arcelus et al., 2011), the family may deny that an actual problem exists. They often attribute severe weight loss or amenorrhea to a stressful phase in their loved one's life (LeGrange, Lock, Loeb, & Nicholls, 2010). Following is one family's experience.

Taylor is a very successful sophomore in high school. Taylor is popular, intelligent, active in extracurricular activities, and enjoys the attention of several boys her age. Still, Taylor complains about her weight and is concerned about her looks. She exercises several hours a day and does not join the family for meals. Taylor's parents received a call that one of her teachers reported seeing her become ill in the restroom following the lunch hour. Taylor's school counselor also noticed she has become more withdrawn. Most striking, Taylor has lost considerable weight and appears unhealthy, as evidenced by dark circles under her eyes and swollen glands. Taylor's counselor is concerned she is becoming bulimic and is involved in binge eating behaviors. After talking to Taylor, the counselor invited her parents to a meeting.

Family Denial

Taylor's parents were hesitant to attend but did so. Their response to the counselor's concern was, "Don't all people care what they look like? Certainly, Taylor is concerned with her looks and isn't eating well these days, but she appears fine. If this is the biggest problem we have with our teenager, we are lucky!" It is common for bulimic clients to hide their behaviors from loved ones (Broussard, 2005). When they are caught or finally reach out to others for help, family members may also deny the existence of a disorder. Parents often feel they would recognize problems with their child. Catching their child or learning of eating disorder symptoms can cause a great deal of cognitive dissonance in these cases, and denial serves to ameliorate this sense of unease.

Denial can easily shift into shock or numbness. Family members, especially parents, are often bewildered to learn of their child's condition and question how their child arrived at this place of suffering. Some parents who hear startling medical facts or mental health symptoms resulting from the eating disorder, such as a severely abnormal EKG, poor bone density, or even suicidal thoughts, react with little affect (Thompson-Brenner, Satir, Franko, & Herzog, 2012). This type of information, in addition to the general state of the child's eating disorder, can greatly overwhelm and shock families. Families often lose their understanding of the world; it is as if the proverbial rug has been ripped out beneath their feet (E. Ciepcielinski, personal communication, August 16, 2013). Families often cannot understand how their once healthy and vibrant loved one became so consumed with an often life-threatening condition. Whether the eating disorder's onset is gradual or not, shock sets in as the family realizes they no longer have the relationships they once had with their child. This awareness can trigger an experience of deep grief (Thompson-Brenner et al., 2012).

Family Anger

Many family members are enraged to learn of their loved one's eating disorder and do not have the tools to negotiate this form of grief. Some parents lock their refrigerators to control their child's access to food. Other family members express their anger and frustration loudly, making comments about their weight and demanding they have weekly "weigh-ins" to hold them accountable (E. Ciepcielinski, personal communication, August 16, 2013). Significant marital discord can result when a child develops an eating disorder. Blame is a common response. "Well, you were always dieting when she was younger!" "You and your friends always made 'fat jokes' in front of him!" Some parents say, "You put too much pressure on her!" Siblings can become angry that family life has become consumed with their brother or sister's eating disorder. Taylor's older sister cried out, "Why are you doing this to us?"

Families may become angry at the family counselor for allegedly brainwashing their child or misdiagnosing an eating disorder. This profound anger often stems from feelings of helplessness and devastation in knowing they truly lack control over their child's life. In that respect, eating disorders can be frightening and completely foreign to parents. Placing blame and displaying anger, although ineffective, are understandable attempts at gaining some modicum of control.

Family Bargaining

To further elicit some feeling of control, families may engage in bargaining with the child and/or the family counselor. For example, both parents began bargaining with Taylor: "If you eat all of your dinner tonight, I'll take you shopping tomorrow," followed by "If you gain up to ___ pounds by next Monday, we'll let you go on that trip with your friends next weekend." These attempts at control may seem understandable for a frustrated and scared parent. However, bargaining is ineffective and detrimental to the counseling process. Individuals with eating disorders must find their own internal motivation for recovery, and mixed messages resulting from attempts at bargaining confuse all family members involved.

Family Depression

For families experiencing a loved one with an eating disorder, the time comes to truly mourn the losses associated with the eating disorder. This mourning can lead to significant feelings of depression and sadness for many family members. While this can be incredibly painful, this grieving process can actually propel the family forward into healing and authenticity. Family members may find some small comfort and relief in knowing that they are in this process together and are not alone in their feelings.

Family Acceptance

When families can acknowledge their feelings of loss and sadness, they can move toward a place of acceptance. Acceptance of an eating disorder means that the individual and the family accept the emergence of the eating disorder and yield to the process of recovery. Recovery becomes a priority, and fighting the recovery process is seen as ineffective. Acceptance involves each family member's willingness to engage in counseling and acknowledge each person's role in the family's functioning. When family members perceive the eating disorder systemically and contextually, rather than assigning blame, genuine acceptance is possible and the true work of recovery can begin. When understanding the context of a child's eating disorder, addictive disorder, or other behavioral issues, families may find that their child experienced early trauma. Children may carry unacknowledged loss and grief of early trauma throughout their lives.

Childhood Trauma as Ambiguous Loss

When a child endures physical, emotional, or sexual abuse, neglect, domestic violence, bullying, or the loss of a parent, the family unit is shattered (Copeland, Keeler, Angold, & Costello, 2007). Many traumatized children develop sub-threshold posttraumatic stress disorder (PTSD). Children who experience repeated trauma and anxiety can develop full-blown PTSD (Copeland et al., 2007). Children are often brought to counseling for behavioral problems and later reveal a traumatic event. Families are urged to seek effective, timely treatment to begin healing from these devastating wounds. These wounds reverberate throughout the family system, and no one is immune to their damage.

Couples and families are often bewildered by the change in affect and behavior following trauma to their child. Some children engage in acting out behaviors, such as age-inappropriate sexual activity and misbehaving at school (Cohen, Berliner, & Mannarino, 2010). They may also express maladaptive or ineffective thought patterns, which can lead to significant anxiety and/or depression. These include the following feelings and concerns:

- Guilt and misplaced responsibility
- Powerlessness to prevent the trauma
- Shame
- Concerns over repeating a similar trauma

In cases of PTS symptoms or PTSD, the child may lose sleep, become irritable, feel emotionally numb, suffer from recurring intrusive thoughts related to the trauma, avoid stimuli involving the trauma, and in some cases, exhibit significant mood swings (Cohen et al., 2010). Other symptoms include fear of going to bed, bedwetting, clinging to parents or guardians, anger toward parents or guardians, declining academic performance, social withdrawal, and altercations at school (Cohen et al., 2010). Children can remain fixated in survival mode, at a time and place when they experienced a trauma and were unable to defend themselves (Levine, 1997; Levine & Kline, 2010). Signs and symptoms of trauma can emerge as defense mechanisms and as seemingly protective factors for traumatized children, despite their ineffectiveness (Cohen et al., 2010).

Getting the Family Involved

Family involvement and grief work is crucial in the aftermath of childhood trauma. Although children experience considerable grief, Steele and Raider (2001) found that some parents experienced greater distress than their afflicted children upon learning of their child's trauma. Many anxiously ruminate on what they could have done differently to prevent the trauma from occurring (Steele & Raider, 2001). Parental grief work is important, particularly given that studies indicate how parental influence significantly supports a child's recovery from trauma (Pynoos & Nader, 1988; Vogel & Vernberg, 1993). Identifying models that support a family's recovery begins the path of recovery.

Trauma-Focused Cognitive-Behavioral Therapy

Trauma-focused cognitive-behavioral therapy (TF-CBT) is one evidence-based treatment used to treat traumatized children and their nonoffending family members (Cohen et al., 2010). TF-CBT demonstrates efficacy in various environments and with diverse cultures. Children and parents receive both individual and family counseling. Parents learn skills in stress management, general parenting techniques, and interpersonal communication. They learn to cope with their grief and difficult emotions. Children learn ways to handle their painful emotions, to modify maladaptive or ineffective beliefs, and to communicate their trauma story. Research suggests that shame can decrease the more times a trauma story is shared (Cohen et al., 2010). In the joint child–parent sessions, the child can share his or her trauma story, and the family can learn ways to keep the lines of communication open within the home. Van der Kolk, McFarlane, and Weisaeth (1996) suggested that children can be profoundly resilient if they have emotionally available parents and caregivers.

Miscarriage as Ambiguous Loss

When couples and families look forward to the birth of a child only to lose the child by miscarriage, they do not often have a body to bury, nor do they have memories of the child to grieve (Werner-Lin & Moro, 2004). Given that women often miscarry during the first 20 weeks of pregnancy, they may not yet share their news with friends or family. As a result, they can be left with feelings of isolation in their mourning (Werner-Lin & Moro, 2004).

Danni and her husband, Matt, were overjoyed when they learned she was pregnant. Both were in their early thirties when they married and deeply wanted to start a family. When Danni's pregnancy results came back positive soon thereafter, they could not have been happier. Not long into the pregnancy, however, Danni experienced complications. She was told she had an "incompetent cervix" (Kimber-Trojnar, Patro-Malysza, Leszczynska-Gorzelak, Marciniak, & Oleszczuk, 2010). Danni focused on the word *incompetent.* The pregnancy ended in miscarriage. Although both Danni and Matt expressed sadness about the loss, Danni felt strangely alone. Matt explained how he felt sadness but did not want to dwell on those feelings. Danni, who liked to live a structured, predictable life, felt stuck in a place of anger. She was angry at the loss, angry at herself, and angry at Matt for not responding in ways she could relate to. Matt described feeling helpless to help her.

Counseling Danni and Matt involved helping them communicate with one another, gain perspective on the other's position, and honor their unique experiences. This presented a particular challenge for Danni, who did not like how Matt grieved and said so. Danni would say, "Everyone just goes on after this as if nothing happened—even Matt. How am I supposed to be okay in knowing no one else cares? It is so easy for people to say, 'try again.' I am and it's not working. This wasn't supposed to happen. I feel so alone in this."

The dream that Danni and Matt shared was shattered with the miscarriage. Their dream to become pregnant again was elusive. They both grieved, but as is often the case, they grieved differently. Danni not only experienced the loss of her child, she lost a sense of her own body's competence. She also lost trust that life would work out if only she did the "right" thing. Matt lost the child he could barely wait to meet. He also lost confidence that he could console his wife during difficult times. Both Matt and Danni used counseling to communicate with one another, to work through their individual and collective losses, and to find a common ground where both could feel supported and valued. Using Kübler-Ross's (1969) model, Danni and Matt were able to identify and normalize their many feelings. Using Bowlby's theory (1969), they saw how their attachment to their unborn child had been real. This was healing for both Danni and Matt and helped reconcile what felt like a shattered dream.

As an unacknowledged loss, a miscarriage can create feelings of loneliness and isolation. When couples and families experience disenfranchised losses devoid of societal sanction, their experiences can be particularly profound. Indeed, grief can be poignantly experienced by members of a family who are also marginalized by the larger community. Couples and families who are also members of marginalized groups, or whose losses are private or socially unacknowledged, deal with ambiguous loss, disenfranchisement, and stigmatization.

SIDEBAR 18.5 CASE STUDY: WHAT IS UNACKNOWLEDGED LOSS?

Imagine you are counseling a couple who recently experienced an early-term miscarriage. Although both spouses share feelings of loss, the wife is particularly devastated and blames herself for the miscarriage. Her doctor assures them that miscarriages at this stage are not uncommon and she is not responsible. Still, she suffers great guilt and feels inadequate to be a mother. She feels foolish feeling grief, which is exacerbated when her family and friends tell her she is lucky she miscarried early on. One message she hears is "it happened for a reason." She feels invalidated and alienated, even from her husband. He is encouraging her to move on. If they became pregnant once, they could do it again. How would you help this couple negotiate their loss together? How would you help the wife come to terms with her loss in the absence of social support?

Disenfranchised and Stigmatized Losses

Managing grief can be complex when couples and families experience unacknowledged or stigmatized losses. Hocker (1990) described this form of grief as unsanctioned and disenfranchised. Disenfranchised grief results from losses for which people do not have a socially recognized right, role, or capacity to grieve. These losses are considered ambiguous in that they are not always publicly sanctioned or socially supported. As a result, some couples and families suffer in silence. Imagine the complications that arise when couples experience an unacknowledged or stigmatized loss, such as death to AIDS. Below is a brief example of how societal and legal marginalization can exacerbate losses experienced by couples and families from a nondominant cultural group.

Issues of Loss With Gay and Lesbian Couples

Members of the lesbian and gay community are particularly vulnerable to suffering in silence. Couples and families with gay or lesbian members may suffer ambiguous losses that, in some cases, also carry social stigmas. For example, Jack had been in a 20-year relationship with his partner, Ben, when disaster struck and Jack lost his job. Ben had relied on Jack for financial security, and Jack enjoyed providing it. When Jack's world fell apart and he was no longer able to sustain his family financially, he withdrew into depression. In fact, he was not able to tell Ben about the reversal of their fortunes for several months. Soon thereafter, Ben left quietly without Jack's knowledge and took considerable funds out of their bank account, leaving Jack with little to live on.

Ben did not express feelings of disappointment, anger, confusion, or bewilderment to Jack. So, when Jack sought counseling, he did not know how to explain the circumstances. From his perspective, Ben left their marriage without explanation. Lesbian and gay couples may not have the same opportunity to marry in ways heterosexual couples do. So, for Ben to leave the marriage under these circumstances was particularly hurtful to Jack. Jack's feelings of loss over losing a job that had at one time brought him so much satisfaction, coupled with the shame he felt at the circumstances, left him with few emotional resources. To have his partner then abandon him and take what little resources they had left was a wound he could not explain. Jack experienced profound ambiguous loss.

When gay and lesbian relationships end, a myriad of losses may be involved. For example, Amy and Brenda were partners for 8 years before Amy was diagnosed with cancer. Both women enjoyed good jobs and good friends. Their relationship with Amy's family was a strong one. Brenda was estranged from hers. In what felt like the blink of an eye, their relationship was turned upside down, as was their life and sense of security. Amy was whisked into the hospital and received treatment. Unfortunately, she was unresponsive to the treatment, and after spending several weeks in the ICU, she died.

Although Amy and Brenda were committed to one another, they were not married. As a result, Brenda did not have the rights and privileges to make decisions, consult with doctors, or play an active role in this life-altering process.

Amy's family did include Brenda in major decision making, and she was grateful for that. But she acknowledged feeling like a teenager who needed a set of parents to direct the situation because she did not have the authority to do so. Brenda's grief was multifaceted. She lost her beloved partner and her best friend. She lost her opportunity to acknowledge their love publicly and legally. As a member of a disenfranchised group, she was reminded of the ways her life has been marginalized, and she still felt the ache for connection with her own family, a desire that had long been elusive.

Jack and Brenda's counselors conceptualized their losses systemically, even though they each sought counseling as individuals. Their struggles, challenges, hopes, and inspirations were couple focused. To consider their situations from that light helped them honor their experiences, look at the context in which they experienced them, and move closer toward healing.

Counselors can be supportive allies as lesbian and gay partners experience unacknowledged or stigmatized losses (Werner-Lin & Moro, 2004). Lesbian and gay partners may not feel comfortable openly discussing the loss of their life partners if their social support systems and the cultural climate in which they live are not conducive to the open sharing of personal information (Werner-Lin & Moro, 2004). Complicating matters, gay and lesbian couples may suffer increased practical hardships. Many are ineligible to secure insurance or social security benefits with their partners. When their losses are a result of AIDS, they may be further stigmatized (Werner-Lin & Moro, 2004). Lesbian and gay couples face unique challenges when one partner becomes ill and unexpectedly dies. How they relay the information and to whom become points to consider. If partners choose to maintain their privacy around the loss, they may grieve privately (Werner-Lin & Moro, 2004). Counselors can be advocates for couples and families who carry additional burdens that can, in some circumstances, challenge their connectedness with the larger world around them. Helping them identify their needs and negotiate them with others is an important first step.

CREATIVITY IN GRIEF AND LOSS COUNSELING

Couples and families often pursue counseling services during times of grief and loss, seeking direction, comfort, and clarity. In the first moments of contact with a counselor, clients need a safe physical and emotional space to share their grief. This space and how each family member experiences grief will vary. Therefore, it is essential that counselors simultaneously conceptualize the systemic reaction to grief and the individual members' reactions and needs. Effective grief counselors bring caring presence, attentive listening, and openness to a family's full experience of pain. In these moments, a counselor's presence, openness, and warmth may matter most. Once a couple or family emerges from the initial crisis, counselors may work with their clients to seek creative ways to find moments of peace and live with their loss.

Counselors work with clients through the confusion, complexity, and deep pain of grief. In addition to presence and compassion, counselors and clients can find other ways to explore and heal from their loss. Innovative counseling strategies are designed to help people navigate grief. When utilizing specific interventions in grief counseling, timing is especially important.

For example, a counselor who is uncomfortable with a client's pain may force interventions prematurely. Grief counseling requires patience. It requires empowering clients to know they have a say in the counseling process. These factors must be considered when employing interventions, which can be helpful given the right context and the right time.

Creative Interventions With Couples and Families Experiencing Loss

Counselors working with couples and families have many resources available to promote healing after loss. Among these are family shared audio recordings, videography, online technology, photo journaling, creating a memory box, bibliotherapy, scrapbooks/paper bag books, and music.

Audio Recordings

Older adults and family members with chronic or terminal illnesses may use audio recordings to communicate with loved ones and leave their legacies. These recordings provide them with opportunities to reminisce and communicate life stories to their loved ones. Listening to these recordings after a beloved family member's death can provide great comfort and connection for grieving family members. Older adults can offer messages that support their loved ones and offer direction, compassion, and inspiration. Alternatively, couples and families record stories they recall about their loved ones, creating an auditory scrapbook. These recordings can be passed on to children and future generations, providing living family legacies.

Videography

Couples and families can also use video equipment to share stories and insights and memorialize their lives together. Music, photographs, favorite quotes, and personal messages may be embedded into the recording. For example, an only surviving daughter created a reminiscence video for her ailing parents. Together, they created a song list of the music that permeated their home throughout the years. They used this music as a backdrop to their video. Longtime friends, the family's pastor, and nieces and nephews all contributed stories and brief vignettes to the video.

Scrapbooks

Creating a scrapbook is another intervention that couples and families can use to organize their life stories and memorialize them. Family members can each contribute their favorite photos, notes, drawings, quotes, recipes, travel receipts and mementos, and other memorabilia. Scrapbooking is a creative outlet for couples and families to document their experiences and shared connections.

Memory Box

Children, couples, and families can create memory boxes that contain special keepsakes and memories. Fabric, paper, paint, or any craft items can be used to decorate the boxes. Family members can store favorite or meaningful objects in the box. A young girl of 8 used a memory box to work through her feelings following her parents' divorce and her subsequent move to another city. She wanted to carry important memories in her box and included a key to their old house and a picture of their backyard and her favorite swing set. She used the memory box to connect with her memories, grieve, and share her experiences with her new counselor.

Online Support Forums

Technology provides couples and families with ample opportunities to learn from others, share information, and process their losses. The Internet is filled with discussion groups focused on specific life events such as divorce support groups, families of children with cancer, and pet loss. Forming connections with virtual strangers during times of loss can appear detached for some. However, sharing experiences with people who relate to one's loss can be empowering and a source of comfort. In turn, family members may be more available to more intimately process their losses with loved ones.

A Musical Chronology

This intervention, described by Duffey (2012), uses music to help couples and families connect with and share their experiences, revisit their perceptions around them, and see them with greater perspective. It also uses music to help couples and families identify their current family functioning and identify goals for the future. Couples in conflict can recall both inspiring moments and current challenges to process their differences.

Stage 1: Compiling music to tell their stories. Couples and families can use music to revisit important life events and grieve unreconciled losses. Family members individually and collectively identify, collect, and compile music that tells their family story. They can use a compact disc, iPod, or flash drive to store their music and then arrange it chronologically.

Stage 2: Reflection. Couples and families tell their stories using music that helps them connect with their feelings and experiences and share them. This allows them to revisit experiences and consider new ways of perceiving them.

Stage 3: The present song. Family members select a song that sets the stage for their process. This is a song that describes what they think and how they feel at the outset of counseling. Later, they compare their thoughts, feelings, and perspectives to those they currently hold.

Stage 4: The future song. Couples and families select a future song or songs. These selections represent their future goals and hopes for the future.

The musical chronology can be especially helpful when couples and family members enjoy music and when they feel "stuck" in an experience. Music can powerfully elicit memories and give words to experiences that family members may not readily have available. With music as a prompt, couples and families can work toward greater understanding and deepened empathy and compassion following family losses (Duffey, 2012).

A musical chronology can be used in other ways to help couples and families. For example, couples who are drifting apart or considering a divorce can use this technique to reconnect with their shared love. Music can also assist with deepening the connections between adult children and their older parents (Duffey, Somody, & Clifford, 2006/2007). Using a musical chronology for reminiscence in a small-group counseling experience was helpful to older adults in dealing with multiple losses and looking to the future with hope (Somody, 2010).

SUMMARY

Counselors work with grieving couples and families every day. Divorce and other losses can create havoc in the lives of couples and families. Understanding the impact that loss can have on a family and the challenges they face can help counselors deliver effective, supportive, and compassionate counseling services. Counselors can offer a safe physical and emotional space for clients to share their grief. Counselors can also assist couples and families by addressing the systemic reaction to loss, as well as each family member's responses and needs. By considering the societal and cultural influences on grief and the patterns that couples and families have in response to grief, counselors can support families in navigating their losses and connecting with one another as they work through them.

USEFUL WEBSITES

The following websites provide additional information relating to the chapter topics.

Ambiguous Loss
http://www.ambiguousloss.com
The Compassionate Friends: Supporting Family After a Child Dies
http://www.compassionatefriends.org/home.aspx
First Candle: Helping Babies Survive & Thrive
http://www.firstcandle.org/grieving-families

Grief Haven: Providing Support and Resources to Parents and Others Who Have Lost a Child
http://www.griefhaven.org/index-firstpage.shtml
GriefLink
http://www.grieflink.asn.au
Journey of Hearts: An Online Healing Place for Anyone Grieving a Loss
http://www.journeyofhearts.org
National Eating Disorders Association
http://www.nationaleatingdisorders.org
Pet Loss Support Page
http://www.pet-loss.net
National SUID/SIDS Resource Center
http://www.sidscenter.org

REFERENCES

Academy for Eating Disorders. (2010). *Prevalence of eating disorders*. Retrieved from http://www.aedweb.org/Prevalence_of_ED.htm

Anastasi, J. M. (Ed.). 2011. *The death of a child, the grief of the parents: A lifetime journey* (3rd ed.). Washington, DC: National Sudden and Unexpected Infant/Child Death and Pregnancy Loss Resource Center at Georgetown University. Retrieved from http://www.sidscenter.org/Bereavement/LifetimeJourney.html

Anngela-Cole, L., & Busch, M. (2011). Stress and grief among family caregivers of older adults with cancer: A multicultural comparison from Hawai'i. *Journal of Social Work in End-of-Life & Palliative Care*, 7, 318–337. doi:10.1080/15524256.2011.623460

Arcelus, J., Mitchell, A. J., Wales, J., & Nielsen, S. (2011). Mortality rates in patients with anorexia nervosa and other eating disorders: A meta-analysis of 36 studies. *Archives of General Psychiatry*, *68*, 724–731. doi:10.1001/archgenpsychiatry.2011.74

Becker, A. E., Franko, D. L., Speck, A., & Herzog, D. B. (2003). Ethnicity and differential access to care for eating disorder symptoms. *International Journal of Eating Disorders*, *33*, 205–212. doi:10.1002/eat.10129

Bissler, J. (2005). Soup, stitches, and song: Helping parents grieve when their adolescent dies. In T. Duffey (Ed.), *Creative interventions in grief and loss: When the music stops, a dream dies* (pp. 123–134). New York, NY: Haworth Press.

Boss, P. (1999). *Ambiguous loss: Learning to live with unresolved grief.* Cambridge, MA: Harvard University Press.

Boss, P. (2004). Ambiguous loss. In F. Walsh & M. McGoldrick (Eds.), *Living beyond loss: Death in the family* (pp. 237–246). New York, NY: W. W. Norton.

Bowlby, J. (1969). *Attachment: Attachment and loss* (Vol. 1). New York, NY: Basic Books.

Bowlby, J. (2005). *The making and breaking of affectional bonds*. New York, NY: Routledge.

Broussard, B. B. (2005). Women's experiences of bulimia nervosa. *Journal of Advanced Nursing*, *49*, 43–50. doi:10.1111/j.1365-2648.2004.03262.x

Byers, D. S. (2012). Review of the book *Devastating losses—How parents cope with the death of a child to suicide or drugs*, by W. Feigelman, J. R. Jordan, J. L. McIntosh, & B. Feigelman. *Clinical Social Work Journal*, *41*(4), 413–415. doi:10.1007/s10615-012-0431-0

Clements, P. T., DeRanieri, J. T., Vigil, G. J., & Benasuttie, K. M. (2004). Life after death: Grief therapy after the sudden traumatic death of a family member. *Perspectives in Psychiatric Care*, *40*, 149–154. doi:10.1111/j.1744-6163.2004.tb00012.x

Cohen, J. A., Berliner, L., & Mannarino, A. (2010). Trauma focused CBT for children with co-occurring trauma and behavior problems. *Child Abuse & Neglect*, *34*, 215–224. doi:10.1016/j.chiabu.2009.12.003

Conway, M. B., Christensen, T. M., & Herlihy, B. (2003). Adult children of divorce and intimate relationships: Implications for counseling. *Family Journal*, *11*, 364–373. doi:10.1177/1066480703255609

Copeland, W. E., Keeler, G., Angold, A., & Costello, E. J. (2007). Traumatic events and posttraumatic stress in childhood. *Archives of General Psychiatry*, *64*, 577–584. doi:10.1001/archpsyc.64.5.577

Doka, K. J., & Martin, T. L. (2010). *Grieving beyond gender: Understanding the ways men and women mourn*. New York, NY: Taylor & Francis. doi:10.1080/08952841.2011.589290

Dowling, E., & Elliott, D. (2012). Promoting positive outcomes for children experiencing change in family relationships. In S. Roffey (Ed.), *Positive relationships: Evidence based practice across the world* (pp. 109–126). New York, NY: Springer. doi:10.1007/978-94-007-2147-0

Dozier, B. (2004). *For the children's sake: Parenting together after the marriage ends*. Bloomington, IN: iUniverse.

Duffey, T. (2005). When the music stops: Releasing the dream. In T. Duffey (Ed.), *Creative interventions in grief and loss therapy: When the music stops, a dream dies* (pp. 1–24). New York, NY: Haworth.

Duffey, T. (2012). Creative interventions in grief and loss counseling. *Advances in Bereavement 2*(5), 8–10.

Duffey, T., Somody, C., & Clifford, S. (2006/2007). Conversations with my father: Adapting a musical chronology and the emerging life song with older adults. *Journal of Creativity in Mental Health*, *2*(4), 45–64. doi:10.1300/J456v02n04_05

Duffey, T., Wooten, R., Lumadue, C., & Comstock, D. (2004). The effects of dream sharing and self-disclosure training on couple intimacy and satisfaction. *Journal of Couples and Relationship*, *3*(1), 53–68.

Dyer, J. E. T., & Hagedorn, W. B. (2013). Navigating bereavement with spirituality based interventions: Implications for non-faith-based counselors. *Counseling and Values*, *58*, 69–84. doi:10.1002/j.2161-007X.2013.00026.x

Dykeman, B. F. (2003). The effects of family conflict resolution on children's classroom behavior. *Journal of Instructional Psychology*, *30*, 41–46.

Friedlander, M. L., Escudero, V., Heatherington, L., & Diamond, G. M. (2011). Alliance in couple and family therapy. *Psychotherapy*, *48*, 25. doi:10.1037/a0022060

Garber, B. D. (2011). Parental alienation and the dynamics of the enmeshed parent–child dyad: Adultification, parentification, and infantilization. *Family Court Review*, *49*(2), 322–335.

Hocker, W. V. (1990). Characteristics of unsanctioned and unrecognized grief, and appropriate helping strategies. In V. R. Pine, O. S. Margolis, K. Doka, A. H. Kutscher, D. J. Schaeffer, M. Siegel, & D. J. Cherico (Eds.), *Unrecognized and unsanctioned grief: The nature and counseling of unacknowledged loss* (pp. 104–117). Springfield, IL: Charles C. Thomas.

Hooghe, A., Neimeyer, R. A., & Rober, P. (2011). The complexity of couple communication in bereavement: An illustrative case study. *Death Studies*, *35*, 905–924. doi:10.1080/07481187.2011.553335

Johnson, V. I. (2011). Adult children of divorce and relationship education: Implications for counselors and counselor educators. *Family Journal, 19*, 22–29. doi:10.1177/1066480710387494

Jordan, J. V. (2010). *Relational-cultural therapy*. Washington, DC: American Psychological Association.

Kenny, M. C. (2000). Working with children of divorce and their families. *Psychotherapy: Theory, Research, Practice, Training, 37*, 228–239. doi:10.1037/h0087667

Kimber-Trojnar, Z., Patro-Malysza, J., Leszczynska-Gorzelak, B., Marciniak, B., & Oleszczuk, J. (2010). Pessary use for the treatment of cervical incompetence and prevention of preterm labour. *Journal of Maternal-Fetal and Neonatal Medicine, 23*, 1493–1499. doi:10.3109/14767051003678093

Kiselica, M. S., & Englar-Carlson, M. (2010). Identifying, affirming, and building upon male strengths: The positive psychology/positive masculinity model of psychotherapy with boys and men. *Psychotherapy: Theory, Research, Practice, Training, 47*, 276–287. doi:10.1037/a0021159

Klerman, G. L., Weissman, M. M., Rounsaville, B. J., & Chevron, E. S. (1994). *Interpersonal psychotherapy of depression: A brief, focused, specific strategy*. Lanham, MD: Rowman and Littlefield.

Kübler-Ross, E. (1969). *On death and dying*. New York, NY: Springer.

Kübler-Ross, E. (2003). *On death and dying*. New York, NY: Scribner's.

Lefley, H. P., & Wasow, M. (Eds.). (1994). *Helping families cope with mental illness*. Newark, NJ: Harwood.

Le Grange, D., Lock, J., Loeb, K., & Nicholls, D. (2010). Academy for eating disorders position paper: The role of the family in eating disorders. *International Journal of Eating Disorders, 43*, 1–5. doi:10.1002/eat.20751

Levine, P. (1997). *Waking the tiger: Healing trauma*. Berkeley, CA: North Atlantic Books.

Levine, P. A., & Kline, M. (2010). *Trauma through a child's eyes: Awakening the ordinary miracle of healing*. Berkeley, CA: North Atlantic Books.

Lewis, J. M., Wallerstein, J. S., & Johnson-Reitz, L. (2004). Communication in divorced and single-parent families. In A. L. Vangelisti (Eds.), *Handbook of family communication* (pp. 197–214). Mahwah, NJ: Erlbaum.

Lindgren, C. L., Connelly, C. T., & Gaspar, H. L. (1999). Grief in spouse and children caregivers of dementia patients. *Western Journal of Nursing Research, 21*, 521–537. doi:10.1177/01939459922044018

Marwit, S., & Klass, D. (1995). Grief and the role of the inner representation of the deceased. *OMEGA—Journal of Death and Dying, 30*, 283–298. doi:10.2190/PEAA-P5AK-L6T8-5700

McConnell, R. A., & Sim, A. J. (2000). Evaluating an innovative counselling service for children of divorce. *British Journal of Guidance and Counselling, 28*, 75–86. doi:10.1080/030698800109628

Neimeyer, R. A. (1999). Narrative strategies in grief therapy. *Journal of Constructivist Psychology, 12*(1), 65–85.

Neimeyer, R. A. (2009). *Constructivist psychotherapy: Distinctive features*. New York, NY: Routledge.

Neimeyer, R. A. (Ed.). (2012). *Techniques of grief therapy: Creative practices for counseling the bereaved*. New York, NY: Routledge.

Neimeyer, R. A., Harris, D., Winokeur, H., & Thornton, G. (Eds.). (2011). *Grief and bereavement in contemporary society: Bridging research and practice*. New York, NY: Routledge.

Newson, R. S., Boelen, P. A., Hek, K., Hofman, A., & Tiemeier, H. (2011). The prevalence and characteristics of complicated grief in older adults. *Journal of Affective Disorders, 132*, 231–238. doi:10.1016/j.jad.2011.02.021

O'Halloran, M., & Carr, A. (2000). Adjustment to parental separation and divorce. In A. Carr (Ed.), *What works with children and adolescents?: A critical review of psychological interventions with children, adolescents and their families* (pp. 280–300). New York, NY: Routledge.

Ott, C. H., Lueger, R. J., Kelber, S. T., & Progerson, H. G. (2007). Spousal bereavement in older adults: Common, resilient, and chronic grief with defining characteristics. *The Journal of Nervous and Mental Disease, 195*, 332–341.

Parkes, C. M. (1993). Psychiatric problems following bereavement by murder or manslaughter. *Bereavement Care, 12*(1), 2–6.

Pynoos, R. S., & Nader, K. (1988). Psychological first aid and treatment approach to children exposed to community violence: Research implications. *Journal of Traumatic Stress, 1*, 445–473. doi:10.1002/jts.2490010406

Rando, T. A. (1993). *Treatment of complicated mourning*. Champaign, IL: Research Press.

Richardson, S., & McCabe, M. P. (2001). Parental divorce during adolescence and adjustment in early adulthood. *Adolescence, 36*, 467–489.

Rodgers, K. B., & Rose, H. A. (2002). Risk and resiliency factors among adolescents who experience marital transitions. *Journal of Marriage and Family, 64*, 1024–1037. doi:10.1111/j.1741-3737.2002.01024.x

Somody, C. F. (2010). *Meaning and connections in older populations: A phenomenological study of reminiscence using "A musical chronology and the emerging life song."* (Doctoral dissertation). Retrieved from ProQuest Dissertations and Theses database. (Order No. 3433230)

Steele, W., & Raider, M. (2001). *Structured sensory intervention for traumatized children, adolescents, and parents: Strategies to alleviate trauma*. New York, NY: Edwin Mellen Press.

Stroebe, M., Schut, H., & Stroebe, W. (2005). Attachment in coping with bereavement: A theoretical integration. *Review of General Psychology, 9*, 48. doi:10.1037/1089-2680.9.1.48

Talerico, K. A. (2003). Grief & older adults: Difference, issues, and clinical approaches. *Journal of Psychosocial Nursing & Mental Health Services, 41*(7), 12–16.

Thompson-Brenner, H., Satir, D. A., Franko, D. L., & Herzog, D. B. (2012). Clinician reactions to patients with eating disorders: A review of the literature. *Psychiatric Services, 63*, 73–78. doi:10.1176/appi.ps.201100050

Trepal, H. C., Boie, I., & Kress, V. E. (2012). A relational-cultural approach to working with clients with eating disorders. *Journal of Counseling & Development, 90*, 346–356. doi:10.1002/j.1556-6676.2012.00043.x

van der Kolk, B. A., McFarlane, A. C., & Weisaeth, L. (Eds.). (1996). *Traumatic stress: The effects of overwhelming experience on mind, body, and society*. New York, NY: Guilford Press.

Vazquez, C. I., & Rosa, D. (2011). *Grief therapy with Latinos: Integrating culture for clinicians*. New York, NY: Springer.

Vogel, J. M., & Vernberg, E. M. (1993). Children's psychological responses to disaster. *Journal of Clinical Child Psychology, 22*, 464–484. doi:10.1207/s15374424jccp2204_7

Wallerstein, J. S. (1991). The long-term effects of divorce on children: A review. *Journal of the American Academy of Child & Adolescent Psychiatry, 30*, 349–360. doi:10.1097/00004583-199105000-00001

Walsh, F. (2003). Family resilience: A framework for clinical practice. *Family Process, 42*, 1–18. doi:10.1111/j.1545-5300.2003.00001.x

Walsh, F. (Ed.). (2011). *Normal family processes: Growing diversity and complexity* (4th ed.). New York, NY: Guilford Press.

Walsh, F., & McGoldrick, M. (Eds.). (2004). *Living beyond loss: Death in the family* (2nd ed.). New York, NY: W. W. Norton.

Werner-Lin, A., & Moro, T. (2004). Unacknowledged and stigmatized losses. In F. Walsh & M. McGoldrich (Eds.), *Living beyond loss: Death in the family* (2nd ed., pp. 247–271). New York, NY: W. W. Norton.

Worden, J. W. (1996). Tasks and mediators of mourning: A guideline for the mental health practitioner. *In Session: Psychotherapy in Practice*, 2(4), 73–80.

Worden, J. W. (2009). *Grief counseling and grief therapy: A handbook for the mental health practitioner* (4th ed.). New York, NY: Springer.

Meet the Editors

David Capuzzi, PhD, NCC, LPC, is a counselor educator and member of the core faculty in clinical mental health counseling at Walden University and professor emeritus at Portland State University. Previously, he served as an affiliate professor in the Department of Counselor Education, Counseling Psychology, and Rehabilitation Services at Pennsylvania State University and scholar in residence in counselor education at Johns Hopkins University. He is past president of the American Counseling Association (ACA), formerly the American Association for Counseling and Development, and past chair of both the ACA Foundation and the ACA Insurance Trust.

From 1980 to 1984, Dr. Capuzzi was editor of *The School Counselor*. He has authored a number of textbook chapters and monographs on the topic of preventing adolescent suicide and is coeditor and author with Dr. Larry Golden of *Helping Families Help Children: Family Interventions With School Related Problems* (1986) and *Preventing Adolescent Suicide* (1988). He coauthored and edited with Douglas R. Gross *Youth at Risk: A Prevention Resource for Counselors, Teachers, and Parents* (1989, 1996, 2000, 2004, 2008, and 2014); *Introduction to the Counseling Profession* (1991, 1997, 2001, 2005, 2009, and 2013); *Introduction to Group Work* (1992, 1998, 2002, 2006, and, with Mark D. Stauffer, 2010); and *Counseling and Psychotherapy: Theories and Interventions* (1995, 1999, 2003, 2007, and 2011). His other texts are *Approaches to Group Work: A Handbook for Practitioners* (2003), *Suicide Across the Life Span* (2006), and *Sexuality Issues in Counseling*, the last coauthored and edited with Larry Burlew. He has also coedited and authored with Mark D. Stauffer *Career Counseling: Foundations, Perspectives, and Applications* (2006, 2012) and *Foundations of Addictions Counseling* (2008, 2012). He has authored or coauthored articles in a number of ACA-related journals as well.

A frequent speaker and keynoter at professional conferences and institutes, Dr. Capuzzi has also consulted with a variety of school districts and community agencies interested in initiating prevention and intervention strategies for adolescents at risk for suicide. He has facilitated the development of suicide prevention, crisis management, and postvention programs in communities throughout the United States. He also provides training on the topics of youth at risk and grief and loss, and serves as an invited adjunct faculty member at other universities as time permits.

An ACA fellow, he is the first recipient of ACA's Kitty Cole Human Rights Award and also a recipient of the Leona Tyler Award in Oregon. In 2010, he received ACA's Gilbert and Kathleen Wrenn Award for a Humanitarian and

Caring Person. In 2011, he was named a Distinguished Alumnus of the College of Education at Florida State University.

Mark D. Stauffer, PhD, NCC, is a core faculty member in the clinical mental health counseling program at Walden University. He specialized in couples, marriage, and family counseling during his graduate work in the Counselor Education Program at Portland State University, where he received his master's degree. He received his doctoral degree from Oregon State University, Department of Teacher and Counselor Education.

Dr. Stauffer is the immediate past co-chair of the American Counseling Association International Committee with Dr. Sachin Jain. He was a Chi Sigma Iota International Fellow and was awarded the American Counseling Association's Emerging Leaders Training Grant. He is a member of the International Association of Marriage and Family Counseling (IAMFC).

As a clinician, Dr. Stauffer has worked in crises centers and other nonprofit organizations working with low-income individuals, couples, and families in the Portland Metro Area in Oregon. He has studied and trained in the Zen tradition, and presents locally and nationally on meditation and mindfulness-based therapies in counseling. His research focus has centered on Eastern methods and East–West collaboration. In private practice, Dr. Stauffer worked with couples and families from a family systems perspective.

He has coedited three textbooks in the counseling field with Dr. David Capuzzi: *Introduction to Group Work* (2010); *Career Counseling: Foundations, Perspectives, and Applications* (2006, 2012); and *Foundations of Addictions Counseling* (2008, 2012).

Meet the Contributors

Jonathan K. Appel, PhD, has worked in the field of behavioral health for almost three decades. He has worked with individuals, groups, families, and organizations as a counselor, psychotherapist, clinical supervisor, director of behavioral health services, consultant, researcher, department chair, IRB director, and educator. He is currently a full professor in the Department of Behavioral and Social Sciences, within the School of Criminal Justice and Social Sciences at Tiffin University in Tiffin, Ohio. Dr. Appel received his bachelor's degree in psychology from Kent State University, a master's degree in community/clinical counseling from Kent State University, a second master's of science in criminal justice/homeland security (Tiffin University), and a PhD in counseling (subspecializing in both marriage and family therapy and organizational psychology) from the University of Akron. He has also received a graduate certificate degree from the Institute of Transpersonal Psychology.

Dr. Appel is a diplomate in psychotherapy and is a clinically certified forensic counselor, a national certified counselor, a certified clinical mental health counselor, a certified career counselor, and an approved clinical supervisor, as well as an internationally certified alcohol and drug abuse professional. He has also received training as a Red Cross mental health disaster worker and a behavioral health disaster responder to state disaster, emergency, and terrorist events. Dr. Appel is currently licensed as an independent marriage and family therapist, an independent chemical dependency counselor, and a supervising professional clinical counselor. His research areas include substance abuse, family issues, mindfulness, and international issues in behavioral health. Dr. Appel has done extensive travel and research in Asia.

Esther Benoit, PhD, received her master's in marriage, couples, and family counseling and her PhD in counselor education from the College of William and Mary in Williamsburg, Virginia. She has worked as a family, couples, and individual counselor in the Hampton Roads, Virginia, area since 2005. Dr. Benoit is core faculty in the Marriage, Couples, and Family Counseling Program at Walden University. She previously directed the New Horizons Family Counseling Center, a university-based family counseling teaching clinic serving the families of students referred by the public schools and providing clinical instruction in marriage and family counseling for both master's and doctoral-level graduate students.

As a licensed professional counselor in the state of Virginia, she continues to work with at-risk youth and their parents through a grant-based prevention program in both group and family counseling settings. Her research and clinical interests include moral development, military families, and counselor education and supervision. Dr. Benoit remains actively involved in identifying and supporting the needs of families and individuals in the greater Hampton Roads community, including work with homeless women and their children.

Brian S. Canfield, EdD, is a counselor educator and practicing counselor specializing in work with couples and families. He received bachelor's and master's degrees from Louisiana Tech University and his EdD from Texas A&M University at Commerce, with a major in counseling and guidance and program emphasis in marriage and family therapy. He is an internationally recognized family counseling educator and has presented workshops and keynote addresses to professional groups throughout the United States, as well as in the United Kingdom, Germany, Turkey, Australia, Cyprus, Rwanda, and China.

Dr. Canfield is a fellow and past president of the American Counseling Association and a past president of the International Association of Marriage and Family Counselors. He currently serves as the IAMFC Director of International Education and Development and is professor and chair of the Department of Counseling, Barry University. He is the father of five children. He and his wife, Irene, reside in Hollywood, Florida.

Montserrat Casado-Kehoe, PhD, is an associate professor of counseling psychology at Palm Beach Atlantic University in Orlando, Florida. She is a licensed marriage and family therapist, a registered play therapist, and an approved supervisor in the state of Florida. She is also Prepare-Enrich certified and EMDR Level II trained. She is coeditor of *Case Studies in Couples Therapy: Theory-Based Approaches.*

As a therapist, Dr. Casado-Kehoe's passion is working with couples, children, and families. In couples therapy, she integrates an experiential strength-based approach that helps couples look at their attachment patterns and find new ways to build intimacy and communication. The exciting part of therapy is helping each partner find ways to reconnect and regain a sense of love and commitment for each other. Loving one another involves work, dedication, and an exercise of forgiveness as they create a new vision of their future as a couple.

Yvonne Castillo, PhD, NCC, LPC-S, is presently employed as director of the Counseling and Training Clinic at the Counseling and Educational Psychology Department at Texas A&M University–Corpus Christi. She is a national certified counselor, a certified school counselor, and a licensed professional counselor-supervisor with 23 years of experience in public schools and higher education systems. Dr. Castillo is also a certified anger resolution therapist and is trained in eye movement desensitization reprocessing therapy.

Today, her work involves facilitating healthy relationship classes and positive parenting programs while also presenting on diverse topics to schools and community agencies. She is director/owner of C^2 Counseling, a Christ-centered counseling and consulting business where she also supervises licensed professional counselor interns. Dr. Castillo is highly involved in serving her community through her participation as an officer of the Coastal Bend Coalition Against Modern Day Slavery.

Ashley Clark, MS, earned a bachelor's degree in psychology from Saint Francis University (2004), a master's in psychology from Mount Aloysius College (2006), a master's in mental health counseling from Walden University (2011), and is currently a doctoral candidate in Counselor Education and Supervision at Walden University. She currently works as a vocational rehabilitation counselor for the Commonwealth of Virginia Department for Aging and Rehabilitative Services supporting individuals with disabilities in increasing employment opportunities, which utilize their strengths to promote independence within the community. Prior to her current position, she worked in several agencies providing family counseling services with at-risk adolescents and their families through systemic means.

Clark is a current member of the American Counseling Association, the National Board for Certified Counselors, the Association for Counselor Education and Supervision, the Association for Lesbian, Gay, Bisexual, and Transgender Issues in Counseling, the Association for Multicultural Counseling and Development, the American Rehabilitative Counseling Association, and the Association for Humanistic Counseling. She is a national certified counselor, distance certified counselor, and is currently pursuing supervision for licensure as a licensed professional counselor. Her research interests include multicultural issues, disability awareness and etiquette, and the integration of these issues within a systemic focus.

Astra B. Czerny, PhD, received her doctorate in counseling from the University of North Carolina at Charlotte in 2014. Dr. Czerny has worked as a counselor at a local domestic violence shelter since 2009, providing individual and group counseling services. In addition, she has a private practice in Cornelius, North Carolina.

Her research areas include substance abuse, women's issues, trauma, and empowerment. Dr. Czerny is the recipient of the 2012–2013 McLeod Institute's Student Fellowship Award. She has been a member of the Domestic Violence Advocacy Council and presents on topics that include domestic violence, empowerment, and working with trauma. She is a member of the National Board of Certified Counselors, the Association of Counselor Educators, and the American Counseling Association. Dr. Czerny is also a licensed professional counselor.

Thelma Duffey, PhD, is professor and chair in the Department of Counseling at the University of Texas at San Antonio, owner of a multidisciplinary group practice, and president elect of the American Counseling Association. She is a licensed professional counselor and licensed marriage and family therapist, serving individuals, couples, and families in Texas for over 23 years. Dr. Duffey chaired a series of conferences focused on creativity in practice and successfully spearheaded an effort to establish a new division within ACA. She was founding president of the Association for Creativity in Counseling and serves as editor for the *Journal of*

Creativity in Mental Health, published by the Taylor & Francis Group. Dr. Duffey is the 2011 recipient of the Association for Counselor Education and Supervision Distinguished Mentor Award and was inducted as an American Counseling Association ACA Fellow in 2010. Dr. Duffey's collaborative work on relational competencies and creativity received the 2010 Texas Counseling Association Research Award. In 2008, an award was established in her name by the Association for Creativity in Counseling. She received the 2006 American Counseling Association Professional Development Award and the 2006 Association for Counselor Education and Supervision Counseling Vision and Innovation Award.

Dr. Duffey has over 50 publications in the areas of creativity, innovations in grief and loss counseling, relational competencies, and addiction. She is editor of *Creative Interventions in Grief and Loss Therapy: When the Music Stops, a Dream Dies*, published by the Haworth Press/Taylor & Francis Group. Dr. Duffey is coediting a book on counseling men with the ACA Press, and was a guest editor for the *Journal of Counseling and Development* for a special issue on counseling men. She is currently serving as a guest coeditor for a *Journal of Counseling and Development* special section on relational-cultural theory. Dr. Duffey is co-chair of the ACA-ACC Creative Interventions and Activities Clearinghouse and chair of the ACA Governing Council New Member Training and Resource Committee. Dr. Duffey served two terms on the Governing Council for the American Counseling Association and is president of the Texas Association for Counselor Education and Supervision.

Nick Erber, MA, LPC, CAADC, is a licensed professional counselor and doctoral student at Walden University in Counselor Education and Supervision, specializing in consultation. Nick has been a counselor since 2008, but has worked in the mental health field since 2002. He is currently the program coordinator and counselor for the Thomas Judd Care Center, a Ryan White funded HIV/AIDS clinic, at Munson Medical Center, in Traverse City, Michigan. He has clinical experience with serious mental illnesses in adults, domestic violence treatment, mindfulness and holistic health, HIV/AIDS, and LGBTQ issues, specifically people who identify as transgender. Nick's dissertation research is a qualitative study of transgender identity development in a rural area. He has worked in agencies and owned a private practice as a counselor.

Nick currently serves as the treasurer of the Michigan Counseling Association and president of the LPCs of Northern Michigan. Nick is a member of the American Counseling Association, Michigan Counseling Association, Association for Counselor Education and Supervision, the Association for Humanistic Counseling, and the Association for Lesbian, Gay, Bisexual, and Transgender Issues in Counseling. He is also a member of the Michigan Association for Counselor Education and Supervision and a member of Chi Sigma Iota since 2007.

Brandé Flamez, PhD, NCC, LPC, is a licensed professional counselor and a professor in the Counseling and Special Populations department at Lamar University in Beaumont, Texas. Currently, she serves on the American Counseling Association (ACA) Governing Council for the International Association of Marriage and Family Counselors. She was elected by the ACA Governing Council to serve on the ACA Finance Committee. She is also the president of the Association for Humanistic Counselors (AHC), chairs the ACA Publications Committee, and was appointed to the ACA Investment Committee.

She is on the editorial board for *The Family Journal* and the *Journal of College Counseling*. She has presented over 100 times nationally and internationally and has authored or coauthored over 30 book chapters and articles. She is the coauthor of the assessment textbook *Counseling Assessment and Evaluation: Fundamentals of Applied Practice* and the upcoming textbooks *Diagnosing and Treating Children and Adolescents: A Guide for Mental Health Professionals* and *Introduction to Marriage, Couples, and Family Counseling: Applied Practice*. She is the recipient of numerous national awards, including the 2014 ACA Kitty Cole Human Rights Award, the 2012 ACA Gilbert and Kathleen Wrenn Award for a Caring and Humanitarian Person, the 2012 AHC Humanistic Advocacy and Social Justice Award, the 2012 IAMFC Distinguished Mentor Award, and the American College Counseling (ACC) Meritorious Award.

Melinda Haley, PhD, received her master's in counselor education at Portland State University (Oregon) and her doctorate in counseling psychology from New Mexico State University (Las Cruces). She is a licensed psychologist in the state of New Mexico. For 5 years, she was an assistant professor at the University of Texas, El Paso, in the Counseling and Guidance Program. Dr. Haley currently works as a core faculty member in the Counselor Education and Supervision Doctoral Program at Walden University. She has written numerous book chapters and journal articles on diverse topics related to counseling. She has extensive applied experience working with adults, adolescents, children, inmates, domestic violence offenders, and culturally diverse populations in the areas of assessment, diagnosis, treatment planning, crisis management, and intervention. Dr. Haley's research interests include multicultural issues in teaching and counseling, personality development over the lifespan, personality disorders, the psychology of criminal and serial offenders, trauma and posttraumatic stress disorder, bias and racism, and social justice issues.

Danica G. Hays, PhD, LPC, NCC, is an associate professor of counseling and chair of the Department of Counseling and Human Services at Old Dominion University in Norfolk, Virginia. She is a recipient of the Outstanding Research Award, Outstanding Counselor Educator Advocacy Award, and the Glen E. Hubele National Graduate Student Award from the American Counseling Association (ACA), as well as the Patricia B. Elmore Excellence in Measurement and Evaluation Award and President's Special Merit Award from the Association of Assessment and Research in Counseling (AARC). Dr. Hays served as founding editor of *Counseling Outcome Research and Evaluation*, a national peer-refereed journal of the AARC, and is editor of *Counselor Education and Supervision*, a national peer-refereed journal of the Association for Counselor Education and Supervision. She served as President of the AARC in 2011–2012.

Her research interests include qualitative methodology, assessment and diagnosis, trauma and gender issues, and multicultural and social justice concerns in counselor preparation and community mental health. She has published over

75 articles and book chapters in these areas. In addition, she has authored, coauthored, or coedited six books to date: *Assessment in Counseling: A Guide to Psychological Assessment Procedures* (ACA), *Developing Multicultural Counseling Competence: A Systems Approach* (Pearson), *Qualitative Inquiry in Clinical and Educational Settings* (Guilford), *Mastering the National Counselor Exam and the Counselor Preparation Comprehensive Exam* (Pearson), *A Counselor's Guide to Career Assessment Instruments* (National Career Development Association), and the *ACA Encyclopedia of Counseling* (ACA).

Janet Froeschle Hicks, PhD, is an associate professor of counseling in the Educational Psychology and Leadership Department and College of Education at Texas Tech University. She is both a licensed professional counselor and a certified school counselor in Texas.

Dr. Froeschle Hicks worked many years in the public school system as a teacher and school counselor as well as in the community before earning her PhD in counseling and becoming a professor. She currently specializes in working with families, children, and adolescents.

Aaron H. Jackson, PhD, has been a providing mental health and substance abuse counseling to clients and families for over 10 years. He began his career in the criminal justice system as a probation officer in North Carolina, where he worked for 6 years before going on to graduate school. He holds a master's degree from Campbell University and a PhD from The College of William & Mary. Over the years, he has presented at local, state, and national conferences, and has provided additional training to the professional counseling community across North Carolina. Jackson is a core faculty member in the Marriage, Couples, and Family Counseling Program at Walden University.

Dr. Jackson is a licensed professional counselor in North Carolina. He is also recognized as a national certified counselor by the National Board of Certified Counselors. In addition to his clinical and academic work, he serves his community in several civic organizations.

Hyeseong Kang, MA, earned her master's degree in clinical and counseling psychology at Korea University in Seoul, Korea. After working as an assistant manager in human resources for LG Electronics in Korea, she came to the United States to advance her training as a doctoral student in the University of Connecticut's COAMFTE-accredited Marriage and Family Therapy Program. Kang's research interests focus on evidence-based, multicultural systemic interventions aimed at bolstering family resilience, particularly among Korea's underrepresented and underserved populations. Her goal is to return to Korea with the research and clinical competencies necessary to promote and evaluate preventive and protective evidence-based health and mental health treatment programs that provide venues for effective and relevant collaboration among family, work, and community systems. On a larger scale, she is committed to expanding the role of couple and family therapists in Korea by incorporating more nontraditional, systemic service models into public family therapy programs to support and empower families at all points across the life span.

DoHee Kim-Appel, PhD, IMFT-S, LPCC-S, ATR, LICDC, NCC, is an associate professor in the Department of Art Therapy and Counseling at Ursuline College in Pepper Pike, Ohio. Dr. Kim-Appel is an American Association for Marriage and Family Therapy (AAMFT)-approved supervisor and a clinical fellow, and an internationally certified alcohol and drug abuse professional. She has also received training as a certified general and divorce mediator, a certified Red Cross mental health disaster worker, and a behavioral health disaster responder to state disaster. Dr. Kim-Appel serves as an editorial board member of the *Journal of Counselor Practice* (JCP), a peer-reviewed national publication published by the Ohio Counseling Association. She is a committee member of the Association for Counselor Education and Supervision (ACES) International Initiative. She has presented papers and training sessions regionally, nationally, and internationally in such topics as workplace violence, family violence, mindfulness, substance abuse and mental illness, and therapeutic jurisprudence.

Dr. Kim-Appel has been published in such peer-reviewed publications as the *Journal of Aggression, Maltreatment, and Trauma;* the *Journal of Elder Abuse and Neglect;* the *Family Journal: Counseling and Therapy for Couples and Families;* the *Journal of Transpersonal Research; Psychology;* the *Journal of Health and Human Services Administration;* and the *International Journal of Mental Health and Addiction.* She coauthored a book chapter titled "Psychology's View of Religion and Spirituality: A Long Short History" in the *Handbook on Spirituality: Belief Systems, Societal Impact and Roles in Coping* (Nova Science, 2012). Her research interests include family differentiation, mindfulness, cultural competency, and international issues in behavioral health. Dr. Kim-Appel has more than a decade of experience in the field of behavior health, working with a diverse population of clients across the spectrum of emotional and substance-related issues, including youth, individuals, couples, and families.

Pamela S. Lassiter, PhD, is an associate professor in the Department of Counseling at the University of North Carolina at Charlotte. She has over 25 years of work experience as a counselor, clinical supervisor, and administrator in substance abuse treatment and community mental health. Dr. Lassiter continues her clinical work in private practice in Charlotte, North Carolina, and holds credentials as a licensed professional counselor, a licensed marriage and family therapist, and a licensed clinical addiction specialist. She serves as director of the Addictions Track and the Substance Abuse Certificate Program at UNC Charlotte. Dr. Lassiter has been the coordinator of the annual Jonnie H. McLeod Institute on Substance Abuse at the UNC Charlotte for 11 years.

Her areas of research include multicultural counseling and supervision, gay and lesbian issues in counseling, GLBT parenting issues, addictions counseling, and women's issues. She is past president of the International Association of Addictions and Offender Counseling (IAAOC), where she served as an officer for 5 years. She is the recipient of the 2011 Addictions/Offender Education Excellence Award from the International Association of Addictions and Offender Counseling (IAAOC); the 2008 recipient of the Dr. Mary Thomas Burke Mentoring Award given by the

North Carolina Association of Spiritual, Ethical, and Religious Values in Counseling; and the 2005 recipient of the JoAnna White Founder's Award given by the Chi Epsilon Chapter of Chi Sigma Iota International.

Colleen Logan, PhD, LPC, LMFT, NCC, serves as the program coordinator for the master's in Marriage, Couples, and Family Counseling, Addictions Counseling, Career Counseling, and School Counseling programs and the PhD in Counselor Education and Supervision at Walden University. Previously, she held academic and administrative positions at Argosy University and the University of Houston–Victoria, serving in the roles of vice president of academic affairs and associate dean, School of Psychology and Behavioral Sciences, respectively. Dr. Logan provided counseling services in a private practice from 1997 to 2009, specializing in HIV services, adolescent intervention, and enrichment counseling.

In addition to acting in such academic and administrative positions, Dr. Logan also served as the president of the American Counseling Association (ACA) in 2008–2009 and president of the Texas Association for Lesbian, Gay, Bisexual, and Transgender Issues in Counseling, a division of the Texas Counseling Association, in 2009–2010. She has been recognized for her contributions to the field of counseling and affirmative therapy with lesbian, gay, bisexual, and transgender individuals and their significant others. Dr. Logan has been instrumental in working with school counselors and administrators to institute and implement zero-tolerance policies toward bullying, with an emphasis on creating an affirmative environment for all students. Dr. Logan has presented locally, nationally, and internationally, including at the American Counseling Association's annual conference and the National Lesbian and Gay Health Conference, among others, on issues related to counseling gay, lesbian, bisexual, and transgender clients. In addition, she has authored or coauthored a number of articles and chapters, as well as a book on how to work effectively with gay, lesbian, bisexual, and transgender clients and their significant others.

Kirsten W. Murray, PhD, is an associate professor in the Department of Counselor Education at the University of Montana. Her interests include couples and family counseling, supervision, counselor wellness, and social justice and advocacy practices.

Dr. Murray has taught graduate-level courses with emphases in system frameworks and couples and family counseling since 2004 and has worked clinically with couples, parents, and families since 2001. Her current research interests include exploring the relational impacts of counselor training.

Marvarene Oliver, EdD, is an associate professor in the Counseling and Educational Psychology Department at Texas A&M University–Corpus Christi. She is coordinator of the Marriage, Couple, and Family Counseling Program as well as the clinical coordinator for both the master's and doctoral programs. Dr. Oliver has over 30 years experience in private practice working with individuals, couples, and families.

Dr. Oliver is a licensed professional counselor-supervisor and a licensed marriage and family therapist-supervisor in Texas. In addition, she holds the approved supervisor and clinical fellow designations in the AAMFT. She serves as the executive editor of the *Journal of Professional Practice: Practice, Theory, and Research*. She is currently the president of the American Association for Marriage and Family Therapy (2015–2016).

Diane Kimball Parker, MS, is a registered mental health counselor intern and a graduate of Palm Beach Atlantic University. She has extensive play therapy training with children and families and integrates the use of expressive arts when working with couples. As a couples therapist, she focuses on integrating an emotionally focused theoretical approach that looks at the importance of attachment when working with couples. She is also EMDR Level II trained.

Kimball Parker brings 30 years of experience as a musician, educator, educational advocate, mentor, and parent into her present work as a therapist. As a counselor in a local agency, she works with largely with families, children, and adults through the use of creative arts, play therapy, and EMDR techniques. She specializes in trauma work with children, adolescents, and adults, as well as working with individuals of all ages diagnosed with Asperger's syndrome and other related disorders. She enjoys working with individuals and couples in creative ways to assist them in rediscovering their strengths, connect with others, and make peace with their past in order to move forward in their relationships and daily lives.

Shawn P. Parmanand, PhD, is a core faculty member in the Marriage, Couples, and Family Counseling Program at Walden University. He received his doctorate in counselor education and counseling from Idaho State University. He is an active counseling practitioner, working at a local child advocacy center in his hometown of Pocatello, Idaho.

Dr. Parmanand's recent publications include the coauthoring of several articles including "Developing Counseling Skill Using the Landro Play Analyzer (LPA): A Grounded Theory" (2012) and "Experiencing Emotion Across a Semester-Long Family Role-Play and Reflecting Team: Implications for Counselor Development" (2011). He was also asked to be a part of a microtraining DVD helping to train beginning practitioners on the use of emotionally focused theory. His research includes gatekeeping, online supervision, and mentoring in counselor education.

Michelle Perepiczka, PhD, LMHC, CSC, RPT, NCC, is a core faculty member in the Clinical Mental Health Counseling Program at Walden University. She is a past president of the Association for Humanistic Counseling (AHC) and serves as the AHC governing counsel representative. Dr. Perepiczka is a journal reviewer for the *Journal of Humanistic Counseling* and the *Journal of Counseling and Development*. Dr. Perepiczka received the Outstanding Humanistic Dissertation Award, Past President Award, and the Counselor Educator and Supervisor Award from AHC.

Dr. Perepiczka's clinical experiences include providing counseling and play therapy services in agency, hospital, and school settings to children who have experienced various forms of abuse and their families. Her specialization with adults is in anxiety and relationship struggles. Dr. Perepiczka's research interests include wellness, humanistic philosophies, and the impact of alternative teaching models in higher education.

Cassandra G. Pusateri, PhD, NCC, is an assistant professor in the Department of Counseling, Special Education, and School Psychology at Youngstown State University in Youngstown, Ohio. Dr. Pusateri received her master's degree in community agency counseling at East Tennessee State University and her PhD in counseling at Old Dominion University. She has experience working in school, hospital, clinic, and community agency settings as well as with grant-funded programs.

Dr. Pusateri was selected as an Association for Counselor Education and Supervision (ACES) Presidential Fellow and Southern Association of Counselor Education and Supervision (SACES) Emerging Leader in 2012. Her research interests include assessment, rural issues and Appalachian cultural identities, and gender issues in counseling. Dr. Pusateri is a member of several professional associations and has presented at many local, state, and national conferences as well as coauthored journal articles and book chapters.

Sandra Rigazio-DiGilio, PhD, is a professor in the University of Connecticut's Marriage and Family Therapy master's and doctoral programs. Her scholarship addresses cultural, contextual, integrative, and multidisciplinary competencies in the domains of theory building, model development, training, and supervision and the clinical adaptation of culture- and context-centered research instruments for interactive assessment and treatment in couple and family therapy. Her work to advance a systemic cognitive-developmental therapy model and corresponding supervisory approach is recognized as addressing cultural and community issues and as organizing traditional and contemporary models while keeping cultural and contextual factors in the forefront of therapy and supervision. Since 2000, she also has been working to identify and operationalize cultural, contextual, integrative, and multidisciplinary competencies and corresponding pedagogical and supervisory methods for the preparation of MFT scientist/practitioners. Dr. Rigazio-DiGilio presents and publishes widely on all of these topics and has coauthored a book, *Community Genograms: Using Individual, Family, and Cultural Narratives with Clients* (Teachers College Press, 2005).

Mark B. Scholl, PhD, LMHC, is an associate professor in the Department of Counseling at Wake Forest University. He is an active member in both the Association for Humanistic Counseling (AHC) and the American College Counseling Association. Dr. Scholl is past president of AHC and past editor of the *Journal of Humanistic Counseling.* He is also former chair of the ACA Council of Journal Editors. He has received the Hollis Award for publishing in the area of humanistic counseling and the Distinguished Reviewer Award from AHC.

Dr. Scholl recently served as the president of the Association for Humanistic Counseling (2012–2013). He is coauthor of the book *Humanistic Perspectives on*

Contemporary Counseling Issues. His research interests include culturally responsive counseling, client preferences for counselor role, and constructivist approaches to counseling. Dr. Scholl currently provides career counseling services to members of the community ex-offender population through partnerships with the North Carolina Department of Public Safety and the Forsyth County Public Library in Winston-Salem, North Carolina.

Stephanie K. Scott, PhD, is a core faculty member in the Mental Health Counseling Program at Walden University. She has her doctorate in human services, with a specialization in marriage and family therapy, which she earned at Capella University. Dr. Scott is a licensed mental health counselor in Florida, and her clinical work includes individuals, couples, and families. Much of her clinical work focuses on adolescents and young adults, with special attention to trauma, identity, and developmental considerations.

Dr. Scott's areas of research include affective training both in counselors and in clients, cultural diversity and conceptualization, systemic family issues, and standards of practice. She is also the founder of a local teen advocacy organization that supports adolescent health and wellness. Dr. Scott has worked extensively in inpatient and outpatient settings and currently maintains a small private practice in Florida.

Kevin C. Snow, MS, MA, is a doctoral candidate in counselor education and supervision in the Department of Counseling and Human Services at Old Dominion University in Norfolk, Virginia. He has been an active regional and national presenter, recently presenting at the Virginia Association of Counselor Education and Supervision (VACES) and the American Association of Counselor Education and Supervision (ACES) conferences. He currently serves as the managing editor for the pending *Encyclopedia of Theory in Counseling*, working with Dr. Edward Neukrug. In addition, he is serving as a CACREP initial reviewer, is secretary of the Omega Delta chapter of Chi Sigma Iota, and served as the codirector of Old Dominion's Student Training Clinic.

His research interests include multicultural issues and social justice concerns in counseling, pedagogy in counselor education, spirituality in counseling, mental health portrayal in popular media, and qualitative research methods. He has over 13 years of clinical community and mental health experience, beginning his career as a domestic violence and sexual assault counselor in a crisis center. In addition to his current doctoral work at Old Dominion University, he studied community counseling at Shippensburg University of Pennsylvania and did postgraduate studies in school counseling at Indiana University of Pennsylvania.

John Sommers-Flanagan, PhD, is a professor of counselor education at the University of Montana. He is also a clinical psychologist and mental health consultant with Trapper Creek Job Corps. He served as executive director of Families First Parenting Programs from 1995 to 2003 and was previously cohost of a radio talk show on Montana Public Radio titled *What Is It With Men?*

Primarily specializing in working with children, parents, and families, he is author or coauthor of over 50 professional publications and nine books. Some of his latest books, cowritten with his wife, Rita, include *How to Listen so Parents Will Talk and Talk so Parents Will Listen* (Wiley, 2011); *Counseling and Psychotherapy Theories in Context and Practice* (2nd ed.; Wiley, 2012); *Clinical Interviewing* (5th ed.; Wiley, 2014), and *Tough Kids, Cool Counseling* (2nd ed.; ACA, 2007). In his wild and precious spare time, Dr. Sommers-Flanagan loves to run (slowly), dance (poorly), laugh (loudly), and produce homemade family music videos.

Lee A. Teufel-Prida, PhD, is currently a core faculty member at Walden University in the Marriage, Couple, and Family Counseling Program. Dr. Teufel-Prida is a licensed professional counselor in California, a licensed mental health counselor in Florida, and a national certified counselor. Her research interests include counseling and advocating for children and families impacted by abuse, trauma, significant life stress, or military service. Additional research interests and pursuits include clinical supervision and the use of Photovoice in advocacy.

Dr. Teufel-Prida teaches numerous courses, serves as a course lead, and participates in the residency program experiences. In addition to her work at Walden University, Dr. Teufel-Prida is active in many state and national counseling organizations. She has presented at several community, state, national, and international conferences and workshops, including the American Counseling Association and the Association for Counselor Education and Supervision.

Michael Walsh, PhD, LPC, CRC, is a practicing licensed professional counselor and rehabilitation counselor, as well as a counselor educator. Dr. Walsh is currently the curriculum development director for the University of South Carolina School of Medicine's Rehabilitation Counseling Program. Dr. Walsh is a two-time past president of the Association for Humanistic Counseling (AHC) and currently serves as AHC's governing council representative.

Dr. Walsh maintains an active practice as an LPC, working with both individuals and families. He prefers humanistic approaches that involve the family as a holistic unit and help the families to develop the skills they need to grow and flourish. He chooses to focus on developing the family's own native resources. This approach helps families to learn and grow while providing sustainable tools for improved family functioning.

Kimberly S. Williams, MA, EdS, LPC, LPC-S, is currently enrolled as a doctoral student in the Counselor Education and Supervision Program at the University of North Carolina at Charlotte. Williams has 10 years of work in the mental health field, providing direct care in homes, schools, and other natural settings, as well as counseling in outpatient and inpatient settings. She has worked primarily in the southern piedmont area of North Carolina as a licensed professional counselor.

Williams's experiences with adolescents include addressing substance abuse issues, family/system challenges, developmental concerns, and transitional stressors. She has worked with adults in inpatient settings primarily focusing on areas of crisis stabilization and grief and loss. Most recently, she has provided outpatient counseling services to individuals, groups, and families, including work addressing developmental issues. She serves as a mentor and supervisor to master's level students seeking to obtain degrees within the counseling field. Her areas of research include working with individuals and families who experience disabilities, as well as multicultural family counseling and adolescent counseling issues.

Dawn M. Wirick, PhD, is a core faculty member of Marriage, Couples, and Family Counseling at Walden University. Dr. Wirick is a licensed professional counselor, a licensed marriage and family therapist, and a national certified counselor. Her research interests include chronic pain issues in cancer survivors, grief processes related to chronic pain, and the effects of female infertility on couple/family functioning.

She currently works with children and families in an intensive in-home family therapy program. She annually participates in a social change project in Mexico designed to assist residents with housing and increased access to community and educational resources. She also coordinates and supervises chronic pain management groups for female cancer survivors in teaching/research hospitals.

Christina G. Yoshimura, PhD, is an associate professor of communication studies at the University of Montana. She earned her bachelor's degree in communication at Syracuse University and her master's and PhD in communication at Arizona State University. She is currently earning a clinical mental health counseling MA degree at the University of Montana.

Dr. Yoshimura specializes in research on the ways in which the family system communicatively responds to challenges. Her published work includes empirical investigations of the kind of interpersonal interactions family members have while watching television; the ways that siblings, siblings-in-law, and spouses experience and communicate envy in their triadic relationship; and the communicative coping strategies of couples navigating work–family tensions. The perspectives of communication studies and counseling each add insight and unique frameworks to her work on how families cope with challenges.

Author Index

Subject Index